# GREAT BRITAIN 1989

# THE CONTRIBUTORS

**Melanie Menagh** wrote the chapters *Traveling to Great Britain in 1989; Orienting Yourself; Priorities;* most of the *London* sections; *Thames, Oxford, and the Cotswolds; The Lake District; The Scottish Lowlands; The Scottish Highlands and Islands;* and *Travel Arrangements.* She is a New York-based writer, who spends much of her time in Great Britain. Ms. Menagh has contributed to books on Italy, Mexico, and New York City and her articles have appeared in *Savvy, Travel & Leisure,* and *Vanity Fair.*

**Stephen Mills,** contributor of *The Southeast, The West Country, East Midlands,* and *West Midlands* chapters, is a London-based journalist who has worked extensively in the British press and contributed to a range of national newspapers and magazines including *The Observer, The Independent, The Face, The Daily Telegraph,* and *Time Out.*

A native of Cheshire in the northwest of England, **James McGeachie,** who wrote the *East Anglia, Northwest,* and *Wales* chapters, currently works as a free-lance researcher and writer in Cambridge, London, and New York. He teaches for the University of Cambridge, has published articles in various academic journals, and is completing a book on the politician and philosopher Arthur Balfour.

**John Davison,** contributor of our chapter *The North Country,* was born in Northumberland and has spent most of his life in the North Country, living in many of its towns and cities, and walking its hills.

The restaurant section of the London chapter was contributed by **Helen Varley,** London restaurant critic and writer on consumer affairs. She has been editor of the annual *Time Out Guide to Eating Out in London* and its offshoots for several years and is a regular contributor to *Time Out* magazine's food columns.

Contributor of the *Business Brief,* **James Louttit,** an author, publisher, and travel writer, was president of Fodor's Travel Guides and David McKay Company, Inc. until he retired to North Carolina in 1986. His experience in "doing business in Great Britain" covers the 15 years that Fodor's/McKay was owned by a British parent company.

**Carl Nagin,** who contributed the *Cultural Timeline,* is a free-lance journalist who teaches writing at Harvard. Mr. Nagin has written for *New York* magazine, the *Christian Science Monitor, Interview, Geo, Reader's Digest, Art and Auction,* and the *Boston Globe.*

The New York editor for the book is Audrey Liounis and the assistant editor is Charlotte Savidge. Maps are by Swanston Graphics and R.V. Reise und Verkehrsverlag.

A BANTAM TRAVEL GUIDE

# GREAT BRITAIN

## England, Scotland, Wales

### 1989

BANTAM
NEW YORK ● TORONTO ● LONDON ● SYDNEY ● AUCKLAND

GREAT BRITAIN 1989
*A Bantam Book / April 1989*

ISBN 0-553-34638-5

*Published simultaneously in the United States and Canada*

---

*Bantam Books are published by Bantam Books, a division of Bantam Double-*
*day Dell Publishing Group, Inc. Its trademark, consisting of the words "Ban-*
*tam Books" and the portrayal of a rooster, is Registered in U.S. Patent and*
*Trademark Office and in other countries. Marca Registrada, Bantam Books,*
*666 Fifth Avenue, New York, New York 10103*

---

PRINTED IN THE UNITED STATES OF AMERICA

0 9 8 7 6 5 4 3 2 1

# CONTENTS

# FOREWORD

Anyone who's ever used a travel guidebook knows how addictive they become when they're good, but how annoying they are when they're bad. We at Bantam launched this new guidebook series because we honestly believed we could improve on, no, that's too weak, we believed we could *significantly* improve on the best of what's already out there. And there are some good guidebooks out there.

It was apparent to us that, unless we improved on the best of what's currently available, there was no sense in producing a new series. More to the point, there'd be no reason for you, the traveler, to buy our guidebooks. We analyzed the guidebooks already on the market, making note of their best features as well as their deficiencies. The single greatest deficiency of most guidebooks is that you have to buy something else to supplement these deficiencies. Usually you need to buy a good map or a guide to hotels or restaurants because your primary guide lacks good detailed maps, has outdated information on hotels or restaurants, or simply doesn't include such information at all—never mind whether it's up-to-date or not.

The Bantam team had one major goal—that of producing the only travel guides that both the experienced and the inexperienced traveler would ever need for a given destination. You're holding an example of how well we succeeded. Can we document this success? Let's take a look.

- One of the first things you'll notice is that Bantam Travel Guides include a full-color travel atlas with maps detailed enough for the most demanding travel needs.
- Upon closer scrutiny you'll find that the guide is **organized geographically** rather than alphabetically. Think of what this means to you. Descriptions of what's available in a contiguous geographical area make it easier to get the most out of a city neighborhood or a country region. For those who still need to locate something alphabetically we provide a detailed index.
- A real convenience is the way that restaurants and hotels in major cities are keyed into the maps so that you can locate these places easily.
- At the end of major city chapters you'll find a feature called City Listings where museums, churches, and major sites

are listed with their addresses, phone numbers and map-location code.

- Bantam guides will be revised every year. Travel conditions change and so do our guides.
- Finally, we think you'll enjoy reading our guidebooks. We've tried hard to find not only well-informed writers, but good writers. The writing is literate and lively. It pulls no punches. It's honest. Most of all it's a good read.

Still, no guidebook can cover everything that's worth seeing or doing—though we believe we come closer than anyone else. We ask you to bear in mind, too, that prices can change at any time, and that today's well-managed restaurant or hotel can change owners or managers tomorrow. Today's great service or food can be tomorrow's disappointment. We've recommended places as they are now and as we expect them to be in the future, but there are no guarantees. We welcome your comments and suggestions. Our address is Bantam Travel Guides, 666 Fifth Avenue, New York, N.Y. 10103.

Richard T. Scott
Publisher
Bantam Travel Books

## Tips On Getting the Most Out of This Guide

Bantam Travel Guides are designed to be extremely user friend-ly, but there are a few things you should know in order to get the maximum benefit from them.

1. You'll find a special **Travel Arrangements** section, easily identified by the black-bordered pages, toward the back of the book. This section can be invaluable in planning your trip.
2. The **Priorities** chapter will insure that you see and do the most important things when you visit your destination. Whether you're spending two days or two weeks there, you'll want to make the most of your time and certainly not miss the musts.
3. Note that in addition to our main selection of important restaurants you'll also find described in the text informal places to stop for lunch, a snack, or a drink.
4. To help you instantly identify restaurant and hotel write-ups, whether they're in a list or mentioned in the text, we've designed the following two little versions of our friendly Bantam rooster. Miniatures of these roosters will appear at the beginning of restaurant and hotel lists and in the margin of the text whenever a restaurant or hotel is described there.

Restaurants

Hotels

# 1

# TRAVELING TO GREAT BRITAIN IN 1989

You couldn't have picked a better time to come to the United Kingdom. Britain is undergoing a radical overhaul, a modern refurbishing; and, as with any nation experiencing extensive, essential change, it is a fascinating place to visit. One assumes you are aware of the traditional reasons for visiting Britain: glorious countryside, amiable citizens, stout ale, wild salmon, cricket, castles, rock and roll, art galleries, roses, Shakespeare, bed-and-breakfasts, royalty, perhaps a hunt for lost ancestors. If any of these reasons intrigue you, you have merely to flip through these pages for a tantalizing foretaste.

The rest of this book is chockablock with places to see, historical facts, anecdotal asides. But in addition to this information on where in Britain you should go and why, it is important to understand a bit about where Britain is going and why. Because if one is at all keen, it will quickly become apparent that there is a lot more going on here than stately homes and revivals of *Macbeth.* In fact, the recent changes in the political, social, and economic scene are largely responsible for the fact that many stately homes are now open to the public. And no British theater company worth its salt would reenact the machinations of the Thane of Cawdor without elucidating the political, social, and economic subtexts.

These subtexts are also to be found between the lines of newspapers, novels, conversations in the street, in pubs, and in Parliament. It is a time of great excitement and advancement. But progress is necessarily fraught with controversy. The debate currently centers on the questions of at what price this progress will be achieved and who will foot the bill. And, as in any time of great excitement and advancement, the answers are subtle, intricate, and complex.

A professor of English history once observed that the British don't like things foreign and they don't like change. The anti-alteration credo was understandable and enforceable during the preindustrial days when foreign ideas could be kept at bay by the watery barriers surrounding the British Isles; and later, during the early days of the Industrial Revolution when the British Empire ruled the world, the world could be made to submit to the Empire's ways.

Now, at the close of the 20th century, preservationism and isolationism are no longer possible for several salient reasons. The first is the Big Bang of 1986, a measure championed by Prime Minister Margaret Thatcher's Tory government that essentially deregulated all money matters and launched Britain into the international financial marketplace. The Big Bang ushered the yuppie ethos of hard work and fast money into a society that had heretofore upheld the legitimacy of an old-money consanguineous upper class. Now the nation's Young Turks are forsaking late nights at the club for power breakfasts, and weekends' grouse shooting for Saturdays at the office.

The next scheduled upset is due in 1992, although preparations are presently in full swing. The establishment of a unified economy for all Europe, an event touted as having earth-shattering effects on all EEC (European Economic Community) nations and on the world, has been given only a lukewarm reception by Mrs. Thatcher, who has publicly dismissed the establishment of a "United States of Europe" as an "airy-fairy notion." Nevertheless, in three years trade and travel barriers will be lifted and a market of 340 million Europeans will swing open for business.

Finally, with multinational money markets and communications networks linking the Island to the outside world over airwaves and computer terminals, a tangible, geographic link will at last connect Britain to the Continent. The Chunnel, a colossal tunnel beneath the English Channel, is scheduled to be completed by the middle of the next decade. Within ten years, Britons will be able to drive to France, and, of course, foreigners will be able to drive to Britain.

The effect of the aforementioned events on Britain has been staggering and will continue to be so for some time to come. But before projecting what is to come, it would do well to rewind the tape just a bit to examine the recent climate of the country and disposition of the people which have permitted this veritable tsunami of extra-national elements to whelm the British Isles. Although the changes seem precipitous, obviously they didn't happen overnight or in a vacuum, but rather they have been a long time coming—and many would argue are long overdue.

Undoubtedly, one of the reasons Britons have been so inhospitable to things foreign is that they have had enough trouble reconciling differences among themselves and haven't needed strangers to further complicate matters. If you stand an Aberdonian next to a Yorkshireman next to a Cornishman next to a Londoner and asked each to read the morning's *Times,* their accents would be as different from one another as they are from that of a Chicagoan or an Aucklander. It is difficult for a traveler from a land as vast as America or Australia to appreciate the differences in accent, ambition, and temperament that exist within the confines of as relatively small a country (about 88,700 square miles) as Britain.

Within an hour's drive you can quit the urbane, cutthroat atmosphere of London and land in a Cotswold village that for all intents and purposes time has forgotten for the past four hundred years, and whose inhabitants are delighted things should remain so. In that same hour you can quit Inveraray Castle, ancestral seat of the Campbell clan, and land on the Isle of Skye, heart of MacDonald country, where descendants of that house still remember vigorously the Campbells' massacre of fifty-odd Highlanders in the snows of Glencoe nearly three hundred years ago.

In centuries past, the differences among the various tribes of Britain amounted to more than mere picturesque local color, as the number of ruined castles littered about the country attests. The chafing between races, clans, and fiefdoms has been the source of massive destruction and human suffering. *Briton* is a term used for convenience; the Cornishman or Welshman would prefer to be referred to by his more specific monicker. And whatever you do, don't call anyone north of Hadrian's Wall or west of the river Wye an Englishman. To this day, the Aberdonian, the Yorkshireman, the Cornishman, and the Londoner will make much of the differences, the accent being the least of which, between them. Northumberland rugby players will tell you that to this day there is a certain keenness of competition when the match concerns themselves and a Scots Borders team, stemming from the days when brigands from north and south made regular raids on their across-the-border brethrens' churches, cattle, castles, and women. But while the old rivalries are reenacted on the playing field, many Newcastle lads will tell you that their disagreement no longer rests with their historical antagonists to the north. These days their argument lies instead with new-sprung adversaries in the south; the southeast, to be more specific, London, to be most particular. Ancient enemies are astonished to find themselves allies in the same camp, united by a sense of dissociation from and disillusionment with Thatcherism, which is largely passing Britain's agrarian and older industrial regions by.

London is the hub of and key to Britain as perhaps no other city is to its nation. Ever expanding, amoeba-like, to engulf the surrounding fields of rape seed and alfalfa, the city of London is yanking the nation (kicking and screaming in many cases) into the modern world of high finance, high technology, and self-sufficiency, promulgating a Wall Street-style work ethic to make the retreat from socialism to capitalism possible.

This is not to say that the Conservative government's policies have failed, or failed to appeal to most of the electorate. On the contrary, Britain in the early 1980s was a backward, economically and spiritually depressed country relative to most other first-world nations—a circumstance extremely unsettling for a kingdom that previous to World War I had been the greatest global power for over a century.

The Conservative government wrested power from the Labour Party in 1979 and has since rigorously championed a policy of helping those who help themselves. The figures show that Mrs. Thatcher's supply-side approach has succeeded in shaking up the nation and shaking the economy out of its doldrums. The GNP has more than doubled in the last ten years from 115,340 million pounds in 1976 to 323,775 million pounds in 1986. Concurrently, the inflation rate has declined from well into double digits during the seventies (24 percent in 1975), to a comfortable 4.4 percent in 1987. From its nadir in 1981, the British economy has posted seven straight years of growth, outstripping all other major European economic powers.

It would appear, then, that things are quite rosy under the Conservatives' green-thumb reforms; however, there is a significant segment of the population that is not at all pleased with the state of the nation. While Thatcherism has proved a boon to New-Age industries like micro-engineering, telecommunications, and especially financial services, it has been anathema to the older, already–declining industries like mining, shipbuilding, agriculture, and heavy manufacturing—all traditionally sources of income for the blue-collar classes, and all traditionally centered in northern cities like Liverpool, Leeds, Glasgow, depressed areas far removed from the economic upsurge being enjoyed in the Southeast. These regional industries, traditionally the heart and guts of the British economy, feel they are being made to bear an unfair share of the cost of Britain's recent fiscal growth, while the Southeast reaps all the rewards.

Unemployment for the nation as a whole is high, 11 percent; but in the Southeast it is closer to 6 percent, whereas in Wales it is 12.8, in Scotland 13.5, and in Northern Ireland a miserable 18.3 percent. While Mrs. Thatcher won a comfortable majority in the government's most recent vote of confidence, she was overwhelmingly defeated in the industrial belts of northern England and Scotland and in the mining regions of Wales.

Mrs. Thatcher's job is not an easy one, for reasons very much tied to the original proposition that Britons don't like things foreign and they don't like change. The Conservatives inherited a fiscal morass of overbloated government and managerial ineptitude from the Labour Party ten years ago. The Conservatives believed that the British economy was collapsing under the double burden of 19th-century antiquated industrialism and a postwar Socialist welfare state. Drastic and speedy changes were needed to resuscitate the economy. High-tech and business-service industries were successfully operating in other countries, so foreign techniques, ideas, and personnel were imported and installed in and around London to create a community sincerely devoted to capital gains.

But elsewhere in the country, the citizenry feel they have been duped into making sacrifices for the common good when in reality they were supporting a small, albeit growing, group of Southeastern entrepreneurs. Thus Yorkshiremen and Border Scots, who've not seen eye-to-eye on anything for millennia, suddenly find themselves united in their battle against the new economics. Organizations as diverse as the coal miners' union (crippled by a horrific strike in 1984–85) and Oxford University (being asked by alumnus Margaret Thatcher to justify in economic terms the practical use of studying Jane Austen, cosmology, or Sanskrit) suddenly find themselves facing the same foe in a fight for survival.

The working classes are not the only ones upon whom Thatcherism has had a dramatic effect; the upper classes are also experiencing far-reaching changes. Travelers from more recently developed democracies are often caught off-guard by the extent and tenacity of class distinction in Britain. Unlike those of non-monarchic new-world nations, Britain's is an aristocracy of blood; so no matter how hard one works, no matter how rich one becomes thereby, one will never be a member of the nobility. In Britain, if you weren't born an aristocrat, with very few exceptions you cannot become one.

In many other developed nations, the upper classes are made up of the rich and powerful, not of the ancient and noble. But in one of the more salient ironies of the Conservatives' free-for-all attitude toward new entrepreneurialism, the nation's attention and fascination are slipping away from aristocratic suspects, and focusing instead on the movers and shakers bustling about the City of London and other expanding financial centers. This development is ironic because Thatcher's Conservative Party has long been a bastion of old-money, old-family British tradition. The public still overwhelmingly approves of the Queen. The revival of a serious work ethic, prodded by the constant encouragement of Mrs. Thatcher, however, has caused many Britons to consider some difficult questions about the purpose and expense of supporting a burgeoning monarchy, questions that would have heretofore been unthinkable. On the one hand, the country obviously takes great pride in the Queen, and she raises morale and money for worthy causes. She maintains a busy schedule of queenly duties and travels extensively as a result. On the other hand, Elizabeth Windsor is easily the wealthiest woman in the kingdom and, in fact, in the world. She and her family own by far the most and the most valuable real estate in Britain. On top of this she receives an annual sum (which amounted to £4.3 million in 1987) from the state to cover expenses incurred from official duties—upkeep on the royal yacht, planes, trains, palaces, and the requisite staff for these. This sets up a bit of a dilemma in the minds of some Britons: The Conservative government is assiduously dismantling the welfare state, arguing that every able-bodied man and woman should get out to work and help themselves instead of relying on the government to support them while they live needlessly at the nation's expense. At the opposite end of the spectrum, despite Margaret's occassional spats with Elizabeth, the Conservative government is also a staunch supporter of the Royals, who have more money than God and who draw fat salaries from the national coffers as well—every quid of it tax free.

All of these questions are bandied back and forth ad infinitum in the national press, which in Britain is more varied in its opinions and more strident in expressing its opinions than anywhere else in the world. The national press in Britain is quite firmly entrenched in London. In Britain you are what you read and vice versa: If you are conservative, you read *The Times* and *The Financial Times* daily; you read *The Economist* and *Private Eye* weekly; you read *Harpers & Queen* and possibly *The Tattler* monthly. If you are liberal, you read *The Guardian* and/or *The Independent* daily, *The Observer* and *The New Statesman* weekly, and you might have a look at *The Face* or *Arena* each month.

If all this talk of politics and economics, of coal miners and royals seems confusing, that's because it is—very confusing, complex, and complicated. It is not possible to give these important and intricate matters a complete going-over in a brief essay; the best way for you to get a clear picture of the country to which you are headed is to do some reading. Aside from the popular press, you can trot over to your library and pull some books off the British history and literature shelves— many stories of the former are hardly less fantastic than those of the latter.

Another great way to immerse yourself in the British scene before you leave home is to rent a couple of British films for the VCR each week. This way you can get some background information, history, and sociology—and have fun while you're about it.

The very best way to understand the current scene in Great Britain is to come and see for yourself. This is obvious, of

course, but what might not be so obvious are the ways of seeing Britain while you are here. The primary source is the people. Talk to your host at the country house hotel, have a chat
with the gas attendant while he's filling up your tank, solicit
a bobby's opinion on Mrs. Thatcher, find out what your rail
companions do in their spare time. The British by and large
are a friendly, chatty bunch; they have strong convictions and
are usually delighted to expound upon them. Another strategy
is to try to see and do things that natives (as opposed to tourists) see and do. Look up long-lost friends you have in the
country, or get names of British friends and relatives from
your friends at home. Watch the telly and listen to the radio
whenever you can. They're different from TV and radio at
home—especially if home is North America. And different
from what you'd expect: It is not all London Philharmonic and
Shakespeare and *Masterpiece Theatre*. There are inane chat
shows, lugubrious soap operas, dull documentaries—the bad
stuff is as important to know about as the good.

This is a terrific time to visit Britain. It is a time of great
change in a nation neither accustomed nor naturally disposed
to such things. The atmosphere has an electricity and the people a vitality not seen on these shores since the lusty days
of the first Queen Elizabeth—days when even the sleepiest
shire was infected by the scent of the winds of change in the
air, and by the belief that they were living at the brink of a
new age in Britain's long and illustrious life.

# A Glossary of British Terms

Many of the words listed here under the "King's" English are not to be found in the OED (the *Oxford English Dictionary,* arbitrator of such things) because many of them are slang—often derived from cockney expressions. We have included them so that visitors will know the correct terms and won't "get the mickey taken out of them" by the locals.

| The "King's" English | North American English |
|---|---|
| ta, cheers | thanks, good-bye |
| chuffed | pleased, happy |
| biscuit or bickie | cookie |
| sacked | fired from work |
| chips | french fries |
| crisps | potato chips |
| cuppa | cup of (usually tea or coffee) |
| loo | toilet |
| copper | cop (police officer) or penny |
| dodgy | dubious |
| flat | apartment |
| knackered | exhausted |
| kip, kipping | sleep, sleeping |
| knickers | undies |
| lorry | truck |
| bonnet | hood of a car |
| boot | trunk of a car |
| return | round-trip ticket |
| single | one-way ticket |
| quid (*never* plural—"two quid") | pound or pounds (sterling) |
| queue, jumping the queue | line (and to wait in line), cutting in line |
| pissed | drunk |
| to take the piss/mickey out of | to tease or make fun of |
| fag | cigarette |
| jumper | sweater (usually a pullover) |
| jumble sale | rummage sale, garage sale |
| telly | TV |
| coach | bus |
| subway | underground passageway |
| bangers | sausages |
| spuds, tatties | potatoes |
| roundabout | traffic circle |
| stalls | orchestra seats |
| jar | glass (usually a pint) of beer |

| The "King's" English | North American English |
| --- | --- |
| hire/let | rent |
| autumn | (never fall) |
| football | soccer |
| American football | football |
| bike | motorcycle |
| push bike | bicycle |

# 2

# ORIENTING YOURSELF

We've all seen the map of Britain—its elongated, bottom-heavy silhouette—since childhood. Not surprisingly, the country's larger-than-life role in creating the history of other English-speaking nations often conveys the impression that the island is considerably larger in size than is, in fact, the case. Britain encompasses some 88,700 square miles, approximately six hundred miles from north to south and three hundred miles at its widest point east to west; and since it is an island, you will never find yourself more than 75 miles from the sea.

Great Britain comprises three distinct entities: England, Wales, and Scotland. The United Kingdom includes these three and Northern Ireland (which we do not include in this volume) as well. England is, of course, the biggest of the three lands of Great Britain, encompassing about fifty thousand square miles. Wales is a large peninsula jutting out from about one-third to one-half of the way up the west coast of the island and covering about eight thousand square miles. Scotland extends from the northern boundary of England upward to the northern extremity of the island and thence to the Orkney and Shetland islands, the latter of which are at the same latitude as Bergen, Norway. Scotland includes over thirty thousand square miles—approximately three-fifths of the area of England.

Great Britain is divided into 66 counties (referred to as regions in Scotland). There are 46 counties in England (including Greater London and Greater Manchester), 8 counties in Wales, and 12 regions in Scotland. We have apportioned these counties among 12 regional chapters, with an accompanying chapter devoted exclusively to London. These regions hang together geographically, geologically, socially, and historically, and they can be taken as discrete entities unto themselves.

## GREAT BRITAIN

miles 50
kilometers 120

N

Indeed, we would encourage you to pick one, or at the most two, of these regions to explore in a fortnight's holiday. Although, as mentioned, Britain is not a particularly large country, especially when compared to giants like the United States and Australia, its history and culture are so rich and dense that each area is rife with gardens, galleries, stately homes, restaurants, theaters, museums, national parks, sports, hotels . . . Naturally, those of you who have not visited Britain before have a long list of sights you've been dying to see for decades. However, if you try to cram London, Stratford, the Yorkshire moors, and the Outer Hebrides all into one visit, you are going to spend entirely too much time on trains, in cars, and packing and unpacking your baggage to appreciate the elegant and subtle intricacies of Great Britain.

Do keep in mind, though, that with the exception of the farthest reaches of Scotland, everything in Britain is an easy day trip from London. So many travelers make the mistake of restricting themselves to the capital with perhaps a quick junket to Windsor or Oxford. Long-distance traveling in Britain is simple and comfortable, and it is most enjoyable by high-speed rail service. We do urge you to set out for the hinter-lands—the Highlands or Cornwall or Mount Snowdon—though all would be too much for one trip. Go to Cornwall and spend your vacation exploring the whole of the West Country from Bristol to Land's End. By so doing, you will have the opportunity to explore the region, to talk to the local folk, to sample the local brew and pastries, to generally get a real sense of place; to relax, enjoy yourselves, and feel like you are beginning to understand what the land and its folk are all about.

When traveling to the more out-of-the-way regions, remember that many places (sights, shops, hotels) are open seasonally—usually April through October. If you plan to tour the countryside out-of-season, check to be sure the place you want to visit will be open.

To give you an idea of roughly where each of our designated regions is located and what it encompasses, we have devised a brief sketch of each to help you decide which might tickle your fancy:

## THAMES, OXFORD, AND THE COTSWOLDS

This area includes the counties of Bedfordshire, Berkshire, Buckinghamshire, Gloucestershire, Hertfordshire, Oxfordshire, and Warwickshire. This is perhaps the most oft-traveled of any region in Britain for several reasons, not the least of which is its proximity to London. Travel westward through the Thames Valley to visit at Windsor, out-of-town address for the Queen et. al., and the Chiltern Hills, among which are some important stately homes. Continue west and make your way to Oxford, whose medieval university has churned out luminary Brits from Chris Wren to Maggie Thatcher. Oxford is on the eastern fringes of the Cotswold Hills, which feature the kind of neat little thatched villages one thinks of as quintessentially English. The Cotswolds include Stratford-upon-Avon (sadly no longer quaint), birthplace of the bard, mecca for bardophiles, and still a most worthy destination—including a must-to-include evening at the Royal Shakespeare Company's theater(s).

## THE SOUTHEAST

This area includes the counties of Hampshire, Kent, East Sussex, West Sussex, and Surrey. As with the previous region, the Southeast is an extremely popular destination: It is close to London yet proffers some lovely countryside and seaside. Kent is in the extreme east on the Strait of Dover, practically within spitting distance of France, which accounted for its attractiveness to foreign invaders in days gone by. Here is Canterbury, whose cathedral is headquarters for the Church of England; southwest are East and West Sussex. In this pair you'll find another great cathedral city, Chichester, as well as the crowded, classic seaside town of Brighton. Continuing west you'll come upon Winchester, whose cathedral once presided over the capital city of England. Along the coast are the towns of Portsmouth and Southampton, busy shipping centers and best skirted for the more tranquil streets of Lymington, or take a ferry across to the Isle of Wight.

## THE WEST COUNTRY

This area includes the counties of Avon, Cornwall, Devon, Dorset, Somerset, and Wiltshire. This region covers a lot of ground and includes a long list and wide variety of sights. Its history includes the magnificent Bronze-Age circles at Stonehenge and Avebury, connections with King Arthur, and a wild rugged coast long- (and currently) favored by smugglers. In the West Country you'll be treated to the Georgian streets of Bath—Britain's most perfect Regency resort—the ancient seafaring town of Bristol, Salisbury Cathedral, the lonely hills of Dartmoor, the populous, luxurious towns of the English Riviera, and the unspoiled, cliff-strewn coast of Cornwall. Here is the place for Devonshire cream with your tea, Cornish pasties, and Somerset cider—with all this to explore, you'll appreciate the hearty fare.

## EAST ANGLIA

This area includes the counties of Cambridgeshire, Essex, Norfolk, and Suffolk. Technically, East Anglia begins in London's East End and travels northeast through the low hills of Essex and the fens of Cambridgeshire to the coastal plain of the Wash and the Norfolk Broads. Here you can thrill to the horse races at Newmarket, and punt your way around the ancient university at Cambridge, or toast the day's sport with any of a slew of real ales for which East Anglia is justly famous. After contemplative Cambridge, continue to Ely and Peterborough, whose cathedrals are an eyeful; then on to Newmarket and Bury St.-Edmunds, which exhibit a range of English architecture from the Middle Ages to the Victorians. Norwich, once the second city of England, retains much of her medieval charm and is a base for visits to the undercrowded Edwardian resort towns of the East Anglian coast.

## EAST MIDLANDS

This area includes the counties of Derbyshire, Leicestershire, Lincolnshire, Northamptonshire, and Nottinghamshire. The Pennine Hills run down through the heart of the East Midlands and include the Peak District, England's first and one of her loveliest national parks. The primary towns are Lincoln and Nottingham, the former a Roman city whose Norman castle and cathedral are among the nation's finest, the latter, of course, of Robin Hood fame with its own castle and brewery-pub set in a cave. On the must-see list are the spa and seaside towns of Buxton in the grand Edwardian manner; Matlock and Matlock Bath, favorites of Lord Byron; Mablethorpe and Skegness, blue-collar beaches with all the usual trimmings. Finally, there is Chatsworth House, 17th-century home of the dukes of Devonshire, with its lavish furniture and art collection and Capability Brown park and gardens.

## WEST MIDLANDS

This area includes the counties of Hereford and Worcester, Shropshire, Staffordshire, and West Midlands. Often overlooked because of its tradition of factories, highways, and economic decline, the West Midlands offer, in addition to these unpleasantnesses, the glorious scenery of Shropshire's "blue remembered hills," the porcelain of Stoke-on-Trent, the ale of Burton-upon-Trent, the Malvern Hills, and quaint, half-timbered towns aplenty. After exploring the important industrial sights—a must for understanding the Industrial Revolution that spread from here around the world—you might like to base yourself in the old market town of Hereford, at Malvern—in the shadow of her spectacular hills—or in Shrewsbury—everything you'd want in a quiet conglomeration of cottages. Add to this the excitement of Birmingham, the bargain-hunting for Wedgewood, the cathedral at Lichfield, and the castles of Shropshire, and you'll be completely taken in by the variety and vitality of the region.

## THE NORTHWEST

This area includes the counties of Cheshire, Greater Manchester, Lancashire, and Merseyside. The Northwest manages to include two of Britain's largest urban areas and some of her prettiest villages and lushest farm country. Liverpool, whose 19th-century fortunes were made on the cotton trade, is now world famous as birthplace of the Beatles, and its docks district is being renovated with shops and museums. Manchester has always been England's second city, culturally, with a host of galleries, theaters, and concerts. The clubs of both cities remain at the forefront of the rock and roll scene. Tudor-timbered Chester is a city oozing charm and shopping possibilities, and the Cheshire plain is the home of neat farms and dairy cows. North of Liverpool is the giddy, gaudy seaside resort of Blackpool, and just east of it are the hills of Lancashire, including the splendid Forest of Bowland and the Ribble Valley.

## THE NORTH COUNTRY

This area includes the English counties of Cleveland, Durham, Humberside, North Yorkshire, Northumberland, South Yorkshire, Tyne and Wear, and West Yorkshire. The industrial towns of the Northeast are picking themselves up, dusting themselves off, and installing boutiques and wine bars in neglected warehouses. Beyond the cities of Leeds, Newcastle, and Sheffield (perfect for cutlery bargain-hunters) is the majestic country of the Yorkshire moors, celebrated by the Brontës and James Herriot. There are four national parks here, complemented by man-made beauty in the perfectly preserved medieval town of York, the cathedral at Durham, the Roman Hadrian's Wall, and the tiny island of Lindisfarne, famous for its Gospel—one of the most important documents from the eighth century.

## CUMBRIA: THE LAKES

This area includes the county of Cumbria. The area known familiarly as "The Lakes" is actually the central portion of the county of Cumbria, but, not surprisingly, the county merits its own chapter owing to its extraordinary natural beauty and the poetic and artistic expression this beauty has inspired. The Lakes' most illustrious citizen was poet William Wordsworth, who was responsible for 19th-century English romanticism. Many of the sights here are connected to his life, most of which was spent here. There are (delightfully) no major cities in Cumbria, only charming large towns such as Winder-

mere right on the lake, Kendal to the south, and Carlisle—
with its splended cathedral and Roman associations north at
the Scottish border. The primary reason to come here, however, is to walk, hike, drive, pony trek through the fells and
pikes, which slide downward through forests (most of the
county is national park) into the silvery lakes.

## WALES

This area includes the counties of Clwyd; Dyfed; Mid, South,
and West Glamorgan; Gwent, Gwynedd and Powys. Despite
the mining and manufacturing for which the country until recently was famous, most of the land is given over to forests
and sheep fields. In the south and west is a marvelous coast
alternating sandy beaches with rocky cliffs capped with heather and gorse. In the southeast are the Usk and Wye river valleys, lined with forests. Central are the Brecon Beacons and
the Black Mountains, full of shepherds and the highest concentration of castle ruins in Britain. Northwest is Snowdonia,
whose magical name only hints at the intoxicating beauty of
the mountains, waterfalls, and wild deer that await here. All
this, and a people whose language is as lilting, ancient, and
proud as they are.

## THE SCOTTISH LOWLANDS

This area includes the regions of Borders, Central, Dumfries
and Galloway, Fife, Lothian, Strathclyde, and Tayside. Although this part of Scotland accounts for less than half of her
land mass, it contains over 75 percent of her population—
centered in an east–west belt connecting Edinburgh and Glasgow, Scotland's two most important cities. These two cities,
longtime rivals separated by a mere forty miles, are blooming
cultural centers. Edinburgh, stately and serene, is a combination of medieval castle town and Georgian city. Glasgow,
down-to-earth and amiable, is a Victorian burg enjoying Britain's most remarkable renaissance. South of these are the low
hills of the border country, favorite of sportsmen who come
for the shooting and fishing. North of these is Stirling, with
its own hill-mounted castle, the Trossach mountains—gentler
than their northern neighbors—and, of course, St. Andrew's,
whose links courses have infuriated the keenest pro since golf
began here five hundred years ago.

## THE SCOTTISH HIGHLANDS AND ISLANDS

This area includes the regions of Grampian, Highland, the
Orkney Islands, the Shetland Islands, and the Western Isles.
Although the farther-away reaches covered by this chapter
require a little extra effort to get to, the time and energy is

well worth it. Quite simply, the Highlands and islands of Scotland are among the most beautiful places on earth and one of the last unspoiled regions in all of Europe. The people are delightful, the food is fantastic, the peace is profound. Royal Deeside—favorite retreat of the Windsors—follows the course of the river Dee through the mountains to the city of Aberdeen, rife with flowers, art, restaurants, beaches, and golf courses. Northwest through the Grampian Mountains travel the whisky trail, along which you can watch the production of the world's finest fiery spirits—and sample the results. Westward from Inverness is Loch Ness, home of the world's most elusive celebrity; then on into the Highland region, at the western reaches of which are the islands comprising the Inner and Outer Hebrides. The whole of northwest Scotland offers some of the most awesome scenery you will ever experience: high scarred crags crashing down into glassy lochs and islands rising dream-like out of the misty sea.

# 3

## PRIORITIES

Undoubtedly, as you hoist this volume, packed with intriguing possibilities, a serious dilemma furrows your brow: How to select the most important items from among the many choices clamoring for your attention. Among the must-see sights of Britain, there is not an embarrassment of riches, it's more like an avalanche. This list could easily be three or four times as long as it is. Compiling a compendium of superlatives in Britain is tricky business: possibilities are as thick as sheep on a Welsh hillside, and no matter how one agonizes over which to keep and which to cut, somebody's favorite is bound to fall into the latter category.

Nevertheless, we have narrowed the immense roster of candidates down to twenty-odd items. These places are, because of their scenic, historic, or cultural import, integral elements of Great Britain, and should be included whenever possible in the program of anybody traveling through the country. The list is in alphabetical order, including the title of the chapter in which you will find a more detailed description, a brief synopsis of each sight, the amount of time you should expect to devote to exploring (this, of course, is our best approximation and will undoubtedly vary from person to person), and a few suggestions of what other interesting things there are to see nearby.

As we continually stress, don't overload your holiday (or your brain cells) with 15 different red-letter sights at one go. Rather, having chosen which region or regions of Great Britain you wish to explore on your journey, consult this list to determine which of the country's most important places fall within the boundaries of your travels. When you are in the neighborhood, here are the places you must see:

### BATH
(The West Country)
From Roman baths to Regency spa, the town has always attracted a fashionable, upscale clientele. Its streets are Geor-

gian, graceful, and of perfect proportions. The city has several museums, top-notch restaurants, and shopping to inspire any latter-day Beau Brummel. Take about two days.

**Nearby:** Bristol, Glastonbury, Wells Cathedral.

## BEATLES TOUR OF LIVERPOOL
(The Northwest)

The Fab Four's favorite haunts are here: Take in the "scouser" scene along Matthew Street where The Cavern once stood, visit the Odeon Cinema where they played bigger gigs, and enjoy a jar at the Grapes or Ye Crack like the lads used to do. Half to a whole day depending on how big a fan you are.

**Nearby:** the Walker Art Gallery, Mersey (boat) cruise, Canning and Albert Docks.

## BRIGHTON
(The Southeast)

From sovereigns to shopkeepers, the natives have always had a special place in their hearts for this quintessential seaside resort. Everything you'd expect is here, from fish-and-chips stands to luxury hotels. Along with the roller coasters you'll find the Royal Pavillion, perhaps the most perfect example of 19th-century Britain's passion for lavish excess. One to two days.

**Nearby:** Arundel, Chichester, Portsmouth.

## CAMBRIDGE
(East Anglia)

A 12th-century university town through which flows the shy, sluggish river Cam—perfect for the novice punter. Treasures you'll find along the city's stone streets are King's College Chapel, the Fitzwilliam Museum, and the Wren Library. One or two days.

**Nearby:** Ely Cathedral, Newmarket, St. Ives.

## CANTERBURY
(The Southeast)

Since that fateful slaying of Saint Thomas à Becket in 1170, pilgrims have been wending their way to Canterbury to have a look at the cathedral where it all happened and at the town that is presently the capital city of the Church of England (Anglican) and home of its primate, Robert Runcie, Archbishop of Canterbury. One day.

**Nearby:** Dover, Margate, and Ramsgate (none are highly recommended).

## CORNWALL, THE NORTH COAST
(The West Country)

Beginning in the town of Bude and heading west to Land's End, northern Cornwall is blessed with a spectacular coastline of high, sheer-faced cliffs, tiny fishing villages, isolated beaches. Most of the land, thankfully, is protected under the National Trust. Two days.

**Nearby:** Bodmin Moor, Land's End, Tintagel.

## COTSWOLD TOWNS
(Thames, Oxford, and the Cotswolds)

When you close your eyes and dream of the perfect English village—geese waddling beside the mill stream, thatched cottages, roses twining around the doorway—you've transported yourself to Burford or Snowshill or one of the Slaughters. The Cotswold Hills enfold the tiny, picture-perfect towns you yearn to find in the English countryside. Two to three days.

**Nearby:** Bath, Oxford, Stratford-upon-Avon.

## EDINBURGH
(The Scottish Lowlands)

Illustrious, exquisite—superlative adjectives tumble out when describing this northern city—half medieval, half Georgian, and all set on high hills overlooking the Firth of Forth. Edinburgh boasts a catalogue nonpareil of museums, theaters, fine restaurants, and chic shops. Of special interest is the International Arts Festival held each August. Three days.

**Nearby:** Glasgow, St. Andrews, Stirling.

## FELL WALKING
(Cumbria: the Lakes)

Not exactly a place, more an activity, a national passion, in fact. Who could blame the Brits for enjoying the ancient hills, crystal glacier lakes beneath, to be found in the central regions of Cumbria? Where and how far to walk is very much a matter of taste and ability, but by all means plan to hike these fells celebrated by Britain's greatest poets and artists. Two to three days.

**Nearby:** Carlisle and Hadrian's Wall, Levens Hall, the Wordsworth Properties.

## GLASGOW
(The Scottish Lowlands)

Scotland's largest and most varied city offers great art and food, and boasts a most urbane, yet sociable citizenry. Charles Rennie Mackintosh, who is to Glasgow what Gaudí is to Barcelona, has left his Art-Nouveau mark all over town. Two to three days.

**Nearby:** Edinburgh, the southern Highlands and islands, the Trossachs.

## GOWER-PEMBROKESHIRE COAST
(Wales)

From the town of Tenby around to Pembroke, this peninsula is a mecca for writers and walkers. The coastal footpath is rarely more than a few dozen yards from the water's edge, but the sea most probably is fifty feet below, pounding against

the towering cliffs. Good hotels and restaurants abound. One
to two days.
**Nearby:** St. David's, Swansea, Tenby.

## HADRIAN'S WALL
(Cumbria: the Lakes, The North Country)
What began as an earthenwork barrier denoting the northern
boundary of the Roman Empire eventually grew into a 15–foot
stone wall stretching 76 miles from Newcastle to Carlisle.
Built between A.D. 120 and 130 much of the wall and its string
of forts is still visible and visitable. Half day.
**Nearby:** Carlisle, Durham, Newcastle-upon-Tyne.

## HIGHLANDS AND ISLANDS OF NORTHWEST SCOTLAND
(The Scottish Highlands and Islands)
Not a single sight, this is a region, and a very large region
at that. It offers eye-popping, jaw-dropping scenery and a
chance to really escape from the rest of the world. The High-
landers are delightful, as are their hotels and restaurants.
Three days.
**Nearby:** (within the region) Ben Nevis, Inverewe Gardens,
Isle of Skye.

## LONDON
(London)
The Thames, the Tower, the theatre, the pomp, the pubs. You
hardly need to be told. See London chapter for in-town priori-
ties. Five days at least.
**Nearby:** Brighton, Greenwich, Windsor, and Eton.

## MALVERN HILLS
(The West Midlands)
Topographical muse to Edward Elgar, the hills and glens
coursed by cattle and speckled with neat villages is a perfect
place to achieve a calm and tranquil state. Less crowded than
the Cotswolds, these hills offer no less charm and no fewer
good hotels and restaurants—just fewer tourists. One to two
days.
**Nearby:** Cheltenham, Hereford, Ross-on-Wye.

## OXFORD
(Thames, Oxford, and the Cotswolds)
A graceful and noble city, Oxford has just about everything:
ancient university, fine museums, concerts and theater, excel-
lent restaurants. Rent a bike or stroll through the tiny streets
redolent with history and romance. Two days.
**Nearby:** Blenheim Palace, the Cotswolds, Stratford-upon-
Avon.

## PEAK DISTRICT
(East Midlands)
England's oldest national park is set in the Pennine Hills of Derbyshire. The Peaks cater to a wide variety of clientele: for the archeologist there are many Stone Age remains, for the speleologist there are caves a-plenty, for the hiker walks abound for all levels of ability, for the art and architectural historian there are five stately homes. Two days.
**Nearby:** Chatsworth (within the Peak District), Stoke-on-Trent, Nottingham.

## ROYAL DEESIDE AND ABERDEEN
(The Scottish Highlands and Islands)
The valley of the river Dee runs down from the mountains to the city of Aberdeen. In between are great fishing, hunting, golf, galleries, the best of Scottish food and lodging, and a half-dozen castles including the Windsors' favorite, Balmoral. Two days.
**Nearby:** Aberdeen Art Gallery, Craigievar and Crathes castles, Malt Whisky Trail.

## SNOWDONIA NATIONAL PARK
(Wales)
Land of druids, knights, and fairies; you can practically picture Merlin wandering about the mist-hung forests of northern Wales. Mount Snowdon is a favorite of serious hikers, and the little villages that ring the park offer cozy pubs and warm beds for the all-day climber. One day.
**Nearby:** Caernarfon Castle, Conwy and Llandudno, Portmeirion.

## STONEHENGE-AVEBURY-SALISBURY
(The West Country)
These three are close enough together that a tour combining them is simple and obvious. Stonehenge and Avebury are mammoth Bronze Age circles, still the site of midnight rituals at the equinox and solstice. Salisbury town, unremarkable in itself, is the home of the great cathedral—try to fit it all in one snapshot—celebrated by numerous Constable studies. A day and a half.
**Nearby:** Bournemouth, Lyme Regis, Shaftesbury.

## STRATFORD-UPON-AVON
(Thames, Oxford, and the Cotswolds)
The town, regrettably crowded and commercial, is still well worth a visit to see the five properties of the Shakespeare Trust and, of course, to spend an evening at one of the Royal Shakespeare Company's theaters.
**Nearby:** Cotswolds, Kenilworth and Warwick castles.

## THE WORDSWORTH PROPERTIES
(Cumbria: the Lakes)

It is impossible to gauge the extent to which poet William Wordsworth's philosophy has informed English (and English-speaking) culture. And it's impossible to understand the man without visiting his stomping grounds—from his birthplace at Cockermouth to his school at Hawkshead to his homes at Dove Cottage and Rydal Mount. Two days.

**Nearby:** Carlisle, Lake District National Park (throughout the region), Steam Yacht Cruises.

## YORK
(The North Country)

In any but an alphabetical list, York would appear at the top, not the bottom. This is one of the best-preserved medieval cities in Europe. England's biggest and best Gothic cathedral, old city wall, half-dozen museums, a slew of hostel and eateries—York really is a city perfect for soaking in the medieval. Two days.

**Nearby:** Castle Howard, Marston Moor Battle site, Ripon.

# Priority Hotels

As with sights, we have selected a couple dozen hotels that are nonpareil. These are those establishments, among the many we have sampled and recommended throughout this guide that are truly outstanding and truly worth the trip and worth the (unfortunately often hefty) price. By region they are:

## Thames, Oxford, and The Cotswolds
**Buckland Manor,** Buckland
**Le Manoir aux Quat' Saisons,** Great Milton

## The Southeast
**Chewton Glen,** New Milton
**The Grand Hotel,** Brighton
**The Mermaid Inn,** Rye
**The Spread Eagle Hotel,** Midhurst

## The West Country
**The George Hotel,** Hatherleigh
**Plumber Manor,** Sturminster Newton
**The Priory Hotel,** Bath

## East Anglia
**The Angel Inn,** Bury St.-Edmonds

## East Midlands
**The Palace Hotel,** Buxton
**The White Hart Hotel,** Lincoln

## The West Midlands
**The Lion Hotel,** Shrewsbury

## The North Country
**Lord Crewe Arms,** Blanchland
**Middlethorpe Hall,** York

## The Northwest
**Chester Grosvenor Hotel,** Chester

## Cumbria: The Lakes
**Farlam Hall,** Brampton
**Sharrow Bay,** Ullswater

## Wales
**Bodysgallen Hall Hotel,** Llandudno
**Hotel Portmeirion,** Portmeirion
**St. Tudno,** Llandudno
**Waterwyneh House,** Tenly

## The Scottish Lowlands
**Auchterarder House,** Auchterarder
**One Devonshire Gardens,** Glasgow

The Peat Inn, Peat Inn

## The Scottish Highlands and Islands
The Airds Hotel, Port Appin
Alt-na-harrie Inn, Ullapool
Culloden House, Inverness
Inverlochy Castle, Fort William

# 4

# LONDON

London is the indisputable hub of its country. Government is here, fashion is here, the Queen is here, the media are here, finance is here, art and music are here. If any young Briton has a notion of making it in the world, he or she must make the inevitable pilgrimage to the capital to seek his or her fortune. It is this convergence of ideas and temperaments that makes London so lively—and so volatile.

As with the opportunists of the nation, so too the opportunists of the (former) Empire have immigrated to the capital in search of employment. Black people from Africa and the West Indies, brown people from India and Pakistan, tawny people from China and Southeast Asia now make up (unfortunately) much of the impoverished classes of London, living in neighborhoods, like the East End and Brixton, once occupied by their predecessors in disenfranchisement, the Jews and the Irish. But the situation is not uniformly depressing; on the contrary, they add to the rich spectrum of cross-cultural cuisine, fashion, music, and philosophy that makes London truly a cosmopolitan city. London is long-practiced in the art of accommodating foreigners, either as visitors or as eventual citizens. London, above all other cities, is supremely complacent about the movements of the populace, be they natives or tourists. The strongest impression many people take away from London is its pleasantness, its amiability, and, oddly enough for the world's largest city by area, its manageability. Much of the center of town is still dominated by four- or five-story buildings built a hundred or more years ago. The vast expanses of the Royal Parks, Regent's Park, Holland Park, and Hampstead Heath provide a verdant sanctuary for birds, bunnies, squirrels, and, of course, the citizenry who flock thither in droves to sun, chatter, row, ride, bike, court, fly kites, play tennis, picnic, and generally disport themselves about the greensward. And the Thames provides a liquid link to the outside world and to the city's past.

Another important factor contributing to the humanness of the city is indeed her human element. Londoners, for the most part, aren't at all the archetypal imperious upper-class twits caricatured in the mind of the rest of the world. The average Londoner is as down-to-earth and sociable (not to be confused with social) as you please. If you pull up next to one in a pub, he or she will most likely favor you with all kinds of suggestions of where to go, what to do, what to think about the prime minister; hold forth with a history lesson, a literary survey, several personal anecdotes; and manage to buy you a pint of beer before you can get your pounds out of your pocket in protest. As mentioned, many if not most Londoners were not born here, and consequently even those with an obviously extra-Britannic accent are simpatico with strangers.

We have divided up London into nine areas. These follow roughly the traditional lines of the towns that have been incorporated into the city of London.

Try as much as possible to do your touring neighborhood by neighborhood so you can get the feel of intellectual St. Marylebone and Bloomsbury or official Westminster and Whitehall or residential South Kensington, Belgravia, and Chelsea. You could easily spend your entire visit exploring the City of London alone and never set foot in another district. So much the better. London is not a city known quickly or easily. It takes time and effort but will reward the traveler whose energy and enthusiasm allow for an intelligent, appreciative approach.

The logical place to begin is **the City,** where the city itself began. Here you'll find the Tower, remnants of the London Wall that surrounded what was then the entirety of Londinium, St. Paul's, and a score of Christopher Wren–designed churches erected after the Great Fire. The City is also London's business address, where you'll find the Stock Exchange, the Bank of England, and all the important financial institutions of Britain.

Next is **Westminster and Whitehall.** Although the City of Westminster is a clearly defined area in London, it is too large and unwieldy to consider touring in a day or two, so our definition of Westminster is the area bounded by Buckingham Palace, the Houses of Parliament, and Trafalgar Square, where most of the country's governmental business is attended to.

**Soho and Covent Garden** are the sensuous and artistic hubs of London where you'll find most of her important commercial theaters, smart shops, and important galleries.

**Belgravia, South Kensington, and Chelsea** are the lands between park and river chosen by Londoners who like green grass and "blue" waters and who can afford to pay for such luxury. Shops and galleries have followed this sybaritic crew here and cater to their costly, capricious needs.

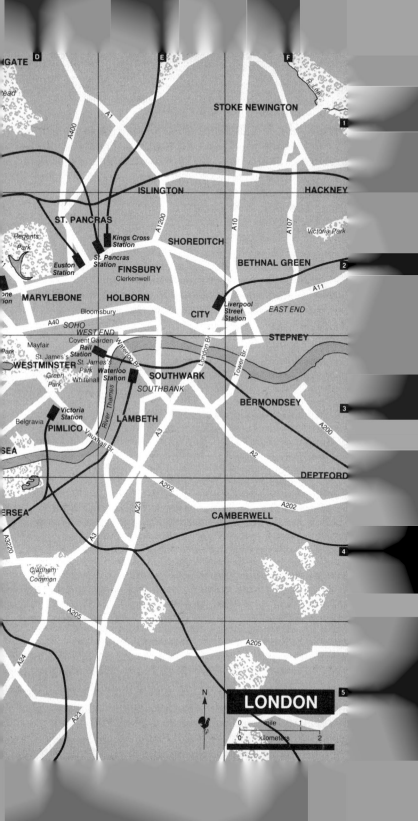

**St. James's, Mayfair, and the Parks** are the areas wherein you'll discover the London repositories of upper-class distinction: elegant architecture, consciously conservative shops, and the quiet assuredness only old (ancient) money can bestow.

**Bloomsbury and Marylebone** are the provinces of lawyers and professors, writers and students. The presence of London University, the British Museum, and several small but important art collections perpetuate the intellectual engagement of this north-central sector.

**Clerkenwell and Holborn** are nuts-and-bolts, no-nonsense neighborhoods full of outspoken tradition, from the monks of the Charterhouse and the knights of the Order of St. John to the lawyers of Gray's Inn to the orations of Marx. Through the years this area has produced a succession of people with a lot to say—and a lot to answer for.

**Kensington** makes up the western reaches of central London and has usually served as a relatively rural outpost, with pretty Holland Park, antiques shops along Church Street and Portobello Road, several period houses and one palace open to the public.

The **South Bank** cuts across the lower margins of the River Thames and is a good place to see high-minded art at the South Bank Centre or low-brow living at the Thames-side pubs and along working-class streets.

## ❦ HOTELS

Finding a good hotel is an especially tricky business in a city: There are thousands, and yet, despite the competition, prices are twice what they are in the country. And ultimately the plethora of choices becomes more of a nuisance than anything else—after all, do you really have time to sift through a couple thousand brochures or do several hundred on-site inspections? So we have worn out countless pairs of shoes pounding endless miles of pavement, examining each property with a keen and critical eye. We sifted through the masses, adding, subtracting, refining the list down to a couple dozen choices to make the decision just a little bit easier for you.

Despite the number of hotels in London, things get crowded, especially during the busy summer season and around holidays like Christmas and Easter. Do plan to make reservations as far in advance as possible (the hotels we've selected are very popular and fill up fast) so you won't be disappointed.

If you would like information and listings of hotels other than those we've selected, write (at least six weeks in advance) to the **London Tourist Board, Accommodation Services Dept., 26 Grosvenor Gardens, London SW1W 0DU.** There are same-day booking services at both **Heathrow** and **Gatwick airports;** and in London at the **British Travel Centre, 12 Regent St., SW1; tel.** (for information only, no bookings) **730-3400.**

To the right of each hotel name, you'll find location information: First is the name of the London neighborhood the hotel is in, followed by a reference to the atlas which will give you a more specific idea of location. For example, the key given for the Beaufort hotel, below, is p. 4, 5A, so you would turn to page 4 in the atlas section and find the square where the coordinates 5 and A meet. A few of London's best hotels are not within the parameters of our map and in these cases just a neighborhood name is given.

All phone numbers for London hotels should be dialed with an 01 prefix. All prices quoted are inclusive of VAT. Many hotels accept credit cards. Our abbreviations are as follows: AE—American Express, DC—Diners Club, MC—MasterCard, and V—Visa.

Here then is our list of the best of London's hotels:

### The Basil Street Hotel          KNIGHTSBRIDGE; P. 4, 4B
Basil St., Knightsbridge, SW3 1AH; tel. 581-3311; telex 28379
**Double room with private bath £101 (without breakfast)**
Around the block from Harrods, the Basil Street is one of those English hotels you thought disappeared with hansom cabs and the Empire. It's British as the British like it, not gussied up and modernized for North Americans. This also means that the rooms can be small, and not all of them have private bath, but when it comes to service, everything is just so, from a morning paper with breakfast to a shoe-shining service overnight. The 103 rooms are cheerily furnished with antiques, some with original 1910 marble baths. The hotel has a restaurant, coffeeshop, wine bar, and lots of repeat customers (who eventually qualify for a discounted rate). All rooms have TV, telephone, and 24-hour room and valet service. All major credit cards.

### The Beaufort          KNIGHTSBRIDGE; P. 4, 5A
33 Beaufort Gardens, SW3 1PP; tel. 584-5252; telex 929200; fax (01) 589-2834
**Doubles from £105 (including a generous Continental breakfast)**
You might easily miss this hotel on one side of a little oval of plane trees tucked just off Brompton Rd. There is only a small brass nameplate to let you know you've arrived. Once inside you may still wonder if you haven't wandered into somebody's house by accident. The point is that the Beaufort wants you to feel completely at home, so it's arranged like a home. Waiting in your room will be a decanter of brandy, chocolate eggs (from Lindt, a family connection with the owners), soft bathrobes, and lots of flowers everywhere. The 29 rooms are country-house chintz given a cosmopolitan context: thick carpets, bleached-wood furniture, strong-print floral drapes, TV, phone, and private bath. All major credit cards.

### The Capital          KNIGHTSBRIDGE; P. 4, 4B
Basil St., Knightsbridge, SW3 1AT; tel. 589-5171; telex 919042 HOTCAP; fax (01) 225-0011
**Single rooms £125, doubles from £150, suites £210 (exclusive of breakfast)**

The Capital is a small, full-service hotel strategically situated for shopping, museums, and Hyde Park. Much work has been done recently to attract the international business traveler. Rooms have been refurbished in a style as comfortable as it is luxurious. Suites have escritoires with desk and hideaway TV; baths with Italian marble, terry robes, and Capital cosmetics. Each room is air-conditioned. TV, radio, and light controls are tucked conveniently next to the bed. The hotel provides 24-hour concierge, room, valet, and laundry services. It is also one of the few small hotels with a restaurant worth bothering about; Michelin-starred chef John Elliot serves French-ish food in a formal French setting that is popular with business lunchers. The wine list is exclusively French and very expensive. Reservations are necessary. All major credit cards.

## Dorset Square Hotel
MARYLEBONE; P. 1, 2B
39/40 Dorset Square, NW1 6QN; tel. 723-7874; telex 263 964 DORSET G; fax (01) 729-3328
**Small doubles £80, luxury suites from £150 (without breakfast)**
Looking at the map, Dorset Square seems a bit out of the way, but it is actually within steps of the Underground and BritRail. Dorset Square is a small hotel in two parts occupying several listed Regency buildings, the double rooms at 39/40 and the suites at 25 Dorset Square. No matter which you choose, you'll find everything jolly good. Rooms have hand-painted trim and details in soft shades, and they are often furnished with antique wardrobes that have heaps of hanger space. Marble and mahogany bathrooms are roomy, with Gilchrist and Soames toiletries littered about. The rooms have lots of extras: mineral water, two separate phone lines (in the suites), and bowls of potpourri. Some of the suites have gas-fired marble fireplaces. Cricket memorabilia is deployed throughout. Credit cards: AE, MC, V.

## Dukes
ST. JAMES'S; P. 5, 4C
St. James's Place, SW1A 1NY; tel. 491-4840; telex 28283; fax (01) 493 1264
**Doubles £168, suites from £245 (not including breakfast)**
Secreted down a little passage off St. James's Place is a courtyard brightened by gas lamps and a cascade of potted flowers. Here you'll find Dukes Hotel. Dukes manages, as it has since its beginnings in 1908, to be located in the middle of everything but at the same time feel private and restful. Its 58 bedrooms and suites, including a penthouse with patio, all still have the feel of a classic gentleman's club. There are humorous sporting prints on the walls, crisp-cased pillows, antique mahogany reproductions, and fresh freesia adding a touch of softness. The baths are mahogany with old-style chrome fixtures. The 40-seat modern-British restaurant with its trompe l'oeil murals and Roland Batchelor watercolors is recommended. Over the years Dukes has had a very loyal following, including Lord Byron, Oscar Wilde, Frédéric Chopin, and Edward Elgar. All major credit cards.

## Durrant's Hotel
MARYLEBONE; P. 1, 2B

George St., W1H 6BJ; tel. 935-8131; telex DURHOT 894919; fax (01) 487-3510

**Singles with shower from £58, twin with bath from £85—request a room with shower if necessary—(prices do not include breakfast)**

Durrant's is steps away from the marvelous Wallace Collection and blocks away from Regent St. shopping in Marylebone. This former coaching hotel celebrates its 99th anniversary in 1989. Fortunately, Durrant's is still privately owned and has had nearly a century to work out the perfect equation of upscale service and modest prices. Rooms are decorated in shades of buff and brown with a smattering of Edwardian furniture, TV, radio, phone, and mirrored armoires. Doubles tend to be smaller than twins, so book the latter if you need room to roam. Singles are small but not skimpy, and they are reasonably priced, hence very popular. Amenities include concierge, room, and business services. Credit cards: AE, MC, V.

## Ebury Court Hotel
BELGRAVIA; P. 4, 5B

26 Ebury St., SW1W O6U; tel. 730-8147

**Single room with shower £40, doubles with bath (but not necessarily shower) £70**

There are several four-poster-bed rooms available for the same price as a standard double, so try to reserve one of these. All prices include full English breakfast served in a sweet little downstairs café. Belgravia is one of London's most exclusive addresses, but surprisingly Ebury Court is neither snooty nor expensive. The atmosphere is old-fashioned, like visiting a favorite aunt whose linens were always fresh and soft and who always made a big fuss over you. This hotel offers a very good value for the money, which people know, so book well in advance. Credit cards: MC, V.

## The Fenja
CHELSEA; P. 4, 5A

69 Cadogan Gardens, SW3 2RB; tel. 589-7333; telex 934272 FENJA G; fax (01) 581-4958

**Single £75, standard double £90, superior twin and suites £140 (additional charge for breakfast)**

The Fenja's drawing room welcomes you with the scent of fresh flowers and mellowed leather. Fix yourself a drink at the honor-tab bar and settle in with *The Times*. The Fenja is the closest you can come to finding a private town house in this cosmo capital city. The 14 grandly sized bedroom suites are named for famous writers and painters who previously chose this part of London for its garden squares, shaded sidewalks, and tranquillity. Your every need is anticipated by a small but superior staff: wonderful J. Floris toiletries, fresh flowers, TV, phone, business services, access to private Cadogan Gardens, and a light-meal room service. Breakfasts are worth the extra money. Among the best in its class, the Fenja is a most welcome addition to the London hotel scene. All major credit cards.

## The Goring Hotel
BELGRAVIA; P. 4, 5C

Beeston Place, Grosvenor Gardens, SW1W 0JW; tel. 834-3211; telex 919166

**Singles from £87.50, doubles from £130 (breakfast is extra)**
Built in 1910, the Goring is one of the best and (sadly) one of the last family-run hotels in this city. The Goring is especially popular with the British—it was Hotel of the Year in 1988. The rooms have deep, rich color schemes, brass beds, and thick royal blue carpets, a shade taken up in the bedspread, canopy, and curtains. Baths are all wood, marble, brass, and Gilchrist and Soames English herb cosmetics. Out back there is a private garden full of flowers and a lawn most spacious for these parts. Rooms overlooking the garden cost no more than others, so request one. Beeston Place is around the corner from Buckingham Palace and Victoria Station, so business in the City is a quick Tube ride away. The 24-hour concierge will arrange golf and tennis nearby, swimming down the street, and provide you with a jogging map of the Royal Parks nearby. All rooms have private bath, TV, phones, and most have air-conditioning. All major credit cards.

## Halcyon                                      KENSINGTON
81 Holland Park, W11 3RZ; tel. 727-7288; telex 226721 HALCYON G; fax (01) 229-8516
**Singles from £115, doubles from £165, suites from £250**
Halcyon occupies a pair of almost-pink town houses with a lacy wrought-iron canopy. Holland Park is London's prettiest, set on the side of a hill in the northwest corner of the city—a supremely secluded location. Halcyon is furnished in a style they call Belle Epoch. What used to be 100 mediocre rooms have been converted into 44 spacious doubles and suites. The walls are covered in fabric hung with Impressionist oils. Bathrooms are elegantly stocked with Czech and Speake toiletries, a scale, bidet, phone, towels, and robes embroidered with the kingfisher; some have Jacuzzis. The Halcyon Suite has its own conservatory. Extras include satellite TV, air-conditioning, 24-hour concierge, laundry and room services, as well as a wine bar and garden restaurant. All major credit cards.

## Hyde Park Hotel              KNIGHTSBRIDGE; P. 4, 4B
Knightsbridge, SW1Y 7LA; tel. 235-2000; telex 262057; fax (01) 235-2000
**Singles from £140, doubles from £160, suites from £250 (not including breakfast); special weekend packages are available**
The Hyde Park is one of the few larger hotels listed; it is special in many ways, principally among which is the staff's ease and confidence in delivering country-inn service at a truly grand hotel. The Hyde Park Hotel is right on Hyde Park, the location is superb. On the opposite front of the hotel is Knightsbridge; Harvey Nichols is across the street, Harrods is down the block. If you've ever had a yen to stay in an Old World grand hotel, this is a good place to do so. Nothing could be more breathtaking than the view up the entrance's marble stairs to explosions of flowers and a ceiling of luxurious detail. Standard rooms are large enough to accommodate delicate plaster moldings, watered-silk wall coverings, curvilinear closets, satellite TV, antiques, minibar and fridge, and bath with telephone. Nothing

could be nicer than watching the horse guards pass by precisely at 10:50 A.M. right outside on their way to Buckingham Palace as you're taking your tea in the Park Room. All major credit cards.

## L'Hotel
KNIGHTSBRIDGE; P. 4, 4B
28 Basil St., Knightsbridge, SW3 1AT; tel. 589-6286
**Doubles are £90, there is one suite for £120 (breakfast is included)**
L'Hotel is a successful hybrid: too luxurious to be called a B&B, too casual to be called a hotel. There are 12 rooms—all with bath, TV, phone, and minibar. The decor is country antique, but the country could be Tennessee or Provence or Wales. In lodging presented by the owners of the Capital up the street, with which there is a reciprocal arrangement for business facilities, laundry, and the like. There is a wine bistro, Le Metro, in the basement where you also can have your breakfast. Credit Cards: AE, V.

## Number Sixteen
CHELSEA; P. 4, 5A
16 Sumner Place, SW7 3EG; tel. 589-5232; telex 266638
**Singles from £40, doubles from £95 (including breakfast)**
Ask six Londoners where they would send a friend looking for a nice hotel in a good location for a reasonable price, and Number Sixteen will be mentioned a half dozen times. The rooms are named for colors, among other things. The Olive Room is just that: soft green complemented by antiques, bargello-pattern fabrics, etchings, and Woods of Windsor soaps in the smallish bathrooms. There are TV, phone, fridge with complimentary mixers, and pots of fresh flowers. But speaking of flowers, try to get a room in back, not too high up, in order to get the best view of Number Sixteen's gem of a garden, a fury of color most of the year. Your breakfast will be delightful served here. Credit Cards: AE, DC, MC, V.

## Pembridge Court Hotel
KENSINGTON
34 Pembridge Gardens, W2 4DX; tel. 229-9977; telex 298363
**Singles from £45, doubles from £55**
Pembridge Court is just off Pembridge Square, a garden bordered by the white 19th-century town houses characteristic of the neighborhood, Notting Hill. Pembridge Court is convenient to the Underground, the market at Portobello Road, and the parks over the hill. The hotel has 25 rooms with phone, TV, hair dryer, trouser press, and private bath or shower. Pembridge Court is ingeniously decorated with framed theatrical costumes, Victorian slippers, fans, and lace dresses. Baths are comfortably sized with pine appointments, striped towels, and L'Avenie soap. Standard twins are on the small side but serviceable. Singles have double-size beds. Breakfast can be taken at Caps, the downstairs bistro named for jockeys' striped headgear. Pembridge Court offers many amenities for which you'd pay twice as much elsewhere. All major credit cards.

## The Ritz
ST. JAMES'S; P. 5, 4C
Piccadilly, W1V 9DG; tel. 493-8181; telex 267200

**Singles £145, doubles from £175, suites from £390**

Cesar Ritz was a willful man. When Cesar decided he wanted to build a hotel to rival the palaces of imperial France, there was just no stopping him. If Versailles or Chambord appeals to you, the Ritz might be just the thing. The public rooms are beneficently Baroque, with gilt chandeliers and statuary, gold-leaf trim, and frivolous murals in the style of Fragonard. Of course afternoon tea at the Palm Court is an institution: young ladies are treated for their 18th birthday, and older ladies look on conspiratorially, remembering when. Luckily a lot of the original turn-of-the-century details have been retained—most especially the Ritz's signature gold leaf gleaming from moldings, cornices, and ceilings. Some rooms have 1906 brass beds, marble fireplaces, and French vanities. The best rooms face west over Green Park. Bathrooms might be a tad smaller than expected but have Ritz royal blue towels and toiletries, bidets, and phones. All hotel services you'd expect at these prices are provided. A special treat is big-band dancing on Friday and Saturday from 10 P.M. to 1 A.M. in the Palm Court. All major credit cards.

## The Savoy COVENT GARDEN; P. 5, 3D

The Strand, WC2R 0EU; tel. 863-4343; telex 24234; fax (01) 240-6040

**Singles from £115, doubles £150, suites from £320**

In the American Bar are hung portraits of famous Savoyards of yore—Fred and Ginger, Bogey and Baby, Hope and Crosby. Looking around the hotel, you can just picture them here, fitting right into the all-out glamour of the place. Garbo stayed here, and the Savoy is very much in the Grand Hotel manner. There is still a system of call lights for every chamber whereby you can summon the waiter (red), the maid (yellow), or the valet (green). Each floor has one of each at the ready at all times. The rooms are decorated in sinuous thirties Deco: rounded closets with space enough for grand tour trunks, vast tubs, and cerulean tiles in the blue bathrooms (many guests request blue bathrooms specifically). Of course the Thames suites offer the most spectacular view of any hotel in London, bar none. Impresario Richard D'Oyly Carte built the hotel with money made from his protégés Gilbert and Sullivan. Its prime location is in the center of London theaters, and it is the best hotel close to business in the City. Indeed, many a gray suit can be spotted power-breakfasting at a river-view table. All major credit cards.

## PRIORITIES

As with every vast and ancient city, London has its list of not-to-be-missed activities—a very long list indeed. If you're new to the city, or if you have only a short time to spend here and don't want to waste it making wrong turns or tracking down dull monuments, have a look at the following suggestions.

**To the right of each entry you will find a reference first to the neighborhood tour, following in this chapter, where you'll find a more detailed description, then, when applicable, a key to the atlas so you can locate the sight.**

## BRITISH MUSEUM

BLOOMSBURY AND MARYLEBONE; P. 2, 2D

This houses collections of objects from ancient civilizations to Beatles' manuscripts, incorporating collections from the British Library. At least a half to a full day to visit. Great Russell St.; tel. 636-1555. Open Mon.–Sat., 10 A.M.–5 P.M., Sun. 2:30–6 P.M.; admission is free. Underground: Russell Square, Holborn, Tottenham Court Rd.

**In the area:** Courtauld Institute Galleries, Percival David Foundation of Chinese Art, Regent's Park.

## CHANGING OF THE GUARD

WESTMINSTER AND WHITEHALL; P. 5, 4C

The bearskin hats and scarlet uniforms and horses and bands fete the assembled masses(!) daily at 11:30 A.M., 10:30 on Sunday; during winter, every other day. May be canceled due to inclement weather or special state occasions. Buckingham Palace, the Mall. Underground: Victoria, St. James's Park, Green Park.

**In the area:** The Mall, Parliament Square and Westminster Abbey, the Tate Gallery, the Royal Parks.

## A TOUR OF THE CITY

London's oldest neighborhood established by the Romans. A tour should include St. Paul's and the Tower (see below), the City churches, the Smithfield Meat Market, the financial district (see *City* section). A good tour should take at least a day. Underground: Temple, Blackfriars, Mansion House, Cannon Street, Monument, Tower Hill, St. Paul's, Bank, Liverpool St.

## HOLLAND PARK

KENSINGTON

London's loveliest—full of flowers and woodlands, an open-air theater, a cafeteria, and a restaurant. Spend an afternoon here, preferably Sunday when Londoners are out in force. Underground: Notting Hill Gate, High St. Kensington.

**In the area:** Linley Sambourne House, Leighton House, Kensington Palace, Portobello Rd. Market (Saturdays).

## MARKETS

To get the flavor of what shopping was like before indoor malls, try an outdoor market. Go early in the morning for the best buys. Some are on the fringes: Brick and Petticoat lanes and Spitalfields are just to the north and east of the City; Camden Lock is north of Bloomsbury; Smithfield Market is in the City; Portobello Rd. is on the northwest edge of Hyde Park in Notting Hill.

**Brick Lane and Petticoat Lane.** Clothes, fruit, records, junk—you name it on Sunday mornings. Underground: Liverpool St.

**Camden Lock.** Beside a canal; crafts and antiques, Sat. and Sun. Underground: Camden Town, Chalk Farm.

**Portobello Road.** Famous for antiques, "antiques," junk; on Sat. 8 A.M.–6 P.M. Underground: Notting Hill Gate.

**Smithfield.** The world's largest meat market is open from midnight until roughly 9 A.M., Mon.–Thurs. Underground: Farringdon, St. Paul's.

**Spitalfields.** London's vegetable market, due to be torn down, so get there before it's gone. 5–9 A.M. weekdays. Underground: Liverpool St.

## MUSEUM OF LONDON
THE CITY; P. 3, 2 F

A tour through the history of the city from geologic to modern times; a great intro, it will probably take two hours to tour. London Wall; tel. 600-3699. Open Tues.–Sat. 10 A.M.–6 P.M., Sun. 2–6 P.M.; admission is free. Underground: St. Paul's, Barbican, Moorgate.

**In the area:** Barbican Centre, St. Paul's, Smithfield Market (mornings only), St. Bartholomew-the-Great.

## NATIONAL GALLERY
SOHO AND COVENT GARDEN; P. 5, 3 D

European and British masterpieces; a stunning collection. Reserve at least an entire morning or afternoon. Trafalgar Square tel. 839-3321. Open Mon.–Sat. 10 A.M.–6 P.M., Sun. 2–6 P.M.; admission is free. Underground: Charing Cross.

**In the area:** National Portrait Gallery, Piccadilly Circus, Covent Garden.

## ORIGINAL LONDON TRANSPORT SIGHTSEEING TOUR

Departs from various points at various hours; phone 227-3456. The original double-decker bus tours to give you a quick run around the city, so you can plan your more intensive touring from here. Fare: £5.

## CHELSEA ROYAL HOSPITAL AND RANELAGH GARDENS
BELGRAVIA, SOUTH KENSINGTON, AND CHELSEA;

A Wren building inhabited by war veterans, the Chelsea Pensioners, set in a Thames-side garden. Lovely. Royal Hospital Rd., SW3. Open Mon.–Sat. 10 A.M.–noon and 2–4 P.M., Sun. 2–4 P.M.; admission is free. Underground: Sloane Square.

**In the area:** Shopping on King's and Fulham roads. Open Wed. and Sun. 2–5 P.M. only.

## ROYAL OPERA HOUSE
SOHO AND COVENT GARDEN; P. 2, 3 D

The Royal Opera, the Royal Ballet, and Sadler's Wells Ballet all call this home; an exquisite European opera house. A night here is a night to remember. Royal Opera House, Covent Garden; tel. 240-1066. Underground: Covent Garden.

**In the area:** For pre-performance visits, Covent Garden Market, the London Transport Museum, the Theatre Museum.

## ST. PAUL'S CATHEDRAL          THE CITY; P. 3, 3 F

Wren's masterpiece with interiors by 17th-century masters, whispering gallery, and crypt. Two or more hours depending upon how high you climb in the dome. Come for a service if you can. Admission charges for crypt, ambulatory, and galleries, and for a conducted supertour. Ludgate Hill. Underground: St. Paul's, Mansion House.

**In the area:** The financial district, the Old Bailey, other City churches.

## SHOPPING IN SOUTH KENSINGTON AND CHELSEA

Along King's Rd., Fulham Rd., and Old Brompton Rd. you will find most of London's top shops and designers. Much more fun than a single department store or, worse yet, a shopping mall. Could take you an afternoon or all week depending on the state of your shoes and your credit cards. Underground: Sloane Square, South Kensington, Knightsbridge, Gloucester Rd.

**In the area:** Hyde Park and Kensington Gardens, Chelsea Royal Hospital, Kensington museums.

## TATE GALLERY          WESTMINSTER AND WHITEHALL; P. 5, 5 D

Britain's collection of British art and modern European art. Most famous for its collection of Turners in the newly opened Clore Gallery. Wonderful restaurant. Half to a whole day. Millbank; tel. 821-1313. Mon.–Sat. 10:30 A.M.–5:30 P.M., Sun. 2–5:30 P.M.; admission is free with the occasional exception of special exhibits. Underground: Pimlico, or Vauxhall and walk across the bridge— great views.

**In the area:** Westminster Abbey and Parliament Square.

## TAXI TOUR BY NIGHT

Any cabbie should oblige your request to take a spin around the capital's monuments and fountains all lit up. A suggested itinerary would be to start on the south side of the Thames (the South Bank Centre is a good place to find taxis), cross over Waterloo Bridge, work west along the Embankment, turn right past Parliament Square down Birdcage Walk to Buckingham Palace, up Constitution Hill to Hyde Park Corner, around to Park Lane, up to Marble Arch, right onto Oxford Street, right again on Regent St., down to Piccadilly Circus, and finish up either at Trafalgar Square or continue down the Mall back to the palace and thence home. The fare should run you £8–10, depending on how loquacious your driver is.

## THAMES CRUISES

Departing for various destinations from various locations. Call the River Boat Information Service, 730-4812, or stop in at any London Tourist Board Information Centre. The Thames is the aorta of London, and there is nothing more eye-opening in many ways than to spend a morning, afternoon, or romantic evening gliding with the tide watching the skyline change and the city's most important monuments slip in and out of view. You haven't seen London till you've seen it from the water. A basic 20-minute cruise departs from Westminster Pier, by Westminster Bridge, to the Tower during spring and summer.

## A NIGHT AT THE THEATER

No, we're not going to send you to the West End, although we won't discourage it. If you really want to get your money's worth and see a production the quality of which is unequaled else-where on the planet, spend a glorious evening with the National Theatre (tel. 982-2252) at the South Bank Centre, or the Royal Shakespeare Company (tel. 628-8795) at the Barbican Centre. Shakespeare and his contemporaries are, of course, featured, but the NT and the RSC also mount wonderful productions of modern plays and are responsible for debuting many important works, so if you don't think you could sit through *King Lear,* not to worry; there is bound to be something to your taste running in repertory. Prices, of course, will vary, but these nationally funded companies' tickets are always well below West End prices. Underground: for the NT, Waterloo, or Embankment and walk across the river—most pleasant. For the RSC, Barbican, Moorgate.

## THE TOWER OF LONDON
THE CITY; P. 3, 3 G

London's most famous sight, complete with beefeaters, halls of armor, the crown jewels, and a grisly history. Very crowded; come early in the day during the week. Should take about three hours to see (almost) everything. Tower Hill; tel. 709-0765. Open Mon.–Sat. 9:30 A.M.–5 P.M.; Sun. 2–5 P.M.; winter hours till 4, closed Sundays. Admission is £4. Underground: Tower Hill.

**In the area:** St. Katharine's Dock, Tower Bridge, London Wall, the financial district.

## VICTORIA AND ALBERT MUSEUM
BELGRAVIA, SOUTH KENSINGTON, AND CHELSEA; P. 4, 5 A

Museum for art and design that was an outgrowth of the 1851 exhibition. *Very* wide variety of paintings, furniture, fashion, etc. At least a half to a full day. Tel. 589-6371. Open Mon.–Sat. 10 A.M.–5:50 P.M.; Sun. 2:30–5:50 P.M.; admission by suggested dona-tion. Underground: South Kensington.

**In the area:** Other Kensington museums (science, natural his-tory, geology . . . ), Royal Albert Hall, Hyde Park and Kensington Gardens, shopping in Knightsbridge, South Kensington, and Chelsea.

## WESTMINSTER ABBEY AND PARLIAMENT SQUARE
WESTMINSTER AND WHITEHALL; P. 5, 4 D

Here are the Houses of Parliament, Westminster Bridge, and Westminster Abbey. Check the Westminster and Whitehall sec-tion for advice on (the difficult task of) getting into the Houses of Parliament. Westminster Abbey is the burial place of many of Britain's kings, queens, and august subjects. Scene of coronations and royal weddings (Andy and Fergie's, for exam-ple). Tel. 222-7110 for abbey tour information. The abbey is open Mon.–Fri. 8 A.M.–6 P.M., Sat. 9 A.M.–2:45 P.M., and for services on Sundays. Try to come for choral evensong weekdays at 5. Admission charge for parts of the abbey or take a supertour. Underground: St. James's Park, Westminster.

**In the area:** Buckingham Palace, the Tate Gallery, the Cabinet War Rooms, Victoria Embankment.

# TRANSPORTATION

## ARRIVING IN LONDON

### AT HEATHROW
Although there are transportation information desks at each airport, it's best to arrive prepared. When you make your reservations, ask your hotel to suggest the best way to get to it from whichever airport.

Heathrow is London's busiest airport, about 15 miles west of the city. The fastest, cheapest way to get into town is by **Underground** (which travels a pleasant aboveground route for much of the journey): follow the signs in the terminal that are indicated by the Underground symbol, a red circle with a horizontal slash cutting across it. For about £2 the Piccadilly line will take you to central London in 45 minutes to an hour's time.

If you prefer to go by **bus,** London Transport runs an Airbus service from terminals 1, 2, and 3 (if you arrive at terminal 4 you will have to take intra-airport transportation to one of the other three). Look for the signs indicating "Airbus" outside the terminal. Airbus Route A1 goes to southwest London, Airbus A2 goes to northeast London. If you're not sure which to take, ask the driver when you get on. The trip takes an hour and costs about £4. If you're arriving at night, go to the Heathrow Central Bus Station—a building in the center of the ring of terminals 1, 2, and 3—and take night buses N56 and N97.

If you must take a **taxi,** the fare to central London will hover around £20, not including tip. There may be extra charges for luggage and nighttime or weekend service. London cabbies are usually quite honest, but it's always best to get an estimate of the total fare before you get into a taxi, so there will be no surprises at the other end.

If you are planning to rent a **car** (and we strongly advise against it, except for out-of-London trips), book it in advance (i.e., at home before you leave) with an international company. You can book a car in the U.S. or Canada and pre-pay in dollars at a guaranteed rate, so you won't have to worry about fluctuating exchange rates. If you wait till you arrive, check with Budget (01-759-2216) or catch the shuttle bus to Swan National Car Rentals. The extra ten-minute ride to their offices could save you considerably (01-897-3232).

### AT GATWICK
Gatwick is London's second airport and popular with many budget carriers. The best way by far to get into town from Gatwick

is the **Gatwick Express,** a train service to Victoria Station in southwest London where you can make connections for the Underground or get a taxi. The trip takes about a half hour and will cost about £7.50.

**Green Line Flightline buses** operate between Gatwick and Victoria Bus Station. The journey takes a little over an hour, depending on traffic, and costs £3. Again, Budget is a good choice of rental car at Gatwick (293-540141), as is Swan (293-513031).

## GETTING AROUND THE CITY

On foot is far and away the best way to see London. Unlike many New World cities dependent on their motor arteries, London is a pedestrian city. It's web of back streets with tiny pubs and local shops tucked along each is an enchanting change from the grid form and freeways of more modern burgs so by all means walk whenever and wherever you can.

Public transportation in London is cheap and reliable. The **Underground** (or **tube**) is London's subterranean rail system (in Britain "subway" means a pedestrian crossing below the street); it is fast and usually quite efficient. The fare within central London is 50 pence for all destinations. Beyond the inner ring, fares increase up to about £2. Be sure you retain your ticket; it will be collected by a machine or an agent as you exit the system. The Underground is open Mon.–Sat. 5:30 A.M.–12 midnight, Sun. 1:30–11:30 P.M. Each station will have a sign posted about an hour before closing listing the departure times for the last trains of the night. For a map of the Underground, see atlas page 7.

**Buses** are slower, but they service more areas and, of course, are a kick to ride if you've got only the single-decker kind at home. Buses run 24 hours, so they are the only cheap mode of transportation after the tube shuts down at midnight. However, the bus routes change completely at night—usually from about 10 P.M.–5 A.M. Night bus routes are denoted by an *N* before the number (i.e., N2, N93, and so on). The best way to catch a bus at night is to go to Trafalgar Square, around the north and east edges of which are bus stops for nearly all the night routes in central London. Many bus stops are "request stops" and will be so indicated on the sign. If you want the bus to pick you up at one of these, you are obliged to step out into the street and wave it down. Likewise, when you are disembarking, you must press the request-bell button to alert the driver to stop.

Your fare will be collected as you get on and will vary according to the number of zones you will be crossing during your journey, beginning at 35 pence. Most drivers will make change; however, handing them large bills makes them testy. Upstairs is reserved for smokers and tends to attract the kids, so it can be the most fun place to sit (especially at night, but it can get rowdy), and, of course, the view is much better.

It is possible to buy a Travelcard for bus and/or Underground that is good for one day (£2) or for periods up to a month. These are worthwhile only if you plan to do a lot of traveling in one day. Passes can be bought at selected travel agents, newsagents (shops), or at bus garages and Underground stations. One good thing about buying a Travelcard is that it comes with a city bus map.

For London Transport Information (bus and tube) call 222-1234 to plan your route. Or phone 222-1200 to find out if there are any delays or changes in service. Information on special routes for disabled travelers is available on the 222-1234 line.

**Taxis** are a good idea if there are two or more of you traveling, if you need to travel a long distance in a hurry, or if you are traveling at night. Do keep in mind, however, that London daytime traffic can be horrific, so if you're just going a short distance, it will probably be much faster to walk or take the tube. There will be extra charges at night and on weekends at a fixed rate. A 10 to 15 percent tip is customary.

The absolute last option is to **drive** in London. As mentioned, London traffic can be dreadful. Additionally, parking is scarce and can be expensive, and the "Lovely Ritas" policing no-parking zones are generous in their distribution of parking tickets. The only possible reason for renting a car in London is for traveling outside the city. In this case, it is better to take the train to your destination and rent a car there, or take the tube to Heathrow and drive from there, thus avoiding the chaos of city driving and the higher prices of hiring a car in town.

## ORGANIZED TOURS OF LONDON

**Original London Transport Sightseeing Tour** is a quick overview of the city, whisking you around on a red double-decker bus. The tours depart daily from various locations at various hours but all follow the same route, take the same amount of time—a painless hour and a half—and charge the same practically painless rate—£5. This tour provides you with a working knowledge of how the city is laid out, what is near what, and what might be worth coming back to for a closer look. For information on times and places of departure convenient for you, call 227-3456.

The other overall sightseeing tours we recommend are those by water. You can chug along the Thames from Hampton Court to Greenwich, during the day's bustle for sightseeing or the night's romance for dinner and music. Although some riverboats run year-round, trips are drastically reduced in number from October to April. For information on all **Thames River cruises,** call the River Boat Information Service at 730-4812.

The other watery part of London not so well known to visitors, but no less intriguing, is her **system of canals.** The Grand Union and Regent's canals converge in a pretty, aqueous triangle in the northwest part of the city known as Little Venice. It is possible to glide through the back streets of town on several different canal barges that service several different destinations. Some boats even offer leisurely dinner cruises. The *Jason* and *Serpens* run along Regent's Canal from Little Venice to Camden Town via Camden Lock daily from Easter to October. Call 286-3428 for details and reservations.

The *Jenny Wren* also plies Regent's Canal on a round-trip excursion from Camden High St. past the London Zoo and Regent's Park to Little Venice and back again daily from Easter through October. Call 485-4433 or 485-6210 for information.

The *Regent's Canal Waterbus* is a fun way to get from here (Camden Lock) to there (the Zoo or Little Venice) daily April to Oct., weekdays only in winter. Trips eastward to the East End and Docklands are also available. Call 482-2550.

Several crackerjack companies operate **walking tours** that concentrate on a small, specific area at a time. The guides are exceptionally well-informed and well-read on their territory and can provide you with a rich impression of the intricacies of a particular neighborhood.

Probably the best of the bunch is **Citisights of London,** 145 Goldsmith's Row, E2 8QR (tel. 739-4853). This company employs archeologists and historians as guides who for £3 will take you on an hour-and-a-half to two-hour stroll through various neighborhoods covering various ages and themes in London's history. Walks depart from either museums or tube stations, rain or shine. They list several dozen different walks: among them are "Lundenwic—in Search of Dark Age London," "London After the Great Fire—the City of Wren & Dr. Johnson," "London and the Big Bang—Brave New World or Rape of London?" "Bawdy House to Opera House: A Covent Garden Pub Walk."

There are also special one-time-only walks geared to holidays such as "William Shakespeare Birthday Walk Special" (April 23), "May Day Radical London Walk Special" (May 1), "Pagan Eostra to Christian Easter in London" (Easter Sunday). The list is very long and intriguing; it's best to write or call for a leaflet.

A similar operation, **Cockney Walks,** 32 Anworth Close, Woodford Green, Essex (tel. 504-9159), also employs teachers and historians and also has a provocative roster of tours, among them "The Jewish East End," "Dickens's and Fagin's Haunts," "St. Thomas Becket's Strange Story." Walks meet outside tube stations usually at 11 A.M. and cost £3.

The tours offered by **London Theatrical Walks,** 16 Ridgedale St., Bow, E3 2TW (tel. 980-5565), are conducted by theatrical types who do as much performing as informing along their one-and-a-half to two-hour routes, which cost £2.50. Choices include "London's Magical Theatreland," "Literary and Theatrical Fleet Street," "Shakespeare's London."

There are also several good neighborhood tours sponsored by various local organizations interested in promoting their area. A trio of good ones are: **Clerkenwell,** Clerkenwell Heritage Centre, Clerkenwell Rd. and St. John's Gate, daily walking tours spring and summer at 2:30 P.M., tel. 250-1039; **St. Bart's and Smithfield,** Main Gate of St. Bartholomew's Hospital, West Smithfield, London EC1, Sun. at 2 P.M., April–October, £2 (no phone), just meet at Main Gate; **Shakespeare's Bankside and Globe Theatre,** Wed. at 2 P.M. outside London Bridge Underground station, Sun. at 10:30 A.M., same meeting point, two-hour tour, £2. Operated by Learning with Pleasure, tel. 868-5055.

For those who like to live in fear, **Tragical History Tours** (tel. 857-1545 or 467-3318) runs a "Bus Trip to Murder," showing the sinister side of London. These tours depart from the Temple Underground station at 7 P.M. Mon.–Fri. in summer, Mon., Wed., and Fri. in winter. The tour lasts three-and-a-half hours and costs £8.50.

# The City

The City of London is the most important part of London; it is the heart of London. Within the City—a constitutionally defined entity granted privileged status in 1215 by King John—the Lord Mayor's position precedes Princes of the Blood and is second only to the reigning sovereign. Of the neighborhoods of London—most of whose parameters have shifted, amoeba-like, from one century to another—only the City has remained unchanged from the almost perfect square mile colonized by the Romans. They named the fishing village they found here Londinium, around which they, as was their wont, erected a wall in the second century A.D.—a wall that remained intact, in one form or another, for the next sixteen hundred years. Among the sites, ancient and modern, are the Tower of London, the Bank of England, the Old Bailey, the Guildhall, St. Paul's Cathedral, St. Bartholomew-the-Great, the Temple, the Barbican Centre, the Museum of London, the Stock Exchange, and the Smithfield Market.

## Smithfield Market

Your day could dawn (literally) at this last, **Smithfield Market.** And you'll have to get up pretty early in the morning to find men who work harder at their business than do the butchers who ply a convivial, cacophonous trade here; in fact, you'll have to get up last night. Servicing these 10 acres, trucks come rattling in at midnight, and Smithfield's "day" begins officially at 5 A.M. You don't have to arrive quite that soon, 7:30 to 8 A.M. (Monday through Thursday) will do.

Smithfield has its own law—a private police force employed by the market owner, the City of London Corporation—and its own time clock, as you'll find announced outside the **Smithfield Tavern,** where a sign states that special license has been granted to serve spirits to those "following their lawful trade at Smithfield" from 6 A.M.–9 A.M. For £4.10 you too can have the Best Breakfast in London of eggs, tomato, mushrooms, and fresh-from-the-market bacon, ham, and sausage—accompanied, as the barrow boys do, by a wasser, or whisky with tea.

Fortified by your rasher and wasser, skirt the market and scoot down Little Britain Street, where, just on your left, you'll see a half-timbered structure above a gateway. This building's true Elizabethan character was revealed by an exploding zeppelin bomb during the First World War. Through

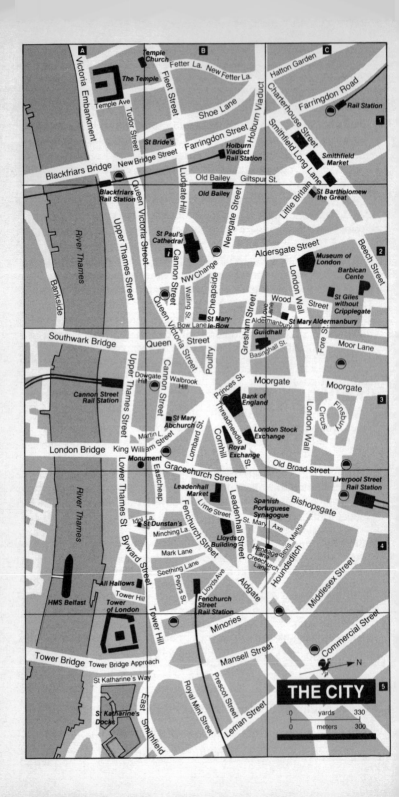

the gateway is London's second oldest church, **St. Bartholo-mew-the-Great.**

The present church, capped by a ceiling upheld by tremendous wood beams, is considerably smaller than the 12th-century original, much of it destroyed during Henry VIII's Dissolution of the Monasteries. The bells in the tower date from 1510 and are rung Sundays from 5:50 to 6:30 P.M. The church is noted for its music: 11 A.M. choral matins, 6:30 P.M. choral evensong. Special programs are staged around holidays. Free lunchtime recitals are held most Thursdays at 1:10 P.M. Schedules of events are available at the shop desk on your right as you enter.

## The Tower

**Her Majesty's Tower of London** (the official title) is open 9:30 A.M. to 5 P.M. Monday through Saturday, 2 to 5 P.M. Sunday; £4 admission. Even if you've been here before, there is something you're bound to have missed, and if you've never been . . . well, you simply must go. The crowds can be tiresome, the guards do rush you past the Crown Jewels too fast to allow for a good gawk, but this should not dissuade you from coming.

You should come armed with a plan of attack. The plan includes arriving around 9:45 A.M., allowing a little time for the preopening line to lessen, and arriving only during the week—don't even think about coming here on a Saturday or Sunday.

During the summer Yeomen Warders (in the black uniforms) give quickie tours that begin at the Bell Tower, or you can gather some background info at the history gallery, down the stairs by the Tower Bridge corner. Nearby are the Tower's infamous ravens. They are maintained for more than ornithological curiosity. From the time of Charles II, it has been said that if the Tower's ravens become extinct, the White Tower will fall and the empire will dissolve.

The site was originally commandeered by the Romans, but it wasn't until after the Conquest that William I, Duke of Normandy, decided in 1078 to hang his helmet here.

Make a beeline for the **Crown Jewels** and join the line twisting through the waiting maze along which they've thoughtfully installed swords of state, candlesticks, punch bowls to beguile the time. Downstairs in the mammoth Chubb vaults you'll have to plow your way through school kids ogling and Parisians ooh-la-la-ing to get a glimpse of Her Majesty's eye-popping baubles. The queue on the lower level next to the display cases must be kept in perpetual motion; the upper level is raised for stopping and staring. No doubt about it, you too will be mesmerized, bewitched by the glitter.

In contrast to this extravagance is what ought to be your next stop, the **Chapel Royal of Saint John the Evange-**

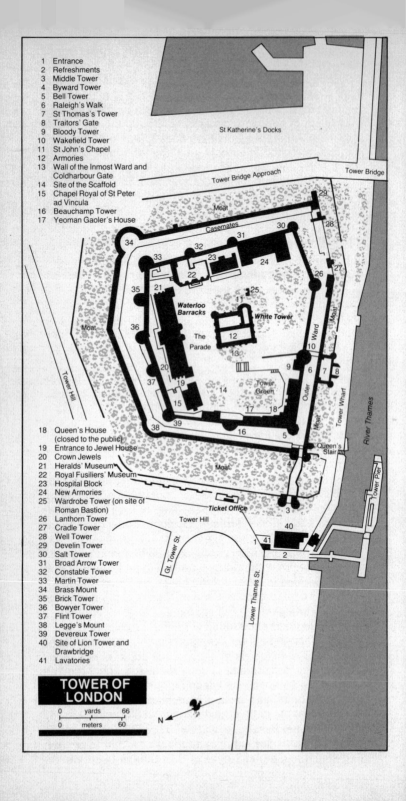

1  Entrance
2  Refreshments
3  Middle Tower
4  Byward Tower
5  Bell Tower
6  Raleigh's Walk
7  St Thomas's Tower
8  Traitors' Gate
9  Bloody Tower
10 Wakefield Tower
11 St John's Chapel
12 Armories
13 Wall of the Inmost Ward and
   Coldharbour Gate
14 Site of the Scaffold
15 Chapel Royal of St Peter
   ad Vincula
16 Beauchamp Tower
17 Yeoman Gaoler's House

18 Queen's House
   (closed to the public)
19 Entrance to Jewel House
20 Crown Jewels
21 Heralds' Museum
22 Royal Fusiliers' Museum
23 Hospital Block
24 New Armories
25 Wardrobe Tower (on site of
   Roman Bastion)
26 Lanthorn Tower
27 Cradle Tower
28 Well Tower
29 Develin Tower
30 Salt Tower
31 Broad Arrow Tower
32 Constable Tower
33 Martin Tower
34 Brass Mount
35 Brick Tower
36 Bowyer Tower
37 Flint Tower
38 Legge's Mount
39 Devereux Tower
40 Site of Lion Tower and
   Drawbridge
41 Lavatories

St Katherine's Docks

Tower Bridge

Tower Bridge Approach

Moat

Casemates

Waterloo Barracks

White Tower

The Parade

Tower Green

Inner Ward

Outer Ward

Moat

Tower Wharf

River Thames

Queen's Stair

Tower Pier

Ticket Office

Tower Hill

Gt. Tower St.

Lower Thames St.

**TOWER OF LONDON**

0  yards  66
0  meters  60

N

**list,** upstairs through the armories in the White Tower (the oldest surviving Norman structure in London). Henry IV invited 46 gentlemen to attend him here on the eve of his coronation and knighted them. Whereupon they bathed, prayed, and spent the night in 46 beds, thus beginning the Ceremony of the Bath.

One of the Tower's most famous components is the **Bloody Tower.** Originally known as the Garden Tower, the more titillating title dates from the time of the Little Princes, the boy-king Edward V and the Duke of York. The brothers were incarcerated here and then murdered, most likely by order of their uncle, Richard III.

---

### The Ceremony of the Keys

If you really want to escape the crowds at the Tower, you can come by at 9:35 P.M., present your pass, and witness the Ceremony of the Keys. This is a seven-hundred-year-old tradition involving the locking of the gates and the setting of the watch, and the half-hour ritual is most impressive and relatively private. To obtain a pass, make application *in writing* to The Resident Governor, Queen's House, HM Tower of London, EC3N 4AB. Include a stamped, self-addressed envelope, and they will send you an application form.

---

## On into The City

Now that you've done the City sights, which must be done early in the day, you're at leisure to reconnoiter what you will in this treasure trove of essential London. If you'd like a bird's-eye-view of the Thames, **Tower Bridge**'s towers and connecting skywalk are now open to the public. If you're hungry, stroll over to **St. Katharine's Dock,** on the other side of Tower Bridge.

Or if you're keen to press on, you might like to set off on the London Wall Walk, which begins its westerly route at a series of explanatory wall panels in a below-ground passageway across the street by the Tower Hill Tube station. Along the Walk you'll come to the **Barbican Centre,** a concrete fortress of a place—built on blitz-leveled land—which incorporates towers of flats, the Royal Shakespeare Company theaters, the London Symphony Orchestra hall, an arts complex, and the Museum of London.

The **Museum of London** is a great place to explore on the first day or two of a visit to London. It begins at the beginning with geologic history and works itself up to the Stone Age, Roman, Saxon, Medieval, Tudor London on up through the present, using artifacts, photos, paintings, dioramas, and multimedia presentations.

As for the other public sections of the Barbican, you'll certainly want to return in the evening to see the Royal Shakespeare Company or hear the London Symphony, and you can pick up tickets while you're here. There are plenty of daytime amusements as well. The Arts Centre is a multifloor building, including several subterranean levels, so you may find yourself walking in from the sidewalk onto Level 5, where you'll find the main lobby with entrances to the main theater, and where there is often free music at lunchtime or after 5 P.M.

The complex has galleries, theaters, restaurants, and shops littered liberally about its precincts. The best way to sort out what's on when and where is to head for the info desk on Level 7, which has a question-answering staff and a board listing the day's events throughout the building.

It is high time to discuss the City's other churches. As you will have learned at the London Museum, after the Great Fire in 1666 only 11 of the City's churches remained standing. Sir Christopher Wren and others built 51 churches on existing property but by the 1930s only 43 were left. During the Axis bombings of London, barely a single one came through unscathed. Today the tally rests at 39 City churches, many heavily restored in the forties and fifties; of this final number, 23 buildings and six standing towers were designed by Wren.

## The 1660s: Contagion and Conflagration

Late in November of 1664 London barbers and physicians were reporting cases of patients taken with fever and delirium who developed a red rash and finally black sores around their joints as the last sign or "token" of impending death. The Great Plague of 1665 was a strain of bubonic plague (named for the "buboes" or black sores, whence also the name "Black Death"). By the spring of 1666 more than one hundred thousand Londoners had succumbed.

The plague was transmitted by infected rats and their fleas, and quickly spread through the crowded, filthy streets of London. There was hardly a single street that didn't have its house with the red cross of quarantine painted on the front door. The inmates of the stricken house were locked inside in appalling conditions (strictly enforced by the constabulary) for forty days after the infected person had died. The aristocracy fled in terror to their country estates, Charles II decamped to Hampton Court, Parliament was suspended. In one week of September 1665, about twelve thousand Londoners died. Thankfully, the winter weather brought the mortality rate down. The court returned to Whitehall in February 1666. The rest of the gentry trickled hesitantly back into London.

Things were just returning to normal by the end of the summer, when on the morning of September 2nd, a little bakeshop in Pudding Lane caught fire (Robert Hubert, a Frenchman, subsequently confessed to arson and was executed). The Great Fire spread as quickly as had the plague in London's cramped, polluted streets. The lord mayor and the king himself pitched in to help pull down houses in the fire's path, transport water, and attend to victims. But the situation was hopeless; by the time the wind changed on September 7th, four hundred acres, two-thirds of the City, had been laid to ruin. To everyone's amazement only nine people had died.

But the double dose of plague and fire in a little over a year had left its mark on the face of London and on the minds of her populace. Eighty-seven churches had been destroyed, and many public buildings were reduced to rubble. Although he wasn't permitted to carry out his master plan for rebuilding London, Sir Christopher Wren—and his cronies Nicholas Hawksmoor, and Grinling Gibbons—did manage to rebuild the town in a Neoclassical, "Enlightenment" style.

The aristocrats had been shaken by the swiftness with which both flames and pestilence tore through the city, and the poor whose houses had been the first to go also felt the need to rebuild away from the dirt and danger. The City of London had burst its seams, it seemed, and the plague and fire were merely a predictable outcome of the massive problems caused by overcrowding and concomitant overtaxing of the water supply, sanitation facilities, and medical and city services. Many citizens chose not to return to the City but instead began to settle in the fields and woods between the City and its satellite towns, filling up the unpopulated, in-between land. This was the beginning of the building of London into the city of many cities that it is today.

All of these several dozen houses of worship within the City's limits are worth visiting, each is architecturally and historically unique, and taken as a group they reveal the marvelous, multifaceted artistic and spiritual life of the City. Obviously, though, most visitors won't have time to see them all, and for those people the following are seven of particular interest: **All Hallows-by-the-Tower,** Byward Street; the **Spanish and Portuguese Synagogue,** Heneage Lane, Bevis Marks; **St. Bride's,** Fleet Street; **St. Dunstan in the East,** St. Dunstan's Hill, Lower Thames Street; **St. Mary Abchurch,** Abchurch Lane, Cannon Street; **St. Mary Aldermanbury,** Aldermanbury and Love Lane; and **St. Mary-le-Bow,** Bow Lane and Cheapside. As mentioned, all have been partially destroyed at one or more points in their histories, so most have been restored several times from the 17th century onward.

These houses of worship are merely a prelude (as they were in Wren's own education and work) to the grandest by far of all London churches, St. Paul's Cathedral.

## St. Paul's

The site of St. Paul's Cathedral alone is fraught with historic significance. Its position atop Ludgate Hill, best appreciated when approached from Fleet Street, has proved irresistible

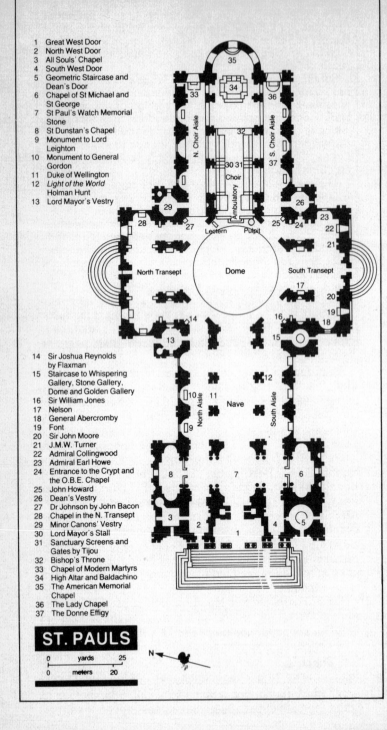

1 Great West Door
2 North West Door
3 All Souls' Chapel
4 South West Door
5 Geometric Staircase and Dean's Door
6 Chapel of St Michael and St George
7 St Paul's Watch Memorial Stone
8 St Dunstan's Chapel
9 Monument to Lord Leighton
10 Monument to General Gordon
11 Duke of Wellington
12 *Light of the World* Holman Hunt
13 Lord Mayor's Vestry

14 Sir Joshua Reynolds by Flaxman
15 Staircase to Whispering Gallery, Stone Gallery, Dome and Golden Gallery
16 Sir William Jones
17 Nelson
18 General Abercromby
19 Font
20 Sir John Moore
21 J.M.W. Turner
22 Admiral Collingwood
23 Admiral Earl Howe
24 Entrance to the Crypt and the O.B.E. Chapel
25 John Howard
26 Dean's Vestry
27 Dr Johnson by John Bacon
28 Chapel in the N. Transept
29 Minor Canons' Vestry
30 Lord Mayor's Stall
31 Sanctuary Screens and Gates by Tijou
32 Bishop's Throne
33 Chapel of Modern Martyrs
34 High Altar and Baldachino
35 The American Memorial Chapel
36 The Lady Chapel
37 The Donne Effigy

N. Choir Aisle
S. Choir Aisle
Choir
Ambulatory
Lectern   Pulpit
North Transept
Dome
South Transept
North Aisle
Nave
South Aisle

ST. PAULS

0   yards   25
0   meters   20

N

to builders of would-be landmarks down through the centuries. There is a tradition that a Roman temple to Diana stood here, making it a focal point in the life of Londinium. The present St. Paul's (properly, New St. Paul's) is actually the fourth or fifth Christian church built here. The first was founded in 604 by St. Ethelbert, King of Kent. It was destroyed by fire and rebuilt later in that century. The second building, in turn, was ransacked by the Vikings in 961. The third and final Saxon church was also destroyed by fire in 1087. Old St. Paul's, erected and amended well into the 14th century, was larger even than its present-day progeny. It was struck by lightning in 1447 and never returned to its original proportions.

Permitted by the Great Fire of 1666 to erect an entirely new edifice, architect Christopher Wren met with trouble at every turn. Having tried and failed twice to produce an acceptable plan, Wren submitted a third model and quite cagily had inserted in his contract a clause granting him license to make "ornamental rather than essential" changes in the accepted model. Obviously given to a broad interpretation of things, among Wren's "ornamental" alterations was the exchange of the spire (echoing the structure of Old St. Paul's) called for in the original plan for an immense Italianate dome. In 1708 the architect's son laid the last stone in the lantern.

You can take an hour-and-a-half-long supertour of the Cathedral Monday through Saturday at 11 A.M., 11:30 A.M., 2 P.M., or 2:30 P.M. for £3.50. This is a good way to begin, especially because tours are taken to areas otherwise closed to the general public. After the tour, or in lieu of it, if those sorts of things don't appeal, you'll want to spend extra time seeing certain things. There is a small (separate) admission charge to circumnavigate the ambulatory, or descend into the crypt, or climb up to the various levels of the dome.

There are prayers and announcements over the public address system on the hour. Sung services are held weekdays at 10 A.M. and 5 P.M. The crypt and galleries are closed on Sundays in deference to services held throughout the day. Note that the outside galleries close early and are usually closed for the winter and inclement weather.

Across St. Paul's churchyard from the cathedral is the **London Information Centre,** stocked with souvenirs and booklets and staffed by Londoners with an encyclopedic knowledge of the city and the City. There are also good listings of daily events, festivals, and sacred and secular music programs.

## A TRINITY OF PUBS

After all this climbing around sacred spaces, you will undoubtedly have worked up a keen thirst. How fortunate that the streets east of the cathedral are full of great little pubs just right for slaking same. The trio we recommend (a half pint at each, perhaps?) is **The Pavillion End,** Watling Street; **Ye Olde Watling,** Watling Street; **The Green Man,** Bucklersbury.

# Big Business

Farther east from St. Paul's begins the hard-core heart of London's financial district. Some guides suggest that you visit here on a weekend, when the business crowd has decamped to the country, so as to get a better view of the buildings. This misses the point entirely. The point of this place *is* the constant coming and going, so by all means come on a weekday. At the intersection of a web of important streets is the **Bank of England,** the base of which was designed by Sir John Soane in 1788. Unfortunately, Soane's masterful facade has been surmounted by several storys designed by Sir Herbert Baker in 1925.

Across the way is the **Mansion House,** the lord mayor's official in-town digs. Built from 1739 to 1752, its Palladian design is the work of Charles Dance the Elder. Admission is by written appointment only: Principal Assistant, Mansion House, Mansion House Place, London EC4. Include alternate dates.

Dominating the eastern front of the intersection is the **Royal Exchange,** home of the London International Financial Futures Exchange (LIFFE). If you've never seen an exchange at work, walk up to the visitors' center, which is open from 11:30 A.M. to 2 P.M., Monday through Friday (free).

At the corner of Leadenhall and Lime streets you'll spot a steel building seemingly with no skin gleaming in the wan light. This 1986 construction is the home of pub master Edward **Lloyd's** insurance company. The visitors' gallery (open during business hours, Monday through Friday; free) is a balcony in the central atrium.

---

Tucked behind all these modern monoliths is a splash of olde London, **Leadenhall Market.** The entrances along Gracechurch Street lead into bricked streets covered by a buff and burgundy canopy. The stores, their signs lettered in gilt, are a tad up-market for the working classes who shopped here of yore—some sell champagne and caviar, Norwegian prawns, *corgettes Provençale.* There are several good choices for lunching; try the **Lutine Bell** at Number 35 for gourmet takeaway or sit-down upstairs. After work—closer to 5 o'clock here than in more hectic cities—the double-breasted brokers stand four deep outside the **Lamb Tavern.**

## . . . and the Law

Needless to note, with all these bankers, brokers, and bishops scurrying about their business in so small a space, disputes were bound to arise. It's only logical, therefore, that the final group of long-term tenants in the City are lawyers. Their bases of operations are the **Central Criminal Court** (Old Bailey and Newgate streets), better known as **The Old Bailey,** where you can hear cases debated; and the **Temple** (south of Fleet Street), whose Temple Church is open daily from 10 A.M. to 4 P.M.

# Westminster and Whitehall

This is the London of officialdom: of princes, peers, and pomp—all those things that bring a flush to the cheeks of British subjects, a lump to the throats of the International Order of Anglophiles, and a gleam to the eye of the British Tourist Authority, which thanks its lucky stars that Geoffrey Chaucer had the good sense to be buried here and that Elizabeth Windsor has the good sense to insist on fresh soldiers daily.

Over the centuries the area has remained the center of all Britain's institutions of government: federal, in the Houses of Parliament and the prime minister's operation at No. 10 Downing Street; royal, at Her Majesty's London address, Buckingham Palace; corporeal, among the officers stationed at Scotland Yard; and clerical, as the ecclesiastics oversee the workings of all the rest from Westminster Abbey.

In fact, the area is almost exclusively devoted to the business of running Great Britain.

## Trafalgar Square

Trafalgar Square is best appreciated from the porch of the National Gallery—the putty-putt of the diesel cabs, the grinding thrum of the double-deckers, the counterpoint of German, Japanese, and English as the tourists stream up the steps, the rhythmic chants of the perpetual anti-apartheid vigil outside Good Hope House (the South African embassy), and above it all the distant hum of Heathrow's flight pattern. It's an unimaginable chaos of sound and motion. Flocks of pigeons fly suicide runs around Nelson's Column and traffic snarls and untangles on its careen through the Admiralty Arch.

## Down Whitehall

As you begin your journey have a look at the statue of Charles I bestride his charger at the head of the road. This is London's oldest alfresco monument, having been constructed in 1633. Immediately beyond the statue are the repositories of Britain's national security. The **Old Admiralty** (1725), on your

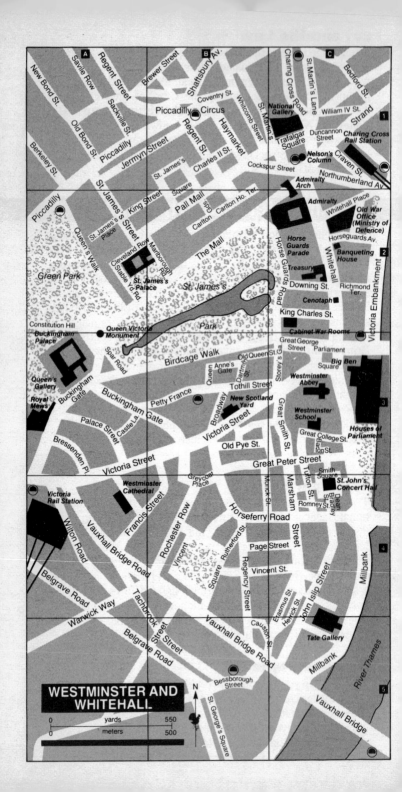

right and across the street the less attractive but no less strategic **Old War Office,** now known as the Ministry of Defence.

Farther on down the road is the headquarters of the **Queen's Life Guard.** The brace of mounted guardsmen, aloft and aloof, patiently permit tourists to pat their steeds and pose for photos.

On the corner across Whitehall is the **Banqueting House,** whose interior is renowned for its grandiose dimensions and most especially for its ceiling and murals by Peter Paul Reubens. Charles commissioned the artist to depict his father, James I, being carried by angels up to his divine rest as reward for all his earthly regal pains. (The Banqueting House is open daily from 10 A.M. to 5 P.M.; admission 80 pence.)

Continuing past the **Old Treasury Building,** now the Cabinet Office, you'll come to a police barricade on the other side of which is Downing Street, designed on the former site of a brew house by Harvard graduate Sir George Downing, MP. Former residents included James Boswell and Tobias Smollett. The house at **No. 10** became the official residence of the prime minister since the tenure of Robert Walpole in the early 1730s.

## Churchill's Underground

During World War I, zeppelin bombings of London caused Britons to pause and consider the implications of air-based warfare. In 1938 the attacks of Hitler's Luftwaffe on civilian targets in Europe confirmed their worst fears. Luckily for the nation, the farsighted soon-to-be PM Winston Churchill had not waited for aviation history to take its terrible course but had, with others, demanded that a fortified facility be built beneath the civil service buildings next to Parliament Square.

From these cramped, stuffy box-like **Cabinet War rooms** the prime minister, his cabinet, and generals ran the war. The museum is still run as the installation was run in the forties: the clocks are kept ticking, and the weather-forecast notices are kept up to date. The War Rooms are open daily from 10 A.M. to 5:15 P.M.; admission is £2.50. Great posters are sold in the gift shop.

## On to Parliament

The square is, in fact, London's first attempt at a roundabout, laid out in 1750 and revamped by Sir Charles Barry in 1868 to provide an impressive open-space foreground for the Palace of Westminster he designed with the assistance of Augustus Pugin.

## The PM and the MPs

One almost hates to describe the glories contained within the neo-Gothic perpendiculars of the **Houses of Parliament,** bolstered by perennial postcard favorite, **Big Ben,** properly called the New Palace of Westminster, because it is so damnably difficult to get inside. There are several ways of doing it, none of which are simple or surefire, but all of which are well worth the effort if you have the good fortune and tenacity to succeed.

1. Write directly to a member of Parliament, each of whom is given an allotted number of tickets per day. If you can't get hold of an office address, write to the MP at the House of Commons, Westminster SW1.
2. Get same-day passes from your own country's embassy or consulate. Most have four such passes available per day. These passes allow you to move to the head of the line but do not guarantee you a seat.
3. Wait in what may be a long queue outside of the Houses for same-day admittance during sessions. Guides will be provided on request if you have a member of Parliament's permit.

If you're at all confused by these instructions (and who wouldn't be?), the Parliament information number is 219-4272, or switchboard 219-3574.

## Westminster Abbey

The abbey you see today through the bobbing heads of the crowds is the result of many tempestuous centuries of building and rebuilding. The first spate of construction was brought about by Edward the Confessor and completed in 1065, just in time for his funeral, a week after its consecration. Edward had chosen a site traditionally associated with churches dedicated to St. Peter, and his new abbey followed suit. After Edward's canonization, there was great cachet in being associated with his abbey, and many princes were generous in their funding for continued work.

There really is so much to see here and so much to understand about the abbey that we strongly urge you to take one of the supertours conducted by vergers. The tours last about an hour and a half and take you to parts of the abbey where you would not be admitted on your own. Supertours run Monday through Friday, at 10, 10:30, and 11 A.M. and 2, 2:30, and 3 P.M.; Saturday 10 and 11 A.M. and 12:30 P.M. (subject to availability). You can book tours in advance by calling 222-7110—probably the best way to ensure that a tour is in fact running and that you will have a place in it. Included in the price of the tour is admission to all the sights.

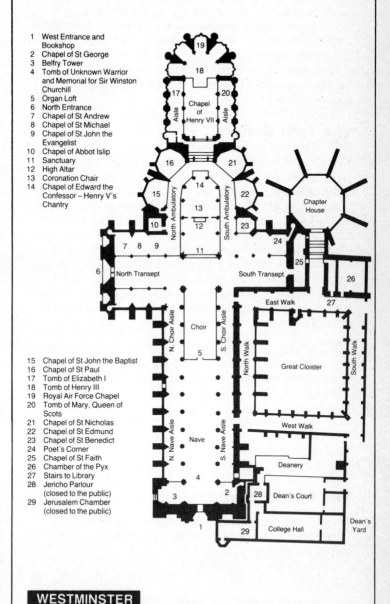

1  West Entrance and Bookshop
2  Chapel of St George
3  Belfry Tower
4  Tomb of Unknown Warrior and Memorial for Sir Winston Churchill
5  Organ Loft
6  North Entrance
7  Chapel of St Andrew
8  Chapel of St Michael
9  Chapel of St John the Evangelist
10 Chapel of Abbot Islip
11 Sanctuary
12 High Altar
13 Coronation Chair
14 Chapel of Edward the Confessor – Henry V's Chantry

15 Chapel of St John the Baptist
16 Chapel of St Paul
17 Tomb of Elizabeth I
18 Tomb of Henry III
19 Royal Air Force Chapel
20 Tomb of Mary, Queen of Scots
21 Chapel of St Nicholas
22 Chapel of St Edmund
23 Chapel of St Benedict
24 Poet's Corner
25 Chapel of St Faith
26 Chamber of the Pyx
27 Stairs to Library
28 Jericho Parlour (closed to the public)
29 Jerusalem Chamber (closed to the public)

**WESTMINSTER ABBEY**

0   yards   33
0   meters  30

N ←

If you are visiting independently, the abbey is open Monday through Friday from 8 A.M. to 6 P.M., Saturday from 9 A.M. to 2:45 P.M.; however, most of the abbey is closed after 4:45 P.M. to allow for evening services. On Sundays most of the abbey is closed to visitors all day except between services. If you have a choice, try to come on a Thursday, the only day the College Garden—at nine hundred years it's probably England's oldest—is open. While it is free to walk into the church, most of the important points of interest—the Choir, Transepts, and Royal Chapels—each charge a separate small admission fee.

## The Tate Gallery

Built on the site of a former jail, this gallery, once you've sampled some of its treasures, will completely captivate you, and you'll be reluctant to depart until you've seen every last item in the collection (a project that could take weeks). Just recently opened is the **Clore Gallery,** a controversial new home for the J.M.W. Turner collection. All the (justifiable) fuss over the Turners has tended to overshadow the other collections of the Tate, which—were they housed in any other museum—would certainly be considered highlights. The Tate collections focus on two areas: British painting from the 16th to the 20th century; and the modern collection, devoted primarily to contemporary British artists but also including the works of foreign artists.

We suggest by all means that you plan to be here at lunchtime to enjoy the treat of eating at the **Tate Gallery Restaurant.** Reservations are urged (834-6754). Lunch only is served from 12 to 3 P.M.

The Tate is open Monday through Saturday from 10 A.M. to 5:50 P.M., Sunday from 2 to 5:50 P.M. Admission is free with the exception of major visiting exhibitions, for which a nominal fee may be charged.

## The Main Event

They're changing guard at Buckingham Palace—
Christopher Robin went down with Alice. Alice is marrying one of the guard.
"A soldier's life is terrible hard,"
says Alice.—*A. A. Milne*

Ever since Mom read you these sing-song verses, you were keen to come to London and see the spectacle of the changing of the guard for yourself. The event, which takes place every other morning in winter and daily during the summer at 11:30 A.M. and 10:30 A.M. on Sunday. For a days-on, days-off listing

of times, check the board outside the Guard Bookshop just
south of the palace on Birdcage Walk.

# Soho and Covent Garden

The area whose high spirits are just barely contained by Oxford Street, Regent Street, Trafalgar Square, the Strand, and
Drury Lane prides itself on the possession of some of London's most sought-after entertainments. This is the place to
go when you're hungering for the larger-than-life wallop that
only the biggest and best of cities can offer.

Theaters, boutiques, boîtes, beautiful people . . . the list
continues with terrific museums like the National Gallery, the
melting-pot feel of Chinatown, and London's primest people-
watching in Leicester Square, Covent Garden, and Piccadilly
Circus. Your head's sure to be set spinning by the overload
of input.

## Oxford Circus

Oxford Circus holds down the northwest corner of Soho, its
easterly radian, Oxford Street, being the northern border and
its southerly radius, Regent Street, being the western. Although the east side of Regent Street could be considered
within Soho proper, its shops owe more to upper-crust Mayfair than trendy Soho, so we will include them in the Mayfair
section.

### Oxford Street

Oxford is that street in all cities where the clothes are cheap
and look that way, where the shops try to distract you from
the tattiness of their merchandise by bright lights, loud music,
and, in some cases, a kick line of mechanical female legs can-
canning up a storm in the front window. This in no way dis-
suades mobs of Londoners from flocking here to pursue their
sartorial business. And in no way should it dissuade you either. You may not find anything you're dying to own, but Oxford Street is a scene unto itself and should be seen, if only
to make a comparison with similar thoroughfares in your own
city. Besides, you just might find a record you're looking for
at the shops for **HMV** or **Virgin**—worth a look in to watch
the videos—or some raspberry ripple bath bubbles at the
**Body Shop.**

### Trafalgar Square

The square itself is so grand and governmental that we have
included it in the Westminster-Whitehall section, where it
most properly fits. The buildings, however, have more to do
with artistic Soho, so we will take up its peripheral elements
forthwith.

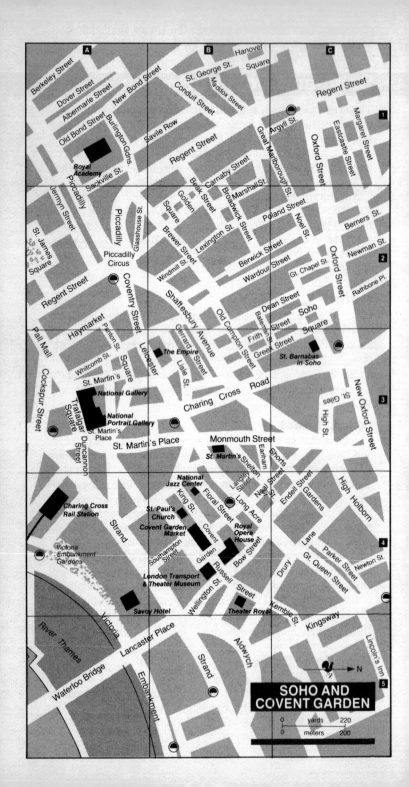

SOHO AND
COVENT GARDEN

## The National Gallery

Along with the Tate and the British Museum, the National Gallery forms London's trinity of transcendent museums. Like the Louvre or the Metropolitan or the Prado, it rather spoils the gallery-goer, spanning the artistic ages with a collection that is not so much large as perfect; each artist is represented by only the finest examples of his or her work.

Hours are Monday through Saturday from 10 A.M. to 6 P.M., Sunday from 2 to 6 P.M. Admission is free. There are guided tours weekdays at 11:30 A.M. and 3 P.M., Saturdays at 2 and 3:30 P.M. Additionally, there are special events daily, lectures and films at 1 P.M. on weekdays, 12 on Saturdays, and audiovisual programs at the Orange Street Theatre, 1 to 5:30 P.M. Tuesday through Saturday. To allay the confusion, pick up a free copy of the month's events at the info desk. There they will also supply you with a map and suggest a tour based on your interests.

Of course you'll find great postcards, art books, and journals in the shop. The cafeteria is pleasant, and the food is brought to you by Justin De Blank of Sloane Square fame.

## Some Old Familiar Faces

The **National Portrait Gallery** on St. Martin's Place is a chronology of the people who have been vital in the creation and promotion of Britain. You can see contemporary portraits of all the characters you've read about and follow their exploits, royal and otherwise, through time. The sitter is vastly more important than the painter here—indeed, many of the tags on Tudor portraits explain that the artist is unknown.

The gallery is open Monday through Friday from 10 A.M. to 5 P.M., Saturday from 10 A.M. to 6 P.M., Sunday from 2 to 6 P.M. Admission to the main gallery is free; occasionally there will be a small charge for a special exhibit. There are gallery talks—usually centering on history and biography rather than art—Tuesday through Friday at 1:10 P.M., Saturday at 3 P.M. Printed schedules are available at the info desk, and daily events are listed on the board in the lobby by the portrait of Mrs. Thatcher.

## Sanctuary on the Square

**St. Martin-in-the-Fields** was originally built in the village of Charing (of Charing Cross fame), which was situated between the City and Westminster. There were several churches previously on the site, the last being completed in the mid-16th century. There are free lunchtime concerts Monday and Tuesday at 1:05, and evening concerts are held twice a month; call 839-1930 for information, or pick up a schedule at the information table. Downstairs in the visitors' center, open 10 A.M. to midnight, you'll find a cavernous restaurant where you can buy beer and cappuccino, salads, hot meals, and sweets in a room loaded with atmosphere. Here is also the new headquarters of the **London Brass Rubbing Centre** with items costing from 50 pence to £6.

# Covent Garden

This used to be the garden of the convent (shortened to covent) of Westminster, and it has always had agricultural associations, most importantly with the fruit and vegetable market that started in the mid-17th century with a few makeshift stalls set up within the square owned by the Earl of Bedford.

By the 19th century the market had grown to be a serious enterprise and the carnival atmosphere of the 19th-century market is still very much a part of the scene.

In the market itself, aside from the permanent-fixture stores—mostly branch offices of big names—stalls are set up that are reminiscent of the former flower and fruit stands. The new tenants sell antiques on Monday, crafts Tuesday through Saturday.

## Museums at the Market

The **London Transport Museum** is located in a building that formerly served as the flower market. Today actual locomotives and Tube cars and double-deckers are parked where the violets and primroses used to be.

Some of Britain's best graphic designers have worked for the transportation authority, and therefore the shop has some of London's best postcards, decals, and posters of vintage Underground, BritRail, etc., adverts. Open daily, 10 A.M. to 6 P.M.; £2.40 adults, £1.10 children.

The **Theatre Museum** is actually underneath the Transport Museum. At the door is a box office where you can get theater tickets for West End plays with a £2.50 per-seat surcharge. Inside is the box office for the museum.

The collection was formerly housed at the Victoria and Albert Museum but quite wisely was moved here to the heart of the neighborhood that made it all possible.

There are constantly changing exhibitions featuring a historic period of theater, or a style of filmmaking, or a particular actor, or a photographer specializing in celebrity photos. There is also a working theater in the building that offers performances, usually evenings at 6:30, and lectures at lunchtime. Check the schedule at the box office. The museum is open Tuesday through Sunday from 11 A.M. to 7 P.M., café till 8 P.M. Closed Mondays. Admission is £2.25.

## The Opera House

What began as a playhouse is now home to the Royal Opera, the Royal Ballet, and the Sadler's Wells Ballet companies. An evening in the 2,158-seat auditorium of the Opera House should be on everyone's must-do list of London.

Tickets are available at the box office, 48 Floral Street, from 10 A.M. to 8 P.M., Monday through Saturday.

---

The area surrounding Covent Garden is wall-to-wall with unusual shops and restaurants. One of the best places to explore is Neal Street, just across Long Acre to the north. Pop down Shorts Gardens to **Neal's Yard,** where the sixties are still flourishing and easing into the New Age. Pick up some natural munchies for the road at the **Wholefood Warehouse** on the corner.

Other unusual stops in the Covent Garden sphere of influence include **The Africa Centre** at 38 King Street, a retail store and galleries for paintings and performances. Downstairs is the **Calabash** restaurant.

**Edward Stanford,** 12–14 Long Acre, is for maps, travel, and picture books of subjects around the world—should you wish to extend your journey outside the boundaries of the valuable book you presently hold in your hands.

The **British Craft Centre,** 43 Earlham Street, sells the best of British artisans in an atmosphere much less hectic than that at Covent Garden.

---

# Leicester Square

Leicester Square and its down-the-street neighbor, Piccadilly Circus, are the kind of precincts the locals love to hate. Crowded with tourists, bright with the imported plastic and neon of McDonald's and Pizza Hut, Londoners strive manfully to boycott the area and leave the armies of visitors to overrun it at will. Yet somehow, the natives never quite succeed in avoiding this designated no-Londoner's-land.

The best reasons to come are the **half-price ticket kiosk** and the glockenspiel at the **Swiss Centre.** The former has same-day returns from most West End theaters and the Barbican and South Bank centers as well. Matinee tickets are sold from noon; evening seats from 2:30 P.M., Monday through Saturday. The queue has been known to stretch around the square, so come early. Tickets are sold on a cash-only basis, and a £1 per-seat service charge will be added.

The glockenspiel chimes on the hour, and so of course is best at midnight or noon, when the business takes a bit longer.

A few blocks north is Gerrard Street, the middle kingdom of London's **Chinatown.** The gates at either end of the street will alert you that you've arrived if the crisp tones of Cantonese and the sour scent of bok choy haven't done so already.

West of the square in Charing Cross Road and most especially on **Cecil Court** and **St. Martin's Lane,** there is a slew of book and print shops, perfect for the browser or the serious collector. A fine print or an illustrated edition of a classic novel can be found at reasonable prices; they make great gifts for the folks back home.

## Piccadilly Circus

It is no accident that this second hub of London has at its center a statue to neither a great statesman, nor war hero, but rather to Eros, the god of, well—you know. And, indeed, this piece of London is the center of the city's sensual scene, with its restaurants, theaters, sex shops, and tourist traps.

A pleasant place to shop is the **London Design Centre,** 28 Haymarket. The shop contains all British-designed items approved by the Design Council of Britain. You can find Beatrix Potter Wedgwood, Taylor's Eye Witness knives, books, stationery, jewelry, toys. Not just for tourists, the center is a means of connecting interested manufacturers with designers, and provides a referral service. There are galleries and a café that has salads, quiche, soup, wine, and claret. Open daily.

### Trocadero

Lord knows whence the Latino lilt to the title of this place, which is primarily designed to get the tourist off the street and give him a place to spend his stray £s. Not to be flip; some of the attractions are pretty amusing in this complex, which is part amusement gallery, part café conglomeration, part shopping mall. Best to see is the **London Experience,** at which five screens trace London's history from Rome through the plague, the Great Fire and the blitz, with emphasis, as you may have gathered, on the melodrama. The 35-minute multimedia presentation includes film, slides, computer-trafficked images, flames, clouds, strobes, smoke, and a roaring sound system. Good fun. (10 A.M. to 11 P.M. seven days; £2.50.)

The other good fun is to be found at the **Light Fantastic,** open 10 A.M. to 9:30 P.M., also seven days, also £2.50. Light Fantastic makes you feel like you're a hologram image as you creep along the catwalk bordered by mirrors and lights entering through a soundless sliding door into a room with intergalactic music. The gallery contains holograms, light sculptures, and other high-tech trompe l'oeil techniques, including a laser that "drips" off your finger and onto the floor.

# Belgravia, South Kensington, and Chelsea

There are three (at least) distinct neighborhoods packed in between the grass of Hyde Park and the waters of the Thames. Belgravia belonged to the Lords Grosvenor, whose name still graces many of the streets and businesses, and was built by them in the 1820s as a locale for the fashionable to rival the mansions of Mayfair.

SW1 post codes still carry the cachet of being some of the toniest properties in London—witness the number of embassies on Belgrave Square—ranged along its gracious streets and around its private gardens.

Just west of this area is Knightsbridge, whose inhabitants bicker over whether it is a neighborhood unto itself or merely the name of the main drag that runs through the area and along which you'll find the redoubtable Harrods. Dropping down from Knightsbridge is Sloane Street, another site of ritual shopping pilgrimages.

West of Knightsbridge is South Kensington (South Ken, if you're too busy to finish your phrases). Shopping mania continues here along Brompton Road. But sartorocentricism does give way to a flurry of culture in the collection of concert halls and museums clustered just south of Kensington Gardens at Kensington Gore. These facilities—among them are the Victoria and Albert Museum and the Royal Albert Hall—are all the descendants of the Great Exhibition of 1851, the Victorians' pardonably excessive revel in their own imperial might.

South of South Ken is Chelsea, which somehow, despite the maze of buildings, has managed to retain a certain scent of her pastoral origins. Chelsea's favorite shopping streets are among London's most important fashion centers these days. Along Fulham Road is a lineup of stores the constituents of which are constantly trying to keep ahead of the well-heeled Londoner whose taste Fulham essays to dictate. South of Fulham is King's Road, formerly the operating theater for London's punks who inspired designers like Katherine Hamnett and Vivienne Westwood to take their street-tough "fashion" up-market.

Not to be missed in Chelsea is the Chelsea Royal Hospital, Wren's second masterpiece in London. It's set in peaceful Ranelagh Gardens, which stretch down to the Thames, and is truly one of the city's most underappreciated, and therefore thankfully undercrowded, showpieces.

The smart thing to do is to plan a morning around museum hopping at the Victoria and Albert and its neighbors, then spend late afternoon exploring the Chelsea Royal Hospital. In between the two you can do a shopping serpentine along Fulham and King's roads.

## Royal Albert Hall

The **Hall** runs a very lively one-and-a-half-hour tour of its interior at regular intervals from 10 A.M. to 8 P.M., for £2.50.

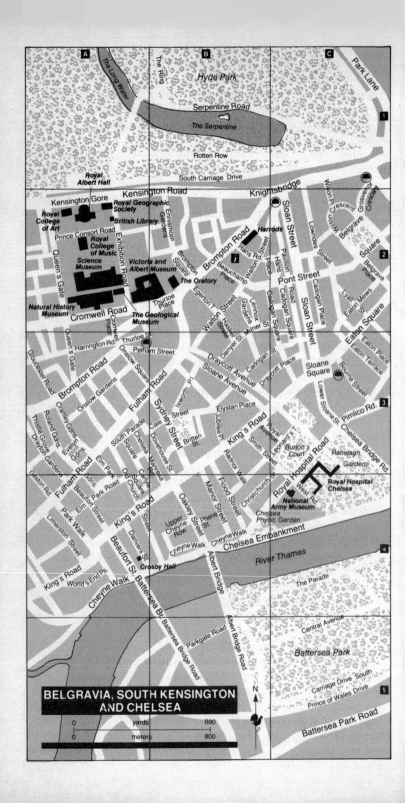

BELGRAVIA, SOUTH KENSINGTON AND CHELSEA

This includes the hall's art collection, which is otherwise closed to the public.

The hall today hosts an incredible variety of events, from basketball and championship tennis to pop concerts featuring the likes of Eric Clapton, Shirley Bassey, and Tammy Wynette. The acoustics are still excellent, making the Albert Hall a favorite among classical musicians as well. For summertime visitors, the Proms—a series of classical-music events—are held here from July. Information on scheduled events can be had by calling the box office at 589-8212. Tickets can be purchased with a major credit card by calling 589-9465.

## Exploring the Sciences

The **Science Museum** (open Monday through Saturday from 10 A.M. to 6 P.M., Sunday from 2:30 to 6 P.M.; admission is free) is immense and needs to be as the national museum for science and industry. Among the first exhibits you'll see is one devoted to steam engines, including a reconstruction of Watt's workshop whence came the industrial revolution, whence came the Empire, whence came the Exhibition, whence came the funds for this collection—get it? The museum covers the history of technology from the invention of the wheel to manned space travel.

The **Geological Museum** is available for inspection Monday through Saturday from 10 A.M. to 6 P.M., Sunday from 1 to 6 P.M. (£1). This museum traces the prehistoric life of Britain when it was part of the Old Red Continent. There are cases of glittering gems and the "World's Oldest Rock" displayed in state as augustly as are the sapphires. The more dramatic aspects of geologic change are illustrated by films of volcanoes and an earthquake simulator that re-creates a 1964 quake in Alaska. Standing on the platform as the tremors climb the Richter scale is like bronco riding—hold on!

You can pay £2 to visit the **Natural History Museum** Monday through Saturday from 10 A.M. to 6 P.M., Sunday from 1 to 6 P.M., or if you would like to sneak in a late-afternoon freebie, there is no admission charge if you arrive after 4:30 P.M. during the week, or after 5 P.M. Saturday and Sunday. The Great Hall as you enter is an impressive 1880s design that is an attraction in its own right. Daily events are listed on the blackboard at the entrance; schedules are available at the info desk to your right. The galleries that are the most popular display the remains of dinosaurs, the origins of man, and a collection of rocks and minerals. In certain galleries you'll find "focus points," manned trolleys for hands-on experience with rocks or animals or flowers. Take a stroll along the museum's arcade of shops before you leave.

## The Victoria and Albert Museum

The Victoria and Albert Museum is eclecticism incarnate. The collection is mammoth and encompasses an astonishing range of literally millions of objects. The museum can embrace such a variety of departments because its stated purpose on the occasion of its opening in 1909 was "to encourage and promote a high standard of excellence among the craftsmen, manufacturers and designers of this country." The museum is open Monday through Saturday from 10 A.M. to 5:50 P.M., Sunday from 2:30 to 5:50 P.M., and you'll need every minute to see what you'll want to see. To simplify things, you might like to take a guided introductory tour, which begins at 11:30 A.M. Monday through Saturday, or a tour of the museum's "treasures," which runs at 2 P.M.

The general layout of the museum runs thusly: The main floor is for general-overview collections, items with a common theme deposited in a particular gallery. The upper floors have corresponding galleries for the main-floor rooms, but the exhibits are aimed at those whose interest in the particular style, period, or genre is more scholarly and specific.

 The **V&A lunchroom** is bright and airy, with blond-wood tables at which you can enjoy a light meal with wine, cider, beer, or tea in the afternoon. The shop is a good place to find gifts supplied by the Crafts Council for your design-conscious friends.

## Old-Style Chic

A half-mile away from the place, you'll begin to notice a smug succession of shoppers with their telltale green and gold bags. Just to drop a few names, the orange façade of **Harrods** boasts the arms of the Queen, the Duke of Edinburgh, the Queen Mum, and the Prince of Wales in larger-than-life relief.

Re Harrods: There is not a great difference between it and many other deluxe department stores here in London and the world over, but try telling that to the millions who sweep in, misty-eyed with the thrill, every year. The most interesting and unusual feature of the store are the food halls—the likes of which you will *not* find elsewhere—but don't get glued to the food; the rooms are all tile and Rococo ceilings. Display is as important as produce; check out the hammerhead shark deftly incorporated in the *tableau vivante montage de la mer.*

If you'd like to find many of the same clothes and furnishings as Harrods in a less manic and melodramatic setting, seek refuge down the street at quietly chic **Harvey Nichols.**

Also frightfully up-market are the shops along **Sloane Street** north of Cadogan Gardens. Clustered here are the European designers.

## The Nerve Center

Terence Conran, the tireless, ubiquitous designer, must have the world's most effective PR machine: Everywhere over the past year travel writers have been gushing ink and purple prose over his renovation of the **Michelin House** at 81 Fulham Road, an address that has become akin to the first step on the Yellow Brick Road to London's Oz of shopping.

On your left as you enter is the **Oyster Bar,** whose aphrodisiacal wares are excessively overpriced, as are most things in the upstairs restaurant—appropriately named **Bibendum** for the pudgy, pneumatic guy. Much more fun (reasonable, if not cheap) is **Grabowski,** a wine bar-cum-gallery behind the funky mosaic directly across Sloane Avenue.

Sir Terence has set up shop in the back. He has collected well-thought-out and well-wrought furnishings from about the globe and serenades your purchasing with thirties pop tunes. Downstairs are more affordable wares and a gourmet department great for hostess gifts.

You can explore along Fulham Road which is currently "Design Center."

## Down-Market Chic

**King's Road** is where the world rediscovered black, black leather, black leather with studs, black leather with studs and black lace.

The days of punk are fading fast, but among the junky leather and T-shirt shops that are still trying to capitalize on the old days are some places that are still interested in taking risks and setting, instead of following, fashion. Drop in at **Jones** (two stores), **the Shop for Boy, Darlajane Gilroy,** and **Manolo Blahnik** (on Old Church Street). One hates to make many further suggestions of where to shop on King's Road because in the first place, prices rocket and fashion swerves, and secondly by the time you make your way back to your favorite boutique, it will have been replaced by a Pizza Hut.

## Chelsea Royal Hospital

One feature of the neighborhood that will certainly continue to stand the test of time as it has done for over three hundred years is Sir Christopher Wren's magnificent building beside the Thames. A quarter mile down King's Road from Sloane Square is an arcade of trees bordered by some very nice houses and a graveled walkway heading toward the river. Beyond the trees of Royal Avenue is the **Royal Hospital,** truly one of London's most breathtaking vistas to this day.

The hospital is not strictly speaking a facility for nursing the sick but is more along the lines of the French institutions built to house their returned and perhaps ailing soldiers.

Within the hospital, the Chapel, Great Hall, and Museum are open Monday through Saturday from 10 A.M. to noon and 2 to 4 P.M.

The hospital enjoys a splendid setting in Ranelagh Gardens. Beyond the avenue of elms is the Chelsea Bridge, and beyond that is a power station due to be transformed into a fun-fest leisure center. The gardens are the site each May of the Chelsea Flower Show, always a most rewarding, if claustrophobic, event.

# St. James's, Mayfair, and the Parks

This is the never-never land of gentlemen's clubs, royal warrants, bespoke tailors, and neighborhood royals-in-residence to keep the uninitiated properly agog. Although the sovereign now lives down the Mall at Buckingham Palace, the Queen Mum's in-town residence is Clarence House in St. James's and foreign envoys to Britain are still styled Ambassadors to the Court of St. James's.

The Royal Parks—Hyde, Green, St. James's, provides Londoners of all ranks with a cool, spacious playground.

Add to this shopping for London's finest on St. James's, Jermyn, Bond, Regent, and South Molton streets, taking a ritual tea at the Ritz or the Dorchester, roaming through the galleries of the Royal Academy or along Cork Street, and you'll find there is plenty of diversion for the traveler who appreciates the best without necessarily having to pay for it.

## The Mall

Probably the best way to begin is to take a leisurely stroll along the esplanade of the Mall.

At the eastern end of the Mall are a group of Georgian terraces designed by John Nash of Regent's Park fame. On the Mall level of **Nash House** (No. 12) is the **Institute of Contemporary Arts (ICA).** The ICA incorporates and celebrates all the modern incarnations of the arts. There is a 75-pence admission charge to the galleries and special events require additional fees, depending upon the program. The shop stocks funky jewelry, postcards, and a good selection of art books and journals. There is a café/bar servicing the theaters and the three galleries. Tickets for all events are available at the box office. All tickets are half price on Mondays. The ICA is open 12 to 9:30 P.M.

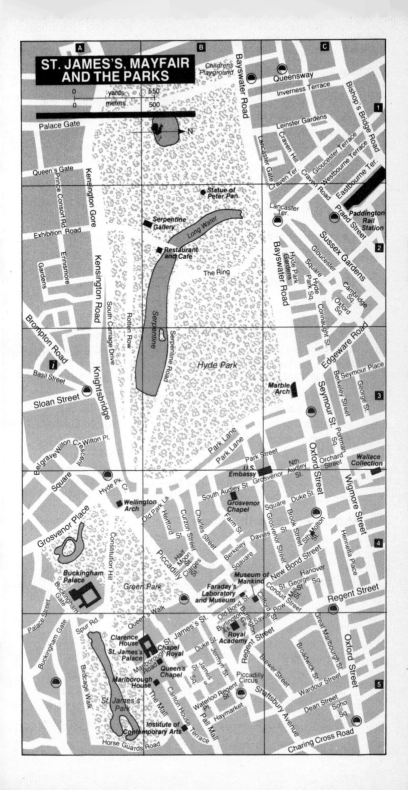

# ST. JAMES'S, MAYFAIR AND THE PARKS

0 yards 550
0 meters 500

N

Palace Gate

Queen's Gate

Kensington Gore

Prince Consort Rd

Exhibition Road

Ennismore Gardens

Kensington Road

Brompton Road

South Carriage Drive

Knightsbridge

Basil Street

Sloan Street

Belgrave Wilton Crescent Wilton Pl.

Square

Grosvenor Place

Constitution Hill

Buckingham Palace

Palace Street

Buckingham Gate

Spur Rd

Birdcage Walk

St James's Park

Horse Guards Road

Childrens Playground

Bayswater Road

Queensway

Inverness Terrace

Leinster Gardens

Leinster Terrace

Craven Hill

Lancaster Gate

Craven Ter. Craven Road

Lancaster Ter.

Statue of Peter Pan

Serpentine Gallery

Long Water

Restaurant and Cafe

The Ring

Rotten Row

Serpentine

Serpentine Road

Hyde Park

Park Lane

Park Lane

Park Street

U.S. Embassy

Grosvenor

Nth Audley St.

South Audley St.

Grosvenor Chapel

Farm St.

Square Duke St.

Old Park La.

Hertford

Curzon Street

Charles Street

Berkeley Square

Davies Street

Grosvenor Street

Brook Street

St Molton

Hay Hill

Half Moon Street

Clarges

Piccadilly

Museum of Mankind

New Bond Street

St. George Hanover St.

Conduit Street

Clifford St.

Faraday's Laboratory and Museum

Old Bond St.

Burlington

Sackville St.

Savile Row

Burlington

Royal Academy

Regent Street

Street Marlborough St.

Green Park

Queen's Walk

Clarence House

St. James's Palace

Chapel Royal

Marlborough Road

Queen's Chapel

Duke St.

St. James's

Jermyn St.

St. James's Sq.

Regent Street

Brewer Street

Broadwick St.

Oxford Street

Marlborough House

Institute of Contemporary Arts

Pall Mall

Carlton House Terrace

Waterloo

Regent St.

Haymarket

Piccadilly Circus

Shaftsbury Avenue

Wardour Street

Dean Street

Soho Sq.

Charing Cross Road

Bishop's Bridge Road

Gloucester Terrace

Westbourne Terrace

Eastbourne Ter.

Praed Street

Paddington Rail Station

Sussex Gardens

Gloucester

Hyde Park Square Sq.

Cambridge Sq.

Oxford Sq.

Connaught St.

Bayswater Road

Edgeware Road

Seymour Place

Berkeley Street

George St.

Marble Arch

Seymour St.

Portman Sq.

Orchard St.

Oxford Street

Wigmore Street

Wallace Collection

Henrietta Place

Regent Street

A    B    C

1    2    3    4    5

### The Heart of St. James's

Up the stairs from the ICA are **Carlton Gardens** and the original **Pall Mall.** For those of a tobaccan turn, **Rothmans** is located at No. 65 and there you can buy, of course, cigarettes, signature crystal, cuff links, and luggage. Although you cannot enter **St. James's Palace,** you are certainly permitted to skirt its exterior, which is full of Tudor architectural detailing, and perhaps the great clock will sound while you are doing so.

Running up from Pall Mall is St. James's Street, boasting some of London's oldest and finest merchants. **Berry Brothers and Rudd, Ltd.** has been selling wines since the 17th century behind its black, glossy façade. **Lock and Company** is as much a museum of old hats as a store for new ones. **D. R. Harris,** self-styled "Purveyors of Toiletries and Medicines to Royalty and the Gentry," will have been in business two hundred years in 1990.

### The Clubs

Perhaps you noticed several smart buildings on either side of St. James's Street. **The Carlton, White's, Boodle's,** and **Brooks's** are among the last of a vanishing breed of gentlemen's clubs that flourished during the 18th and 19th centuries. At the close of the 17th century the coffee and chocolate houses of St. James's were famous for their gatherings of men discussing subjects of a political, social, or amorous nature. They tended to be segregated according to political affiliation, the Whigs favoring St. James's and the Tories preferring the Cocoa Tree. A rhyme of the day runs, "About 12 o'clock I go to the Cocoa Tree where I talk treason, then to St. James's Coffee House where I praise the Ministry, thence to White's where I talk gallantry."

### Shirtmakers to the Stars

Jermyn Street is known as the premier place for gentlemen's haberdashers. The most famous on the block is the redoubtable **Turnbull & Asser,** who are responsible for keeping the Prince of Wales in starch and looking smooth. There are cherubs and polychrome bunting to greet you at the door and an army of solemn salesmen ready to initiate you into the mysteries of custom-shirt selection.

## Piccadilly

Piccadilly sweeps down from the statue of Eros at its circus to the statue of Wellington at Hyde Park Corner. It's also full of fine shops, the most fun of which is certainly **Fortnum & Mason.** With its sage green and gold façade and green and white chandeliered interior, this shop has been supplying London with the finest comestibles and dry goods for years.

Another fun place to shop is the **Burlington Arcade.** Get the Regency feel of browsing along this covered galleria of 39 shops with storefronts downstairs, more space up. You can find cashmere, tobacco, diamonds, handkerchiefs as Beau Brummell undoubtedly did in his day.

Hard by the Burlington Arcade is the **Royal Academy** (R.A.) at the far end of Burlington House Square. Sir Joshua Reynolds, the R.A.'s first president, stands in bronze at its center, brush and palette poised. Founded in 1768 to "promote the arts of design," the Royal Academy serves many functions. It is an art school, a public gallery, and an institution devoted to showcasing new and established talent. The R.A. is open daily from 10 A.M. to 6 P.M. Admission prices vary according to the exhibits you are interested in visiting. The shop has unusual books, periodicals, art supplies, even R.A. wines and champagne. There is a coffeeshop and also a lovely restaurant (open from 11:30 A.M. to 2:30 P.M.) with murals, special academy paper napkins and plates, a huge salad bar, and a hot and cold buffet.

## Art of Your Own

If you prefer to bring art appreciation into your very own home, the north end of the Burlington Arcade runs into Cork Street, a collection of galleries featuring primarily the work of modern artists. **Browse and Darby** concentrates on 20th-century Europeans with an emphasis on British painters. **Redfern** sells Hockney, Miro, Chagall. **Waddington Graphics** has prints, some for as little as £75, by Alex Katz, Milton Avery, Jasper Johns, Jim Dine, Robert Motherwell. Even if you're not in the market for a £10,000 "investment," the street as a whole is a modern-art mall perfect for browsing.

## Savile Row

Just to the east is Savile Row, decorated with more coats of arms than Windsor Castle. Underlings are out polishing the brass, and through the railings you can peer down to the basement workrooms, where the tailors look anything but fashionable in their bifocals with a tape measure as cravat. Savile Row is, of course, the home of correct gentlemen's clothing—although Hardy Ames, the Queen's dressmaker, has a shop at No. 14 in a building once occupied by playwright Richard Brinsley Sheridan, whose fops and dandies certainly patronized the street's tailors.

## Regent Street

Regent Street was part of John Nash's master plan for an imposing Continental-style avenue between Regent's Park and St. James's Palace, where the Regent (George IV) resided. Although the street doesn't quite cut a straight line as originally intended, the breaks and curves make for interesting strolling. And its high-minded plan has attracted a group of distinctly up-market shops. South from Oxford Circus is **Laura Ashley's** flagship store, with aisles of flowers and ruffles, little girls stuffed into sailor dresses, and boyfriends collapsed resignedly into chairs. Clothes are considerably cheaper here than overseas, especially during sales (January and August). Just down from there is **Dickins & Jones,** a department store so soigné that a pianist by the door serenades you as you make your perfume purchases.

## At Long Last, Liberty's

Perhaps the best department store in the world, certainly the best in London, is **Liberty's.** It's most impressive to enter at the main door on Great Marlborough Street into a five-story atrium—built before anybody else had the idea. Throughout the store you'll enjoy the Tudor-style architecture, which incorporates timbers from two of the British Navy's last sailing ships

After buying a precious smocked dress for the little one at Liberty's, visit **Hamley's,** Her Majesty's own toy merchant. When the Queen needs a Barbie or a Master of the Universe, this is where she calls. Planes zoom overhead and a terrific model railroad chugs around the room. This is a great place to get an official, from-London Paddington Bear.

At the curve in Regent Street known as the Quadrant is **Garrard and Co.,** crown jewelers. Plush carpets muffle any disturbance, and the air is perfumed by sprays of fresh flowers as you select your own regal gems. In the rear are sculptures in gold, amethyst, and diamonds—*caravelles* and magic mountains—large and massively ugly (no accounting for taste).

# The Royal Parks

The welcome triumvirate of air and space that make up the Royal Parks has been called the lungs of London; certainly after the fumes and noise and fuss of town it is a most delightful, nay essential, relief to take to the paths of Hyde, Green, St. James's, or Kensington Gardens by foot, bike, or horse.

The parks have their distinctive characters. **St. James's** is floral and faunal with bunches of daffodils in spring and lots of waterfowl paddling past the geyseresque fountain. **Green Park** is trees and grass—there is a legend that flowers won't grow here because it was formerly used as a burial ground for the patients at St. James's Hospital (for lepers).

**Hyde Park** is by far the largest and most diverse. Its eastern end has contoured topography and a random planting of trees. The Serpentine lake snakes its way through the center, and beyond it the land flattens out to the more formal tree-lined walkways of **Kensington Gardens.**

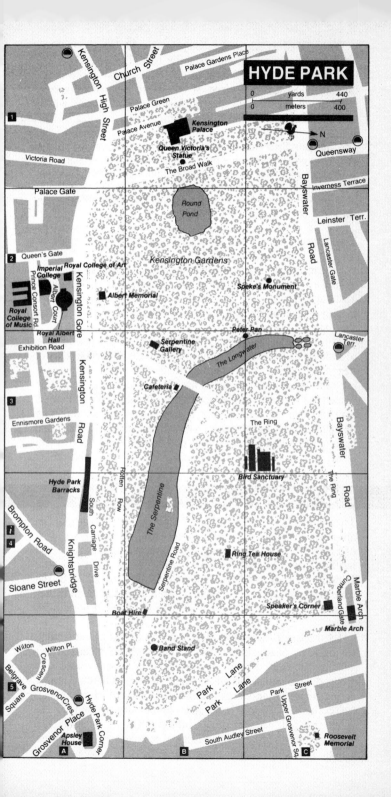

# HYDE PARK

0 yards 440
0 meters 400

N

Kensington High Street
Church Street
Palace Gardens Place
Palace Green
Palace Avenue
Kensington Palace
Queen Victoria's Statue
The Broad Walk
Victoria Road
Queensway
Inverness Terrace
Bayswater Road
Leinster Terr.
Palace Gate
Round Pond
Lancaster Gate
Queen's Gate
Imperial College
Royal College of Art
Prince Consort Rd
Albert Court
Kensington Gore
Royal College of Music
Kensington Gardens
Albert Memorial
Speke's Monument
Royal Albert Hall
Exhibition Road
Kensington Road
Peter Pan
Serpentine Gallery
The Longwater
Lancaster Terr.
Cafeteria
Ennismore Gardens
The Ring
Bird Sanctuary
Bayswater Road
Hyde Park Barracks
Rotten Row
South Carriage Drive
The Ring
Brompton Road
Knightsbridge
The Serpentine
Serpentine Road
Ring Tea House
Sloane Street
Cumberland Gate
Marble Arch
Boat Hire
Speaker's Corner
Marble Arch
Wilton
Wilton Pl.
Crescent
Band Stand
Belgrave Square
GrosvenorCres.
Grosvenor Place
Hyde Park Corner
Apsley House
Park Lane
Park Lane
Park Street
Upper Grosvenor Street
South Audley Street
Roosevelt Memorial

1
2
3
4
5
A
B
C

Within Hyde Park is the **Serpentine Gallery,** set back from the southeastern shore of the lake. It's open Monday through Friday from 10 A.M. to 6 P.M. Saturday and Sunday till 7 P.M.; admission is free. If you'd like a bit of culture to go with your nature, wander through the sunlit space, which tends to display the work of modern artists.

The **Serpentine Restaurant** is not worth the money unless you get a window seat. It's better for cocktails. Better still is the **Café Pergola** take-away or outdoor buffet next door. This way you can position yourself according to your desires to watch the boaters, the ducks, and perhaps a game golden retriever sallying into the drink after the latter.

You can rent a boat and enjoy the watery part of the park at the boathouse on the south bank.

During the summer a bandstand is used for concerts held from 3 to 4:30 and 6 to 7:30 P.M. Sundays and bank holiday Mondays from the end of May through August. Programs are usually posted on the large you-are-here maps deployed about the park.

At the Marble Arch corner of the park is a place where all of London is welcome to vent its hostilities. **Speakers Corner** was so designated after a particularly fiery orator preaching anti-government policies was hauled off to prison. The citizenry rose up in protest, and the powers that be thought it prudent to set aside a spot in the city where anyone was permitted to hold forth on any view. Its proximity to the traffic roar of Park Lane insures that not even the most powerful lungs or ideas could possibly be discerned above the din.

# Bloomsbury and Marylebone

These precincts have somehow always managed to attract the attention and patronage of an interesting crowd. Like most of London's more extreme margins, they began as farm and hunting land. The reason such a large space as close to central London as Regent's Park remained "unimproved" until the 19th century was that previously the Royals had been rather jealous about parting with any of their convenient outlets for sport.

By the late 19th century, the most important of the several generations of artists and philosophers who had chosen this serene atmosphere took up residence in north London and were duly dubbed the Bloomsbury Group. Famous among them, for example were Virginia and Leonard Woolf.

To this day, Marylebone and Bloomsbury are among the most tranquil, attractive, cerebral patches of London. The area around Bloomsbury and Russell squares is the traditional habitat of lawyers and professors, the latter of whom practice their trade at the University of London nearby. The university, of course, lends gravity and purpose to the region even as its students inject a bit of fun and energy into what otherwise might become an area drowsy with its own ease.

To keep the intellectuals keen there are some of London's best museums, great and small, tucked away in primarily residential streets. Principal among them, of course, is the incomparable British Museum, home of the Elgin Marbles, the Rosetta Stone, the Diamond Sutra, and various other treasures pirated back to the mother country by British explorers in the name of preservation.

There are plenty of pursuits of a less serious nature as well: a tour through Madame Tussaud's waxworks, a game of cricket at Lord's—world headquarters of the sport—or perhaps a visit to the London Zoo.

## The British Museum

The British Museum and Library was begun in 1753 with the art and scientific collections of Sir Hans Sloane, whose will directed they should be sold to the nation at bargain-basement prices.

Today, the museum has ninety—count 'em, ninety—galleries full of treasures brought here by the unflagging zeal of the same people who brought the world the empire upon which the sun never set.

The most fascinating aspects of the museum are its holdings devoted to ancient civilizations. It is possible to travel from the galleries of ancient Egypt, where you'll find the Rosetta Stone to the Ninevah Galleries, in which are reconstructed Assyrian temples, and finally to the Duveen rooms, inhabited by the warriors and steeds of the Elgin Marbles, "rescued" from the frieze of the Parthenon in Athens.

Among the British Library collection of documents and manuscripts important to the British people there are two of the remaining copies of the Magna Carta of 1215, complete with the signature of King John, next to which is another, more fabulously famous work by another British John, an original copy of Mr. Lennon and Mr. McCartney's "Yesterday," on loan with several of their manuscripts. The museum is open Monday through Saturday from 10 A.M. to 5 P.M., Sunday from 2:30 to 6 P.M. Admission is free. Gallery talks run daily at 11:30 A.M. except Sunday; lectures are given daily at 1:15 P.M., except Sunday and Monday. Additionally, there is a perpetual whirl of films, videos, and special events. Pick up a listing leaflet at the information desk, and be sure to consult the information video listing daily features.

## The Galleries at University of London

The northerly reaches of Bloomsbury are occupied by the **University of London.** The university has been the beneficiary of several great art collections over the years.

The **Courtauld Institute Galleries,** located on the southwest corner of Woburn Square, are open Monday through Saturday from 10 A.M. to 5 P.M., Sunday from 2 to 5 P.M.; admission is £1.50.

Samuel Courtauld was a textile industrialist who pioneered the development of such synthetics as rayon. He and Mrs. Courtauld collected all the important Impressionists and donated to the university their holdings along with their town house on Portland Place, which was endowed for use as an institute for the study of art history. The institute's collection was aggrandized by the posthumous donation of several other important private collections, including one of old master paintings and drawings.

The **Percival David Foundation of Chinese Art** is located nearby at 53 Gordon Square and is open Monday through Friday from 10:30 A.M. to 5 P.M. Percival David was a great scholar and collector of things Chinese. The collection begins with ceramics from the Sung Dynasty—nearly one thousand years old—and continues through Ming and Ch'ing into the 18th century.

## ST. MARYLEBONE FOR SHOPPING AND LUNCHING

The sights discussed thus far have been in Bloomsbury; continuing westward WC1 gives way to the W1 addresses of St. Marylebone. **Marylebone High Street** is a good shopping route; better still is smaller, sinuous **Marylebone Lane,** which snakes its way southward to Oxford Street.

Stop in for lunch at No. 35, **Paul Rohe and Son Deli.** They have super-cheap sandwiches to take away or eat at their lo-tech tables; save room for a custard tart.

The most fun shopping street, however, is tiny **St. Christopher's Place** just west of Marylebone Lane off Wigmore Street. There is **Mulberry and Co.** (with correct clothes and luggage), **The Changing Room** (casual, constructed clothes), and **Droopy and Browns** (romantic frocks for the ladies).

## The Wallace Collection

After a bout of shopping seek refuge in the glorious sanctuary of the Wallace Collection on Manchester Square. The building, Hertford House (1776–88), has served as the Spanish and French embassies but was built as a residence by the Dukes of Manchester and acquired eventually by the Marquesses of Hertford, the first of whom was a patron of Reynolds and who founded a long line of art lovers and collectors.

The collection is open Monday through Saturday from 10 A.M. to 5 P.M., Sunday from 2 to 5 P.M. and is free. There is an abundance of riches here. Upstairs are painting galleries. There is also a room of European and Persian armors, and French and English porcelain and furnishings.

## A Visit to Madame Tussaud's

Marylebone's second museum—certainly more famous than the first—is **Madame Tussaud's Waxworks,** and connected to the waxworks is the **London Planetarium.** Admission to Madame Tussaud's is £4.30; to the planetarium, £2.50; or buy a combo ticket for £5.60. Lines stretch around the block, especially on the weekends and bank holidays, so come early and during the week. (Open daily 10 A.M. to 5:30 P.M.)

Since pre-revolutionary Paris, Madame Tussaud's has been entertaining the masses. Today new figures are made in a workroom at the top of this building, which has stood here for over one hundred years. The tour begins as a history lesson with Pepys at his diary, Mary, Queen of Scots, at her execution, and a petite, barely postpubescent Victoria receiving news of her accession. At the center of the room is the Sleeping Beauty tableau, with a "breathing" princess. There is a room of famous rulers and downstairs a chamber of horrors. At Legend's Café, you may want to pass on the food, but don't miss the figures of Brando, Elvis, Marilyn, Chaplin, and Bogey. Additionally, you might enjoy the evening laser concerts accompanied by different rock tunes at the planetarium (nightly, £3.75).

## The Home of Cricket

West down Marylebone (you'll pass Sherlock Holmes's Baker Street), then north on Gloucester Place you'll come to Dorset Square, which was the site of Thomas Lord's (a self-made merchant magnate and sportsman from Yorkshire) original cricket ground, **Dorset Fields,** which has since 1787 been the home of the Marylebone Cricket Club. Continuing up Gloucester Road, left onto Park Road and left again onto St. John's Wood Road—a good twenty minute hike—will bring you to Dorset Fields' vast and venerable descendant, **Lord's Cricket Ground.** Both the Marylebone and the Middlesex County Cricket clubs play matches here that last from one to five days, April through September. For information about scheduling and tickets, call 289-1611. If you're a fan, or care to become one, there is the **Cricket Memorial Museum** and a tour of the grounds. For more information, call 289-1611. The **Lord's Shop** sells sweat- and T-shirts, towels, brollies, books, prints, sweaters, mugs, bats, balls, and rule books.

## Regent's Park

In the early 19th century John Nash was chosen to develop and landscape the site. He ringed the park with eight terraces—named for the king's brothers—that were distinct groupings of milk-white to ecru town houses connected behind a unifying Greek-revival façade. Nash's plan incorporated residences, shops, and a farmers' market surrounding a huge area of green, producing the ultimate inner-city suburb. A circumambulation of the park's perimeter is a most satisfying stroll. If you can, plan to do the circuit at dusk, just when they're ringing the closing bells at the zoo, making the coyotes howl. The skylight diminishes and the city lights come up along the arcade of Park Square and Park Crescent just south of the park; it is one of London's prettiest and most romantic promenades.

At the northern end of the park is the **London Zoo.** The descendant of the Tower of London Menagerie, this is the oldest zoo in the world. It is decidedly not old-fashioned, however; cages have given over to natural-habitat environments. Join the stroller traffic jams or ride the steam train through the animals of Asia. The elephants bathe at 3:45 P.M., and feeding times range from 1:30 to 3 P.M. There are lots of special events on weekends and bank holidays. Open daily 9 A.M. to dusk, winter hours from 10 A.M.; admission is £3.90.

# Clerkenwell and Holborn

Both of these neighborhoods have names associated with London's gone and nearly forgotten water supply. Holburne stream was a tributary of the Fleet River. The Clerkes Well was an underground source used by the worshipful company of parish clerks, a guild whose "craft" was to assist priests in their official tasks and who put on mystery plays around the well during the Middle Ages. The area has seen many changes and gone through various incarnations—from savory to sordid and back again.

Today, Holborn and Clerkenwell have much to tantalize the traveler who is interested in looking beyond the pretty parks and imposing museums and into the lives of working-class Londoners. There is a wide variety of professions and dispositions to be found here. Three of London's Inns of Court—Staple, Gray's, and Lincoln's—and the Public Record Office Museum, representing the law, are here. Vestiges of the days when the fields and farms were owned by powerful ecclesiastical orders are the Charterhouse, St. John's Gate and Museum, and St. Etheldreda's Cathedral—London's oldest Catholic church. Legacies left behind by former residents are Sir John Soane's Museum, the Dickens House and Museum, and the Old Curiosity Shop where Little Nell plied her pitiful trade.

Clerkenwell is getting bullish on itself: witness the Clerkenwell Heritage Centre at Clerkenwell Road and St. John's Square. It promotes these regions as a unified, important entity within London. Daily walking tours begin here during spring and summer, usually at 2:30 P.M. To be sure they are departing the day you want to go, call 250-1039.

## Monks and Knights

**The Charterhouse** has limited hours: a one-hour guided tour runs only on Wednesday afternoons at 2:45 P.M. from April through July; it is wise to call ahead to book a place on the tour (253-9503). It is also difficult to find; the entrance is on Charterhouse Square at the Aldersgate Street end of Charterhouse Street.

The name Charterhouse is a mangling of Chartreuse, the place from which came the Carthusians, the order of monks for whom the place was originally built in 1371. The buildings served as a priory until they were taken over during the Dissolution of the Monasteries, by Henry VIII, who ordered the prior and his monks executed for refusing to recognize him as head of the new (Anglican) church.

The path of the tour wends its way through beautiful walled gardens patrolled by legions of cats to keep the city vermin down. The interiors contain some of the only Elizabethan appointments remaining in London (including a charter granted to Sutton, signed by the queen herself). The Great Hall is rich with Tudor wood paneling, charred in the war but splendidly restored. There is furniture from the original monastery throughout, and some of the original Carthusian cells can still be seen. The Chapel walls are from the 14th century and contain a 17th-century memorial to Thomas Sutton. In the Gallery are English-made Tudor tapestries and an original, most unusual Jacobean fireplace. For years residents assumed it was black, but renovation after the bombing revealed that it had in fact been brightly painted with the Royal Coat of Arms, an Annunciation, and a Last Supper.

Before you take your tour here, you might like to take some luncheon in the **Café du Marché,** down a little alley at the far end of Charterhouse Square. Wood-paneled and beamed, it serves French food with an emphasis on the freshest and best meats brought from Smithfield next door.

## The Dissolution of the Monasteries

Henry VIII, primarily remembered for his proclivity to switch spouses, more importantly should be remembered for solidifying and aggrandizing the Tudor monarchy in Britain. One of Henry's primary means of securing power was through transfering power from the church to the state. The first step in this process was Henry's break with Rome over the decision to divorce his first wife, and the concurrent establishment of the Church of England with himself at its head, as mandated by the Act of Supremacy in 1534.

In 1535, under the direction of his minister, Thomas Cromwell, a volume, *Valor Ecclesiasticus,* was presented to Henry, describing in minute detail the wealth of the various ecclesiastic organizations in the realm. This was the final impetus needed to convince Henry to do what many of his court tacitly supported: confiscate church holdings for himself, and sell off or grant in favor the excess.

The nobility largely approved of the move because many of them already leased monastic lands, and saw this as their chance to own the properties outright. Henry's special allies naturally received the primest plots, and their fealty was thus bought and secured. The common folk often had little love for the inhabitants of the monasteries or abbeys, many churchmen and women were foreigners—French or Italian—spoke little English and had little to do with the neighboring communities. Indeed, the medieval monastic life of contemplation and charity had largely disintegrated, and there was no longer the need or tolerance for those who would perpetuate the sham of piety which monastic life had largely become.

The Dissolution of the Monasteries was effected in two stages between 1538 and 47. In 1536 a Court of Augmentations was appointed to disband any order whose annual income was less than £200. Cromwell's plan was to "practice" on the smaller, less influential orders in order to increase monies in the royal coffers, and also to gauge public opinion and quell any resistance, before advancing on the wealthy and powerful churches. Brother and sisterhoods were disbanded and occasionally their members were executed for refusing to accept the Act of Supremacy, art treasures were destroyed or sold off, lands were broken up, and churches were partially or totally razed, their stones often serving as building materials for manor houses constructed by the new landowners. By 1547 it is estimated that Henry raked in between £800,000 and 1.5 million, halving again his net worth, and providing much needed funds for his grandiose palace–building schemes and (largely unsuccessful) foreign military campaigns.

**The Museum of the Order of St. John** is located at St. John's Gate—you can't miss it, straddling as it does a pedestrian street below St. John's Square.

The name is today famous in Britain and throughout the world for the St. John's Ambulance Service, one of the first groups to utilize modern transport—first autos and now heli-

copters—to rescue accident victims speedily and get them to a hospital.

The origins are ancient, beginning with the Military Knights Hospitalar. The tradition of attending the sick began during the Crusades, after which the knights set up hospitals along the routes to the Holy Land and in Jerusalem itself to care for exhausted, wounded, and diseased pilgrims. The museum is open Monday through Friday from 10 A.M. to 5 P.M., Saturday from 10 till 4 P.M. The rest of the buildings (the best part) can only be seen by taking an hour-and-a-half guided tour on open days at 11 A.M. and 2:30 P.M.

## Dickens at Home

The **Dickens House,** 48 Doughty Street, is open Monday through Saturday from 10 A.M. to 5 P.M.; admission is £1.50. Charles Dickens, who was paid by the word and waxed loquacious thereby, lived here for most of his adult life, from 1812–70. It is a modest, unassuming house. If you're not a Dickensian by nature, you may find the exhibits a bit dense and disappointing. There are knickknacks from his life, prints of favorite characters, curtained cases of correspondences, first editions, illustrations, reading-tour texts. The shop has rare and old editions and bits of repro-Victoriana for sale.

## On to the Inns

**Gray's Inn,** rather unremarkable rectangles of buildings built in the 14th through 16th centuries, saw a lot of service during the wars. Members of the local army corps drilled here for the First World War, and the complex was heavily bombed during the Second. The Chapel is rather nondescript, with studies of modern heroes of the church and jurisprudence in stained glass.

The most pleasant part of Gray's Inn are its gardens, entrance from Gray's Inn Place, open to the public for alfresco lunching Monday through Friday from 12 to 2:30 P.M.

South of High Holborn is another barristorial bastion, **Lincoln's Inn.** The only part of Lincoln's Inn regularly open to the public is the Chapel (hours: 12 to 2:30 P.M., Monday through Friday). It was built to an Inigo Jones design between 1619 and 1623. It is here that John Donne, preacher to the Honorable Society of Lincoln's Inn, gave the chapel's first sermon to a large and eager crowd.

## A Curious Museum

At No. 13 Lincoln's Inn Fields is **Sir John Soane's Museum,** open Tuesday through Saturday from 10 A.M. to 5 P.M.; admission is free. Sir John Soane, R.A., lived here from 1813–37, having popped over from next door at No. 12, where he originally lived and which he designed along with this house and No. 14.

Soane was a painter and primarily an architect and a collector of a most unusual sort indeed. His interests were eclectic and so, therefore, are the contents of this house. The rooms have works by Veronese, Rubens, and Turner. Soane's personal, quirky collection of books, paintings, sculpture, architectural fragments, fungi samples, notebooks, et al., is indeed fascinating, but you wouldn't want to dust it.

### A Curious Shop and Pub

Just south of Lincoln's Inn Fields at 13–14 Portsmouth Street you'll recognize **Dickens's Old Curiosity Shop.** The author's first editions are for sale here at exorbitant prices. Escape the crush of souvenir seekers upstairs, where a case of Dickensiana and junkish antiques are sagging out from under the beams.

If you crave more Dickensian flavor, down the passage at 145 Fleet St. is perennial favorite pub and chop house, **Ye Olde Cheshire Cheese,** circa 1667.

In the chop room is a first edition of Dickens's *A Tale of Two Cities* opened to the page that refers to this establishment. Steaming joints are carried past you, sawdust scrunches underfoot, the church-pew benches have been worn down to a comfortable smoothness. The place is large, so do some exploring.

## A Final Inn and a First Church

East down High Holborn is the **Staple Inn,** the last of the Inns of Court. Its most interesting aspect is the row of Tudor frontages along High Holborn.

Just past Holborn Circus on Ely Place is **St. Etheldredas,** London's oldest Catholic church, built in 1293.

It is possible to have some of your earthly appetite slaked here at the **Pantry,** which serves cheap, cheap food at lunch: meat pies with two veggies for £1.70, lasagne for £2 to eat in or take away. If you prefer something alcoholic, down twisty Ely Place is **Ye Olde Mitre Tavern,** a neighborhood fixture since the 17th century. Picnic tables hoard every available scrap of sunlight in the tiny alley.

# Kensington

The Royal Borough of Kensington received its regal status in 1901 in consideration of the fact that Queen Victoria had been born at Kensington Palace, still occupied by some of the Royals when they are in town. In 1965 Kensington was incorporated with Chelsea, a mammoth merger, which properly included Kensington, Earls Court, South Kensington, and Chelsea. It would be sheer silliness to suggest that one could cover an area so vast and varied as this mega-borough in one go, so we've broken it down into a brace of touring centers, with the logical boundary between them being Kensington High Street.

Kensington is a beauty of a borough worth a long, lazy savoring—so you should be sure to give it all the attention due accorded a royal borough.

## Kensington Palace

A good place to begin your peregrinations is at Kensington Palace, the only palace in London of which a major portion is open for public inspection. It is, relative to other palaces you may have seen on the Continent or elsewhere in Britain, surprisingly understated. John Evelyn pronounced the house "very noble tho not greate"—an epithet quite appropriate to the place.

Until the reign of George III, Kensington was the preferred palace of British monarchs, who made various alterations to the interior and grounds. The palace then fell out of favor and was used by lesser members of the royal family until 1819, when the Duke of Kent, recently married to Princess Victoria of Saxe-Coburg, moved in with his pregnant wife, who in May of that year gave birth to a daughter, also Victoria. Victoria was raised here but moved to Buckingham Palace upon her accession to the throne.

There is quite a lot to see at the palace: private royal apartments, an exhibit explaining court protocol, and a terrific collection of finery, including Princess Di's wedding dress. The exhibits are open from 9 A.M. to 5 P.M., from 1 P.M. on Sunday. Admission is £2.60.

## A Slice of Victoriana

Continuing westward from the Palace is Kensington High Street. Make a right up Argyll Road and a quick left down Stafford Terrace. Number 18 is the **Linley Sambourne House.** It is only open from March through October, Wednesday from 10 A.M. to 4 P.M. and Sunday from 2 to 5 P.M., so be sure to schedule yourself accordingly. Admission is £1.50.

The house's 19th-century owner, Edward Linley Sambourne, drew satirical cartoons for *Punch* magazine. He filled his home with photographs and paintings he created or collected to use as inspiration for his own work, many examples of which are also hung around the house.

This is the only Victorian house in its original form in London. Sambourne's granddaughter Anne lived here till the end of her life and changed very little in the house. All the wallpaper, furniture, plumbing, and pictures remain untouched, as they appeared in 1875, right down to the walking sticks in the entry. The heavy, overstuffed furniture in the overstuffed

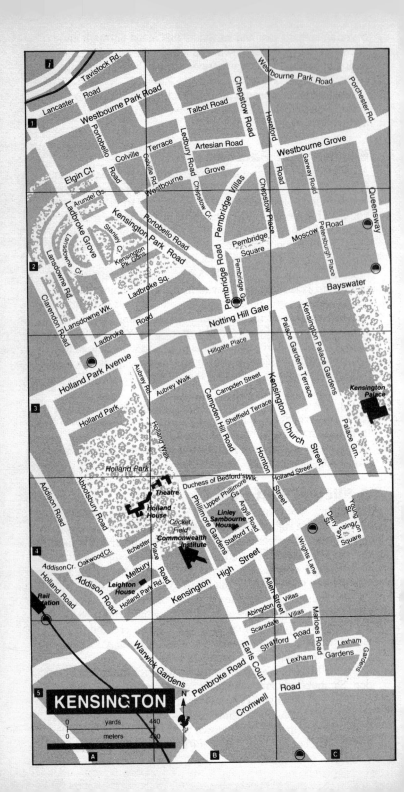

**KENSINGTON**

rooms preserves precisely the flavor of life for the artistic Kensingtonian of the Age of Empire.

Turn right off Kensington High Street onto Melbury Road and left on Holland Park Road. At No. 12 is **Leighton House,** the legacy of a second Victorian artist, Frederick Lord Leighton, painter and one-time president of the Royal Academy. Obviously concerned with making a bold aesthetic statement, Leighton worked with architect George Aitchison to create a residence the likes of which had not been seen before. Outside is a sculpture garden and lawn studded with daffodils and bluebells in the spring. The house is open Monday through Saturday from 11 A.M. to 5 P.M.; admission is free.

Leighton House is also the home of the Kensington and Chelsea Music Society. Most Thursday evenings at 7:30 concerts featuring chamber, vocal, and piano music are held in the upstairs studio. Tickets are £3.50 and can be reserved by phoning 602-6040. The combination of art and music makes for a most enjoyable evening.

## Holland Park

Holland Park is easily the prettiest park in central London. Its hillside topography and thick planting of trees and shrubs is the closest you'll come to finding the countryside in the city. **Holland House** and its grounds are the last of a lost era when Kensington was a town of country gentlemen's estates.

The park covers nearly 55 acres and preserves some of its original splendors in the 17th-century gateway attributed to Inigo Jones, a Dutch Garden full of tulips, the ballroom (which has been turned into a restaurant), an iris garden, a rose walk, the former ice house (now an exhibition space), 28 acres of woodlands called the Wildernesse, and several tennis courts. During the summer, the Open Air Theatre mounts productions of operas and Shakespeare, and other spectacles. Check the arts section of the daily papers for listings.

## To Market, to Market

London's most famous alfresco shopping is at the **Portobello Antiques Market.** Portobello Road is best reached from Notting Hill Gate. Right by the Underground station, on the north side of the street, is Pembridge Road, a left-hand fork off of which is Portobello Road. If you come for the Saturday market, you can't get lost, because you'll notice the streams of people heading in that direction. Today on any Saturday, the streets are just jammed with would-be bargain spotters rummaging through the old silver, jewelry, furniture, clothing, and knickknacks.

# The South Bank

The regions south of the Thames have for some time been viewed as *terra incognita* by generations of visitors to London. No doubt about it, compared to the river's northern shore, the things to see and do to the south are few and far between. It's had the unfortunate reputation of being a bombed-out, badly rebuilt working-class neighborhood with little color and less elegance. But inevitably, as space on the other side of the Thames is filling up, developers are looking back across at the South Bank as a logical place to deposit London's burgeoning population of yuppies so they can walk to work across Southwark or London Bridge to their jobs in the City. To amuse these new arrivals, a huge complex of stores, restaurants, and offices, called Hays Wharf, has just opened east of London Bridge. Hays Wharf does for southside London what the South Street Seaport did for New York and Quincy Market did for in Boston—revitalized a neighborhood needlessly neglected.

Hays Wharf joins another complex of new buildings designed to take advantage of underutilized space. Farther west at the river's great bend southward is the South Bank Centre, a most festive home of the arts that includes the Royal National Theatre Company's theaters, the National Film Theatre, the Hayward Gallery, Royal Festival Hall, and several other stages and galleries. Southwark (pronounced "suttuck" by locals) was once the home of brothels, breweries, prisons, and theaters. The most famous of this last group was of course the Globe, which was home to the Chamberlain's Men, a company whose principal asset was their playwright, son of a Cotswold glovemaker, William Shakespeare. The Globe was only one of a slew of theaters that favored the public with highbrow entertainment like *King Lear* but also some less cerebrally taxing fare such as bearbaiting, cockfighting, bullbaiting, and dogfighting.

Although the Puritans in a fit of righteous indignation had the theaters destroyed in the mid-17th century, Southwark, and its neighboring borough Rotherhithe, are still great places to go for a pint. All along the bank are wonderful pubs with great views and outdoor decks upon which you can enjoy the aquatic traffic plying Father Thames.

Ranged along the southern shore of the Thames are three boroughs: from east to west, Southwark, Bankside, and Lambeth. It is difficult to suggest the best way to tour the area because, as mentioned, the sights are spread far apart, and if you're on foot you will be obliged to walk through long stretches of run-down neighborhoods.

As for the Thames-side pubs, some will be along your route; two notable exceptions are The Mayflower and The Angel to the east in Rotherhithe. These places are great for lazy Sunday afternoon lunches, so you can catch them then (see "Pubs," below). Learning with Pleasure (868-5055) runs walking tours of the Bankside and Southwark area Sunday mornings at 10:30 and Wednesday afternoons at 2; admission is £2. The two-hour tours meet outside the London Bridge Underground station and hit all the vital spots, so you might like to do the Sunday tour before your lunch. Be sure to call first to confirm times.

## Galleria on the River

The Hays Wharf installations are being built and opened piece bypiece, and when it's all finished it will be a mini city unto itself. Of interest to the visitor is the **Hays Galleria,** a Milan-styled atrium with an overarching of glass, an unobstructed view to the river, and a sculpture depicting a humongous, improbable battleship. The galleria is full of up-market shops ranged around the high-gloss polished floors; offices line the atrium up above.

The **Horniman** is a pleasant restaurant overlooking the water populated by business folk at lunchtime.

Next door is the **Cottons Centre,** with another riveroverlook atrium replete with palm trees, waterfalls, and plenty of polished-granite floor space to accommodate exhibitions and cocktail parties for the nabobs.

## Southwark Cathedral

A Roman villa once stood on this site that was later to support a nunnery in 606. The official name of **Southwark Cathedral** is the Cathedral Church of St. Savior and St. Mary Overie ("over the river"). It has gone through many incarnations and many renovations.

There are a few vestiges of a 12th-century Norman priory within the 13th-century Gothic St. Mary Overie, which was begun in 1220, making it the first Gothic church in London and the only significant Gothic building in London besides Westminister Abbey. Because the church has been subject to fires, roof cave-ins, and the pleasure and displeasure of various monarchs, much of the Gothic construction has been replaced or obscured.

There are organ recitals on Mondays and concerts on Wednesdays at 1:10 P.M. after the Eucharist. Check the schedule by the info desk.

Just south of the cathedral, under the BritRail trestle, is the **Borough Market.** If you happen to be here before midmorning, you can catch the jaunty, agricultural atmosphere of the greengrocers and florists. Proceedings are presided over by a congenial dalmation who keeps an eye on the fruit and cress vendors.

---

Down a little alley at 77 Borough High St. is one of the few National Trust properties in London, the **George Inn.** Luckily, the inn has not become a look-but-don't-touch fossil but is still doing delightfully what it was always meant to do, provide customers with cheer and libations.

The George was built in 1676 on a site that has probably offered hospitality to travelers since the Middle Ages. It is the only galleried inn left in London, a picturesque pair of wood-railed porches running—and sagging—along the length of its façade.

A good meal can be had for £6–8 on picnic tables set out in the courtyard or on the sturdy ones inside, upstairs and down. Just shy of Southwark Bridge is the **Anchor Bankside,** a pub and restaurant with an outdoor barbecue patio right on the water. It is tourist-traveled but nonetheless a most pleasant place of respite along the way. The present building was erected in the late 18th century after a fire had destroyed the original a hundred years earlier.

---

## The Bear Gardens

Proceed in your progress along the river till you come to Bear Gardens, a street on your left just beyond the bridge. With all the construction going on (to result in a replica of the Globe Theater), you'll have to walk down to Park Street and double back to No. 1 Bear Gardens, where you'll find **The Bear Gardens Museum of the Shakespearean Stage.** On the site of the last bearbaiting ring in operation (1662–82), the Bear Gardens were frequented by Samuel Pepys and Ben Jonson, some of whose plays were performed nearby.

The museum traces the history and importance of Elizabethan and Jacobean theater with models and relics and text. The small theater hosts dramatic and musical workshop performances. Open Tuesday through Saturday from 10 A.M. to 5:30 P.M., Sunday from 2 to 6 P.M., closed Monday; admission is £1.

## The Arts Along the River

In 1951, spiritually and financially depressed by the aftermath of World War II, as London was still digging itself out from under the rubble, some game souls sought to boost the city's morale by staging a Festival of Britain. It was also a good excuse for some organized fund-raising to finance some badly needed concert space after several halls had been destroyed by the blitz. One of the centerpieces for the festival was **Royal Festival Hall,** to be built in a bombed-out riverside neighborhood.

Royal Festival Hall has become the home of the London Philharmonic and also plays host to visiting classical and pop musicians. **Queen Elizabeth Hall** and the **Purcell Room** are smaller venues more suited to chamber music, New Age music, recitals, folk music, and some theater pieces. For general information and schedules, phone 928-3002. To reserve tickets with a major credit card, phone 928-8800. The **National Film Theatre** (928-3232) produces festivals of cinematic achievement built around the work of a particular director, performer, period, or theme. The **National Theatre Company** has three venues in the complex: the **Cottesloe,** in-the-round seating for 400; the **Lyttelton,** a proscenium theater with 890 seats; and the **Olivier,** with a thrust stage into the audience of 1,160. For information and schedules, phone the information desk, 633-0880. To buy tickets with any major credit card, phone 928-2252.

## PUBS

There are three terrific pubs on the South Bank—**The Angel,** 26 Rotherhithe St.; **The Mayflower,** 117 Rotherhithe High St.; and **The Goose and Firkin,** Borough and Southwark Bridge roads—all especially good for Sunday lunch. Unfortunately, they are not on your exploring route and inaccessible from just about anywhere on foot so plan to take a taxi.

# Short Trips From London

The following excursions—Greenwich, Hampstead, Hampton Court, and Kew Gardens—are all within or just outside the city limits and easily reached by Underground, riverboat (call River Boat Information Service, 730-4812), or other public transport. All four of these can be explored within the confines of a day and do not call for an overnight stay.

## Greenwich

BritRail from Cannon Street, Waterloo, Charing Cross, and London Bridge to Greenwich. Underground: Docklands Light Railway, then cross at the pedestrian tunnel. Best way in spring and summer is to take the ferry from Westminster or Tower Piers.

Greenwich (pronounced "grennich") is a little town by the riverside a few miles east of London. There are great buildings to see here. The **Naval College** was designed by Wren, Hawksmoor, and Vanbrugh; some of its rooms, including the Painted Hall and the Chapel, are open to the public. The **National Maritime Museum,** whose most important asset is the **Queen's House,** is the work of Inigo Jones. On the same watery theme, there are two ships to explore. The most impressive is the *Cutty Sark,* built in Glasgow in 1869. She

is a sleek, still fully rigged clipper ship. Nearby is the *Gypsy Moth IV,* the first yacht to be raced around the world, a feat accomplished in 1969 by Sir Francis Chichester.

Nearby is the **Royal Observatory,** also Wren-designed, full of astronomical instruments, the center of the globe at 0 degrees longitude, and the keeper of Greenwich Mean Time.

Also on view is a beautiful park and the Thames Flood Barrier, a short walk downriver which is a group of enormous, *Twilight Zone* gates used to regulate the flow of water.

The place to eat is **Goddard's Eel and Pie House,** which has been offering up these local delicacies since 1890, or for even more atmosphere, stroll among Greenwich's famed fishmongers.

## Hampton Court Palace
BritRail from Waterloo Station to Hampton Court, then walk across the bridge; or by riverboat from Westminster Pier in spring and summer.

The easy journey by rail or river takes you out to Henry VIII's palace set in a spectacular park of formal gardens. This, the finest Tudor mansion in England, was built by Cardinal Wolsey and was later confiscated by the king. After the Tudors, the court preferred Whitehall until the time of William and Mary, who, notorious for their lack of fondness for that palace, commissioned Christopher Wren in 1699 to do renovations. The State Apartments were severely damaged in 1986, when a fire broke out in the flat of one of the grace-and-favor wards who lived here. Thankfully, much of the furniture and artworks were saved. There are paintings by De la Tour, Tintoretto, Lely, and Verrio among stunning architectural details spanning the centuries. The gardens are laid out with strictly trimmed hedges and tended beds. Get lost in the maze or visit the Great Vine, a two-hundred-year-old creeper still going strong. Bring a picnic or try one of the riverside pubs.

## Hampstead Heath
Underground: Hampstead or Golder's Green, then take bus 210 from either station to Kenwood on Hampstead Lane.

The Heath is situated in northeast London and is a huge, surprisingly rural plot overlooking the city. In fact, it provides one of the city's best-loved vistas at the top of Parliament Hill, London's highest point, with a sweeping panorama of the Thames valley. At the north edge of the Heath is **Kenwood,** a wonderful art museum housed in a former private mansion largely designed by Robert Adam. The house ended up in the hands of Edward Cecil Guinness, First Earl of Iveagh, who deposited his great art collection here, eventually bequeathing it, along with the house and grounds, to the city. The paintings include works by Gainsborough, Rembrandt, Vermeer, Turner, and Reynolds in a truly lovely setting. Evening music recitals and poetry readings are given in the Orangery. Call (01) 348-1286 for info on Kenwood House; (01) 734-1877 for concert info. There is a pleasant restaurant connected to the house.

In the town of Hampstead is another wonderful residence operated by the National Trust, **Fenton House.** A William and Mary structure, its collection features—aside from paintings and period furnishings—the musical instrument collection of George Henry Benton Fletcher. The instruments are all in working order and are used to give concerts at the house periodically throughout the year. There is also a neat, quiet walled garden in which Shakespeare's plays are produced several times a summer. For news of these events, phone the National Trust Office at (01) 222-9251; call (01) 435-3471 for Fenton House info.

## Kew Gardens
Underground: Kew Gardens, or by riverboat from Westminster Pier in summer.

Technically called the Royal Botanic Gardens, these are just that. Outdoors, laid out in precise, precious beds, or indoors, displayed in huge hothouses, they are spread out over three hundred acres on a peninsula formed by a lazy oxbow in the Thames south and west of the city proper. The garden was begun in 1731 by the Prince of Wales and was continued by his widow. Their house, Kew Palace, is also open for inspection and retains its original Georgian furniture. The greatest work on the garden was done during the reign of George III by the brilliant landscape architect Capability Brown. The gardens are an important center for botanic and scientific research. Their public attractions include the 18th-century Orangery; Queen Charlotte's Cottage, a rustic tea house a la Marie Antoinette's petite ferme at Versailles; the Japanese Pagoda, copying one in Kyoto; and of course the fantastic 19th-century greenhouses, some large enough to contain fully grown palm trees.

## SHOPPING

Shopping in London, as in all chic European cities, is an event and an entertainment unto itself. We can't pretend to cover all the interesting places to put your plastic through its paces; however, we have selected a few dozen places which are unique and/or uniquely British. For hard-core shoppers, we suggest picking up the *Time-Out Guide to Shopping in London* (available at many newssellers) which has thousands of listings.

**To the right of each listing you'll find location information: first the name of the London neighborhood the store is in, followed by a key to the atlas.**

### Clothing, Traditional English

Whether you're heading to the City for a business appointment or to the country for grouse shooting, the following stores are recommended to supply you with everything in sartorial corrections.

**Aquascutum**                                  MAYFAIR; P. 5, 3C
100 Regent St., tel. 734-6090

**Burberrys**                                   SOHO; P. 5, 3D
18–22 Haymarket, tel. 930-3343

**Droopy and Browns**                MARYLEBONE; P. 2, 3B
16–17 St. Christopher's Place, tel. 935-3198

**Fenwick of Bond Street**                      MAYFAIR; P. 5, 3C
63 New Bond St., tel. 629-9161

**Hardy Ames**                                  MAYFAIR; P. 5, 3C
14 Savile Row, tel. 734-2436

**Jasper Conran**  SOUTH KENSINGTON; P. 4, 5A
37 Beauchamp Place, tel. 589-4243

**Laura Ashley**  MAYFAIR; P. 2, 3C
256–258 Regent St., tel. 734-5824

**Marc O'Polo**  COVENT GARDEN; P. 5, 3D
3–7 Southampton St., tel. 831-1501

**Naturally British**  COVENT GARDEN; P. 2, 3D
13 New Row, tel. 240-0551

**Paul Smith**  COVENT GARDEN; P. 2, 3D
41–44 Floral St., tel. 379-7133

**The Scotch House**  SOUTH KENSINGTON; P. 4, 4B
2 Brompton Rd., tel. 581-2151

**Tommy Nutter**  MAYFAIR; P. 5, 3C
19 Savile Row, tel. 734-0831

**Turnbull & Asser**  ST. JAMES'S; P. 5, 3G
Jermyn St., tel. 839-5133

## Clothing, Modern Design

If you'd like something a bit more daring and hot off the press-
es, you'll find Britains established and rising stars at:

**Academy**  CHELSEA; P. 4, 6A
188A King's Rd., tel. 352-0507

**Arkitect**  COVENT GARDEN; P. 2, 3D
No. 1 Langley Court, tel. 240-5071

**Boy**  CHELSEA; P. 4, 6A
153 King's Rd., tel. 351-1115

**Brown's**  MARYLEBONE; P. 1, 3B
South Molton St., tel. 491-7833

**Christopher New**  SOHO; P. 2, 3D
52 Dean St., tel. 734-5363

**Darlajane Gilroy**  CHELSEA; P. 4, 6A
327 King's Rd., tel. 352-2095

**Ice Station**  CLERKENWELL; P. 2, 1E
294 Pentonville Rd., tel. 278-0230

**Joseph Bis**  BELGRAVIA; P. 4, 5B
166 Sloane St., tel. 235-6117

**Katherine Hamnett**  CHELSEA; P. 4, 5A
264 Brompton Rd., tel. 584-1136

**World's End**  CHELSEA
430 King's Rd., tel. 352-6551

**Workers For Freedom**  SOHO; P. 2, 3C
4 Lower John St., tel. 734-3767

**Zandra Rhodes** MAYFAIR; P. 5, 3C
14A Grafton St., tel. 499-6695

## Department Stores

For the most part, we'd steer clear of department stores—
they're much the same as at home. A few with something special are:

**Dickins & Jones** MAYFAIR; P. 2, 3C
224–244 Regent St., tel. 734-7070

**Harrods** BELGRAVIA; P. 4, 4B
Old Brompton Rd., tel. 730-1234

**Harvey Nichols** BELGRAVIA; P. 4, 4B
Old Brompton Rd., tel. 235-5000

**Liberty's** MAYFAIR; P. 2, 3C
200 Regent St., tel. 734-1234

**Selfridges** MARYLEBONE; P. 1, 3B
400 Oxford St., tel. 629-1234

## For Bargains

From army surplus to half-off on better designers, the economist in you will find happy hunting at:

**The Constant Sale Shop** CHELSEA; P. 4, 5A
56 Fulham Rd., tel. 589-1458

**Hyper Hyper** KENSINGTON
Kensington High St., tel. 937-6964

**Monsoon** MARYLEBONE; P. 1, 3C
67 South Molton St., tel. 499-3987

**A Shop Called Sale** COVENT GARDEN; P. 2, 3D
28 Bedfordbury, tel. 240-9730

**Thomas Pink** THE CITY; P. 3, 3G
16 Cullum St., tel. 929-1405

**Warehouse** MARYLEBONE; P. 1, 3B
27 Duke St., tel. 486-5270

**Zap** EAST END
413 Mare St., tel. 985-2491

## Furnishings

For fitting your home up in chintz and knickknacks fit for
country gentlefolk:

**Colefax & Fowler** MAYFAIR; P. 4, 3B
39 Brook St., tel. 493-2231

**The Conran Shop**  CHELSEA; P. 4, 5A
81 Fulham Rd., tel. 589-7401

**Designers Guild**  CHELSEA; P. 4, 5B
King's Rd., tel. 351-5775

**Freuds**  SOHO; P. 2, 3D
198 Shaftesbury Ave., tel. 831-1071

**Gered Wedgwood**  ST JAMES'S; P. 5, 3C
173 Piccadilly, tel. 629-2614

**Halcyon Days**  MAYFAIR; P. 4, 3B
14 Brook St., tel. 629-8811

**Liberty's**  MAYFAIR; P. 2, 3C
200 Regent St., tel. 734-1234

**Ogetti**  CHELSEA; P. 4, 5A
133 Fulham Rd., tel. 581-8088

**Sanderson**  MARYLEBONE; P. 2, 2C
52 Berners St., tel. 636-7800

**Watts & Co.**  WESTMINSTER; P. 5, 5D
7 Tufton St., tel. 222-7169

**Zoffany**  MAYFAIR; P. 4, 3B
327 South Audley St., tel. 226-8643

## Antiques

English antiques are pricey for the most part but try your luck at:

**Bennison**  BELGRAVIA; P. 4, 5B
91 Pimlico Rd., tel. 730-3370

**George Johnson Ltd.**  KENSINGTON
120 Kensington Park Rd., tel. 229-3119

**H. C. Baxter and Sons**  CHELSEA; P. 4, 6A
191–95 Fulham Rd., tel. 352-9826

**Harvey and Co.**  MAYFAIR; P. 5, 3C
5 Old Bond St., tel. 499-8385

**Hoff Antiques Limited**  KENSINGTON
66A Kensington Church St., tel. 229-5516

**Mallett and Son**  MAYFAIR; P. 2, 3C
40 New Bond St., tel. 499-7411

**Norman Adams Ltd.**  BELGRAVIA; P. 4, 4B
8–10 Hans Rd., tel. 589-5266

**Stair & Co Ltd.**  MAYFAIR; P. 4, 3B
120 Mount St., tel. 499-1784

Bargain hunters can try their luck around Portobello Rd. and Camden Lock on market days (see "Priorities" section). Red-letter days for antiquers come in April for the Chelsea Antiques

Fair held at Chelsea Old Town Hall; in June at the Fine Art &
Antiques Fair at the Olympia Exhibition Centre; and twice in September, again at Chelsea Old Town Hall, and at the Burlington
House Fair at the Royal Academy.
Or you can sit in on an auction at:

**Bonhams**  SOUTH KENSINGTON; P. 4, 4A
Montpelier Galleries, Montpelier St., tel. 584-9161

**Christie's**  ST. JAMES'S; P. 5, 4C
                CHELSEA; P. 4, 5A
8 King St., tel. 839-9060
and 85 Old Brompton Rd., tel. 581-7611

**Phillips**  MAYFAIR; P. 5, 3C
Blenstock House, 7 Blenheim St., tel. 629-7702

**Sotheby's**  MAYFAIR; P. 2, 3C
34–35 New Bond St., tel. 493-8080

## Cosmetics and Toiletries
Terrific for gifts or for yourself. Pick up some potions at:

**The Body Shop**  SOHO; P. 2, 3C
32–34 Great Marlborough St., tel. 437-5237

**Crabtree and Evelyn**  KENSINGTON
6 Kensington Church St., tel. 937-9335

**Czech and Speake**  ST JAMES'S; P. 5, 3C
Jermyn St., tel. 439-0216

**D. R. Harris & Co. Ltd.**  ST. JAMES'S; P. 5, 4C
29 St. James's St., tel. 930-3915

**J. Floris**  ST. JAMES'S; P. 5, 3C
89 Jermyn St., tel. 930-2885

**Neal's Yard Apothecary**  COVENT GARDEN; P. 2, 3D
Neal's Yard, tel. 379-7222

**Penhaligon**  COVENT GARDEN; P. 2, 3D
41 Wellington St., tel. 836-2150

# RESTAURANTS

Diversity is the theme of London restaurants. In the city's two
central square miles alone you can choose from 25 international
cuisines.

But in London planning is the key word for successful eating
out. If you don't plan and your luck is out or your instinct fails
you, mealtimes could become a study in culinary mediocrity, sullen service, and even dubious hygiene—in all the price brackets,
right up to the highest. Discerning Londoners themselves avoid
their city's worst eating places by using a restaurant guide.
There are many good ones: *Egon Ronay's Lucas Guide* covers
all of Great Britain while *The Time Out Guide to Eating Out in
London* is the only one dedicated just to London restaurants.

On the next few pages you'll find guidance to help you choose a restaurant in London followed by our selections. Several options are mentioned but not all made our selections list. Pertinent details for these establishments are given as they come up.

## DISTRICTS TO EAT IN

If you had no restaurant guide and wanted to know what district to head for where you'd be pretty sure of finding a good place to eat, the answer would be: Covent Garden or Soho in the West End. Covent Garden is the center of London's theaterland. You can sit in the sun at one of the tables out on the piazza and watch street entertainers perform in front of St. Paul's (The Actors') Church. In the streets around are many excellent restaurants.

Up until two or three years ago Soho, which starts on the west side of Charing Cross Road, was the sleazy part of London, unequivocally the red-light district, with peep shows and strip clubs taking every available space for rent. Thanks to a dedicated cleanup campaign on the part of residents, business interests, and the municipal authority (Westminster Council) most of its pornographic clientele has been squeezed out in favor of enthusiastic new businesses—Soho now has a settlement of young, up-and-coming fashion designers whose shops you should visit. The effect of the new local regime on the restaurant trade in this, its historical center in London, has been electrifying.

## RESTAURANTS TO BE SEEN IN

It's fair to say that London's most fashionable restaurants—the restaurants the glitterati go to be seen in—are now in and around Soho, specifically on Frith St., W1. The oldest of these is **L'Escargot,** on Greek St., which has been fashionable since it was taken over and reopened by restaurateur Nick Lander. Downstairs is a brasserie, the main attraction between 6–7 P.M. because you can buy drinks without accompanying food; but the restaurant upstairs is also very much patronized by media people and politicians.

London's trendiest restaurants are not all in Soho. The opportunity to buy one of the capital's most beautiful buildings—the Michelin Building at the junction of Knightsbridge, South Kensington, and Chelsea—inspired designer Terence Conran to open his new restaurant. The Michelin Building is now beautifully restored and **Bibendum** is currently the capital's trendiest place to eat. The chef is the revered Simon Hopkinson, who cooks basic French food. You'll have to book about one week in advance.

## CHEFS YOU SHOULD KNOW ABOUT

Over the last five years or so London has seen the emergence of a new generation of inspired chefs/patron some of them brilliant, some self-taught, few trained in the techniques of classic French cuisine, all anxious to develop their own style. Various names have been given to this new cooking: "new British" is one; "modern European" another. Eclectic and progressive is what everyone agrees it is.

Chefs you should not only know about but whose cooking you should try while in London include such luminaries as Alastair Little of **Alastair Little** and Simon Hopkinson, mentioned earlier. Equally fashionable is chef/patron Sally Clarke, who serves her innovative brand of West Coast food at **Clarkes** in Kensington Church St., W8. Another woman chef, Carla Tomasi, operates from **Frith's,** on fashionable Frith St. in Soho.

Chef of the year, however, is indisputably the flamboyant Marco White of **Harvey's,** south of the river in untrendy Tooting. This young chef, still in his twenties, won a Michelin star within a year of opening his little restaurant. His cooking is complex, interesting, and expensive. You'll have to book *at least one month ahead* to sample it—and you'll be safest if you write some weeks ahead from the States.

Other award-winning chefs include the notorious Nico Ladenis, owner of **Simply Nico** in Pimlico; Pierre Koffman, holder of two Michelin stars, at **Tante Claire,** in Chelsea; and Albert Roux at **La Gavroche** in Mayfair. All are listed below

## CUISINES IN THE NEWS

Not all fashionable food in London is French or modern British—in fact, French food is currently rather out of the news. Highest in the cuisine charts are Spanish, Lebanese, Thai, Vietnamese, Indonesian, and Korean. Spanish tapas bars are opening at quite a rate. There is one in Waterloo conveniently near the South Bank Arts Centre—**Meson Don Felipe** (53 the Cut, Waterloo; tel. 928-2327; lunch noon–3 P.M., dinner 5:30–11 P.M. Mon–Fri., dinner only, 6:30–11 P.M. Sat.; average £5). (See also **Guernica** listed below.)

The most exciting Italian restaurant event this year was the opening of the pretty **Ziani Dolci** on the Thames embankment in Chelsea.

The Lebanese restaurant you should be seen eating in is possibly **Al Sultan** in Mayfair (52 Hertford St.; tel. 408-1155; Underground Hyde Park Corner; open noon–midnight daily; average £16), a new, elegant place serving a bright, trendy crowd. But if you genuinely love Middle Eastern food, don't stop there. Head for Edgware Rd., where the Arab community is based, and walk into almost any restaurant or juice bar along there.

For Indonesian food try the **Rasa Sayang,** on Frith St., an excellent restaurant we recommend for the authenticity of its food. For Thai food, arguably the best place in town is the **Bahn Thai.** The prettiest and most elegant Korean restaurant is **Korea House,** off Bond St., with a pretty patio garden upstairs. The Vietnamese restaurant to eat in is the delightful **Mekong** in Victoria, not far from the station.

## EATING ETHNIC

London is full of Indian restaurants and you don't have to walk far to find a good one. Currently the best is the **Jamdani,** on Charlotte St., opened by chef Amin Ali, who has been responsible for a whole chain of excellent Bengali restaurants across central London. Jamdani is notable for its modern decor and its eclectic menu, which incorporates dishes from all over India. There are little clusters of vegetarian Indian restaurants on Westbourne Grove (Notting Hill Gate Underground/bus 31) and in Drummond St. (Euston Tube/BR or Warren St. Tube).

Brixton is an exciting place to just walk around (cautiously at night, however), with its marvelous daily market (at the junction of Brixton Station Rd. and Electric Ave.), full of stalls selling West Indian vegetables, textiles, and music. Notable among the restaurants around there is **Taste of Africa,** where the food is as hot as it should be.

London's Chinatown is just south of Soho in a pedestrian area centered on Gerrard St. If you want to eat after midnight you can confidently head here, knowing there will be somewhere open if you want to dine at 5 A.M. Gerrard St. and Wardour St. are lined with restaurants serving Cantonese, Sichuan, and Peking food, but in fact, the better ones are discreetly tucked away on Lisle St. (parallel to Gerrard St. and just to the south): **Mr. Kong,** the **New Diamond,** the **Fung Shing,** and the tiny **Poons** are the best Chinese restaurants in Chinatown.

There are few kosher or Israeli restaurants around central London (most are around Finchley Rd. and in Golders Green), with one noble exception: **Grahame's Seafare,** a superb fish and chips restaurant on Poland St. in Soho, where you can ask for your fish to be deep-fried in kosher batter (made from matzo meal) or ordinary batter.

## EATING BRITISH

The taste for fish and chips is an acquired one. Most Americans find them greasy, but that's mainly because in the cheaper places they often are. It's worth searching out a good one. Besides Grahame's there is the **North Sea Fish Restaurant** up in Bloomsbury, the university quarter. It's well worth walking up to if you're shopping around Covent Garden.

What most visitors love about English food is the roast beef. So do the English, and most restaurants oblige by abandoning their daily menus and individual cooking styles and serving up a roast at Sunday lunchtime. The most famous restaurant in London for its roast beef is **Simpson's Grand Divan Tavern,** where the roasts are indeed good, but you'll find the restaurant expensive.

Our tip for a roast served in the correct atmosphere at a reasonable price would be either the **St. James's Restaurant**—on the fourth floor of Fortnum & Mason's department store on Piccadilly—or a carvery.

In the listings below the times given are first and last orders. Most restaurants close an hour to an hour and a half after last orders. The prices are strictly average prices of a three-course meal without wine; you could spend 25 percent more or less depending on what you order.

**Tipping is usual in London restaurants: 10 percent of the bill in the smaller, cheaper restaurants; 15 percent in the more expensive establishments.**

The following credit-card abbreviations are used: AE for American Express; MC for MasterCard; V for Visa; CB for Carte Blanche; DC for Diners Club. Keep in mind that not all restaurants accept traveler's checks.

To the right of each listing you'll find location information: first the name of the area the restaurant is in, followed by, when applicable, a key to the atlas section.

## Ajimura
COVENT GARDEN; P.2, 3D

51 Shelton St. (tel. 240-0178). Covent Garden Underground.

A picturesque and informal little Japanese restaurant, notable for especially cheap lunches (£6.50) and pre-theater dinners (served 6:30–7:30 P.M.). Ajimura is also noted for sushi. The menu is carefully translated, and the staff either are or speak English. Lunch noon–3 P.M. Mon.–Fri. Dinner 6–11 P.M. Mon.–Sat., 6–10:30 P.M. Sun. **Average £15.** Credit Cards: AE, DC, MC, V.

## Alastair Little
SOHO; P.2, 3D

49 Frith St. (tel. 734-5183). Piccadilly Circus Underground.

A small, unpretentious restaurant—you can see right into the kitchen—run by a young, ingenious, self-taught chef who changes his menu twice a day and the emphasis of his cooking as often as the spirit moves him. Alastair has a well-deserved reputation for being good with offal and with fish. His Frith Street restaurant is one of London's most fashionable. Lunch 12:30–2:30 P.M., dinner 7:30–11 P.M., Mon.–Fri. **Average £20.** No credit cards.

## Apollonia
FITZROVIA; P.2, 2C

17A Percy St. (tel. 636-4140). Tottenham Court Rd. Underground.

One of Charlotte St.'s many Greek restaurants, selected as one of the best for a plate-smashing, party ambience at night. The ground-floor dining room is a calm place in which to try some decent Greek food and Keo beer; downstairs there is dancing (on dance floor and table), bouzouki playing, singing, and plate-smashing until the early hours. Lunch noon–3 P.M., dinner 6 P.M.–1 A.M., Mon.–Sat. 6 P.M.–midnight, Sun. **Average £11.** Credit Cards: AE, DC, MC, V.

## L'Arlequin
BATTERSEA

123 Queenstown Rd. (tel. 622-0555). Clapham Common Underground/Queenstown Rd. BritRail station.

People for whom nouvelle cuisine can never be passé will love chef Christian Delteil's fine cooking, exquisitely arranged. The food at L'Arlequin is simple in preparation and beautifully presented. It's expensive, but at £15.50 the set lunch is a bargain. Lunch 12:30–2 P.M. Mon.–Fri. Dinner 7:30–10 P.M. Mon.–Sat. **Average £31.** Credit Cards: AE, DC, MC, V.

## Bahn Thai
SOHO; P.2, 3D

21A Frith St. (tel. 437-8504). Piccadilly Circus Underground.

One of London's oldest Thai restaurants run by an English-Thai couple. The downstairs room is crowded and noisy; the softly decorated, green room upstairs has a hushed, meditative atmosphere. The food is superb (the emphasis here is on sea-food) and authentic—but the chef will spice down your curry if you ask when you order. Lunch noon–2:45 P.M. Mon.–Sat.; 12:30–2:30 P.M. Sun. Dinner 6–11:15 P.M. Mon.–Sat.; 6:30–10:30 P.M. Sun. **Average £11.** Credit Cards: AE, MC, V.

## Bibendum                    SOUTH KENSINGTON; P.4, 5A
Michelin House, 81 Fulham Rd., SW3 (tel. 581-5817). South Kensington Underground.

British design baron Terence Conran effected a coup when he bought the lovely old Michelin Building here, restored it, and opened Conran (his new lifestyle shop) and Bibendum in it. Bibendum is beautiful, its clientele is stylish and fashionable, and the food is superb. The chef is the hallowed Simon Hopkinson, renowned for his classically balanced modern French food. It's pricey, and you'll have to book to eat here, well in advance. Lunch 12:30–2 P.M. Mon.–Fri.; 12:30–3 P.M. Sat. Dinner 7–11 P.M. Mon.–Fri. **Average £30.** Credit Cards: AE, DC, MC, V.

## braganza                              SOHO; P2, 3D
56 Frith St. (tel. 437-5412). Piccadilly Circus Underground.

A restaurant/brasserie complex on three floors, the work of famous restaurant designers Fitch & Co., who have used sculpture in the decor to great effect. A year after its opening it is still popular, though no longer at the peak of fashion. The ground-floor brasserie is busiest; the food is good: French with Californian inspiration. The wine list is eclectic. Open noon–11:30 P.M. Mon.–Fri.; 6–11:30 P.M. Sat. **Average £6.** Credit Cards: AE, DC, MC, V.

## Brilliant                              SOUTHALL
72–74 Western Rd., Southall, Middlesex (tel. 574-1928). Southall RR.

A small, functional, and atmospheric café, a family concern that best captures the ambience of the many café/restaurants in this Asian center west of London. Don't expect chic decor or unctuous service, but do expect good food. Non-Asians are made welcome. Lunch noon–2:45 P.M. Tue.–Fri. Dinner 6–11:15 P.M. Tue.–Thur., Sun.; 6–11:45 P.M. Fri., Sat. **Average £8.50.** Credit Cards: AE, DC, MC, V.

## Calabash                    COVENT GARDEN; P2, 3D
The Africa Centre, 38 King St. (tel. 836-1976). Covent Garden Underground.

This dark, atmospheric restaurant in the basement of the Africa Centre. The menu lists dishes from all points of the pan-African compass; the daily specials take care of any region, cuisine, or ingredient that's been missed out. Respect is paid to Caribbean cooking. The food is consequently varied and very nicely cooked—but the service is an exercise in the kind of patience you need in Africa. Dinner Mon–Sat. 6 P.M.–12:30 A.M. in summer, 6–11 P.M. in winter. **Average £9.** Credit Cards: AE, DC, MC, V.

## Casper & Giumbini's
MAYFAIR; P.2, 3C

6 Tenterden St. (tel. 493-7923). Oxford Circus Underground.

Most so-called American restaurants in London should be re-classified American-style, but this vast new restaurant is authentic. The meat dishes are good and the brunch (£6 including a drink) is great. Brunch 11:30 A.M.–12:30 P.M. Mon.–Fri., noon–3 P.M. Sat., Sun., lunch 11:30 A.M.–3 P.M., Mon.–Fri., dinner 5:30 P.M.–midnight daily, brunch 11:30–12:30 P.M. Mon.–Fri., noon–3 P.M. Sat., Sun. **Average £15.** Credit Cards: AE, DC, MC, V.

## Chez Solange
COVENT GARDEN; P5, 3D

35 Cranbourn St. (tel. 836-0542). Leicester Square Underground.

The French proprietor can remember when Chez Solange was one of only two restaurants in Covent Garden and he catered then, as he does now, to a mainly thespian clientele. This is a classic pretheater venue. The menu ranges from simple omelettes to traditional dishes of great complexity.Eat in the restaurant, the brasserie behind it with tables out on St. Martin's Court, or in the downstairs wine bar. Open noon–12:15 A.M. Mon.–Sat. **Average £20.** Set lunch and pre-theater menu £13.50. Credit Cards: AE, DC, MC, V.

## Clarke's
WEST KENSINGTON

124 Kensington Church St. (tel. 221-9225). High St. Kensington Underground.

As a result of her period of pupilage under Alice Waters, the kind of food Sally Clarke cooks is an interesting blend of what Londoners now call "new British" or "modern European," with Californian overtones: colorful salads, perfectly composed pizzas. Her food is simple, with gourmet touches and accompanied by California wines. Sit downstairs, where you can watch Sally at work in her kitchen. Lunch 12:30–2 P.M., dinner 7:30–11 P.M., Mon.–Fri. **Set lunches £14; £16. Set dinner £25; supper** (10–11 P.M.) **£19.** Credit Cards: MC, V.

## L'Escargot
SOHO; P.2, 3D

48 Greek St. (tel. 437-2679). Tottenham Court Rd. Underground.

A former Soho landmark, the brainchild of Nick Lander and his wife Jancis Robinson, who writes the superb wine list, L'Escargot is one of the most fashionable places to be seen in London. Not least of its attractions is the discreet Elena Salvoni at the front of the house in the first-floor dining room, who may no longer be young but who is still the darling of the media world. Downstairs is a popular brasserie and upstairs is the restaurant. Eat here while you can since Nick Lander is retiring due to ill health and the future of L'Escargot is in doubt. Brasserie: Lunch 12:15–3 P.M. Mon.–Fri. Dinner 5:30–11:15 P.M. Mon.–Fri., 6–11:55 P.M. Sat. **Average £20.** Restaurant: Lunch 12:30–2:15 P.M. Mon.–Fri. Dinner 6:30–11:15 P.M. Mon.–Sat. Brasserie: Lunch 12:15–3 P.M. Mon.–Fri. Dinner 5:30–11:15 P.M. Mon.–Fri, 6–11:55 P.M. Sat. **Average £20.** Credit Cards: AE, DC, MC, V.

## Fortnum & Mason's
## St. James's Restaurant ST. JAMES; P.5, 4C
Fortnum & Mason PLC, 4th floor, 181 Piccadilly (tel. 734-8040). Green-Park Underground.

Three pleasant restaurants with cheerful service are to be found inside Fortnum & Mason's department store on Piccadilly. The food is trans-Atlantic, so there are English pies and grills, and American chowders, BLTs, and lobsterburgers. There's a whole menu of ice creams, frappés, sundaes, and other delights. Open 9 A.M.–5 P.M. Mon.–Sat. Breakfast served 9:30–11:15 A.M. Lunch served noon–2:30 P.M. Mon.–Sat. Tea served 3–5 P.M. Mon.–Fri.; 3–4:30 P.M. Sat. **Set breakfasts £4.45 (English), £2.95 (Continental). Afternoon tea £5.50; high tea £7.50.** Credit Cards: AE, F&M, DC, MC, V.

## Frith's SOHO; P.2, 3D
14 Frith St. (tel. 439-3370). Tottenham Court Rd. Underground.

Carla Tomasi is chef-proprietor of this pretty little Soho restaurant, where she serves a monthly changing menu of simply cooked meats and fish, plus wonderful things for vegetarians. All her cooking exhibits diverse influences—from France, Italy, and Southeast Asia. Her breads and cheese board are all frequently praised, and her wine list is well chosen. Lunch noon–2:30 P.M. Mon.–Fri. Dinner 6:30–11:30 P.M. Mon.–Sat. **Average £25–30** (drinks and wines are also expensive). Credit Cards: MC, V.

## Fung Shing CHINATOWN
15 Lisle St. (tel. 437-1539). Piccadilly Circus Underground.

Cantonese gourmet food is served in elegant, comfortable surroundings here. The menu is varied and imaginative, and the food cooked flawlessly. Booking is usually necessary. Open noon–11:30 P.M. daily. **Average £15.** Credit Cards: AE, DC, MC, V.

## Le Gavroche MAYFAIR; P.4, 3B
43 Upper Brook St. (tel. 408-0881). Marble Arch Underground.

Albert Roux (brother of Michel, proprietor of the Waterside Inn in Berkshire) is justifiably revered as the first chef in Britain to have won three Michelin stars. His restaurant is not a place to come to see or to be seen. The clientele is not necessarily famous but consists mainly of well-off people who want to spend money on gourmet food. There's a very good-value set lunch for under £30, but if you eat à la carte be prepared to spend up to £100. The wine list is more like a book than a list and the markup is high. Lunch noon–2 P.M., dinner 7–11 P.M. Mon.–Fri. **Average £22 (lunch), £50–£100 à la carte; minimum £40 (dinner).** Credit Cards: AE, DC, MC, V.

## Grahame's Seafare SOHO; P.2, 3C
38 Poland St. (tel. 437-3788/0975). Oxford Circus Underground.

London's gourmet fish and chip shop is a kosher restaurant, and one of its attractions is that you can get fish fried in crisp matzo meal. The range is wide—from salmon to rock salmon—and prices are high, though portions are massive. The takeaway counter is inside the rather old-fashioned, green-upholstered restaurant. Open noon–2:45 P.M. Mon.; noon–2:45 P.M., 5:30–8:45 P.M. Tue.–Thur., Sat.; noon–2:45 P.M., 5:30–7:45 P.M. Fri. **Average £10 (evenings).** Credit Card: V.

## Guernica                                    OXFORD ST.; P.2, 3C
21A Foley St. (tel. 580-0623) Oxford Circus or Great Portland Street Underground.

Traditional Spanish dishes are given a new light twist in the new style of Basque cooking currently sweeping through Spain. This, the first serious Spanish restaurant to open in Britain since before World War II, boasts a notable Basque chef Danat Arroyabe, who trained in the kitchens of one of the Basque country's leading restaurants. Lunch noon–3 P.M. Mon.–Fri. Dinner 7–11 P.M. Mon.–Sat. **Set lunch £12. Average à la carte £18.**

## Harvey's                                               TOOTING
2 Bellevue Rd. (tel. 672-0114). Clapham Common Underground.

Within a year of opening his own restaurant in London's outback south of the river, Marco Pierre White became the youngest chef to be awarded a Michelin star. This year he's extending his restaurant to cater to the foodie pilgrims who trek out there in such numbers that you must now book about a month in advance for dinner. The enfant terrible of English gastronomy produces an Italian-influenced cuisine, of which his *tagliatelle* of oysters is a classic. Lunch 12:30–2:15 P.M. Mon.–Fri.; 7:30–11 P.M. Mon.–Sat. **Set lunch £15. Set dinner £26.** Credit Cards: AE, MC, V.

## Inigo Jones                              COVENT GARDEN; P.2, 3D
14 Garrick St. (tel. 836-6456). Leicester Square Underground.

Long heralded as a brilliant chef, Paul Gaylor is a master of nouvelle cuisine and his presentations were among the first to be described as "art on a plate." Rich foods, such as duckling, Norfolk pigeon, and pig's trotter, are transformed by his masterful touch into feather-light creations—but vegetarian gourmets are graced with their own separate menu at £32.50. The wines here are chosen from all wine-producing regions of France. Lunch 12:30–2:30 P.M. Mon.–Fri. Dinner 5:30–11:30 P.M. Mon.–Sat. **Average £39. Minimum £7.50.** Credit Cards: AE, DC, MC, V.

## Jamdani                                     FITZROVIA; P.2, 2C
34 Charlotte St. (tel. 636-1178). Goodge St. Underground.

Chef Amin Ali, creator of a number of outstanding London restaurants serving Bengali food (Last Days of the Raj in Drury Lane, Covent Garden; Last Days of the Empire in Soho), has surpassed himself with this, his latest venture. Relaxed enough not to feel the need to stick to one cuisine and confident enough to call in celebrated restaurant designers Fitch & Co., he has founded a unique restaurant, a work of art decorated with *jamdani* (woven Indian prints) and with a wonderful menu. Its dishes come from all over the subcontinent and include the innovative *Khargosh achari* (hare cooked in vinegar and spices), to pick out one. London is now a center for the development of Indian Asian cooking, so you should try it while you're here and the best place to do so is at Jamdani. Lunch noon–2:30 P.M. daily. Dinner

6–11 P.M. Mon.–Sat.; 6–10:30 P.M. Sun. **Average £20.** Credit Cards: AE, DC, MC, V.

## Joe Allen
COVENT GARDEN; P.2, 3D

13 Exeter St. (tel. 836-0651). Aldwych Underground.

Assuage those pangs of homesickness at Joe Allen, still one of London's most fashionable American restaurants after all these years. It's a place you can safely be seen in while indulging in a good hamburger or perhaps a huge American salad and definitely one of Joe Allen's wonderful puddings. If you come from Chicago you'll miss the Cadillac, though. Open noon–1 A.M. Mon.–Sat.; noon–midnight Sun. **Average £13.** No credit cards.

## Kensington Place
WEST KENSINGTON

201 Kensington Church St. (tel. 727-3184). Notting Hill Gate Underground.

This brasserie, opened a year ago by super-successful restaurant management team Nick Smallwood and Simon Slater, is glass-walled and cool gray and white. The menu is full of both cheap and pricey dishes thought up by chef Rowley Leigh, an award-holding former Roux Brothers trainee. Go for lunch. The evenings are often overrun and the kitchen cannot always cope. Open noon–11:45 P.M. Mon.–Sat.; noon–10:30 P.M. Sun. **Average £15.** Credit Cards: MC, V.

## Korea House
MAYFAIR; P.2, 3C

10 Lancashire Court, 122–123 New Bond St. (tel. 493-1340/491-4762). Bond St. Underground.

The prettiest place in London to try out the newly fashionable Korean cooking. The restaurant is very hard to find—down a small alley off Bond St. (walk down from Oxford St. on the western side and look for a gap between the buildings on your right)—but worth it. On the ground floor is a bar and a pretty patio, and there's a cozy restaurant in the basement. The manager speaks perfect English and takes pains to explain the cuisine and the menu to his customers. Korean food is not unlike Japanese food, with lots of raw fish and cook-at-the-table stews, but it's hotter, spicier, and very strongly flavored. Lunch noon–2:30 P.M. Mon.–Sat. Dinner 6–10:30 P.M. daily. **Average £8.50 lunch, £17 dinner.** Credit Cards: AE, DC, MC, V.

## Mekong
PIMLICO/VICTORIA; P.5, 6C

46 Churton St. (tel. 834-6896). Victoria Underground/BR.

The best Vietnamese food in London is served here, which may explain the celebrity-studded clientele. There's a restaurant downstairs and a wine bar upstairs where snacks are served. Tastes are understated, flavors extracted, and aromas released to linger everywhere, enticingly. Presentation is beautiful. Lunch noon–2:30 P.M., dinner 6–11 P.M. daily. **Average £15.** Credit Cards: MC, V.

## Mr. Kong
CHINATOWN

21 Lisle St. (tel. 437-7341). Piccadilly Circus Underground.

The respected Mr. Kong is one of the few celebrity chefs of London's Chinatown. Prices in this part of London are now quite high, but for all his fame Mr. Kong doesn't overcharge. This isn't the place to come for chicken and sweet corn—though it's on the menu for anyone who wants it. Order from Mr. Kong's special menu and you'll have a wonderful meal. Booking isn't always necessary, and the restaurant serves very late. Open noon–1:45 A.M. daily. **Average £11.** Credit Cards: AE, DC, MC, V.

## New Diamond                                                    CHINATOWN
23 Lisle St. (tel. 437-2517). Piccadilly Circus Underground.

Risen this year like a phoenix out of the ashes of the old Diamond, the new version has benefited from the opportunity to refurbish with a pretty decor and more spacious environment. The food is as good, if not better, and just as varied. This is the Chinatown restaurant that serves duck webs with fish lips. Open 3 P.M.–3 A.M. daily. **Average £13.** Credit Cards: DC, MC, V.

## North Sea Fish Restaurant               BLOOMSBURY; P.2, 1D
7–8 Leigh St. (tel. 387-5892). Russell Square Underground.

You'll have to travel to find an outstanding fish and chips shop in London, but this one's worth the pinching shoes. In the front it's just a chippie—but what a chippie, with a whole range of different fish deep-fried in plain or kosher batter, or grilled, or baked in milk and butter, and served with nice, waxy chips. At the back is a small restaurant. Portions are huge. Lunch noon–2:30 P.M., dinner 5:30–10:30 P.M., Mon.–Sat. **Average £5.** Credit Cards: AE, DC, MC, V.

## Orso                                    COVENT GARDEN; P.2, 3D
27 Wellington St. (tel. 240-5269). Covent Garden Underground.

This fashionable Chicago-Italian restaurant was opened a year or two ago by Joe Allen. Like his eponymous restaurant around the corner, Orso is in a basement, though it's brightly painted in clinical white. The food is outstanding for London, where Italian food has, until recently at least, been generally mediocre. Ingredients such as buffalo mozzarella are flown in from Italy. The chic dish to order is a small pizza, ludicrously overpriced at £3.50. Open noon–midnight daily. **Average £15.** No credit cards.

## Park Room                                    BELGRAVIA; P.4, 4B
Hyde Park Hotel, 66 Knightsbridge (tel. 235-2000). Knightsbridge Underground.

A beautiful hotel restaurant with a beautiful view across the park to lift the spirits in the mornings. You can have a light breakfast of fruits, cereals, and yogurt, or an English breakfast that will see you through the day. There's no breakfast dish they don't have, from porridge to kedgeree and kippers, corned beef hash and grilled lambs' kidneys. Dress in style. Breakfast served 7–10:30 A.M. Mon.–Sat.; 8–11 A.M. Sun. Tea served 4–6 P.M. daily. **Set breakfasts £9.95 (English), £7.95 (Continental). Cream teas £8.50.** Credit Cards: AE, DC, MC, V.

## Poons                                    BLOOMSBURY; P.2, 1D
50 Woburn Place (tel. 580-1188). Russell Square Underground.

Opened in the heart of Bloomsbury—the university quarter and the site of a good number of tourist hotels—is this, the latest in the Poons chain. The decor is slick, designed around a series of moon gates, and the menu is extraordinary, with the likes of dried tiger lilies and wood ears flavoring the casseroles. Poons's food is always good. Lunch noon–3 P.M., dinner 6–11:30 P.M. daily. **Average** £15. Credit Cards: AE, DC, MC, V.

## Rasa Sayang
SOHO; P.2, 3C

10 Frith St. (tel. 734-8720). Leicester Square Underground.

One of London's nicest Indonesian-Malaysian restaurants (in fact, the Rasa concentrates on Singaporean, or Straits, cooking). The restaurant is large and stylish, and the food is beautifully flavored with lemon grass and other authentic herbs and spices. Be prepared for lukewarm dishes—that's how they like them in the tropical Straits. Lunch noon–2:45 P.M. Mon.–Fri. Dinner 6–11:30 P.M. Mon.–Thur.; 6–11:45 P.M. Fri., Sat. **Average** £15. Credit Cards: AE, DC, MC, V.

## Saigon
SOHO; P.2, 3C

45 Frith St. (tel. 437-7109). Tottenham Court Rd. Underground.

A prettily decorated, light, and stylish Vietnamese restaurant with an intimate atmosphere upstairs. Vietnamese cooking has only recently become fashionable in London, and the food here is a tribute to the cuisine: light, imaginative, and subtly and distinctly flavored. Outstanding dishes are the refreshing green papaya salad with nuoc mam sauce and grilled fish with chili, coriander, and spring onions. Open noon–11:30 P.M. Mon.–Sat. **Average** £15. Credit Cards: AE, DC, MC, V.

## Sichuen
SOHO; P.2, 3D

56 Old Compton St. (tel. 437-2069). Piccadilly Circus Underground.

Chef Tsoe-Bing, who opened up here after moving from the Dragon Gate in Gerrard Street, Chinatown, a year or so ago, claims to have introduced Sichuan cooking to London and so, consequently, to the U.K. Sichuan food in London is not outstanding, but Tsoe-Bing's pun pun chicken and tea-smoked duck stand up to scrutiny. Lunch noon–11:45 P.M., daily. **Average** £15. Credit Cards: AE, DC, MC, V.

## Simply Nico
VICTORIA/PIMLICO; P.5, 5C

48A Rochester Row (tel. 630-8061). Victoria Underground/BritRail station.

A tiny restaurant owned and run by Nico Ladenis and his wife and daughter. Nico is a self-taught chef, winner of two Michelin stars, author of a successful book, *My Gastronomy*, and notoriously uncompromising with the press, the foodie trade, and his customers. He gets away with it all because his cooking is sublime. Lunch 12:30–2 P.M., dinner 7:30–11 P.M. Mon.–Fri. **Average** £45. **Price-fixe lunch** £19.50. Credit Cards: AE, DC, MC, V.

## Simpson's Grand Divan Tavern
COVENT GARDEN; P.5, 3D

Simpson's-in-the-Strand, 100 Strand (tel. 836-9112). Charing Cross Underground/BR.

An old English restaurant, justifiably famous for its roasts, which are wheeled around on trolleys and carved at your table. The menu is an interesting list of old English dishes: tripe and onions, boiled beef and carrots, and daily specials (braised oxtail on Wednesdays), but only the roast beef is really good. The wine list includes several New World labels, a concession, no doubt, to the predominantly American clientele. This place is formal to the point of stuffy. Lunch noon–3 P.M., dinner 6–10 P.M., Mon.–Sat. **Average £25.** Credit Cards: AE, DC, MC, V.

### Taste of Africa                                    BRIXTON
50 Brixton Rd. (tel. 587-0343). Brixton Underground.

One of the newest African restaurants in Brixton, the center of London's black community. The food is eclectic and authentic—"as hot as it should be," said my African guest—and the list of drinks is diverse. Open noon–midnight daily. **Average £8.** No credit cards.

### Tate Gallery Restaurant           WESTMINSTER; P.5, 4D
Millbank (tel. 834-6754). Pimlico Underground.

A restaurant for wine buffs and art buffs, for the Tate Gallery Restaurant is best known for its outstanding cellar; for its many wines bought *en primeur;* and for its murals by Whistler. The food is typically English (roasts, steak and kidney pie, or pudding and fried fish, all £6 to £8) and not outstanding. Lunch noon–3 P.M. Mon.–Sat. **Average £15.** No credit cards.

### La Tante Claire                          CHELSEA; P.4, 6A
68 Royal Hospital Rd., SW3 (tel. 352-6045). Sloane Square Underground.

A pretty restaurant run by Pierre Koffmann, a respected and dedicated chef who specializes in modern French cooking, for which he has won two Michelin stars. Prices are high, but like most of London's highly creative chefs, M. Koffmann offers a set price lunch for under £20 and a house wine for under £10. Don't miss them. Lunch 12:30–2 P.M., dinner 7–11 P.M., Mon.–Fri. **Average £34.** Credit Cards: AE, DC, MC, V.

### The White Tower                        FITZROVIA; P.2, 2C
1 Percy St. (tel. 636-8141). Goodge St./Tottenham Court Rd. Underground.

The oldest Greek restaurant in London opened in 1938, when eating Greek was not fashionable and only the rich and/or famous ate out. Consequently the restaurant's name hardly gives away its ethnic identity: the menu is half French, half Greek with some good English game in season, and the prices are high. The standards of cooking are, however, excellent and the restaurant is always busy. Lunch 12:30–2:30 P.M., dinner 6:30–10:30 P.M. Mon.–Fri. **Average £20.** Credit Cards: AE, DC, MC, V.

### Ziani Dolci                              CHELSEA; P.4, A6
112 Cheyne Walk (tel. 352-7534). Buses 19, 39, 45, 49.

This elegant Chelsea restaurant epitomizes a new wave of Italian food in London. The chef is Venetian and his menu an eclectic selection of regional dishes, all given a light touch. Nothing is stodgy, everything is authentic and interesting. Lunch 12:30–2:45 P.M. daily. Dinner 7–11:30 P.M. Mon.–Sat. **Average £19.** Credit cards: AE, DC, MC, V.

# ENTERTAINMENT

As far as we're concerned, and as far as you're concerned, everything you do on your trip should be classified as "Entertainment." Just walking around absorbing all the new stuff-should wear you out every day. London is not a city for relaxing. There's simply far too much to do all the time. And all of it is entertaining.

However, you do need to know about more specific types of entertainment.

## Sports

Sport in Britain can be endlessly entertaining (the races at Ascot) or merely endless (cricket).

You can go to **horse racing** (try Kempton Park, tel. 0932-782292) or **greyhound racing** (try Wimbledon, tel. 946-2662). You can see **cricket at Lord's** (tel. 289-1611/1615) or at the **Oval** in Kennington (tel. 582-6600). Naturally you'd like to score some tickets for **Wimbledon** beginning the last week in June. Here's how, if you're a plan-aheader: Write in August or September of the *preceding* year for tickets (you'll have to write for 1990 tickets this year) to All England Lawn Tennis and Croquet Club, Box 98, Church Road, Wimbledon, SW19 5AE (tel. 946-2244). A limited number of seats are available on the day; however, people have been known to camp out early (i.e., 5 A.M.) to get them. There are also **regattas** (for rowing sculls) on the Thames, the most famous of which are the Oxford-Cambridge match around Easter and the international competition at Henley-on-Thames (about 15 miles northwest of town), which invariably coincides with Wimbledon. You don't need tickets for either of these events; just find yourself a spot on the riverbank and break open a picnic. The daily papers include advice on the best vantage points from which to watch the races.

You can let somebody else do the running for you in Hyde Park with a mount supplied by Bathurst Riding Stables (tel. 723-2813), Lilo Blum's Riding School and Stables (tel. 235-6846), or Ross Nye's Riding Establishment (tel. 262-3791). Or you can glide on your own two feet at the Queen's Ice-Skating Club (tel. 229-0172).

If you need more info about such matters, call the Sports Council (388-1277), or talk to the concierge at your hotel.

## Theater

Undoubtedly you don't need reminding that London is one of the most important centers for theater of all sorts in the world. The West End is the heart of London's commercial theater scene.

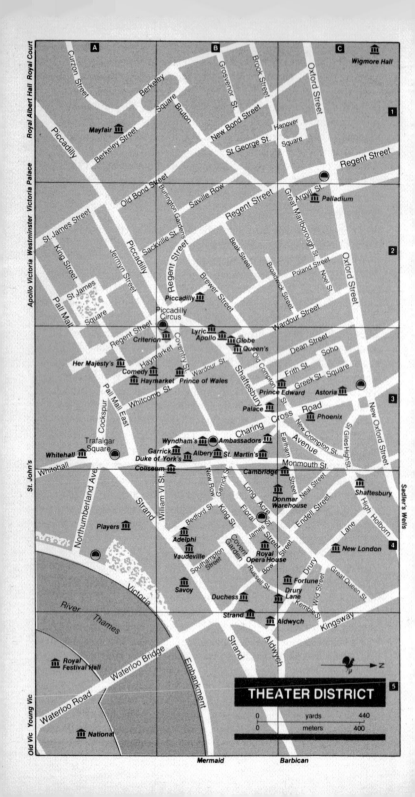

Another can't-miss bet is to head for the National Theatre's theaters at the **South Bank Centre** or the Royal Shakespeare Company's theaters at the **Barbican Centre.** You can also take an out-of-town overnight junket to the RSC's theaters at **Stratford.** To keep in-town prices down, buy tickets at the half-price booth in Leicester Square. But keep in mind, the hottest shows won't be available there, and there will be a line (very long in summer). There is a lot of great experimental or "fringe" theater in London. Check out the offerings at the **Battersea Arts Centre** (tel. 223-2223), **Bloomsbury Theatre** (tel. 389-9629), **Donmar Warehouse** (tel. 240-8230), **Hackney Empire** (tel. 985-2424), **Holland Park Theatre** (tel. 602-7856), **ICA Theatre** (tel. 930-3647), **Lyric Hammersmith** (tel. 741-2311), **Open Air Theatre, Regent's Park** (tel. 486-2431), **Royal Court** (tel. 730-1745), or **Young Vic** (tel. 928-6363).

## Music and Dance

In the world of dance, London's premier companies are the **Royal Ballet** and the **Sadler's Wells Ballet.** Both call the Royal Opera House (Covent Garden, tel. 240-1066/1911) home. The Sadler's Wells Theatre (tel. 278-8916) is also noted for its dance programs, as are various theaters at the Barbican and South Bank Centres. London's two most important opera companies are the **Royal,** which performs at Covent Garden (see above), and the **English National,** which performs at the London Coliseum (tel. 831-3161; 240-7200). The **Royal Choral Society** often performs at the Royal Albert Hall (tel. 589-3203), as do many other groups.

In the last ten years London has produced a bumper crop of important dance companies. Among the many, *Michael Clark* and *DV8* are ones to look out for.

There are concert and recital halls all over town. Heavy hitters include the **Royal Philharmonic** at the Barbican (tel. 628-8891) and Royal Festival Hall (tel. 928-3002), the **London Symphony Orchestra** at the Barbican, and the **Academy of St. Martin-in-the-Fields** at Royal Festival Hall and at the church whence comes its name. **Queen Elizabeth Hall** and the **Purcell Room** (tel. for both 928-8800) at the South Bank Centre and **Wigmore Hall** (tel. 935-2141) are places for smaller-scale concerts and recitals.

## Nightlife

The pop music scene is a highly visible and highly volatile component of London nightlife. Check out the daily listings in *Time Out* and *City Limits* for up-to-the-minute news. The best fun is to be had by catching some live music at one of the dozens of music-halls-turned-rock-clubs in town. They feature rhythm-and-blues greats, new wavers, pop stars, reggae, and African bands—London is BIG on ethnic music. Check listings and posters to see what's on tap at the **Academy,** Brixton (tel. 274-1525), the **Astoria** (tel. 434-0403), the **Bass Clef** (tel. 729-2476), **Dingwalls** (tel. 267-4967), **Hammersmith Odeon** (tel. 748-4081), **100 Club** (tel. 636-0933), **Rock Garden** (tel. 240-3961), **Town & Country Club** (tel. 267-3334).

If jazz is your gig, man, check out the jams at the Bass Clef and 100 Club (see above), **Jazz Cafe** (tel. 359-4936), **Pizza Express** (tel. 439-8722), and **Ronnie Scott's** (tel. 439-0747).

As far as nightclub/life spots go, the top spot changes nearly minute by minute. If you attend well to your *Face* and *Arena* magazine gossip columns, you should have a fair idea of what's the newest hot joint in town. Lots of the clubs feature a different music/entertainment/theme/sexual orientation program each night of the week. Some dance clubs that are fixtures on the scene and that have consistently served up good entertainment to satisfy the capricious tastes of London's latenighters: **Fridge** (tel. 326-5100); **Heaven** (gay) (tel. 839-3852); **Limelight** (tel. 434-0527); **Stringfellows** (tel. 240-5534); **Wag Club** (tel. 437-5534).

# CITY LISTINGS

## Churches

**All-Hallows-by-the-Tower**                                          THE CITY; P. 3, G3
Byward St.; tel. 481-2928; Mon.–Fri. 9:30 A.M.–5:30 P.M., Sat.–Sun. 10 A.M.–5:30 P.M.

**Lincoln's Inn Chapel**                                          HOLBORN; P. 2, 2E
Lincoln's Inn, Lincoln's Inn Fields; tel. 405-6360; tour Mon.–Fri. 9 A.M., 11 A.M.

**Southwark Cathedral**                                          SOUTH BANK; P. 6, 4G
1 Montague Pl.; tel. 407-2939

**Spanish and Portuguese Synagogue**                                          THE CITY; P. 3, 3G
Heneage Lane, Bevis Marks

**St. Bartholomew-the-Great**                                          THE CITY; P. 3, 2F
Little Britain St.; tel. 606-1575

**St. Bride**                                          THE CITY; P. 3, 3E
Fleet St.; tel. 353-1301

**St. Dunstan in the East**                                          THE CITY; P. 3, 3G
Idol Lane, St. Dunstan's Hill, Lower Thames St.

**St. Etheldredas**                                          HOLBORN; P. 4, 2E
14 Ely Pl.; tel. 405-1061

**St. Martin-in-the-Fields**                                          SOHO; P. 5, 3D
5 St. Martin's Lane; tel. 930-0089

**St. Mary Abchurch**                                          THE CITY; P. 3, 3F
Abchurch Yard, Cannon St.; tel. 626-0306

**St. Mary Aldermanbury** THE CITY; P. 3, 2F
Aldermanbury and Love Ln.

**St. Mary-le-Bow** THE CITY; P. 3, 3F
Bow Lane and Cheapside; tel. 248-5139

**St. Paul's Cathedral** THE CITY; P. 3, 3F
Ludgate Hill; tel. 248-2705

**Temple Church** THE CITY; P. 3, 3E
Fleet St.; tel. 353-1736

## Museums and Galleries

**Barbican Centre Art Gallery** THE CITY; P. 3, 2F
Silk St.; tel. 638-4141; Mon.–Sat. 10 A.M.–6:45 P.M., Sun. 10 A.M.–5:45 P.M.

**Bear Gardens Museum** SOUTH BANK; P. 6, 3F
**of the Shakespearean Stage**
1 Bear Gardens; Tues.–Sat. 10 A.M.–5:30 P.M., Sun. 2–6 P.M.

**British Museum** BLOOMSBURY; P. 2, 2D
Great Russell St.; tel. 636-1555; Mon.–Sat., 10 A.M.–5 P.M., Sun. 2:30–6 P.M.

**Courtauld Institute Galleries** BLOOMSBURY; P. 2, 2D
Woburn Sq.; tel. 580-1015 or 636-2095; Mon.–Sat. 10 A.M.–5 P.M., Sun. 2–5 P.M.

**Cricket Memorial Museum** MARYLEBONE; P. 1, 1A
Lord's Cricket Ground, St. John's Wood Rd.; tel. 289-1611; Mon.–Sat. 10:30 A.M.–5 P.M.

**Dickens House** HOLBORN; P. 2, 2E
48 Doughty St.; tel. 405-2127; Mon.–Sat. 10 A.M.–5 P.M.

**The Geological Museum** SOUTH KENSINGTON; P. 4, 5A
Exhibition Rd.; tel. 589-3444; Mon.–Sat. 10 A.M.–6 P.M., Sun. 1–6 P.M.

**Institute of Contemporary Arts** ST. JAMES'S; P. 5, 4D
12 Carlton House; tel. 930-6393; 12–9:30 P.M.

**Kenwood** HAMPSTEAD
Hampstead Lane; tel. 348-1286; daily 10 A.M.–5 P.M.

**Light Fantastic** SOHO; P. 5, 3D
Trocadero, Piccadilly; tel. 734-4516; 10 A.M.–9:30 P.M.

**London Experience** SOHO; P. 5, 3D
Trocadero, Piccadilly; tel. 439-4938; daily 10 A.M.–11 P.M.

**London Planetarium** MARYLEBONE; P. 1, 2B
Marylebone Rd.; tel. 486-1121; daily 9 A.M.–5:30 P.M. in summer, 10 A.M.–5:30 P.M. in winter

**London Transport Museum** COVENT GARDEN; P. 2, 3D
Covent Garden; tel. 379-6344; daily 10 A.M.–6 P.M.

**Madame Tussaud's** MARYLEBONE; P. 1, 2B
Marylebone Rd.; tel. 935-6861; daily 10 A.M.–5:30 P.M.

**Museum of London** THE CITY; P. 3, 2F
150 London Wall; tel. 600-3699; Tues.–Sat. 10 A.M.–6 P.M., Sun. 2–6 P.M.

**The Museum of the** CLERKENWELL; P. 3, 2F
**Order of St. John**
St. John's Gate, St. John's Lane; tel. 253-6644; Mon.–Fri. 10 A.M.–5 P.M., Sat. till 4 P.M.

**National Gallery** SOHO; P. 5, 3D
  Trafalgar Sq.; tel. 839-3321; Mon.–Sat. 10 A.M.–6 P.M., Sun. 2–6 P.M.

**National Portrait Gallery** SOHO; P. 5, 3D
  St. Martin's Pl.; tel. 930-1552; Mon.–Fri. 10 A.M.–5 P.M., Sat. 10 A.M.–6 P.M., Sun. 2–6 P.M.

**Natural History Museum** SOUTH KENSINGTON; P. 4, 5A
  Cromwell Rd.; tel. 589-6323; Mon.–Sat. 10 A.M.–6 P.M., Sun. 1–6 P.M.

**Old Royal Observatory** GREENWICH
  Greenwich Park; tel. 858-1167; Mon.–Sat. 10 A.M.–6 P.M., till 5 P.M. in winter, Sun. 2–6 P.M., till 5 P.M. in winter

**Percival David Foundation of** BLOOMSBURY; P. 2, 2D
**Chinese Art**
  53 Gordon Sq.; tel. 387-3909; Mon.–Fri. 10:30 A.M.–5 P.M.

**Queen's House, National Maritime Museum** GREENWICH
  Romney Rd, Greenwich; tel. 858-4422; Mon.–Sat. 10 A.M.–6 P.M., Sun. 12–6 P.M.

**Royal Academy** MAYFAIR; P. 5, 3C
  Burlington House Sq.; tel. 439-7438; daily 10 A.M.–6 P.M.

**Science Museum** SOUTH KENSINGTON; P. 4, 5A
  Exhibition Rd.; tel. 589-3456; Mon.–Sat. 10 A.M.–6 P.M., Sun. 2:30–6 P.M.

**Serpentine Gallery** HYDE PARK; P. 4, 4A
  Kensington Gardens, Hyde Park; tel. 402-6075; Mon.–Fri. 10 A.M.–6 P.M., Sat. and Sun. 10 A.M.–7 P.M.

**Sir John Soane's Museum** HOLBORN; P. 2, 2E
  13 Lincoln's Inn Fields; tel. 405-2107; Tues.–Sat. 10 A.M.–5 P.M.

**South Bank Crafts Centre** SOUTH BANK; P. 5, 4E
  Royal Festival Hall; tel. 928-0681; Tues.–Sun. 12–7 P.M.

**The Tate Gallery** WESTMINSTER; P. 5, 5D
  Millbank; tel. 821-1313; Mon.–Sat. 10 A.M.–5:50 P.M., Sun. 2–5:50 P.M.

**Theatre Museum** COVENT GARDEN; P. 2, 3D
  Russell and Wellington sts.; tel. 836-7891; Tues.–Sun. 11 A.M.–7 P.M.

**Victoria and Albert Museum** SOUTH KENSINGTON; P. 4, 5A
  South Kensington; tel. 589-6371; Mon.–Sat. 10 A.M.–5:50 P.M., Sun. 2:30–5:50 P.M.

**The Wallace Collection** MARYLEBONE; P. 1, 2B
  Hertford House, Manchester Sq.; tel. 935-0687; Mon.–Sat. 10 A.M.–5 P.M., Sun. 2–5 P.M.

# Historic Sites
**Bank of England** THE CITY; P. 3, 3G
  Threadneedle St.; tel. 601-4444; by appointment only

**The Banqueting House** WHITEHALL; P. 5, 4D
  Whitehall; tel. 930-4179; daily 10 A.M.–5 P.M.

**Big Ben** WESTMINSTER; P. 5, 4D

**Buckingham Palace** WESTMINSTER; P. 5, 4C
  The Mall; Changing of the Guard, Mon.–Sat. 11:30 A.M., Sun. 10:30 A.M.

**The Central Criminal Court** THE CITY; P. 3, 3F
  Old Bailey and Newgate sts.; tel. 248-3277; galleries Mon.–Fri. 10:30 A.M.–1 P.M., 2–4 P.M.

**The Charterhouse**                     CLERKENWELL; P. 3, 2F
Charterhouse Sq.; tel. 253-9503; tours Apr.–Jul., Wed. 2:45 P.M.

**Gray's Inn**                              HOLBORN; P. 2, 2E
Gray's Inn Pl.; tel. 405-8164; gardens open Mon.–Fri. 12–2:30 P.M.

**Hampton Court Palace**                  HAMPTON COURT
East Molesey Surrey, Hampton Ct.; tel. 977-8441; daily 9:30 A.M.–6 P.M.

**Her Majesty's Tower of London**
(see the Tower of London, below)

**Houses of Parliament**              WESTMINSTER; P. 5, 4D
Palace of Westminster; tel. 219-4272 or 219-3574

**Kensington Palace**                        KENSINGTON
Kensington Gardens; tel. 937-9561; Mon.–Sat. 9 A.M.–4:15 P.M., Sun. 1–5
P.M.

**Leighton House**                           KENSINGTON
12 Holland Park Rd.; tel. 602-3316; Mon.–Sat. 11 A.M.–5 P.M.

**Linley Sambourne House**                   KENSINGTON
18 Stafford Terrace; tel. 937-0663; open May–Oct., Wed. 10 A.M.–4 P.M.,
Sun 2–5 P.M.

**Lloyd's**                              THE CITY; P. 3, 3G
1 Lime St.; tel. 623-7100; Mon.–Fri. 9 A.M.–5 P.M.

**Mansion House**                        THE CITY; P. 3, 3G
Mansion House Pl.; tel. 626-2500; by written appt. only

**Old Bailey**                           THE CITY; P. 3, 3F
(see The Central Criminal Court, above)

**Old War Office**                       WHITEHALL; P. 5, 4D
Whitehall; tel. 218-9000

**Parliament Square**                 WESTMINSTER; P. 5, 4D

**Royal Exchange**                       THE CITY; P. 3, 3G
Cornhill and Threadneedle sts.; tel. 283-7101 Mon.–Fri. 11:30 A.M.–2 P.M.

**Royal Hospital Chelsea**                      CHELSEA
Royal Hospital Rd.; tel. 730-0161; Mon.–Sat. 10 A.M.–12 P.M., 2–4 P.M.

**Royal Opera House**             COVENT GARDEN; P. 2, 3D
Covent Garden; tel. 240-1066;

**Smithfield Market**                    THE CITY; P. 3, 2F
Mon.–Thurs. 5–10 A.M.

**Staple Inn**                             HOLBORN; P. 2, 2E
High Holborn; tel. 242-0106

**The Temple**                           THE CITY; P. 3, 3E
Crown Office Row; tel. 353-4355

**The Tower of London**                  THE CITY; P. 3, 3G
Tower Hill; tel. 709-0765; Mon.–Sat. 9:30 A.M.–5 P.M., Sun. 2–5 P.M., winter Mon.–Sat. til 4 P.M., closed Sun.

**University of London**              BLOOMSBURY; P. 2, 2C
Montague Pl.

**The War Rooms**                        WHITEHALL; P. 5, 4D
Clive Steps, King Charles St.; tel. 930-6961; daily 10 A.M.–5:15 P.M.

**Westminster Abbey**                 WESTMINSTER; P. 5, 4D
Parliament Sq.; tel. 222–7110; Mon.–Fri. 8 A.M.–6 P.M., Sat. 9 A.M.–2:45
P.M., Sun. for services

## Parks and Gardens

**Dorset Fields** MARYLEBONE; P. 1, 2B
 Dorset Square

**Green Park** P. 5, 4C

**Holland Park** KENSINGTON
 Kensington High St.

**Hyde Park** P. 4, 3H-A, B

**Kensington Gardens** P. 4, 3–4A

**London Zoo** MARYLEBONE; P. 1, 1B
 Regent's Park; tel. 722-3333; daily 9 A.M.–dusk, winter from 10 A.M.

**Lord's Cricket Ground** MARYLEBONE; P. 1, 1A
 St. John's Wood Rd.; tel. 289–1611; Apr.–Sept.

**Ranelagh Gardens** CHELSEA
 Royal Hospital Rd.

**Regent's Park** MARYLEBONE; P. 1, 1A, B, C

**St. James's Park** WESTMINSTER; P. 5, 4C-D

# 5

# THAMES, OXFORD, AND THE COTSWOLDS

Gentlemen, start your engines, rev them high, and push them fast into overdrive. You'll need speed and skill to cover the course laid out in this chapter, which cuts a westward swatch from London almost to Wales and includes seven shires: Warwick, Gloucester, Oxford, Buckingham, Bedford, Hertford, and Berk. The area also includes four of Britain's most visited neighborhoods: Windsor and Eton, Oxford, the Cotswolds, and Stratford-upon-Avon. As Oxonian Lewis Carroll remarked in another context, it will take all the running you can do just to keep in place.

For the sake of simplicity, we have divided this complicated area into four regions: East, Central, Southwest, and North. The East is centered in Windsor/Eton and includes some of Britain's most celebrated stately homes and gardens—that of the monarch included. Central is based around Oxford, an ancient seat of learning and culture. Southwest is the heart of Cotswold country, with its quintessential half-timbered towns enveloped in English roses. North is hard-core Shakespeare country at Stratford, whose crowds you can escape to Warwick and Kenilworth castles.

You may have noticed that we have cited cities as the core of three out of four of these areas. This is a device to assist you in orienting yourself, and should be used merely as a frame of reference. It would not do at all for you to head straight for these centers of activity and feel thereby that you had gotten to know the Thames Valley and the Cotswold Hills. On the contrary, if you stick to the more urban centers, you miss the point entirely. Far too many people come to this region and "do Windsor-Stratford-Oxford," then shuffle back to London scratching their heads and wondering at all the fuss about the Cotswolds. The fuss is about the tiny villages, the twisting back roads, the acres of sheep meadows and wheat fields. Sadly, many formerly precious preserves of Thames and Cotswolds antiquity have been overrun by visitors trampling gardens, demanding chichi boutiques, littering film wrappers, and generally overthrowing the very charm and character they came (in droves) to enjoy. Towns like Moreton-in-Marsh, Stow-on-the-Wold, Broadway, and, most obviously, Stratford itself have gone hog-wild to attract customers, failing to proceed with care and caution for preserving the special quaintness that the visitor was coming to enjoy in the first place.

Because there is such a slew of things to see, we tried to avoid the usual tour routes through this magnificent countryside. Of course we will help you assess what there is to see and do in Oxford and Stratford and Windsor, but we don't recommend that you stay in any of these towns; better to install yourself in a terrific hotel in the country—with which this country is fraught—and visit these towns on day trips. Keep to the back roads—the B roads, and the unmarked roads. While the latter may be lacking numerical classifications on your map, they are usually well marked and are often the fastest way to get from place to place, since the A roads tend to get clogged with slow-moving traffic. And, if you should get lost, distances here are not too great; more than likely you will discover some of the primest scenery of your trip while getting your route disentangled.

## TRAVEL

The Thames Valley stretches directly west from London and is, therefore, a cinch to get to. Heathrow is twenty minutes east of Windsor, so if you're heading straight to the country upon arrival, you can pick up a car at the airport. Even if you're spending time in London, you might want to take the Underground out to Heathrow and pick up a car there to save the hassle of city driving and the expense of city leasing. Other options include taking BritRail to one of the centers—Oxford, Windsor, or Stratford—and hiring a car from there. Trains servicing this area depart from London's Paddington Station (tel. 01-262-6767). As mentioned, the best way to see this region is by back road, avoiding major towns when possible. That's why we recommend a train/drive combination; otherwise you're restricted by rail schedules and to towns with stations in them—which tends to automatically turn them into tourist magnets. Additionally, the hotels we suggest and many of the restaurants are usually well off the beaten track and can be patronized feasibly only by car.

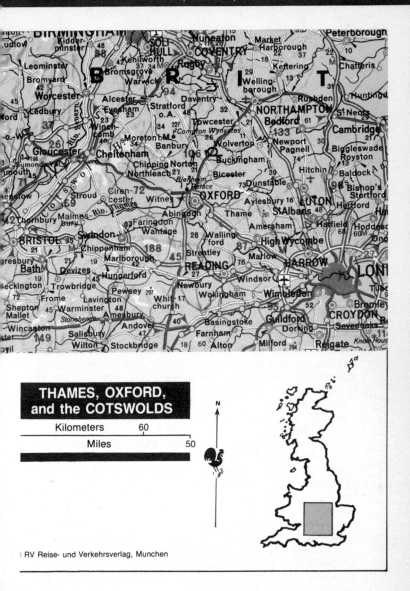

# 🐓 HOTELS

This stretch of English countryside has for centuries been a favorite country address for the gentry whose estates still prolifer-
ate, and for the more common folk looking for a bit of fresh air
and green away from the steaming streets of London and Birmingham. Since the local folks have been at the business of
hospitality for so long, they've got it down not so much to a science as to an art. Without question, some of the finest inns,
country house hotels, and restaurants in the kingdom are nestled in the Thames River Valley and in the Chiltern and Cotswold

hills. As mentioned, the division of this chapter into directional sections with Stratford, Oxford, and Windsor as heads is merely a device for our convenience and yours. Accommodations in these towns are generally far inferior to those found just a short distance out of city centers in the country. With few exceptions, all the hotels we recommend for this area are blissfully situated on multi-acre estates with gardens and parks for you to luxuriate in.

If you prefer accommodations on a simpler scale, may we suggest staying on a farm in the Cotswolds. Many working farms—you know, cows, sheep, chickens, the works—offer bed-and-breakfast lodgings. Some farmhouses are upwards of four hundred years old and will envelop you in low-key comfort: fresh eggs for breakfast, home-cured bacon, milk fresh from the Frisians, and a sense of what it's like to live here, not just merely visit. Gloucestershire, the county that encompasses most of the Cotswolds, offers several dozen farmhouse B&Bs. Call (0453) 810348 for Gloucestershire farmhouse information.

As mentioned, this chapter covers a large area and a large roster of must-see sights. You'll need a week at the very least to begin to see all that's worth seeing. Probably the best program would be to spend half the time at an inn in the eastern part of the region—either near Windsor or Oxford—and the other half in the north and/or western parts—near Stratford or in the Cotswold Hills. This way you can work within two different easy-touring radii. For the Windsor/Eton area consider staying in Ashton Chaton, Egham, or Mapledeerham. Around Oxford try Great Milton and Woodstock. If you're staying in the heart of the Cotswolds good hotels are to be found at Buckload, Cheltenham, Tetbury, Upper Slaughter, and Winchcombe. Alderminster is near Stratford.

Unlike many other parts of Britain where good restaurants tend to be connected to hotels, there is a plethora of great places to eat in this region, so definitely plan to check out some of our gastronomic suggestions and to solicit others from your hotelier or from the man on the street. Many hotels do expect you to eat in their dining room unless you inform them otherwise. If you plan to eat elsewhere, be sure to make a point of telling reception, or they will automatically save you a table (and may make you pay for it). You will find the Thames Valley and the Cotswold Hills among the loveliest, most carefree places you have ever visited. Most definitely so if you choose to stay at any one or several of the following.

**Credit card abbreviations used in hotel and restaurant listings are as follows: AE for American Express, CB for Carte Blanche, DC for Diner's Club, MC for MasterCard, and V for Visa.**

# Alderminster

**Ettington Park Hotel,** Alderminster, Warwickshire CV3 8BS; tel. (0789) 740740; telex 311825 EJ PARK G. Ettington Park, about 15 minutes outside of Stratford, is the only answer to that town's crowds and noise. Ettington Park is a grand hotel housed in the manor of the Shirley family, built between 1858 and 1862. The house is a dream for lovers of the Victorian; it is chock-full of carved paneling, polychrome stonework, Gothic touches. A pianist entertains in the drawing room every evening and makes a perfect parenthesis to dinner at Ettington's fine restaurant under the practiced palate of Patrick McDonald. Diversions are many: gardens reproduced from their 1827 plan, a full-fledged riding school, clay-pigeon shooting, tennis courts, indoor pool and Jacuzzi, sauna, tanning bed. There are 48 rooms; the ones in the main house are of course more interesting than those in the extension, but all are decorated with faux antiques and have TV with video selection, some baths come with Jacuzzi and telephone, and all rooms have a garden or parkland view. A double room with full breakfast begins at £105; suites, at £140. AE, DC, MC, V.

## Ashton Clinton

**The Bell Inn,** Ashton Clinton, Buckinghamshire HP22 5HP; tel. (0296) 630252. The Bell Inn is just outside of Aylesbury on the A41, rather a busy thoroughfare; however, the courtyards and gardens of the Bell feel serenely removed from the comings and goings of the world. A member of Relais & Château for some years now, the Bell is a hotelier's hotel: every detail is attended to perfectly, as has been done under several generations of the Harris family. The main building is a 16th-century coaching inn, and it retains its antique feel with candlelight whenever and wherever possible. Rooms are full of extras like fresh flowers, fruit, toasty terry robes, wheat-germ and millefleurs toiletries. The dining room is a source of special pride and the best of English cooking is produced perfectly time after time. The wine list is extensive and expensive, with an emphasis on burgundies. A double room including breakfast begins at £83. MC, V.

## Buckland

**Buckland Manor,** Buckland, Gloucestershire WR12 7LY; tel. (0386) 852626. Adrienne and Barry Berman are pleased that the town of Buckland (tiny as it is) is situated on a non-through road—it keeps the place quiet. Yet the Bermans have done much to put the town on the map with their gracious country house hotel, portions of which have been standing since the 13th century on an estate whose records date back to the seventh century. They quit their London life and moved here with truckloads of fabulous antiques and paintings. The house has bounteous wood—wood floors with rugs scattered to accentuate their beauty, wood paneling, wood beams. The four-poster rooms have working fireplaces, and all rooms have special touches like hand-painted furniture, Victorian fixtures, chinoiserie wallpaper, Gilchrist and Soames soaps, and panoramas of the formal gardens, the Malvern Hills, the tennis court, putting green, heated pool, and croquet lawn. Dinner is a most special affair; it is complemented by a wine list that is very fine and de-

tailed indeed. Double room including breakfast begins at £105.
MC, V.

## Cheltenham

**The Greenway,** Cheltenham, Shurdington GL51 5UG; tel.
(0242) 862352; telex 437216. Green Way is the name given to
a sheep path used since Roman times, and the Lawrence family
that originally owned the estate made their living in the wool
trade. The present hotel is set back from the A46 just outside
of Cheltenham behind a field of daisies and buttercups. Built in
1584, the house is 405 years old. It stands in pretty gardens,
and its conservatory dining room overlooks the lily pond. Guest
rooms are *very* large, with thick sandy carpets, demi canopies,
Queen Anne furnishings, and dressing rooms. Coach-house accommodations look new on the outside but actually are refurbished from 200-year-old stables, with many of the old beams
and brickwork left intact to enhance the ambience. Double
rooms including breakfast and morning paper begin at £95 and
increase to £170. AE, DC, MC, V.

## Egham

**Great Fosters Hotel,** Egham, Surrey TW20 9UR; tel. (0784)
33822. Great Fosters is technically just outside this region, in
Surrey; however, it is very close to Windsor and Eton, so we're
giving it special dispensation to be included here. And special
dispensation indeed is due this Tudor mansion house set in
acres of park including period topiary and water gardens. From
the massive doors to the walk-in fireplaces to the tithe-barn dining room with its tiers of beams, all the 16th-century details have
been perfectly preserved. Special rooms include the tapestry
room—Charlie Chaplin's favorite—with tapestries, of course,
and a magnificent fireplace. The Italian Room has Baroque appointments and a heavily carved gilt bed. The Queen Anne
Room is simpler and has a four-poster with views into the garden. Tennis and swimming are available, as is golf a short distance away. Double rooms including breakfast begin at £65.00.
AE, DC, MC, V.

## Great Milton

**Le Manoir aux Quat' Saisons,** Great Milton, Oxfordshire
OX9 7PD; tel. (08446) 8751. One feels quite confident in saying
that Le Manoir is the finest establishment in the region, if not
in the whole of Britain. The rooms in this elegant country house,
portions of which date from the 14th century, are all named and
color-schemed in honor of various flowers to be found in the surrounding acres of formal gardens. M. and Mme. Blanc are nothing if not generous in their inclusion of amenities: Madeira in a
cut-glass cruet, fresh exotic fruits, flowers, luxurious bathrobes,
Manoir signature soaps, shampoos and bath gels, Limoges ash-
trays. Even the smaller rooms are amply sized and give the illu-
sion of extra space because they're furnished elegantly, not

overly. A heated pool and tennis court are available to assist you in disposing of some of the extra pounds you'll undoubtedly acquire eating at Raymond Blanc's restaurant nonpareil. A native of Besançon, Blanc came to Britain to learn English and seek his fortune. He has become a major fixture in the culinary firmament of his adopted country. Dining at Le Manoir ought to be a must on anyone's list. Having sung the praises of both hotel and restaurant, it must be admitted that prices at each are high even for this up-market neighborhood. We can only assure you that whether you devote a fortnight or merely have a dinner here, it will be well worth the expense. Double rooms including breakfast begin at £110, suites at £250 (there are good midweek rate breaks). All major credit cards.

## Mapledurham

**Mapledurham Cottages,** Mapledurham Estate Office, Mapledurham, Reading RG4 7TR; tel. (0734) 723350. The cottages at Mapledurham are simple and rustic, with just the basic necessities in each. Mapledurham House is part of an ancient fiefdom and these cottages are farmhouses or village residences owned by the estate and converted into self-catering accommodations. The little houses are most charmingly situated on the 2,500-acre property with its Tudor mansion house, water mill, and Thamesside setting—a little English village all to yourself. The houses are simply furnished with beds, basic furniture, and fully operational kitchens for you to putter about in, or you can drive to any of many great restaurants nearby. Television and telephone are available if requested. The cottages are perfect for families or groups of friends traveling together; of the ten cottages available, the pretty Thatch Cott (with thatched roof) sleeps two, and the Queen Anne Mill House sleeps seven, with other properties sleeping any number in between. Prices are very reasonable and are arranged on a per-house, per-week basis and vary according to season, so write or phone for complete tariff listings. No credit cards, but will accept a personal check.

## Tetbury

**Calcot Manor,** Near Tetbury, Gloucestershire GL8 8YJ; tel. (0666) 89227; telex 437105. Brian and Barbara Ball have coaxed their son, Richard, to join them in this delightful venture, refurbishing and bringing brilliantly back to life a 15th-century manor farmhouse and outbuildings including one of Britain's oldest tithe barns, originally built to serve the Cistercian monks of Kingswood Abbey nearby. The service is warm and solicitous as you choose your dinner from chef Raymon Farthing's classical English and French menu while seated by the fireplace attended by any of several yellow Labradors who will beg shamelessly for a nibble of the petits hors d'ouevres served with your cocktail. Whatever you choose for dinner—you can hardly go wrong—do take advantage of their wonderful assortment of British farmhouse cheeses for dessert. The rooms are comfortably furnished with a mixture of antiques and newer pieces; the stables have been quite cleverly converted into guest rooms, some of which are the manor's most popular. There is a secluded, garden-enveloped swimming pool; shooting, riding, golf, and fishing can be arranged nearby. A standard double including full breakfast and a newspaper is £80. All major credit cards.

**Snooty Fox,** Market Place, Tetbury, Gloucestershire GL8 8DD; tel. (0666) 52436; telex 437334 HATCRTG. Unlike most of these hotels, the Snooty Fox is smack in the center of town, but you'll be delighted to find yourself surrounded by a place as pretty as Tetbury—after all, the Prince and Princess of Wales live right down the road. The Snooty Fox was a 16th-century coaching inn whose former owner, a Jew, was not permitted to join the prestigious local hunt for reasons of his religion. He thus named his hotel as a permanent reminder of the silliness of the local aristocrats. Try to reserve one of the deluxe guest rooms: king-size bed, fruit, fresh flowers, and Malvern water are all standard equipment. In all the rooms you'll find nice details like exposed beams, Woods of Windsor toiletries, oil paintings, and potpourri. The dining room serves the best of the season's local produce, thoughtfully enhanced by chef John Waldron. A standard double room is £71.50, a superior is £78, including breakfast and morning paper. AE, DC, MC, V.

## Upper Slaughter

**Lords of the Manor Hotel,** Upper Slaughter, Cheltenham, Gloucestershire GL54 2JD; tel. (0451) 20243; telex 83147 VIAOR G. This unlikely titled town is one of a pair of the most engaging in all of the Cotswolds, and Lords of the Manor is a hotel befitting its fairy-tale setting. The 17th-century house was originally owned by the Witts family, one of whose members, the Reverend F. E. Witts, wrote "Diary of a Cotswold Parson," a 19th-century journal describing an oftentimes charmed existence here that you can still enjoy during your stay in any of the hotel's 15 sumptuous bedrooms overlooking the gardens and rolling meadows. The rooms are almost all suite-size, with large beds clothed in sweet-scented sheets. Wall coverings tend toward the floral; paintings and prints tend toward the rural; baths tend toward the colossal, with almond oil and seashell cosmetics from Crabtree and Evelyn. Dining is by candlelight and features a heady selection of local fish and game arranged table d'hôte or à la carte. Try a bottle of Cloud Bay Cabernet Sauvignon from New Zealand—lighter than air. Double rooms begin at £75 and work their way up to £105 for four-poster master rooms, all including an ample breakfast. AE, DC, MC, V.

## Winchcombe

**Sudely Castle Cottages,** The Secretary, Sudely Castle and Gardens, Winchcombe, Gloucestershire GL54 5JD; tel. (0242) 604103; telex 83343 ABTELX G. Like the cottages at Mapledurham, Sudeley Castle's are part of a much larger estate and are self-catering properties in centuries-old houses. Unlike Mapledurham, Sudely cottages are quite luxuriously furnished with all the amenities, including period and modern furnishings, with housekeeping available at a small extra charge. The cottages and flats sleep from two to seven people and are rented on a weekly basis, with various prices for each of the 17 available properties, whose costs change from season to season. Write for a complete rate schedule. No credit cards.

## Woodstock

**The Feathers Hotel,** Market Street, Woodstock, Oxfordshire OX7 1SX; tel. (0993) 812291; telex 83138 TELKAY G. Gordon Campbell-Gray began his career working in Bangladesh and Nicaragua for Save the Children, and perhaps it is no paradox that he now runs this 16-room inn catering to the needs of the more privileged with great care and congeniality. The hotel is a conglomeration of three town houses in the most picturesque town of Woodstock, famous for Blenheim Palace and its Churchill connections. The Feathers rooms are hardly palatial, but they are certainly most luxurious, with modern takes on traditional designs in furnishings, decorated in soft pastels. The public rooms are a tremendous asset, a collection of taxidermied birds is in keeping with the house theme, and drinks are to be had in the paneled bar with its free-standing fireplace. The Sheraton-style dining room is enhanced by the inspired cooking of chef Sonya Kidney, who hails from Barbados, a heritage endowing her with a great flair for trying and succeeding with unconventional combinations as well as with standards of Modern British Cooking. Double room with breakfast begins at £68. AE, DC, MC, V.

# The Chiltern Hills and Royal Windsor

To the north and west of London are Hertfordshire and the three Bs: Bedfordshire, Buckinghamshire, and Berkshire. It is an area of gentle countryside which inspired a slew of Britain's finest stately homes and the studied nonchalance of the quintessentially English country park—the passion and profession of Capability Brown (whose real name was Lancelot)—celebrating the natural contours and native trees of the countryside.

## The Country Houses

We have chosen nine of literally dozens of fantastic dream houses in this region, each with its own particular atmosphere and attraction. Taken as a group, they represent the best in English baronial architecture from the Tudors through the Victorians. Working westward from Hertfordshire they are:

**Hatfield House,** on the A1000 from London in Hatfield. This is a Jacobean mansion built in the early 17th century, with a

15th-century wing where Elizabeth I spent some of the more pleasant years of her childhood. An important Tudor garden is the scene of a Festival of Gardening at midsummer. Elizabethan banquets are held in the old palace most nights. Open daily except Monday from 12 to 5 P.M., Sunday from 2 to 5:30; £2.60).

**Knebworth House,** on the A1 by Stevenage. A Tudor mansion transformed into a Gothic fancy by the Victorian writer Edward Bulwer-Lytton. You might recognize the Jacobean banqueting hall from a painting by Churchill or the gardens laid out by Edwin Lutyens—also painted by Churchill—or the house as a whole, which was used as a location for the movie *The Shooting Party.* (Open weekends only from March to May, open daily except Mondays during the summer from 12 to 5 P.M.; admission to house and gardens £3.)

**Luton Hoo,** off the M1 in Luton. Luton Hoo has it all: Capability Brown gardens, a Robert Adam house, and, probably the most remarkable of all, the Wernher collection of fine art, including paintings by Rembrandt, Titian, and other old masters, and a stunning collection of Fabergé jewelry smuggled out of Russia by Lady Zia Wernher, who was the daughter of a grand duke. (Open daily except Monday, mid-April to mid-October from 2 to 5:45 P.M.; admission to house and gardens £2.50.)

**Woburn Abbey,** off the M1 in Woburn. Woburn is also rich in architectural interest, having been renovated in the mid-18th century by Henry Holland. The art collection includes works by Canaletto, Holbein, Velazquez, and Rembrandt. If the kids get bored with the indoor amusements, take them on a drive through the Wild Animal Kingdom on the abbey grounds and Britain's largest drive-through park, with lions and tigers and bears—oh my! (Woburn Abbey is open from April through October, Monday through Saturday from 11 A.M. to 5:45 P.M., Sunday from 11 A.M. to 6:15 P.M.; Wild Animal Kingdom is open mid-March through October, from 10 A.M. to dusk.)

**Cliveden,** off the M40 at Taplow. Only the most magnificent palace would do for the Astors, who bought this stunning 19th-century mansion built by Charles Barry of Palace of Westminster fame. The house is rivaled only by its 375-acre park, landscaped with parterres and water gardens. The National Trust is now operating the house as a hotel and restaurant (tel. 06286 5069 for information and reservations). It is also the site of the Cliveden Festival of open-air theater in June and July. (The house and grounds are open April through October, Thursday and Sunday only, from 3 to 6 P.M.; admission to house and grounds £3.)

**Stonor Park,** on the B480 off the A423 near Henley-on-Thames. Portions of this house, owned by the Stonor family for eight hundred years, date back to 1190. The family's staunch support of Catholicism through thick and thin is attested to and celebrated by fine works of medieval religious art. (Open May through September, Wednesday, Thursday, Sunday (and Saturday in August from 2 to 5:30 P.M.; £3.)

**Waddesdon Manor,** on the A41 near Aylesbury. Baron Ferdinand de Rothschild built a French château here in the late 19th century and filled it with his collection of paintings by Romney, Gainsborough, Rubens, illuminated manuscripts, Savonnerie carpets, and much French imperial furniture. (Open April through October, Wednesday through Saturday from 1 to 6 P.M., Sunday from 11:30 A.M. to 6 P.M.; from £3 to £4.)

**Mapledurham House,** off the A4074 from Reading. It's tricky to find, so call (0734) 723350 for directions; or, better yet, take a ferry on the Thames from Reading (call same number for particulars). Mapledurham is more than a house; it's a lovely little village, a Norman church, and a water mill that served as a setting for *The Wind in the Willows.* Other literary connections include Alexander Pope, who was a great friend of the Blount family that has lived here since 1580. The Blounts, also staunch Catholics, were sorely taxed for their religion, but this very lack of funds meant that the house was not fussed with and modernized over the years but stands much as it did in the 16th century. (Open Easter through September, Saturday, Sunday, and holidays from 2:30 to 5 P.M.; separate admissions for various parts of the estate.)

**Basildon Park,** on the A329 near Pangbourne. This 18th-century manor is built of the famous yellow Bath stone in the Georgian style on 406 acres of parks and gardens. It is most famous for its Octagon Room, unique in Britain, as well as for other Neoclassical detailing and the Shell Room, which contains rarities from around the world. (Open April through October, Wednesday through Saturday from 2 to 6 P.M., Sunday from 12 to 6 P.M.; admission to house and grounds £2).

## Windsor and Eton

Of course all of these homes are merely a prelude to the main event in the eastern part of the Thames Valley: Windsor Castle, out-of-town lodgings for the Queen et al. The town of Windsor is pleasant enough, with its hillside/Thameside location. It does, however, get frightfully full during the summer months, and the usual suspects—McDonald's, Pizzaland, etc.—have been rounded up to service the masses hungry for a glimpse at the Royals and perhaps a Coke and some fries. Across the Thames by way of a thoughtfully placed footbridge is Eton, home of the famous public (meaning private or prep, here) school for boys upon whose playing fields, the Duke of Wellington observed, the flower of British officership learned all the skills necessary to assure victory at Waterloo. Be that as it may, the quiet, contemplative streets of Eton are a welcome respite from the overtrammeled High Street of Windsor, and once you have seen the castle, we suggest seeking refuge here amid the 15th-century architecture. The college buildings and grounds are open to the public at various times; check at the tourist office at the Station approach off Windsor High Street. Usually open is the chapel, with its marvelous paintings of the Virgin to whose service Eton was originally dedicated by Henry VI in 1440.

The best restaurants in town are also in Eton—the **Eton Wine Bar** at 82 High St. for light lunches, or the **House on the Bridge** just over Windsor Bridge for fancier fare in a more formal setting.

**For a map of Windsor/Eton see atlas page 10.**

## The Queen Out of Town

Windsor is the largest inhabited castle in the world and as such easily offers a day's worth of things to see and do. It is free to walk around the grounds and into the **Albert Memorial Chapel;** these open daily at 10 A.M. and close at dusk. The chapel is a not-unpleasant study in Victorian excess. **St. George's Chapel** (admission £1.50) is the burial site for several monarchs, including Henry VIII, and was completed in 1528. The **Curfew Tower** (admission 20 pence) is remarkable primarily for its view, which is not much better than other views from elsewhere on the grounds that are free. The most important sights are in the castle itself. The State Apartments (admission £1.80); Queen Mary's Dolls' House (80 pence); and Exhibition of Old Master Drawings (80 pence) are open Monday through Saturday from 10:30 A.M. to 3 P.M. in the off-season, till 5 and on Sundays during the summer.

As you go up the stairs to Queen Mary's Dolls' House and the Exhibition of Old Master Drawings, take a closer look at the fanciful carvings around the pillars; the masons had a free-for-all depicting men and beasts from life and mythology. One particularly jocund stonecutter, perhaps in an editorial comment on the castle's prospective residents, included a mannequin on the topmost left pillar as you are ascending who has dropped his trousers and is here caught in the act of relieving himself.

**Queen Mary's Dolls' House,** designed by Sir Edwin Lutyens, is always a favorite; it is as well attended as the Crown Jewels and rightly so, for it is really every little girl's dream: with incredible detail, leather-bound volumes in the library, cars in the garage, portraits of monarchs copied from the originals in the royal collections, carved friezes, painted ceilings—the works.

The **Exhibition of Old Master Drawings** is less popular but even more wonderful. The Queen's art collection is among the finest in the world, and its contents are rarely seen other than here and at the Queen's Gallery in London. The pictures are rotated frequently, but usually on display are some Holbeins, hauntingly realistic, conveying a whole world of personality through a few lines; Leonardo studies; paintings by royal family members; architectural drawings of royal properties, etc.

The **State Apartments** are as rich and ornate as one would wish of a royal residence: gilt and grandeur prevail, richness and Rococo run as rampant as our purple prose.

Last is the exhibition of the Queen's presents and royal carriages, just outside the main gate: Her Majesty's coaching regalia and gifts bestowed on her to mark various auspicious occasions. It is open the same hours as the castle proper; admission is 80 pence.

## In The Shadow of the Castle

Occasionally throughout the summer, the gardens and mausoleum at Frogmore—the latter containing the bodies of Victoria and Albert—are open for public inspection. Call the Windsor Tourist Information Centre at (0753) 852010 for dates.

There are several other things worth checking out while you are inspecting the Greater Windsor area, and several of these have a seasonal sporting theme. The Royals, partial as they are to spectacle of an equestrian sort, are always on hand for the Royal Meeting at **Ascot Racecourse** in June. There are meetings (races) held throughout the summer season; for information write The Racing Information Bureau, Winkfield Road, Ascot, Berkshire SL5 7HX or phone (0990) 25912. The Royals' other passion is of course for polo, and His Royal Highness can be seen enjoying many a spiffing chukka throughout the season at The **Guards Polo Grounds** in Windsor Great Park; contact the Windsor Tourist Information Centre (phone number above) for schedules. Finally, although not specifically equestrian, but certainly terribly "upper," is the **Royal Regatta** at Henley-on-Thames just north of Windsor. Held annually from the last week of June into the first week of July, rowing teams from around the world now race against the original competitors, Oxford and Cambridge. Tailgaters prevail—champers, strawberries and cream served by the butler from the rear of the Rolly—as do men in boaters and old school ties, women in gossamer frocks and sunhats, and plenty of the hoi polloi drinking pints.

## The Magna Carta

King John, who reigned from 1199 to 1216, had grown dreadfully unpopular with his barons. The late 12th century was a time of unusual prosperity in Britain; the barons were growing richer, but the king's access to the country's new wealth was restricted. John tried to devise ways to circumvent the restrictions and raised money by selling heiresses in his care, levying inheritance taxes, charging for waivers of military service, etc. Many of these practices had been pursued by his predecessors, but not with the same rigor and not at the expense of barons as powerful as these had become.

In 1214 the king returned from an ignoble defeat in France. This emboldened the barons, who gathered in Bury St. Edmunds with Stephen Langton, former archbishop of Canturbury. Langton, and had no love for John, who had stripped him of his post and banished him, and proposed to the barons that temporal law should apply to kings just as canonical law applied to the clergy. So resolved, the barons prepared to confront the king, who knew something was afoot and tried to placate the rebels, stalling for time even as he raised troops. After several unsuccessful attempts at capturing castles, the barons persuaded the citizens of London to their side. With the capital in their pocket, the king was at their mercy. On June 15, 1215, the barons met with the king at Runnymede. Negotiations and revisions were complete by the 19th, and the Magna Carta, signed by the king and the assembled barons, was proclaimed in every shire.

The original version of the Great Charter was primarily concerned with this particular group of barons' specific grudges, and most of it addressed their needs, not necessarily those of the common man. However, two important chapters, the 12th and the 39th, were enough to ensure the document's reputation as a major step forward in establishing the rights of men. Chapter 12 states that the crown cannot raise men and money for the military service without the consent of an assembly of nobles—i.e., the barons. The assembly stipulated grew into the House of Lords and thence into Parliament. This statute (and in fact the entire document generally) indicates that the King acknowledged his submission to (temporal) law. Chapter 39 states that no free man can be assessed, imprisoned, fined, etc., except by judgment of his peers or of the land. This statute guaranteed, therefore, every citizen's right to due process of the law. Although representing a relatively small portion of the entire charter, these ideas represented a revolution in politics, and the Magna Carta is credited with the germination of modern democracy.

Nearby Windsor are a couple other points of interest, including a very special meadow and a great garden. Just to the side of the A308, a mile from the M25 Egham intersection, is a field yellow with dandelions and buttercups beyond which on a little hill is a marble pavilion given by, of all groups, the American Bar Association, representatives of which return every 14 years to this meadow to renew the association's pledge to the ideals of the Magna Carta. For indeed it was at this very Thamesside spot, known as **Runnymede,** that, in 1215, 25 barons "persuaded" King John to sign the document that would forever alter the fate of all free men in Britain (see box). Also here is a memorial to John F. Kennedy, including an acre of land donated to the United States by the British people in Kennedy's honor.

Across the A308 from these monuments is the boathouse for French Brothers, which operates launches on the Thames from here to Windsor to the west or Hampton Court to the east; call (0753) 851900 for details.

Just down the road the A308 intersects with the A328, which in turn runs into the A30. Just after this junction on the right is Wick Rd., which leads to Wick Lane. On Wick Lane you'll find **The Sun,** a two-hundred-year-old cottage that has served as a most congenial pub for about half that time; it presently features Courage on tap, a garden out back, and a menagerie for the kids—all supervised by your host, Vernon "Slippery" James.

Down Wick Lane is the entrance to **Savill Garden,** 36 acres of Great Windsor Park, half of which are formal beds, half of which are woodland. (Open daily from 10 A.M. to 6; £1.80.) The gardens were a favorite of Queen Elizabeth during her childhood. In fact, so delighted was she that she knighted the gardens' chief creator, Eric Savill, to express her appreciation.

## ❦ RESTAURANTS

While you're here, if you're serious about food and don't mind paying for it, you must sample the riches at the **Waterside Inn** in Bray (tel. 0628-20691 and 22941; reservations a must). The Waterside Inn is the sylvan extension of the empire of the Brothers Roux. While Albert sees to Le Gavroche in London, Michel is in charge here beside the Thames. The dining room is painted with orchids and hung with apple blossoms, and it affords a sweeping panorama of the Thames, usually populated with sculls around twilight. A five-course *menu exceptionnel* clocks in at £40.50 per head, or you can choose a possibly even more costly dinner from the exclusively French à la carte menu. The wine list is equally expensive, and the service borders on the imperious; however, it is one of the finest country restaurants in Britain, so try to ignore the hauteur and the prices and enjoy the food and the view. AE, DC, MC, V.

# Oxford and Environs

In addition to the oceans of ink spilled by scholars in the city, there has been an equally deep and wide amount of ink spilled by writers on the subject of the city. This circumstance undoubtedly accounts for the presence of two rivers, the Cherwell and the Thames—known in Oxford as the Isis—to accommodate this dual outpouring. And, as luck would have it, this circumstance provides the town with perfect conditions for punting and sharing white wine and Yeats with your mates beside the rivers. You can rent a punt (or a rowboat if you're timid) and get the sensation yourself. Try Salters, Folly Bridge, St. Aldate's (tel. 0865-51160) for the Thames (a larger and trickier river); or Howard, Magdalen Bridge Boat Station, Bardwell Road (tel. 0865-559780), for the Cherwell. Other than by water, Oxford is only and utterly worthwhile on foot or by bike—rent one from Broadribbs at 6 Lincoln House, Market Street, off Turl Street next to the Covered Market.

The university is actually a conglomeration of colleges, thirty-odd in all, that began in the 12th century. Oxford's first scholars were monks and priests who came together here to study and debate points of theosophy in a sheltered, celibate, cerebral atmosphere. Indeed it was only in the 19th century that faculty were permitted to be laymen and to marry. The presence of women and the laiety has done little to dispel the heavy mantle of arcane tradition and asceticism that hangs around the medieval quadrangles and the tiny back streets.

**For a map of Oxford see atlas pages 12–13.**

## Ancient Academia

For the visitor, the university is first and foremost. Colleges have to walk the tightrope of providing peace and quiet for their students while maintaining an open-door policy to the public, the British element of which pays for the joint to run in the first place. Colleges tend to be open afternoons on various days during the week, although Sunday is usually a good bet. When exploring a college check out the grounds and gardens—but quads (quadrangles) usually have very stiff keep-off-the-grass policies, so watch where you step. If buildings are open, most interesting are usually the college's dining hall—many with 16th-century hammer-beam roofs—library, and chapel.

The best place to commence your touring is at the Oxford Information Centre on St. Aldate's up from the post office. The center is an amiable and knowledgeable resource for anything and everything Oxford. Do take advantage of its box-office service offering tickets for just about every musical and dramatic event in Oxford (and London, Stratford, and Birmingham as well). The Guild of Oxford Guides—best in the business—offers morning and afternoon walking tours that begin from the center and provide a most informative and efficient use of two hours in Oxford (tel. 0865-72071). Also of interest is the **Oxford Story,** a multimedia event tracing the history of the town, located at 6 Broad Street (0865-728822; open 9 A.M. to 7 P.M. in summer, till 5:30 in winter; £3).

If you plan to tour around yourself—and we do endorse it—trot over to **Blackwells**—*the* bookstore in town, if not in the English-speaking world—at 50 Broad Street and pick up a copy of *Vade Mecum* (Latin for "Come with Me"), a steal at 50 pence. This invaluable publication is revised quarterly by Oxford students and is the authoritative guide to the town. And while you're here, do have a browse around Blackwells; if you're at all interested in books and things British, you'll think you died and went to heaven.

Back on the university beat, there is the roster of standards among the colleges that everyone agrees the first-time visitor should pursue. The "A" list includes:

**Christ Church:** It's immense Tom Quad (named for the tower, which was named for the bell, Great Tom, clocking in at seven tons) will be recognizable from salad-days scenes of *Brideshead Revisited*. The college has one of the best art collections among the colleges, portions of which are on display at its picture gallery, reached through the entrance on Oriel Street. Christ Church Chapel is a favorite for Sunday services (Church of England, to be sure); outside enjoy its gardens and especially its adjacent meadow (see "Oxford Greenswards," below).

**Magdalen College:** Pronounced "maudlin," although it is a decidedly cheery place, with its tower—a full six inches higher than Christ Church's—and most especially its deer park and Cherwell-side path, Addison's Walk. Magdalen is also known for its calliopal as well as its natural beauty, and Magdalen Choir concerts are always worth attending.

**New College:** But only relatively so, having been established in 1379. The college itself is one of the prettiest, with its 14th-century cloister, treasure-filled chapel, and secluded gardens. But it also provides a good excuse for passing under the Venetian Bridge, just off Broad Street, and snaking down past the old city wall along New College Lane—of all the city's streets, the most redolent with the scent of medieval monasticism.

**St. John's College:** Also one of the university's best endowed (rumor has it that only God and the Windsors have more assets in Britain). In any case, the cash has been well spent, and the buildings and gardens—including a venerable rock garden—are easily among the university's most splendid.

If you've got a few extra hours to spend college-hopping, we would also suggest looking in on the following:

**Merton College:** Vying for the title of Oxford's oldest with University College, which, despite much evidence to the contrary, staunchly insists on its primacy. Merton's garden overlooks Christ Church Meadow, and its 14th-century library overlooks Mob Quad, which set the trend for tetrahedric design here at Oxford.

**Worcester College:** A bit off the Broad/High Street route, it's worth the minor detour for the lovely gardens and willows trailing their tresses in the Thames.

**Queen's College:** The regent in question is Caroline, wife of the second George. The college is relatively newer than many here but was built with no expense spared by Chris Wren, Nick Hawksmoor, and their cronies.

Of course one cannot leave the university precincts without paying homage to the **Bodleian Library,** various portions of which are open at various times. The best way to see it is to take a tour, times and information for which are available at the shop—along with some great postcards—just in from the Bodleian Quad.

## Oxford Greenswards

All the while you're touring the university, look up, up, up. The most elegant and whimsical features of the town are the minarets and spires and roofs and gables and chimney pots and gargoyles. You can climb up the **Carfax Tower** and get the pigeon's eye view—an excellent idea.

From there you'll notice that there are tremendous stretches of green, not surprisingly, bordering the rivers—and the canal we forgot to mention. The closest patch is right down St. Aldate's beside the Thames, Christ Church Meadow—full of cows and Italian teenagers on school trips having a picnic. If you take the meadow's path along the Thames, you'll come to a fork, the right hand of which goes over a high-arched bridge. Take a stroll down here around twilight every night— or early in the morning, if you've the strength of character— and watch the Oxford eights on down to single-man sculls ply their poised way across the river. It's a very pretty sport, and this is a perfect setting for it.

Along the east end of the meadow is the Cherwell, and just north of the meadow on the Cherwell is the **Botanic Garden,** another glorious retreat—as if Oxford needed one. Unlike the colleges, admission is free, and it's open more often than not. It's great for picnics (pick up provisions at the **Covered Market** on Carfax Street between Turl and Cornmarket).

Another great picnic alternative is **University Parks** down Parks Road, north from Broad Street. The parks are wide open spaces bordered by the Cherwell and perfect for cricket, football, rugby, dog walking, baby strolling, jogging, and the like.

## Museums—Ancient and Modern

Oxford has two terrific museums that almost deserve to go at the top of the list, just to impress upon you the importance of getting to them. First is the **Ashmolean Museum** on Beaumont Street at the corner of St. Giles. The Ashmolean is peerless among smaller museums in Britain. Its collections include art works from ancient civilizations to the Ming Dynasty, and into the moderns. (Open Tuesday through Saturday from 10 A.M. to 4 P.M., Sunday from 2 to 4 P.M.)

Across the street is the **Randolph Hotel,** overpriced and stuffy in general. But that's the sort of place you want for your afternoon tea, and the Randolph's soothing Edwardian salon is the best place in town to take your Darjeeling and fresh scones, clotted cream, and jam. £2.50 per person.

The **Museum of Modern Art,** at 30 Pembroke Street, provides a very full and eclectic schedule of events and exhibitions. Films, workshops, dance, visiting artists, lectures, a great café, and one of Oxford's best shops—there are plenty of reasons to come. (Open Tuesday through Saturday from 10 A.M. to 6 P.M., Sunday from 2 to 6 P.M.; admission is a mere 50 pence.)

### A COURSE IN PUBS

Another of Oxford's perennial sources of entertainment are her pubs. There are dozens of great ones in town; however, the best ones are just out of town. They are probably best reached by bike or car but are a bit tricky to find, so get good directions before you set out. **The Perch** has a backyard garden overlooking the Thames and is in Binsey village. Family barbecues are held on Sundays in summer. **The Trout** is in Wolvercote and has views of the Thames, a bridge and some rapids from its patio. The **Isis** is also on the Thames by the Iffley Lock. In town, try the **Bear** on Alfred St., wallpapered with school ties from around the planet; the **Turf** in a mews off Holywell St., a 15th-century pub with outdoor tables; the **Head of the River** on St. Aldate's at Folly Bridge is perfect for watching expert eights or amateur punters; and the **Eagle and Child** on St. Giles is where Oxonians Lewis (C. S.) and Tolkein (J. R. R.) concocted their tales of the extranatural for thirty years.

## Blenheim Palace

One of Oxfordshire's most important repositories of art and history actually lies outside the city proper, in the town of

Woodstock, just to the north of Oxford on the Woodstock Road (the A34). Here is Blenheim Palace, resplendent in its acres of exquisite formal gardens and park. While not a palace in the strictest sense of its being inhabited by princes, the home of the dukes of Marlborough couldn't be considered anything less than palatial. Blenheim can easily take and easily merits a day, so do give yourself enough time to see everything. The property and fortune to support Blenheim were given to the first duke by a grateful Queen Anne for his victory over the French in the Wars of the Spanish Succession at Blenheim in 1704. Every year on the anniversary of the battle, the Blenheim standard must be sent to the sovereign by way of rent. If the duke forgets, the palace and grounds revert back to the crown. The first duke of Marlborough's name was John Churchill, and his most illustrious progeny, Sir Winston, was born here at Blenheim in 1874.

This was not at all a bad place to grow up. The house is considered to be the masterpiece of English Baroque architecture and of its creator, John Vanbrugh; and the two hundred acres of parkland, some of the finest work of Capability Brown. Inside the palace, the (Winston) Churchill connection is emphasized by a special exhibition, most delightfully by young Winston's collection of toy soldiers, several thousand strong. The interiors are rich with tapestries, French furnishings, fine paintings, and a foison of gilt, cherubs, painted ceilings, etc.

## ❦ RESTAURANTS

Oxford is a veritable gold mine for restaurants—so proud parents can take their undergrads out for a celebratory splurge. Unquestionably, the best in the area is **Le Manoir aux Quat' Saisons,** 12 miles away in Great Milton (see "Hotels," at beginning of chapter). **Fifteen North Parade** (at 15 North Parade, tel. 0865-513773), now owned by Georgina Woods, it is cool creams and ecrus and light wood. Chef Duncan Huitson's light touch is evident in the salmon tort and monkfish terrine, the scallops of veal with a sage and port sauce, and apple-stuffed quails with an onion cream. Desserts are as lush and gooey as you please. MC, V. **Restaurant Elizabeth** upstairs at No. 84 St. Aldate's (tel. 0865-242230) is an Oxford fixture and has managed to maintain standards without caving in to every new food fad to come along in the past 25 years. Chef Antonio Lopez presides over the 16th-century dining room with its views over Christ Church. The thankfully old-style menu includes steaks, breast of chicken in butter with cognac and cream, fresh river trout with white wine and fish fumé sauce. AE, DC, MC, V. For something completely different, cruise out to the **Hi-Lo Jamaican Eating House,** 70 Cowley Rd. (tel. 865-725984). It's a great place to let your hair down, enjoy the kids skampering around, some Bob Marley on the airwaves, and have a cosmic discussion with your amiable if abstruse host. There's jerked chicken, funky fish with lots of hot sauce, vegetables, and the obligatory Red Stripe to wash it all down. Not cheap precisely, but fun. No credit cards. Also of import is **The Features** in Woodstock (see Hotels earlier).

## At Night

Nightlife-wise there's lots to do here, with concerts from the old masters to new wave, theater galore, festivals, lectures, films (try the Penultimate Picture Palace, Jeune St., tel. 0865-723837 for classics). While you're at the Information Centre, pick up a copy of "This Week at Oxford," a pastel-colored broadsheet with all the listings you need.

# The Core Of The Cotswolds

How many times can one employ "quaint" or "picturesque" or "charming"? As many times as there are villages in the southwestern reaches of this area, the hard-core heart of the Cotswolds. Have your camera cocked at all times and your sunroof open so that you can pop up for a snapshot at a moment's notice. The ticklish thing about the Cotswolds is that there are plenty of other Nikon-happy shutterbugs crawling around the place. No town here is "undiscovered," but some are more discovered than others, so we will avoid mentioning most of those; if you really want to find out about the busier hamlets, consult any of the local tourist offices. As far as we're concerned, you should be plowing through a flock of sheep, not a flock of tourists, while you're in the Cotswolds, and pursuant to this we'll suggest some less-tramped-through towns, some more-out-of-the-way sights, and a few unmarked routes to help you get from one to another. Consult your map, chat with your innkeeper or tapster or grocer or waiter, stay off the marked roads (you can even avoid B roads here) in favor of the narrow over-hill-and-dale routes, and give yourself extra time to get lost and discover things even we don't know about.

## The Towns

**Burford** on the B4425 just off the A40. The town's sand-colored stone houses sidestep down the hill of the High Street and cross over the Windrush before heading uphill and out of town again.

Little Burford is home to a couple of good inns, **The Golden Pheasant Hotel** on the High Street (tel. 099382-3223) and **The Lamb Inn** (tel. 099382-3155).

**Cheltenham,** best approached from the south on the B4070, which runs along a ridge with a great view. Cheltenham is actually a major city in this area but warrants including for its graceful Regency and Edwardian facades and its luxe shopping along the Promenade and Montpellier Walk. By all means do sample the spring water that made this spa possible—Great Britain's only naturally alkaline brew—at the Town Hall in Imperial Square.

❦ And to really give yourself a lift, by all means take a meal at **Redmond's** (see "The Restaurants," below).

**Chipping Campden,** take the B4081 in from the south or the B4035 from the north. *Chipping* is the local word for "market," and at the center of this village is a stone-and-timber market hall built in 1627. The town is geared for visitors, with an information center and a local history and crafts museum in a former wool-stapler's abode.

❦ Try a light, inexpensive lunch at the **Badger Bistro and Wine Bar** in the center of the High Street (with a bottle of Budweiser beer from Czechoslovakia), or stop in at **Willmotts** for picnic fixings and **Bennetts** for a bottle.

**The Slaughters, Upper and Lower,** reached by a number of unmarked roads off the B4068. A pair of the prettiest towns, Upper Slaughter is more of a working village—rustic and agricultural. Lower Slaughter is crisscrossed by footbridges, which are in turn crisscrossed by geese.

❦ A great hotel/restaurant lurks in each of the Slaughters: **Lords of the Manor** (see "Hotels," earlier) in Upper, and **The Manor** (0451-20456) in Lower; both are fancy and pricey.

**Snowshill,** take unmarked roads from the A44 or A46 or the B4077. Clinging to and sallying up a hillside, Snowshill has some good, snug pubs and **Snowshill Manor,** a Tudor house with an 18th-century exterior. Inside are collections of objects of local importance or ownership.

**Stanton,** use unmarked roads off the A46. Stanton is a two-street town with cottages and gardens among the trees.

❦ One cottage is called the **Vine** and is a 16th-century B&B (tel. 038673-250) run by Mrs. Gabb.

Mrs. Gabb also runs the best stables in the county and has a terrific reputation among the locals for having true-blood hunters, not just hacks. You can ride over the hills for hours with your guide and not once come upon a road. A mere £7 per hour, it's about the best time you'll have in the Cotswolds, so make a point of it (same phone number as above).

**Tetbury,** arrive on the A433 or the B4014. Chuck and Di, Princess Anne and Mark all live in the neighborhood of this busy market town. The medieval market hall is still put to use on Wednesdays for a crafts, plants, antiques market. Skip down the Chipping Steps, terraced with cottages and gardens, or peek in any of the numerous antique shops.

🐾 Have an ale at the **Crown Inn** or a meal at any of several of the town's new bistros, like **Gibbons.**

## The Sights

**The Cotswolds Way.** The Cotswolds' finest sight isn't a single entity but a string of beautiful vistas, running streams, thick woods, and sunny meadows. The Cotswolds Way is a footpath that runs for nearly a hundred miles through the western hills. The trail is clearly marked with its own set of signs, but it's best to arm yourself with a good map, available at area tourist boards. It's a fairly easy hike as hikes go, but as even easy hikes go, go prepared with water, sturdy shoes, and extra warm, dry clothing.

**Chedworth Roman Villa.** Follow ROMAN VILLA signs on unmarked roads off the A40 or A429. In a glen surrounded by larches and firs are the foundations of one of the largest and best-preserved villas in Britain, dating back to the second through fourth centuries. Mosaics and heating and sanitary systems have all been exposed and maintained. (Open Tuesday through Sunday from 11 A.M. to 6 P.M.; admission £1.70 including a ten-minute film in the information center.)

🐾 After your visit, hike over the hill for lunch at the **7 Tuns** pub in Chedworth.

**Cotswold Countryside Collection,** on the A429 in Northleach. A 19th-century House of Correction has been wonderfully reincarnated into a museum devoted to—not surprisingly—local contributions to prison reform but, most importantly, devoted to an exposition of farm life, habits, buildings, villages. (Open daily April through October from 10 A.M. to 5:30 P.M., Sundays from 2:30; admission 60 pence.)

**Hailes Abbey and Church,** off the A46 or, better still, take unmarked roads east then north from Winchcombe. Founded in 1242 for Cistercians, Hailes was one of the richest, grandest, and most important abbeys in western Britain. Only ruins remain, but the visitor's center is full of artifacts and information. (Open daily till 6:30 P.M.; £1.) Just across the way is a 12th-century parish church, truly a tiny gem. It's black-and-white timbered roof and medieval oak rood screen are out-shone only by the marvelous wall paintings of saints, animals, arms, and a hunting scene. (Open same times as the abbey; free.)

**Rollright Stones,** off the A34. On the brow of a hill are seventy stones set in a ring one hundred feet in diameter. The Bronze Age installation consists of a group of larger stones, the King's Men, and a smaller group consisting of the King and his Whispering Knights.

**Sudeley Castle,** a wonderful drive on an unmarked road from the A40 near Whittington north to Winchcombe, or take the easy way on the A46. Sudeley was the home of Catherine Parr, Henry VIII's last wife. It has seen much history and contains much attesting to this. Painters represented include Van Dyck and Rubens, Turner and Hogarth. Gardens are extensive. Best of all are the falconry demonstrations. The falconer's charges are put through their paces several times daily on Tuesday, Wednesday, and Thursday—depending on weather, of course. In fact, you can take a two-day course in falconry here, scheduled at various times from March through November. There is also a crafts center for demonstrations and sales. (The castle is open April through October from 12 to 5 P.M.; £2.)

## ❦ THE RESTAURANTS

**Oakes,** 169 Slad Rd., Stroud; tel. (04536) 79950. Chris Oakes's popular eatery is housed in a former girls' school; returning alumni are universally delighted with the change, as will you be. The menu lists Oakes's all-local suppliers. Each of the three-course menus are priced, according to costliness of ingredients and intricacy of preparation, from £19 to £25. Try the sliced breast of duck served with apricots flavored with thyme, or a slice of salmon garnished with zucchini and tomato served with a lemon sauce. Finish with a hot cinnamon soufflé served with Drambuie cream. A three-course lunch is a steal at £11.50. MC, V.

**Redmond's,** Malvern View Hotel, Cleeve Cheltenham; tel. (0242) 580323. Hayward Redmond is a self-taught chef save for "the most basic catering course known to man." He and his wife, Pippa, bought a "dilapidated, hideously decorated shop," fixed it up, and clocked in their first Michelin M in only eight months. Lemon-ice walls, rattan chairs, white damask, marbel-ized plates, a potpourri of pictures, and of course splendid food. Viz? A warm salad of calf sweetbreads and mange tout with roasted pine kernels and an herb dressing to start, saddle of wild rabbit in puff pastry with a chive and champagne sauce or maize-fed chicken with a timbale of saffron rice and a wild mushroom sauce for the main course, perhaps rhubarb and honey ice cream with a cinnamon—flavored crème anglaise for dessert.

From two courses at £16.50 to four courses at £20.50. Redmonds is not to be missed. MC, V.

**Wickens,** Market Place, Northleach; tel. (0451) 60421. Christopher and Joanna Wickens are sincerely devoted to the promotion of fine English cuisine, and their four-course dinner menu (£14 to £17) is a celebration of local produce and traditional recipes with some modern complications for added interest. Start with a comice pear with smoked salmon pâté or a veal and lamb terrine with spiced oranges, continue with a char-grilled leg of spring lamb with mushroom and sherry sauce or a terrine of wild rabbit with plum chutney, and be sure to save space for Joanna's puddings. All this in a Cotswold-stone dining room with bentwood chairs, silver candlesticks, and cushions to match the drapes, right in the center of town in a little gabled row house. V.

# Stratford And The North Cotswolds

If the bard were here today, doubtless he'd get a mighty chuckle and perhaps a plot or two from the money-making machinery clinking and grinding away in this erstwhile woolmarket town. They arrive in droves on buses, trains, by car, bike; pore over the town; buy Will tea towels, postcards, pencils, drinking glasses; take rolls of photos; and collapse, exhausted and elevated by the experience, at the Pizza Hut with the half-timbered façade.

And yet despite the continual traffic jam, the row of B&Bs, and the World of Shakespeare wax museum, if you're among the English-speaking races, no matter how many times you've been here, there is a certain charge, a little surge of adrenaline when you drive across the Clopton Bridge and into Stratford at last. The Shakespeare Birthplace Trust has done an excellent job maintaining crowd control even as it maintains the shrines in its care.

The Trust owns five properties, all staffed with knowledgeable guides who know just about all there is to know about life in an important Cotswold wool center during the 16th century. If you visit all five, you'll know a great deal more than you did not only about Shakespeare but also about the life of his neighbors and contemporaries.

**For a map of Stratford-upon-Avon, see atlas page 11.**

## The Shakespearean Scene

The best approach is to get an early start visiting the various houses—as the tour buses tend to arrive early in the afternoon—and buy an all-inclusive ticket at £4.20, which will save you considerably if you plan to visit all five places, as we suggest. All are open weekdays from 9 A.M. to 6 P.M., Sundays from 10 P.M., and till 4:30 only during the winter.

The logical place to begin is **The Shakespeare Birthplace,** Henley Street. John Shakespeare, the bard's dad, originally rented this house, which formerly was one of a row of houses. As John Shakespeare's wool-trading and glove-making businesses prospered, he eventually bought the house and garden, and here his son William made his debut circa April 23, 1564. The place has been a mecca for some time, as the upstairs window attests: the signatures of Sir Walter Scott, Henry Irving, and Thomas Carlyle, among others, are carved into the glass. It had been converted into an inn and a butcher's shop until it was bought for the nation for £3,000 in 1847.

Next stop is **Nash's House** and the foundations and gardens of **New Place** on Chapel Street. Nash's House is a museum of the history of Stratford from prehistory onward. Shakespeare bought New Place in 1597 but didn't live here until his retirement, from 1610 to 1616. Unfortunately, the house was demolished in 1759. Just behind where the foundations were laid is an Elizabethan knot garden, so named because the flower beds are arranged to look like knotted ribbons.

Along your way down Church St. past the almshouses is the **Windmill Inn,** a pub probably attended by the man himself when he lived up the street. There are theater posters on the wall, Flowers on draft, and Stratford's best lunchtime bargain, at £2.50 for a hot or cold meal from the serve-yourself counter.

Turn left off Church Street onto Old Town, where the third Shakespeare property, **Hall's Croft,** is located. John Hall, a wealthy physician, married a Shakespeare daughter and installed her in this, by far the nicest of the five stops. For its day it was a very grand house, with high ceilings, lots of timbers, stone fireplaces, and 17 rooms. The house is furnished in the style of the 15th and 16th centuries, including some of Hall's personal effects. You can have luncheon or tea at the tearoom, which is a club for locals (who are allowed to have spirits here as well), but non-members may stop in for non-alcoholic refreshment.

Continue down Old Town to **Holy Trinity Church** beside the Avon. Although it's not operated by the trust, it is important to the story owing to the fact that Shakespeare's tomb is here.

If you backtrack a little up Old Town to Southern Lane, eventually you'll spot the Royal Shakespeare Company's theater complex, across from which is another favorite pub, whose identity is undecided. On one side of the sign it's called the **Black Swan,** on the other it's known as the **Dirty Duck,** but what's in a name? You are perfectly welcome to bring your pint or your lunch outside and sit on the wall, feet dangling, and watch the traffic go by on the river. Or try the restaurant across the street right in the theater complex and on the river.

The last two properties are a bit out of town, so you'll need to drive to them or take the shuttle buses, information on which is to be had at the Information Centre at the corner of Bridge and High streets. **Anne Hathaway's Cottage** is in Shottery, a mile from the center of Stratford. Undoubtedly you've seen photos of this cunning thatched house in the middle of a wildflower garden. The oldest part of the house dates back to the 1470s, when it was known as Hewlands Farm. The Hathaways, a prosperous farming family, arrived in 1520 and stayed here through 13 generations, until 1911. Happily this circumstance accounts for the presence of some of the original furniture, including a courting settle whereon Mr. S. is supposed to have wooed Miss H., who was perhaps persuaded more by the discomfort of the bench than by the eloquence of the suitor. Upstairs is Anne's parents' four-poster; the children slept on straw bedding on the floor.

Five miles out of town in Wilmcote is **Mary Arden's House,** where Shakespeare's mother spent her childhood. The house and some of its furnishings date back to the 15th and 16th centuries. Unlike the other properties, it is definitely a farmhouse, with a barn and all the outbuildings. Outside you'll see the straddle stones, two stones put together that look like a mushroom. These were used to raise barns off the ground to keep the grain dry and the rats at bay. Inside the house you'll see an arcane rat trap. The rats taken were saved in a holding pit and when the farmer got enough together, he invited the neighbors over; they set their Jack Russell terriers on the rats, one at a time, and bet on the outcome.

## A Bit of the Bard

All of this touring could and should take the better part of a day. In the evening, of course, you have tickets to see one of Shakespeare's or one of his contemporary's theatricals at the Royal Shakespeare Company. While architecturally no great shakes from the outside, the three theaters—Royal Shakespeare, Swan, and Other Place, in descending order of size—are truly magical places to see the world's best English-speaking actors. The Avonside view at intermission only adds to the dreamy quality of actually seeing the bard at his best in his hometown. If you're interested, there are backstage tours during the day and at night after the performance. For booking information for theater tickets call (0789) 295623; for tours call (0789) 296655. A suggestion: The theater shops usually have copies of all the plays currently in repertory; try to pick up a copy of the one you're seeing so you can, well, brush up your Shakespeare.

## Stratford Escapes

Because of the crowds, you'll probably not want to spend too much of your time right in Stratford; a day and an evening should suffice. And there's plenty to do in the area. Just up the A46 from Stratford are Warwick and Kenilworth, each town containing an eponymous castle.

**Warwick Castle** is touted as being the finest medieval castle in England, and its attractions include a long history and an important role during the War of the Roses. The castle apartments have been done up by Mme. Tussaud's as an 1898 garden party, with figures appropriately dressed and posed. For those strong of stomach there is a dungeon and torture chamber underground. For more pleasant views, climb to the top of the 14th-century Guy's Tower for a splendid panorama. (Open daily from 10 A.M. to 5:45 P.M., till 4:45 in winter; £2.)

If you like, there are medieval banquets held in the castle most evenings at £17.50 a head. Phone for reservations—a must—(0926) 495421. Or if you prefer just a bite, stop in at **Charlotte's Tea Rooms** on Jury St. Sunday lunch is roast beef and Yorkshire pudding for £3.95.

Down Jury Street is **Lord Leyster Hospital,** open weekdays, built in the 14th century as a home for veterans and their wives and widows. Across the street is the **Friends' Garden,** with birds atwitter and benches slipcased in moss. The **Collegiate Church of St. Mary's** on Church Street features music in the evenings; try to catch their boys' choir, active since 1123.

Before or after, stop in at the **Zetland Arms Pub,** garden out back, for a pint of Davenports.

**Kenilworth Castle** is the former home of John of Gaunt and is mentioned in the Domesday Book. Only ruins of the castle remain today, attesting to a long career of attacks and sieges. The ruin of rusty stone against a cloudy sky is most evocative, as Sir Walter Scott felt back in 1821 when he wrote a book imagining its original inhabitants. (Open daily 9:30 A.M. to 6:30 P.M., until 4 in winter; £1.20.)

Across Castle St. is **George Rafters**—the food is tasty and not too pricey.

South from Stratford off the A46 is **Hidcote Manor Garden,** which should be very high on everyone's list of things to see here (open April through October, daily except Tuesdays and

Fridays from 11 A.M. to 8 P.M.; £2.70). The 287-acre estate has been given to the National Trust and its ten acres of gardens are the labor of love of Lawrence Johnston, who lived here at the turn of the century. As Johnston's allowance grew, so did his garden. He envisioned his garden as a house: as a house has its separate rooms, so should a garden have its separate spaces of color and character. There is a red border and a white garden; the hedges are given a tapestry effect by combining holly and copper beeches. Its philosophy is devotion to aesthetics, sensuality, and an unabashed combining of all the gardener's arts and artifices to create a place of beauty. Hidcote is very popular, so try to come during the week.

Southeast of Stratford on the A422 is **Upton House,** also a National Trust property, set in 37 acres of wysteria and rose gardens. The William and Mary house is a gold mine for porcelain fanatics, containing an important collection of Sèvres china and Chelsea figures. There are also paintings by several of the Old Masters. (The house and grounds are open Saturdays and Sundays from 2 to 6 P.M. in April and October, Saturday through Wednesday from 2 to 6 P.M., May through September; £2.)

East of Banbury just off the B4525 is **Sulgrave Manor,** a great mecca for busloads of the Daughters of the American Revolution who flock here to pay their respects to the home of George Washington's ancestors. The manor is a bit out of the way, and if you arrive when a tour is not in progress—it is normally very quiet here—you can have the whole place to yourself. The stars and stripes are flying proudly outside in the garden, with its apple trees, chestnuts, roses, and topiaries. The house was built in 1539, and three generations of Washingtons lived here until John, George's great grandfather, left for America in 1657. The house is furnished in the 16th century and 18th century style to denote the newer wing, which was added circa 1700. Some of George's own effects are on display, sent here by Americans and British alike, who also jointly maintain the house. (Open April through September, daily except Wednesday, from 10:30 A.M. to 1 P.M. and from 2 to 5:30 P.M. until 4 in the winter; £1.20 includes a guided visit through the house; just ring the bell and you're shown around.)

# 6

# THE SOUTHEAST

The Southeast is easily the most traveled region in the country. For many, it is the epitome of England, with its snug rural villages, majestic castles, stately country homes, magnificent cathedrals, historic battlefields, rich maritime history, and popular seaside resorts.

The region includes the counties of Hampshire, once the ancient kingdom of Wessex when the magnificent cathedral town of Winchester was the capital of England; Sussex, with another fine cathedral at Chichester, the outstanding castled village of Arundel, the seaside resort of Brighton, and the legendary battlefield of Hastings; Surrey with the ancient market town of Guildford in the heart of idyllic countryside beloved by everyone for its classic half-timbered houses; and Kent, the home of Canterbury Cathedral—the Mother Church of England—and the defensive shoreline against Continental invaders known as the Cinque Ports.

To see the best the region has to offer, we suggest you travel first to Winchester in the southwest, then head south to the coast, and then travel west to east along the coast, from Lymington to Rye. Surrey, in the center of the region, and Kent, to the east, should be tackled as separate visits because of their easy access from London.

The region is easily divided into five areas centered in towns which make good bases from which you can easily see the rest of the surrounding attractions, and we also recommend that you make several different overnight stops.

Winchester, located in the heart of Hampshire to the southeast, is a superb base from which to explore the historic kingdom of Wessex and the attractions to the south—including Lord Mountbatten's home at Romsey, Beaulieu Abbey and Palace House with its National Motor Museum, the ancient Norman hunting ground of the New Forest on the coast, and the country's premier naval base at Portsmouth. Chichester, further east, is ideally situated for exploring the beautiful

THE SOUTHEAST

Not all roads shown

0 miles 20
0 kilometers 20

N

The Channel

GREATER
LONDON

OXFORDSHIRE

BERKSHIRE

HAMPSHIRE

SURREY

KENT

SUSSEX

Salisbury
Middle Wallop
Andover
Newbury
Reading
Maidenhead
Twyford
Slough
Windsor Castle
Farnborough
Woking
Guildford
Dorking
Westerham
Rochester
Chatham
Maidstone
Sheerness
Southend
Basildon
Whitstable
Canterbury Cathedral
Margate
Ramsgate
Sandwich
Dover
Folkestone
Hythe
New Romney
Ashford
Romney Marsh
Rye
Rye Bay
Winchelsea
Hastings
Pevensey Bay
Pevensey
Bexhill
Battle
Bodiam Castle
Royal Tunbridge Wells
East Grinstead
Gatwick
Horsham
Petworth
Midhurst
Singleton
Petersfield
Farnham
Aldershot
Basingstoke
Stockbridge
Winchester Cathedral
Eastleigh
Southampton
Fareham
Portsmouth
Chichester
Chichester Harbour
Selsey Bill
Bognor Regis
Arundel
Findon
Worthing
Brighton
Lewes
Newhaven
Seaford
Beachy Head
Eastbourne
Romsey
New Milton
Lymington
Yarmouth
The Needles
Cowes
Newport
Isle of Wight
Shanklin
Ryde
Bembridge
Beaulieu Abbey
Buckler's Hard
New Forest
The Solent
Sheppey
R. Medway
R. Thames

KENT

A2
A20
M20
M2
M26
M25
M23
M3
M27
M4
A4
A34
A33
A31
A281
A325
A272
A264
A265
A21
A27
A259
A283
A3
A343
A342
A3057
A327
M2
A256

West Sussex countryside, its popular coastal resorts, and the magnificent village of Arundel.

Brighton, further east—probably the most popular seaside resort in Britain—is near the many attractions along the southeast coast, including the site of the epic 1066 battlefield near Hastings—a superb overnight stop—and still further east, the fascinating history of the Cinque Ports, at Rye. Guildford, located in the heart of the region directly south of London, is a splendid market town with good access to the surrounding countryside and its many picturesque villages.

Canterbury, located in the far east of the region, is wellplaced for traveling to the popular seaside resorts at Margate and Ramsgate further east, and to view Britain's rich maritime history to the northwest at Chatham.

# TRAVEL

There are several ways to approach the region. You can take either intercity **rail services** from Victoria and Waterloo stations (call 01-928-5100) to the main cities (Brighton, 0273-206755; Canterbury, 0227-454411; Hastings, 0424-429325; Portsmouth, 0705-825771; Southampton/Winchester, 0703-229393) or the fast regular coach service from Victoria Bus Station. Alternatively, hire **a car** in London and drive direct: to Winchester via the M3; Portsmouth via the A3; Brighton via the M23/A23; Hastings via the A21; Canterbury via the A2/M2. It should be remembered that heavy traffic to the major coastal ports, particularly the Continental ferry services at Dover and Folkestone, together with seasonal traffic to the seaside resorts, means delays. If the main roads are heavily congested, set out early in the morning to travel to your next destination before commercial traffic gets onto the roads; or travel on minor roads. For car hire: Budget Rent a Car—UK Central Reservations Freefone 0800-181181; 87 Preston St., Brighton 0273-27351; 256 Vouxhall Rd., Canterbury 0227-470293; 41 Arlington Square, Margate 0843-296604; 14 The Tricorn, Tricorn Center, Portsmouth 0705-862226.

# ❦ HOTELS

**Credit card abbreviations used in hotel and restaurant listings are as follows: AE for American Express, CB for Carte Blanche, DC for Diner's Club, MC for MasterCard, and V for Visa.**

## Arundel

**The Norfolk Arms Hotel,** High St., Arundel, West Sussex BN18 9AD; tel. (0903) 882101. A superb overnight stop, this 200-year-old Georgian coaching inn situated in the heart of the picturesque village offers a comprehensive menu (£15–20), good wines, and large comfortable rooms, from £40 for a single, £56 for a double. All major credit cards.

# Battle

**The Beauport Park Hotel,** Battle Rd., East Sussex TN388AE; Hastings, tel. (0424) 51222. Situated in beautiful countryside between historic Battle and Hastings, this is one of the finest country houses in the southeast. It's set in 33 acres of outstanding woodland and gardens with many rare trees, heated pool, golf course, and riding stables, and offers exquisite haute cuisine (£15–30), selected wines, and luxurious rooms, from £48 for a single, £58 for a double. All major credit cards.

# Brighton

**The Grand Hotel,** Kings Rd., Brighton, BN12FW; tel. (0273) 21188. Now fully refurbished after the IRA bombing during the 1985 Conservative Party Conference, this outstanding hotel overlooking the seafront offers exceptional standards and service, a comprehensive set menu (£17.50), good wines, and spacious, luxurious rooms, from £90 for a single, £125 for a double. All major credit cards.

# Canterbury

**The County Hotel,** High St., Canterbury CT1 2RX; tel. (0227) 66266. This exceptional 400-year-old, large, half-timbered hotel in the heart of town offers well-prepared specialty dishes (£15–20), vintage wine list, and charming Tudor and Georgian rooms, from £49 for a single, £59 for a double. All major credit cards.

# Chichester

**The Dolphin and Anchor Hotel,** West St., Chichester PO19 1QE; tel. (0243) 785121. Directly opposite Chichester Cathedral, this large Georgian hotel offers a comprehensive set menu (£10) and à la carte (£10–15), a varied wine list, and modern comfortable rooms, from £50 for a single, £65 for a double. All major credit cards.

# Guildford

**The Angel Hotel,** High St., Guildford GU1 3DR; tel. (0483) 64555. This large half-timbered hotel with courtyard, popular bars, and atmospheric crypt restaurant formerly connected to the town's castle serves specialty English dishes (£7–12) and varied wines; comfortable rustic rooms start at £53 for a single, £68 for a double. All major credit cards.

# Midhurst

**The Spread Eagle Hotel,** South St., Midhurst GU29 9NH; tel. (073081) 6911. A highly recommended overnight stop, this ancient medieval hotel positively exudes character, with its stunning timbered features, and offers delightful bars, delicious cordon bleu dishes (£15–25) and fine wines, and enchanting crooked rooms, from £52 for a single, £60 for a double. AE, DC, MC, V.

## New Milton

**Chewton Glen Hotel,** Christ Church Rd., New Milton, Hampshire BH25 6QS; tel. (04252) 5341. A recommended overnight stop, this outstanding country hotel is situated in the New Forest and set amid beautiful wooded parklands with a golf course and heated pool. It offers exceptional levels of comfort and service, superb French and English cuisine (£30), vintage wines, and lavishly furnished rooms, from £115 per person, suites £250. All major credit cards.

## Rye

**The Mermaid Inn,** Mermaid St., Rye TN31 7EU; tel. (0797) 223065. The largest medieval building in Rye (rebuilt in 1420), this fascinating timbered hotel offers a romantic atmosphere, a choice set menu (£8.50), à la carte menu (£10–15), excellent wines, and quaint rooms (including four-poster beds), from £24 for a single, £34 for a double. All major credit cards.

## Winchester

**The Royal Hotel,** St. Peter St., Winchester 5023 8BS; tel. (0962) 841582. A large, comfortable hotel, formerly a convent, the Royal is set in a secluded street. It has an intimate bar, a conservatory, a peaceful garden, and offers a choice selective menu (£10–15), varied wines, and modern pleasant rooms, from £54 for a single, £64 for a double. AE, DC, MC, V.

# Winchester—the Cathedral and Historic Hampshire

Once the capital of England, Winchester was formerly occupied by the Romans, who established a fort and later an important town here known as Venta Belgarum. It was during Saxon times that Wessex and Winchester became the predominant kingdom and capital of England, and the first Saxon cathedral, known as Old Minster, was built in about A.D. 645. During the ninth century the city was threatened by Viking raids, but under the leadership of King Alfred, the English successfully fought off the Danes. Alfred then established a network of fortified towns, of which Winchester was the largest: its Roman walls and gates were repaired and rebuilt.

During the reign of peace that followed, Alfred encouraged the revival of learning and monastic life, and laid the foundations for the single kingdom of England, of which Winchester was the capital. The arrival of the conquering Normans in

1066 marked a new era for Winchester, with the building in 1079 of the Norman cathedral and a castle in which the Domesday Book was compiled and kept. Even after London became the capital in about 1278, Winchester remained a royal city—the birthplace of Henry III and the setting for the marriage of Mary Tudor to Philip of Spain in 1554. The castle, largely rebuilt by Henry III, was besieged by Cromwell in 1645 and demolished in 1651—only the Great Hall, housing the famous Arthurian Round Table, remains.

Many of Winchester's traditions persist today. The curfew bell has rung out at 8 P.M. each evening for the last nine hundred years, and Winchester College, founded six hundred years ago, remains one of the country's leading boys' public schools. Today, High Street follows the line of the original Roman road through the town. At the bottom end can be seen the imposing bronze statue of King Alfred by Hamo Thornycroft erected in 1901, set against St. Giles Hill, where medieval fairs famous throughout Europe were held. The top end of High Street is guarded by **Westgate,** originally built by the Romans, rebuilt in the 13th century, and fortified in the 14th century. From the 16th century, the upper room was used as a prison. Today it houses the **Westgate Museum** (0962-69864; open April through October, Monday through Saturday from 10 A.M. to 5 P.M., Sunday from 2 to 5 P.M.; November through March, closed Mondays, Sunday open only 2 to 4; 20 pence for adults, 10 pence for children), featuring a ceiling of painted wooded panels made for the warden of Winchester College, John White, before he became bishop of Lincoln in 1554. The huge, stout, bonded wooden chest was the new strongbox made after a raid on the city coffers in 1590. Splendid views of the city can be seen from the roof. Nearby lie the carefully preserved ruins of the castle and the only surviving building, the **Great Hall.** Here you will find the legendary Round Table of King Arthur and his knights, although according to scientific tests, it was made six hundred years later, possibly by King Edward (1272–1307), who is known to have been very interested in the Arthurian legends. Originally the table had 12 legs and a large central support. It is 18 feet in diameter, weighs over a ton, and was made out of 121 separate pieces of oak. It was hung from the wall of the hall in the 15th century and painted in Tudor colors during King Henry VIII's reign. The hall itself is considered by many to be the finest medieval hall in the country after Westminster. It has a magnificent roof constructed of open timber and spanning the 110-foot raised aisle. The wall opposite the Round Table is decorated with the chronological tree of the knights of the shire between 1283 and 1868, and there are magnificent early windows, fine stained glass, and a re-creation of a 13th-century garden outside. (0962-841841;

open March through October, daily from 10 A.M. to 5 P.M.;
November through February, closes at 4 P.M.; free.)

## The Cathedral

The arrival in A.D. 643 of Bishop Birinus of Genoa, sent by
Pope Gregory to convert the pagan Saxons, marked the start
of the first cathedral. Winchester was then the capital of
Kinegils, king of the West Saxons. While on his way to marry
his daughter to Oswald, king of Northumbria, Kinegils met
the Pope's envoy and was converted to Christianity. Kinegils
then built the first church in Winchester, which Birinus consecrated in 648. The bishop's throne subsequently moved to
Winchester from Dorchester, and the church was converted
to a cathedral. Its most famous bishop was Swithun, who wit-
nessed King Egbert's crowning as the first king of all England,
and was adviser to King Aethelwulf and tutor to his sons, one
of whom was to become King Alfred the Great.

Swithun had been bishop for ten years when he died in 862;
he had asked to be buried outside so that "the rain of heaven
might fall on him." Contrary to his wishes, one hundred years
later, Bishop Aethelwold decided Swithun's remains should
be dug up and placed in a shrine as holy relics. But the day
the removal took place, the heavens opened, and it rained for
forty days! Under Bishop Aethelwold, the famous Winchester
School of Illuminated Manuscript flourished in the Benedictine monastery of St. Swithun. In 1079, the Normans began
the 500-foot long cathedral; it took 14 years to build, with the
Norman tower added in the 12th century. Much of the original
structure remains today, together with the beautiful 14th-
century remodeled Gothic nave by Bishops Edington and
Wykeham. After the Dissolution, only a few columns of the
Chapter House at St. Swithun's Monastery remained. The cathedral also had much of its medieval glass destroyed during
the civil war, together with many of its records, although the
12th-century Illuminated Bible survived and can be seen today
in the cathedral library.

The Restoration saw the cathedral flourish again, and preserved stained glass was rearranged to kaleidoscopic effect
in the Great Western Window. But perhaps the greatest tribute to the cathedral's survival should go to one man, William
Walker, the diver. In 1906 it was discovered that six-hundred-
year-old tree-trunk foundations were disintegrating and sink-
ing because of improved drainage of the marshy land here.
Walker spent six years immersed in pitch black conditions beneath the cathedral replacing the rotting wood with bags of
cement.

# Winchester's Ancient Sights

Many of Winchester's ancient monuments remain today. A walk from West Gate down High Street will take you past the rebuilt ancient manor of **Godbegot,** presented by Edward the Confessor to his mother, Queen Emma. Farther along is the beautifully carved 15th-century **City Cross** midway in High Street, and behind it, a 15th-century timber house. The adjacent overhanging row of shops known as **The Pentice** stands on the former site of William the Conqueror's palace and leads to the Square, where you will find the **Eclipse Inn,** a good stop for light bar lunches. Formerly the old rectory of the nearby St. Lawrence Church, it was named the Eclipse to oppose its rival, the Sun, which stood opposite. Also in the Square is **The City Museum** (0962-63064; open April through September, Monday through Saturday from 10 A.M. to 5 P.M., Sunday from 2 to 5 P.M.; October through March, Tuesday through Saturday from 10 A.M. to 5 P.M., Sunday from 2 to 4 P.M.; free), with Roman remains, brief histories of Winchester, and a complete Edwardian bathroom and chemist's shop. To the south of the cathedral lie the **Cloisters;** the buildings of **Priory of St. Swithun,** which now form the Deanery; and the **Pilgrims' Hall,** with its remarkable 14th-century hammer-beam roof. Move on to view the 12th-century **Kings Gate,** the only remaining city gate besides West Gate. In nearby College Street is the house where Jane Austin died—she is buried in the cathedral—and **Winchester College** (0962-64242; open April through September, Monday through Saturday from 10 A.M. to 6 P.M., Sunday from 2 to 6 P.M.; £1 for adults, 75 pence for children). At the bottom of College Street is the river Itchen, running parallel with the city wall and behind which can be found the ruins of **Wolvesey Castle** and **Old Bishop's Palace** (0962-54766; open April through October, Monday through Friday from 9:30 A.M. to 6:30 P.M., Sunday from 2 P.M. 70 pence for adults, 35 pence for children).

On Bridge Street is the 1744 **Winchester City Mill,** now leased to the Youth Hostel Association (0962-53723; open April through mid-October, Tuesday, Wednesday, Thursday, and Saturday from 1:45 P.M. to 4:45 P.M.; 40 pence for adults, 20 pence for children).

 Nearby is the city's oldest surviving house, the **Old Chesil Rectory Restaurant** (0962-53177), dating from 1450, which takes its name from Cheesehill (now St. Giles Hill), where cheese fairs used to take place. Occupied many times as tearooms and a restaurant, it now offers a superb choice of classic English dishes (£10–15) and fine wines in delightful crooked-beam surroundings.

Back across Bridge Street is King Alfred's statue in Broadway, leading back into High Street. For guided tours of the town, contact the tourist office in Broadway at (0962) 840222.

Other nearby attractions include the oldest charitable institution in the country, founded in 1136 and still offering the "wayfarer's dole" of bread and ale on request: the Porters Lodge in **The Hospital of St. Cross** (0962-51375; open April to October, Monday through Saturday from 9:30 A.M. to 12:30 P.M., and 2 to 5 P.M.; from October to April, Monday through Saturday from 10:30 A.M. to 12:30 P.M., and from 2 to 3:30 P.M.; £1 for adults, 25 pence for children). Monthly exhibitions of modern art and crafts can be seen at the **Winchester Gallery** in Park Avenue (0962-842500; open Monday through Friday from 10 A.M. to 4:30 P.M., Saturday from 9 A.M. to 12 P.M.; free).

Winchester is superbly placed for traveling outward in any direction to see the many surrounding attractions, most of which lie to the south and along the coast.

## A List of Northern Excursions

**Wellington Country Park,** Risley (0734-326444; open March through October daily from 10 A.M. to 5:30 P.M., November through February, weekends only; £1.70 for adults, 90 pence for children).

**Jane Austen's House,** one mile southwest of Alton off the A31 near Chawton; (0420-83262; open April through October, daily, November, December, March on Wednesday and Sunday, January and February on Saturday and Sunday, from 11 A.M. to 4:30 P.M.; £1 for adults, 50 pence for children). Where the author lived and wrote most of her books between 1809 and 1817, with many personal and family items on display, and a pleasant garden for picnics.

**Museum of Army Flying,** Middle Wallop, Stockbridge (0264-62121, ext. 421; open January through December, daily from 10 A.M. to 4:30 P.M.; £2 for adults, £1 for children). Features the history of British army flying from the 19th century to the Falklands War, with models, photographs, films, moving exhibitions, and aircraft.

**The Hawk Conservancy,** Weyhill, near Andover (026477-2252; open March through October, daily from 10 A.M. to 4 P.M.; £2 for adults, £1 for children). The largest sanctuary in the south of England for birds of prey from all over the world—the birds are allowed to fly completely free daily at noon, 2 P.M., 3 P.M., and 4 P.M., weather permitting.

**The Vyne,** Sherborne St. John, Basingstoke (0256-881337; open April through October daily except Monday and Friday;

house from 1:30 to 5:30 P.M., garden and tearoom from 12:30 to 5:30 P.M.; £2.20). An impressive National Trust 16th-century house of diaper brickwork extensively altered in the 17th century, a Tudor chapel with Renaissance glass, Palladian staircase, and beautiful gardens, lawns, and lake.

**Whitchurch Silk Mill,** 28 Winchester Street, Whitchurch (025689-2065; open Tuesday through Friday from 10:30 A.M., to 5:30 P.M., Sunday from 11 A.M. to 4 P.M.; open Saturdays as well May through September from 10 A.M. to 4 P.M.; £1.20 for adults, 40 pence for children). The last silk mill in southern England operating powered looms, with a working millrace, silks on sale, and pleasant grounds by the river

# Southward

### Lord Mountbatten's House

Turning south from Winchester, nearby is the grand home of Lord Mountbatten, at Broadlands, near Romsey. Your visit will combine both the spectacular Palladian house and Capability Brown grounds with background on one of the most important military and political figures of the 20th century. Capability Brown is largely responsible for the transformation of the earlier Tudor and Jacobean manor house to the neoclassical Palladian style during its ownership by the 2nd Viscount Palmerston. Considerable landscaping, planting, clearing, and work on the river completed the overall effect of elegance and harmony. Inside, the house is a masterpiece of design and decoration, from the octagonal domed entrance hall to the spectacular delicate white and gold neoclassical decorative leaf by Joseph Rose in the Saloon. Four magnificent Van Dykes grace the dining room. The Drawing Room, favorite of Lord Mountbatten and his wife, Edwina—through whom the house was inherited in 1939—continues to be the center of family life for the present Lord and Lady Romsey. Equally impressive is the Wedgwood Room, with stylish friezes and moldings in the characteristic blue and white decoration of Wedgwood pottery. Normally this room is used for tea, while the Drawing Room, the Saloon, and the Wedgwood Room are also used for receptions. During the last war, Broadlands was used as a hospital annex, and the Wedgwood Room and the Saloon were in constant use as wards. The Library was doubled in size by the 3rd Viscount, Prime Minister Palmerston, and contains the famous painting *The Iron Forge* by Joseph Wright. Distinguished visitors to Broadlands have included Florence Nightingale, the Queen and Prince Philip, and the Prince and Princess of Wales, who started their honeymoons here, in 1947 and 1981, respectively. There is also the dazzling Imperial Collection of Crown Jewels of the World (in perfect facsimile) in the house, and a film and displays of

Mountbatten and Broadlands in the exhibition center. (0794-516878; open April through September, Tuesday through Sunday plus Mondays in August and September from 10 A.M. to 4 P.M.; £3.40 for adults, £1.80 for children.)

## New Forest

Farther south lies the New Forest, famous as the popular hunting ground of Norman kings and an ideal spot near the coast for camping (call 042128-3771 for information). Nearby, you will find the **National Motor Museum** at Beaulieu (0590-612345; open May through September, daily from 10 A.M. to 6 P.M.; October to May from 10 A.M. to 5 P.M.; £4.75 for adults, £3.25 for children). Situated in the grounds of Beaulieu Abbey and Palace House, the museum is a superb collection of cars: vintage and 1930s, veteran, postwar, sports and racing, world land speed record holders, commercial vehicles, and motorcycles. Little remains of the abbey church today apart from one wall and the pillar bases, but when it was completed in 1226, it was the largest of all Cistercian churches in England, with an overall length of 336 feet and a width of 182 feet. Dissolution saw it ruined, along with many of the buildings in the great abbey complex, although parts of the cloisters and the living quarters of the Lay Brothers are still intact. The original palace house was altered extensively when Lord Henry received it as a wedding present from his father in 1867. The resulting Victorian Gothic style included monastic remains such as rib vaulting and ready dressed stone being incorporated as features. Today, it serves as the home of Lord Montagu and his family, and contains much family history of the last four hundred years. Also within the area is the indoor tropical butterfly garden, housing some of the world's rarest species, plus dragonfly ponds, and insectarium, at the **New Forest Butterfly Farm,** Longdown, near Ashurst (042129-2166; open Easter through October, daily from 10 A.M. to 5 P.M.; £2.20 for adults, £1.30 for children).

## The Coast

Within striking distance of the New Forest are the many attractions of the Hampshire coastline. Nearby Lymington is a delightful seaside port and popular boating marina where you can enjoy lunch looking out across the harbor to the **Isle of Wight.** You can make the short trip from here across the Solent to Yarmouth with Sealink Ferries (call 0590-72875).

On the quay you will find a welcoming pub, **The Ship Inn,** and on nearby Quay Hill, **The Kings Head,** both serving inexpensive meals. The newly refurbished **Stanwell House Hotel** in the busy High St. is popular for cocktails and for its delicious varied table d'hôte menu (£15) and fine wines.

# Lord Mountbatten

Lord Mountbatten was born at Frogmore House, next to Windsor Castle, on June 25, 1900, the younger son of Prince Louis of Battenburg and Princess Victoria of Hesse, granddaughter of Queen Victoria, who was the young infant's godmother and held him at his christening. His father was first sea lord from 1912 to 1914, and like him, Mountbatten was to reach the same position in the navy, the only instance ever of father and son to do so. Strangely enough, Winston Churchill made both appointments. On leaving university, the young Mountbatten accompanied his cousin Edward, Prince of Wales, on tours of Australia and New Zealand, and India, Japan, and the Far East. In New Delhi on his second tour, he became engaged to Edwina Ashley, daughter of Lord Mount Temple and granddaughter of Sir Ernest Cassel. They married in London in 1922. After six months' leave of absence from duty on half pay, Mountbatten returned to the naval career that was to catapult him to the top of the nation's military command.

"Dickie," as he came to be known, had joined his first ship, H.M.S. *Lion,* in July 1916, and served three years at sea during World War I. He first made a name for himself with wireless operations, and wrote two handbooks for the navy. At the outbreak of war in 1939, he was put in command of the 5th Destroyer Flotilla. His command ship, H.M.S. *Kelly,* was subsequently mined off the Tyne River in 1939, but it was quickly repaired. In May 1940 the ship was torpedoed in the North Sea but was successfully towed back for repairs despite repeated air attacks. H.M.S. *Kelly* capsized during efforts to escape dive bombers during the Battle of Crete in 1941. Mountbatten survived with less than half the crew, and then quickly rose through the ranks to join Combined Operations in 1941, becoming its chief in 1942 and a member of the Chiefs of Staff Committee, and helping to plan campaigns in North Africa, Italy, and France. By D-day, he was far away as supreme Allied commander of the newly formed South East Asia Command, which successfully routed the Japanese against all the odds and in appalling conditions. He was the one to accept the Japanese surrender at Singapore Town Hall after the atomic bombings. Showered with awards, he was then appointed last viceroy of India, to oversee the transition to independence, and was invited by India to stay on as governor general or first head of state.

In 1948 Mountbatten rejoined the navy, and in 1953 formed NATO. In 1955 he attained the highest rank as first sea lord and chief of naval staff. He retired in 1965 after fifty years of service but continued to work as an adviser and through the United World College education program. On August 27, 1979, Mountbatten was killed together with his granddaughter and a local boatman in an IRA bomb attack while cruising on his boat, *Shadow V,* in Ireland. Moutbatten lies buried in the beautiful 12th-century Romsey Abbey near Broadlands.

The best place to swim is at the expansive **Hordle Beach** near Barton-on-Sea.

From nearby Keyhaven, you can catch the ferry (£1.20 for adults, 70 pence for children) or walk the half mile along the pebble spit to **Hurst Castle.** This most impressive of Henry VIII's coastal defenses could, together with the forts on the Isle of Wight, effectively close the Solent. The Tudor castle was built in 1541 and was extensively modernized during the Napoleonic wars and in the 19th century. The castle was garrisoned in both world wars. Its huge guns now silent, it remains a foreboding place of isolation and a graphic reminder of the hardships endured here.

## Southampton

Southampton dates from Roman times as the famous port of Clausentum and has long been associated with Atlantic crossings, which began with the Pilgrim Fathers, who left from here (although they docked again at Dartmouth and Plymouth for repairs before sailing on). Its huge dock area remains the most important industry, although the town suffered severe bombing in the last war. Today it remains a busy commercial center, with good shopping.

Attractions include: **The Bargate,** Above Bar (0703-224216; open Tuesday through Friday from 10 A.M. to 5 P.M., Saturday from 10 A.M. to 4 P.M., Sunday from 2 to 5 P.M.; free), originally the north gate of the walled medieval town, now a museum with local history displays; **Southampton Museum of Archaeology,** God's House Tower (0703-220007; open Tuesday through Friday from 10 A.M. to 12 P.M., and 1 to 5 P.M., till 4 on Saturday, Sunday from 2 to 5 P.M. only; free), containing impressive collections of Roman, Saxon, and medieval finds; and **Southampton Hall of Aviation,** Albert Road South (0703-635830; open Tuesday through Saturday, from 10 A.M. to 5 P.M., Sunday from 12 to 5 P.M.; £1.50 for adults, 75 pence for children), featuring the exciting history of experimental flying and military aircraft development, including the work of R. J. Mitchell, who designed the Spitfire.

## Portsmouth

Portsmouth boasts a fascinating history as the country's premier naval port. Badly bombed in the last war, much of the town has been rebuilt and is commercial and crowded. Of greatest interest is the area around **The Hard,** where you will find the Royal Naval Base, which contains some of the country's most famous warships. They include *The Mary Rose,* the legendary Tudor warship that capsized off Portsmouth with the loss of nearly everyone on board during an engagement with a French invasion fleet in 1545. King Henry VIII's flagship remained perfectly preserved in deep mud until the site of the wreck was discovered in 1836. It was rediscovered in 1965, and after considerable research and excavations, the Mary Rose Trust, with Prince Charles as president, was formed: the hull was recovered from the seabed in 1982. Today it can be seen in dry dock a few hundred yards from where it was built, kept in carefully controlled conditions to prevent it from deteriorating, and there is an extensive museum nearby of finds aboard. (0705-839766; open daily from 10:30 A.M. to 5:30 P.M.; £2.80 for adults, £1.80 for children.) Adjacent is perhaps the most famous battleship, Lord Nelson's flagship at the Battle of Trafalgar in 1805, H.M.S. *Victory.* Built in 1758 at Chatham, the country's principal shipyard near Rochester, she saw continuous service, particularly in the blockade of the French port of Toulon. In the Battle of Trafalgar, Nelson was shot on deck by a sniper from an enemy ship and died below decks; both spots are marked by commemorative plaques. The guided tour of the ship is fascinating. (Tel. 0705-839766; open Monday through Saturday from 10:30 A.M. to 5:30 P.M., Sunday from 1 to 5 P.M.; £1.80 for adults, £1 for children.) Also nearby is H.M.S. *Warrior*, the first ironclad steam-driven warship, built in 1859 to combat the growing menace of French warships under Napoléon. Once built, she reestablished Britain's supremacy at sea, and in fact never fired a shot in anger. Of the 45 ironclads built between 1861 and 1877, she is the only survivor. (0705-839766; open Monday through Saturday, daily from 10:30 A.M. to 5:30 P.M.; £3 for adults, £1.50 for children.)

A full history of Portsmouth's naval glory can be seen in the adjoining **Royal Navy Museum** (0705-733060; open daily from 10:30 A.M. to 5 P.M.; 75 pence for adults, 50 pence for children). Also nearby is the **Charles Dickens Birthplace Museum,** 393 Old Commercial Road—look for the Oliver Twist pub just off the dual carriageway (0705-827261; open March through October, daily from 10 A.M. to 5:30 P.M.; 50 pence for adults, 25 pence for children). Restored in 1970, this modest terraced house recalls Dickens' humble beginnings, together with displays of his personal possessions. Across the harbor at Gosport, you will find more naval history, together with tours of the large submarine H.M.S. *Alliance* at the **Submarine Museum,** Haslar Pontoon Road (0705-529217; open March through October daily 10 A.M. to 4:30 P.M.; till 3:15 other times; £2 for adults, £1.20 for children). At Southsea, there is the full story of the Normandy landings in the **D-Day Museum,** Clarence Esplanade (0705-827261; open daily from 10:30 A.M. to 5:30 P.M.; £1.75 for adults, £1.25 for children). Portsmouth's Roman beginnings can be traced at nearby **Porchester Castle** (0705-378291; open March to October, Monday through Saturday from 9:30 A.M. to 6:30 P.M., Sunday from 2 to 6:30 P.M.; October to March, Monday through Saturday from 10 A.M. to 4 P.M., Sunday from 2 to 4 P.M.; £1 for adults, 50 pence for children), where there are the /emains of a castle built by Henry II in the late 12th century, set inside the walls of an impressive third century Roman fort.

# Chichester

## The Roman Sights

The Roman city of Regnum, founded at the intersection of two important roads—marked by the impressive stone-carved Butter Cross, built in 1501—is most noted for its magnificent Norman **cathedral** built on the site of a Saxon church. First started in the 12th century, the cathedral is a blend of Romanesque, Decorated, and Perpendicular styles, with some of the best medieval carvings in Britain, and an Aubusson tapestry designed by John Piper. Virtually traffic-free, the town center offers excellent shopping, an annual arts festival in July, and a popular marina and harbor.

Chichester's Roman history can be studied at two of the finest Roman sites in Britain: the nearby **Fishbourne Roman Palace,** Fishbourne (0243-785859; open May through September, daily from 10 A.M. to 6 P.M.; March, April, and October, daily til 5 P.M.; November, til 4; December through February, Sundays only 10 A.M. to 4 P.M.; £1.80 for adults, £1 for children), the largest Roman residence found in the country, with fabulous mosaic floors, rooms, corridors, courtyards, and a bath suite; and **Bignor Roman Villa,** Bignor (07987-259; open April through September, from 10 A.M. to 6 P.M., March and October from 10 A.M. to 5 P.M.; closed Mondays except bank holidays and during the months of June through September; admission £1.50 for adults, 75 pence for children), with the largest single mosaic (eighty feet long) in Britain, and a museum containing models and other interesting finds.

Of special interest is the **Mechanical Music and Doll Collection,** Church Road, Portfield, featuring the most important collection of working barrel organs, musical boxes, street pianos, and pianolas in the country—a truly wonderful experience (tel. 0243-785421; open Easter through September daily from 10 A.M. to 6 P.M.; October through April, Saturday and Sunday from 10 A.M. to 5 P.M.; £1.50 for adults, 75 pence for children).

# Arundel

To the east lies Arundel, an absolute must. An outstanding castle, an exceptional cathedral, and an idyllic half-timbered town overlooking the River Arun combine to make this one of the most rewarding visits in the county. Towering over the town, **Arundel Castle** (0903-883136; open April through October, Sunday through Friday from 1 to 5 P.M.; £3 for adults, £2 for children) has been the seat of the dukes of Norfolk for over seven hundred years. Built in the 11th century, badly damaged in 1643 during the civil war, and restored in the 18th and 19th centuries, the castle is of exceptionally stout construction and on a huge scale. Inside it is a veritable treasure house of design and furnishing. Special features include the beautiful chapel, the vaulted oak hammer-beam roof in the Baron's Hall, and the richly paneled Gothic library. Nearby is the gigantic **Catholic Cathedral of Our Lady and St. Philip Howard,** designed by Joseph Hansom, the inventor of the Hansom cab, begun in 1869 and taking just over three years to complete. Built of Bath stone in the French Gothic style, and situated on the highest point in Arundel, it is a landmark for miles around and quite breathtaking inside, with its nave 97 feet long and 71 feet high. The town itself is no less pleasing, running steeply down to the river, with many charming crooked buildings, attractive shops, and inviting cafés and restaurants.

The **Cafe Violette Restaurant** near the castle exit is recommended for cream teas and exotic dishes (£5–8).

Whether sightseeing, wandering through the lanes, or feeding the ducks, geese, and swans at the nearby Wildfowl Trust, Arundel has something for everyone.

## To the Shore

Of the seaside towns along the coast, **Bognor Regis** and **Worthing** are the most popular for their expansive safe beaches, good shopping, and leisure facilities. Worthing, popularized by Oscar Wilde, who wrote *The Importance of Being Earnest* here and named its chief character after the town, is particularly attractive, with its pier and fashionable boutiques. But as always in summer, crowds can be a problem wherever you go, and it's best to trawl the coastline in search of a quiet spot. Care should be taken not to swim near the point of Selsey Bill because of fast currents, but nearby East Beach is safe and retains much of the atmosphere of the old fishing port of Selsey, popular for local seafood.

## . . . And the Countryside

Turning inland, **Cissbury Ring,** north of Worthing near Findon, is a remarkable prehistoric hill fort with good views to the Isle of Wight and Beachy Head. Farther north, the **Mid-**

**hurst–Petworth** area offers beautiful countryside with a range of stunning attractions.

🐾 Midhurst has many fine ancient timbered buildings and some superb restaurants, which include the **Olde Manor House** and **Maxines Restaurant,** both in Red Lion St., offering cordon bleu dishes (£8–12) and good wines in rustic settings.

A short walk from the village duck pond along the river will take you to the romantic **Cowdray House,** a former fortified Tudor mansion built in 1542 but destroyed by fire in 1793; it is situated in the extensive Cowdray Park, the venue for polo matches occasionally attended by Prince Charles when Windsor is playing. A short drive away, Petworth House, Petworth, is a magnificent 17th-century house in a deer park landscaped by Capability Brown. The house contains an exceptional art collection, including many Van Dycks, and a whole room of Turners, a sculpture gallery, and Grinling Gibbons carvings (0798-42207; open April through October, daily, from 1 to 5 P.M. except Monday and Friday; £2.50). The adjoining **St. Mary's Church** is notable for its nave ceiling of 126 molded panels and list of rectors dating from 1268.

🐾 In the village, the 15th-century **Tudor Cottage** restaurant is recommended for light lunches and cream teas.

Also in the area is the highly recommended **Weald and Downland Open Air Museum,** Singleton (north of Chichester on the A286) a fascinating collection of rescued historic buildings reconstructed on the site, including houses, barns, rural craft workshops, a market hall, working windmill, and village school. (Tel. 024363-348; open March through October, daily from 11 A.M. to 6 P.M., £2.20 for adults, £1.10 for children.)

# Brighton and Beyond

A curious blend of culture and candy floss, excellence and eccentricity, Brighton has quickly risen to the status of Britain's most popular seaside resort. The town began as the tiny but thriving fishing village of Brighthelmston, favored by fashionable London society from 1750 onward, after Dr. Richard Russell published a book extolling the virtues of sea bathing for the treatment of glandular diseases. Brighton's attraction surged with the arrival of the prince regent, later George IV, in 1783 to take the cure for a glandular swelling in the neck. He liked Brighton so much that he decided to live there, and commissioned the building of the fabulous Oriental-style Royal Pavilion palace. The arrival of the railway in 1840 transformed the town as London day-trippers made the journey to what was affectionately dubbed London-by-the-Sea.

## The City and the Seafront

The town has expanded enormously to accommodate the millions of visitors who come each year but somehow manages to make everyone feel at home. **The Palace Pier,** built in 1899, with its 1,760 feet of promenade deck and classic domes, continues to be the focus of the seafront, while sadly, its sister, the **West Pier,** has fallen into disrepair and is now closed.

Behind the Royal Pier is the fascinating warren of winding streets known as The Lanes, packed with small shops, boutiques, and restaurants—a favorite of antique collectors. In Ship St. is **Bexes Bistro,** where the delicious seafood and home-made specialty dishes (£10–15) more than make up for the somewhat spartan decor. Nearby, **Food for Friends** in Prince Albert St. is a favorite meeting place, serving cheap but wholesome vegetarian meals throughout the day, and at 7 Pavilion Buildings **Al Duomo** is a popular inexpensive pizza–pasta house where meals are cooked in an old-fashioned log oven. The choice, however, is extremely wide: there are dozens of restaurants in the area, and most hotels offer equally attractive menus.

Behind The Lanes you will find the **Theatre Royal** in New Road (0273-28488), renowned for its many productions that precede major box-office success in London's West End. Opposite, across the green, is **the Royal Pavilion**. Originally a modest mansion designed by architect Henry Holland in 1787, it was transformed in 1820 by Beau Nash to its present Oriental fantasy in the style of the mogul palaces. The lavish Chinese decor inside is even more stunning. Everything from the decorative wallpapers to the specially woven carpets, the bamboo ceilings to the cane furnishings, is styled according to authentic Chinese designs and colorfully reflects the prince regent's deep love of the arts. Not to be missed. (Tel. 0273-603005; open daily, October through May from 10 A.M. to 5 P.M., June through September from 10 A.M. to 5 P.M.; £2.30 for adults, £1.20 for children.)

The **Brighton Art Gallery and Museum** in Church Street (0273-603005; open Tuesday through Saturday from 10 A.M. to 6 P.M., Sunday from 2 to 5 P.M.; free) houses the astonishing Willett pottery and porcelain collection, depicting British social history, together with impressive collections of 20th-century fine and applied art, Art Deco and Art Nouveau. The mammoth **Brighton Center** in Kings Road (0273-203131) is the country's largest entertainment and conference complex, seating up to five thousand and hosting concerts, sporting championships, and exhibitions.

The seafront and Esplanade, however, remain the main attraction of Brighton for many visitors. The pebble beach, which gives way to sand near the water's edge, offers safe bathing at all times. On the seafront is the country's largest aquarium, the **Brighton Aquarium and Dolphinarium** (0273-604233; open daily, April through September from 10 A.M. to 6 P.M., October through March from 10 A.M. to 5 P.M.; £2.40). Regular shows are held throughout the day in the one-thousand seat dolphinarium, and other features include exotic fish, a reptile pool, and the country's biggest shark tank. Nearby, you can take a ride to **Brighton Marina** on the world's first electric railway, completed in 1883: the **Volk's Seafront Railway** (0273-681061; open daily March through September; 60 pence for adults, 30 pence for children). The marina, the largest in Europe with seventeen hundred berths, has recently been transformed into a major pleasure resort complete with shopping village, ten-cinema complex, restaurants, cafés, and shops. The imposing building on the cliffs nearby is Roedean, one of the country's top private girls' schools. Popular events in Brighton throughout the year include Model World in March, the International Arts Festival in May, the Brighton Marine Yacht Club Regatta in August, and the London-Brighton Veteran Car Run in November. Nearby Hove, two miles away, is inextricably linked with Brighton, but it's a good deal quieter and more sedate than its sister resort. Its attractions include the popular **King Alfred Leisure Center,** Kingsway (0273-734422; open Monday through Thursday from 10:15 A.M. to 8:45 P.M., Friday from 10:15 A.M. to 5:45 P.M., Saturday and Sunday from 8:15A.M. to 5:45 P.M.; £1.20 for adults, 65 pence for children), one of the first leisure centers to be built on the south coast, offering swimming, a water chute, ten-pin bowling, and a health center; the **Hove Museum and Art Gallery** (0273-779410; open Tuesday through Friday from 10 A.M. to 5 P.M., Saturday from 10 A.M. to 4:30 P.M., Sunday March through September only from 2 to 5 P.M.; free), housing impressive collections of ceramics and British art, and a popular children's museum; the **Briths Engineerium,** Neville Road (0273-559583; open daily from 10 A.M. to 5 P.M.; £1.80 for adults, £1 for children), housed in the old Goldstone Water Pumping Station, which supplied Brighton and Hove with over four million gallons of water a day; it contains over two thousand models and full-size exhibits of various engines, including the massive 16-ton Corliss Engine; the **Sussex County Cricket Club,** Eaton Road (0273-732161); and the **Brighton and Hove Stadium,** Neville Road (0273-204601).

## Along the Coast

To travel farther east along the coast is to encounter some breathtaking scenery. Beyond the commercial port of Newhaven and the relatively isolated seafront at Seaford you come to the three-hundred-acre **Seaford Head Nature Reserve.** From the car park here you can walk along the path to Hope's Gap to view the towering chalk cliff faces known as Seven Sisters, which rise to five hundred feet in places. Stretching back from the cliffs is the seven-hundred-acre **Seven Sisters Country Park,** and behind it the dense two-thousand-acre **Friston Forest.** More dramatic views can be found farther along the coast at **Beachey Head,** where the cliffs rise to over five hundred feet.

Nearby **Eastbourne** is another busy seaside resort with a three-mile seafront, pier, and bandstand popular for its summer concerts. **Pevensey Bay** is reputedly the spot where William the Conqueror came ashore in 1066, and at **old Pevensey,** a mile inland, there are the substantial ruins of **Pevensey Castle** (0323-762604; open March to October, Monday through Saturday, 9:30 A.M. to 6:30 P.M., Sunday from 2 to 6:30 P.M.; October to March, Monday through Saturday from 9:30 A.M. to 4 P.M., Sunday from 2 to 4 P.M.; £1 for adults, 50 pence for children), an immense Roman fort reoccupied by the Normans.

Adjacent is the **Royal Oak and Castle pub,** a good stop for light lunches.

**Bexhill** is worth a visit to view the impressive **De La Warr Pavilion,** built in 1935.

## Hastings

And so to Hastings, which lends its name to the most famous battle in English history, in 1066—the last time England was invaded—although the event in fact took place six miles inland, at Battle. Hastings and adjoining St. Leonards are popular seaside resorts in summer, with the usual seafront entertainments.

Hastings, situated between West Hill and East Hill cliffs, offers the interesting George Street precinct in the old town, where you will find the rustic **Katie's Pantry** for delicious cream teas, and **Ye Olde Pump House,** a fascinating leaning-timbered pub five hundred years old that was badly damaged forty years ago and completely rebuilt using old ship's timbers—recommended for excellent pub lunches.

The main interest centers around the nearby harbor, identified by its unique tall, wooden net-drying huts, where you will find three thousand years of maritime history at the quaint

**Shipwreck Heritage Center** (0424-437452; open daily June through September, from 11 A.M. to 5 P.M.; £1 for adults, 50 pence for children). Nearby is the **East Hill Railway** to the cliffs above; the **West Hill Railway** will take you up to the remains of the **Norman Hastings Castle** and the mysterious Whispering Dungeons (open daily March through October from 10 A.M. to 5 P.M.; 65 pence for adults, 35 pence for children). Also of interest are the four acres of underground smugglers' warrens under West Hill at **St. Clement's Caves** (open daily from 10 A.M. to 5:30 P.M.; 85 pence for adults, 40 pence for children). In town you can see the outstanding **Hastings Embroidery** at the Town Hall, Queens Road (0424-722022; check opening times; 75 pence for adults, 40 pence for children), a colorful tableau commissioned on the nine hundredth anniversary of the Battle of Hastings in 1966 and executed by the Royal School of Needlework. The 27 panels chronologically depict 81 major events in British history from 1066 to 1966. In the Middle Ages, Hastings was one of the federation of fortified towns along the southeast coast, together with Rye, Winchelsea, Dover, Hythe, and Sandwich, to repel invaders (see the Cinque Ports, Kent, discussed below).

## Battle

Battle itself, six miles to the north, is fascinating. Little more than a High Street of shops and houses, it marks the spot of the most significant change in English history. Start with a visit to the **Battle Museum** in High Street (04246-389; open Easter through September, Monday through Saturday from 10 A.M. to 1 P.M., and from 2 to 5 P.M. from Sunday from 2:30 to 5:30 P.M.; 30 pence for adults, 10 pence for children), to view a copy of the Bayeux Tapestry depicting the battle. Nearby is **Battle Abbey** (04246-3792; open March through October, Monday through Saturday from 9:30 A.M. to 6:30 P.M., Sunday from 2 to 6:30 P.M., October through March from 9:30 A.M. to 4 P.M.; Sunday from 2 to 4 P.M.; £1.25 for adults, 60 pence for children), erected by William the Conqueror to commemorate his victory and ruined during the Dissolution, although parts still standing are today occupied by a girls' school. The spot where Harold fell is marked by a stone plaque, and there are good views of the battlefield. Harold, the self-proclaimed king after the death of Edward the Confessor, was unlucky to lose the battle. He had already defeated the invading forces of Hardrada of Norway a month earlier at York before he was forced to march back again to the coast to face the Normans on October 14, 1066. Despite the superior strength of the Normans, Harold's battle-weary, foot-sore troops managed to split their ranks and put them to flight. Recklessly, Harold's troops pursued them, only to be cut down when the Normans turned and charged again. Harold was reputedly hit in the face (though some say the eye) with an arrow and then cut down by four horsemen. He was buried under an inscribed stone on the shore near Hastings. The outcome of the battle was significant because of the order and development throughout the land that followed under Norman rule.

## East Sussex Historic Sights

Other attractions around the county include: **Bodiam Castle,** at Bodiam (058083-436; open April through October, daily from 10 A.M. to 6 P.M.; November through March, Monday through Saturday from 10 A.M. to sunset; £1.30 for adults, 70 pence for children), built in 1385 in fear of French invasion; it is considered by many to be the most attractive castle ruin in the country, with its romantic castellated drum towers surrounded by a picturesque moat. **Bateman's,** Burwash, Etchingham (0435-882302; open April through October, Saturday through Wednesday from 10 A.M. to 6 P.M.; £2.50 for adults, £1.30 for children), was Rudyard Kipling's home from 1902 to 1936, built by a local ironmaster in 1634, with Kipling's rooms and study as they were during his lifetime. The water mill in the garden grinds corn for flour, and Kipling's 1928 Rolls Royce is on show. **Alfriston Clergy House,** The Tye, Alfriston (0323-870001; open April through October; daily from 11 A.M. to 5:30 P.M.; 80 pence for adults, 40 pence for children), the first building acquired by the National Trust, in a delightful down-land village, is a half-timbered and thatched 14th-century priest's house with medieval hall and attractive garden. **Lewes Castle,** Lewes (open Monday through Friday from 10 A.M. to 5:30 P.M.; April through October, also Sunday from 11 A.M. to 5:50 P.M.; 65 pence for adults, 35 pence for children), is the remains of a Norman castle with panoramic views of the county town of Lewes and exhibitions by the Museum of Sussex Archeology.

## The Cinque Ports

A defense system of fortified ports, the Cinque Ports along the south coast were built up during the Middle Ages to combat Continental invaders. In return for certain privileges, the ports provided men and ships for the Crown. The original Cinque Ports were Dover, Sandwich, Romney (now New Romney), Hythe, and Hastings, and later, Rye and Winchelsea in neighboring East Sussex.

### Rye

Rye is probably the most picturesque of them all—a delightful town with twisting cobbled streets that has long since seen the sea recede. Rye Harbour is a completely separate village over two miles south of Rye, where the sea has now receded to Rye Bay beyond the harbor.

Rye became notorious for smuggling when Edward I imposed duties on wool, cloth, leather, and wine. But new Victorian moral attitudes and cuts in levied duties put an end to the trade.

Mermaid St. is a particularly attractive steep, cobbled street lined with crooked buildings. Here you will find the outstanding medieval **Mermaid Inn,** once the famous haunt of the Hawkhurst Gang, a bloodthirsty group of smugglers known to have bribed officials and killed informers. Today it is Rye's most popular pub, hotel, and restaurant serving local seafood (£10–15).

The top of Mermaid Street leads into West Street and past **Lamb House,** where the authors Henry James and E. F. Benson lived. At the top of West Street is **St. Mary's Church.** Built in 1150, it was reduced to a smoldering ruin together with much of the town by the French in a raid in 1377, and rebuilt between 1400 and 1500. The inhabitants of Rye and Winchelsea made a retaliatory raid on Normandy in 1378, setting fire to two towns and also recovering Rye's church bells, which the French had seized. The church also contains one of the oldest clocks in the country, dating from about 1513, with a huge pendulum that swings overhead inside the doorway.

Adjacent to the church is the **Old Vicarage Guest House** (0797-222119), a superb, quaint B&B that makes a perfect overnight stop.

## Winchelsea

Nearby Winchelsea suffered even more than Rye, not just at the hands of the marauding French, who destroyed the town on several occasions, but also from the erosion by the sea of the shingle spit on which the old town stood until it disappeared altogether in the 13th century. New Winchelsea began as a planned town but was never completed, and the sea that had destroyed the old town through erosion began returning the shingle, which effectively, like at Rye, ended the town's seafaring trade. The same fate has befallen Hythe, Sandwich, and New Romney. The surrounding 50,000-acre **Romney Marsh** is popular walking country, famous for its long-wooled sheep, while the coastal path between Folkestone and Dover provides dramatic views of the monumental concrete defenses against the continual erosion of the famous chalky cliffs of this shore.

# Around Guildford

An ideal base for exploring the surrounding attractions in Surrey, the county town of Guildford takes its name from a Saxon phrase meaning "ford of the golden flowers"; it is the point where Harrow Way, an ancient track along the North Downs escarpment, crossed the river Wey. The earliest occupation by the Saxons in the sixth century saw the town develop as a series of tenements, with narrow frontages onto the picturesque cobbled High Street and long strips of land to the rear and long passages, or "gates," leading off the High Street. Much of the layout remains today, making Guildford an interesting and rewarding town to explore. A few minutes' walk from High Street is the remaining **Keep of Guildford Castle** on Castle Street (0483-505050; open April through September from 10:30 A.M. to 6 P.M.; 40 pence for adults, 20 pence for children). Originally built by Henry II as a fortress, the walls are 15 feet thick in places and stand 63 feet high, with excellent views. Adjoining it is **Guildford Museum,** Castle Arch, Quarry Street (0483-503497; open Monday through Saturday from 11 A.M. to 5 P.M.; free), containing the history and archeology of Surrey, with a special focus on Guildford.

On the corner of Quarry and Castle sts. is the half-timbered **Kings Head pub** (good for lunches). Also in Quarry St., the intimate **Cafe de Paris** offers specialty dishes (£8–12) and good wines.

Nearby is **St. Mary's Church,** Guildford's oldest building (dating from 1050); the simplified Gothic **Guildford Cathedral** on Stag Hill is the only modern cathedral in southern England. There are many ancient buildings in High Street, including **The Angel Hotel,** established before 1527 and the only survivor of Guildford's five large coaching inns, and **The Guildhall,** built in 1683, with a lovely projecting clock John Aylward made for the town before being allowed to set up shop. Dozens more half-timbered buildings can be found in the surrounding streets, many of them occupied by modern shops and boutiques that continue to make this former important market town a busy shopping center.

Within easy driving distance of Guildford are: the three hundred-acre experimental **Royal Horticultural Society Gardens** at Wisley (0483-224234; open daily from 10 A.M. to 7 P.M.; £2.50 for adults, £1 for children); the outstanding 18th-century **National Trust country house,** built for the 2nd Lord Onslow, with a fine marble hall and Gubbay collection of furniture, pictures, and porcelain, at Clandon Park, West Clandon (0483-222482; April through October, every-

day except Thursday and Friday from 1:30 to 5:30 P.M.; £2.30
for adults, £1.20 for children).

## Runnymede

To the north of Guildford is Runnymede, where the signing
of the Magna Carta by King John took place in 1215, the spot
marked by the domed classical temple built by the American
Bar Association at the foot of Cooper's Hill. Halfway up the
hill is the **John F. Kennedy Memorial,** and at the top of
the hill, the **Air Forces Memorial** commemorates twenty
thousand airmen who died in the Second World War. Magnificent views of nearby Windsor Castle and seven counties can
be seen from here.

## Dorking

To the east lies Dorking, where the new has been fashionably
blended with the old to retain the atmosphere of this ancient
town. Traces of the Stone Age, Iron Age, and Roman occupation have been found, and there is early reference to the town
in the Domesday Book. Principally a farming town, it also had
the most prosperous lime pits in the country, which provided
the lime to build London docks. The town has famous associations with Churchill and Benjamin Disraeli, who both stayed
at the old Deepdene mansion in Dorking, and with the military
engineer General Sir Arthur Cotton, who pioneered irrigation
schemes in India.

The **White Horse Inn** in High St. is a particularly attractive
Dickensian coach house that serves a good lunch.

One mile north of Dorking is the popular **Box Hill,** named
after the box trees that grow all over the hill. Rising 400 feet
from the river Mole, it comprises eight hundred acres of
woods and chalk down land with magnificent views to the
South Downs. South of Dorking, near Coldharbour, is the
18th-century **Leith Hill Tower,** the highest point in southern England at 1,029 feet, which provides magnificent views
of the North and South downs. And a little over a mile to the
southwest is the beautiful **Rhododendron Wood,** best seen
in April and May. A peaceful enough spot today, Leith Hill
was the site of one of the most ferocious battles against the
invading Danes, who were defeated by the West Saxon King
Ethelwulf, father of Alfred the Great, in 851.

On the northwest slopes of Leith Hill is the enchanting tiny
hamlet of **Friday Street,** with a lake buried among the trees.
Also nearby, three miles northwest of Dorking, is **Polesden
Lacey,** where King George VI and the Queen Mother spent
part of their honeymoon. Originally an 1820s Regency villa,
it was remodeled in 1906 and lavishly furnished; it also has
extensive grounds and a walled rose garden (0372-58203;
open April through October, Wednesday through Sunday

from 1:30 to 5:30 P.M.; March through November, Saturday through Sunday from 1:30 to 4:30 P.M.; £2.50).

Between Guildford and Dorking is Shere, a superb stop for delicious home-cooked lunches at the 1471 **White Horse Inn** overlooking the river.

Nearby are exhibitions of local history at the **Shere Museum** (048641-3245; open April through September, Monday, Tuesday, Thursday, Friday, from 1 to 6 P.M., Sunday from 11 A.M. to 7 P.M.; 30 pence for adults, 10 pence for children). The idyllic tranquillity of Shere belies a fascinating history. The nearby Silent Pool is the spot where Stephen Langton and his cousin Alice were attacked by Prince John and his men, and Alice was carried off. Langton managed to rescue her but thought she was dead. In grief, he became a monk, vowing to avenge her, and was eventually made archbishop of Canterbury by the Pope in Rome. On his return to England, King John was forced to humbly receive him. Alas, his love, Alice, had become a nun, thinking him dead, and when she was presented to him, she collapsed and died. The Silent Pool is also said to be haunted by a local girl named Emma, who drowned while bathing when surprised by Prince John. It is said that if you come on a moonlit night, you can see a white form dipping in and out of the water.

### Farnham

To the west is one of Surrey's prettiest villages, Farnham, where you will find the former bishop's palace with many Norman features at **Farnham Castle,** on Castle Hill (0252-721194; open Wednesday only from 2 to 4 P.M.; free), and **Farnham Castle Keep,** a motte and bailey castle and former residence of the bishop of Winchester (0252-713393; open April through September, Monday through Saturday from 9:30 A.M. to 6:30 P.M., Sunday from 2 to 6 P.M.; 75 pence for adults, 35 pence for children).

# Canterbury and the Coast

Canterbury is undoubtedly the main attraction in Kent and probably the most visited city in Britain outside of London. Dating back to the former Roman city of Durovernum Cantiacorum, it has long been famous for Chaucer's *The Canterbury Tales* and the destination of pilgrims visiting the shrine of Thomas à Becket in this most hallowed of cathedral cities.

## The Cathedral

Canterbury renewed its Roman links in A.D. 597 when a company of Benedictine monks from Rome arrived in response to a royal plea for missionaries. The conversion of the Saxon

King Ethelbert of Kent and his Queen Bertha was followed by the consecration of St. Augustine as archbishop and the rebuilding of a ruined church dating from Roman times that served as the first Canterbury cathedral. The Norman Conquest marked the rebuilding of the cathedral, after a fire in 1067, on a magnificent scale. After the murder of Thomas à Becket inside the church in 1170 on the orders of Henry II, it became the greatest religious center of pilgrimage in northern Europe and the Mother Church of England. Features inside the cathedral include the shrine to Becket, the Black Prince's Tomb, the Norman crypt, the fan vaulting under Bell Harry Tower, the beautiful stained glass, and the unusual tiering of the choir and the altar above the nave.

Canterbury continued to develop and prosper through the ages with the influx of skilled Protestant refugees, or Huguenots, from across the Channel after the Reformation, followed by two centuries of peace after Restoration, and with the coming of the Victorian railway. The town suffered considerable air-raid damage in 1942, although the cathedral escaped almost unscathed; much work has been done since to rebuild the town as a center of religious pilgrimage. Today Canterbury is inundated with worshipers and tourists throughout the season, and its modern pedestrian precincts make it a busy center for shopping.

Much of Canterbury's illustrious history can be traced through two fascinating exhibitions: **Canterbury Pilgrims Way,** St. Margaret's Street (0227-454888; open daily from 9 A.M. to 5:30 P.M.; £2.50 for adults, £1.50 for children); and **Canterbury Heritage** (0227-452747; open Monday through Saturday from 10:30 A.M. to 4 P.M.; Sunday June to October only 1:30 to 4 P.M.; £1 for adults, 50 pence for children).

# Chatham

The Kent coastline has always played a vital part in British maritime history, from the days of the first great warships built at Chatham in the north to the famous Cinque Ports in the south, cross-Channel traffic at Dover and Folkestone, and now the building of the Anglo-French Channel Tunnel.

The importance of the Royal Dockyard at Chatham began in about 1547, when a storehouse at "Jillingham Water" was rented to service the king's ships at anchor on the Medway. The launch of Chatham's first ship, the *Sunne,* in 1586 was followed by over four hundred warships. In the 17th century, Chatham became the principal building yard and fleet anchorage of the Royal Navy. It was in the front line during the Dutch wars (1652 to 1674), when the port was attacked and ships were sunk and captured. In 1759, the shipwrights laid down perhaps the most famous of all British ships, H.M.S. *Victory,* Nelson's flagship at the Battle of Trafalgar, and in 1863 the first ironclad, H.M.S. *Achilles,* was built. The massive Victorian extension at St. Mary's Creek was followed by the launch of Chatham's largest battleship, H.M.S. *Africa.* In 1908 the first of 57 submarines to be built here was launched. Chatham continued to refit and service ships, including nuclear submarines, until the dockyard closed in 1984. Today the dockyard and buildings have been carefully preserved by the Chatham Historic Dockyard Trust, and they provide a fascinating journey through every stage of shipbuilding over the centuries. Tel. 0634-812551; open March to October, Wednesday through (Sunday from 10 A.M. to 6 P.M.; October to March, Wednesday, Saturday, Sunday from 10 A.M. to 4:30 P.M.; £1.75 for adults, £1 for children.)

## Rochester

Nearby Rochester is closely linked with Chatham and the defense of the Medway. Originally the site of a Roman walled city, the Normans built one of their finest castles here as well as the magnificent cathedral. The castle was ruined by King John's siege in 1215, but it still has the tallest keep—at 113 feet—in the country, offering superb views. The cathedral is a curious blend of Norman and Gothic (funds for rebuilding ran out in about 1300). Rochester is also famous for its associations with Charles Dickens, which are celebrated annually during the week-long Dickens's Festival in May. His home at nearby Gad's Hill can be seen together with dramatic audiovisual presentations of his life's work at the **Charles Dickens's Center,** Eastgate House, High Street (0634-44176; open daily from 10 A.M. to 12:30 P.M. and from 2 to 5 P.M.; £1.50 for adults, 90 pence for children).

The High St. is a charming collection of ancient timbered buildings with many cafés, tearooms, and restaurants, making this the ideal lunch spot. Recommended is **Farthings** for delicious specialty dishes (£7–12) and selected wines.

---

Kent's best **beaches** are to be found on the east coast, at the wide expansive sands of **Sandwich Flats,** and at the popular seaside resorts of **Margate** and **Ramsgate.** Also here is Deal, reputedly the spot where Julius Caesar stepped ashore in 55 B.C., and just offshore, the treacherous Goodwin Sands, one of the most dangerous areas in the world for shipping (it has claimed countless lives).

---

## Other Kent Attractions

At the busy county market town of **Maidstone** you'll find **Leeds Castle** (0622-65400; open April through October, daily from 11 A.M. to 5 P.M.; November through March, Saturday and Sunday from 12 to 4 P.M.; £4.50 for adults, £3 for children), named after Led, chief minister of King Ethelbert of Kent in A.D. 857. Originally a Norman stronghold, it was later converted into a royal palace by Henry VIII. It is considered by many to be one of the most beautiful castles in the world. The castle was built on two islands in the middle of a lake within landscaped, wooded parkland, and is magnificently furnished with French and English furniture, tapestries, and Impressionist paintings.

The once fashionable 18th-century spa town of **Tunbridge Wells,** famous for its sweeping colonnaded promenade known as the **Pantiles,** is now a busy commercial center. Nearby is the childhood home of Anne Boleyn, second wife of Henry VIII and mother of Elizabeth I, at **Hever Castle** (0732-865224; open April through October, daily from 12 to 5 P.M.; £3.40 for adults, £1.70 for children).

The home of Winston Churchill from 1924 till his death, at Chartwell, Westerham, is now a museum; the rooms are left as they were in his lifetime, with documents, personal mementos, and a garden studio that contains many of his paintings. (0732-866368; house open April through October, Tuesday through Thursday from 12 to 5 P.M., Saturday and Sunday from 11 A.M. to 5 P.M.; March and November, on Wednesday, Saturday, and Sunday 11 A.M. to 4 P.M.; the garden and studio are only open April through October, from 11 A.M. to 5 P.M.; house and garden £2.50, garden alone £1, studio 40 pence.)

# 7

# THE WEST COUNTRY

The West Country is the first choice of many British vacationers: its legendary past, seafaring traditions, scenic countryside, ancient monuments, historic towns, and relaxed atmosphere make this a most stimulating region to explore.

This is the land of King Arthur—a land of smuggling, tiny fishing villages, famous trading ports, superb beaches, stone circles, castles, fine cathedrals, country homes, thatch villages, and rugged landscapes. It includes the counties of Avon, with the ancient port of Bristol and the country's premier spa resort, Bath; Somerset, the home of cider, Glastonbury, and the country's smallest cathedral city, Wells; Wiltshire, with the magnificent cathedral town of Salisbury, stone circles at Stonehenge and Avebury, chalk hill figures, and open countryside; Dorset, the heart of Thomas Hardy's Wessex, and the popular seaside resorts of Bournemouth, Poole, and Lyme Regis; Devon, of clotted cream tea fame, Dartmoor, and the "English Riviera" seaside resorts; and Cornwall, with its Celtic traditions, tin mining, and majestic coastline.

Keep in mind that this area is a popular summertime destination. To avoid the problems of congestion and crowds, to witness the spring and autumn seasonal changes, and for those who dislike the heat and humidity of this particularly warm region in midsummer, it's best to visit the region either pre- or post-season.

Touring the region at random can be difficult because the land is elongated and long distances are involved. To really get the most out of your visit, it would be better to see a few of the main attractions and then head for the coast. We recommend you begin at Bristol or Bath, from where you can visit the ancient stone monuments of Stonehenge and Avebury in Wiltshire, and Cheddar Gorge, Wells Cathedral, and Glastonbury before heading for the best of coastal attractions to be

THE WEST-COUNTRY

© RV Reise- und Verkehrsverlag, Munchen

Kilometers    Miles

0    60    50

found in Cornwall. Then if you have time, return via Dartmoor, Lyme Regis, Bournemouth, and Salisbury for a round trip that will have included the very best the region has to offer.

There are several towns that make good bases for staying and from which you can travel outward to see surrounding attractions. The size of the region means it will not always be possible, or feasible, to return to base, so we also suggest a number of overnight stops.

Bath is a superb base in an idyllic town that has a rich history as a fashionable spa dating from Roman times. From here, it is but a short drive to see the cathedral and waterfront of Bristol and the large, if overrated, seaside resort of Weston-super-Mare to the west; the spectacular crags of Cheddar Gorge, the picturesque cathedral town of Wells, and ruined Glastonbury Abbey to the south in Somerset; and Castle Combe—voted the prettiest village in England—the impressive stately homes of Corsham Court and Bowood House, and Avebury stone circle to the east, and Stonehenge farther south, in Wiltshire.

St. Ives/Sennen Cove boast some of the best beaches in Britain, and these two spots are ideally situated for exploring Cornwall's stunning north coast, including the quaint miniature natural harbor of Boscastle, the legendary site of King Arthur's castle at Tintagel, and the charming fishing village of Padstow. Land's End—the most westerly tip of England—has been horribly commercialized by recent development; instead visit Cape Cornwall just five miles north along the coast for equally spectacular views out across the ocean and that feeling of isolation at "the end of the world," before the voyages of Drake and Columbus discovered that the earth was, in fact, round. Cornwall's south coast attractions include the magnificent island fort of St. Michael's Mount at Penzance and the popular "Cornish Riviera" seaside resorts and fishing villages.

The nearby naval port of Plymouth, on the south Devon coast, associated with the poineering voyages of Drake, Raleigh, Cooke, and the Pilgrim Fathers, was heavily bombed in World War II; much rebuilt, it is heavily commercialized, a nightmare for drivers, and is not recommended. Hatherleigh, strategically placed in the middle of Devon as you return, is a delightful isolated market village in beautiful countryside just north of Dartmoor. Its central location makes it ideal for striking out in any direction: in particular, to the rocky granite mass of Dartmoor to the south, and to Devon's popular seaside resorts in the southeast along the "English Riviera."

Dawlish, a continuation of your journey east, is one of the smaller, more managable seaside towns on the northeast Devon coast. From here, you can travel north to the county's ancient cathedral town, Exeter; south to Teignmouth's attractive harbor, the "English Riviera" seaside resorts of Torquay, Paignton and Brixham, and to Dartmouth Castle; and east to Dartmoor.

Lyme Regis, conveniently situated on a southeast swing of the region, is an ideal overnight stop in an enchanting, ancient seaside town noted for smuggling, and the scene of the book and film, *The French Lieutenant's Woman*.

Continuing east from here, just north of the coast, you will find the Elizabethan manor of Parnham House, the chalk hill Cerne Abbas Giant, and the home of author Thomas Hardy at Dorchester.

Bournemouth, your final stop as you travel east and south back to the coast, is the country's second most popular seaside resort offering excellent leisure and entertainment facilities, and just two miles to the west, one of the world's largest natural harbors, at Poole.

Salisbury, directly to the north, is a magnificent cathedral town, somewhat spoilt by modern development, but still worth a visit. An easy drive from Salisbury are the former site of the town at Old Sarum, two miles north, the outstanding country home of Wilton, also close by, and further north, the historic Stonehenge and Avebury stone circles; the zoo and fabulous house at Longleat, exotic gardens at Stourbridge, and Sherborne Abbey and nearby Sir Walter Raleigh's castle, to the west; and chalk hill horses and other figures common to Wiltshire throughout the county.

## TRAVEL

There are a couple of ways to approach the region. One is to take intercity **rail services** from London's Paddington and Waterloo stations to the main centers such as Bath, Bristol, Salisbury, Bournemouth, Exeter, and Plymouth.

**By Rail:** London Paddington (tel. 01-262-6767); London Waterloo (tel. 01-928-5100); Bath (tel. 0225-63075); Bristol (tel. 0272-294255); Bournemouth (tel. 0202-292474); Exeter (tel. 0392-33551); Plymouth (tel. 0752-221300); Salisbury (tel. 0722-27591). **National Express Coaches** also operate regular services from London's Victoria Station to the main towns. But because many of the attractions are far-flung, you will need a car to see the rest of the region. Alternatively, **hire a car** in London and drive direct: to Bath and Bristol via the M4 or the A4; to Salisbury via the M3/A30; to Bournemouth via the M3/M27/A31/A338; to Exeter via the M3/A303 or the A30; to Plymouth via the M3/A303/A38.

The A30 is a particularly attractive route, running right through the heart of the West Country all the way to Land's End. The A303, which runs parallel to it through Wiltshire, is often heavily congested and less scenic, and should be avoided.

Many roads throughout the region become congested at the height of the season, and traveling can become slow and tiresome. A useful tip is to set off for your next destination early in the morning, after the initial rush-hour traffic, when the roads clear for a time. By midday, much of the commercial traffic is on the roads, together with many holiday travelers, and delays can be expected. Alternatively, wait until early evening, after the rush-hour home. We recommend a combination of both tactics. If you have to travel when the roads are busy, the B roads are quieter and often quicker than the A roads.

**Car hire:** Budget Rent a Car—UK Central Reservations Freefone 0800-181181; locations—Royal York Hotel, George St., Bath 0225-60518; 25 Ave. Road, Bournemouth 0202-296163; Gibbs Garage, Jacobs Wells Rd., Clifton, Bristol 0272-277614; Exeter Workshop, Unit 15, 39 Marsh Green Rd., Marsh Barton's Exeter 0392-72223; One Enterprise, Somerset Place, Stoke, Plymouth 0752-556800; Brunel Rd., Salisbury 0722-336444.

# HOTELS

Remember that the popular sights like Bath, Salisbury, and the South Dorset, East Devon, and Cornish coasts are particularly busy and crowded during summer. If you are planning to stay in the region, you should book accommodations well in advance. If you are unable to plan ahead, and find that hotels in the main centers are all booked, try the smaller hotels, guest houses, and B&Bs in the surrounding countryside.

**Credit card abbreviations used in hotel and restaurant listings are as follows: AE for American Express, CB for Carte Blanche, DC for Diner's Club, MC for MasterCard, and V for Visa.**

## Bath

**Harrington's of Bath Hotel,** 8/10 Queen St. Bath, Avon BA1 1HB; tel. (0225) 61728. Located in a quiet city center street close to the Theatre Royal, this is a small, pleasant hotel comprising several 18th-century houses, with comfortable, pretty rooms, and a choice, selective menu (£12–15) but limited wine list, in intimate surroundings, from £24 for a single to £30 for a double. MC, V.

**The Priory Hotel,** Weston Rd., Bath, Avon, BA1 2XT; tel. (0225) 331922. Located one mile from the city center, near the Royal Crescent and Victoria Park, the Priory is a superb Georgian country-style hotel standing in 2 acres of beautiful private gardens with heated swimming pool, luxurious, antique-furnished rooms (including four-poster beds), a superb cordon bleu menu (£20–30), and fine wines. From £65 for a single to £99 for a double and £130 for a deluxe double. All major credit cards.

## Bournemouth

**The Carlton Hotel,** East Overcliff, Bournemouth BH1 3DN; tel. (0202) 22011. A grand, Edwardian hotel ten minutes from the town center, with luxurious surroundings overlooking the sea, the Carlton has a heated swimming pool and health facilities, an elegant restaurant with excellent French and English cuisine (£20–30) and fine wines, and spacious, air-conditioned rooms. From £91 for a single, £130 for a double, and £152–199 for suites. All major credit cards.

**The County Hotel,** Westover Rd., Bournemouth BH1 2B1; tel. (0202) 22385. Located in the center of town overlooking the pier, with a limited restaurant menu (£7–10) and wine list, but clean, spacious rooms, from £35 for a single, £56 for a double. AE, MC, V.

# Bristol

**The Hawthorns Hotel,** Woodland Rd., Clifton BS8 1UB; tel. (0272) 738432. A large, comfortable hotel in the fashionable leafy suburb of Clifton, Hawthorns is close to the city center and dockyards, with modern, spacious rooms, comprehensive à la carte menu (£15–20) and wine list, from £38 for a single, £55 for a double. All major credit cards.

# Castle Coombe

**The Castle Hotel,** Castle Combe, Chittenham, SN14 7JN; tel. (0249) 782461. A charming Cotswold stone and timbered building, the Castle also has a 13th-century bar, intimate dining room, specialty menu prepared by Young Chef of the Year regional finalist Ivan Reid (£17–23), selected wine list, excellent choice of over 20 cheeses, and with quaint, timbered rooms, from £52 for a single, £92 for a double. AE, MC, V.

**The Manor House,** Castle Coombe SN14 7HR; tel. (0249) 782206. Located in a tiny hamlet voted the prettiest village in England. The Manor House is set in 26 acres of beautiful gardens surrounded by parkland, offering both luxurious suites and delightful terrace cottage rooms, comfortable lounges and bar, small secluded dining rooms, exsquisite English and French dishes (£20–30) and fine selected wines. From £80 single, £90 double, £120 suites. All major credit cards.

# Dawlish

**Langstone Cliff Hotel,** Dawlish Warren, South Devon EX7 ONA; tel. (0626) 865155. This large cliff-top hotel overlooks the sea near superb beaches and has indoor and outdoor heated swimming pools and sports facilities, spacious bars, lounges, a restaurant with a comprehensive menu (£10–15) and wine list, and comfortable, modern rooms. From £24 for a single, £50 for a double. All major credit cards.

# Glastonbury

**Hawthorns Hotel,** Northload St., Glastonbury BA6 9JJ; tel. (0458) 31255. Originally a row of cottages dating back to the

17th century, this is a reasonable overnight stop with a popular bar, newly opened restaurant with varied menu (£10) and wines, and basic, comfortable rooms. From £15 for single, £32 for a double. No credit cards.

## Hatherleigh

**The George Hotel,** Market St., Hatherleigh, Devon EX20 3JN; tel. (0837) 810454. This is a rustic 15th-century timber-framed and thatched former monk's rest home and coaching inn that has retained its original charm. It's set around a delightful courtyard with popular bars, an inviting lounge with huge open fireplace, a pleasant restaurant with a selective menu (£12–15) and good wines, and enchanting timbered bedrooms (including four-posters). From £45 for a single, £60 for a double. AE, MC, V.

## Lyme Regis

**The Mariner's Hotel,** Silver St., Lyme Regis, Dorset DT7 3HS; tel. (02974) 2753. A suitable overnight stop, Lyme's most picturesque hotel is a former 17th-century coaching inn with modern facilities, a pleasant lounge, a spacious restaurant with table d'hôte menu (£12) and comprehensive wine list, and old world crooked rooms with distant sea views. From £33 for a single, £66 for a double. All major credit cards.

## Salisbury

**The King's Arms Hotel,** 9-11 St. Johns St., Salisbury SP1 2SB; tel. (0722) 27629. The town's oldest hostelry, it predates the building of Salisbury Cathedral by almost a century and is a marvel of ancient timbered construction, offering popular bars, an intimate restaurant with a selective menu (£10–15) and good wines, and tastefully modernized rooms (including four-poster beds). From £32 for a single, £48 for a double. All major credit cards.

**The Red Lion Hotel,** 4 Milford St., Salisbury SP1 2AN; tel. (0722) 23334. Located in the heart of town, this former coaching inn was originally a hostelry dating back to the 13th century. Numerous additions have been made since then to form its attractive courtyard structure, but the Red Lion offers rustic beam interiors throughout, numerous antique furnishings, an attractive bar and restaurant, a table d'hôte menu (£10.50) and a varied wine list, and comfortable rooms including four-poster beds. From £45 for a single, £65 for a double. All major credit cards.

## St. Ives

**Longships Hotel,** Talland Rd., St. Ives, Cornwall, TR26 2DS; tel. (0736) 798180. Located around the bay from the harbor, this is a modernized, comfortable hotel with its own bar and restaurant serving basic English fare with a limited wine list. It has spacious, clean, airy rooms with good sea views. From £21 for a single, £42 for a double. MC, V.

## Sturminster Newton

**Plumber Manor,** Sturminster Newton, Dorset D T10 2AF; tel. (0258) 72507. Although situated in isolated Wiltshire country-side three miles south of Sturminster Newton, this fine 17th-century family country home is well worth a visit. It's set in extensive gardens with a river, croquet lawn, and tennis court, an intimate lounge/bar and restaurant, superb French and English cuisine (£16–20), a vintage wine list, and a luxurious main house and stable cottage rooms. From £45 for a single, £45–70 for a double. All major credit cards.

## Wells

**The Crown at Wells,** Market Place, Wells BA5 2RP; tel. (0749) 73457. A former coaching inn dating from 1450, the Crown is modernized inside, with a selective menu (£10–15) and good wines and tastefully furnished rooms (including four-poster beds). From £30 for a single, £43 for a double. All major credit cards.

**The Red Lion Hotel,** Market Place, Wells BA5 2RX; tel. (0749) 72616. Once an early 15th-century timbered coaching inn and temperance hotel, the Red Lion has modernized its interiors, and now has a popular bar and restaurant, a comprehensive menu (£10–15) and wine list, and comfortable rooms. From £30 for a single, £44 for a double. AE, MC, V.

**The Star Hotel,** High St., BA5 244; tel. (0749) 73055. A former 16th-centure coaching inn set around a cobbled courtyard, the Star has an intimate bar and restaurant, table d'hôte and à la carte menus (£10–20) and varied wines, and quaint rooms. From £25 for a single, £35 for a double. AE, MC, V.

# Bristol

Bristol and Bath are the two principal towns at the heart of Avon, one of the smallest and newly created counties of England under the Local Government Act of 1972. Divided by the Avon River it is named after, the county includes parts of southern Gloucestershire and northern Somerset. Situated in lowland bordering the Severn Estuary, which gives Weston-super-Mare its expansive beaches, Avon lacks a spectacularly diversified landscape, but it is near enough to the Cotswolds across the Gloucestershire border and to Somerset's Mendip Hills to the south for the visitor to experience some variety. Avon is essentially urban in character, largely due to the development of Bristol over the centuries as one of the country's premier trading ports, and to Bath's two-thousand-year history as a world-famous spa.

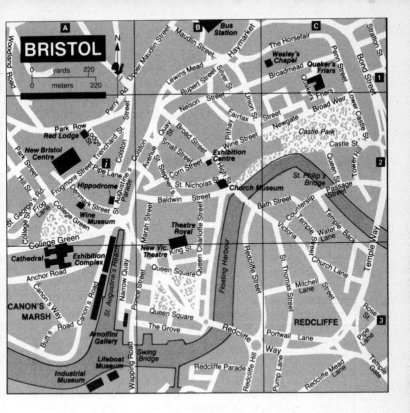

The largest city in southwest England, Bristol has for centuries been one of the country's principal ports and, as early as 1337, was the country's richest provincial town due to its seafaring trade. In the 15th century, trade with Ireland, France, Spain, and Portugal was primarily through exporting cloth and importing wine; it later expanded to fishing, then, with the discovery of the New World, rum, slaves, sugar, and tobacco. After the decline in trade caused by England's Industrial Revolution and the American Revolution, Bristol's fortunes were revived by the advent of steam power and heavy industry, which made possible trans-Atlantic travel to New York—through the Great Western Railway link between London and Bristol—and the construction of steam-powered iron ships—all notably the work of one man, Bristol's brilliant engineer, Isambard Kingdom Brunel. One of his most enduring achievements, and Bristol's most distinctive landmark, is **Clifton Suspension Bridge** across Avon Gorge. Although it won him the designer's prize in a competition in 1829–31, when he was still in his early twenties, the bridge was not opened until 1864, five years after his death. It is 245 feet high with a total span of 702 feet. The most remarkable story attached to the site concerns Sarah Ann Henley, who jumped off it in 1885 after a lover's quarrel; fortunately, her petticoats billowed open and she parachuted safely down to the mud below. She married and lived to 85! Although Bristol's importance as a port has declined again, the city continues to thrive as an engineering center and a popular tourist attraction.

## The New World

It was from Bristol that John Cabot, an Italian navigator who had settled in England, sailed in 1497 to America. Aboard the *Matthew,* a ship of fifty tons, with a company of between 18 and 26 men, he sighted land on June 24, after 52 days at sea, and disembarked. There, the crew erected a cross and the banners of Henry VII, the Pope, and St. Mark of Venice, claiming for the King of England this "new found land," the spot later to become known as Newfoundland. Thus, the mainland of America had been discovered five years after Columbus reached the West Indies. Re-embarking, Cabot sailed nine hundred miles along the coast and returned to Bristol. After a second voyage in 1498 (though details are scarce), Cabot sailed again in 1499 with a bigger fleet, met a storm, and drowned. In 1897, to mark the four-hundredth anniversary of his discovery, the people of Bristol erected the Cabot Tower at Brandon Hill overlooking the sea in memory of his achievements. His pioneering voyages were to lead to many subsequent expeditions, and numerous places throughout America bearing the name Bristol are further recognition of the part the English port played in that continent's development.

## The Harbor

Despite the obvious dereliction of the city dockyards, the waterfront—or **Floating Harbour,** as it is known—is the focal point of the town and continues to draw many visitors. Of particular interest is Brunel's SS *Great Britain,* the first steam-powered, propeller-driven iron ship, which made many voyages to America and Australia; it is now fully restored to its original condition and located at the site on which it was originally built, at Great Western Dock, Gas Ferry Road (open daily from 10 A.M. to 6 P.M. summer, from 10 A.M. to 5 P.M. winter; admission £1.70 for adults, 80 pence for children). We recommend you visit this maritime museum piece, also good for its view of Clifton Bridge, to gain a clear insight into Bristol's outstanding engineering achievements, both at sea and on land, through the centuries. The attractively refurbished waterfront in the heart of Bristol is a natural extension of the dockyards, and its stout iron fixtures, ancient cobbled streets, timber-framed buildings, and inland waterways dotted with small boats and tugs provide much atmosphere.

❦ Savor the surroundings by lingering in one of the many pubs and restaurants near the water's edge, particularly at night, when the reflected city lights give it a romantic air. Recommended is the rustic **Old Duke** pub in King St. for a lunchtime drink and live jazz every night of the week.

Nearby are the **St. Nicholas covered market** in St. Nicholas Street; **Theatre Royal** in King Street (0272-277466), the country's oldest continuous (since 1766) working theater; and **The Watershed,** One Cannon's Road (0272-276444), the country's premier provincial avant-garde arts establishment, which features seasons of films, satellite TV broadcasts, theater, and live music.

## City Sights
In the center of town, just behind the waterfront, the main attractions include the city's two principal churches, **Bristol Cathedral** and **St. Mary Redcliffe.** The cathedral, at College Green, dates from 1542 and includes earlier portions of the original St. Augustine's Abbey dating from 1140 and a magnificent stone vaulted hall designed by the great Victorian architect George Edmund Street in 1867. St. Mary Redcliffe, in Redcliffe Way, is known, in the words of Queen Elizabth I, as the "fairest, goodliest and most famous parish church in England"; it dates from the 14th century and has a magnificent 12th-century octagonal north porch, 292-feet spire, and one of the finest organs in the country.

Other attractions include the **City Museum and Art Gallery,** Queen's Road (0272-29971; open Monday through Saturday from 10 A.M. to 5 P.M.; free), with magnificent art collections, displays of archaeology, geology, and natural history, and outstanding collections of European ceramics and glass.

The **Bristol Industrial Museum,** Princes Wharf, tel. 0272-299771 (open Saturday through Wednesday from 10 A.M. to 1 P.M. and from 2 to 5 P.M.; free), has displays of local vehicles, Bristol aero-engines, and a mock-up of the Concorde cockpit.

For shopping in Bristol, there's the Broadmead center in the heart of town, attractive stores in Park Street and Queen's Road, and the small boutiques and antique shops of Clifton Village.

The **Bristol Zoo,** Clifton Down in Clifton (0272-738951; open Monday through Saturday from 9 A.M. to 6 P.M., Sunday from 10 A.M. to 6 P.M.; admission £3.20 for adults, £1.60 for children), is set in 12 acres of gardens and houses over one thousand exotic animals and many rare species, including tigers, apes, tropical birds, reptiles, and marine life. The **Mari-**

time **Heritage Center,** Wapping Wharf (0272-260680; open daily from 10 A.M. to 6 P.M.; free), illustrates the history of shipbuilding in Bristol since medieval times.

## Nearby Attractions

Recommended visits out of town include the quiet Victorian seaside town of **Clevedon,** south of Bristol, with Clevedon Court, a 14th-century fortified manor house containing the Eltonware pottery collection and a display of local Nailsea glass (0272-873180; open April through September, Wednesday, Thursday, Sunday from 2:30 to 5:30 P.M.; £1.70 for adults; 90 pence for children).

**Weston-super-Mare** is a popular seaside resort with two piers, seaside attractions and rides, and safe expansive beaches, although the tide retreats far out, exposing mud that releases an ozone said to make the air so healthy here.

## ❦ RESTAURANTS

Bristol has restaurants to suit all tastes, particularly up Park St. from the town center to Bristol University. **Wheeler's Fish Restaurant** (0272-221336) and the **Mauretania Brasserie** (0272-265148), both at 9 Park St., are recommended—the former serving special fish dishes in secluded, intimate surroundings (£9–15), the latter specializing in Continental cuisine in a wine bar setting (£5–8). Both accept all major credit cards. **Vincenzo's Italian Restaurant,** 71a Park St. (0272-260908), offers delicious pizzas, pastas, and grills (£5–8); MC, V; and the **Glass Boat Restaurant,** Welsh Back (0272-290704), is a superb, converted floating restaurant on the waterfront (£10–15). DC, MC, V.

# Bath

Bath is undoubtedly one of the most beautiful cities in Britain. For centuries, it has been a place of pilgrimage for the fashionable, artists, writers, and sightseers alike, to take the curative waters, admire the Georgian and neoclassical Palladian architecture or simply bask in the glory of the city's noble history. As the train from London approaches Bath Spa rail station (designed by Brunel) there is a particularly fine view of the town, with its graceful rows of staggered, terraced houses, seemingly white in the distance, but in fact built of the familiar local honey-colored Bath Stone, set against the rich green of the surrounding gentle hills. Once seen, the magic of Bath that everyone talks about has an instant effect. On close inspection, Bath is a beautifully proportioned city, with many fine buildings, cobbled streets, a superb abbey, glorious river frontage, and fine gardens. There has been considerable new development, too, with many smart boutiques and shops carefully blended in with the old so that the overall feeling of harmony and unity remains.

## Spa History

For thousands of years, the bubbling waters have gushed from this site at a constant temperature of 46.5 degrees Celsius and at a steady flow of two hundred sixty thousand gallons a day. Recent excavations have established occupation of the site by both Stone and Iron Age settlers. The Celts, who worshiped water—particularly springs, where they believed gods resided—believed the hot springs were sacred to Sulis, the Celtic word for *sun,* possibly referring to the heat of the water. When the Romans arrived in the first century, they build magnificent baths and temples around the hot springs and named the site Aquae Silus after the Celtic deity. They also brought their own goddess—Minerva—whose temple now lies under Stall Street. Bath flourished for four hundred years before the Roman empire collapsed and the site was abandoned. Under Saxon rule, Christian monks built new baths around the thermal springs and a great abbey nearby, where Edgar was crowned first king of all England in A.D. 973. Pillaging Norman barons subsequently destroyed much of the town before it was again rebuilt, and work started on a vast Benedictine cathedral priory, now the site of Bath Abbey. In medieval times, Bath was the center of a flourishing cloth trade. By the early 18th century, the spa town was again considered fashionable, and Beau Nash brought civilized life to the town through a carefully planned series of glittering social events. Cornishman Ralph Allen was then charged with restructuring the region's notorious postal service. The world's first postage stamp was mailed from Bath on May 2nd, 1840. The service became a huge success, a model for the rest of the country and hugely profitable for Allen, who bought stone quarries at nearby Claverton and Combe Down to supply the building of a new town. Yorkshireman John Wood, a classicist inspired by Bath's Roman past, drew up a new plan for the town, which was again to become a model for the rest of the country, and in particular designed Queen's Square and King's Circus. After his death, his son continued the grand design with the monumental Royal Crescent, considered to be one of the finest architectural achievements in Europe.

For a map of Bath, see atlas page 16.

## A Walking Tour of Bath

If you go first to the **Abbey Church Yard,** where you will find the tourist office; they can also arrange guided tours of the town.

Begin with the **Roman Baths and Museum** in nearby Stall Street (0225-461111; open daily from 9 A.M. to 5:30 P.M., £2.50 for adults, £1.25 for children), which have been fully restored, allowing the visitor to walk right down to the water's edge of the central bath. It is surrounded, around the balcony above, by classic Roman statue figures. The central bath was originally lined with over eight tons of lead mined from the nearby Mendip Hills, and the same lead has been identified in a similar Roman bath at Pompei. The tour of the museum takes you through the excavated remains of the original temples with their stone and mosaic floors, surviving decorative stonework, and to the fountainhead of the hot springs.

❧ Back at street level, the adjacent restored **Pump Room** is open all day for morning coffee, buffet lunch, and delicious afternoon cream teas in a superb, elegant Georgian setting with background piano music. You can even sample a glass of the purified spa water from the fountain.

Move on to view magnificent **Bath Abbey,** dating from 1500 and completed only last century, with flying buttresses and crocketed pinnacles outside, and fan vaulting inside by Robert and William Vertue, designers of the vaulting in the Henry VII Chapel at Westminster Abbey. Bath Abbey occupies the former site of a vast Benedictine cathedral priory that was never completed. Move round to the left of the abbey into Orange Grove, past the beautiful Parade Gardens on your right fronting the river Avon, and around to your left along Grand Parade, where there is a good view of the enchanting Pulteney Bridge, designed by Robert Adam, with its small shops, and onto Bridge Street. Looking right, down Argyle Street to the end of Great Pulteney Street, you will see the **Holburne of Menstrie Museum** (0225-66669; open February through December, Monday through Saturday from 11 A.M. to 5 P.M., Sunday from 2:30 to 6 P.M.; £1 for adults, 50 pence for children), which has good collections of Old Masters, English and Continental silver and porcelain, furniture and glass, and a craft study center. From Bridge Street, continue up Northgate, past New Bond Street on the left with its expensive boutiques, and bear left into Broad Street, where you will find, at No. 8, the **Bath Postal Museum** (0225-60333; open Monday through Saturday from 11 A.M. to 5 P.M., Sunday 2 to 5 P.M.; £1 for adults, 50 pence for children). The first letter was posted through from here, then Bath's main post office, on May 2, 1840. Displays and films tell the story of letter writing and mail carrying through the ages, and there are working postal machines and a life-size Victorian post office.

Walk back down Broad Street, turn right onto Green Street, and right at Milsom Street, where you will find the **National Centre of Photography** in the Octagon (0225-62841; open daily from 9:30 A.M. to 5:30 P.M.; £1.50 for adults, £1 for children), the oldest photographic society in the world, with four galleries showing major exhibitions, a fascinating museum of photographic history, workshops, a bookshop, and a restaurant. Continue up Milsom Street, across George Street, onto Bartlett Street, and across Alfred Street to the **Museum of Costume** in the Assembly Rooms in Bennett Street (0225-462111; open Monday through Saturday from 9:30 A.M. to 6 P.M., Sunday from 10 A.M. to 6 P.M.; £1.50 for adults, 95 pence for children), one of the largest museums of its kind covering the history of fashion from the late 16th century to the present day, with special sections on jewelry, millinery, underthings, baby clothes, royal and ceremonial dress, dolls and toys. There are also guided tours of the 18th-century Assembly Rooms designed by John Wood. From here, turn left into Bennett Street, and walk down to **The (King's) Circus** to view the splendid architecture, bearing right to walk up Brock Street to the Royal Crescent, where No. 1 is open to the public (0225-28126; open Tuesday through Saturday from 11 A.M. to 5 P.M., Sunday from 2 to 5 P.M.; £1.50 for adults, 80 pence for children) and has been fully restored and furnished in 18th-century fashion.

Below the crescent and to the right is the **Royal Victoria Park.** Retrace your steps from the Circus via Gay Street to see Queen Square along the way, and down Barton Street to the Theatre Royal in Saw Close (0225-65065), one of the most beautiful theaters in the country—recently restored and the focus of the annual Bath International Festival of the arts in late May/early June, probably the best time to visit Bath.

### Special Museum Stops

The **Museum of English Native Art** is at the Countess of Huntingdon Chapel, The Vineyard, Paragon (0225-446020; open Monday through Saturday from 11 A.M. to 6 P.M., Sunday from 2 to 6 P.M.; £1.50 for adults, 75 pence for children). We highly recommend this fascinating and amusing collection of work from the 18th and 19th centuries by itinerant and skilled artists depicting scenes from everyday life—livestock, country sports, and market towns—in a vanished England.

**The American Museum,** Claverton Manor, two miles south of Bath, near Claverton (0225-60503; open April through October, daily except Monday from 2 to 5 P.M.; £3 for adults, £2 for children). Founded in 1961 in a handsome 1820 manor, it offers a unique re-creation of American history and life. Sir Winston Churchill made his first political speech here in 1897. Eighteen authentically furnished rooms detail the changes in American homes between the 17th and 19th centuries, and there are displays of the American Indian, the Old West, American Folk Art, and a replica of George Washington's garden at Mount Vernon.

### Castle Combe

Castle Combe, 12 miles northwest of Bath off the A420, was voted the prettiest village in England.

Though it consists of no more than a collection of a few stone houses dominated by the the Manor House, a luxury hotel, it's well worth a visit just for its picturesque setting and a light lunch and drink at the **Castle Hotel.**

Nearby are Castle Combe Race Track, and Badminton, where the annual Badminton Horse Trials are held over three days in early May.

**Corsham Court,** near Corsham, off the A4 between Bath and Chippenham (0249-712214; open daily except Monday and Friday from 2 to 4 P.M., June through September from 2 to 6 P.M.), is a spectacular royal manor dating from Saxon times, rebuilt in 1582, and purchased by Paul Methuen in 1745. The house and park, principally the work of Capability Brown, John Nash, and Thomas Bellamy, are somewhat disappointing because of the limited access to the house, but there are magnificent state rooms, outstanding decorative work, furniture attributed to Chippendale, pictures by Van Dyke and Rubens, and superb gardens.

## ❦ RESTAURANTS

There are many choices when it comes to dining out, with the city's many restaurants, wine bars, cafés, and tearooms. The **Popjoys Restaurant,** next to the Theatre Royal, in Saw Close (0225-460494), is recommended for haute cuisine (dinner £19, lunch £14) and vintage wines in luxurious surroundings. MC, V. The **Beaujolais Restaurant,** Chapel Row (0225-23417), has superb nouvelle cuisine (£10–15) and fine wines in more intimate surroundings. MC, V. Try **The Wife of Bath,** 12 Pierrepont St. (0225-61745), for tasty bistro dishes (£5–8) and varied wines in a candlelit basement setting. MC, V. **The Canary tea shop and restaurant** in Queen St. is particularly recommended for light snacks and delicious scented specialty teas in genteel surroundings.

## Somerset County

The most tranquil county in the region, Somerset is dense, flat, and fertile farming country. But it is also rich in legends as the birthplace of Christianity in Britain and the land of King Arthur. Most of its attractions lie to the north and west and so make the ideal motor trips from Bath.

### Cheddar Gorge

Best approached from Bristol via the A38, or via the A39/A368 from Bath, the town of Cheddar has been a center for cheese making since 1170, although little is made here today. You can view the dairy process in the village at the **Cheddar Cheese Museum** (0934-742810; open Easter through November, daily from 11 A.M. to 5 P.M.; 50 pence for adults, 25 pence for children). The real attraction here is the spectacular limestone gorge, which runs from the village to the top of the Mendip Hills. **Gough's and Cox's caves** (0934-742343; open daily from 10 A.M. to 5:50 P.M.; £2.95 for adults, £1.60 for children), considered to be among the most impressive caverns in the world, are richly decorated by stalactites and stalagmites, and display inside the remains of prehistoric man dating back twelve thousand years. If you have time, climb the 322 steps of Jacob's Ladder from the foot of the gorge to the plateau above, or drive slowly up the steep ravine, to admire the breathtaking scenery and views. Be warned, though: the gorge is extremely crowded in season.

## Wells

England's smallest city is a charming ancient market town dominated by its magnificent Gothic **cathedral.** Wells was occupied by the Romans, but it was the West Saxon King Ine who built the first church near its wells in nearby Bishop's Palace, which give the city its name. The cathedral and the palace were originally separated by a road, which now serves as a marketplace, the center of town, and where any tour should begin. The outstanding cathedral has many features of special interest—its 150-foot west front supporting nearly three hundred statues, the scissor-arched nave designed to counteract subsidence, and a six-hundred-year-old astronomical clock. The seven-hundred-year-old adjoining fortified and moated **Bishop's Palace** was destroyed by Reform Act rioters in the 19th century. Also adjoining the cathedral is the 14th-century Vicars' Close, Europe's oldest complete street, a fine example of classic English set-piece architecture. Close by, the charming **Wells Museum** in Cathedral Green (0749-73477; open daily Easter through October, Monday through Saturday from 10 A.M. to 5:30 P.M., Sundays from 11; October to Easter, Wednesday through Sunday from 11 A.M. to 4 P.M.; 50 pence for adults, 10 pence for children) has displays on the archeology of the Mendip Hills, local history, and a collection of one hundred needlework samplers. The town's many old coaching inns down High Street retain their original character and continue to make this an inviting overnight stop for today's traveler. Many offer attractive set-course meals, lunchtime bars, and afternoon teas.

A walk farther down High St. into Broad St. and Priory Rd., past many of the town's bustling shops, will take you to **The Good Earth,** an excellent whole-food restaurant for delicious meals, snacks, and teas.

Two miles from Wells are the popular **Wookey Hole Caves** (0749-72243; open daily from 9:30 A.M. to 5:30 P.M.; £3.35 for adults, £2.25 for children), a group of subterranean fissures and caverns; nearby is a paper mill and collection of ghoulish exhibits by Madame Tussaud.

## Glastonbury

The legendary birthplace of Christianity in Britain and the focus of fabled King Arthur (see box in "Cornwall" section, below) combine to make this a place of special interest. The town itself, approached on the A39 from Wells, is a simple affair, namely a bisected High Street; the real attractions are the ruined **Glastonbury Abbey** and nearby **Glastonbury Tor,** soaring to over 500 feet, its medieval church tower a symbolic landmark for some distance around. There is also the **Somerset Rural Life Museum** at Abbey Barn, Bere Lane (0458-32903; open Monday through Friday from 10 A.M. to 5 P.M., Saturday and Sunday from 2 to 6 P.M.; 70 pence for adults, 20 pence for children), a fully restored Cotswold stone barn housing a fascinating history of local rural life, willow growing, peat digging, and cider making.

Glastonbury is thought to have been originally an island or peninsula rising from a vast inland lake, known as the Isle of Avalon. It is said that in about A.D. 30, Joseph of Arimathaea brought the Holy Grail, reputedly the chalice used by Christ at the Last Supper, to Glastonbury, where, upon driving his staff into the ground on the hill, it took root and grew into what is now known as the Glastonbury Thorn. Taking this to mean that his wanderings were over, Joseph is said to have buried the chalice on the nearby Chalice Hill beneath a natural spring, now called Chalice Well, which then flowed red. He also built a wattle and daub church on the site of today's ruined abbey. The injured King Arthur, mortally wounded at the Battle of Camlann, is said to have been buried together with his queen, Guinevere, in the abbey grounds; the spot is now marked by a plaque. Glastonbury's importance as the center of Christianity led to reconstruction of the abbey from about A.D. 943 until it was destroyed by a fire in 1184. Reconstruction started almost immediately but was not completed until 1524. Its unhappy demise in 1539, with the Dissolution of the monasteries, saw it ruined again, its stone scavengered for local houses and roads, and the last abbot, Richard Whiting, put to death on the Tor.

The spread of the church throughout Somerset, typified by the addition of tiered towers with pinnacles, marked a considerable phase of rebuilding between the 13th and 16th centuries. Fine examples include **St. John's Church** in Glastonbury and the beacon of **St. Mary Magdalene** in Taunton, the county town.

As you travel farther south through what is largely rural Somerset, the landscape is dominated by the drained wetlands—or Somerset Levels, as they are known—which make this a rich farming region.

## Taunton

Originally a Saxon town, Taunton was an important and prosperous cloth center lying at the heart of a huge estate owned by the bishops of Winchester. Its castle keep dates from 1138, and later additions included halls, chambers, and kitchens. In 1873, the Somerset Archaelogy and Natural History Society bought the castle as a home for its museum and library. Today it is the home of the **Somerset County Museum** and the **Military Museum of the Somerset Light Infantry** (0823-255504; open Monday through Saturday from 10 A.M. to 5 P.M., 70 pence for adults, 20 pence for children), featuring displays of ceramics, pottery, local history, a doll emporium, and military exhibitions. Taunton was besieged three times during the civil war and was also the focus of the Pitchfork Rebellion, when the ill-fated Duke of Monmouth, the illegitimate son of Charles II, returned to England four months after his father's death. After landing at Lyme Regis he marched to Taunton to gather his many supporters there. He was proclaimed king before marching on to his defeat in a massacre near Bridgwater at the Battle of Sedgemore in 1685. Monmouth was caught two days later and executed on Tower Hill. The battle was followed by the Bloody Assizes conducted by Judge Jeffreys, which saw 144 rebels in Taunton condemned to hang and hundreds more banished to the West Indies, Taunton today maintains its importance as the county town, but it is very commercial. Its attractions include the ancient street of shops in **Bath Place** and **St. Mary Magdalen's Church,** with its 190-foot tower.

The outstanding wisteria-draped **Castle Hotel** offers excellent cuisine (lunch £9.50, dinner £19.90). Visit the elegant **Victorian Tea Room** in the County Hotel for delicious snacks and cream teas.

The surrounding area, known as Taunton Deane or the Vale of Taunton, is pleasant touring country with attractive towns, including Bishop's Lydeard, Combe Florey, Milverton, and Wellington—a landmark for miles around with its 175-foot obelisk dedicated to the Duke of Wellington. Farther afield, Exmoor on the north Somerset coast is a popular attraction for its varied scenery and tiny villages. To the west lies **King Arthur's Camelot** at South Cadbury; and **Montacute House** in Montacute Village (0935-823289; open April through October, Wednesday through Monday from 12:30 to 5:30 P.M.; £2.80), one of the finest Tudor mansions in the country, with extensive Jacobean gardens, built in 1597 by Speaker of the House and Master of the Rolls Sir Edward Phelips. Fully restored by the National Trust, the rooms are gems of antiquity, while the top floor Long Galley, the longest in existence at 172 feet, has a fascinating collection of ninety pictures of Tudor and Jacobean kings and queens on loan from the National Portrait Gallery.

# Cornwall

The mere mention of Cornwall conjures up the boom of the Atlantic, towering cliffs, fishing communities, smuggling, tin miners, desolate moorland, Celtic folklore, and the legend of King Arthur. The perfect end to a holiday must be a few days spent roaming leisurely along Cornwall's majestic coastline— if you really want to relax, why not skip the rest of the region altogether and come straight here? Cornwall makes you want to write "Decided to stay—forever!" on your postcard home. The reason is evident: much of the Cornish coast has been designated an area of outstanding natural beauty and is protected by the National Trust. But there is also an irresistible sense of mystery to Cornwall. Its stunning beauty almost begs a question, but whatever it is, the answer is sure to lie lost in the mists of time. For the uninitiated, the effect will be swift, dramatic, and memorable. The north coast is particularly spectacular, and we suggest you start here, with the occasional foray inland to Bodmin Moor and the heart of the tin-mining industry. The south coast is warmer and more sheltered, but it is also more commercial.

## The North Coast

From Bude to Land's End, the north Cornish coast is one of the wonders of Britain, the meeting point of land, sea, and air with epic results. Bude has been described as the "Bondi of Britain" by Australians because of its superb surfing at Summerleaze and Crooklets beaches. The small town overlooks a wide bay of firm golden sand flanked by cliffs and protected by a breakwater. Nearby is Bude Castle, built in 1830 on a concrete raft to resist the shifting sands and today housing council offices. More sandy beaches can be found at Sandy Mouth to the north and Widemouth Sand to the south.

### Bude

Bude's popularity as a seaside resort dates from Victorian times, when it was notorious for wreckers who plundered more than eighty ships between 1824 and 1874. Its importance as a port rose with the building of the Bude Canal in 1823 that linked the town with Launceston 35 miles inland. A remarkable feat of engineering, the canal has only one sealock, at Breakwater, although the canal rises 350 feet. The change in levels was achieved by a series of inclined ramps up which wheeled tugboats were pulled on rails.

❧ The imposing **Falcon Hotel** overlooking the canal in Bude offers a mouthwatering range of inexpensive international dishes
(£1–7).

## Launceston
You can reach Launceston via the Launceston Steam Railway
(for details call 0288-5665). Well worth a visit for its antiquity,
the former county town offers excellent views of Bodmin
Moor from the tower of the former assize court and jail at
**Launceston Castle** (open March through October, Monday
through Saturday from 9:30 A.M. to 6:30 P.M., Sunday from
2 to 6:30 P.M., winter close 4 P.M.; £1 for adults, 50 pence
for children). A fascinating history of the town can be found
at the **Local History Museum** (0566-2833; open April
through September, Monday through Friday from 10:30 A.M.
to 12:30 P.M., 2:30 to 4:30 P.M.; free).

## Boscastle
Continuing farther down the coast is an absolute must. The
tiny stone harbor of Boscastle, formed by a natural twist in
the cliffs, is a perfect seaside retreat and a spectacular setting
in a gale.

❧ A superb spot for lunch or an overnight stop, the rustic stone
**Wellington Hotel** (0840 5203) overlooking the jetty offers
pleasant modern accommodations at give-away prices (from
£19 per person), an à la carte menu (£8–12), and good wines.
Also recommended is the creative home cooking at **The Old
Mill Restaurant** (£7–10), or try the 16th-century stone-roofed
**Valency House Hotel** for light lunches and delicious cream
teas in the garden by the stream.

Thomas Hardy restored the village church here while working
as an architect. Nearby is an extensive gory exhibition of the
history of witch-hunting at **The Witches House** (open Easter through October, daily from 10 A.M. to 6 P.M.; 75 pence
for adults, 45 pence for children).

## King Arthur's Castle
And so to Tintagel, undoubtedly the showpiece of Cornwall.
**Tintagel Castle** (0840-770328; open March through October, daily from 9:30 A.M. to 6:30 P.M.; winter close 4 P.M.;
£1.25 for adults, 50 pence for children), the legendary birthplace of King Arthur, is a jagged ruin in a truly romantic setting astride spectacular cliffs. Approached from the village
bookshop along a broad path, it is divided into two distinct
parts—the mainland area and the island site. They were originally connected by a natural bridge, but it collapsed, leaving
a chasm later spanned by a drawbridge that made the castle
impenetrable when raised. Today it is linked by a flight of one
hundred steps. Below is **Merlin's Cave,** reached by stair-
way, and at low tide you can walk right through the cave to

the rock-strewn beach on the other side of the causeway to view the waterfall cascading over the cliff. Back on the cliff-top, there are many tearooms and restaurants offering refreshment, and nearby the fascinating story of King Arthur depicted in stained glass at **King Arthur's Hall** (0840-770526; open April through October from 10:30 A.M. to 5:30 P.M.; £1 for adults, 50 pence for children). Opposite is the fully restored 14th-century stone **Tintagel Old Post Office** (0840-770256; open April through October from 11 A.M. to 6 P.M.; 90 pence), formerly the main post office for the district. There are small beaches below Tintagel Head and south of the island.

## Bodmin and Beyond

The 150 square mile **Bodmin Moor** is a granite mass rising to over one thousand three hundred feet at Brown Willy and Rough Tor to the north of the A30. At Bolventor, near the center of the moor, you will find **Jamaica Inn,** famous as the setting for Daphne du Maurier's novel of the same name, and from here you can walk to the tors for spectacular views, and to **Dozmary Pool,** believed to be the site where King Arthur received Excalibur. The ancient town of Bodmin still claims to be the county town after the transfer of the assize court from Launceston (which lost it to Truro for refusing to allow the Great Western Railway through). At **Camelford,** you will find a comprehensive collection of implements used in Cornish industries, at the **North Cornwall Museum of Rural Life** (0840-212954; open April through September, Monday through Saturday from 10:30 A.M. to 5 P.M.; 50 pence).

From Bodmin, the river Camel flows down to Wadebridge, where the annual Royal Cornwall Show is held in June, and on to the charming fishing port of Padstow.

Surrounded by three quays, the enchanting stone harbor is an ideal spot for lunch. You can sample local seafood at **The Skipper's Restaurant;** also try **The Fo'c's'le** for cream teas and **The Chough** for delicious Cornish ice cream.

Farther south is **Newquay,** Cornwall's biggest coastal resort, once famous for its pilchard catch and its old harbor at **Sandy Haven,** with large sheltered beaches and good surfing, but very crowded in summer. Quieter beaches to the south are the sheltered **Porth Joke cove** and **Holywell Bay dunes.** At **St. Agnes Head** you can see for miles along the coast. The local tin mine was once the county's biggest producer, but the real heart of the industry lies inland around **Camborne and Redruth,** littered with the gaunt ruins of over three hundred chimney stacks, engine-pumping stations, and pitheads. Tin is still mined here today. The phrase "Nineteen

## King Arthur

The fables surrounding King Arthur, his Queen Guinevere, Camelot, Sir Lancelot, and the knights of the Round Table have long held a special place in English history. However, much of the Dark Ages—the two centuries between the Roman retreat in about A.D. 410 and the settlement of the Saxons—remains shrouded in mystery.

Legend recalls that King Arthur was born at Tintagel Castle on the north Cornwall coast, the illegitimate son of Uther Pendragon and Ygerne, wife of Gorlois, duke of Cornwall. Merlin the Magician is said to have enabled Uther, who was obsessed with the beautiful Ygerne, to take on the likeness of Gorlois, enter his castle at Tintagel, and seduce her. He then killed Gorlois and married Ygerne. When Arthur was born, he was given into the care of Merlin until he was age 15. He was proclaimed king after withdrawing the sword embedded in stone. Arthur the warrior is said to have defeated the English in 12 battles, culminating in the great Battle of Badon Hill in about A.D. 490. Although Badon Hill has never been found, it is thought likely to be Lymington Castle near Swindon, or Badbury Rings in Dorset. During battle, Arthur had broken the sword drawn from the stone, and Merlin took him to a lake, believed to be Dozmary Pool on Bodmin Moor, where Arthur was given the magical sword Excalibur by the Lady in the Lake. Arthur's downfall was apparently cast when he seduced Morgause, the wife of Loth of Lothian who was sent to make peace with Arthur. She was one of three daughters born to Ygerne and Gorlois—and therefore Arthur's half sister. The boy born—Mordred—would destroy the kingdom, Merlin predicted.

The kingdom of Camelot is widely believed to be the site of a Neolithic hill fort previously occupied by the Romans, Saxons, and Danes at South Cadbury on the Somerset/Dorset border and now nothing more than a huge earthwork (free access at any reasonable time). The Round Table (which can be seen in Winchester) was a wedding present from Guinevere to Arthur, and the exploits of its knights, and their quest for the Holy Grail, are legendary. After Sir Lancelot and Guinevere's love affair was discovered, they fled to France, pursued by Arthur. In the king's absence, Mordred raised an army and seized the crown, and upon Arthur's return, they met at the Battle of Camlann, believed to be on the banks of the River Camel on Bodmin Moor. Mordred delivered a fatal blow to Arthur before being slain by his father. Dying, Arthur ordered that Excalibur be returned to the lake, where a ghostly arm rose from the water, caught it, and vanished. Arthur then sailed for the Isle of Avalon—believed to be Glastonbury—where he was joined by Guinevere, and where they died and were buried.

to the Dozen" comes from the pumping engine's rate of work with a beam engine lifting nineteen thousand gallons of water from the mine for every 12 bushels of coal burned. You can make the underground journey yourself at the reopened **Poldark Mine** to the south near Wendron (0326-573173; open

Easter through October from 10 A.M. to 5 P.M.; £3.20 for adults, £1.90 for children). To the north, **Truro Cathedral** with its three distinctive towers dates from 1850, the time when it began to expand with the arrival of the railway and the transfer from Bodmin of the county offices, library, and museum (0872-72205; open Monday through Saturday from 9 A.M. to 5 P.M.; 50 pence for adults, 25 pence for children).

### . . . To Land's End

South from **Newquay** is a particularly fine stretch of coast with cliff views of the savage breakers down to the secluded **Basset's Cove** and the former port and surfer's beach at Portreath. Across Godrevy Point is **St. Ives,** one of the most beautiful north coast resorts, with superb crescent beaches at **Porthmeor** for surfers, and Portgwidden and **Porthminster** for children. Between Porthmeor beach and the attractive stone harbor is the old town, with an astonishing jumble of tiny streets packed with a crooked array of colorful shops and houses.

Here you will find the basement **Bistro Sauvage** in Fore St.— for seafood and continental cuisine (£7–10).

Worth a visit to see the sculpture of one of the many artists to patronize St. Ives is the **Barbara Hepworth Museum** (0736-796226; open Monday through Saturday from 10 A.M. to 6:30 P.M.; Sunday from 2 to 6 P.M. 50 pence). Not unexpectedly, St. Ives is very popular in summer, when you will be asked to leave your car in the parking lot at the top of the town and take the bus down. The legend of the mermaid enchanted by the singing of a local chorister who then vanished into the sea will take you to the tiny nearby village of **Zennor,** perched precariously three hundred feet above the waves. In the area are a number of the eerie, isolated massive raised stone grave shelters peculiar to Penwith—at Zennor Quoit, Chysauster, and Lanyon Quoit—dating from around 2500 B.C. This hard granite peninsula in the toe of Cornwall marked the end of the known world five hundred years ago. Cape Cornwall, reached by road and on foot from St. Just, is identified by its soaring mine chimney, which provides panoramic views, and its contemplative isolation. It is a welcome alternative to **Land's End** just five miles away and the most westerly tip of Cornwell, which has been spoiled by massive commercial development.

Between the two is seven hundred-year-old **First and Last Inn in England** (depending on which way you are traveling), one of three pubs in the area bearing the same name, although this claims to be the oldest; it's famous for its smuggling connections. But the last stop should be saved for a visit to nearby Sennen Cove. Its sweeping crescent of bleached sand is the perfect spot to relax, enjoy a pub lunch at **The Old Success Inn** over-looking the bay, or just watch the sun go down.

## The South Coast

Across the point from Land's End is the **Minack Theatre** at Porthcurno (0736-810471; open May through September Monday through Friday 8 P.M. evenings, 2 P.M. matinee Wednesday and Friday only; £3 for adults, £1.50 for children), an open-air amphitheater, terraced into the side of the cliffs, featuring a variety of opera, musicals, and drama. Inland on the road to Mousehole and Penzance, the squat and tall standing stones are the Merry Maidens to the south, turned to stone for dancing to the tune of the Pipers to the north. Mousehole lives up to its name as a cute cluster of fishermen's cottages round a small stone harbor where The Lobster Pot does a brisk trade in local seafood.

### Penzance and the Isles of Scilly

At the heart of the "Cornish Riviera" is Penzance, once a major port that now serves as a pleasure craft center and harbor for ferry services operated by the Isles of Scilly Steamship Co. (0736-62009). You can also fly to the Islands from the Heliport with British International Helicopters Ltd. (0736-63871).

Separating a low stone cliff to the west and a wide stretch of sandy beach to the north, the seafront is somewhat restricted by the quay. Behind it are the principal shopping areas in Market Jew and Chapel streets, while other flower-filled streets create a Continental atmosphere.

The timbered 15th-century **Admiral Benbow,** a favorite haunt of smugglers, is the perfect drinking spot.

A treasure trove of sea relics can be found at **the Museum of Nautical Art** (0736-68890; open April through October, Monday through Saturday from 10 A.M. to 5 P.M.; 90 pence), and exhibitions of local history at **The Local Museum** (0736-36125; open Monday through Saturday from 10:30 A.M. to 4:30 P.M.; free). The main attraction along the beach is the island stronghold across the bay at **St. Michael's Mount** (0736-710507; open Monday through Friday from 10:30 A.M. to 4:45 P.M.; £2.30 for adults, £1.15 for children). Originally the site of a Benedictine chapel established by Edward the Confessor, this outstanding castle dates from the 14th century. Access is via a causeway at low tide, or by boat, from the beach at Marazion. Formerly the Roman island of Ictis, St. Michael's Mount was the European center of the tin trade in 4000 B.C.

## Smugglers Coast

The pattern of infinitely varied small coastal villages continues around **Lizard Point,** the most southerly tip of England, where Cornwall's first lighthouse was built in 1619. This treacherous coastline has long been plied by smugglers, particularly near the offshore underwater rocks at the Manacles, which have claimed thousands of lives. The peninsula is renowned for its beautiful serpentine stoneware, favored by Queen Victoria, which can be bought in Lizard village. The Helford River is a favorite for small pleasure boats and safe-sheltered bathing, and in Gweek at the mouth of the estuary, you can enjoy the antics of the occupants rescued by the **Seal Sanctuary** (0326-22361; open daily from 9:30 A.M. to 6:30 P.M.; seals are fed 11 A.M. and 4 P.M.; £2.80 for adults, £1.40 for children ). Falmouth offers a very picturesque harbor with attractive shops behind it in Church Street.

Enjoy a drink in the **Old Kings Head** pub, and delicious pastries and snacks at the **Wynn's Coffee Shop.** Or try **Bon Ton Roulet** for varied Continental and vegetarian dishes (£3–5).

The Carrick Roads estuary is protected by the formidable defenses at **Pendennis Castle** (0326-316594; open March through October, daily from 9:30 A.M. to 6:30 P.M., Sunday from 2 to 6:30 P.M.; £1 adults, 50 pence children) and across the bay, at **St. Mawes Castle** (0326-270526; open March through October, daily from 9:30 A.M. to 6:30 P.M.; 75 pence for adults, 35 pence for children). More attractive fishing villages extend to the real attraction of the "Cornish Riviera," **St. Austell,** a rich seaside town that has prospered through local clay mining, the world's biggest supplier—at three million tons annually—for the potteries as well as for the chemical, paper, and medical industries. The favorite local bathing spots include **Carlyon Bay** to the east and **Mevagissey Bay** to the south. Farther east, **Fowey** shares the busy coastal traffic in clay exports with pleasure craft and is an enchanting town to explore.

# Exeter and the English Riviera

Superb beaches, stunning scenery, a great cathedral town, picture-postcard villages, a rich maritime history—the county of Devon has much to attract the millions who flock here each summer. Be warned—the "English Riviera" seaside resorts of Torquay, Paignton, and Brixham around Torbay on the east coast are particularly popular and crowded in season.

Alternatively, the granite mass of Dartmoor at the heart of the county is a breathtaking contrast of isolation and beauty. The cathedral in the county town of Exeter is one of the finest

## The English Riviera

So called because its subtropical flora and palm trees resemble its French counterpart, this twenty-mile stretch of coastline offers no less than 18 superb beaches centered around the commercial resort of Torquay, the family holiday town of Paignton, and the quaint port of Brixham—collectively known as Torbay. It was here at Kent's Cavern in Torquay that was found the earliest evidence of man twenty-five thousand years old, in Britain. It was also the closest Napoléon got to England, aboard a ship anchored offshore following his first period of exile on the island of Elba; during his brief stay in the bay he was told he was being sent to St. Helena. Paignton Sands, Broadsands, and Torre Abbey Sands are safe beaches for children; Oddicombe and Redgate beaches are the cleanest; Elberry Cove is popular with skiers, and if you are feeling really adventurous, Petit Tor beach is for nudists! Brixham is the most attractive town, with its old buildings and narrow cobbled streets running down steeply to the ancient fishing port where William of Orange landed in 1668 and seized the British crown. Here you will find a full-size replica of the *Golden Hinde,* the surprisingly small ship in which Sir Francis Drake made his three-year circumnavigation of the world in 1577. Torquay offers superb shopping facilities, particularly in the Pavilion on the quay, where you can enjoy light refreshments on the terrace of the Continental-style Boulevard café-bar-restaurant. For a unique experience, try the horse-drawn open carriage ride to the thatched-cottage village of Cockington on the outskirts of Torquay for a drink or lunch at the Drum Inn before returning to the seafront.

in the country, although the town suffered in the last war. Similarly, Plymouth was badly bombed and completely rebuilt, but it is also the country's most historic port through the voyages of Drake, Raleigh, Cook, the Pilgrim Fathers, and the Falklands War. Essentially, though, Devon remains that green and pleasant land of flora and fauna, rich farming valleys, idyllic stone thatch cottages, cider, and, of course, clotted cream teas!

# Exeter

Strategically placed at the mouth of the river Exe, Exeter is the former Roman stronghold of Isca Dumnoniorum, its walls still visible today. Since then, Exeter has been embattled by the Danes, the Normans, and during the War of the Roses and the Monmouth Rebellion. The present cathedral, with its distinctive twin Norman towers, began as a Saxon abbey and further evolved between 1100 and 1400 with the building of the spectacular three hundred feet rib-vaulted nave decorated with carved colorful bosses. Nearby is the ancient Ship Inn in St. Martin's Lane, and Mol's Coffee House in Cathedral

Close, favorite haunts of Drake. Exeter also boasts Britain's oldest municipal building, the **Guildhall** in High Street, dating from 1160, still in regular use for council meetings and functions. Exeter Heritage Tours of the town can be arranged by calling (0392) 265212. Principal attractions include the Quay, where you will find the largest collection of ships in the world, from a dugout canoe to a Chinese junk, at **Exeter Maritime Museum,** the Haven (0392-436031; open daily from 10 A.M. to 6 P.M.; £2.80 for adults, £1.50 for children), and the **Royal Albert Memorial Museum and Art Gallery** in Queen Street (0392-265858; open Tuesday through Saturday from 10 A.M. to 5:30 P.M.; free), with exhibitions of local history, collections of Exeter silver, porcelain, and glass, and ethnographic displays of the Eskimo and North American Indian.

Nearby, to the east of **Exeter,** can be found the beautiful two-mile sandy beach of **Exmouth; Budleigh Salterton,** famous for its fresh scallops; **Axminster,** the famous carpet-weaving town; and the perfect Saxon stone thatched village of **Colyton.**

To the north are **Bickleigh,** another delightful village with a mill craft center and farms; **Honiton,** a household name for lace and pottery; and the famous wool town of **Tiverton.**

To the south lies **Dawlish,** delightfully set around Dawlish Water with its series of weirs, and the extensive pleasure boat harbor of Teignmouth—both skirted along the red sandstone cliffs common to this coastline by Brunel's Great Western Railway, a considerable engineering feat.

### Dartmouth

Across the scenic river Dart estuary from Brixham the town is famous for its naval college and for **Dartmouth Castle** built in 1481, the first to fire cannon and one of the great maritime defenses on Britain's south coast (08043-3588; open March through October, Monday through Saturday from 9:30 A.M. to 6:30 P.M., Sunday 2 to 6 P.M.; other times til 4 P.M.; 75 pence for adults, 35 pence for children). At the mouth of the Dart is Totnes, stony, hilly, and sporty with its mega-collection of vintage cars at the **Motor Museum** (0803-862777; open Easter through October from 10 A.M. to 5:30 P.M.; £2.25 for adults, £1.50 for children). Cool off at the near-by superb **Blackpool Sands beach.** Fifteen miles south, Salcombe, the southern most point of Devon, nestled on the Kingsbridge estuary, is a yacht haven and quite beautiful. Thousands of Americans sailed from here on D-day.

# Around Bournemouth

Dorset has something for everyone—fine beaches, rich coastal history, great scenery, Roman remains, ancient castles, chalk hill figures, magnificent country houses, delightful villages, and literary acclaim as the heart of Thomas Hardy's Wessex.

## Bournemouth

A popular south coast seaside resort, Bournemouth makes an ideal base from which to explore Dorset's attractions, which lie mainly to the west along the coast and in the beautiful hinterland behind it.

Bournemouth itself began as a fashionable resort in the mid-1800s, a new town started by the retired Captain Lewis Tregonwell, who used to patrol the coastline here. He built a holiday mansion estate known as Tregonwell's Bourne, which was leased out in the family's absence to people wanting to enjoy the new popularity in spa centers and the seaside. The development of the town and seafront flourished with the arrival of the railway. Its miles of safe, sandy beaches are still its greatest asset, while the town offers extensive shopping facilities and entertainment. The beautiful Winter Gardens, the Pavilion, and the Pier separating East and West Cliff beaches are the focus of the town. Bookings for a variety of musical and theater performances can be made by calling the **Winter Gardens Theater,** Exeter Road, at (0202) 290-765; the **Pavilion Theatre,** Westover Road, at (0202) 297-297; the **Pier Theatre,** Bournemouth Pier, at (0202) 764-500, and the nearby modern **Bournemouth International Center,** Exeter Road, at (0202) 22-122. There are hundreds of hotels with numerous restaurants which compete heavily for diners—the choice is yours.

Popular annual events include the July flower festival, the regatta and carnival at the end of July, the August folk dance festival, and the powerboat festival at the end of September.

Attractions in town include the **Russell-Cotes Art Gallery and Museum,** East Cliff (0202-21009; open Monday through Saturday from 10 A.M. to 5 P.M.; 50 pence for adults, 10 pence for children), with its wide range of 17th- to-20th-century oil paintings and watercolors, Japanese and Italian art, sculpture, ceramics, furniture, keyboard instruments, an armory, theatrical relics, a Maori room, marine collection, and shipwreck finds. The **Shelley Museum,** Beachwood Avenue, Boscombe (0202-303571; open Monday through Saturday from 10:30 A.M. to 5 P.M.; 20 pence for adults, 10 pence for children), is the only museum in the world devoted to the poet Shelley, and includes a Romantic period reference library. The **Bournemouth Transport Museum,** Mallard Road Bus Depot, Castle Lane (0202-21009; open Wednesday only from 10 A.M. to 3:30 P.M.; 50 pence for adults, 10 pence for children), houses restored tramcars, trolleybuses, and historic diesel buses.

# Poole

Just three miles to the west is Poole, inextricably linked with Bournemouth and an ideal complement, being one of the largest natural harbors in the world. Superb bathing can be found at nearby **Sandbanks** and on the wildlife sanctuary within the harbor, **Brownsea Island** (0202-707744; open April through October, daily from 10 A.M. to 8 P.M.; £1). Contact Harveys Pleasure Boats at Fish Shambles Steps on Poole Quay (0202-666226) for details of harbor cruises. The attractive quayside is a haven for pleasure craft and, together with the old town, the focus of the better pubs and restaurants. Behind it is the modern, commercial Arndale shopping center. Poole is the perfect destination for a day's outing, lunchtime drink, or evening meal.

There are many pubs along the quay. Recommended restaurants in nearby High St. include the **Topogigio Italian Restaurant** for delicious seafood, pasta, and grills (£7–10), and **Scalpens Restaurant** for seafood and specialty dishes (£5–10).

The efficient tourist office on the quay is a useful source of local information. Three nearby museums charting the history of seafaring Poole and the development of the town include the **Guildhall Museum** in Market Street, the **Maritime Museum** and **Scalpen's Court Museum** on High Street (all inquiries at 0202-675-151, ext. 3550; all three are open Monday through Saturday from 10 A.M. to 5 P.M., Sunday from 2 to 5 P.M.; 50 pence for adults, 25 pence for children).

Another popular attraction is nearby **Compton Acres,** Canford Cliffs Road, near Sandbanks (0202-700778; open April through October from 10:30 A.M. to 6:30 P.M., £2.20 for adults, 95 pence for children), an exotic collection of set-piece gardens of the world, including Japanese, Italian, and Roman.

Ten miles west across the bay are the impressive ruins of **Corfe Castle** (0929-480921; open March through October, daily from 10 A.M. to 5:30 P.M., £1.50 for adults, 75 pence for children), which dominates the skyline and offers good views. The **Blue Pool** at Furzebrook (0929-551408; open year-round except December, daily from 9 A.M. to 7 P.M.; £1 for adults, 50 pence for children) is a famous spot for its water-filled clay quarry, which is often bluer than the sky overhead. There also are **Wareham,** a pleasant old town that has suffered more than its fair share of destruction and disastrous fires through the ages, now at last at peace; **Lulworth Cove,** a beautiful secluded sheltered beach on the coast, scene of Troy's suicide swim in Hardy's *Far From the Madding Crowd;* and **Swanage,** the famous quarry town and harbor that supplied the stone to rebuild much of Victorian

London, now a popular yachting achorage with a good sandy beach for bathers.

To the north lies the ancient **Wimborne Minster,** dating from 1043. Nearby is **Kingston Lacy** (0202-883402, open March through October, Saturday through Wednesday, house from 1 to 4:30 P.M., park from 12 to 6 P.M., £3.50 for adults, £1.75 for children), a magnificent Renaissance palazzo built by the son of Sir John Bankes to replace Corfe Castle, which was ruined in 1646 during the civil war; it is filled with an outstanding collection of master paintings, furniture, and antiques, and is surrounded by 250 acres of wooded park. **Milton Abbas,** a picturesque model 18th-century hamlet, may rival Castle Combe, near Bath, as the prettiest village in England. **Blandford Forum** is another attractive Georgian village, rebuilt within thirty years after being destroyed by fire in 1731. Nearby is the **Royal Signals Museum** at Blandford Camp (0258-52581; open Monday through Friday from 8:30 A.M. to 5 P.M., Saturday through Sunday from 10 A.M. to 4 P.M.; weekends only in Summer; free), a fascinating history of telecommunications from the days of Morse code.

**Shaftesbury,** on the border with Wiltshire, is one of the most photographed hilltop views in Britain; its steep, cobbled, cottage-lined Gold Hill frequently appears in television commercials as the epitome of the classic English village—the place with "nowt takin owt."

## West of Bournemouth

Traveling west from Bournemouth is to head for Hardy country, around Dorchester. Attractions along the way include the **Tank Museum,** Bovington Camp (0929-463953; open daily from 10 A.M. to 5 P.M.; £2 for adults, £1 for children), one of the world's largest collections of fighting vehicles, with over two hundred exhibits.

T.E. Lawrence (Lawrence of Arabia) bought the idiosyncratic cottage **Clouds Hill,** near Wareham (April through September, Wednesday, Thursday, Friday, Sunday from 2 to 5 P.M.; October through March, Sunday only from 1 to 4 P.M.; £1). He lived in it until his untimely death in a motorcycle accident in 1935, and it contains his personal possessions from when he joined the RAF in 1925.

**Athelhampton,** near Puddletown (030584-8363; open March through October, Wednesday, Thursday, Sunday, also Monday and Tuesday in August, from 2 to 6 P.M.; house £1.25, garden £1, children free), is an exceptional example of Gothic architecture (built in 1485), with a fine furniture collection and outstanding individual gardens.

Continuing toward Dorchester, you may also want to take in **St. John the Baptist Church** in Bere Regis, considered to have the finest wooden parish church roof in the country, and **Tolpuddle,** the village that forged the trade union movement in the 1830s after the transportation of the Six Martyrs, who were banished to Australia after a wage protest.

## Dorchester—Thomas Hardy Country

The county town of Dorset, long associated with Thomas Hardy, is in fact the settlement created when the Romans expelled the inhabitants from the nearby colossal **Maiden Castle** (free access at any reasonable time), now nothing more than a huge earthwork, although the finest in Britain. There is a considerable collection of finds in the town at the **Dorset County Museum** in High West Street (0305-62735; open Monday through Saturday from 10 A.M. to 5 P.M.; £1 for adults, 50 pence for children), together with a re-creation of Thomas Hardy's study from his former house, Max Gate, in town. The real attraction, though, **Hardy's Cottage,** lies two miles away at Higher Bockhampton (0305-62366; open April through October, daily except Tuesday from 11 A.M. to 1 P.M., 2 to 5 P.M.; £1.30), a classic small, thatched country cottage where Hardy was born in 1846. A plaque in the room reveals how Hardy was cast aside for dead until the nurse exclaimed: "Dead! Stop a minute, he's alive enough, sure!" Subsequently revived, and though delicate as a child, he lived 88 years. In *The Mayor of Casterbridge,* Hardy referred to Dorchester and its Bloody Assize of 1685, when Judge Jeffreys hanged 74 people and transported hundreds more to the West Indies for supporting the Monmouth rebellion. The reference by Hardy's character Buzzford, spoken to his cronies in The Three Mariners (without too much attention to accurate dates), reads: " 'tis recorded in history that we rebelled against the King one or two hundred years ago, in the time of the Romans, and that lots of us was hanged on Gallows Hill, and quartered and our different jints sent about the country like butchers' meat." "Jints sent about the country" was correct. Allocations of human quarters and heads were dispatched to various villages and towns to act as a warning. Heads were impaled on the railings of St. Peters Church in Dorchester's High West Street. Judge Jeffreys's lodging house in Trinity Street is still a landmark in the town, and the venue for the court, the Oak Room in the Antelope Hotel in Cornhill, is little changed. Dorchester was also the scene of the trial of the Tolpuddle Martyrs. Today, Dorchester remains a bustling, if crowded, market (Wednesday) town.

## Weymouth and the Channel Islands

To the south lies Weymouth's ferry services to Cherbourg and the Channel Islands, as well as Britain's largest chalk hill figure (323 x 280 feet), the **Osmington White Horse,** believed to be either of Weymouth patron King George III on his horse or of the Duke of Wellington; the Isle of Portland produced the pure white limestone to build Buckingham Palace and St. Paul's. The four-mile peninsula has been a maritime stronghold for centuries, since Henry VIII built the finest of his coastal defenses here—the now ruined **Portland Castle** (0305-820539; open April through September, Monday, Thursday, Friday, and Saturday from 10 A.M. to 6 P.M., Wednesday and Sunday 2 to 6 P.M.; 75 pence for adults, 35 pence for children). Portland Harbour is today the home of the Admiralty Underwater Weapons Establishment. The Bill (peninsula) at the tip of Portland offers fine views and sunsets.

**Abbotsbury,** with the ruins of an abbey that includes the country's largest stone tithe barn (272 x 30 feet), has a popular swannery containing five hundred birds, exotic subtropical gardens, and the inland Fleet Lagoon abutting the peculiar pebble Chesil Beach, unusual for the significant decrease in pebble size from west to east. Visible for miles just inland is Hardy Tower, the 70-foot octagonal stone tower at the top of Black Down, dedicated in fact to Sir Thomas Hardy, commander of Nelson's flagship HMS *Victory* at the Battle of Trafalgar; he lived in Portesham, the town at the foot of the hill.

## North of Dorchester

To the north of Dorchester is the amusing 180-foot celtic **Cerne Abbas Giant** chalk hill figure, complete with 120-foot club and 30-foot appendage; it is said that any barren woman who prostrates herself before him will have her every wish granted!

 Cerne Abbas itself is a fabulous tiny stone village, the perfect lunchtime or evening-drinks spot, at either the thatched **Royal Oak**—dating from 1430 and near the site of the ruined Benedictine abbey founded in 987—or at the **New Inn**—believed to be the abbey guesthouse and shouldering a two-hundred-ton stone roof.

**Sherborne Abbey** is a rich Benedictine abbey amidst medieval buildings in an ancient market town. Nearby is **Sherborne Castle** (0935-813182; open Easter through September, Thursday, Saturday, Sunday from 2 to 6 P.M.; £2.50 for adults, £1.25 for children), home of Sir Walter Raleigh, who first tried to rebuild the ruined fortified bishop's palace and then built the lavishly furnished Sherborne Lodge (now Sherborne Castle); the lake and park are by Capability Brown.

## To the West

On the border with Devon is the workshop of **John Makepeace,** maker of fine furniture, at his home in the magnificent Elizabethan house and gardens of Parnham, on the A3066 near Beaminster (0308-862204; open Easter through October,

Wednesday, Sunday from 10 A.M. to 5 P.M.; £2.20 for adults, £1 for children).

**Forde Abbey,** five miles to the northwest off the B3162 near Winsham (0460-20231; open April through October, Wednesday, Sunday 2 to 5 P.M.; gardens open daily year-round from 10:30 A.M. to 4:30 P.M.; £1 house, £1.50 garden, children free) is a former nine-hundred-year-old Cistercian monastery transformed into a grand country house with beautiful gardens.

## Lyme Regis

One of the most memorable seaside towns on the south coast, this is an ideal overnight stop in enchanting surroundings. Lyme remains an irresistible mesh of bright, colorful buildings on steep hills sloping down to the ocean swell, set against high cliffs famous for their fossils. **The Cobb,** a 600-foot-long sweeping stone jetty, has long been Lyme's landmark, the dramatic focus of Jane Austen's *Persuasion* and the novel *The French Lieutenant's Woman* by John Fowles. In 1980, the town was the location for the film of the same name. Fowles was well-placed to write the book—he lives on the road leading to the Cobb. Lyme is also the point where the Duke of Monmouth disembarked in 1685 before marching to his defeat at the Battle of Sedgemore. Twelve supporters were executed on Monmouth Beach where he landed. Lyme also boasts a rich history of smuggling tobacco, rum, whisky, tea, and silks throughout the centuries. A walk around the town should include Broad Street, Bridge Street, along the river Lym, and along Marine Parade to the Cobb.

There are many pubs in which to enjoy a lunchtime drink, and the tiny **Bistro Restaurant** on Bridge St. offers superb sea dishes and other specialties (£5–10).

# Salisbury and the Stone Circles

Often overlooked by travelers on their way to other parts of the West Country, Wiltshire possesses the country's most ancient monuments at Stonehenge and Avebury, possibly the country's finest cathedral at Salisbury, grand country homes at Wilton and Longleat, beautiful open countryside, and the strange chalk hill figures peculiar to the county.

Another convenient base for approaching the region, within easy reach of London via the M3/A30, Salisbury lies near the heart of most of Wiltshire's attractions.

## Salisbury Cathedral

Salisbury Cathedral is the supreme example of classic early English Gothic church architecture. The highest spire—404 feet—in the country, its awesome proportions are more apparent when seen from the original site of the town, two miles away at Old Sarum. Salisbury Cathedral is, in fact, the third attempt at a cathedral. The first, at Old Sarum, was destroyed in a storm soon after its consecration. It was rebuilt, but problems with its inhospitable location and conflicts with the local military garrison made a new site desirable.

Work on the new cathedral began in 1220, and it was consecrated in 1258. The cloisters, chapter house, tower, and spire were built during the next fifty years. On display inside are the oldest existing clock in England, dating from about 1386, and a copy of the Magna Carta. In 1327, the cathedral at Old Sarum was demolished and much of the stone was used to build the wall around the new cathedral close, the largest in England. The town built around the cathedral developed along the classic grid pattern; it is divided into two distinct areas—the buildings in the cathedral close, and the commercial area around Market Place where markets are held on Tuesday and Saturday. Much new development has taken place in the town, and the combination of shoppers and visitors means the town is often crowded.

Visit the **Salisbury and South Wiltshire Museum** in the Kings House, Cathedral Close (0722-332151; open April to October, Monday through Saturday from 10 A.M. to 5 P.M.; July through August, Sunday from 2 to 5 P.M.; October to April, Monday through Saturday from 10 A.M. to 4 P.M., £1.50 for adults, 50 pence for children), for its superb collections of archeological finds (including Pitt-Rivers) from Stonehenge, Old Sarum, and the surrounding area; and the **Salisbury Giant** or St. Christopher, the only surviving example in this country of the medieval pageant figures. **Mompesson House,** Chorister's Green, the Close (0722-335659; open Saturday through Wednesday from 12:30 to 6 P.M.; £1.50 for adults, 70 pence for children), is one of the most distinguished houses in the close, with a large collection of 18th-century drinking glasses. Salisbury also has many historic inns: the oldest, the **King's Arms** in St. John Street, where Charles II planned his escape after the Battle of Worcester; the **Haunch Inn,** opposite the town's only surviving market cross, famous for its timbered features and 14th-century fireplaces; and the **Red Lion** in Milford Street, also from the 14th century.

## ❦ RESTAURANTS

Suggested restaurants include the intimate **Manuel's** in Oatmeal Row, near Market Place, for superb cordon bleu (£8–12) and table d'hôte (£8) menus, and a comprehensive wine list (all credit cards accepted), or the spacious **Don Giovani's** in Catherine St., for classic Italian dishes (£5–9) and superb wines (all credit cards). For delicious home-cooked bar meals at lunchtime, try the 16th-century **Wig and Quill Inn,** New St.

## Entertainment

You can enjoy film at the ancient timbered cinema in New Canal (0722-22080), theater at the **Salisbury Playhouse** in Malthouse Lane (0722-20333) and multimedia events at the **Arts Center in Bedwin Street** (0722-21744). Annual events include the July Southern Cathedrals Festival and the September Salisbury Festival.

## Trips Out of Town

Out-of-town visits to be considered include the outstanding four-hundred-year-old home of the earls of Pembroke, **Wilton House,** Wilton (0722-743115; open Easter through October, Tuesday through Saturday from 11 A.M. to 6 P.M., Sunday from 1 to 6 P.M.; £2.50 for adults, £1.25 for children), considered by James I to be the "finest house in the land." Shakespeare played here, Winston Churchill painted here, and D-day was planned here. Highlights include the eight superb state rooms designed by Inigo Jones, including the Double Cube Room with Van Dyck portraits, the children's model railway and dolls' house, and the expansive garden with its Palladian bridge and large cedars. The nearby **Wilton Royal Carpet Factory** in King Street (0722-742441; open Monday through Saturday from 9 A.M. to 5 P.M. £1.60 for adults, £1.15 for children) is where carpet weaving began as a cottage industry, with original machinery and modern Wilton and Axminster looms on display.

**Old Sarum** (0722-335398, open March to October, Monday through Saturday from 9:30 A.M. to 6:30 P.M., Sunday from 2 to 6:30 P.M.; October to March, Monday through Saturday from 9:30 A.M. to 4 P.M., Sunday from 2 to 4 P.M.; 75 pence for adults, 35 pence for children) is the fascinating outline of the Neolithic hill fort occupied by the Saxons, Romans, and Normans, and the ruins of the former castle and cathedral, with good views of Salisbury and the surrounding area.

To the north lie the stone circles of Stonehenge and Avebury (see box, below), and Swindon, the county town, once the central workshop of the Great Western Railway in its day, now a busy commercial and light-industry center.

## Stonehenge and Avebury Stone Circles

Stonehenge—located two miles west of Amesbury at the junction of the A303 and A344/A360 (open daily March through October from 9:30 A.M. to 6:30 P.M., October through March from 9:30 A.M. to 4 P.M.; £1.30 for adults, 65 pence for children)—has long been regarded as the most fascinating prehistoric monument in Europe. Its isolated position on the rolling Salisbury Plain deepens the sense of mystery surrounding this relic of Neolithic ritual. But numerous excavations have revealed much about the long formation of the site and its religious importance. It first began between 3000 and 2500 B.C. as a ditch and chalk bank, the entrance flanked by a single pair of small stones, but was abandoned after five hundred years. In about 2000 B.C., the inner circle of bluestones (so called because of their color when first hewn) was begun. They weighed up to four tons each and originally numbered about sixty. Incredibly, they were transported from the Preseli Mountains in south Wales, it is believed, by boat and raft along the coast and upriver from Bristol, and finally dragged on rollers to the site—a distance of some almost 240 miles. Before the bluestone circle could be completed, however, the plan changed, and between 2000 and 1500 B.C., a more elaborate temple was built of larger hard sandstones—or sarsens, as they are known—weighing up to fifty tons each, from the Marlborough Downs, 15 miles to the north. Thirty uprights were arranged in a continuous circle linked by lintels, with five gigantic free-standing pairs with lintels inside the circle, an inner horseshoe of bluestones, and finally the altar stone at the center. The odd stone near the road is the Heel Stone, over which the sun appears exactly in its most northerly position on midsummer's day to anyone standing at the center of the circle. This, and other lost sight lines, which suggest a considerable knowledge of astrology, have led to one theory that Stonehenge may have been not only a religious shrine but also a primitive . . . observatory!

Avebury—on the A361, just off the A4 midway between Calne and Marlborough (free access at any reasonable time)—is a superb contrast to the isolation of Stonehenge, and—dare one say it?—more rewarding. The rings and avenue of upright stones, constructed in about 2400 B.C., almost completely encircle the tiny village. Originally consisting of about 180 stones weighing up to 40 tons on a 28-acre site—the largest in the world—it was surrounded by a large earthen bank and ditch, with two smaller circle formations within. The Avenue of stones, about one hundred pairs in alternating sizes, is thought to form a road leading to the burial site known as the Sanctuary. Most of the hard sandstone sarsens came from the nearby Malborough Downs and were not shaped by man but were selected for being either thin and straight (male) or diamond-shaped (female). Numerous intrusions on the site over the centuries have greatly reduced the number of stones remaining—some were broken up for local building, others were removed altogether—but enough remain, together with careful restoration where possible, to gain a good knowledge of the original structure.

The **Avebury Museum** (06723-250; open March to October, Monday through Saturday from 9:30 A.M. to 6:30 P.M.,

Sunday from 2 to 6:30 P.M.; October to March, Monday through Saturday from 9:30 A.M. to 4 P.M., Sunday 2 to 4 P.M.; 75 pence for adults, 35 pence for children) has one of the most important prehistoric archeological collections in Britain. Nearby, the **Museum of Wiltshire Rural Life** at the Great Barn (06723-555; open March to November, daily from 10 A.M. to 6 P.M.; November to March, Saturday 1 to 5 P.M., Sunday 11 A.M. to 5 P.M.; 90 pence for adults, 45 pence for children) features displays of the traditional rural crafts of the saddler, the blacksmith, wheelwright, thatcher, and barrel maker, housed in a hugely impressive thatched tithe barn.

Opposite the museum is the excellent **Stones Restaurant,** open between March and October, for delicious vegetarian meals, herbal wines, and cream teas.

Also nearby, two miles west of Avebury on the A4, is earthen **Silbury Hill,** dating six hundred years earlier than Avebury, covering over five acres and 130 feet high, and the largest man-made hill in Europe. But numerous excavations have failed to identify its purpose—it remains a complete mystery!

Additionally, the **Bowood House,** near Chippenham, off the A342, midway between the villages of Derry Hill and Sandy Lane (0249-812102; open March through October, daily from 11 A.M. to 6 P.M.; £2.70 for adults, £1.60 for children), has a spectacular ninety acres of gardens and lake landscaped by Capability Brown between 1762 and 1768; it is considered to be one of the most beautiful parklands in the country, with over four hundred trees, three hundred shrubs and climbers, cascades, caves, and grottoes. The house, the family home of the earl of Shelburne since 1754, has magnificently decorated ground-floor rooms designed by Robert Adam, including a library with five thousand volumes, the laboratory where Dr. Joseph Priestly discovered oxygen gas in 1774, the Orangery picture gallery, and the family chapel built by Sir C. Cockerell.

## Western Wiltshire

To the west of the county lies the ruined 14th-century **Wardour Castle** off the A30 south of Tisbury (0747-870487; open April to September, Monday through Saturday from 10 A.M. to 5:30 P.M., Sunday 2 to 6:30 P.M.; September to April, Saturday 9:30 A.M. to 4 P.M., Sunday 2 to 4 P.M.; 75 pence for adults, 35 pence for children), set against the landscaped grounds of New Wardour Castle, a 1770 Palladian mansion designed by James Paine, now a girls's school. **Stourhead Gardens,** in the village of Stourton off the B3092 near Warminster (0747-840348; open daily from 8 A.M. to 7 P.M.; £1.50 for adults, 80 pence for children), is an idyllic landscape of lakes, temples, trees, and shrubs designed by Henry Hoare II and dating from 1700. **Longleat House and Zoo** on the A362 between Warminster and Frome (09853-551; House, open Easter to September, daily from 10 A.M. to 6 P.M.; September to Easter, daily from 10 A.M. to 4 P.M., £2.80 for adults, £1 for children; zoo, open March through November, daily from 10 A.M. to 6 P.M.; £3.50 for adults, £2.50 for children; combined ticket £7 for adults, £5 for children) was, the first stately home to open its doors to the public. This is a magnificent Elizabethan house in superb Capability Brown gardens, a treasure of architectural design, decoration, pictures, and furnishings; the safari park boasts elephants, rhinos, giraffes, zebras, lions, and tigers.

Throughout Wiltshire county can be found the peculiar phenomenon of chalk hill figures. Although the most famous of these is the **Uffington White Horse,** across the border into Oxfordshire, many others in Wiltshire include: the **Alton Barnes Horse** at Old Adam Hill, Pewsey; **Broad Town Horse** at Wootton Bassett; **Cherhill Horse** at Cherhill, near Calne; **Hackpen Horse** at Hackpen Hill, Marlborough; **Marlborough Horse** at Marlborough; **Pewsey Horse** at Pewsey; **Westbury White Horse** at Bratton Down; and the **military badges** at Fovant.

# 8

## EAST ANGLIA

East Anglia comprises the counties of Essex, Suffolk, Cambridgeshire, and Norfolk. It starts with the East End of London and ends with the Wash and the Norfolk Broads. The name East Anglia refers to the Eastern Angles, Germanic settlers who came to the region in the fifth and sixth centuries after the Roman withdrawal. To this day there is a pronounced Germanic look to many of the natives of the region, the result of centuries of trade and commerce between the East Anglian ports and Germany, Scandinavia, and the Low Countries. East Anglia is also one of the lowest parts of Britain. Much of the fen land north of Cambridge is below sea level; the coast is flat and sandy. Often it is this very starkness and flatness that gives the area its distinctiveness. South Cambridgeshire, north Essex, inland Norfolk and Suffolk are gentler, more rolling and pastoral, dotted with villages of half-timbered, thatched cottages, and medieval stone churches.

In the Middle Ages, East Anglia was one of the wealthiest parts of Britain, its wool and cloth being exported across the North Sea to Flanders. This is why many small villages in Norfolk and Suffolk possess huge churches. (A good deal of medieval wealth was invested in buildings dedicated to the saving of souls.) Despite this history of prosperity, however, much of the region has always been notable for its isolation. The Fens have mostly now been drained, but in medieval times they were almost entirely underwater except for outcrops of land, literally "islands"—the Isle of Ely, namely—where people lived in villages. Something in the starkness of the landscape seems to have lent itself to the fundamentals of a fierce Protestant faith. Of the two ancient universities Oxford nestles in the cheery Thames Valley while Cambridge is the puritan one. Its theologians were the intellectual driving forces of the English reformation; from this region came the Pilgrim Fathers and Oliver Cromwell.

Puritanism and isolation are only one part of the picture, however. Against Cromwell's Roundheads and New Model

EAST ANGLIA

0       Kilometers      60

Miles          50

N

© RV Reise- und Verkehrsverlag, Munchen

Army has to be set Newmarket, mecca of the English horse racing world and headquarters of the Jockey Club. During the summer, Newmarket Heath echoes to the thunder of horses' hooves, the cries of racing punters, and the popping of celebratory champagne corks. Economically, too, the region has regained the prominence it lost for two centuries to the industrial North and Midlands. Cambridge, with its science park and information technology, is now also "Silicon Fen," and it boasts one of the lowest unemployment rates in the country. In recent years property prices have soared to levels rivaling those of London. With its huge expanses of intensively farmed land Norfolk is a center of "agribusiness." Peterborough is a thriving shopping center to which people come from far and wide, some even from the Continent, taking advantage of frequent ferry sailings across the North Sea. The Anglian ports—Harwich, Felixstowe, and Lowestoft—have prospered with Britain's membership in the European Economic Community and with the decline of Liverpool as England's major port.

Improvements in transport facilities are also breaking down the region's traditional isolation. With the opening of the M11 motorway from London to Cambridge, high-speed trains from Peterborough to King's Cross Station, and the electrification of the line from Liverpool Street Station to Cambridge, Cambridgeshire and some parts of Norfolk are becoming increasingly viable as areas within commuting distance to London. Harwich is the main ferry port for travelers to northern Europe through the Hook of Holland, with boat trains serving it twice daily from Liverpool Street station. And Stanstead Airport is soon to be expanded into the third London airport and will have extensive international links.

Last but not least, East Anglia is one of the great areas for beer, for the rhapsodically hoppy taste of what the English call real ale—beer served from wooden barrels in which it continues to ferment right up to the time of serving, an eye-opener and taste-sharpener to those whose palates have grown accustomed to the pasteurized lager beer of Milwaukee or New South Wales! East Anglia is fortunate in possessing several small family-run breweries that serve the area—notably Greene King, based in Bury St.-Edmunds, and Adnams, in the old-fashioned seaside resort of Southwold on the Suffolk coast. (Greene King beer has been eulogized in Graham Swift's novel *Waterland,* a powerful evocation of life in the Fens. The novelist Graham Greene is related to the Greene King brewing family, and in 1984 the brewery celebrated his eightieth birthday by producing a bottled beer named after him!) East Anglian villages and towns are full of beautiful old pubs, many of them also serving food. In the Middle Ages the region was also noted for the wine production of its monasteries, and in recent years there has been something of a revival in this area. Chilford Hundred is one local wine to look out for.

# TRAVEL

Cambridge makes an ideal base from which to explore East Anglia. The trains that leave London's Liverpool Street Station at thirty-five minutes past the hour take just over an hour to reach their destination, traveling out through the urban sprawl of northeast London into the lush Essex countryside. By car you drive up the M11 motorway from east London. There is also a direct motorway link across London from Gatwick Airport, and there are direct coach services from both Gatwick and Heathrow airports. Coach services from London leave from Victoria and Aldgate coach stations. From Cambridge there are frequent train services to Ely, Peterborough, Norwich, and King's Lynn. Newmarket, Bury St.-Edmunds, Aldeburgh, and the Suffolk coast make an excellent drive due east. Peterborough is served by high-speed Inter-City trains on the east coast mainline to York, Durham, and Scotland.

For all its delights, however, Cambridge gets *very, very crowded* with visitors between May and September. One way of enjoying it to the full *and* getting away from the crowds afterward is to stay in nearby Newmarket or Bury St.-Edmunds. Both are short train or car rides from Cambridge and also have much to offer in themselves.

Norwich complements Cambridge both as an ancient and beautiful city and as the best place to center yourself in the eastern half of East Anglia. It now has excellent rail links with London's Liverpool Street station—two hours on Inter-City trains leaving hourly during weekdays—and there is also frequent service northeast from the city out by the beautiful Norfolk Broads and up to the Victorian coastal resorts of Cromer and Sheringham. The A11 road to London has been vastly improved, and Norfolk has an airport with daily flights to Amsterdam and Frankfurt.

To get to Norwich from Cambridge by rail takes nearly two hours in a fairly basic train that stops at every station in some of the bleakest and most desolate countryside you will find this side of the Russian steppes. We would therefore recommend making the journey only once—say, out from Cambridge to Norwich and later returning from Norwich to London. Alternatively, you might go straight to Norwich from London, do Cromer and the Norfolk coast, then go back to Norwich and take the train down to Cambridge, perhaps breaking the journey at Ely. By car you might choose to carry on by the coast through Wells-next-the-Sea to King's Lynn, and then down from there to Ely.

King's Lynn is your best base for the most northerly part of East Anglia. From Norwich it can be reached directly by the A47 or, more indirectly, through Cromer, the coast road to Hunstanton, and then the A149 to Lynn itself. From Cambridge it's an hour's ride on the train or a straight drive up the A10. You can make forays out from Lynn to Hunstanton, Wells, and other coastal locations, and it's also well worth a visit in its own right.

Consider purchasing East Anglia Rail Rovers, tickets that give you seven days' unlimited rail travel within the region for £32. (available from any railway station)

Premier Travel in Cambridge (tel. 0223-7262) operates a coach service directly to and from London's Gatwick and Heathrow airports—departing every two hours—and to Stanstead Airport in Essex.

Another option: River and Norfolk Broads Cruises from Norwich, operating daily from May to October by Southern River Steamers (tel. 0603-501220).

## ✿ HOTELS

**Credit card abbreviations used below are: AE for American Express, CB for Carte Blanche, DC for Diner's Club, MC for MasterCard, and V for Visa.**

## Cambridge

**All Seasons Guest House,** 219–221 Chesterton Rd., Cambridge CB4 1AN; tel. (0223) 353386. A real bargain if you're on a tight budget. This nine-room guesthouse is meticulously clean, extremely good value, and a short walk from the center of town. Room rates are £11 per person per night with English breakfast. Half-price for children under ten; babies free and cots provided. No credit cards. Tea or coffee served free at any time.

**Arundel House Hotel,** 55 Chesterton Rd., Cambridge CB4 3AN; tel. (0223) 67701. A 90-room family-run hotel overlooking Jesus Green and the river, the Arundel has been put together from six adjacent Victorian terrace houses, each with its own staircase, a short walk from the center of town. The bay-window rooms overlooking Jesus Green are particularly recommended. The Arundel offers a restaurant that has won the Cambridge City Council Clean Kitchen Award for five consecutive years and also the national Heartbeat Award for healthy vegetarian, low-fat food and non-smoking seat allocations. At the rear of the hotel, across the 75-space parking lot, is the Coach House. In 1894 this wooden building was the stables of the Cambridge Coach Company. Now it contains further accommodation and two conference rooms with facilities for up to 35 people. Rates in all of the houses are £22.50 (single)–51 (double room with bathroom) and include Continental breakfast, service, and VAT. The Arundel has a good reputation for food, serving classic English and French dishes (£6.85–8.65 for a main course). Its house wines are of good quality and extremely reasonable at £3.60 for a half-carafe. Meals can be had in the bar, lunch and evenings, for £2–4, and there is also a children's menu. All major credit cards.

**Ashley Hotel,** 74 Chesterton Rd., CB4 1ER; tel. (0223) 35009. A superior 10-room guest house, owned by the same family that owns the Arundel, the Ashley is opposite the lively Old Spring pub, near the river and Midsummer Common, and only a ten-minute walk from the town center. Room rates run £18.50 (single)–32 (double). All rooms have private showers except for the two single rooms, which share a bathroom. Price includes breakfast, service, and VAT. Parking for 16 cars. Credit Cards: MC, V.

**Garden House Hotel,** Granta Place, Mill Lane, Cambridge CB2 1RT; tel. (0223) 316605, telex 81463, fax 0223-316605. A stylish modern brick building, adjacent to the river and near to the Backs and King's Parade, the main "drag" of the colleges, this 117-room hotel has its own riverside garden in which you can feed the ever hungry local ducks and watch people go by in punts. On the other side of the river through the trees you can see the Granary, a lovely old house formerly the home of one of Charles Darwin's family and now part of Darwin College. It's well worth paying the £5 supplementary charge for a river-view room. Some rooms have balconies; all have ceiling-to-floor sliding windows. Rates run £55 (singles)–160 (suites), including Continental breakfast and VAT. Conference and banqueting facilities are available for groups of twenty to two hundred. The hotel also has conference and meeting rooms at adjacent Peterhouse, Cambridge's oldest college. Photocopying, secretarial, and translation services are available by arrangement. Afternoon teas can be had in the Riverside Lounge for £2–4. A low/non-alcohol drinks section is being built into the bar area. Le Jardin Restaurant is spacious and light, opening onto the riverside garden. Dinner there is £14–50. A two-course lunch is £9–25; three courses are £12–35. Vegetarian dishes are also available. There is parking for 160 cars. All major credit cards.

**Gonville Hotel,** Gonville Place, Cambridge CB1 1LY; tel. (0223) 66611. Cricket buffs should note that the Gonville is adjacent not just to Parker's Piece but also to Fenner's, the university cricket ground where the first-class counties come to play during May and June. The 62-room hotel was built 16 years ago to cater primarily to the commercial trade. Room rates are £42 (single with bath)–77 (family room with three beds). Weekend rates are available. Rates include breakfast, service, and VAT. There are two conference rooms with facilities for up to fifty people and an air-conditioned restaurant with a three-course set menu for £7.45 (lunch) and £9.50 (dinner). There are ample parking facilities. AE, MC, V.

**University Arms Hotel,** Regent St., Cambridge CB2 1AD; tel. (0223) 351241, telex 817311, fax 0223-315256. Although the entrance on Regent St. is through a 1960s addition, the greater part of the University Arms is solid, stately, and Victorian, flanked by four towers. The 114-room hotel dates back to 1834 and has been owned by the Bradford family since 1891. Gillian Bradford, the managing director's wife, has designed the room interiors in the old building, giving each an individual character. One wing is said to be haunted by six dogs—each room door has a picture of a different dog on it. Go for a room facing Parker's Piece. In the summer you'll be able to look out from your window at one of the many cricket matches played out there. Rates run £42(single)–95 (suite). Children sharing parent's room, £4.50–7.50. Prices include full English breakfast. Special weekend rates are available throughout the year. There are conference facilities for up to one hundred people in the Churchill Suite or the Newton, Darwin, Byron, and Cromwell rooms. These rooms are also available as private suites for dinners. A definitive afternoon tea (£3.50) is to be had in the Octagon Lounge. Before or after dinner you might relax in the Whisky Galore Bar; with over a hundred different brands available, this justly claims to be Cambridge's best stock of malt whisky. Dinner in the wood-paneled Parker's Lounge overlooking Parker's Piece is £10–20. The hotel has free parking. All major credit cards.

# King's Lynn

**Duke's Head Hotel,** Tuesday Market Place, King's Lynn, Norfolk PE 30 1JS; tel. (0553) 774996, telex 817349. The leading hotel—with a pink Baroque, rather German façade—is located in King's Lynn's largest square, the Tuesday Market Place. Parliamentary candidates used to address the electors from the hotel windows, and you should try to get a room overlooking the marketplace—unless you're staying during the second half of February, when there is an extremely noisy fun fair taking place outside. The main entrance is where stagecoaches pulled into the yard at the back, and Queen Victoria once stayed in what is now Room 12. It's now part of the Trusthouse Forte chain, and there has been considerable refurbishment in recent years to cope with the growing numbers of overseas visitors, including many from Holland, a country that has a traditional affinity with this area.

Room rates £47 (single)–£69 (double), don't include breakfast. Room service will serve Continental breakfast for £4.75, but you would probably want to go to the Coffee Shop, which does a Continental (£4.50) or full English breakfast all day (9:45 A.M.–10 P.M.). There is a buffet counter in the bar at lunchtime, and the restaurant is open 12:15–2 P.M. and 7–9:30 P.M. The set menu is £13.45 and includes such local specialities as Fen Dyke eel. The hotel can arrange for baby-sitters, and there is also a baby-listening service for while you are in the restaurant. The hotel also offers conference facilities for up to 225. Parking for forty cars. All major credit cards.

**The Globe Hotel,** Tuesday Market Place, King's Lynn, Norfolk PE30 1EZ; tel. (0553) 772167. Also on the Tuesday Market Place, the Globe dates back to 1645. Oliver Cromwell once signed an important declaration within its walls. Now part of the Berni Inn chain, it offers forty rooms, two bars, and a restaurant open 12–2:30 P.M. and 6–10:30 P.M. A three-course lunch can be had for £3.99. Rooms are £32 (single), £45 (double). Weekend rates £19.50 per person per night. There is parking for ten cars with a public parking lot nearby. All major credit cards.

**Tudor Rose Hotel,** St. Nicholas St., King's Lynn, Norfolk PE30 1LR; tel. (0553) 76284.

See the section on King's Lynn for the local seafood and steak dishes that Ian and Christine Carter produce in their restaurant. The Tudor Rose is a friendly little 12-room hotel just off the Tuesday Market Place by the magnificent chapel of St. Nicholas. The bar has medieval beams in its ceiling and local fishermen among the patrons sampling its real ale. Ian takes great pride in his wine list, and this can also be explored in the bar. Rates run £19.95 (single)–£35 (double). All major credit cards.

# Newmarket and Bury St. Edmunds

If you stay in the best and most interesting hotels in the highest priced category—the Rutland in Newmarket and the Angel in Bury—you need go no farther in terms of eating. Should you choose to stay elsewhere, we recommend visiting these hotels for the sheer delight of the sturdy English dishes that they offer.

**Angel Hotel, Angel Hill, Bury St. Edmunds,** Suffolk IP33 1LT; tel. (0284) 753926, telex 81630, fax (0284) 750092. This is the doyen of old coaching inns as far as East Anglia is concerned! Ivy-clad walls overlook Angel Hill and the Abbeygate; a harpist plays at afternoon teas on Wed. afternoons, and a piano player does the same on Sat. and Sun. King Louis Philippe of France died there. The room in which he stayed contains a four-poster bed once owned by the Duke of Sutherland; its bedposts contain individually set china pieces. Charles Dickens stayed there when he was in town, and his old room (number 15) is mentioned in *The Pickwick Papers*. The room is said to be haunted by a vision that appears on the panel behind the dressing table! The room to ask for if you're a single male traveler is number 52, "The Man's Room," all done out in blue and overlooking the back. But all the 37 rooms in the Angel are special, different, and spacious, with solid oak furniture and the oak beams exposed in many of the ceilings. Rates are £50 (single)–85 (double). Louis Phillippe room, £90. Weekend rate, £30 per person per night, with breakfast. Full English breakfast costs £5.50; light breakfast £3.50.

Another ghost is said to haunt the Vaults, one of the hotel's two restaurants. The Vaults is in the basement and has a Norman undercroft. It is thought to have been the abbey's charnel house for the laity during the Middle Ages. There are supposed to be tunnels going from the Vaults to the abbey, and down one of these a pig was once sent to explore. When the pig did not return, a fiddler was sent on his trail, but he, too, failed to return. Now the plaintive sounds of a fiddler are said to be heard during the night from behind where the wine refrigerator now stands!

Every three months literary dinners are held in the Regency. Past speakers include the earl of Lichfield and Hammond Innes. At these dinners annual prizes are awarded to East Anglian authors, like the thriller writer P. D. James. Musical evenings are also held at the Angel, and its friendly and informative manager, Mr. Donovan, can provide details of these along with further snippets about the hotel's history. Parking for fifty cars. All major credit cards.

*U.S. Representative:* Josephine Barr: tel. 800-223-5463; telex 286778.

**Chantry Hotel,** 8 Sparhawk St., Bury St.-Edmunds, Suffolk IP33 1RY; tel. (0284) 67427. In medieval times a chantry was a chapel in which masses were said for the souls of individuals after their deaths. The Chantry Hotel is a moderately priced hotel with a rendered Georgian façade on a much older building, built on the site of a chantry chapel. To the rear of the hotel was a coach maker's yard, and the deeds to the building are displayed on the dining room wall. It's also central (around the corner from Angel Hill), friendly, and has interesting individual rooms, many of which contain antique furniture. One room has a four-poster double bed. It has a bar and a small restaurant in which evening meals are served (£9–10 for three courses) with vegetables fresh that day. Of the 13 rooms 10 have either baths or showers. All have color television, coffee/tea-making facilities, and telephones. There is a family room with two bunks, suitable for children. Room rates run £20 (single)–36 (double). Children, £5 per night when sharing family room with parents. Parking space for every room. Credit cards: MC.

**Rutland Arms,** High St., Newmarket, Suffolk CB8 8N3; tel. (0638) 664251, telex 329265. Dominating the eastern end of the High St., as you go from the Horseracing Museum to the Clocktower, this Georgian, former coaching inn is British horse racing's oldest hotel. It is built of red brick and opened a few months after the Battle of Waterloo, but there has been an inn on the site since the 15th century. The three-story hotel has 45 rooms, with corridors running around a courtyard. Because it is an old hotel, no two rooms are the same, although all have had their original half-timbered ceilings restored. Room rates: £46 (single), £57 (double), £65 (family room). Weekend rates are available during spring and summer.
The old stables have been converted into a conference room; the Georgian Room, available for groups or for lectures, has original 17th-century paintings on the walls.
The Aga Kahn used to maintain a suite at the Rutland all year round, although he only used it during race meetings. This suite is currently being refurbished.
The bar serves Adnams beer, snacks in the evening, and a range of hot lunches at around £1.75. They estimate they sell around forty portions a day of their locally produced steak and kidney pie. The restaurant, which is partly built in the old entrance to the courtyard for stagecoaches, does a three-course Sun. lunch for £6.95 and a daily set lunch or dinner, also three courses, for £9.50. The roast Suffolk pork is particularly good. The hotel has parking space for 34 cars. All major credit cards.

**White Hart Hotel,** Newmarket, Suffolk CB8 8JP; tel. (0638) 663051. Located across the High St. from the National Horseracing Museum, this is a 17th-century 24-room hotel that has recently been refurbished. Like the Rutland, it very much caters to a racing clientele. The hotel has a cocktail bar and a lounge bar, which operates a food counter (£1.20 for a sandwich; £4 for a hot dish) at lunchtime. The restaurant serves vegetarian main courses for around £6 and house specialties from £7.15 upwards. Oak Plank fillet steak (£12.50) is the showpiece dish. The hotel provides minimal room service and no telex or fax facilities but does welcome families and supplies cots and high chairs. The Suffolk Room has a four-poster bed and a whirlpool bath. Rooms run £38 (single)–48 (double). Parking for 25 cars. MC, V.

# Norwich

**Crofter's Hotel,** 2 Earlham Rd., Norwich NR2 3DA; tel. (0603) 613287/620169. This small, 15-room, family-run hotel is currently being refurbished. It is a short walk from the marketplace up St. Giles St. and then along Earlham Rd., immediately after the Catholic cathedral. There is a terrace with chairs and tables overlooking the hotel garden. A three-course evening meal with coffee can be had for £5.75. Although there is no room service, the hotel kitchen is open all night, serving bread, cold meats, cheese, salads, tea, and coffee, with a kettle for guests who fancy a midnight snack. A cup of tea is brought to your room at around 7:30 A.M. Rates run £15 (single)–33 (triple). Includes English breakfast, service, and VAT. Family rates are available on request. Free parking. No credit cards.

**Hotel Nelson,** Prince of Wales Rd., Norwich, NR1 1BX; tel. (0603) 628612, telex 975203, fax 0603–628612. Situated on the river directly across from the railway station, the Nelson combines informal hospitality with a new, three-story building and is now Norwich's premier hotel. It attracts both a business and a leisure clientele and offers facilities for small and medium-sized conferences (up to ninety people). The hotel has 122 rooms with private bath, two restaurants, two bars, a sauna and exercise room, and parking facility for 180 cars. River moorings are available for boats.

Rooms fall into two categories: Executive State Rooms with luxury fittings, refrigerator, trouser press and Teletext service; and standard rooms with tea- and coffee-making facilities, fitted hair dryer, telephone, and color television. Rooms in the newer executive wing open onto the hotel's river garden. For families, Room 121 connects with two other rooms. With standard rooms, those on the river side are noisier but the view is prettier (the river and at night the illuminated Victorian station front); the parking lot side rooms are quieter. Rates for Executive State Rooms run: £59.50 (single), £69.50 (twin/double), £99.50 (suite); rates for standard rooms run: £51.50 (single), £61.50 (twin/double), £69.50 (suite). Rates include English breakfast, VAT and service. Special rates are available for weekend and midweek.

The Quarter-Deck Buttery is the more informal of the Nelson's two restaurants, and main courses are mostly under £4 with vegetables or salad included. The Quarter-Deck bar also serves snacks; Norfolk Ploughmans for £1.60; pâté, salad, and rolls for £1.60. The nautical, Lord Nelson associations are also carried through into the main restaurant, the Trafalgar, and the Cannon Bar, which is at river level by the terrace. At lunchtime the Trafalgar does an Admiral's Table Lunch (two courses and coffee for £7.50). In the evenings, three courses and coffee can be had for £9. These prices include VAT and service. All major credit cards.

**Maid's Head Hotel,** Tombland, Norwich NR3 1LB; tel. (0603) 628821/32, telex 975080, fax 0603–613688. Arguably super-seded in recent years by the modern conveniences of the Hotel Nelson, the Maid's Head remains the mecca for visitors who want to steep themselves in traditional Norwich. In a superb lo-cation by the Erpingham Gate to the cathedral close, the Maid's Head has seven hundred years of tradition to offer. Queen Eliza-beth I is said to have stayed here, and a meeting was held in the hotel in 1778 to raise men to fight against the rebellious American colonies. Service is formal but friendly, and the hotel is still the preferred meeting place of the county set. Because it is such an old building, none of the 79 rooms will be exactly the same, but all have either baths or showers, television and in-house videos, fresh fruit on your arrival, and hospitality trays. The showpiece room is the Queen Elizabeth Double, with its four-poster bed and slightly sloping floor, another sign of the hotel's age. There are three bars and two restaurants specializ-ing in local Norfolk dishes. Go for the Carvery in the old court-yard; it's light and airy with a glass roof. Two suites can be used for conferences or business meetings. The hotel has an ar-rangement with a nearby health and fitness club. Room rates are £40 (single)–86.75 (triple). Rates include full English break-fast, VAT, and service. Special rates are available for two to three nights at weekends. Free parking within hotel grounds. All major credit cards.

# Cambridge

Coming into Cambridge by road or rail is very much a matter of spotting landmarks. From the north or the east the tallest college chapels—King's and St. John's—stand out above the buildings of Britain's flattest town. Coming north from London on the M11 it's the 1930s tower of the University Library. But the best entry into Cambridge by far is by the London train. Flat open fields are suddenly interrupted by two hills, the Gogmagogs, to the right of the train as you face north. They are almost immediately followed by the 1960s edifice of Addenbrooke's Hospital, also to your right. A succession of college playing fields on either side of the track gives way on the left to the Cambridge University Press building, and then Cambridge station—one long platform. Outside the latter a bus or a cab ride toward the center of Cambridge goes past another notable Cambridge landmark, the 19th-century Gothic revival spire of the Catholic church of Our Lady and the En-glish Martyrs. From there it's a short ride to the center of town and the concentrated beauties of the ancient colleges.

Cambridge is a much more compact university than Oxford. This means that its four most interesting colleges—Queens', King's, Trinity, and St. John's—can be comfortably visited in a morning or an afternoon. They are all near one another in the middle of town, and they back onto the river. One of Cambridge's most distinctive features is the "Backs," the green open spaces and gardens by the river Cam onto which these and other colleges *back*. As well as offering picturesque views of the colleges and the river, the Backs also provide a means whereby visitors can stroll in and out of the colleges, visiting each one in turn.

The river Cam is a crucial element in the identity and coherence of Cambridge. Some of the city's fans would compare its water-centered beauty to that of Venice, and, indeed, Cambridge is as much the city of its river as is Venice the city of its canals. Up until quite recently the Cam used to be the principal means by which those two essential accompaniments to scholarly life in the English climate—coal and wine—were brought down by barges from King's Lynn. The wharfs and warehouses by Magdalene College have been replaced by designer apartments, but the Cam continues to provide the means of engaging in two quintessential Cambridge activities—punting and boat rowing. From the weir on Jesus Green, past the Backs, and out to Grantchester, the Cam is too shallow for any vessels other than (flat-bottomed) punts and canoes. During the summer, students and visitors take to the river en masse.

**For a map of Cambridge see atlas pages 14–15.**

## The Punts

No visit to Cambridge is complete without a ride in a punt with a group of friends and, weather permitting, a bottle or two of champagne or chilled white wine. Brave souls can attempt to stand up at the back of the punt and steer it without jamming the punt pole in the muddy bed of the Cam and drifting away without it. Others may prefer to hire one of the chauffeur-driven punts that can be gotten by the bridges at Garret Hostel Lane and Silver Street. From Scudamoore's boatyard, next to the Garden House Hotel, you can punt out through the beautiful Grantchester Meadows, which Pink Floyd celebrated on their *Umma Gumma* album in the sixties, to the village of Grantchester, justly celebrated for Byron's Pool and the church clock, which still stands at ten to three as in Rupert Brooke's poem.

Grantchester was where Brooke lived while a Fellow of King's, and the honey he hoped for at tea can be had in the Orchard tea garden. Alternatively, go out there at lunch time or in the evening for a reasonably priced meal or snack washed down with Tolly Cobbold beer at the **Green Man.**

Punts can be moored both at the Orchard and the Green Man. Grantchester is also an attractive walk through the meadows and takes no more than half an hour to reach from the city center.

Ah God! to see the branches stir
Across the moon at Grantchester!
To smell the thrilling-sweet and rotten
Unforgettable, unforgotten
River-smell, and hear the breeze
Sobbing in the little trees.
Say, do the elm-clumps greatly stand
Still guardians of that holy land?
The chestnuts shade, in reverend dream,
The yet unacademic stream?

Oh, is the water sweet and cool,
Gentle and brown, above the pool?
And laughs the immortal river still
Under the mill, under the mill?
Say, is there Beauty yet to find?
And Certainty? and Quiet kind?
Deep meadows yet, for to forget
The lies, and truths, and pain? . . . Oh! yet
Stands the Church clock at ten to three?
And is there honey still for tea?

From "The old vicarage, Grantchester," by
Rupert Brooke

Below the weir on Jesus Green the Cam becomes the river of boat crews. One side of the river is dotted with the clubhouses from which boat crews emerge to practice for the Bumps, the twice-yearly boat races between the colleges. These take place at the ends of Lent and Easter terms. Because the Cam is relatively narrow, it is not possible for boats to overtake each other, so instead you bump the boat in front of you and then you are considered to have outraced it. The finish to the Bumps can be viewed from the vantage point of the Pike and Eel pub in Chesterton.

The river apart, the best way to get around Cambridge is on foot or by bicycle. Cambridge is not a city that is sympathetic to the driver. It's got a crazy one-way system, and where cars are allowed the traffic jams are horrific. Public transportation to and from the train station is good, but otherwise forget it. Virtually every place worth visiting can be gotten to on foot or by bicycle. The number of cyclists will be one of the first things you notice about Cambridge, and as a pedestrian you need to watch out for cyclists every time you step into the road. Students ride fast and tend not to ring their bells—they're in too much of a hurry to get to that lecture or garden party! A particular hazard of high summer is the hordes of students who cruise the streets four abreast on pink bicycles, often going the wrong way up one-way streets. The pink bicycles they ride are hired from the same firm and you, too, can hire a bicycle for the day or longer from firms like Mike's Bikes.

*Two words of warning:* never leave your bike unlocked, because stealing bikes is a local sport; never ride at night without lights, because the Cambridge police are very wary of this and you could be fined.

# Cambridge University and its Colleges

Cambridge University is said to date from the end of the 12th century, when there was a migration to Cambridge of a number of unruly scholars who had made Oxford too hot to hold them. The origins of its colleges were as hostels for students. Peterhouse, the oldest of these, was founded by a Bishop of Ely in 1281. Many of them were founded by royal benefactors, notably King's (Henry VI in the 15th century) and Trinity (Henry VIII in the 16th).

A college consists of a master, mistress, or president; fellows engaged in research and teaching; and students. Every Cambridge student has to be a member of a college, and much of the teaching provided for undergraduates is within their own college.

The oldest colleges were monastic foundations, and so at the center of their communal life is a chapel, where there are daily services in the Anglican rite, and a dining hall, where the college comes together to eat twice a day. The fellows sit at a high table on a dais raised above where the students eat. At certain, more formal meals, gowns are worn and Latin grace is said at the beginnings and ends of meals.

Up until the second half of the 19th century Cambridge colleges were entirely male and entirely Anglican. The first women's colleges, Girton and Newnham, were founded at that time, and religious tests for graduation were abolished. There are now 32 colleges. The most recent of them, Robinson College on Grange Road, was founded by a local millionaire in 1977.

Visitors are generally welcome on the grounds, and in the courts and chapels of colleges, except during student examinations from May to the middle of June. Guided tours leave from the Tourist Information Centre on Wheeler Street (0223-322640). Be sure to go with a blue-badged guide, otherwise your party will not be allowed into the colleges.

The three grandest colleges are King's, Trinity, and St. John's. They are all near one another, in the middle of town, and all back onto the river. **King's** 15th-century chapel, built in the perpendicular style, is the most magnificent building in Cambridge. It has all its original stained glass and Rubens's painting of *The Adoration of the Magi* is behind the altar. King's has its own choir school, and at Christmas their rendering of Nine Lessons and Carols is broadcast by the BBC. Try to get there for evensong (times are posted on the chapel door). Watch the serpentine line of choir boys approach the chapel from the river, walking by the stately Georgian Gibbs building. The chapel acoustics have a three-second echo, and the ethreal sound of the choir singing medieval plainsong and psalms will send shivers up your spine.

**Trinity** is the largest and wealthiest of the colleges. It is the college of Francis Bacon, Sir Isaac Newton, and the poets Dryden, Byron, and Tennyson. Entering through the Great Gateway brings the visitor into the huge expanse of the Great Court, with the chapel to the right of the gate, a stone fountain in the center of the court, and at the opposite side, the dining hall. Here fellows and students dine under the watchful eye of Holbein's portrait of Henry VIII, the college's founder. Continue through the passageway from the Great Court past the hall, and you are in the 17th-century Nevile's Court facing the wondrous library designed by Sir Christopher Wren. Raised from the ground by pillars, through which you can see the river and the Backs, the Wren Italianate library appears to be floating on air. Go there during visiting hours and you can see the stately interior with bays of mahogany bookcases flanked by busts of the world's great scholars.

Passing out under the library, you can cross the river by Trinity bridge. Turning right from Trinity bridge, a short walk along the Backs gives access to the adjacent college of **St. John's,** where William Wordsworth once studied. St. John's has its own Bridge of Sighs based on the original in Venice. Stand on the bridge in the cool of a summer's evening and watch the punts glide by underneath. At the rear of St. John's is the **School of Pythagoras,** the oldest house in Cambridge. At its front is a beautiful early 16th-century **gatehouse** with a painted statue of the college founder, Lady Margaret Beaufort, over the gate.

On a smaller scale but also worth a visit is **Queens' College,** so called because it was founded by two 15th-century queens, Margaret of Anjou and Elizabeth Woodville. The 16th-century President's Lodge is half-timbered and evokes the ghosts of Elizabethan courtiers. In the old hall of Queens' is some woodwork by the Pre-Raphaelite craftsman William Morris. The oldest parts of Queens' are probably the most compact medieval buildings in Cambridge. At the river end they back onto what is, after the Bridge of Sighs, Cambridge's second most famous bridge, the **Mathematical Bridge.** This was originally put together in the 18th century without any nails. During the Victorian period it is said to have been taken apart to see how it could work without nails and bolts. Unfortunately, it could not be put back together without them.

In addition to the colleges, the university also has buildings of great beauty and architectural interest. Look out particularly for the Baroque-style **Senate House** (1722–1730) on King's Parade, where students and distinguished scholars line up in gowns and mortarboards to be awarded degrees by the head of the university, the vice-chancellor. Behind the Senate House are the **Old Schools** (1350), the medieval heart of the university and now its administrative center. On Trumpington Street is the **Fitzwilliam Museum** open Tuesday through Saturday from 10 A.M. to 5 P.M., Sundays from 2:15 to 5 P.M.) This dates from 1834 and has a notable collection of paintings, antiquities, ceramics, and armor. Also worth a visit are the **Scott Polar Research Institute** (open Monday through Saturday from 2:30 to 4 P.M.), the **Museum of Classical Archaeology,** (open Monday through Friday 9:15 A.M. to 1 P.M.; 2:15 to 5 P.M.) and the **Whipple Museum of Science** (open Monday through Friday from 2 to 4 P.M.). Folk art and modern art can be found in the collections of the **Folk Museum** (open Monday through Saturday from 10:30 A.M. to 5 P.M., Sundays from 2:30 to 4:30 P.M.). and **Kettle's Yard** (house open daily from 2 to 4 P.M.; gallery open Tuesday through Saturday from 12:30 to 5:30 P.M., Thursday til 7 P.M., Sundays 2 to 5:30 P.M.), at the foot of Castle Hill. A day could be allocated to visiting these buildings.

## A Church and Pub Crawl of Cambridge

Having spent the morning going round colleges, why not spend the rest of the day combining the sacred and the profane! In addition to its college chapels the city of Cambridge is dotted with beautiful old churches and cozy pubs. And as far as having lunch is concerned, several pubs give much better value than anything to be found in restaurants.

Principal among pubs serving lunch is **The Free Press** on Prospect Row, near Parker's Piece. This is one of the few establishments in Cambridge, restaurants included, to have gotten into Egon Ronay's *Good Food Guide,* but for our present purposes it is a charming little pub with a sporty clientele that serves wonderfully cool pints of Greene King IPA. IPA stands for "India Pale Ale" and was beer that used to be brewed for British soldiers in India, so it's an ideal thirst quencher on a hot day. Green King makes another, stronger draft beer called Abbott. This is to be treated with extreme caution. You have been warned!

From The Free Press, cross Parker's Piece to the **Catholic Church,** a fine example of Victorian Gothic from the 1840s. Adjacent to that on Lensfield Road is the **Scott Polar Research Institute** (see above), whose museum collection commemorates Scott of the Antarctic. Down where Lensfield Road meets Trumpington Street is **Hobson's Conduit.** Originally in the market square, this fountain commemorates the 17th-century horse seller whose horses were all equally good or bad—the origin of the saying "Hobson's choice is no choice at all." Turning right onto Trumpington Street, past the Fitzwilliam Museum and Peterhouse, the oldest college, you come to **Little St. Mary's.** This is a High Anglican church that has strong associations with the cavalier cause during the English civil war. The metaphysical poet Richard Crashaw used to meditate before the high altar through the small hours of the night. These meditations eventually led him to exile with the court of Charles I's wife, Henrietta Maria, and conversion to Roman Catholicism. Although the church was consecrated in 1352, parts of its tower date back to the 12th century. The interior is pervaded by the aroma of the incense used during the rituals accompanying high masses, and there is a fine lady chapel on the south side complete with Madonna and votive candles. Near the entrance of the church is a memorial tablet dedicated to Godfrey Washington, a parish priest who died in 1729. George Washington was a descendant of his, and the arms of the Washington family can be seen on the table.

From Little St. Mary's go down Little St. Mary's Lane and turn right by the University Centre and Scudamore's boat yard. You are now by the river and near two pubs, where you can sit outside and watch the river: **The Anchor** on Silver Street and the **Granta** on Newnham Road. Of the two the Granta, overlooking a former mill pool, has the better views, out over Coe Fen toward the Fen Causeway. Alternatively, go toward King's Parade from Little St. Mary's, turning right after Corpus Christi College onto Bene't Street. The street is named after the Benedictine monks who once used **St. Bene't's Church.** This is the oldest church in Cambridgeshire, with a squat Anglo-Saxon tower and an austere barestone interior. It is now served by Anglican Franciscans. Facing St. Bene't's is the most historically interesting pub in Cambridge, the **Eagle Inn.** It's an old coaching inn with a galleried courtyard dating from the early 19th-century but based on a much older original. There are tables and benches in the cobbled courtyard and two cozy bars in the larger, at which hot food—cottage pie, chili con carne, etc.—can be had for lunch and sometimes in the evenings.

Going back from the Eagle onto King's Parade in the direction of the market square soon brings you to the university church of **Great St. Mary's.** The latter can also be reached from the Anchor by going up Silver Street and turning left onto King's Parade, or from the Granta by going along the Backs and cutting through the rear gate of King's College.

As befits the official church of a traditionally puritan university, Great St. Mary's has a somber, protestant, and official air to it when compared with the high-church, ritualist air of its smaller namesake. It is used for university sermons and other devotional purposes. The building dates from the 13th century, with 18th-century galleries over the aisles. During the Reformation, Great St. Mary's was at the center of the age's turbulent religious controversies. The reformers Erasmus, Cranmer, Latimer, and Ridley all preached from its pulpit. At one point the works of Martin Luther were ceremonially burned outside its door. During the civil war, Oliver Cromwell reputedly came into the church and had the *Book of Common Prayer* torn up in front of him. Climb to the top of the 15th-century tower to get a panoramic view of the city from the tower of the University Library beyond the Backs to Castle Hill, and then toward Newmarket Heath to the east and over to Addenbrooke's Hospital to the south.

One final ecclesiastical edifice now awaits you. This is the famous **Round Church.** To get to it you need to walk between the tower of Great St. Mary's and the Senate House and along Trinity and St. John's Streets, past the colleges of those names, but perhaps pausing to browse in **Heffer's,** the main university bookstore facing Trinity Great Gate. You will find the Round Church where St. John's Street meets Bridge Street. Probably dating from the 12th century, its round shape is based on the Church of the Holy Sepulcher in Jerusalem. Its parish is the oldest in Cambridge. Churchmanship is low or evangelical, and so the east end of the church has a wooden communion table decorated with flowers as opposed to an altar with candles like at Little St. Mary's. Architecturally its great glory is the interior of the Round, a dome supported by eight Norman pillars, each with its own individually carved heads. Above these is a gallery with double Norman arches, and then a tower with Victorian stained-glass windows.

By now the afternoon is probably turning into evening, and it's "attitude-adjustment time." What better than a ten-minute stroll through Jesus Green, just round the corner from the Round Church, crossing Victoria Avenue to Midsummer Common and the **Fort St. George.** There are tables outside by the common and river and bar snacks should you be hungry.

## Country Pubs Around Cambridge

The villages surrounding Cambridge abound in delightful country pubs, many of which also serve food. Here are a few suggestions.

**Green Man,** High Street, Grantchester (0223-841178)

**Pike and Eel,** Water Street, Chesterton (0223-350521)

**Plough Inn,** Green End, Fen Ditton (Teversham 3264)
   These three pubs are all adjacent to the river and can be reached by punt from Cambridge.

**Queen's Head,** Fowlmere Road, Newton (0223-870436)—wooden benches, open fires, roast beef sandwiches, and Adnam's beer.

**Tickell Arms,** The Village Green, North Road, Whittlesford (0223-833128)—good food, a garden with a fountain, and a landlord who constantly plays Wagner tapes.

## Side Trips in the Cambridge area

**American Military Cemetery,** in Madingley, is the resting place for 3,811 American servicemen and has a memorial wall to 5,125 troops lost in action.

**Anglesey Abbey** in Lode, is a 16th-century country house with gardens and **Audley End,** Saffron Walden—itself a beautiful old market town—is a Jacobean mansion.

**Imperial War Museum,** Duxford, is a former Battle of Britain airfield with an extensive display of civil and military vehicles.

**Wimpole Hall,** in New Wimpole, is the most spectacular 18th-century mansion in Cambridgeshire, on three hundred acres of landscaped parkland.

**Wicken Fenn,** Wicken, is an undrained peat fen and wildlife reserve.

## ❦ RESTAURANTS

In comparison with Oxford, Cambridge can seem to be a gastronomic desert. There are several good restaurants in the higher price range, but often the food does not match the quality that similar prices would command in London. Eating cheaply in the middle of town is increasingly a thing of the past, as the restaurants that formerly catered to the student population are continually having to raise their prices to cover the astronomical rent increases that their college landlords continually impose on them. Better value, especially for lunch, is often to be found in pubs. As is the case elsewhere, Indian restaurants can be both inexpensive and delightful. We recommend the Meghna on Mill Rd. Otherwise Hobbs Pavilion, Pizza Express, and Brown's give good value in the middle of town; Michel's Brasserie on Bridge Street is a focal point for those whose tastes are a little more elaborate and up-market.

Always make a telephone reservation in Cambridge for Saturday evenings.

**Brown's,** Trumpington St., tel. (0223) 461655. Amazingly reasonably priced and spacious for Cambridge. It's housed in the former outpatients' waiting room of Addenbrooke's Hospital! The best value is spaghetti with Brighton Seafood Sauce, which comes with garlic bread and salad for less than £4, but at £7.95 the steaks are worth trying. No credit cards.

**Fort St. George,** Midsummer Common, tel. (0223) 35432. A riverside pub with restaurant and outside tables that let you enjoy the view. Lunchtime specials like cottage pie or lasagne, served with salad and chips, run about £3. Evening snacks, served 7–10:30 P.M. all week, include soups, pâté, cheese, and salads. Hot dishes like chicken breast or deep-fried scampi are served with chips. Restaurant open 12–2 P.M. all week during summer, Sat. and Sun. the rest of the year. No credit cards.

**Hobbs Pavilion,** Regent Terr., tel. (0223) 67480. Various savory and sweet crêpe combinations (£2.50–£4.75). No credit cards.

**Meghna Tandoori,** Mill Rd., tel. (0223) 312702. This place features Tandoori specialties from around £4. The Biryani dishes, which come with rice, are a great value for around £3, or pay a little more and delight in the chicken masala. MC, V.

**Michel's Brasserie,** Bridge St., tel. (0223) 64961. Two-course dinner, £11.25; three courses, £12.95. Lunch (three courses) for £7.65. AE, DC, MC, V.

**Pizza Express,** St. Andrews St., tel. (0223) 61320. The Cambridge location features their standard menu. You can help to save Venice by ordering the *Veneziana* (around £4 with salad). Does not take phone bookings. AE, MC.

**The Free Press,** Prospect Row, tel. (0223) 68337. This restaurant offers great values on hot food and salads (12–2 P.M., 6–9:30 P.M.). Soup with bread costs £1, and hot dishes run £2.50. Pies or cold meats and cheese with salad are no more than £3.80 We particularly recommend the duck and game pies. No credit cards.

# Cathedral Stops: Ely and Peterborough

A day trip by car or train from Cambridge can comfortably combine both these cathedrals. Alternatively, Peterborough might be your stopping-off point en route from East Anglia to the north of England and Scotland. If you are making them a day trip from Cambridge, then we would suggest going to Peterborough first, since it's farther away (an hour by train across the prairie-like flatness of the Fens) and you might want to combine the cathedral with some shopping. Ely Cathedral is open until 6:30 P.M. during the winter and 7 P.M. during the summer. The cathedral apart, Ely has wonderful views of the cathedral close and the adjoining King's School, both of which can be visited in the early evening.

**Ely Cathedral** looms large on the horizon, rising out of the surrounding Fens as you drive north on the A10 or ride the train. The word *Ely* means eel island, and up until the Fens were drained in the 17th and 18th centuries it was an isolated island. So isolated, in fact, that the Saxon Hereward the Wake was able to hold out here against the Normans until the monks of Ely betrayed his whereabouts. Today it is a small market town with timbered houses and medieval gateways, dominated, as it has been since the 14th century, by the octagonal lantern tower of the cathedral. Ely is unique among English cathedrals in having the corona of the lantern tower as its center and by having only one tower at its west end. Walk through the cathedral, stop underneath the lantern tower, look up, and catch your breath. Follow that with the exquisitely carved choir stalls and the Lady Chapel, the walls of the chapel lined with the figures of saints. Each of these had its face carefully smashed at the time of the Reformation. On your way out from the west door pause in the south porch to read the Victorian inscription on the tombstone of William Pickering. Entitled "The Spiritual Railway," it's all about life and death as a journey on a steam train:

> Come then poor Sinners, now's the time
> At any Station on the Line.
> If you'll repent and turn from sin
> The Train will stop and take you in.

Food for thought if you're now taking the train to Peterborough!

Like Ely, **Peterborough Cathedral** was originally a Benedictine abbey. Henry VIII gave it cathedral rank in 1541, and it's said to have the finest west front of any cathedral in Europe. When the BBC filmed Anthony Trollope's *Barchester Towers* a few years ago, they used the exterior of the cathedral and its close for their outdoor shots. The 12th-century cathedral has been at the center of many significant moments in British history. Henry VIII's first wife, Catherine of Aragon, is buried within its walls. So, too, for a time was Mary, Queen of Scots until her son James I arranged for the transference of her body to Westminster Abbey. Peterborough the town goes back to Roman times. Today its prize-winning Queensgate shopping mall is at the center of a thriving modern city.

# Newmarket and Bury St.-Edmunds

Driving from Cambridge to Newmarket on the A45, you start to gain height as you approach Newmarket Heath. Between gaps in the tree-lined road you catch glimpses of racing stables and stud farms. Before you reach the town of Newmarket you will pass the Rowley Mile, where race meetings are held in April, May, September, and October. The heath has another course, the July, not visible from the main road. Meetings are held there from June to August. As the center of English horse racing, Newmarket dates back to the reign of Charles II (1660–1685). Charles used to move the royal court (and Nell Gwynn!) up to Newmarket during the racing season, and the Rowley Mile is named after his horse Old Rowley.

The town of Newmarket is built around its long, wide High Street. Try to be there between 7 and 9 in the morning, when the horses are being taken for their morning gallop on Warren Hill. This is at the Bury St. Edmunds end of the High Street, beyond the Victorian clocktower. Climb to the top of the hill for a panoramic view of the horses and the town. At any one time there are over two thousand horses in training around Newmarket, and that means a lot of horses in movement each day. The **National Horseracing Museum** does tours of Warren Hill using as a guide a local Newmarket person who has worked with one of the top racers. The museum itself is on the High Street and is a must in itself for any visitor. Ideally you would go to the museum in the afternoon, having seen the horses in the morning. One of the first things you see on entering is a painting of Warren Hill from 1736. That makes a good introduction to the history of racing, its heroes and great characters, jockeys, trainers, bookies, and punters right up to the present day, and a unique collection of racing art. Live races can also be watched on television in the cafeteria. A salutary story to ponder during your visit is that of Henry, the 4th marquis of Hastings, who lost over £120,000 on the 1867 derby laying his money against a win in pursuit of his rivalry with a horse's owner, whose wife he had also stolen. He died bankrupt and broken at the age of 26. The National Horseracing Museum is at 99 High Street (0638-667333). It is open Monday through Saturday from 10 A.M. to 5 P.M., Sunday from 2 to 5 P.M.; various tours from £5.50 to £10.

Next door to the Museum is the headquarters of the **Jockey Club,** the "Holy of Holies" of horseracing. The Museum's tours include a visit to the Jockey Club Rooms, and also to the famous stallions kept at the National Stud. More informally, racing talk can be heard in the many pubs around the High Street like The Bull or The Bushell, in the Rookery just off it. The bar of the Rutland Hotel is also worth a visit (see below).

## Main Newmarket Races
General Accident 2000 Guinea Stakes: late April
Norcross July Cup: early July; the top sprint race in Europe
Dubai Champion Stakes and Tote Cesarewitch Handicap: mid-October

# Bury St. Edmunds
A short train ride or drive along the A45 east from Newmarket brings you to Bury St. Edmunds. Where the 17th and 18th centuries predominate at Newmarket, Bury bears the imprint of the Middle Ages juxtaposed with those of Georgian and Victorian periods. It is an ancient market town that grew up around the great abbey of St. Edmundsbury. Founded in the 11th century, it became one of the four or five greatest Benedictine monasteries in England. All that remains now is the

mighty Abbey Gateway on Angel Hill and the Norman Gate, adjacent to the cathedral.

The large open space of **Angel Hill** is the most natural orientation point for Bury. It is also the location of the Tourist Information Office. Here you will find the 18th-century Angel Hotel and the Athenaeum assembly rooms facing the **Abbey Gate** (14th century) and **St. Edmondsbury Cathedral** (12th century), the former abbey church. Thomas Carlyle compared his own age unfavorably with that which produced the abbey in *Past and Present* (1843). Another great Victorian, Charles Dickens, used to give readings from his works at the Athenaeum while staying at the Angel, where his room is preserved.

From Angel Hill you can either wander into the delightful abbey gardens or proceed up Crown Street past the Norman Gate, then **St. Mary's Church** (14th century) to Westgate Street. Here, facing the end of Crown Street, is the **Theatre Royal** (1819), after Brighton and Bath the third oldest theater in England still performing. Surrounding it on both sides of Westgate Street and on Crown Street are the buildings of the Greene King brewery.

An excellent place to sample the beer on its own doorstep is the **Dog and Partridge** on Crown St. Tours of the brewery can be arranged, and they include a visit to the brewery's own private taproom, where freshly brewed IPA and Abbot can be sampled.

Also of interest on Westgate Street is the Grecian-fronted Catholic church of **St. Edmund** (1837). Unusually for a Catholic church in England, this contains wooden box pews.

From this end of town go back to Angel Hill and cut up Abbeygate Street to the Buttermarket. Here you will find **Moyses Hall Museum,** which most people visit for the relics of the Maria Marten murder. This was turned into a highly successful Victorian melodrama called *Murder in the Red Barn.* Corder, a local farmer, who murdered Maria Marten, the mole catcher's daughter, was hanged in Bury. His skeleton used to be used for teaching purposes at West Suffolk Hospital but is now at the Hunterian Museum in London. Moyses Hall also contains much local history and archeology, including ferocious mantraps left for poachers, an aeolian harp, Cromwellian cavalry helmets,12th–century swords and the remains of the Stone Age Isleham Founder's Hoard.

From here you can quench your thirst in two distinctive local hostelries, both on the Traverse, across from Moyses Hall. The first of these, the Baroque-style **Cupola House,** once belonged to a 17th-century apothecary, and Daniel Defoe is alleged to have stayed there. Next door is the **Nutshell,** which claims to be the smallest pub in England.

# ☙ RESTAURANTS

If you are staying overnight in Bury St.-Edmunds you may be esconced already at the Angel. If not, you can still sample its first-rate cuisine: the hotel welcomes non-residents in its bars and restaurants.

**The Vaults** and the **Regency Restaurant** serve lunch and dinner. Generally speaking, the Vaults is more popular at lunchtime, the Regency in the evenings. Window tables at the Regency overlook the Abbey Gateway. The Regency staff is highly attentive; they have been there for the last twenty years, and this gives their relationship with clientele a terrific feeling of continuity. The set menu is the one to go for (£9.50 for two courses; £11.50 for three). Start with a home-made chicken-liver pâté with red currant dressing and then move on to the house specialty, a sirloin joint carved before you on a trolley and served with local vegetables picked that morning. One should never underestimate the feeling of well-being that comes after English food when it is done well! There is a dessert tray to choose from, or perhaps you would favor a selection of English cheeses—all farm-house with rind and served with biscuits, radish, spring onion, and celery. The wine list is wide-ranging. The Angel has its own, specially labeled champagne, and the two house wines, a Macon-Villages and a Beaujolais-Villages (both 1986), are fine. There are also many tempting Premier Cru burgundies and a very superior 1985 Chateau Trinite (£9.50, or £5 for a half-bottle). A sweet or cheeses may be eased on their way by a 1985 Taylor's Crusted Port, followed by a sharp, bitter Hennessey XOL brandy to aid the digestion. Both take AE, DC, V.

# Norwich

Until the 18th century Norwich was the largest and most important city after London. It remains the premier city of East Anglia, with two cathedrals and a wealth of beautiful old buildings, and it claims to possess the largest number of standing medieval churches—31 of them—of any city in Europe. Unlike most other English towns, it largely escaped the destructive attentions of the Luftwaffe during World War II and property developers afterward. Its old center remains intact, with many streets now pedestrianized. Geographical isolation probably assisted its preservation, although today Norwich basks in the reflected glow of the economically booming southeast of England.

Norwich is situated at the upper end of the **Norfolk Broads,** and from May to October there are boat cruises to them along the river Wensum, leaving from Elm Hill in the heart of the city.

Norwich boasts a number of "firsts." The international Round Table movement began in the Louis Marchesi pub opposite the Anglican cathedral. The first canaries in Britain were brought to Norwich by Dutch Protestant refugees during the 16th century. Canaries kept them company while they worked at their crafts of weaving and lace making. Canary yellow is the city's color; its soccer team members wear a green-and-yellow stripe and are known as "The Canaries." Norwich was the birthplace of the author George Borrow, the prison reformer Elizabeth Fry, and Edith Cavell, the Red Cross nurse shot by the Germans during World War I. Lord Nelson was born nearby. And Norwich is a lively, friendly and safe city that comes into its own at night with the floodlighting and illumination of buildings and picturesque streets.

If you do go to Norwich from London, your journey will be one of masked and interesting transitions. By train you move out through Stratford and Ilford and watch east London gradually give way to the lush, slightly rolling countryside of Essex, villages of neat, well-kept cricket pitches and squat stone churches, Queen Anne farmhouses, and manor houses. After London the first major town is the Old Roman garrison center of Colchester. This is the oldest recorded town in England, with Roman walls, a Norman castle, and a Dutch merchants' quarter. Farther north past Ipswich the village churches get larger and more elaborate, remnants of the region's medieval wealth. The countryside also gets a little hillier and the fields get larger, almost prairie-like. Stowmarket station has an almost Jacobean-mansion look to its brick exterior. Into Norfolk after Suffolk the country again becomes flatter, and then you pull into Norwich's Thorpe Railway station, a small terminus at which you will probably notice the green-painted trains that go up to Cromer and the coast.

The hotels we recommended in Norwich—the Nelson, the Maid's Head, and the Crofter's—are all centrally located, and you can comfortably walk to most places in the city from any of them. If, on the other hand, you are just in Norwich for the day, make for the Castle Meadow. This is a short bus ride from the train station. If you are driving, there is a multistory garage nearby on Rose Lane. With Norwich Castle on the hill above it, Castle Meadow makes one of three orientation points around which you can explore. The other two are the Market Place (look for the 1930s clocktower of City Hall) and the spire of the Anglican cathedral.

## Castle Meadow

Assuming that you are in the Castle Meadow, a curved street with Georgian shop fronts on one side and the side of the castle hill on the other, and assuming that it's lunchtime, then we would suggest that you repair forthwith to the **Bell Inn** on the corner of Castle Meadow and Bell Ave. This can be particularly recommended for its real ale (go for the Adnams) and its hot and cold buffet bar. Those of a more abstemious turn of mind may prefer **Brampton's Sandwich Bar** on nearby White Lion St.

Suitably refreshed, you can now stride up the ramp over what used to be a moat and take a look at the **Castle Museum** (open Monday through Saturday from 10 A.M. to 5 P.M., Sunday from 2 to 5 P.M. The core of the castle is the squarish Keep, which used to function as the county jail, with public executions being carried out by the main gate. By the entrance to the museum is a plaque commemorating one of those executed there, Robert Kett. Kett was a yeoman farmer from the nearby village of Wymondham. He was hanged in 1549 for having led a rebellion of farmers against the crown. His followers were hung in chains from church towers all over the county. The plaque was placed by the citizens of Norwich in honor of "a notable and courageous leader in the long struggle of the common people of England to escape from a servile life into the freedom of just conditions." For some years Norwich has elected a Labour Council, making the city a Socialist oasis in a rural Conservative heartland.

Inside the museum be sure to look for the paintings of the Norwich School. Norwich is unique among English cities in having its own school of painting, like an Italian Renaissance city-state. To study the landscape paintings of John Crome, John Sell Cotman, and George Vincent is to whet your appetite for the waterways and windmills of rural Norfolk. Although the Norwich School produced most of their work in the early 19th century, they were heavily influenced by 17th-century Dutch painting, and the museum also contains several notable examples of this. Look especially for Pieter Brueghel the Younger's *The Rent Collectors* and Tobias Verhaecht's *The Tower of Babel.* The museum also has an interesting collection of local fossils, a shop, and a cafeteria.

Nearby, in the Haymarket, is also the 17th-century overmantel from the home of the famous physician Sir Thomas Browne. Browne, author of *Religio Medici* (1642), is buried in the church of St. Peter Mancroft (see below).

## The Market Place

Locals say of their city that it has no tall buildings, and, with the exception of church spires and the City Hall tower, this is certainly the case in this city center. Unlike Cambridge, Norwich has real hills interspersed with irregular squares known as plains, an anglicization of the Dutch work *plein,* another reminder of strong local ties with the Netherlands. To locate yourself in the historic heart of all this, go back to Castle Meadow, crossing it at the Bell Inn corner. Walking through Arcade Street will bring you into the Royal Arcade, an exquisite late-Victorian indoor shopping mall that looks as if it ought to be in Vienna rather than in Norwich. Pause to admire the marble floor, the wood-framed bay shop windows, the ceiling lamps, and the green tile walls. At the Arcade

Street end the entrance is topped by a stained-glass window. Stained glass of an altogether earlier time awaits you beyond the Royal Arcade in **St. Peter Mancroft church.**

In order to reach the latter you come out of the Royal Arcade and cross the Market Place. This contains Britain's largest open-air market, a wealth of stalls under colored awnings.

Should you be in need of a snack at this point, there is a fish stall facing the Royal Arcade at which you can acquire jellied eels, whelks, and shrimps for immediate consumption, or whole crabs and oak-smoked kippers if you have access to cooking facilities. Here, too, is the **Sir Garnet Wolseley pub,** named after a local soldier who failed to make it to Khartoum in time to save General Gordon.

Behind the Wolseley is St. Peter Mancroft itself. Virtually the size of a cathedral, the church dates from the 1430s. In the 18th century John Wesley noted that he had seldom seen a more beautiful parish church:

> . . . the more because its beauty results not
> from foreign ornaments, but from the very fine
> form and structure of it. It is very large, and of
> an uncommon height, and the sides are
> almost all window; so that it has an awful
> venerable look, and, at the same time,
> surprisingly cheerful.

The 15th-century stained glass in the east window is one of St. Peter Mancroft's great glories, but look also for the 16th-century Flemish tapestry of the Resurrection on the west wall by the font, and the arch that frames the Ringing Chamber at the west end. Sir Thomas Browne's Memorial is to the right of the altar, and there is also a statue commemorating him in a small garden outside the church.

Many of Norwich's churches are faced with gray flintstone, and this can look very impressive in wet weather. Another medieval building faced in flint is the **Guildhall,** on the opposite end of the Market Place to St. Peter Mancroft. At the end of the Guildhall facing Jarrold's store is a plaque in honor of Thomas Bilney, Norwich's first Protestant martyr. Bilney was imprisoned in the vault below the Guildhall before being burned in the Lollards' Pit on August 19, 1531. The Guildhall now contains the local tourist information office, which deals not just with Norwich but also with the whole of the country of Norfolk. Fans of 1930s architecture will go for the City Hall, which occupies the whole of one side of the Market Place. Those interested in the Flemings will also note that the street between St. Peter Mancroft and the Sir Garnet Wolseley is called Weavers Lane.

## Wartime Memorials

During World War II there were numerous air bases in Norfolk. The land was flat, and it was near the North Sea and German targets. In the Roman Catholic Cathedral of St. John the Baptist, under a representation of Our Lady of Czestochowa, is a memorial to the Polish airmen who served in the area. The U.S. Air Force used Norfolk as a base for its Liberators and Flying Fortresses, and the main public library in Norwich, located at the western end of St. Peter Mancroft, has within it an **American Memorial Library.** The contents of this were donated by families of the Second Air Division (2AD) as a memorial to their comrades. Each book in the collection is dedicated to a particular family, and there is also a roll of honor listing all the American servicemen who served in the area.

## Elm Hill

The main shopping area of Norwich is to be found between the Market Place and Castle Meadow. It's still the medieval street pattern, and there are lots of winding streets and alleys to wander down, quite a few of them closed for traffic. We suggest making for Bridewell Alley and the **Colman's Mustard Shop.** Although now part of a large corporation, Colmans, the mustard manufacturers, are a local firm, and this shop is their showpiece. It is open during normal shopping hours except for half-day closing on Thursdays. There are designer mustard pots for sale, some based on Victorian originals, and they would make equally good presents or souvenirs of your visit. Various different flavors of mustard are available, either in powder or in pots. Particularly recommended are "Chive" and "Sage and Onion." The shop also contains a pictorial exhibition on the history of the Colmans firm. In the 1920s they ran a newspaper advertising campaign called the Mustard Club. Dorothy L. Sayers, the detective writer, wrote the advertising copy for this.

Just beyond Bridewell Alley is **Cinema City,** Norwich's art-house movie theater. Unique as a movie theater, it is housed in a 14th-century merchant's house, Suckling House. The theater bar was the former banquet hall of the latter.

Turning right onto Prince's Street will bring you to the top of Norwich's showpiece street, Elm Hill. Before going down there take a look at the **Museum of Church Art** in the former church of St. Peter Hungate on the corner. A large number of Norwich's medieval churches have been deconsecrated and turned into museums. This one (free admission) contains medieval vestments, statues, altar vessels, bells, croziers, and screen panels. From the 17th and 18th centuries there are the remains of wooden pews and the musical instruments used during services—pump organs, a bass, and fiddles. For an example of a parish church still functioning there is **St. George's Tombland** at the corner of Prince's Street and Tombland. This can be visited after Elm Hill as you walk up Tombland toward the Cathedral Close. St. George's is a 13th-century building with 15th-century alterations. The pulpit is 17th-century, with a canopy in laid with ivory. Victorian high church influences are apparent, with statues of Our Lady and of St. George. The Lady Chapel at the west end is dedicated to Our Lady of Walsingham and contains a replica of the medieval shrine at Walsingham.

Now a quiet cobbled street, Elm Hill was once a busy medieval street. Exteriors of buildings are a mixture of Tudor, 17th century, and Georgian. Look especially for the Strangers' Club, from whose windows Queen Elizabeth I once watched a pageant, and the thatched 15th-century Briton's Arms coffee shop. This used to house weavers and shoemakers. Elm Hill is especially beautiful when it is illuminated at night.

After descending Elm Hill, turn right onto Tombland and walk toward the gates to the Cathedral Close. On the corner facing the 15th-century Erpingham Gate is the Maid's Head, Norwich's oldest hotel. Georgian and mock-Tudor façades front a much older building. The Norwich Machine, the first regular stagecoach to London, left from the Maid's Head in 1762. It is traditionally the hotel patronized by Norfolk county society and is mentioned in L. P. Hartley's novel *The Go-Between*. You may like to pause there for morning coffee, afternoon tea, or lunch in the Carvery.

There are several pubs and restaurants in the area adjoining the Erpingham and St. Ethelbert's gates to the Cathedral Close (see "A night out in Norwich," below). Of particular interest may be the Louis Marchesi pub, where the world's first Round Table group is said to have met.

## The Cathedral

Entering the Cathedral Close by the Erpingham Gate you will find the old building of **Norwich School** to your left. The medieval school was founded in 1240, and it became a royal foundation, like so many other old grammar schools in 1547 during the reign of Edward VI. The present Norwich School is behind it next to the cathedral. The cathedral itself, founded in 1096, is magnificent. The best and most dramatic view of its exterior is probably that of its east end from the footpath that crosses from Bishopgate to the Lower Close by the school's playing fields. The spire, with its two smaller towers, appears to be thrusting itself out of the steep flying buttresses that support it like a missile being launched from a bunker. Sit down in the long nave in order to appreciate the interior combination of the Norman and Perpendicular styles, as your eye soars up to the Romanesque galleries and the carved roof bosses; then take a close look at the carved wooden choir stalls where Benedictine monks once performed their daily offices. In the chapels of St. Saviour and St. Luke there are medieval painted reredos over the altars. Don't miss also the 12th-century cloister outside the south wall, reminiscent of the cloister of St. John Lateran in Rome.

Outside the south transept door of the cathedral stands the grave of Edith Cavell, a local woman shot by the Germans in 1915 for allowing Allied prisoners to escape from the Belgian hospital where she was matron. Following the footpath around to the Lower Close and then through to Bishopgate will give you that superb view of the east end of the cathedral from the playing fields. This path brings you onto Bishopgate across from the 13th-century Great Hospital. Originally built to provide hospitality for the poor, it is now a nursing home.

Following the curve of Bishopgate away from the river you come to the **Adam and Eve pub,** the oldest in Norwich, with seats and tables outside—an ideal place to visit for lunch. The Adam and Eve (look out for them along with the serpent on the pub sign) used to be patronized by the wherrymen who sailed wherries (small, light barges) on the river.

There is an exceedingly pleasant stroll to be had along the river from the Adam and Eve round the bend of the river Wensum past the Bishop Bridge, dating from the 13th century and the oldest in Norwich. Nearby is the **Lollard's Pit** where heretics were burned at the stake during the 15th and 16th centuries. Eventually you will come to the beautiful **Pull's Ferry,** a 15th-century water gate. When you walk along the path that leads from there back to the Cathedral Close you are on top of the canal, along which stone used for building the cathedral was ferried. The path also leads you into the world of Trollope's Barchester, stately and homely 17th- and 18th-century houses, beyond which lie the ruins of the Benedictine refectory and infirmary.

## A Side Trip to the Sainsbury Centre for Visual Arts

Located on the campus of the University of East Anglia in a spectacular 1970s building designed by Dennis Lasdun, architect of the National Theatre in London, this houses the Robert and Lisa Sainsbury Collection of modern, ancient, classical, medieval, and ethnographic art. Also here are the Anderson Collection of Art Nouveau and the University Collection of Constructivist Art. Throughout the year there is a varied program of temporary exhibitions. Open noon to 5 daily (closed Mondays). Served by buses 4, 5, 8, 26, and 27 from Castle Meadow.

# ❦ RESTAURANTS

Substantial English lunches of a traditional bent—carved joints of meat and fresh vegetables—are to be had in the **Courtyard Carvery** of the Maid's Head Hotel for under £5.

For vegetarian food go to **The Treehouse** at 16 Dove St., just off the Market Place, open 11:30 A.M.–3 P.M., Mon.–Sat. No liquor or smoking is allowed. The food is prepared fresh each day with organic produce whenever possible. Soup is £1.10; main dishes, many of which are vegetarian, come with a salad. Cakes are vegetarian, gluten and sugar free. Try the pineapple honey rice cake. Meals here cost only a few pounds.

At 39 St. Giles St., beyond the Market Place, is the **Waffle House** (tel. 0603-612790). Friendly, informal and inexpensive, this is good for lunch or dinner. Both savory and sweet courses are waffle-based. Savories are large Belgian waffles, plain or whole-wheat, served with hot toppings like cheese sauce and mushrooms, or cold ones such as tuna mayonnaise. Sweet, golden waffles with maple syrup or honey can be topped with the likes of walnuts, chocolate mousse, or black cherries. Although wine is available, you may choose to be wholesome and try a milk shake or one of the several fruit juices available. No credit cards.

For an evening meal that is rather more substantial and hedonistic go farther up St. Giles St. toward the Catholic cathedral. Facing each other across the street are Green's Sea Food Restaurant and Brasserie l'Abri. **Green's Sea Food Restaurant** (tel. 0605-623733) serves lunch 12–2:30 P.M. and dinner from 7–10 P.M., Mon.–Sat. It is light and roomy with a Mediterranean atmosphere. Starters are in the £3–7 range; main courses £5–10. Sea bass, shark, and angel fish are sometimes available. Credit cards: V, MC. **Brasserie l'Abri** (tel. 0603-63352) is open Mon.–Sat. 8 P.M.–midnight and has a friendly, stylish environment in which to indulge yourself in French nouvelle cuisine with starters £2–4, main courses for around £9, and desserts for around £2.75. Try the smoked salmon wrapped around cream cheese with radicchio salad for a starter and then the venison pieces cooked with green peppers, served with an exquisitely tart selection of vegetables—carrots, zucchini, French beans, and red cabbage cooked in sugar—as your main course. The wine list is excellent, and the Grand Moules 1986 Côtes du Rhône can be especially recommended with the venison. Joyfully regress with your dessert and have Tom Browne's Schooldays, a homemade hot steamed sponge cake served with real custard (made with extra vanilla and egg yolks). All major credit cards.

## A Night Out in Norwich

This may be done either before or after you have dined at one of the recommended restaurants on St. Giles Street (see "Restaurants," above). It's probably better after a brisk stroll to aid the digestion! One such stroll might take you over the walkway at the top of St. Giles to admire the Anglo-Norman exterior of the **Roman Catholic Cathedral of St. John**

**the Baptist.** This was built between 1884 and 1910 as a gift from England's leading Catholic layman, the duke of Norfolk, to the Catholics of Norwich. Returning past the fish restaurant and Brasserie l'Abri you come to the 15th-century parish church of **St. Giles on the Hill.** This stands eighty feet above sea level, and a beacon used to be lit from its tower in Elizabethan times. A curfew bell is still rung nightly following the terms of a 15th-century will. Turning down Cow Lane by St. Giles and then switching back up Willow Lane, you pass the house of George Borrow, the 19th-century author and friend of gypsies. **Willow Lane** is a pleasant back street of brick Georgian houses and also contains a former dissenting chapel, fronted with classical arches and now functioning as an auction room.

Willow Lane brings you back onto St. Giles Street. As you reach the marketplace two options present themselves to you. One is to retrace your steps to Castle Meadow, perhaps visiting the **Bell Inn** if you have not already done so, and then passing up Timberhill to **the Murderers,** so-called because a murder once happened outside its door. The other option involves turning up Exchange Street onto Bedford Street. Those with a taste for wine can go to **Skippers Wine Centre,** while those with a taste for pub conviviality should make for **The Wild Man**—both on Bedford Street. Those with a taste for all things yuppy should go through to Queen Street and the elegant pastel shades of **Drummond's Cafe Bar.** Serving booze during pub hours, Drummond's is also open throughout the day as a coffee shop, and has a hot and cold buffet.

Whichever (or both) of the two options has been taken, those whose perambulatory inclinations are as vigorous as their thirsts may now go to explore the old mercantile quarter of Colegate and Wensum Street. Where puritans and unitarians formerly had their meetinghouses, real ale now reigns supreme. Cross by Cinema City and the imposing medieval halls of St. Andrews and Blackfriars onto George Street and drop in at the **Red Lion.** Then cross the river and turn left onto Colegate. On Muspole Street, just off Colegate to your right, is the **Woolpack,** where live jazz can often be heard. Retracing your steps along Colegate toward Wensum Street you pass near the **Congregational Meeting House** (1642) and the **Octagon Chapel** (1756), where distinguished unitarians like Harriet Martineau were wont to gather. Your priorities, however, are different. Like an 18th-century Tory raising his glass to "confound enthusiasm," you head for **Merchants Bar** on the opposite side of the street. Sometime later you emerge and resume your journey toward Wensum Street. When you reach it you take a right. There are pubs on either side of the river. We especially recommend the **Ribs of Beef** on the Elm Hill side of the river. This is a "free house" (not franchised to a particular brewery) and serves a meaningful pint of Woodford's Norfolk Wherry bitter, named after the ubiquitous wherrymen.

By this time you are probably in need of a gentle stroll in the open air. What could be more agreeable than to walk up illuminated Elm Hill or by the front of the floodlit cathedral gates. If, however, you really want to make a night of it, then you can go clubbing, for Norwich, unlike Cambridge, *does* have a nightlife. **Henry's** in Rose Lane and **Le Valbon** on Prince of Wales Road cater to singles. **Le Valbon** and **Rick's Place** in Anglia Square, at the end of Magdalen Street, cater to a slightly older clientele—a thirties as well as twenties crowd.

# King's Lynn

If you have traveled north from Cambridge to King's Lynn, then you'll really feel that you've come to the end of the line, or the road, or even the world itself! After the immense flatness and big skies of the Fens and the west Norfolk heath and woodland there's nothing now but the river Ouse, the Wash, and the North Sea. The beautiful medieval buildings in the middle of town are deceptive. To the north of them lies an extensive private dock area to which merchant ships from all over the world pay call. But as a thriving port Lynn dates back to the 11th century. King John stayed here the night before he lost his treasure in the Wash, and the Trinity Guildhall contains a priceless 14th-century chalice known as King John's Cup. The town is unique in having two merchant guildhalls, a measure of its medieval importance. The second of these, the Guildhall of St. George, is the largest of its kind in England and now houses the Fermoy Arts Centre and the Museum of Social History. During the civil war the ownership of the town's harbor rights by the Catholic LeStrange family ensured that Lynn became a royalist enclave (hence *King's* Lynn) in a largely parliamentary area. Captain George Vancouver, the surveyor of Hawaii and British Columbia, was born here in 1757.

## Around Town

A word to the wise: To get your orientation you shouldn't ask for the Guildhall (remember, there are two of them) but the **Custom House.** This elegant 1683 building is where George Vancouver's father worked, and it's still used by the Department of Customs and Excise. It's the focal point of the old part of the town and is all the more striking when you come across after walking through the decidedly unhistorical Vancouver shopping mall. Suddenly you are back in the world of the Hanseatic League and the Baltic shipping trade. Indeed,

Lynn became a Hansa port in late medieval times, and this explains the pronounced north German look to the buildings. If you go left from the Custom House along Queen Street you will come into the **Saturday Market Place** (the town also has another, Tuesday Market Place). To the left is the **Trinity Guildhall,** with its Regalia Rooms museum and the local tourist information office. (Try to talk to Mrs. Angela Cribb here. She'll give you a wealth of fascinating information about the locality.) Dominating the Saturday Market Place are the twin towers of the 12th-century **Church of St. Margaret's.** This contains England's two largest brasses and a tide clock on the south tower. Facing it is a former Hanseatic warehouse, dating from the 15th century. Walk down to the quay to appreciate it. Its windows weren't put in until Elizabethan times. Before then the Hansa crowd was too resented by the locals, as Germans, and, after the Reformation, as Protestants, to risk windows! Just beyond here on the corner of Nelson, stands Hampton Court, a pink-painted courtyard surrounded by medieval merchants' houses. Don't miss it!

Thirsts can be slaked with the Greene King beer served at the **Wemm's,** a lively pub on the Saturday Market Place popular with the young crowd. A hot or salad lunch also can be had for around £2.50.

From Saturday Market Place go down College Lane and take a right along South Quay as far as you can go. There are long views here down to the mouth of the Ouse. Back by the Custom House turn left and you're on King St., by another medieval merchant's house and St. George's Guildhall. Morning coffee, afternoon tea, scones, and sandwiches can be had here in the **Undercroft Coffee Shop,** open until 5 P.M.

Next door is the **Museum of Social History,** well worth half an hour or so of your time. There's a brass-rubbing center where you can do your own, a display of Lynn glass, and a marvelous collection of dolls and dolls' houses. Look for the 1912 Google-eye doll, a wire at the back of the head can make the eyes do flirting movements!

For a major fishing port King's Lynn is surprisingly disappointing in terms of locally available fish. This is because most of the fishing is done to contract and is effectively sold before it is caught. All the shrimp, for instance, go to France. Any surplus fish that gets tangled up with the nets is sold off by the fishermen in the local pubs that they frequent.

One final word about King's Lynn. Every year in late July it has a **festival of music and the arts.** In 1988 this was devoted to English and German composers, with concerts given by the Royal Philharmonic and Halle orchestras and a recital by Mstislav Restropovich. Festival details are available from the Fermoy Centre (tel. 0533-773578).

## ❧ RESTAURANTS

If you don't know any fishermen, then you should make for the **Tudor Rose.** Ian and Chris Carter run this combined pub and restaurant, and they are very good for locally caught fish and seafood. Their steaks, which come from a butcher in Downham Market who is said to be the best in the region, are also very good. Everything on the menu is homemade, including ice cream and sauce stocks. Ian Carter delights in discussing the specialty wines currently available. At the time of this writing he reckoned that the Rioja he was selling for £15 a bottle was comparable in quality to a £100 bottle of Bordeaux. To find the Tudor Rose from the Museum of Social History, you continue along King St. to the open expanse of the Tuesday Market Place. To your left will be the Corn Exchange, a building curiously redolent of churches you come across in the streets around the Trevi Fountain in Rome. To your right you seem to be in Germany, with the pink Baroque façade of the Duke's Head Hotel. Go diagonally across the marketplace between Rome and Germany and then go right at St. Nicholas St. There is the Tudor Rose, across the road from the magnificent chapel of St. Nicholas, the largest perpendicular chapel in England. All major credit cards.

# The Suffolk and Norfolk Coasts

Although there are cliffs at Hunstanton and Cromer, much of the region's coastline is flat. North Norfolk beaches are big and the sea goes out for miles; those of Suffolk tend to be narrower. Coming to the sea at **Aldeburgh** is always a surprise. After leaving Bury St.-Edmunds you passed through a succession of small towns and villages similar to the one you are approaching. Suddenly, at the end of the main street of this one, without any warning, you come to the North Sea.

**Great Yarmouth** in Norfolk is a busy modern resort but the places to head for are the largely unspoiled, small Victorian and Edwardian resorts like **Hunstanton, Wells-next-the-Sea, Cromer, and Southwold**. Southwold can now be reached from London in about two hours on the A12. Cromer is a thirty-minute train ride from Norwich. Hunstanton and Wells can be reached by the A149 from either Cromer or King's Lynn. Aldeburgh, about two hours' drive from Cambridge, was the home of the composer Benjamin Britten, and his opera, *Peter Grimes,* is set there. Between there and Southwold lies the submerged village of **Dunwich** whose church bells are said to be audible from beneath the waves.

## ❧ RESTAURANTS

Southwold is the home of the Adnams brewers and wine importers, and has a center of gastronomic elegance and sophistication in the **Crown Restaurant and Hotel** on High St. (0502-722275; AE, MC, V). Farther south the old docks of Ipswich are now a place to eat out. Throw back oysters in **Mortimer's fish**

**restaurant** as you watch the boats pull out. The East Suffolk railway, from Ipswich to Lowestoft, takes you through the countryside painted by Constable and Gainsborough. Over the border in Essex, at Coggeshall near Colchester, Peter Langan has followed up his brasseries in London and Los Angeles with a lively restaurant that offers particularly good value lunches at £6.50 for two courses and £8.50 for three. **Langan's Restaurant** is at 4–6 Stoneham St. in Coggeshall (0376-61453). All major credit cards.

# 9

# EAST MIDLANDS

The East Midlands comprises what are known as the five Shire Counties of Derbyshire, Nottinghamshire, Lincolnshire, Leicestershire, and Northamptonshire. Much of it is open country with distant regional centers that make this one of the most isolated and beautiful regions in Britain.

Travel can be particularly difficult in this part of the world except by intercity rail services to the main towns. A car will then be needed. Traveling from west to east, highlights within the region include Derbyshire's fascinating Peak District, the legendary Robin Hood country around Nottingham, and Lincolnshire's famed cathedral city and seaside resorts.

There are two ways of tackling the region. One is to pick a particular area to visit, like Nottingham or Lincoln, travel directly from London by train, and then hire a car if you want to see more of the region. Nottingham is the most central base from which to see the whole region, and it is an attractive city in and of itself. Alternatively, you can follow a meandering line from Stoke-on-Trent (easy access via the M6 in the west, heading east through the Peak District; also easy access from Birmingham via the A38) to Derby and Nottingham, in the center of the region, and then continuing east to Lincoln and the coast—a route that will include most of everything worth seeing, but you will need a car and it is a long drive. On balance, the region is best seen on day trips from London if cost and time are important factors.

We suggest you center your trip around the spa towns of Buxton, Matlock, and Matlock Bath, located near the heart of the Peak District; Nottingham, probably the most central, a sophisticated city with good access to Derby and the Peak District to the west, Lincoln to the east, and the rural attractions of Leicestershire and Northamptonshire to the south—although the attractions here are few and far-flung; and Lincoln, a fascinating Roman and cathedral town with good access to the surrounding rural countryside and popular sea-

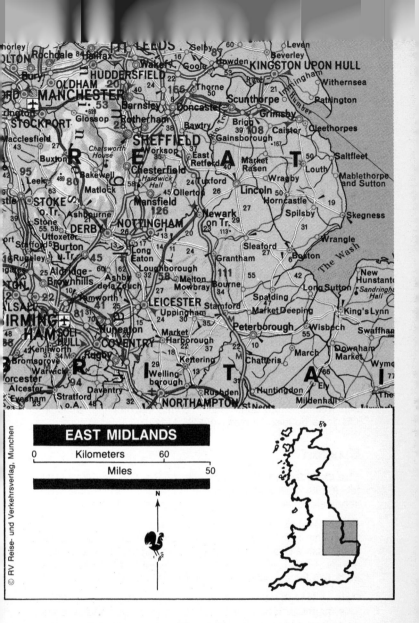

side resorts at Mablethorpe and Skegness. Other good overnight stops are noted under "Hotels," below.

## TRAVEL

There are flights from Heathrow to the East Midlands Airport
(0332-810621) near Castle Donnington for £50 one way, £100
round-trip, £69 with a three-day stay. Trains travel between London St. Pancreas (01-387-7070) and Leicester (0533-29811),
Derby (0332-32051), and Nottingham (0602-476151); and be-

tween London King's Cross (01-278-2477) and Northampton (0788-60116), and Lincoln (0522-39502).

If you are traveling by car, use the MI/M6 for Birmingham and Stoke-on-Trent; the MI for Northampton, Leicester, Derby, and Nottingham; the M1/A46 for Lincoln. To rent a car, try Budget Rent a Car—UK Central Reservations Freefone (0800-181181); Prestage House, Holloway Head, in Birmingham (021-643-0493); Hanger Motors, Aylestone Road, in Leicester (0533-553571); and London Rd., in Northampton (0604-762841). Only local agencies operate in Lincoln, and the best of these is Centurion Leasing, a ten-minute walk from the cathedral, at 276 Wragby Rd. (0522-39537), offering exceptionally low rates.

## ❦ HOTELS

**Credit card abbreviations used in hotel and restaurant listings are as follows: AE for American Express, CB for Carte Blanche, DC for Diner's Club, MC for MasterCard, and V for Visa.**

## Boston

**The New England Hotel,** Wide Bargate, Boston, PE 216SH; tel. (0205) 65255. A good overnight stop, this hotel offers modern facilities, an appetizing carvery (£8–12) and varied wines, and well-furnished comfortable rooms, from £41 for a single, £51 for a double. All major credit cards.

## Buxton

**The Griff Guest House,** 2 Compton Rd., Buxton, SK17 9DN; tel. (0298) 3628, a comfortable home-away-from-home B&B very well priced running from £9 per person. No credit cards.

**Grove Hotel,** Grove Parade, Buxton, SK17 6AJ; tel. (0298) 3804. This 18th century hotel is a reasonably priced alternative. It also has a popular à la carte bistro offering Continental-style dishes (£6–12), varied wines, and pleasant comfortable rooms, from £28 for a single, £36 for a double. AE, MC, V.

**Palace Hotel,** Palace Rd., Buxton SK17 6AG; tel. (0298) 2001. This magnificent hotel, with its stately Victorian frontage dominates the town. inside you'll find grand interiors, ballroom restaurant, conservatory, comprehensive health facilities, and offering choice table d'hôte and à la carte menus (£15–25) and fine wines, and with newly refurbished comfortable rooms, from £54 for a single, £74 for a double. All major credit cards.

## Grantham

**The Angel and Royal Hotel,** High St., Grantham NG31 6PN; tel. (0476) 65816. A good overnight stop, this 750-year-old inn, thought to be the oldest in the country, retains its historic chivalrous and royal atmosphere, with superb bars, a comprehensive menu (£10–15) and good wines, and bright, airy rooms, from £47 for a single, £58 for a double. All major credit cards.

# Lincoln

**Avon Guest House,** 9 Ashlin Grove, Lincoln LN1 1LE; tel. (0522) 20674. An excellent low-cost alternative, this beautifully maintained inn is a ten-minute walk from the cathedral, and offers home-away-from-home atmosphere at just £14 per person. No credit cards.

**The White Hart Hotel,** Bailgate, Lincoln LN1 3AR; tel. (0522) 26222. An outstanding 600-year-old timber-framed hotel frequented by Royalty over the ages, the White Hart has an elegant Georgian restaurant serving gourmet dishes (£15–30) and fine wines, and luxurious rooms, from £59 for a single, £79 for a double. All major credit cards.

## Mablethorpe/Skegness

These two popular Lincolnshire seaside resorts offer a variety of accommodations. In Mablethorpe we recommend:

**The Admiralty Guest House,** 22 Admiralty Rd., Mablethorpe LN12 2AB; tel. (0521) 72820. The hotel overlooks the seafront promenade and offers simple but beautifully kept facilities, home-cooked evening meals on request (£4), and clean, pleasant rooms, at £10 for a single, £18 for a double. No credit cards.

**The Coxswain's Cabin,** 27 Admiralty Rd., Mablethorpe LN12 2AA; tel. (0521) 78037. This is a compact family-run hotel with a small bar and restaurant, selective à la carte menu but limited wine list, and comfortable rooms, from £11 for a single, £20 for a double. No credit cards.

Skegness has an abundance of seaside hotels. We suggest:

**The Crawford Hotel,** 104 South Parade, Skegness PE25 3HR; tel. (0754) 4215. A pleasant family hotel near the seafront, the Crawford has good facilities, an indoor heated pool, spa bath, games room, traditional English cooking (£5–10), house wines, and modern comfortable rooms, from £19 per person. MC, V.

# Matlock

**Riber Hall,** Riber Village, Matlock DE4 5JU; tel. (0629) 582795. An outstanding Elizabethan manor house hotel in a superb secluded country setting ten minutes by car from Matlock, Riber Hall offers exquisite interiors, an excellent restaurant serving gourmet dishes (£20–30) and vintage wines, and romantic lavishly furnished four-poster bedrooms, from £49 for a single, £69 for a double. AE, DC, MC, V.

## Matlock Bath

**The New Bath Hotel,** New Bath Rd., Matlock Bath DE4 3PX; tel. (0629) 3275. Situated in landscaped gardens overlooking the river Derwent, this large modern hotel has two pools filled by warm spa waters and offers a comprehensive menu (£7–12) and wine list, with comfortable well-furnished rooms, from £40 for a single, £60 for a double. AE, MC, V.

## Nottingham

**The George Hotel,** George St., Nottingham NG1 3BP; tel. (0602) 475641. A former coach house popularized by Dickens and conveniently situated in the heart of the city, the George has comfortable surroundings, a pleasant intimate restaurant with a good à la carte menu (£7–15) and choice wines, and modern coordinated rooms, from £39 for a single, £47 for a double. AE, MC, V.

Two miles out of town on the Mansfield Rd. is a wide range of B&B accommodations. We recommend:

**The Woodville,** 340 Mansfield Rd., Carrington NG5 2EF; tel (0602) 606-436. Also has good bars and restaurant serving traditional dishes (£7–10) and varied wines; rooms are from £14 per person. MC, V.

# The Peak District and The Derbyshire Dales

Derbyshire is a county of extremes, sweeping down from the rugged northern Pennine range down to the rich pastures of the Trent valley, and dominated at its center by the spectacular hills and views of the Peak District. About twelve thousand years ago, Stone Age man lived in "the peaks," as they are known, in caves in the northeast (the best of these caves are at Cresswell Crags), and grazed sheep in the northwest. These are some of the earliest known homes of man in the British Isles. Roman occupation left a framework of major roads across the county, including Ryknield Street, running north-south through Lincolnshire. The Anglo-Saxons and Vikings cleared forest from the plains and were responsible for the present pattern of rural parishes in the south. Numerous archeological remains include the eerie stone circles at Arbor Low, Eyam, and Stanton Moor, and the hill fortress of Mam Tor—which have outlasted the later Norman castles—now just mounds.

Many of the great houses built and rebuilt in the 16th and 17th centuries are still intact; they include Haddon Hall, Hardwick Hall, Bolsover Castle, Sudbury Hall, and Chatsworth House. Many ancient customs and traditions have survived, like well dressing (floral decoration of wells) at Tissington on Ascension Day (believed to celebrate the village escaping the Black Death of 1348), and Ashbourne's Shrovetide football match, involving hundreds of players. Quarrying, mining, smelting, wool, and tanning were the mainstay of working life before the industrial revolution, followed by the expanding water-powered cotton spinning industry, and the iron and steel industries. Today, Derbyshire is still a center for dairy farming, iron smelting, textile (rayon) manufacture, plastics, and engineering, particularly around Derby, also home of the world's most luxurious car, the Rolls-Royce (no longer made here) and its engines, which power many of the world's aircraft and naval vessels.

## The Peak District

England's first designated national park offers the contrast of the windswept heather moors and grit-stone outcrops of the north; the caves and valleys of the west, including the famous Derbyshire dales; the rural coal belt to the west, and pastoral lowlands to the south—a riveting, jagged mixture of breathtaking heights and deep gorges sheltering a wealth of fauna and marine life. Your activities here can include walking, cycling, fishing, swimming, rock climbing, pot holing (spelunking), and visits to ancient sites and grand country houses. The position and size of the Peak District makes it the ideal day trip in stunning countryside, just a short journey from Stoke-on-Trent, Manchester, Sheffield, Chesterfield, or Derby, Ashbourne, Buxton, and Matlock are the main towns to aim for, forming a triangle across the southern and most varied section of the peaks.

Ashbourne and Leek are the southern gateways leading to the heart of the area near Buxton. Between them, to the south on the A50, is the richly decorated Restoration house **Sudbury Hall,** with its parade of state rooms, gardens, and lake—well worth visiting before moving on. The approach to Buxton from Leek (on the A53) offers panoramic views of the rising hills and valley floors far below. The road from Ashbourne (the A515) is deceptively tranquil as it follows the lush line of the river Dove before the landscape begins to dramatically unfold. The road (the A6) from Derby to Matlock is less inspiring—and congested. Once within the Peak District, traffic thins considerably, civilization seems to disappear, and a more leisurely pace allows time to savor the attractions.

## Buxton and Environs

Famous for its waters (known even by the Romans), Buxton has prospered as a spa town, offering grand architecture, elegant parades, the fine **Pavilion Gardens,** the elegant **Ed-**

**wardian Opera House,** Water Street (0298-72190), and an international music festival.

Other attractions in town include the **Peak Rail Steam Centre,** Buxton Midland Station (0298-79898; open Monday through Friday from 9 A.M. to 5 P.M., Saturday and Sunday from 9 A.M. to 5 P.M.; rides are 60 pence for adults, 30 pence for children); the intriguing miniature world of microscopic plant life at the **Buxton Micrarium,** The Crescent (00298-78662; open March through October, daily from 10 A.M. to 5 P.M.; £1.80 for adults, 90 pence for children); modest local history displays and art exhibitions at the **Buxton Museum and Art Gallery,** Peak Buildings, Terrace Road (0298-4658; open Tuesday through Friday from 9:30 A.M. to 5:30 P.M., Saturday from 9:30 A.M. to 5 P.M.; free); **street markets** on Tuesdays and Saturdays; and a chance to take the waters in the local pool.

Situated on high ground with superb views, Buxton offers a good base for exploring nearby sites, including the glacial features of **Poole's Cavern,** Green Lane, Buxton (0298-6978; open Easter through November, daily from 10 A.M. to 5 P.M.; £1.85 for adults, 95 pence for children); **Blue John Caverns,** Castleton (0433-20638; open daily from 9:45 A.M. to 6 P.M., £2 for adults, £1 for children), famous for their blue gemstones; and the **Ladybower Dams** (scene of the filming of *The Dam Busters*).

## The Grand Houses

Undoubtedly the jewel of the peaks, **Chatsworth in Bakewell**—a 175-room palace—is the home of the Duke and Duchess of Devonshire and was built between 1686 and 1708 for William Cavendish, the 1st Duke of Devonshire. The house is lavishly furnished and decorated throughout with magnificent collections of paintings, sculpture, silver, and porcelain. The special features of the exotic sweeping gardens are the cascade fountain (a favorite with children, who enjoy splashing in it) and the one thousand acres of surrounding parkland landscaped by Capability Brown. Facilities include an adventure playground, farmyard, gift shop and tea shop—an unbeatable experience. Guided tours by prior arrangement (024688-2204; open April through October, daily from 11:30 A.M. to 4:30 P.M.; £3.50 for adults, £1.75 for children).

The beautifully preserved 14th-century **Haddon Hall,** Bakewell (062981-2855; open March through September, Tuesday through Saturday from 11 A.M. to 6 P.M. £2.50 for adults, £1.40 for children) is popular for its authentic medieval entertainment. **Hardwick Hall,** Doe Lea, near Chesterfield (00246-850430; open April through October, Wednesday, Thursday, Saturday, Sunday from 1 to 5:30 P.M.; £3 for adults, £1.50 for children) is a supreme example of Elizabethan architecture built in 1591 for Elizabeth, countess of Shrewsbury

(Bess of Hardwick), and noted for its furniture, tapestries, contemporary furniture, Cavendish family portraits, and country park.

Special all-inclusive tours can be booked through the Jackie Cowlish Travel Bureau, 5 Market Place, Buxton (0298-71387). Local events in Buxton during the year include the May antiques fair, well dressing in July, and the international festival of music and arts in July/August.

☛ Ten minutes' walk up High St. toward London Rd. will take you to Buxton's popular pubs and clubs, and beyond to the **Cheshire Cheese pub** (0298-5371), which offers excellent wine-bar food at lunch and in the evenings. No credit cards.

## The Spas—Matlock/Matlock Bath

Both Matlock and Matlock Bath have long histories as popular spas. Matlock Bath, made famous by Lord Byron, began in 1698, when baths were built to catch the spa water springing from the hillside opposite the river Derwent. With its rugged setting, riverfront, botanical gardens, and landscaped Heights of Abraham towering above, it quickly became the fashionable spa resort in middle England. For breathtaking views of the town and surrounding area, take the cable car to the **Heights of Abraham,** Matlock Bath Station (0629-582365; open Easter through October, daily from 10 A.M. to 5 P.M.; £2.95 for adults, £1.95 for children). Also nearby is the popular children's theme park **Gulliver's Kingdom and Royal Cave,** Temple Walk (0629-580540; open Easter through September, daily from 10:30 A.M. to 5 P.M.; £2.75). A couple of eclectic museums: The grueling history of local mineral extraction is exhibited at the **Peak District Mining Museum,** The Pavilion (0629-583834; open daily from 11 A.M. to 5 P.M.; 80 pence for adults, 50 pence for children), and there are underground tours of **Temple Mine,** Temple Road (0629-3834; open Easter through October from 11 A.M. to 5 P.M.; 70 pence for adults, 40 pence for children). Also visit the Aquarium and Hologram Gallery, North Parade (0629-583624; open April through October, daily from 10 A.M. to 6 P.M.; 80 pence).

☛ The **Fishpond pub and restaurant** in the center of Matlock Bath is a good spot for lunch, with a varied, inexpensive grill menu (£5).

Matlock boasts the fabulous former **Smedley's Hydro** overlooking the town, now home to the Derbyshire County Council. Established in 1853, the imposing baths and hotel complex greatly added to the town's fortunes as a local tourist resort before closing in 1954. Overlooking Matlock are the ruins of **Riber Castle,** Riber Village (0629-3834; open daily from 10 A.M. to 5 P.M.; £2.20 for adults, £1.20 for children), built by spa owner John Smedley in 1862. But he had problems getting water up the hill and sold it to a clergyman, who used it as a boys' school. Commandeered by the army to store sugar in the last war, it was later vandalized and fell into ruin. It now houses a wildlife park of rare and endangered birds, cats, foxes, and deer. Also worth a visit is the world's first successful water-powered **Caudwell's Mill** at nearby Rowsley (0629-734374; open daily from 10 A.M. to 6 P.M.; 80 pence for adults, 40 pence for children).

## Derby

The Romans first settled in Chester Green to the north of the present city center in the first century, and it was later named Deoraby—"city of the deer"—by the Danes. During the Middle Ages, Derby was granted a number of royal charters, establishing it as an important administrative and trading center. The first successful English silk mill was established here in 1717, followed by the beginnings of the Royal Crown Derby Porcelain Company. Derby's claim to fame came in 1745 during the Jacobite Rebellion, when Bonnie Prince Charlie halted his march on London here. In the 19th century, the city became one of the major railway centers in the country, and one of the world's leading producers of cars and engines at Rolls-Royce.

Derby has many interesting features, mostly centered around the **Cathedral of All Saints** in Iron Gate at the top of the town. The cathedral itself, with its 16th-century tower rising from an 18th-century body built by James Gibbs, is in the classical idiom and includes a magnificent wrought-iron screen by Robert Bakewell and many statuesque sculptures, the largest being of Bess of Hardwick. Nearby, off Iron Gate, are the picturesque cobblestone Sadler Gate and East Street, with their timbered buildings and exclusive boutiques, leading down to the **Derby Museum and Art Gallery,** The Strand (0332-293111; open Tuesday through Saturday from 10 A.M. to 5 P.M.; free). In the center of town are the produce and fish markets, modern shopping precincts, and entertainment centers—the **Assembly Rooms,** Market Place (0332-293111) and **Derby Playhouse,** Eagle Center (0332-363275). Nearby attractions include one of the finest Norman parish churches in England, the **Church of St. Michael and St. Mary** at Melbourne, with its 1130 cruciform, grand interior, and massive nave pillars; the extensive **Royal Crown Derby Porcelain Company Museum,** Osmaston Road (0332-47051; open Monday through Friday from 9 A.M. to 12 P.M., and from 2 to 4 P.M.; free); the **Derby Industrial Museum,** The Silk Mill, off Full Street (0332-31111; open Tuesday through Friday from 10 A.M. to 5 P.M., Saturday from 10 A.M. to 4:45 P.M.; free); and the **Midland Railway Center,**

Butterly Station, Ripley (0773-47674; open March through December, Saturday and Sunday; July through August, daily from 10 A.M. to 4 P.M.; £2.25 for adults, £1.10 for children).

# Nottingham and Robin Hood Country

The land of Sherwood Forest is dominated by the myth and legend of its three most famous characters; outlaw Robin Hood, poet Lord Byron, and author D. H. Lawrence. It is also a region with immense geographical variety, from the hilliest scenery in the west near Belvoir, the mines and quarries to the north near Newark, and the fertile valley south of the meandering Trent. In fact, mining limestone (for cement), alabaster (for church monuments and plasterboard), and coal (for industry and heating) has long been the backbone industry of the county. There is a long history of feudal barons who ruled the land and built huge houses (of which only Welbeck and Thorseby remain) and created fine parks at Clumber and Rufford. Nottingham is ideally situated to explore the region, and is an attractive, modern city in itself worth visiting.

## The City

Nottingham is famed as one of the best shopping cities in the country, with nine markets plus the huge Victoria and Broad Marsh indoor centers, north and south of Old Market Square—the center of town. Excellent town planning has meant the pedestrian is almost completely unhindered by traffic congestion, and the city has a spacious, cosmopolitan feel. Museums, galleries, theater, and nightlife are in abundance, while the city's historic castle and its association with that bounder of the byways Robin Hood create an air of grandeur and importance.

There is a concentration of antiquity around **Nottingham Castle Museum,** Castle Road (0602-483504; open daily from 10 A.M. to 5:45 P.M.; free). Nearby, the nearby rich pageantry of costume and lace, for which the city is famous, is on show at the **Museum of Costume and Textiles,** 51 Castlegate (0602-483504; open daily from 10 A.M. to 4:45 P.M.; free) and at the **Lace Center shop,** in one of the city's oldest buildings (dating from the 15th century), in Castle Road.

The two world-famous tumbledown timber pubs, **The Old Salutation Inn** on Maid Marian Way, dating from 1240 (a renowned watering hole for motorcycle clubs around the country), and **Ye Old Trip to Jeruselum** in Castle Road, an ancient brewery cut deep into the rock below the castle to serve its inhabitants—are

## Nottingham Castle

Although a castle here dates from 1068, built by William the Conqueror, the original has been destroyed and rebuilt many times over. It must be said that the current edifice is not truly representative of the great forts that once occupied the site, and has been described as "that monstrosity." The present building was a residence erected in 1674 by William Cavendish, 1st duke of Newcastle, which was burned down by Reform Bill rioters in 1831. The roofless shell was restored by the city corporation in 1875 and converted into the first municipal gallery for fine and applied art outside London. Many archeological finds reveal the progressive changes made, while on a small green below the castle walls the bronze statue of Robin Hood and reliefs depicting his life with Maid Marian and Friar Tuck commemorate the castle's most celebrated adversary.

a fascinating way to enjoy a pint, a reasonable lunch, and the city's history.

The legend continues twenty miles north on the A60 in Sherwood Forest, where the imposition of laws controlling hunting led to the many conflicts popularized by the tales of Robin Hood robbing the rich to give to the poor. Sherwood and its hunting were favored by many monarchs, including King John, who died in 1216 at **Newark Castle,** Castlegate (0636-79403; open Easter through September, daily except Monday and Thursday; free), during one of his many visits here.

## Robin Hood

There is no hard evidence to confirm Robin Hood's existence, and historians believe he could have been one of six or more men who chose the life of an outlaw. But the myth persists, inherited through countless fables, ballads, and games that speak of his bravery, wit, revolt against unjust laws, and legendary skirmishes with the sheriff of Nottingham. Sir Walter Scott in his novel *Ivanhoe* portrayed the outlaw as a bearded figure clad in Lincoln green, although the attire of the statue outside Nottingham Castle is probably more accurate.

Identifying Robin Hood has been difficult, with as many as six characters of the same name found in a forty-year period between Edward I and Edward III. Some link him with Richard I, while others say he was born about 1160 in the unknown town of Locksley, fought Friar Tuck at Fountaindale, married Maid Marian in the 12th-century St. Mary's Church at Edwinstowe, and died at Kirklees Priory in Yorkshire, reputedly shooting his last arrow to mark the burial spot. Whatever the truth, there were certainly many real outlaws who echoed his exploits, particularly between 1270 and 1340, when highway robbery was rife, but there are no records of handouts to The poor. Still, the legend lives on.

## Entertainment

Popular nightlife venues include: the **Theatre Royal,** Theatre Square (0602-482626); **Nottingham Playhouse,** Wellington Circus (0602-419419); **Odeon Cinema,** Angel Row (0602-417766); **ABC Cinema,** Chapel Bar (0602-475260); **Nottingham Film Theater,** George Street (0602-470096); and **Rock City disco and nightclub,** 8 Talbot Street (0602-412544).

Nottingham is also noted for its **Trent Bridge cricket ground,** Trent Bridge (0602-821525), **Nottingham Forest Football Club,** City Ground, Trent Bridge (0602-822202), and the **National Water Sports Center,** at Holme Pierrepont (0602-821212).

## Literary and Historic Stops

Short trips out of town will take you to Lord Byron's home at the eight-hundred-year-old **Newstead Abbey,** near Linby (0623-793557; open Easter through September, daily from 1:30 to 6 P.M.; £1.20 for adults, 20 pence for children), and the small mining village of Eastwood, with its **D. H. Lawrence Birthplace Museum,** 8a Victoria Street (0773-763312; open April through October, daily from 10 A.M. to 5 P.M.; till 4 P.M. other times; 50 pence for adults, 25 pence for children)—both with comprehensive museums of these men's lives and work. Other popular sites to visit include the four-hundred-year-old **Woolaton Hall,** Woolaton Park, Nottingham (0602-281130; open April through September, Monday through Saturday from 10 A.M. to 7 P.M.; free), with its spectacular stonework, 50-foot-high windows, statues, and natural history and industrial museums; the textile town of **Mansfield; Sherwood Forest Visitors Centre,** Edwinstowe, near Mansfield (0623-823202; open daily from dawn to dusk; free); **Southwell,** with its impressive Norman minster; the **Saracen's Head Hotel,** where Charles I surrendered to the Scots in 1646 to end the civil war, and site of the original Bramley apple tree; and **Clumber Chapel,** Clumber Park, near Worksop, the superb Gothic medieval "Cathedral in Miniature," situated in nearly four thousand acres of beautiful National Trust parkland.

## ⚜ RESTAURANTS

The restaurant choice in Nottingham is varied but can be expensive. **Cafe Punchinello** (602-411965), in Forman St. opposite the concert hall, offers a superb range of homemade dishes and vegetarian recipes at low cost (£3–7). No cards. Also try **The Shires Room** (602-413311), opposite the entrance to the castle, for brunch, light lunches, and afternoon teas. MC.

# Lincoln Cathedral and The East Coast

The overwhelming impression you'll have of Lincolnshire is of a place where the plowed earth meets the sky, broken only by the occasional farm building on the distant horizon. Those in search of variety may be disappointed by mile after mile of fertile flat farmland, with the rise of Lincoln and its cathedral providing the only dramatic contrast in an otherwise monotonous picture. The feeling is one of intense isolation, broken briefly by a colorful riot of tulip fields blossoming in summer before the skies leaden again and isolation returns. But for those who enjoy simple farming life, lots of fresh air, and the chance to explore the largest, oldest, unspoiled rural backwater in Britain, this is the place to be.

There is some variety—in the hills between Lincoln and the popular seaside resorts. The Fens District, which features a crisscross network of flood barriers around the Wash, and the marshland between the Wolds and the sea have both been reclaimed over a one-thousand-year period. The roads are often as straight as the land is flat, like Roman Ermine Street, which runs north through the heart of Lincoln. Welcome breaks on the landscape include the larger market towns of Grantham and Boston. Grantham, the birthplace of Margaret Thatcher, has some historic hotels and is close to the spectacular, stately Belvoir Castle and nearby Woolsthorpe Manor, birthplace of Isaac Newton and site of the apple tree that provided him with his theory of gravity. Boston, from which the American town takes its name, is visible from twenty miles away—its famous St. Botolph's Church with its awesome 272-foot spire, affectionately known as the Stump, is the largest parish church in England. Wherever held, market day in Lincolnshire is a big event. The banks and mounds are all that remain of dozens of villages throughout the county that were deserted over four hundred years ago. But there are many more tiny villages offering refuge, picturesque churches, and rural life. They include Stamford, a fine stone village with the nearby Elizabethan splendor of Burghley House and Rutland Water, the largest man-made lake for water sports in Europe with 27 miles of shoreline; Spalding, home of spring flowers, and tulips in particular, with its May flower festival; Louth, with its 1441 parish church of St. James, boasting the tallest spire (295 feet) of any parish church in England; and Heckingham, with its unique eight-sail windmill; and Inge's bed-and-breakfast/restaurant, voted one of the best independent establishments in the entire northeast of England. Lincolnshire remains essentially rural—at its heart lies the fascinating city of Lincoln, the best base from which to see the rest of the region.

## The Cathedral and Castle

The Normans first built their cathedral in 1072, and work carried out by Bishop Alexander is still evident on the west front. After losing its roof in a fire in 1141, the main structure fell into ruin following an earth tremor in 1185. Between 1186 and 1200, St. Hugh rebuilt the east end and joined it with the Norman west front, although they meet irregularly. Of the two magnificent round stained glass windows, Dean's Eye dates from 1225, and Bishop's Eye from the 14th century. The splendid central tower (271 feet) was originally crowned by a lofty spire of wood and lead, taking it to a total of 525 feet. Lincoln Cathedral is the only three-tower cathedral in the country. The Wren Library was added in the 17th century, and one of the four original remaining copies of the Magna Carta is kept here. Outside the east end of the cathedral stands the statue of Lord Alfred Tennyson, Lincolnshire's Victorian poet laureate, born at Somersby in 1809.

Lincoln Castle, built in 1068 by the Normans, has the unusual feature of two mounds and includes the Keep known as Lucy's Tower, the 14th-century Cobb Hall, 19th-century Observatory Tower, and 19th-century Prison Chapel. It was besieged several times and in 1644, during the Civil War, Parliamentary soldiers stormed the castle after two days, using ladders to climb the ramparts and walls. The castle is now home to the town's courts.

# Lincoln

Lincoln was one of the finest Roman cities in Britain, still much in evidence today. The Romans built this fortress in A.D. 48 to command the meeting of two great highways, Ermine Street and Fosse Way. Later Lincoln became a walled town and a settlement area for retired legionary soldiers. Bailgate Street, which separates the cathedral and castle, takes its name from the outer bailey walls and follows the original line of Ermine Street, down the hill to High Street and the town center.

The Romans introduced an aqueduct that supplied drinking water pumped from a source one and a half miles away, and built fine colonnaded streets and a canal system. Lincoln became a thriving commercial city under the Danes after the Romans left, and a major wool center in the Middle Ages before its decline between the 14th and 19th centuries. Its fortunes rose as an industrial center with the arrival of the railways. Today, Lincoln's major industries include heavy engineering, electronics, and food products.

The Roman inland port around Brayford Pool still survives as the main inland waterway of the East Midlands. Fine examples of major building through the ages are the famous 12th-century Jew's House in Steep Hill, St. Mary's Guildhall in High Street, and the timber-framed Green Dragon Inn, Cardinal's Hat, and City Information Office in Castle Square. Lincoln is a busy commercial center with most of its interest focused around the **Cathedral** and **Castle,** Castle Hill (0522-511068; open summer, Monday through Saturday from 9:30 A.M. to 5:30 P.M., Sunday from 11 A.M. to 5:30 P.M., winter, Monday through Saturday from 9:30 A.M. to 5 P.M.; 50 pence for adults, 30 pence for children).

You may also want to visit the **City and County Museum,** Broadgate (0522-30401; open Monday through Saturday from 10 A.M. to 5:30 P.M., Sunday from 2:30 to 5 P.M.; 25 pence for adults, 10 pence for children); or examine agricultural and industrial machinery on view at the **Museum of Lincolnshire Life,** Burton Road (0522-28448; open daily from 10 A.M. to 5:30 P.M.; 60 pence for adults, 30 pence for children). The **Usher Gallery,** Lindum Road (0522-27980; open Monday through Saturday from 10:30 A.M. to 5:30 P.M., Sunday from 2:30 to 5 P.M., 30 pence for adults, 15 pence for children), filled with paintings, antique watches, silver, porcelain, and glass; and the **National Cycle Museum,** Brayford Wharf North (0522-45091; open daily from 10 A.M. to 5 P.M.; 50 pence for adults, 25 pence for children). Five miles west is **Doddington Hall,** Doddington (0522-694308; open May through September, Wednesday and Sunday from 2 to 6 P.M.; £2.10 for adults, £1.05 for children), a romantic Elizabethan mansion with gardens and a maze. Spectacular painted ceilings and fine Italian paintings, tapestry, silver fireplaces, china, and a Capability Brown park can be found at 16th-century **Burghley House,** near Stamford (0780-52451; open Easter through October from 11 A.M. to 5 P.M.; £3 for adults, £1.70 for children).

## ❧ RESTAURANTS

Restaurant choice is comprehensive, with **Le Papillon Bistro** (0522-511284) in St. Paul's Way near the cathedral offering delicious wine-bar dishes (£5–9) and good plonk in spacious warm surroundings. MC, V. Steep Hill leading down to the town has numerous cafes and tearooms, of which the **Steep Hill Coffe Shoppe** (0522-37909) is probably the best, despite being cramped and often full. V. Try also the **High Bridge tearooms** (0522-513825) overlooking the river in High Street for delicious light lunches, tea, coffee, and snacks. The 12th-century bridge is the oldest bridge to carry buildings in Britain. No cards.

## Mablethorpe/Skegness

During the summer months, the seaside towns of Mablethorpe and Skegness become the playground of thousands of migrating Midland factory workers. Skegness is particularly crowded, with its awesome Disneyland-esque theme parks, although the town center itself is quite small and manageable.

Mablethorpe is particularly neglected in appearance, but its beaches are cleaner and quieter.

# Leicestershire/Northampton-shire

The least popular of the East Midland counties because of the busy motorways running through them, Leicestershire and Northamptonshire fail to offer many points of interest to the visitor. Northampton, the home of Church's very English shoes, is a quiet market town, and Leicester is a busy urban sprawl, a center for shoes and hosiery. The attraction here is in the exploration of isolated countryside churches, ruined monuments, and small country homes.

## Auto Racing and Other Recreation

**Silverstone Race Circuit** (0327-857271) is situated here, 12 miles north of Northampton on the A43; it features the annual British Grand Prix in July. There is also motor racing at **Castle Donnington,** near East Midlands Airport (0332-810621). The **Waterways Museum** at Stoke Bruerne, near Towcester (0604-862229; open April through October from 10 A.M. to 6 P.M.; othertimes, till 4, closed Monday; £1.20 for adults, 60 pence for children), is a colorful display, beside the Grand Union Canal, featuring the two-hundred-year history of canal life.

Much dominated by mining both deep underground and open cast, Leicestershire is popular hunting country, the home of Melton pies, and Stilton and Red Leicester cheeses, featuring the addition in 1974 of Rutland, the smallest of English counties—and with it Rutland Water, a favorite for water sports.

## Architecture Tour

Architectural highlights include Leicester's seventh-century church of **St. Nicholas** and the Norman **St. Mary de Castro,** the 1180 castle hall at Oakham, and castles at **Ashby-de-la-Zouch** (0530-413343; open March to October, daily from 10 A.M. to 6 P.M.; October to March, Tuesday through Sunday from 10 A.M. to 4 P.M.; 75 pence for adults, 35 pence for children), and **Kirby Muxloe** (0533-386886; open October through March, Monday through Saturday from 9:30 A.M. to 4 P.M., Sunday 2 to 4 P.M.; other months open to 6:30 P.M. but closed Wednesday after 1 P.M. and on Thursdays; 75 pence for adults, 35 pence for children). Houses include **Bradgate Park,** Newton Linford, near Leicester (0533-362713; open April through October, Wednesday, Thursday, Saturday from 2 to 5 P.M., Sunday from 10 A.M. to 12:30 P.M.; free), home of the tragic Lady Jane Grey (1537-1554), nine-day queen of England; and the palatial **Belvoir Castle,**

Belvoir, near Grantham (0476-870262; open March through October, Tuesday, Wednesday, Thursday, Saturday from 11 A.M. to 6 P.M., Sunday from 11 A.M. to 7 P.M.; £2.50 for adults, £1.40 for children), seat of the dukes of Rutland since Henry VIII's time, with notable pictures, state rooms and military museum, and special jousting tournaments or other special events every Sunday.

## Saxon Tour

Northamptonshire has much Saxon work in churches at Brixworth, Wittering, Brigstock, Barnock, Earls Barton. The early English **Warmington Church** and unfinished 15th-century **Fotheringhay,** where Richard III was born in 1452 and Mary, Queen of Scots, was executed in 1587, are of special interest. Houses include **Althorp,** Harleston Village, six miles northwest of Northampton on the A428 (0604-769368; open July, August, September, daily from 1 to 6 P.M.; October through June, Monday through Saturday from 1 to 5 P.M., Sunday from 11 A.M. to 6 P.M.; £2.50 for adults, £1.25 for children), with a spectacular collection of masters, porcelain, and rare English and French furniture; and **Holdenby House,** Holdenby, off the A50 (0604-770241; open April through September, and Thursday, July through August from 2 to 6 P.M.; £1.50 for adults, 75 pence for children), featuring the remains of one of the largest Elizabethan gardens in Britain, a new falconry center, and rare breeds of farm animals— both near Northampton.

# 10

## WEST MIDLANDS

To gain an insight into the way working Britain was shaped, and discover how the Great was put into Great Britain, the West Midlands is the place to start. At first sight, it is an area devastated by industrial revolution, war, and economic decline. With the progression from steam power to electricity, the postwar building boom in roads and houses, and the recent recession, much of the region has suffered environmentally. However, despite widespread dereliction, the area possesses both a rich industrial heritage and exquisite landscapes to explore; nowhere else in Britain is the variety and contrast between the two greater.

Geographically, and for the convenience of traveling, the West Midlands region in this guide also includes Shropshire's immortal "blue remembered hills" and the magnificent Tudor town of Shrewsbury to the west; the acclaimed potteries of Stoke-on-Trent, Burton-upon-Trent breweries, and the cathedral city of Lichfield in Staffordshire to the north; and the scenic Malvern Hills and countryside of Hereford and Worcester to the south. This is where the real treasures of the region lie. Here you will find historic charm and rural splendor, ancient timbered towns, cobbled streets, fine churches, fields, rivers, and hills. Various leisure interests include boating, swimming, golf, fishing, sailing, and walks. This is when you might need a car to see magnificent country houses and tiny villages. Hotels and guest houses are reasonably priced and comfortable, and time should be spent absorbing the local atmosphere.

Birmingham, located in the heart of the region, is probably the most central location to stay but can be expensive, and once in the surrounding countryside, the desire is to linger. We suggest you begin with visits to the region's industrial showpieces around Birmingham and in the Beach Country industrial belt to the west, and the breweries and potteries to the north. Some recommended centers to stay in: Birmingham, ideally situated to strike out in any direction to see most of the region, with all the advantages of a major city and excellent travel connections; Lichfield, just half-an-hour north of Birmingham, is a delightful small cathedral city with pleasant rural market town atmosphere, and good access to the Burton breweries and Stoke potteries further north; Shrewsbury, lying to the southwest on the return leg of your tour of the region, is a historic castled town in glorious countryside, close to the Welsh border and picturesque half-timbered villages in the surrounding area, and offering many rural leisure pursuits to be found in the west of the region; Malvern, further south, with the nearby Malvern hills providing the perfect setting to relax in gloriously scenic surroundings, with nearby attractions including Malvern's famous spa town, and further south, the cathedral towns of Hereford and Worcester, and the pretty market towns of Ross-on-Wye and Evesham.

## TRAVEL

Getting there is the easiest part. Birmingham is the best place to start, lying at the hub of the nation's road and rail network with easy access from London. **By rail,** Birmingham New St. (021-643-2711) is just ninety minutes from Euston (01-387-7070); also serving Shrewsbury—call 0743-64041—and Stoke—call 0782-411411—direct, two and one half hours or Coventry—call 0203-555-211—one hour and ten minutes, or less conveniently from Paddington (01-262-6767) to Hereford (0432-266534; allow two and one half hours with change. There are rail stations also in Burton (0283-68121), Lichfield (call Birmingham), and Worcester (0905-27211). With over 40 trains a day from Euston, it is possible to see many parts of the region without having to stay overnight. Faresaver and cheap-day return tickets from as little as £15 are available. You can also go by road in two hours on the motorway (the M1/M6 from London, the M6 from Manchester, the M5 from the West Country, or the A40/A34 from Oxford and Stratford-upon-Avon). **Car hire:** Budget Rent a Car—UK Central Reservations Freefone (0800-181181); Prestage House, Holloway Head, Birmingham (021-643-0493).

National Express **coach** from London Victoria to Birmingham's Digbeth bus station is as little as £9 round-trip. **Coaches and buses:** London Victoria coach station (01-730-0202); Birmingham Digbeth coach station, Digbeth Rd. (021-622-4373); West Midlands Passenger Transport Information, Chamberlain Sq., Birmingham (021-200-2601).

**By air:** Birmingham International Airport (021–767–5511; connecting with the National Exhibition Centre and Birmingham International rail station) is just 45 minutes from Heathrow (01-759-4321), or an hour from Gatwick (01-668-4211 or 293-31299)—fares range from £50 single, £100 return, or £70 three-day return—and can be reached from most European airports. Once you get to Birmingham, rail is still the best way to see the region, and there are good local bus services.

From Birmingham, the main centers to be reached by road are Lichfield and Burton-upon-Trent via the A38; Stafford via the M6; Shrewsbury via the M6/M54/A5; Malvern via the A38/A449; and Hereford via the A38/A4103.

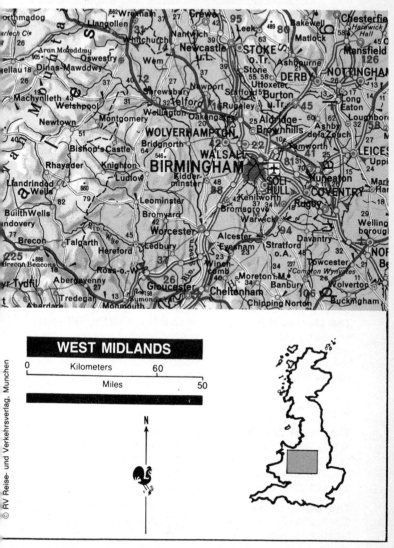

WEST MIDLANDS

© RV Reise- und Verkehrsverlag, Munchen

# 🍴 HOTELS

**Credit card abbreviations used in hotel and restaurant listings are as follows: AE for American Express, CB for Carte Blanche, DC for Diner's Club, MC for MasterCard, and V for Visa.**

# Birmingham

**The Copthorne,** Paradise Circus, Birmingham B3 3HJ; tel. (021) 200-2727. This is a new hotel that has a pleasant bar, indoor pool, health facilities, varied menus (£15–25), and modern comfortable rooms, from £61 for a single, £69 for a double. All major credit cards.

**The Grand,** Colmore Row, Birmingham B3 2DA; tel. (021) 236-7951. The Grand lives up to its name as one of the oldest and biggest hotels, with its magnificent ballroom, banqueting facilities, choice of two restaurants with set menus, carvery (£15–30), and good wines, and modernized comfortable rooms, from £58 for a single, £68 for a double. All major credit cards.

**The Midland,** New St., Birmingham B2 4JT; tel. (021) 643-2601. Situated in the heart of town, the Midland has popular bars, a secluded gourmet restaurant serving specialty dishes (£15–25) and fine wines, and with spacious comfortable rooms, from £63 for a single, £72 for a double. All major credit cards.

**Stephenson's Hotel,** Station St., Birmingham B5 4DY; tel. (021) 643-1134. Conveniently situated near New Street Station Stephenson's also has popular bars, traditional Victorian cooking (£7–12), and a good wine list, as well as well-furnished rooms, from £31 for a single, £42 for a double. AE, MC, V.

# Hereford

**The Merton Hotel,** 28 Commercial Rd., Hereford HR1 2BD; tel. (0432) 265925. A large Georgian hotel offering good bars, a popular restaurant with varied choice menu (£15–20) and good wines, the Merton has modern comfortable rooms, from £20 for a single, £33 for a double. AE, DC, MC, V.

# Lichfield

**The Angel Croft Hotel,** Beacon St., Lichfield WS13 7AA; tel. (0543) 258737. This is a secluded hotel in the square outside Lichfield Cathedral with pleasant facilities, selected menu (£10–15) and wines, and quiet comfortable rooms, from £40 for a single, £50 for a double. DC, MC, V.

**The Duke of York,** Church St., Lichfield WS13 6DY; tel. (0543) 255171. This is a centrally located pub offering modern facilities, varied menu (£5–10) and wines, and comfortable rooms, from £17.50 for a single, £29 for a double. No credit cards.

# Malvern

**Malvern Hills Hotel,** Wynds Point, Malvern WR13 6DW; tel. (0684) 40237. This small hotel has beautiful views of the surrounding hills and offers modern facilities, table d'hôte and à la carte menus (£10–20) with varied wines, and well-furnished comfortable rooms, from £30 for a single, £50 for a double. AE, MC, V.

## Shrewsbury

**The Lion Hotel,** Wyle Cop, Shrewsbury 5Y1 1UY; tel. (0743) 53107. A 14th-century coaching inn popularized by Dickens, the Lion Hotel has excellent facilities, an intimate restaurant serving traditional and exotic dishes (£15–25) and fine wines, plus spacious comfortable rooms, from £45 for a single, £70 for a double. AE, DC, MC, V.

**The Lion and Pheasant Hotel,** 49–50 Wyle Cop, Shrewsbury, SY1 1XJ; tel. (0743) 236288. This delightful small half-timbered hotel offers intimate dining facilities with selective menus (£10–15) and reasonable wines, and has pleasant comfortable rooms, from £27 for a single, £42 for a double. AE, MC, V.

# Birmingham and the Black Country

The heart of the industrial belt, Birmingham and its environs have been the home of metal bashing for centuries. Dubbed the greatest workshop in the world, everything from a needle to a railway carriage is made here. Once the backbone of manufacturing Britain, it has suffered from the twin evils of urban decay and economic collapse. Despite these ills, it remains an important industrial center. Busy commercial markets include automaking, light manufacturing, business conference facilities, technology, and tourism. A visit to any major industrial museum will provide an insight into the immense power and production the region once generated. Manufacturing has added huge acreage to the area, particularly in the Black Country of iron, leather, canals, and enamels. But you will have to look beyond to Ironbridge Gorge in Shropshire to trace the earliest beginnings of the industrial revolution—a short step to the past.

**For a map of Birmingham, see atlas page 17.**

The country's first provincial city is a deceptively large place and has the appearance of a major capital. High-rise office buildings, shopping-center complexes, and an awesomely busy road network are daunting for the first-time visitor. In fact, the city center is surprisingly small; it is contained mostly within the inner ring road, which acts as a steel band preventing further expansion. It is possible to walk around most of the city center in an hour. The city is particularly busy on Saturdays and should be avoided.

The giant Smithfield market can still be seen on Tuesdays and Thursdays.

*A word of caution for motorists*—if you are unfamiliar with the city's confusing ring road and one-way system, you should park your car and walk. A car is not needed in the city center anyway, and public transportation is excellent. Your approach to Birmingham by car will most likely be through Spaghetti Junction (so named by local journalist Roy Smith, who said plans for it looked like a plate of spaghetti!). It is Europe's biggest motorway interchange, handling nearly half a million vehicles a day. From it, the Aston Expressway, running past the famed Gothic-style Jacobean Aston Hall on the right, is a short drive before reaching the inner ring road and the signs for the city center.

## The City Center

For all visitors, the junction of New Street and Corporation Street, outside New Street Station (a constant point of reference), is the best place to start your tour. The other two principal streets are High Street and Colmore Row in what is a packed shoppers' paradise. Looking up Corporation Street, to your right along New Street leads into the pedestrianized High Street, James A. Roberts's landmark **Rotunda,** and down the subway to the bustling **Bull Ring,** the rebuilt 19th-century **St. Martin's Church,** and **Smithfield (Rag) Market**—all on the site of the original settlement. Nearby is the city bus station, the Digbeth coach station, and the **Crown pub** (built in 1368) on the road to Solihull and Warwick.

Corporation Street leads to the travel information center in the city arcade down Union Street to the right, and to **Rackhams** and **Lewis's,** the city's leading department stores. Continuing over Old Square Priory via subway (underground walk) leads down to the magnificent **Victoria Law Courts** by Sir Aston Webb and Ingress Bell (opposite is the similar Methodist Hall), **Hawkins café/restaurant, Aston University** campus and its new technology science park, the avant-garde **Triangle Cinema** (021-3593979), and the quaint **Slug and Lettuce pub.**

Up New Street to the left is **The Midland Hotel, Bobby Brown's restaurant,** and the **Royal Birmingham Society of Artists** (est. 1807), 69a New Street (021-643-3768; open Monday through Friday from 10:30 A.M. to 5 P.M.; 25 pence), which holds regular exhibitions of local art for sale. At the top of the street is the **civic center** surrounding Chamberlain Square; it is dedicated to Prime Minister Neville Chamberlain, who was lord mayor from 1915 to 1917. **The Town Hall** (built 1832 to 1849) was modeled on the classic temple of Castor and Pollux in Rome by Hansom (of Hansom cab fame) and Welch; it is home to one of the country's best ensembles, the City of Birmingham Symphony Orchestra (CBSO), conducted by Simon Rattle. The hall also has one

## The Industrial Revolution

In about the seventh or eighth century, a Germanic tribe sailed into England from the North Sea by way of the River Trent and its tributary, the Tame, settling on the banks of the River Rea, where they began working metals. Thus began Birmingham's history of manufacturing. In the 12th and 13th centuries, charters allowing markets in the town attracted many farm laborers to service the growing boom in crafts and industries. Trade agreements were made with neighboring counties, for the import of iron and coke (made by roasting coal), but it was the tannery and cloth industries, because of plentiful water supplies, that flourished first, then were overtaken by the use of local sands for metal-molding. Although caught up in the anti-Royalist sweep across the country in 1642, the city escaped relatively unscathed apart from the siege of Sir Thomas Holte at his Jacobean mansion, Aston Hall.

Birmingham produced many of the weapons used in the conflict. In the 18th century, specialization led to huge industrial development from Birmingham to Wolverhampton, Walsall to Stourbridge, in mining, metalwork, glass, ceramics, and bricks. In 1769 the canals of engineer James Brindley linked Birmingham with the Staffordshire coalfields, followed by extensions to Wolverhampton (Hereford and Worcester Canal), and the river Severn to the Bristol ports. Between 1708 and 1888, gun manufacture in Birmingham rose to over fifteen thousand weapons a year and heavily supplied the American Civil War. Its pots and pans were also highly sought after in the New World. The Birmingham Small Arms factory at Small Heath subsequently supplied most of the armaments in the First World War and half the entire small arms fire in the Second World War. Other metal-finishing processes led to the birth of the city's Jewelery Quarter (the biggest in Europe), and the award of both the anchor hallmark for precious metals and crown and swords for weapons. The Birmingham Mint also exports coins to over one hundred countries. But the most important development was the steam engine by Matthew Bolton and James Watt, who transformed Birmingham's fortunes through mechanization and steam power. Other eminent residents included Joseph Priestly (who discovered oxygen), William Murdoch (who developed gas lighting), and city father Joseph Chamberlain, who did much to improve conditions for workers and redeveloped the city center. Despite the destruction caused by 77 German air raids on the city during World War II, Birmingham has continued to flourish in the 20th century, owing to famous names such as Cadbury-Schweppes, Dunlop, and electrical giants Lucas and GKN. The scientific and medical research facilities (which include the site where the smallpox virus was isolated) at Birmingham and Aston universities are also widely recognized.

of the finest organs in the country, but getting tickets for any performance is hard, so book ahead: 021-236-3889. Opposite are the **Council House** and **Art Gallery and Museum** (021-235-2834; open Monday through Saturday from 9:30 A.M. to 5 P.M., Sunday from 2 to 5 P.M.; free), both designed by Yeoville Thomason, in 1885. The **Council House,** with its amphitheater chamber, Big Brum clock, and lord mayor, is home to the Birmingham City Council. The splendid art gallery and museum has various displays of fine art (including Renaissance works), costumes, jewelry, ceramics, and local history, a shop, and refreshments served in the Edwardian Tea Room. Across the square is the city's renowned **library,** with over one million volumes. Nearby is the new **Copthorne Hotel,** and across the ring road into Broad Street is the spectacular new (1989) **Hyatt Hotel** conference center and leisure complex, adjacent to the **Repertory Theater** (021-236-4455)—the country's first. Off to the left is Gas Street canal basin, leading down to **Bobby Brown's nightclub** (021-643-0691). Beyond is Hagley Road, with a number of small businessmen's hotels, and the road south to Hereford and Worcester. Back in Chamberlain Square, and down Colmore Row—or from New Street up Temple Street—you come to **St. Philip's Cathedral,** built in the English Baroque style by Thomas Archer, and consecrated in 1715. Opposite on the left is the **Grand Hotel,** overmodernized in parts, but you should take a peek at the magnificent friezes in the ballroom.

Behind the hotel is one of the better pubs for lunch, **The Old Contemptibles** in Edmund St.

Nearby, across the ring road, is the **Museum of Science and Industry,** Newhall Street (021-236-1022; open Monday through Saturday from 9:30 A.M. to 5 P.M., Sunday from 2 to 5 P.M.; free), which includes a Victorian machine shop, and historical displays of steam power and the motor car.

## Auto Racing

Undoubtedly the best time to visit is over the August Bank Holiday, when the city is taken over by Birmingham Grand Prix fever and sealed off for a high-speed Formula 3 race around the city streets, à la Monaco. Now in its fourth year (1989), the city hopes to eventually stage the World Championship Formula 1 race.

## Barge Tours and Other Recreation

One pleasant way to explore the Birmingham area—famous for having more canals than Venice—is by barge, with **Brummagen Boats,** Sherborne Street (021-455-6163; trips £3.50 for adults, £2.50 for children). Other nearby recreational facilities include: the peaceful **Cannon Hill Park and Midland Arts Centre,** Edgbaston Road, Moseley (021-440-3838);

## Motor History

In 1905 Herbert Austin bought a two-acre site at Longbridge, five miles south of the city center, to begin car manufacture. The first car left the works the following year, and the Birmingham motor industry was born. During the twenties and thirties, the Austin Seven pioneered popular motoring in Britain. At the same time (1910), William Richard Morris began planning his first car, the Morris Oxford, at the converted military academy at Cowley, on the outskirts of Oxford. The Morris Minor was launched in 1928. In 1951 the merger of the two companies was followed by the launch of the unbeatable Mini, designed by Sir Alec Issigonis, in 1959 (five million have been sold, and the car is still in production). Its success has also been prolonged by its sister, the Metro.

Rover was begun by cycle manufacturers John Kemp Starley and William Sutton in Coventry in the 1880s. The first car arrived in 1904 and went on to become a symbol of excellence in motoring. After being bombed during the war, the Coventry factory moved to Solihull and went on to produce the Land Rover (1948), based on four-wheel drive army jeeps, and the luxury Range Rover (1970). In 1967 Rover merged with Leyland, the country's main truck and bus manufacturer. A year later, Austin, Morris, MG, Rover, Jaguar, Triumph, and several other famous names joined forces to become BL, and in 1986, the Rover Group. Jaguar, in keeping with a policy to privatize the whole industry, has had considerable success since it went solo in 1984, particularly in the American market. Rover continues to dominate the British market with the Metro, Rover 200 and 800 series, and recent joint ventures with the Japanese and Honda.

Recession and political division have led to stoppages, layoffs, and massive automation. Longbridge is no exception, and visitors to the giant assembly plant will witness the technological revolution in manufacture. Two-hour tours throughout the week can be arranged by calling (021-475-2101).

A visit to the **National Motorcycle Museum** (6755-3311) at Bickenhill, near the National Exhibition Centre (021-780-4141), site of the biannual Motor Show, will also give some idea of Birmingham's former glory in the world of motorcycles; the museum has more than four hundred models of famous names like BSA, Triumph, Norton, Sunbeam, Enfield, Vincent, and many more.

The enduring symbol of Birmingham's checkered history as the home of the motor car is the annual Grand Prix around the city streets, like circuits at Monaco and Detroit. It is a thrilling two days of practice and racing over the August Bank Holiday weekend—fun for the whole family. A large section of the city, including part of the Bristol Road and much of the Chinese quarter, is closed to traffic as Formula 3 and Thundersports cars, among others, dice with death at 180 mph on 30 mph streets. It is the result of twenty years of petitioning by the city for an Act of Parliament to celebrate its history with a grand prix. One day, it hopes to stage the Formula 1 world championship.

**Edgbaston cricket ground**—home of the Warwickshire County Cricket Club, Edgbaston Road, Moseley (021-440-

4292); the city's two football teams—**Aston Villa Football Club,** Witton Lane, Aston (021-328-1722), and **Birmingham City Football Club,** St. Andrews Street, Bordesley Green (021-772-2689); and the **Alexander Stadium sports complex,** Walsall Road, Perry Barr (021-356-1015).

## Side Trips

Short trips out of the city will take you to the beautifully tended Oriental-style **Botanical Gardens,** Westbourne Road, Edgbaston (021-454-1860; open Monday through Saturday from 9 A.M. to 6:30 P.M., Sunday from 10 A.M. to 6:30 P.M.; £1.70 for adults, 85 pence for children); the imposing Gothic-style **Jacobean Aston Hall,** Aston (021-327-0062; open March through October, daily from 2 to 5 P.M.; free). The fascinating history of train travel can be seen at the **Birmingham Railway Museum,** 670 Warwick Road, Tyseley (021-707-4696; open daily from 10 A.M. to 5 P.M.; £1 for adults, 50 pence for children). The bygone era of the industrial age is extensively reconstructed at the **Black Country Museum,** Tipton Road, Dudley (021-557-9643; open daily from 10 A.M. to 5 P.M.; £3 for adults, £2 for children). Also recommended are the Elizabethan timber-framed house at **Blakesley Hall,** Blakesley Road, Yardley (783-2193, open March through October, daily from 2 to 5 P.M.; free); the exceptional collection of rescued and reconstructed medieval and farm buildings at the **Avoncroft Museum of Buildings,** Stoke Heath, Bromsgrove (0527-31886; open March through November daily from 11 A.M. to 5:30 P.M.; £1.90 for adults, 95 pence for children); **Edgbaston Reservoir** for water sports; **Sutton Coldfield Park** for scenic walks; and the **Clent and Lickey hills** for panoramic views of the surrounding countryside.

## ❦ RESTAURANTS

Restaurant choice in Birmingham is limited, dominated by basic English fare, with only foreign influences offering real variety. **Hawkins** café/wine bar/restaurant, at 215–219 Corporation St. (021-236-2001), offers a good choice of simple dishes (£5–10) throughout the day in Continental surroundings; crowded at lunchtime by journalists and lawyers, it is transformed at night by lasers and loud music when the young take over. AE, MC, V. **Bobby Browns in Town,** New St. (021-643-4464) offers Continental cuisine by candlelight in its cellar retreat, and many pubs serve good, reasonable lunches. All major credit cards. At night, the city's **China Town** offers the best in exotic fare: delicious Cantonese at both **Chung Ying** (probably Birmingham's best restaurant, £8–12), 16 Wrottesley St. (021-622-5669) and at the very reasonable Both take all major credit cards. **House of Mr. Chan,** 167 Bromsgrove St. (021-622-1725). Both take all major credit cards. **The Maharaja,** 23–25

Hurst St. (021-622-2641) is the best Indian restaurant (£8–12), and a short trip south will take you to **Balsall Heath's** popular colony of cut-price curry houses. AE, DC, MC, V.

## For Entertainment

In China Town near the Bull Ring, where you'll find the **Birmingham Ice Rink,** Pershore Road (021-622-4325; £1 plus skate hire), and the best nightclubs: the **Powerhouse,** Hurst Street (021-643-4715) for live music, and glitzy discos at **Pagoda Park,** Small Brook (021-643-6696) and **The Dome,** Bristol Road (021-622-2233). Here you will also find the popular family entertainment center **The Hippodrome Theater,** Hurst Street (021-622-7486). For cinema, there is **The Odeon,** New Street (021-643-6101), which also has live music, and **The Futurist,** John Bright Street (021-643-0292). The city's *What's On* guide (free) contains details of all venues and events.

## Coventry

The road (the A45) to Coventry from Birmingham has a few memorable villages off it, notably Barston and Meriden (reputedly the center of England), which only serve, on your approach, to highlight the fate Coventry suffered as the phoenix city of Britain in the last war. Once the city of Lady Godiva (who rode naked through the streets) and the center of the cloth industry, Coventry is now literally a shell of its former self. Once the second home of motor cars in the Midlands, the destruction of most of the city center during the war also claimed the Rover works, which moved to Solihull after the war. Massive concrete redevelopment and recession have further stricken the city. Its new cathedral, risen out of the ruins of the old, is a grim reminder of the past; it features John Piper's 80-foot baptistry window and the largest tapestry in the world, by Graham Sutherland. Historic buildings include **Bond's and Ford's hospitals,** and the **Charterhouse;** other attractions include the **Belgrade Theatre,** Corporation Street (0203-553055), the **Herbert Art Gallery and Museum,** Jordan Well (0203-832381), and—within the city boundary—the excellent **University of Warwick Arts Centre,** Gibbet Hill Road (0203-417417).

## Lichfield

The unusual three-spire **Lichfield Cathedral** is undoubtedly the star attraction of the town. First built in A.D. 700, it was replaced after four hundred years by a Norman cathedral, and the present Gothic cathedral one hundred years later. Its treasures include the priceless eighth-century illuminated Lichfield Gospels, the 14th-century Lady Chapel, and its vaulted Chapter House. Badly damaged in the civil war, it was restored by Bishop Hacket. It is now the focus of the Lichfield Festival in July. Across the square is the delightful timber-framed Vicar's Close.

Across Stowe Pool is **St. Chad's Church,** where the bishop of Lichfield, St. Chad, had his cell. In Market Square is **St. Mary's Church Center** (rebuilt twice), and **Samuel Johnson's Birthplace Museum** in Broadmarket Street (0543-264972; open Monday through Saturday from 10 A.M. to 4 P.M., May through September from 10 A.M. to 5 P.M.; 50 pence for adults, 25 pence for children).

The house in which Dr. Johnson was born was built by his father,Michael Johnson, in 1709, about a year before his son's birth. An unusually fine four-story building with basement and 13 rooms, it presently houses a fulsome exhibition of Johnson's work, including his masterpiece, the first English dictionary. Johnson spent his early life here until 1737, after which the house was rented out but remained in Johnson's possession until his death in 1784. Then auctioned, the house changed hands several times until 1900, when it was bought by the Lichfield city council. In 1969 the house was restored and the collection organized. Outside stands a statue of Johnson and nearby, James Boswell. Lichfield also has overone hundred sixty listed buildings.

We recommend the **Lichfield Heritage Exhibition and Treasury** in Market Square, and the **Lichfield Art Galley,** above the library on Bird Street.

## 🦐 RESTAURANTS

Lichfield is the perfect town for lunch or dinner. We suggest the **Corn Exchange Carvery** in Market Sq. for traditional English dishes (£8–15) in a delightful, airy timber-roofed setting. Varied reasonable three-course lunches (£3–8) can be had at the 15th-century **Tudor of Lichfield** restaurant, and at the intimate **Elizabeth Tea Rooms** in Dam St. you can get delicious hot dishes (£3–6).

## The Breweries

The home of names like Bass, Ind Coope, and Carling Black Label, **Burton-upon-Trent** has been brewing for over nine hundred years, due to the quality of the water in deep wells beneath the town. Situated on the River Trent, it is one of the most prosperous per capita towns in the country—but you wouldn't know it to look at it sometimes. Relatively little seems to have been plowed back into the town, and it suffers from a lack of cultural facilities. Highlights of the town include tours (by appointment) of the **Bass Museum and Shire Horse Stables,** Horninglow Street (0283-45301/42031, weekends), the **Ind Coope Brewery,** 107 Station Street (0283-31111), and **The Heritage Brewery Museum,** Anglesey Road (0283-63563).

Other areas of interest are the **town hall,** with its decorative council chamber and tourist information center; the **market hall** (open Monday through Saturday); the **Meadowside Leisure Centre off High Street;** and the **river garden area.**

🐾 Take the Ferry footbridge across the river to the **Boat House pub** for good lunches.

Four miles away are the ruins of **Tutbury Castle,** where Mary, Queen of Scots, was once imprisoned, and the **Tutbury Glass factory.**

🐾 Near there, **Ye Olde Dog and Partridge** timbered pub is also a good spot for lunch.

## Stoke-on-Trent—the Home of Wedgwood

Stoke has been the home of fine pottery since the 17th century and is synonymous with names like Wedgwood, Spode, Copeland, and Minton. Many of the old salt-glazing processes provoked chronic illnesses in both workers and local inhabitants alike, and devastated the landscape. Similarly, mining and sprawling urban growth have claimed large areas of land and depressed the area. Today, much of the grime and labor have been removed from the pottery trade, which more than ever sustains the region and continues to fascinate visitors.

Of the potteries, **Wedgwood** remains at the forefront of the industry, which at one time boasted over five hundred potteries. The company's huge factory at Barlaston, just two miles from Stoke, has a special museum of Wedgwood history, active displays of hand-turned and embossed pottery, an informative film center, and a well-stocked shop, including Waterford Crystal, which now forms part of the company. Guided tours of the Wedgwood factory may be made. (Tel. 0782-204218; open Monday through Friday from 9 A.M. to 5 P.M., Saturday and Sunday from 10 A.M. to 4 P.M.; £1 for adults, 50 pence for children.)

Many other examples of the local craft can be seen at the comprehensive Stoke Art Gallery and Museum, Hanley (0782-202173; open Monday through Saturday from 10:30 A.M. to 5 P.M., Sunday from 2 to 5 P.M.; free), and bought at the town's factory shop and visitor center next to the rail station. Special tours can also be made of Spode, Stoke (0782-744011; open Monday through Friday from 10 A.M. to 4 P.M., Saturday from 10 A.M. to 1 P.M.; £1), and of smaller potteries

## Josiah Wedgwood

The youngest of 13 children, Wedgwood was born at Burslem in 1730. Apprenticed as a potter to his elder brother at the age of nine, he first joined the Cliffe Bank pottery works of Thomas Elders. After two years, he went into partnership with Thomas Whieldon of Fenton, the greatest potter of his time. After five years, Wedgwood started his own firm at the Ivy House Works in Burslem and then moved to Brick House, where he produced his famous Queen's Ware earthenware, a new highly popular, inexpensive tableware. In 1766 Wedgwood teamed up with Liverpool merchant Thomas Bentley, forming a lifelong partnership that was to lead to new processes, including Wedwood's smooth Black Basalt pottery.

But it is Wedgwood's Jasper pottery that is best remembered, an unglazed vitreous stoneware that could be stained blue, lilac, yellow, maroon, or black, and featured white classical reliefs of the famous Dancing Hours, among other things. The perfection of this technique was crowned by Wedgwood's replica of the famous Portland Vase—the motif adorning all Wedgwood products.

Wedgwood died in 1795. He is now remembered as the father of English potters. The bicentenary of his birth was marked by the moving of the factory, followed by great expansion at the present-day Barlaston works in 1938.

at nearby Burslem, Tunstall, and Hanley. Also at Tunstall is the fascinating Chatterley Whitfield Mining Museum (0782-813337; open daily from 10 A.M. to 6 P.M.; £2.95 for adults, £1.85 for children), with its enormous rustic bottle ovens and the chance to travel underground to see the work of a miner.

It is worth a visit out of town to lunch at **The Wharf,** a canal-side restaurant off the A52 from Stoke, on Foxt Rd., Frognall (053871-486). Or dine on delicious homemade vegetarian dishes or à la carte (£5–12) aboard their horse-drawn barge along some of Staffordshire's ancient canals, once essential to the pottery trade.

There are walks along the ninety-mile **Staffordshire Way,** a long-distance footpath spanning the length of the county between Mow Cop and Kinver Edge, through some of its finest scenery, and linking some of its prettiest villages. Or take an excursion to **Alton Towers,** Alton (0538-702200; open March through November, daily from 9 A.M. to 7 P.M.; £7.99 for adults, £5.99 for children), one of the country's finest Disneyesque fun parks.

# Shrewsbury and the Shropshire Hills and Castles

Shropshire has been rightly described as the Queen of Counties, the land of hills and castles immortalized by Worcestershire man A. E. Houseman in *A Shropshire Lad*. Less than an hour away from Birmingham by road or rail, the county is bound by the Black Country to the east, the Roman ruins of Oswestry and the Ellesmere lakes to the north, Offa's Dyke and the Welsh border to the west, and Ludlow to the south. Particularly impressive is the Welsh border range with its line of castles, the best of which are at Shrewsbury and Ludlow, Shropshire's two finest towns. Other castle ruins lie at Acton Burnell, Bridgnorth, Moreton Corbet, and Stokesay.

## The Estates

Superb country houses include **The Lawns,** at Broseley (0952-882557; open April through October, Thursday through Sunday from 11 A.M. to 5 P.M.; £2), the former home of ironmaster John Wilkinson and John Rose, founder of Coalport china; and **Weston Park,** near Shifnal (095276-207; from Easter through October the house is open from 1 to 5 P.M., the park from 11 A.M. to 7 P.M.; £2.50 for adults, £1.80 for children for the house and park), with its superb early Restoration house and Capability Brown parkland. Shropshire also lays claim to being the cradle of the industrial revolution at Ironbridge Gorge, where iron was first smelted with coke in 1709 to produce a harder metal for bridges, railways, steam engines, boats, and buildings.

## Shrewsbury

Shrewsbury is God's gift to the visitor—a perfectly sited hilltop town, moated by a natural loop in the river Severn sixty feet below, with its historic Shrewsbury Castle, a famous wool center with a wealth of timbered buildings, and natural beauty that has won it the title Town of Flowers. The strategic importance of the town and its fortifications is due to the proximity of the Welsh border just 12 miles away, and it was the capital of the Welsh dominion of Powys in the seventh century. Shared history is marked by both English and Welsh bridges across the river Severn. But its origins follow the retreat in the fifth century of the Romans from Viroconium, at Wroxeter, five miles southeast of Shrewsbury, the largest unspoiled Roman excavations in Britain. It is likely that local inhabitants, seeking security against Saxon invaders, chose Shrewsbury for its natural defenses and commanding height. It only remained to secure the "landward" approach just three hundred yards wide to the north. This began with a watchtower, on the site where Laura's Tower now stands, and is how the castle and settlement started.

## The Castle

At first sight, Shrewsbury Castle on Castle Street (0743-58516; open Monday through Saturday from 10 A.M. to 5 P.M., Sunday also Easter through October from 10 A.M. to 5 P.M.; 60 pence for adults, 25 pence for children) appears curiously small considering its vital position. But it was only one of the town's defenses; the rest of the town, surrounded by the river and further encircled by walls, provided the additional space and protection needed for troop garrisons, stables, and stores. The castle's size meant it was largely unoccupied. The Normans realized its strategic importance in attacking Wales, and in 1074 William the Conqueror's kinsman Roger of Montgomery enlarged the original wooden structure. Henry II rebuilt it in the late 12th century in stone, still evident in parts today. After attacks in 1212 and 1234, the walls were reinforced. Edward I, who finally crushed the Welsh rebellion led by Llewellyn II, enlarged the castle hall in 1300. It fell into ruin during the next two hundred years, until the civil war, when Richard Onslow added the upper-story Tudor features in 1565. Fresh repairs were made but in vain, when the Roundheads broke through a gap in the wall and captured the town. After the return of the monarchy, the castle was privately owned between 1663 and 1924, and it remained fortified until 1686, when its outer defenses were removed. By 1780, it belonged to Sir William Pultney, MP, who got Thomas Telford, then county surveyor, to redesign the interior and windows. The octagonal tower on the mound was built as a summerhouse for Pultney's daughter; hence the name Laura's Tower. In 1924 the Shropshire Horticultural Society purchased and presented the castle to the town. Telford's internal partitions were removed, and the original entrance was restored. Today it is cluttered by the museum of the King's Shropshire Light Infantry, made up of the 53rd (Shropshire) Regiment and the 85th King's Light Infantry. The fifty-third first saw action in the 1775 American War of Independence, and in 1814, the 85th defeated the Americans at Bladensburg, occupied Washington, and burned down the White House, which takes its name from efforts to cover up the damage by whitewashing it.

## Exploring the Town

For many visitors, though, the real attraction of the town is its winding cobbled streets, drunkenly leaning black and white timber houses and pubs, and its fine churches. Famous houses include: the 16th-century timber-framed **Rowley's House Museum,** Barker Street (0743-231196; open Monday through Saturday from 10 A.M. to 5 P.M., Sunday Easter through October, from 12 to 5 P.M.; 50 pence for adults, 20 pence for children), with its Roman and medieval exhibitions; **Clive House** (of Clive of India fame), on College Hill (0743-54811; open Monday from 2 to 5 P.M., Tuesday through Saturday from 10 A.M. to 1 P.M. and from 2 to 5 P.M.; 30 pence for adults, 15 pence for children), has impressive collections of Coalport and Caughly porcelain; and Ireland and Owen's mansions in High Street. Visit the churches, which include **St. Mary's Church,** with its 202-foot spire and the fine stained glass, including a magnificent Jesse window, the imposing **Shrewsbury Abbey,** and the unusual circular **St. Chad's Church.**

Other impressive buildings include the Victorian façade of Shrewsbury rail station, the old grammar school opposite the castle (founded in 1552, now the library), and the new school dominating the horizon across the river, which is crossed by no fewer than ten bridges.

Famous names associated with Shrewsbury include naturalist Charles Darwin, author Mary Webb, horticulturist Percy Thrower, and military men Sir Philip Sydney, Lord Hill, Admiral Benbow, and Clive of India.

## Shopping Stops

Walking about Shrewsbury, there are many famous brand names to attract the ardent shopper, from the shops in the busy High Street to more select ones in The Square. The St. Julian Craft Centre for Shropshire, Fish Street, situated in one of the town's oldest churches, offers originality in local woolens, shoes, painting, and pottery. Markets are held in Market Hall in The Square on Wednesday, Friday, and Saturday.

### Charles Darwin

Undoubtedly Shrewsbury's greatest son, Charles Robert Darwin was born at The Mount on February 12, 1809. The son of Dr. Robert Waring Darwin and Susannah, the eldest daughter of Josiah Wedgwood of pottery fame, he was the fifth of six children. The family interest in botany and zoology rubbed off, and he began collecting samples from an early age, encouraged by his mother, who died when he was aged eight. His interest expanded through chemistry and geology, and studies of the local countryside. Educated at the former grammar school opposite the castle (founded in 1552, and now the library outside which Darwin's statue stands), Darwin went on to study medicine without success at Edinburgh before transferring to Cambridge, where he renewed his interest in natural philosophy.

On Darwin's return to Shrewsbury, a letter awaited him that would determine the course of his life forever: an invitation to travel as a naturalist on the five-year voyage of the *Beagle* in 1831, which resulted in his famed theory of evolution. Darwin died in 1882 at the age of 73 and is buried in Westminster Abbey. The Natural History Museum in London has an exceptionally large exhibition of his life and work.

## Side Trips

Out of town, there are walks at Offa's Dyke (best between Bishop's Castle and Clun Forest); the enchanting **Butterfly World** at Pockleton (0743-84217; open April to October, daily from 10 A.M. to 6 P.M.; £2.30 for adults, £1.30 for children); the **Hill Valley Golf and Country Club** at Whitchurch (0948-3584); the two-hundred-acre **Roman City of Viroconium** excavations at Wroxeter (0743-75330; open March to October, daily from 9:30 A.M. to 6:30 P.M., Sunday from 2 to 6:30 P.M.; October to March daily til 4; 75 pence for adults, 35 pence for children); shire horses and ancient farming methods at the **Acton Scott Working Farm Museum,** Wenlock Lodge, Acton Scott, near Church Stretton (06946-307; open March through October, Monday through Saturday from 10 A.M. to 5 P.M., Sunday from 10 A.M. to 6 P.M.; £1.20 for adults, 60 pence for children); and the historic Roman town of **Much Wenlock**—all within five miles of Shrewsbury.

Farther afield, recommended visits include: ancient timbered **Ludlow,** considered by many to be England's prettiest town; the **Ironbridge Gorge Museum** (095245-3522; open daily from 10 A.M. to 6 P.M.; £4.95 for adults, £3.25 for children), with its famous cast-iron bridge slung across the River Severn as well as the nearby collection of six museums housing original foundries and a fifty-acre reconstructed village of the industrial revolution; the attractive hilly town of **Bridgnorth,** with its Severn Valley Railway, Railway Station (07462-4361), and a collection of over one hundred classic cars at the **Midland Motor Museum,** Stourbridge Road (0746-761761; open daily from 10 A.M. to 5 P.M.; £2.50 for adults, £1.20 for children); the attractive **Ellesmere lakes,** offering camping and water sports (contact the Ellesmere Visitor Centre, The Mere, Ellesmere, tel. 069171-2981); and the nearby **Iron Age** fort at Oswestry.

## ❧ RESTAURANTS

The restaurant choice in town is poor, with the hotels offering the best of traditional English cooking. Alternatively, there is the excellent **Unicorn Restaurant** in Wyle Cop, tel. (0743) 66890 (£5–7), and the savory **Pancho's Mexican Eating House,** 16 Castle Gates, tel. (0743) 58807 (£4–7). Most pubs are good for lunch.

### Entertainment

For your leisure interests there's theater in the **Music Hall,** The Square (0743-50761); the **Empire Cinema,** Mardol (0743-62257); the **Gateway Arts Centre;** football at **Gay**

**Meadow;** or just walking in the delightful gardens at Quarry Bank beside the river. Local events include the regatta in May, the flower show in August, and the horse and tractor plowing trials in October.

# The Countryside

## Hereford

The home of cattle and cider, Hereford is the sort of place where time stands still and your feet really touch the ground. But the tranquillity belies a stormy past of countless sieges, raids, battles, and defeats. It has seen its cathedral burned, its castle bombarded, and its streets occupied during civil war. But its fortunes have flourished in the rich surrounding pastureland that makes this one of the best touring areas in the country.

**Hereford Cathedral** dates from the 11th century and is dedicated to St. Mary and King Ethelbert. It reputedly has the oldest chair in England, one of the oldest maps, a chained library (to prevent it from becoming a lending library) of over 1,440 volumes, and fine stained glass.

Other churches of interest include the 13th-century **All Saints** and the 15th-century **St. Peter's,** with canopied stalls and early English chancel. Look for the remains of 13th-century city walls in Victoria Street and West Street, and the Wye bridge with six arches dated from 1490. There are numerous specialized museums including steam engines at the **Bulmer Railway Center,** Whitecross Road (no phone; (open April through September, Saturday and Sunday from 2 to 5 P.M.; 50 pence for adults, 25 pence for children); and Hereford's history as the home of the county's famous tipple at the **Bulmer Museum of Cider,** The Cider Mills, Ryelands Street (0432-54207; open April through October, daily from 10 A.M. to 5 P.M.; other months Wednesday and Saturday only. £1 for adults, 70 pence for children). A busy market town—butter market daily and general markets Wednesday (livestock, too) and Saturday—Hereford empties equally quickly and returns to serenity.

Leisure activities include a variety of sports at the **Hereford Leisure Center,** Holmer Road (0432-271959). Annual local events feature the regatta and river raft race in May, and the antiques fair in October.

Out and about, the many rural attractions include visits to the attractive town of **Ross-on-Wye,** with its superb location and market traditions, the Roman town excavations at **Kenchester,** and the glorious **Malvern Hills,** with its spa town and classical festival. Though the cathedral city of Worcester is also nearby, you may want to bypass it because of its unbearable traffic noise and congestion.

A trip to Leominster will take you to **Croft Castle** (056885-246; open May through September, Wednesday through Sunday 2 to 6 P.M.; in April and October, Saturdays and Sundays only 2 to 5 P.M.; £1.70), the Capability Brown park and stately home at **Berrington Hall** (0568-5721; same hours and fees as Croft Castle), and the finest black-and-white villages at **Weobley, Eardisland, Pembridge,** and **Dilwyn.**

**Hay-on-Wye** boasts the largest secondhand bookshop in the world and fine views from the Black Mountains.

## ☙ RESTAURANTS

The choice is varied, so try pot luck or stick with your lodgings. **Saxty's Wine Bar** in Widemarsh St. (0432-57872) has a wide range of hot and cold food, and a comprehensive à la carte evening menu (£5–12). Most settle for lunch in their favorite pub.

# 11

# THE NORTH COUNTRY

The Northeast of England, in popular British thought, is an area associated with coal mines, heavy industry, social hardship, and people with incomprehensible accents. The air is thick with curses and effluents, so the image goes—the men all wear flat caps, race dogs, and drink huge amounts of beer; and the women know their place.

On the face of it, then, it might not seem to promise too many riches for the traveler—even one of the local tourist boards describes its patch, rather self-deprecatingly, as "Britain's Best Kept Secret." But to leave the country having absorbed only this impression of the Northeast would be to do yourself, and the region, a great injustice.

The major towns and cities of the area, concentrated in three large conurbations, all grew out of the rapid development of the textile, steel, coal mining, and shipbuilding industries in the 19th century. And these certainly bear scars—not least in the high levels of unemployment brought about by the recent decline of those industries. But between these concentrated centers of population is some of the most beautiful countryside in England. The richness of the region's pre-industrial history is second to none, and even the industrial areas themselves are now actively exploiting their past with the tourist in mind.

The region, for the purposes of this guide, encompasses virtually the whole country lying east of the Pennine Chain of mountains and moors, known as the "backbone of England." It stretches from the steel-making center of Sheffield in the south right up to the Scottish border, and it covers no less than eight different counties—South Yorkshire, Humberside, West Yorkshire, North Yorkshire, Cleveland, Durham, Tyne and Wear, and Northumberland. Included in this enormous area are the commercially important centers of Leeds and Bradford, which once clothed the world in woolen textiles; Newcastle-upon-Tyne, of "coals to Newcastle" and ship-building fame; as well as Sheffield itself, whose high-class cutlery still graces tables all over the world. But it also takes in four of England's ten national parks—areas designated as being of outstanding natural beauty; York, which has one of the best-preserved medieval city centers in Europe; and Durham, whose cathedral was recently voted a "World Heritage Site." In Hadrian's Wall, in the far north, the region boasts Britain's most important Roman monument, and scattered throughout it are more ruined castles and abbeys than you will find anywhere else—reflecting both a turbulent and a pious past. In short, it is an area of sharp contrasts.

Lumping it all together, however, is not simply an arbitary move, since in the Dark Ages it formed the basis of a single, unified kingdom—the Kingdom of Northumbria. Established in the sixth century by Ida, the great Angle invader, its lands stretched from the river Humber north to the Firth of Forth, on which Edinburgh, the capital city of Scotland, now stands—hence the name North–Humber–ria. From pagan beginnings it was quickly converted to Christianity, and in its seventh-century "golden age" Northumbria grew to be not only the most powerful of English kingdoms, but under the influence of both Celtic missionaries and Benedictine monks from Rome, it led the Western world in learning and the arts.

At the heart of this great kingdom stood York, its main trading and administrative center, and indeed Northumbria disintegrated as a political force after York was captured by the Vikings in 866. So it is that Yorkshire forms the heart of the northeastern region to this day.

Until local government reorganization in 1974, Yorkshire was a single county, by far the largest in the country, and retaining broadly the same boundaries and subdivisions, or "Ridings," established by those Danish invaders over a thousand years before. However, these have now been swept away and replaced with the five new counties, a move that still rankles with proud Yorkshiremen. For the sake of simplicity and tradition, we will treat Yorkshire as a whole and deal similarly with the old counties of Durham and Northumberland, which were also carved up in the same reorganization.

Apart from York itself, and cricket, Yorkshire is perhaps most famous as the home of the Brontë sisters. The village of Haworth, where they lived and mostly died, is a place of pilgrimage for thousands of ardent readers every year, and surrounding the village are the wild moors of West Yorkshire that figure so dramatically in the Brontë novels. Rather less revered, but probably now even more widely read, is the author/veterinarian James Herriot, whose stories of country matters (in books such as *All Creatures Great and Small* ) are set in the Yorkshire Dales. This area is one of the undoubted

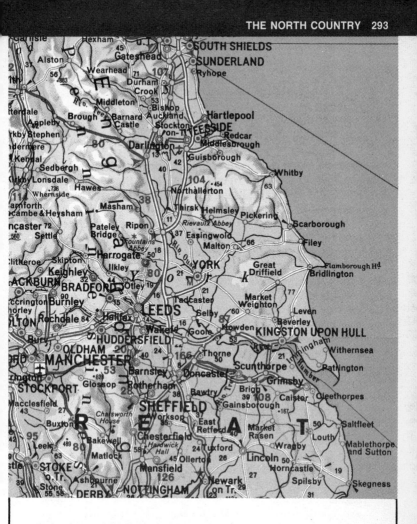

## THE NORTH COUNTRY

| 0 | Kilometers | 60 |
| Miles | | 50 |

N

glories of the region—with lush, green valleys nestling between brooding hills and dotted with quaint, stone-built villages. Farther to the east are the North York Moors, an area of rolling highland covered in heather—in late summer becoming a dramatic blanket of purple—that descends sharply into a beautiful coastline.

The border county of Northumberland boasts some of the least populated country, and some of the biggest skies, in England. Stretched across it is Hadrain's Wall, the northernmost frontier of the Roman Empire, and off its superb coastline lies the island of Lindisfarne, or Holy Island, one of the cradles of European Christianity. Newcastle-upon-Tyne, until reorganization the county's "capital," remains one of the North Country's major cultural centers, and for those in search of nightlife it offers a very distinctive blend of attractions.

Between the two lies the county of Durham, its coastline and eastern landscape largely ruined by centuries of coal mining, but which still has many beautiful spots, a rich history, and its own famous novelist—Catherine Cookson. The city from which it takes its name remains totally unspoiled, with its castle and cathedral rising dramatically on a plateau and dominating the surrounding countryside. Nearby is the unique open-air museum of Beamish, which re-creates life and industry from the last century and offers a working memorial to the forces that shaped the area.

Outside the great historical and industrial cities of the Northeast, and away from the beauty of the wildest landscapes, the most immediately striking characteristic of the region is the enormous number of ruined castles and abbeys. They form a constant and magnificent backdrop to the whole region, cropping up—in some areas, it seems—in almost every little town and beautiful valley. This is no accident; it gives a clear insight into the history of the region—with the most turbulent and pious past of anywhere in England—and whether you are a serious student of English history or just someone who likes to soak up the feeling of times long ago, visits to at least the most spectacular of these ruins must form an important part of any trip to the Northeast.

A far more recent development throughout the area, but equally important to the visitor, is the rapid growth in the numbers of museums and "heritage centers." Again, these seem to be sprouting everywhere; they now form a major part of the effort to promote the region as a tourist center. Here you can find a museum devoted to just about anything—from the Roman army to bagpipes, from great collections covering every aspect of the region's recent past to the National Museum of Photography, Film and Television. As well as giving further evidence of the richness of the area's history, these also mean that there is plenty to do when the occasionally savage northern weather keeps you out of the hills.

# TRAVEL

The easiest and quickest way of getting to the region from London is **by rail.** It lies right on the main East Coast line, where the fast trains to Edinburgh run very regularly. Always one of the fastest lines in the network, this is the route of the old *Flying Scotsman;* it currently is undergoing electrification, which will mean even shorter journey times in 1989. The quickest trains to York currently take just two hours; to Durham and Newcastle, three hours. There are also direct trains to Bradford and Leeds, which take three hours and two hours and 20 minutes, respectively. All services are from London King's Cross, tel (01) 278-2477. For those who are thinking of taking a lot of trains, there are Rover tickets, which allow you to travel freely on the whole British Rail network. But BritRail passes, which must be bought in the U.S., work out to be the cheapest of all: for example, an Eight-Day pass costs $166 standard.

Well worth considering if cash, not time, is the most important factor—are **long-distance coaches** from London to the area; they take longer but are considerably cheaper. Once very much the poor-man's option, standards of both speed and comfort have recently improved a lot, with all long-haul express services now having on-board toilets and refreshments. Journey times are: to York, four hours; to Durham, four hours and 45 minutes; to Newcastle, five hours and 15 minutes; and to Bradford, four hours and 10 minutes. All services are from London Victoria Bus Station, tel. (01) 730-0202.

**Road links** to the region also are excellent. Simply take the M1 motorway as far as Sheffield and then turn off onto the M18, which links up with the A1 Great North Road. This goes right past York, Durham, and Newcastle; the M1 continues on to Leeds and Bradford.

Once there it is possible to get around on local bus and rail services, but these are often slow and don't always go where you want to. Easily the best way of seeing the sights, and a must if you want to get to the most remote and beautiful areas, is to hire a car from one of the regional centers. The biggest operators are **Hertz** and **Godfrey Davis,** which have comparable rates and offices at or close by the main-line railway stations.

Alternatively, there are a number of companies that run coach trips from these centers, and if you don't mind being organized and told what to look at, these are probably the best way to see a lot quickly and cheaply. **Yorktour,** tel. (0904) 641737, runs a selection of tours from York to the Dales and the North York Moors, to Castle Howard and Whitby, to Brontë country and to Herriot country—all at £9 for a full day or £5 for a half-day. They also run a driver-guide scheme, whereby you can hire a car and guide for the day to take up to four people on individually tailored tours—costing £105 for a full day, £65 for a half-day. **Reynard Pullman,** tel. (0904) 229922, also runs a similar range of tours from York at similar prices.

## ❦ HOTELS

Across the region there is a full range of accommodation to suit all pockets and preferences—from plush country house and large "chain" hotels to farmhouse bed-and-breakfast accommodations. Apart from price, choice will depend very much on the time available for touring the region and whether you need quick-in, quick-out efficiency or something a bit more restful and "off the beaten track."

For Yorkshire, there is no better touring base to start with than York itself. Quite apart from its own many attractions, and those of the surrounding Vale of York, both the Dales and the North York Moors can be reached easily by car. The market town of Skipton traditionally is dubbed the southern "Gateway to the Dales," and it also can be used for exploring Haworth and the Brontë moors. To the north, Richmond is the best center for the more isolated dales of the real "Herriot country," and it also gives access to some of the most attractive areas of county Durham. The North York Moors all can be easily covered from Helmsley, a small town on their southern fringe; but for those who want a bit of sea air to complement the moorland winds, Whitby should also be considered.

The small and historic town of Corbridge is a good center for exploring southern Northumberland and the wilder parts of Durham, as is Durham city itself. The rugged town of Alnwick is the natural center for the English borders and the Northumbrian coast.

These, however, are only broad guidelines, and some of the best places to stay are tucked away in less likely spots. The number of places offering inexpensive bed-and-breakfast accommodations are literally too numerous to mention—there are over 200 in York alone—and the best way to choose from these is to consult the local Tourist Information Office. All provide a booking service, for a fee of 90 pence, and will even book you a "bed ahead" at your next destination for £1.90. Official campsites are rather sparse, but many farmers in the region will take campers, and Tourist Information Offices also will advise on where these can be found.

**Credit card abbreviations used in hotel and restaurant listings are as follows: AE for American Express, CB for Carte Blanche, DC for Diner's Club, MC for MasterCard, and V for Visa.**

## York

**Hudson's Hotel,** 60 Bootham, Y03 7B2, York; tel. (0904) 621267. A four-minute walk from the minster, this compact but comfortable hotel was converted from two Victorian houses with extra buildings and courtyard behind. There is also a restaurant. Double with bathroom, £58 (with fireplace, £68); single, £32 including breakfast. With dinner: £75 (£85), £40. AE, DC, MC, V.

**Middlethorpe Hall,** Bishopthorpe Rd., YO2 1QP York; tel. (0904) 641241. Located one and a half miles outside the city, by the racecourse, this is quite simply one of the very best places to stay in the whole of the region—but expensive. Built in 1699, it retains all the atmosphere and character of a traditional English country house, complete with shelves full of antiques and beautifully manicured gardens. It also has the best restaurant in York. The service is efficient, helpful, and courteous without being servile, and the rooms are all individually decorated. A double room with bathroom costs from £95–100 per night (room with four-poster, £130), a single costs £70–80, and a full English breakfast is an extra £7.50 per person. The three–course à la carte dinner is around £32 per head, including wine (the set dinner menu is £24). AE, DC, MC, V.

**The Royal Hotel,** Station Rd., the York YO2 2AA; tel. (0904) 653681. A grand old station hotel, right next to the York railway station and a ten-minute walk from the city center. The impressive main staircase leads down to the large lounge and restaurant. While it is generally very spacious, the rooms can vary greatly in size and quality, which is reflected in the prices. A double is £54; with bath, £70–105. A single is £32; with bath, £48–54. All include breakfast. Dinner costs around £20. AE, DC, MC, V.

## Yorkshire Dales

**Hilltop Guest House,** Starbotton, by Skipton, North Yorkshire, Kettlewell BD23 5HY; tel. (075 676) 321. One of the new breed of guest houses currently being encouraged by the tourist authorities to provide high-quality accommodation at a reasonable price. This converted farmhouse and barn, which has been in the family of the owner since it was built in the 17th century, is situated on a hillside in beautiful Upper Wharfedale. It provides comfortable bedrooms, a large lounge and dining room with open fires, and a genuine warm welcome. The emphasis is on good home cooking, complemented by a respectable wine cellar. A double with bath is £31; a single, £20.50. Dinner runs £8.75, without wine. No credit cards.

**Howe Villa,** Richmond, North Yorkshire DL10 4TJ; tel. (0748) 850055. A delightful small hotel/guest house in a riverside setting located a half mile outside Richmond with splendid views and good, home-cooked food. The villa only does a dinner, bed-and-breakfast package, and has only six rooms, so booking is essential. A double with bath/shower and dinner costs £25–26. No credit cards.

## Calderdale, Brontë Country, and West Yorks

**The Carlton Hotel,** Albert St., Hebden Bridge, West Yorkshire HX7 8ES; tel. (0422) 844400. Recently opened, this privately owned hotel is in a converted Victorian department store. Hebden Bridge is situated at the head of the once industrial, now beautiful, Calder Valley—just 11 miles over the moors from Haworth and well situated for the rest of the relatively new Calderdale tourist area. The hotel has tasteful, modern interiors and an attentive and friendly staff as well as a good restaurant. A double with bath costs £65; a single, £45 (including breakfast). AE, MC, V.

**Old White Lion Hotel,** Main St. Haworth, BD22 8DU West Yorkshire; tel. (0535) 42313. Located right in the center of historic Haworth, close to the Brontë Museum, parsonage and church, this 300-year-old hotel provides comfortable but unfussy accommodation. The popular restaurant and bars tend to be very crowded in high season. A double with bath costs £34.50; a single, £24 (including breakfast). No credit cards.

## North Yorkshire Moors

**Barnards Hotel,** 5 East Terr., Whitby, North Yorkshire YO21 3YB; tel. (0947) 606167. This unpretentious family-run hotel is perched on the cliff overlooking the harbor and abbey. It is small but comfortable; most bedrooms have private bathrooms. The cellar restaurant has three different menus. Bed-and-breakfast costs £9.50 (with bath, £12.50; with seaview, £10.50 and £13.50) per person. AE, DC, MC, V.

**The Black Swan,** Market Place, Helmsley, Y06 5BJ North Yorkshire; tel. (0439) 70466. This is a superb 400-year-old country inn, expanded to include Tudor and Georgian houses and a modern extension. The hotel is patronized by Princess Anne during shooting season. Antiques, oak beams, log fires, period lounges, and good food add to the charm of this fine establishment. A double with bath costs £85; a single, from £54. Breakfast is £6.50 extra. Dinner is from £16.50. AE, DC, MC, V.

**The Feathers Hotel,** Market Place, Helmsley, North Yorkshire YO6 5BH; tel. (0439) 70275. A small, family-run hotel, also fronting onto Helmsley's picturesque marketplace, the Feathers has more oak beams and two bars furnished with "Mouseman" furniture made by local craftsmen. Dine at the restaurant or on one of the cheap, high quality bar meals. Bed-and-breakfast is £16 (£19 with bath) per person. With dinner, £25 (with bath £27.50). AE, DC, MC, V.

## Durham

**Lord Crewe Arms Hotel,** Blanchland, by Consett, Durham DH8 9SP; tel. (43 475) 251. Definitely an off-the-beaten-track gem, the Lord Crewe Arms is situated in the tiny stone-built village of Blanchland, which nestles in a isolated valley in the Durham/Northumberland fells. Originally a guest house for Blanchland Abbey, since demolished, the hotel has been offering hospitality for centuries and has expanded to a large house across the village square. Both are well furnished, with a faithful period atmosphere, and include three special rooms of particularly high quality—including one that is supposed to be haunted.

It also has an excellent restaurant. A double with bath costs £53.80; a single, £38.90 (including breakfast). Special rooms can be had for an additional £8. AE, DC, V.

**Jersey Farm,** Darlington Rd., Barnard Castle, Durham DL12 8TA; tel. (0833) 38223. This ever-expanding hotel started by offering bed-and-breakfast on a working farm and now has taken over most of the farm buildings as well. The farm still has a herd of hairy Highland cattle. The basis of its attraction is the restaurant which serves enormous no-nonsense meals with an emphasis on roast meat; it is run by the equally no-nonsense, but jolly, farmer's wife. The hotel offers a range of different sized rooms and suites looking out onto the beautiful Teesdale countryside. A double with bath costs £34–38; a single, £27–30 (including breakfast). Dinner is around £8. No credit cards.

**Royal County Hotel,** Old Elvet, Durham. DH1 3JN Tyneside; tel. (091) 386-6821. This is a large, luxurious chain hotel providing mid- to high-price comfort in the heart of the historic city of Durham. It has a fully air-conditioned restaurant, on the theme of the local regiment—the Durham Light Infantry—and a well-appointed bar and coffeeshop, a sauna, and a hairdressing salon. A double with bath is £68; a single, £54.50 (including breakfast). AE, DC, MC, V.

# Northumberland

**Langley Castle,** Langley-on-Tyne, Hexham, Northumberland, Haydon Bridge NE47 5LU; tel. (0434 84) 8888. Housed in a genuine 14th-century castle, recently converted into this luxurious hotel, Langley Castle is set on its own grounds, with seven-foot-thick walls and the best examples of 14th-century garderobes (medieval toilets) in Europe—certainly something different. The magnificent drawing room has stained-glass windows and a huge log fire. It is situated six miles from Hexham—head west on the A68 and turn left at Haydon Bridge. The restaurant is good but not brilliant. A double with bath is £49–79; a single, £36–59 (including breakfast). Dinner runs about £13.75. AE, DC, MC, V.

**Manor House Hotel,** Holy Island, Berwick-upon-Tweed, Berwick TD15 2RX; tel. (0289) 89207. Situated on beautiful Lindisfarne Island off the Northumberland coast, known as the "cradle of Christianity," this family-run hotel is anything but pious; it is, in fact, rather rough-and-ready. But it is exceptionally friendly, with the owners holding court in the bar every night—all night if necessary. The hotel offers dinner and also bar meals. A double costs £26 (£30–35 with bath); a single, £17 (including breakfast). MC, V.

**Riverside Hotel,** Main St., Corbridge, NE 45 5LE Northumberland; tel. (043471) 2942. This is a small, attractive, and friendly hotel, situated in the middle of one of Northumberland's most beautiful villages. The pleasant lounge overlooks the river Tyne, and the restaurant specializes in good food. Rates run: double,

£28–35; single, £19–25 (including breakfast). Dinner will cost about £10.25. No credit cards.

**White Swan Hotel,** Bondgate Within, Alnwick, NE66 1TD Northumberland; tel. (0665) 602 109. A pleasant, well-appointed chain hotel, just inside the medieval walls of the historic market town of Alnwick. The White Swan offers good standard bedrooms, a coffee house, and a bar on the theme of angling—plus a restaurant. A double with bath is £58; a single, £43 (including breakfast). AE, DC, MC, V.

# York

"The history of York is the history of England," said George VI, and it is this uniquely preserved past—stretching back over nineteen hundred years—that makes the ancient city of York one of Europe's richest tourist gems. Traditionally the northern capital of England, its development faithfully charts every significant period of the country's history, and buildings and relics from each of these can be encountered by simply walking around York's beautiful streets.

York was built by the Romans, conquered by the Anglo-Saxons, and ruled by the Vikings, and in medieval times it grew into a great religious and commercial center. It played a vital role in the course of the English civil war, enjoyed a period as a major social center in Georgian times, and became a great railway center in the 19th century. Today it is just itself—a place to be visited and savored, and one that rewards much careful examination.

For a map of York, see atlas pages 22–23.

## Walking Around the City

Standing magnificent at its center is **York Minster**—the largest medieval cathedral in northern Europe and Britain's finest example of Gothic architecture. A great church has stood on this site since 627, but the present minster was built over a 250-year period between the 13th and 15th centuries and incorporates the Early English, Decorated, and Perpendicular styles. One of its greatest glories is the Great East Window, whose panels depict scenes from the story of Creation and from Revelation—the beginning and the end. The 15th-century stone Choir Screen shows the kings of England from William I to Henry VI, while the 13th-century Five Sisters Window has five giant lancets over fifty feet feet tall.

A major joy of York is that it is so compact, still surrounded by its medieval city walls with their grand gates, or Bars. It all can be easily covered on foot, and guided tours are run from the tourist information center in Exhibition Square, close to the minster.

Any visit should take in such magnificent buildings as the **Treasurer's House,** with its beautiful rooms furnished from the 17th and 18th centuries; the timber-vaulted **Merchant Adventurers' Hall,** where York merchants have transacted business and held banquets since the 14th century; and **Fairfax House,** one of England's finest Georgian town houses, filled with one of the country's best collections of mid-18th-century furniture. Also walk down the **Shambles,** the perfectly preserved medieval butchers' street, with its closely packed, half-timbered shops and houses.

## An Eclectic Collection of Museums

York also boasts a superb selection of museums. Most recent, and perhaps most exciting, is the **Jorvik Centre,** on Coppergate, where visitors are literally whisked back in time one thousand years and taken in "time-cars" through a detailed reconstruction of a Viking street—complete with sights, sounds, and smells. The archeological dig from which the evidence for this came is itself carefully preserved, and there is an exhibition of the thousands of artifacts found. (Open daily April through October from 9 A.M. to 7 P.M.; November through March from 9 A.M. to 5:30 P.M.) The **Yorkshire Museum** in Museum Gardens has some of the finest Roman, Anglo-Saxon, Viking, and medieval treasures ever discovered in Britain—including sculptures, jewelry, and mosaics, and even the preserved auburn hair of a Roman lady. (Open Monday through Friday from 10 A.M. to 5 P.M., Sunday from 1 to 5 P.M.)

There are reconstructions of Victorian and Edwardian streets in the **Castle Museum,** off Tower Street, Britain's most popular museum of everyday life. This vast collection includes fully furnished period rooms right up to the 1960s, all manner of household objects, period costumes, old agricultural and craftsmen's implements, and even a working water mill. It also includes a huge military collection, where pride of place goes to the Coppergate Helmet—the finest example of an Anglo-Saxon helmet ever found. (Open Monday through Friday from 10 A.M. to 5 P.M., Sunday from 1 to 5 P.M.) The **National Railway Museum** on Leeman Road features 25 magnificent, original locomotives—including the *Mallard,* which holds the world steam speed record of 126 miles per hour—and 20 historic pieces of rolling stock, including Queen Victoria's saloon. It also has displays on the development of railways and a "cutaway" steam locomotive to show how these monsters worked. (Open Monday through Friday from 10 A.M. to 6 P.M., Sunday from 2:30 to 6 P.M.) The **City Art Gallery,** on Exhibition Square, has paintings spanning seven centuries, including a world-renowned collection of Old Masters.

## The Vale of York

York itself sits at the center of the Vale of York, an area of lush green land between the Dales and the North York Moors that is dotted with interesting and historic places worth visiting in their own right. At the top of any list must be **Castle Howard** (open daily from the end of March through October from 11 A.M. to 4:30 P.M.) designed by Vanbrugh and one of the most stunning private residences in England. Just 15 miles north of York and easily accessible by bus, this superb 18th-century stately home is surrounded by beautiful parks and gardens, and has a fine collection of period costumes. Castle Howard was the principal location for the television dramatization of *Brideshead Revisited*.

Taking the A59 west from York takes you past the site of the Battle of Marston Moor, the decisive battle of the civil war, and on to **Knaresborough**—set astride a dramatic river gorge, with a Tudor and Georgian marketplace and the cave-home of ancient prophetess Mother Shipton—who foresaw steam engines five hundred years ago. It then goes on to **Harrogate**—a large former spa town with many elegant buildings, superb gardens, vast green open spaces, and many fine shops. North of Harrogate is Ripon—dating from 886, one of the oldest towns in England with its own Gothic cathedral—and nearby are the beautiful ruins of Fountains Abbey.

## ❧ RESTAURANTS

**Middlethorpe Hall,** Bishopthorpe Rd., York; tel. (0904) 641241. Arguably York's best restaurant in a superbly restored 1699 country house hotel, with a small, beautifully paneled dining room. Food broadly French, and at its best when not too fancy. Service friendly, helpful and efficient. À la carte dinner is around £32, including wine; set dinner from £19.50 without wine. AE, DC, MC, V.

**Old Deanery,** Minster Rd., Ripon (Vale of York); tel. (0765) 3518. Rambling old deanery house right next to the cathedral, with a delightful dog-eared informality and excellent Swiss cuisine. Smart dress preferred; no bookings taken. Dinner is around £18, with wine; set dinner £11, without wine. No credit cards.

# Bronte Country and West Yorkshire

The moors of West Yorkshire are very definitely Brontë country—bleak and yet beautiful, they ooze with the spirit of the famous sisters' best-known novels and are full of places thought to have inspired them.

## Haworth

The central point of literary pilgrimage is Haworth, the little stone village where the Brontë family lived and mostly died. At the top of High Street you'll find the **Brontë Parsonage Museum,** furnished with a wealth of family relics—including Patrick Brontë's Bible, Charlotte's wedding bonnet, Anne's writing desk, the sofa where Emily died, and an extensive collection of original manuscripts. (Open daily April through September from 11 A.M. to 5 P.M., October through March from 11 A.M. to 4:30 P.M.) Next to it is the **Haworth Parish Church,** containing the Brontë family vault, where all the family, apart from Anne, are buried. A three-mile footpath from Haworth leads right onto the moors to **Top Withins,** a ruined farmhouse thought to have been the inspiration for *Wuthering Heights.* While always crowded in the tourist season, the village is an attraction in itself with its steep, stone-flagged main street running down the hill through pubs, craft shops, and tearooms to the famous Worth Valley steam railway, where such films as the *Railway Children* and *Yanks* were made.

## Calderdale

The A6033 moorland road leads south from Haworth, through stunning moorland views, into Calderdale—a valley important for both the beginnings of industrialization and the development of nonconformist religion. It was here that the water power of the swift-running river was harnessed to create some of the world's first factories, and it was also here that John Wesley began his wandering ministry that was eventually to result in the creation of the Methodist Church. **Hebden Bridge** is the most central and lovely jumping-off point for this area, with its old stone mills and houses and delightful riverside walks. Nearby **Heptonstall** is one of the most unspoiled Pennine villages, with its famous octagonal chapel where Wesley often preached, while at **Mytholmroyd** there is a working clog factory. Continuing down the river brings you to the town of **Halifax,** a major textile center famous for its guillotine-like gibbet, its magnificent Town Hall, and the Piece Hall. This dramatic building, built around a huge square, is where wool traders haggled over prices from the 18th century; today it has a market, many craft shops, and a museum that charts textile production from preindustrial days. Halifax also has the **West Yorkshire Folk Museum,** housed in a 15th-century manor house—Shibden Hall (in Shibden Park; open daily April through September from 2 to 5 P.M.; March, October, and November from 10 A.M. to 5 P.M., Sunday from 2 to 5 P.M.); the National Museum of the Working Horse in Dobbins Yard (open 10 A.M. to 5 P.M.), and the award-winning **Calderdale Industrial Museum** on

Square Road (open Tuesday through Saturday from 10 A.M. to 5 P.M., Sunday from 2 to 5 P.M.)

## Airedale

Going north from Haworth takes you into Airedale, another great center of textile production and early industrialization. Like Calderdale, many of its mills are now closed, giving its natural beauty a chance to reassert itself, but they stand as monuments to a wealthy past. Most outstanding is **Salts Mill** at Saltaire near Shipley, built on a huge scale by the famous philanthropist Sir Titus Salt, complete with a model village for its workers and now incorporating an art gallery. The city of **Bradford,** once the wool capital of the world, boasts a fine cathedral and a Victorian City Hall and Wool Exchange— appropriately the world's largest wool market. It also has an **Industrial Museum** (Moorside Road, Eccleshill; open from 10 A.M. to 5 P.M. everyday except Monday); the **West Yorkshire Transport Museum,** with a large collection of buses, trams, and commercial vehicles (Ludlam Street; open from 12 to 5 P.M., first Sunday of the month only); and is the home of the **National Museum of Photography, Film and Television** (Princes View; open from 11 A.M. to 6 P.M. daily except Monday). This very popular museum allows "hands-on" experience of how television programs are made, has an unrivaled photography collection, and boasts an Imax Cinema with the largest screen in Britain. Next door the superbly restored **Alhambra Theatre** features seasons by the National Theatre and London Festival Ballet.

## Leeds

Nearby Leeds, Britain's second-largest provincial city, is also a major cultural center, with an international concert season, a music festival, and an internationally famous piano competition—all in its magnificent Victorian Town Hall. It also has two theaters, one the home of the renowned Opera North company, and a City Art Gallery famous for its collection of work by sculptor Henry Moore; there are many more Moores to be seen at the Yorkshire Sculpture Park near Wakefield. The Jacobean stately home of Temple Newsam, near Leeds, is set in a nine hundred-acre park landscaped by Capability Brown.

## ❧ RESTAURANTS

**Holdsworth House,** Holdsworth, Halifax; tel. (0422) 240024. Elegant but comfortable conversion of 1435 manor house with original paneling, antiques, and open fires. Diverse French/English menu with fish a strength. Excellent, if expensive, wine list. Dinner around £23 with wine; set dinner, £12 without. AE, DC, MC, V.

**Kashmir,** 27 Morley St., Bradford; tel. (0274) 726513. Very cheap and cheerful, this sets the standard for Bradford's many Indian curry houses. Don't expect any frills, or even a knife and fork, but do expect excellent, freshly prepared food. Lunch/dinner around £4. No liquor license, but bring your own. No credit cards.

# The Yorkshire Dales

First, to the hills—and arguably the most beautiful hills in the whole region, the Dales. Stretching north from Skipton to Richmond, with an area of 680 square miles, the **Yorkshire Dales National Park** is characterized by rolling limestone hills crisscrossed with dry-stone walls and leading down to lush green valleys and lovely old villages. Today it is mostly concerned with the two businesses of farming sheep and catering to tourists, but part of its charm is that despite being a regular playground for the Yorkshire and Lancashire conurbations, and attracting an increasing number of foreign visitors, it is largely unspoiled and uncommercialized. The national park has strict controls over planning, caravan, and camping sites, meaning that it retains much of the feel and atmosphere it has always had—and, of course, its stunning scenery. The area was first settled by the Vikings, and the local dialect word *dale,* which simply means "valley," comes from their language.

Walking really is the way to see the Dales at their best—there are over one thousand miles of footpaths in the national park, and guided walks are available. The local tourist office will advise on which to attempt, depending on your ability and ambition.

The best place for information on the whole area is the Yorkshire Dales National Park Information Centre in Grassington; call (0756) 753083.

**Skipton** itself is a good place to start—a charming market town based around a broad main street, where sheep and cattle were sold until the beginning of this century. It has a very good selection of shops, as well as a bustling market on Saturdays and many places to eat, and has a very well-preserved 14th-century castle, which is open to visitors every day. There is also a 13th-century **corn mill,** restored to working condition, and the **Craven Museum,** which covers the farming and lead-mining past of the area and has Roman relics as well as the oldest piece of cloth in Britain—recovered from a Bronze-Age coffin found nearby. (The Corn Mill is on Chapel Hill and is open April through September, Monday, Wednesday, Friday, and Saturday from 12 to 5 P.M., Sunday from 2

## The Norman Castles

The incessant fortification of the Northeast, which carried on from the Norman invasion of 1066 right up until the end of the 16th century, can be divided into two distinct phases; first, the initial castle building of the Normans immediately following invasion—both to suppress the particularly rebellious northerners and to form a bulwark against the marauding Scots; and second, following the Scottish revolt of 1300, the massive castle-building program in Northumberland and Durham to protect the north from the constant threat of Scottish invasion.

The first northern rebellion against the Normans came in 1068, when two Yorkshire earls who had previously sworn allegiance to William the Conqueror rose against him. William marched north to York, sacked the town, and killed hundreds of the inhabitants before building a fort (almost certainly on the mound where Clifford's Tower now stands) and garrisoning the town. The next year there was another uprising, this time backed by the Danes, in which York was captured and three thousand Normans were killed. After William retook the city, he proceeded to lay waste to the whole area between York and Durham, in a process that came to be known as the "Harrying of the North." Towns and villages stood empty, with bodies rotting in the streets, and the land was left uncultivated. It was generations before the area recovered economically.

Norman barons were then ceded areas of the region to administer, and they started to build their castles. The normal pattern for these was a tower, or keep, standing on a mound and surrounded by a ditch, or moat. Originally built of wood, these were later rebuilt out of stone and strengthened by huge walls, erected between the keep and the moat.

The best surviving example of this kind of structure is at Richmond. The castle was first built in 1071 and never suffered a serious siege. It still retains its 11th-century walls and 12th-century stone keep, and in its original hall, built in 1080, there is a rare example of Norman domestic architecture. Other particularly fine Norman castles can be found at Scarborough, which saw more recent action when besieged during the English civil war, and at Conisbrough, which is immortalized in Sir Walter Scott's *Ivanhoe*.

to 5 P.M.; October through March, Saturday and Sunday only 2 to 5 P.M.. The Craven Museum is at Town Hall on High Street; it is open April through September, weekdays except Tuesday from 11 A.M. to 5 P.M., Saturday from 10 A.M. to 5 P.M., Sunday from 2 to 5 P.M.; October through March, weekdays except Tuesday from 2 to 5 P.M., Saturday from 10 A.M. to 4:30 P.M., closed Sunday.)

## Wharfedale

Just to the east are the beautifully isolated remains of **Bolton Priory,** sitting on the banks of the river Wharfe at the very entrance to the national park, which housed an Augustinian community until the Dissolution in the 16th century. It features some famous stepping-stones, and a delightful walk through the tree-lined river gorge.

Continuing north up Wharfedale into the hills, either by car or on another footpath, you come to **Burnsall**—one of the loveliest of all Dales villages. It is centered on a fine stone bridge and a classic English village green—complete with maypole—where annual "feast sports" are held in August, including a strenuous fell race. Still farther up is **Grassington,** sitting at the crossing of two important Dales roads, and with good bus services to many parts of the area. Once a prosperous lead-mining center, it now thrives as a natural touring center for this part of the Dales, with a number of good pubs and small, friendly hotels, and has one of the six national park centers. A small art gallery, selling local pictures, now occupies **Pletts Barn,** where John Wesley used to preach, and there is also the **Upper Wharfedale Folk Museum** in the square, made out of two miners' cottages, which shows how life used to be lived in the Dales. (Open April through September, daily from 2 to 4:30 P.M., weekends only in winter.)

From Grassington the winding Wharfedale road (the B6160) continues up over the steep climb of **Langstrothdale Chase,** and down into Wensleydale. But a still more spectacular route is to turn left onto the single-track road through Hubberholme, which goes right over Dodd Fell to give breathtaking views in all directions. Tiny **Hubberholme** itself is worth a quick look; its delightful church has a pre-Reformation rood loft and pews made by "Mouseman" Thompson, and J. B. Priestley described it as "one of the smallest, pleasantest places in the world." Other roads from Grassington lead to gentle Nidderdale and the glory of Fountains Abbey in the east (the B6265), past the dramatic show caves of Stump Cross Caverns, and to Ribblesdale in the west (follow signs to Settle)—both have outstanding scenery.

## Malham

The latter route also goes past Malham, a small village huddled between the steep fells, which is a popular center for climbers and gives access to some of the most stunning and geologically interesting landscape in the whole area. Created by a feature called the Craven Fault, this escarpment culminates in Malham Cove, three quarters of a mile north of the village—a massive vertical exposure of limestone and the source of the river Aire, one of Yorkshire's great rivers. A walk from the village up to and around the cove is well worth the effort; the energetic perhaps can go on up Dry Valley to the waters of Malham Tarn. For the very energetic, but not the fainthearted, this is also the starting point for one of the Dales' best walks—following the Pennine Way long-distance footpath from Malham, past the Tarn, over Fountains Fell and then the spectacular flat-topped Penyghent, before dropping down to Horton-in-Ribblesdale—a distance of about 15 miles.

## Ribblesdale

Just down the dale from Horton, famous for its Three Peaks fell race over three of the highest fells, is the quaint market town of **Settle.** Notable for its old Shambles (originally a row of butchers' homes, they are now shops) and its collection of fine Georgian buildings—including one with a lintel carving of a naked old man, now a café of the same name—the town is also the beginning of the most celebrated and controversial railway line in England, the Settle to Carlisle line. Much fought over by conservationists, who see it as the highest achievement of Victorian railway engineering, and British Rail, who say it is too expensive to maintain, it undoubtedly provides the country's most spectacular train ride over high viaducts and through dramatic scenery. At present it is closed for normal services, but the National Park Committee runs "Dalesrail" excursions one weekend a month during the summer, allowing walkers and other visitors to get on and off at the out-of-the-way Dales stations of Horton, Ribbleshead, Garsdale, and Dent. The line also connects with the main network at Skipton. Details of trains can be gotten from BritRail there, or through the National Park Office at Grassington.

## Wensleydale

Back up Ribblesdale and over the "tops" to **Hawes,** you are in the higher, harder atmosphere of Wensleydale. Hawes, which gets its name from the Anglo-Saxon word for "mountain pass," is Yorkshire's highest market town and the second highest in the country. A fabulous base for walking, surrounded by some of the highest fells in the Dales, Hawes is also the start of what has come to be known as "Herriot country" after the famous writing vet who practiced in Wensleydale and neighboring Swaledale. The town is a relative newcomer to this part of the world—its history can only be traced back to the 15th century—but it is now the thriving center of a huge sheep and cattle farming area, with its market handling over one hundred thousand sheep and twelve thousand cattle each year. It is also the home of Wensleydale cheese, whose original factory still survives and can be visited by appointment.

### Herriot Country

From Hawes the road west takes you across mountainous country to Sedbergh on the Cumbrian border, or east down the dale to the famous waterfalls at Aysgarth—three different falls, all of a different character. But the best way out is over the top again on one of the several routes leading to Swaledale for breathtaking views. One of these passes Hardrow Force, the highest single-drop waterfall in England, and another goes through Askrigg, where much of the filming for the Herriot TV series *All Creatures Great and Small* was done.

## Swaledale

Swaledale, the most northerly and most isolated of the Dales, is narrower and more sparsely populated than its southern neighbor, but perhaps even more attractive for it. A single, winding road makes its way down through lovely little villages like Keld, Thwaite, and Muker, between the steep-sided fells that rise on either side, and on to the dale's old "capital" of Reeth. Another market town whose prosperity was based on lead, Reeth has gradually declined in importance and now has no market. It does, however, have a folk museum in the old Methodist Sunday school, just off the spacious green.

Back the other way, the road out of the top of the dale will take you to Kirkby Stephen in Cumbria, while a single-track road will take you up to the highest pub in England—the **Tan Hill Inn,** at 1,732 feet above sea level—a good lunch stop with a wide selection of beers and food.

The road from Reeth continues down to Richmond, which stands at the head of the dale and is its undisputed focus. A charming Georgian town, and a tourist attraction in its own right, Richmond offers elegant streets, a huge cobbled marketplace, a restored Georgian theater, and the museum for Yorkshire's famous regiment, the Green Howards, in a 12th-century church. More than anything, however, it is dominated by the magnificence of **Richmond Castle,** whose perfectly preserved Norman keep towers one hundred feet above the town and commands the northern entrance to the Dales.

## RESTAURANTS

**Cockett's,** Market Place, Hawes; tel. (09697) 312. Small, Wensleydale hotel providing adventurous menu as well as many old favorites. Many dishes priced as extra, above set-meal cost. Reserve by 5 P.M. Set dinner is around £16 with wine; from £12, without wine. MC, V.

**Howe Villa,** Whitcliffe Mill, Richmond; tel. (0748) 2559. Cordon Bleu cooking in a small, delightful riverside setting—all prepared by the hostess. Early booking is essential. Set dinner is from £8. No liquor license, but bring your own. No credit cards.

**Sportsman's Arms,** Wath-in-Nidderdale, North Yorkshire; tel. (0423) 711306. Rated as one of the three best restaurants in the county, this features a traditional menu with local game a specialty. Deightful off-the-beaten-track setting. Service informal. Dinner is around £20 with wine; set dinner, £7.50 without wine. AE, DC, MC, V.

# The North York Moors

The third abbot of Rievaulx, St. Ailred, described his life here as a "marvellous freedom from the tumult of the world," and it is a sentiment that could well be used as a motif for the whole North York area. Smaller, less well-known, and less-visited than the Dales, it nevertheless offers a charm and tranquillity all its own and equally fine landscapes, with mile upon mile of wild, open moorland, green peaceful dales, and a dramatic coastline.

The main information point is the Danby Lodge National Park Centre, Lodge Lane, Danby, tel. (02876) 654.

## Rievaulx

Rievaulx Abbey itself, lying on the southern fringe of the North York Moors National Park, is an excellent place to start exploring the area. Splendidly situated in a tree-lined valley on the river Rye, the huge white arches of its graceful structure reach to the heavens, and its impressive nave stretches for 170 feet. It is reached down a little winding road off the road from Helmsley, but probably the best way to see it first is from Rievaulx Terrace—a great sweep of lawn between two mock-Grecian temples—which was created in the 18th century to give the best, most romantic view to the visiting aristocracy.

## Helmsley

The abbey also can be reached by footpath from Helmsley, a charming market town three miles away and standing on the same river, with an old market cross and square, a 17th-century–style town hall, and the 13th-century ruins of its own Norman castle. With a number of pleasant hotels and attractive stone shops and cottages, it makes an excellent touring base. The road to the east leads past Rievaulx through a beautiful valley between the moors and the Hambleton Hills, and on to the Cleveland Hills. The A170 leads south to the dramatic viewing point of Sutton Bank, where you can see right across the Vale of York to the Dales. There is also a fine walk along the top of this escarpment to the White Horse carved in the hillside.

## The Moors and Moorland Villages

Going east on the A170 takes you to the picturesque town of **Pickering,** and then to the coast at Scarborough. But if you turn off at the village of **Keldholme,** on the Castleton road, you are taken right through the middle of the moors and to some of the most spectacular views in the area. It also

## The Abbeys

The story of the region's great religious houses closely follows that of the castles—with communities beginning to appear shortly after the Norman conquest and continuing to grow in number, size, and power until Henry VIII's Dissolution of the Monastaries in 1536–40. The great focus of this activity eventually lay in Yorkshire, although the initial impetus was farther north.

The Christian conversion of the Northeast took place in two distinct phases—first in the 7th century and then in the 11th century, separated by the invasion of pagan Vikings—and the great ruins we see now are all from that second period. During the time of Viking rule in the region, monastic life had all but disappeared; the achievements of the early Northumbrian saints Bede, Wilfred, Hilda, and most importantly Cuthbert were wiped out. It was a wish to rescue and rehabilitate these saints, and the houses where their relics had been honored, that brought monks back to the region.

First came the Benedictines, who reestablished communities at Jarrow, Bede's old home, in 1074, then at Monkwearmouth (1075), Whitby (1077), and York (1087). Most significantly, monks from Jarrow and Monkwearmouth were entrusted with the care of Cuthbert's shrine at Durham Cathedral in 1083, from which position their prior rose to preeminence among landowners of the area and became a great magnate as much as a priest. Next came the Augustinian canons, with a more practical mission to care for ordinary "souls" in the parishes and to run almshouses, hospitals, and schools. Their great centers at Bolton, Bridlington, Guisborough, and Kirkham were all built within a decade of one another (between 1113 and 1122), and all leave impressive remains.

But it was the Cistercians, coming from France in 1131, who made the greatest and most enduring impact. With a reputation for great piety and discipline, and with a policy for recruiting lay brethren to handle much of the practical running of their estates, the Cistercians attracted followers in huge numbers both from England and abroad, and established no less than eight major houses in Yorkshire—Rievaulx, Fountains, Byland, Jervaulx, Meaux, Roche, Kirkstall, and Salley. Meaux has left few remains, but of the others, Rievaulx and Fountains are the most magnificent of any abbeys in the county—many would say of any in England.

In the end, and after almost five hundred years of constant building and rebuilding activity to create all these opulent houses, the orders fell victim to their own success and became seen as a threat to the power of the Crown. Martin Luther's Reformation and Henry VIII's break with Rome provided the trigger for their destruction. The Act of Dissolution was passed in 1536, and by 1540 only the ruins we see today remained.

takes you past **Ralph's Cross,** the most famous of the many ancient stone crosses that stand on the moors to guide travelers. Ralph's Cross is almost exactly in the middle of the moors and is used as the national park's emblem. Down to the east of this road is **Farndale,** which in the spring glows with many thousands of wild daffodils; to the west is the equally beautiful **Rosedale,** with the lovely village of Rosedale Abbey—built from the stone of another ruined monastery—and huge kilns built into the hillside from the days when it was an iron-ore mining center. At Castleton you meet the **Eskdale** road, which runs east to **Whitby.** The main coast road runs along the top at the other side of the valley, but it is well worth meandering through villages like **Danby,** where the main visitor center for the national park is housed at Danby Lodge.

At **Egton Bridge** you can play quoits (a game like horseshoes) outside the riverside pub—**The Board,** a good way to pass a sunny lunchtime.

## Scenic Railways

A BritRail line from the industrial center of Middlesbrough to Whitby also runs through the valley, providing a leisurely way of taking in the scenery. At Grosmont it links up with the privately owned North Yorkshire Moors Railway, which runs steam-train services back through the moors to Pickering and is the single biggest tourist attraction in the area. As well as providing the pleasure of seeing old steam trains working again, this line runs through the beautiful valley of **Newtondale,** which is otherwise inaccessible. At least a short trip should be taken, and there are signposted walks from all of the stations. The best place to see a variety of engines at work is at the **Goathland depot,** in an isolated moorland village worth a visit on its own, and overlooking the rather eerie sight of the "Three Golfballs" early-warning system on Fylingdales Moor.

# The Coast

## Whitby

And so to Whitby, the picturesque resort and fishing port at the mouth of the river Esk, dominated by the clifftop grandeur of **Whitby Abbey.** Originally founded by St. Hilda in 657, it is one of the earliest sites of Christianity in Britain, and the 664 Synod of Whitby was held there to determine the dates for Easter. Following destruction of the Vikings, it was resettled in 1077 and then rebuilt to its current scale over the one hundred years from 1220. The east end still survives to its full height, rising gaunt and magnificent above the sea, and those with strong legs will want to visit it by climbing the steep, stone stairs from the town. The harbor is an attraction in itself, with a mixture of traditional fishing boats and modern yachts, while the town itself is full of gift shops selling Whitby jet jewelry and other, less valuable bits of nonsense. There is also a traditional British seafront, with amusement arcades, candy-floss stalls, and a pier, while across the bay from the abbey stands a pair of whale's jawbones to commemorate the time when the town was an important whaling center. Next to it stands a statue of Captain James Cook, the great explorer who discovered Australia. He was born in the area, had his ships built in Whitby, and is undoubtedly the town's most famous son. Any local tourist office will provide details of a "Captain Cook Trail," which will take you around the places associated with this famous voyager.

## Fishing Villages
One of the spots on the Captain Cook Trail is the fishing village of **Staithes,** just up the coast, which has not changed dramatically from the time Cook was apprenticed to a local draper and grocer in the 1740s. Set in a steep ravine, it still retains a charming Old-World atmosphere and, like all the places along this coast, has a marvelous fish-and-chips shop. Farther up are the cliffs at **Boulby,** which are the highest in England. Between Staithes and Whitby is the delightful little cove of **Runswick Bay,** with a sandy beach and a village that is constantly, and literally, threatening to fall into the sea. Just south of Whitby is **Robin Hood's Bay,** probably the most delightful place on the coast with its oddly shaped houses clinging to the cliff, the dramatic three-mile sweep of the bay, and its romantic past of smuggling. All these places can be reached by car or bus from Whitby, or by foot along the cliff-top track, which is part of the Cleveland Way long-distance footpath. Those making the effort would be rewarded with the spectacular sea views and fresh air.

## Scarborough
Taking the main A171 road from Whitby leads you to **Scarborough**—a spa since 1662 and England's first-ever seaside resort. Straddling two large bays with vast expanses of flat beach, it still is a favorite for traditional family holidays—kids build sandcastles and play at the shore's edge while Mum and Dad contemplate the world from a deck chair. The only thing that can interrupt this idyll is the unpredictable weather, but the North Sea provides one constant—the constant cold. The south bay has the harbor and the inevitable amusement arcades and fun fair on the one hand, and landscaped clifftop gardens and grand hotels on the other; the north bay has neat guest houses, a park and golf course, and a pool. Standing on the massive headland between the two is the imposing castle, thought to have been a defensive stronghold point since the Bronze Age. The town also has the **Stephen Joseph Theater** (0723-37054), the first to be built "in the round," which premieres all the plays by Britain's most popular playwright, Alan Ayckbourn.

## ☙ RESTAURANTS

**McCoy's,** The Tontine, Staddlebridge, North Yorkshire; tel. (060982) 671. Another highly rated Yorkshire eatery, with a nostalgic jumble of a decor and flamboyant French food. Attached bistro with cheaper menu. Dinner is around £32 with wine and all trimmings; about £23, without. AE, DC, MC, V.

**Magpie Cafe,** 14 Pier Rd., Whitby; tel. (0947) 602058. Georgian café, overlooking the harbor. One of the very best places to sample excellent, simply cooked, local fish. Dinner is around £14 with wine; £10 without. Set lunch from £4.75. No credit cards.

# Durham

Over the northern boundary of Yorkshire lies the county of Durham, bearing more industrial scars than most but still with a wealth of beauty and interest.

## Durham City

Guarding the tight neck of a loop in the river Wear, set on a high plateau, is Durham Castle. Behind it rises the magnificent structure of Durham Cathedral. Together they form the focus of the historic city and county of Durham, and one of the most impressive sights in England.

The old city itself is spread out below and between the two arms of the river, with steep narrow streets full of old stone shops and houses leading to a large marketplace. The modern city spreads out both east and west, one way into the smart Georgian houses of Elvet, and the other to Victorian terraced streets of workers' houses—reflecting its development as both a fashionable university city and as the center of the local coal-mining industry.

The naturally defended site was chosen as the eventual resting place for the bones of St. Cuthbert in 995, when the first church was built, and it has been a place of pilgrimage and fortification ever since. It is surrounded on three sides by the steep-sided river gorge, densely wooded and with delightful riverside footpaths. The river itself is a popular spot for rowers, both serious crews from the university and people who just want a leisurely afternoon. Boats can be easily hired.

The present cathedral and castle both date from after the Norman invasion, when the city became an important seat of civil, military, and ecclesiastical power as the home of the prince bishops. These men ruled until 1836 with a power and independence unique in English history. Their lands stretched from the Tees to the Scottish border, forming a buffer state against the Scots, and within these the prince bishops exercised all the powers normally held by the king—with their own army, nobility, courts, and coinage. Their seal is now used as an emblem by the local tourist authority.

## Durham Cathedral and Castle

The cathedral, started in 1093, is the finest example of early Norman architecture in England and was recently voted a "World Heritage Site." It is still the resting place of the remains of St. Cuthbert and the bones of the Venerable Bede, and retains beautiful cloisters and a monks' dormitory from the time when it also housed a great Benedictine monastery. From the top of its great tower, there are magnificent views across the whole of the country. Locally, however, the cathedral is perhaps best-known for its grotesque Sanctuary Knocker—with a large ring to which criminals could cling and claim safety from a pursuing "hue and cry." The original is in the Cathedral Treasury, along with other great treasures including the Durham Gospels, but a replica is still on the cathedral's main doors. (Open May through September, daily from 7:15 A.M. to 8 P.M.; October through April from 7:15 A.M. to 4:45 P.M.)

The castle, which doubled as the palace of the prince bishops, is now part of Durham University—the fourth oldest in the country. It can be visited throughout the year on guided tours, and is particularly notable for its Norman Chapel, dating from 1080, its kitchens, and Great Hall, dated 1499 and 1284, respectively (open July through October, daily from 10 A.M. to 5 P.M.; November through June, Monday, Wednesday, Saturday from 2 to 5 P.M.).

## Beamish: The Past Re-created

Ten miles north of Durham city is the **North of England Open Air Museum** at Beamish—a unique collection of working displays that records in a marvelously effective way how life was lived in the region during the early part of this century. The first of its kind in Britain, and voted European Museum of the Year in 1987, Beamish re-creates whole areas of this life that visitors simply wander through. There is a colliery complex, complete with pit headgear, miners' cottages, and a drift mine you can actually go down; the whole main street of a 1920s town; a 1910 railway station; and a fully stocked farm that charts agricultural developments in the area from the end of the 18th century. All the exhibits are completely original, collected from all over the region and reassembled on-site, and all are connected by a fully operational tramway. (Open April through October from 10 A.M. to 6 P.M., November through March from 10 A.M. to 5 P.M., closed Mondays.)

## The Original Washington

A few miles to the east of Beamish lies **Washington Old Hall,** the family seat of George Washington's ancestors. (To get there go east on the A693, then north on the A1 to the next junction. Then take the A1231 to Washington and follow signs for District 4 Washington Village. The hall is open April through September from 11 A.M. to 5 P.M., closed Fridays; open Wednesdays, Saturdays, and Sundays only in October.)

## Darlington: Birthplace of the Railway

To the south of the county is Darlington, a lively regional center with some fine Georgian architecture, and notable as being the destination of the world's first passenger railway—the Stockton to Darlington—which was built by the great local engineer George Stephenson and first ran in 1825. There is a railway museum there to mark this, with pride of place given to Locomotive No. 1, which hauled that very first train.

# The Durham Dales

Darlington also offers easy access eastward to the northern Pennines, the continuation of the Pennine Chain from the Yorkshire Dales, and itself designated an area of outstanding natural beauty. A tour of this area should start in **Barnard Castle,** the bustling market center of Teesdale, with market stalls and a livestock sale every Wednesday. The village gets its name from its own brooding Norman castle. Just outside the town is the **Bowes Museum,** a magnificent mansion built in 1892 by a local coal baron to the pattern of a French château. On display there is an internationally renowned art collection, including paintings by El Greco, Goya, and Canaletto, and fine furniture, ceramics and tapestries. (Open May through September, Monday through Saturday from 10 A.M. to 5:30 P.M.; Sundays from 2 P.M. to 5 P.M.; March, April, and October, Monday through Saturday from 10 A.M. to 5 P.M.; November through February, Monday through Saturday from 10 A.M. to 4 P.M.; Sunday from 2 to 4 P.M.)

## Flowers and Lead

The road north takes you to the delightful little town of Middleton-in-Teesdale, once a thriving lead-mining center, but now famous for the beautiful countryside that surrounds it, with its wealth of wild flowers. Marvelous walking country, this, especially up the valley to **High Force**—England's most spectacular waterfall. Alternatively, High Force can be reached on the B6277 road north from Middleton. Then the small, but spectacular, road to St. John's Chapel should be taken "over the top" into the almost equally beautiful Weardale. The history of lead mining, which has left old workings dotted all over this part of the country, is charted at the **Killhope Wheel centre** in Upper Weardale—the most complete lead mining site in Britain. Dominated by the 34-foot-high water wheel of the lead crushing mill, it features restored

## The Northumbrian Castles

When the great Scottish leader William Wallace took on the might of Edward I in the Scottish War of Independence in the early 1300s, it raised the curtain for over two hundred years of constant war between the two countries which devastated the border lands. The first chapter of this conflict ended with Robert the Bruce's momentous victory over Edward II at Bannockburn in 1314, but it did not finally end until the Scots were crushed at Flodden in 1513, when they lost ten thousand compared to the English casualties of fifteen hundred.

It was during this period that most of the Northumbrian castles were built. One of the best preserved is Langley Castle, now a country house hotel (see "Hotels," at beginning of this chapter), while the most dramatic is at Dunstanburgh—where the ruins stand isolated on a rocky platform that rises steeply from the sea. Raby Castle, in county Durham, was built in the 14th century, but most of the interior dates from the 18th and 19th centuries. Still the home of Lord Barnard, it is set in spacious walled parkland with herds of deer, follies, and beautiful gardens.

The border wars also led to the appearance of fortified pele towers—often used for the protection of Catholic priests, such as the fine example in Corbridge marketplace—and fortified manor houses. Aydon Castle, just to the north, is a perfect example of this, and one of the most important historical buildings in Northumberland. Strife continued throughout the 16th century, with smaller-scale but equally vicious border feuds, when Bastle houses where built as protection against raiders. Resembling large barns, with living accommodation on the upper floor and space for livestock below, these are almost exclusively found in Northumberland, and all lie within twenty miles of the border. Blackmiddens Bastle House, three miles north of Bellingham, is an excellent example.

The Elizabethan fortifications at Berwick, begun in 1555, were the last great defensive work to be built on the border. Their ramparts and bastions represented the first time this technique was introduced in Europe, but these fortifications became obsolete after 1603, when the English and Scottish crowns were finally united.

buildings and exhibitions on the life of lead miners, and a three-quarter-mile walk through the forest linking mining remains.

# The Durham Coast and Cookson Country

Much of the Durham coast has been ruined by centuries of coal mining, and there are still a number of deep mines that go out under the seabed. But the northernmost tip at **South Shields** has remained largely unspoiled, with dramatic limestone cliffs, broad sandy beaches, and a wealth of bird life. Its main attraction is Marsden Bay, with the one-hundred-foot-high **Marsden Rock** that stands off the shore like a great battered arch. All of this area is, in fact, busy promoting itself on the back of Catherine Cookson—Britain's popular novelist, who also writes under the names of Catherine Marchant, Catherine Fawcett, and Katie McMullen. She was born here, lived here until she was 23, and her most famous novels, *Our Kate, The Gambling Man,* and *Katie Mulholland,* are set here. There is a **Catherine Cookson Trail,** run by the local tourist office, to a number of sites associated with the writer and her work. (The tourist office is at the South Shields Museum and Art Gallery on Ocean Road, call 091-454-6612.) Also opened last year is a full-scale reconstruction of the Roman Fort that once stood in South Shields, complete with a museum and tours around the continuing excavations of the site. The fort was built in A.D. 208 as a supply center for campaigns in Scotland, and it is the only stone-built supply base known to the Roman Empire. Relics in the museum include sculptures and tombstones, jewelry and weapons.

Perhaps the most historically significant place in this part of the region, however, is **St. Paul's Church** in neighboring Jarrow. This is one of the oldest churches in Britain; its monastery was one of the dominant centers in the eighth-century intellectual life of Europe, and it was the home of the great northern saint the Venerable Bede.

## ☙ RESTAURANTS

**Stile,** 97 High St., Willington, Durham; tel. (0388) 746615. An old country cottage with Victorian-style conservatory, this is one of the few really good places to eat in the area. Traditional menu, including game. Dinner is around £14 with wine; £10 without. Set lunch is £5.75. MC, V.

**Market Place Teashop,** 29 Market Place, Barnard Castle; tel. (0833) 690110. All-day tea shop with excellent traditional cooking—including a Yorkshire cheesecake made to a medieval recipe. Good lunchtime specials. Meals are about £8 with wine; £5 without. No credit cards.

# Northumberland

## Newcastle

On the north bank of the river Tyne, 12 miles from the sea, stands Newcastle—a major industrial, commercial and recreational center and the undisputed capital of the "real" Northeast of England.

# Early Christianity in Northumbria

Before reaching its eighth-century pinnacle as a great center of learning, Northumbrian Christianity had undergone over a century of development, resulting in the conversion of the whole of northern England and producing an unparalleled number of saints.

The first of these was a Roman missionary, Paulinus, who accompanied Augustine to Kent in 601. Having been consecrated as a bishop in 625, he set off with a mission to convert the north, and at Easter 627 he baptized Edwin, King of Northumbria, in a wooden chapel on the site of the present York Minster. That same year, in the river Glen west of present-day Wooler, he baptized over three thousand people in 36 days and went on to conduct more mass baptisms in the river Swale near Catterick. For these achievements he was appointed the first archbishop of York.

Much of his work, however, was wiped out in an invasion of Northumbria by the pagan Welsh and Mercians in 633, when Edwin was killed and Paulinus forced to flee back to Kent. Christianity was firmly reestablished only after 634, when Oswald, Edwin's successor, won a decisive victory over the Mercian king Cadwalla at Heavenfield, on the uplands north of Hexham. The spot is still marked by a wooden cross and St. Oswald's chapel, on the B6318 east of the Brunton crossroads. Oswald had spent his early life at the monastery of Iona, off the west coast of Scotland, and it was from here that he now summoned Aiden to reintroduce Christianity to his kingdom. Created bishop of Northumberland, this austere monk established a monastery on the island of Lindisfarne in 635, from which he went on hugely successful missions through the remote hills, often accompanied by Oswald himself.

Aiden had brought with him the particular brand of Celtic Christianity, distinct from that of Rome introduced by Paulinus, that had flourished in virtual isolation from the rest of the world since the end of the fourth century—when the Romans left Britain, the empire was largely ended—and the country was overrun by Germanic tribes. It emphasized simplicity and teaching by example, and continued to be dominant in Northumbria after Aiden's death in 651. Then in 664 the great Synod of Whitby was convened to decide on the true date of Easter, calculated differently by Celtic and Rome-influenced monks, and it quickly turned into a direct conflict over two very different ways of life. The word of Rome, with its more worldly emphasis on building magnificent churches and amassing treasure, won the day, and from this date the Celtic tradition declined in influence.

Very much in this tradition, however, was perhaps the best-remembered and most spiritual of all English saints, Cuthbert. Born in 635, he was instructed at Melrose Priory and, like Aiden, would travel for months at a time to visit the most remote villages and farmsteads. He continued this work after moving to Lindisfarne as prior in 664, but he wished more and more for solitude. Eventually, in 676, Cuthbert withdrew completely to the tiny, uninhabited island of Inner Farne, where he stayed for eight years. He was briefly bishop of Hexham but soon returned to Lindisfarne, and then again to Inner Farne, where he stayed until his death in 687. Cuthbert, despite his isolation, became an early folk hero, and it was in his memory—"for God and St. Cuthbert"—that the greatest flowering of Celtic Christianity was produced—the Lindisfarne Gospels. The original is now in the British Museum, but a copy can be seen in the Parish Church of St. Mary on the island.

Living at about the same time, but very much in the Roman tradition, was Wilfred. He was a major figure at the Synod of Whitby and became first the bishop of Ripon and then of York, with much of Northumbria under his influence. He was removed in 678 by the king, who feared his power, and even was briefly imprisoned. During his life he introduced music and ceremony into the British church and rebuilt many wooden churches with stone. He built the first church at Hexham—said to be the finest north of the Alps—and his throne, the Frith Stool, can still be seen in the present Hexham Abbey.

In 674 Benedict Biscop, a cultured Northumbrian nobleman, founded a monastery at Monkwearmouth, on the north bank of the river Wear. To it he brought books from Rome to establish a center of learning and to teach its monks to worship in the Roman fashion, and then in 684 he founded a sister monastery at Jarrow. Fragments of both original buildings can be found in the present-day churches there, and Jarrow's dedicatory inscription, dated April 23, 685, is the oldest surviving in England. It was in that year that the 12-year-old Bede entered Jarrow priory, and over the next fifty years there he produced a stream of books on history, theology, poetry, grammar, and natural science that made him the greatest scholar in Christendom. Most famous among these were the earliest English version of the Gospel, a life of St. Cuthbert, and his *Ecclesiastical History of the English People*, which traced the story of England from Roman times.

A guarded river crossing since the time of the Romans, who built the fort Pons Aelius here, the city takes its name from the "new castle" built by William the Conqueror's son in 1080. This was itself rebuilt in the 12th century by Henry II; that Norman keep still stands and is one of the best preserved in the country, with fine views from its battlements. The city grew from river trade, particularly the coal trade to London, which gave rise to the "taking coals to Newcastle" saying, and at one time two hundred pits operated west of the city center. As a result, the oldest part of the city is the **Quayside,** along the river front, which has the city's most historic buildings, including some medieval houses. It is also the site, every Sunday morning, of a vibrant market.

The classic view of this compact city is from one of the six road and rail bridges that now span the river, including the most famous of all—the **Tyne Bridge,** which was built in the 1920s as a prototype for the Sydney Harbour bridge in Australia. The modern city climbs up from the river through fine Victorian architecture, including the magnificent curving Grey Street, which is regarded as one of the most graceful streets in Europe, and onto Eldon Square—one of Europe's largest indoor shopping centers.

Newcastle is a major cultural center, boasting three theaters that host the Royal Shakespeare Company each year, the Laing Art Gallery, and a new dance center. And it is also the focus of nightlife for the whole of Tyneside, with a host of clubs and restaurants and the Bigg Market—whose many pubs are thronged every Friday and Saturday night in a weekly, beer-swilling "fiesta."

The best place to start any visit to the city is at **Blackfriars** on Monk Street, a converted 13th-century monastery that now houses the tourist information center, a museum, a craft center, and workshops. (Open April through September, daily from 10 A.M. to 5 P.M.; October through March, Tuesday through Saturday from 10 A.M. to 4:30 P.M.) Trips down the river, past the sites of the Tyne's proud shipbuilding past, are run by River Tyne Cruises, based on the Quayside; call (091) 232-8683.

## Tynedale

The gateway to the rest of Northumberland is Hexham, easily reached along the beautiful Tyne Valley railway line. Dominated by the 12th-century abbey, with the finest Saxon crypt in England, this charming little town huddles around its ancient market square—which still bustles on Tuesdays, when there is also a large livestock mart. Its tourist information center is in the 14th-century Manor Office (through the archway on the eastern side of the marketplace), the country's first purpose-built jail, where there is also a small museum dedicated to the history of the lawless Border Reivers, or raiders, who laid waste to much of the county in the 16th century.

Three miles downriver is the even more ancient town of **Corbridge,** largely built from the stones of its Roman forebear Corstopitum—a supply center for Hadrian's Wall dating from A.D. 80. Now genteel and residential, Corbridge was once the capital of Northumbria where King Ethelred was killed in 796. The town was burned down three times by the Scots, and **St. Andrew's Church,** one of the oldest in the country, still bears the traces of fire. Next to it in the marketplace is the pele tower, built around 1300 to protect the local clergy. At nearby **Newton,** the award-winning **Hunday National Tractor and Farm Museum** has Europe's most extensive collection of agricultural machinery. On the site of Corstopitum itself there is an excellent museum of Roman remains and the best-preserved Roman granaries in Britain.

## Hadrian's Wall

Roman remains, and in particular the great sweep of Hadrian's Wall, are the major historical attractions for tourists visiting this area. For three hundred years Northumberland was the northernmost frontier of the great Roman Empire, and military sites of international importance are dotted all over it. These, of course, are focused on the wall itself—the great feat of engineering that stretched the 76 miles from Wallsend on the Tyne to Solway Firth on the west coast—to divide, in the words of a contemporary chronicler, "the Romans from the barbarian." Started in A.D. 120 on the orders of Emperor Hadrian, it eventually stood 15 feet high and 6 to 10 feet wide, with regular turrets, mile castles, and major forts along its entire length.

In the centuries after it was abandoned, the wall was regularly plundered for building materials by local people. But much of it still remains, particularly in the central section amid some of Northumberland's wildest and most dramatic scenery, and intensive excavation over the last one hundred years has uncovered much more. The best-preserved and most impressive of its forts is at **Housesteads,** on the B6318 near Haydon Bridge, which covers a five-acre site and was once home for a one-thousand-strong infantry regiment. Traces of all its buildings remain, including a well-preserved latrine, as well as evidence of a large civil settlement to the south. Farther west on the same road, **Vindolanda**—with an excellent museum and a fully reconstructed section of wall—should also be visited. The Steel Rigg car park, just above Once Brewed, gives access to a walk on one of the wall's best sections to enjoy some of its best views. All these sites, and more, can be visited using special buses that run from Hexham during the summer months. (Housesteads is open April through September, daily from 9:30 A.M. to 6:30 P.M., from 2 to 6 P.M. on Sundays; October through March, Monday through Saturday, from 9:30 A.M. to 4 P.M., Sunday from 2 to 4 P.M. Vindolanda is open July and August from 10 A.M. to 6:30 P.M., May and June from 10 A.M. to 6 P.M.; April and September from 10 A.M. to 5:30 P.M.; March and October from 10 A.M. to 5 P.M.; and November through February from 10 A.M. to 4 P.M. For information see the tourist center in Hexham, noted above.)

# The North Tyne

Heading north from Hadrian's Wall, the B6320 goes up the beautiful North Tyne Valley to **Bellingham,** on the edge of the enormous Kielder Forest and close to the water-sport center of **Kielder Reservoir,** the biggest man-made lake in western Europe. Alternatively, the A68 Roman road, Dene Street, charges straight over spectacular high ground on its way to Edinburgh. Either way, you should then go on to **Otterburn,** site of the famous battle of Chevy Chase, and then to **Rothbury,** an attractive stone-built town straddling a broad high street. One and a half miles east of Rothbury on the B6341 is the splendidly restored **Cragside House,** built by the Tyneside industrialist Lord Armstrong; it was the first house in the world to be lit by electricity. Around it he planted seven million trees and shrubs to create a nine hundred-acre park, ablaze with rhododendrons in early summer. Both are open to the public. (The house is open daily except Monday, April through September from 1 to 5 P.M.; and in October only on Wednesdays, Saturdays and Sundays. The gardens are open April through September from 10:30 A.M. to 6 P.M., in October till 5 P.M., and during the winter till 4.)

### Alnwick: Lion of the North

The road north continues past one of the most spectacular views in the county, to Alnwick—a former county town and home of Northumberland's greatest family, the Percys. Their family seat, **Alnwick Castle,** rises gray above the river Aln and dominates the town—with its stone figures of soldiers perched on the battlements intended as a threat to advancing enemies. The interior was redecorated in the last century in the style of the Italian Renaissance, with paintings by Titian, Van Dyck, and Canaletto, and has a famed collection of Meissen china. It is surrounded by three thousand acres of parkland, party landscaped by the great Capability Brown, who was born in Northumberland. (Open last day of April through September from 1 to 5 P.M. except Saturdays.)

The town's cobbled market square is the setting for the week-long **Alnwick Fair** in June, when the townspeople dress up in medieval costumes.

## The Perfect Northumberland Coast

East of Alnwick is Alnmouth, a delightful little resort ideal for anyone wanting a bit of peace and quiet. And from here, north to the Scottish border, is one of the least spoiled and most beautiful coastlines in Britain, with a succession of sandy bays, low headlands, and little fishing villages. Head north through Craster, famous for its kippers, past the haunting ruin of Dunstanburgh Castle, and on to Beadnell and Seahouses. Regular boat trips run from Seahouses out to the uninhabited **Farne Islands,** sanctuary of unparalleled numbers of sea birds and gray seals, and giving spectacular views back to the coast and over to the brooding Cheviot Hills.

### Bamburgh

Then it is on to Bamburgh, now a picturesque village facing a manicured green, but once the royal capital of Northumbria where kings were crowned and held court with noblemen and saints. Above the village, and backed by the sea, rise the dramatic red sandstone walls of **Bamburgh Castle.** The present castle dates from the Norman period, but it was restored in grand style at the end of the last century by Lord Armstrong (of Cragside). It is still the Armstrong family home, but it is open to the public and contains a museum dedicated to the achievements of the great industrialist. (Open daily April through June and in September from 1 to 5 P.M.; in July and August till 6 P.M., and till 4:30 in October.)

Bamburgh also is the birthplace of Victorian heroine Grace Darling, who rowed out to rescue shipwrecked sailors, and there is a museum commemorating her as well.

## Holy Island

Going north again brings you to Lindisfarne—or Holy Island, as it is more commonly known—cradle of northern Christianity and now also an important nature reserve. The chief attractions are the gaunt ruins of the 11th-century **priory,** the 13th-century **St. Mary's Church,** and the 16th-century **Castle**—converted into a private home by Sir Edwin Lutyens. There is also a charming harbor, miles of deserted sand dunes, and the famous Lindisfarne Mead—a honey-based liquor made from the monks' ancient recipe.

Visitors here fall into a strange mixture of pilgrims, bird-watchers, and plain holidaymakers, who are all cut off together twice a day when the tide comes in (any local tourist office will give safe crossing times). Whatever the interest, however, a night on the island makes a fine finale to any trip to the northeast. The locals are incredibly friendly, and once the waters do close in, the pubs and bars just refuse to shut.

# ☞ RESTAURANTS

**Fisherman's Lodge,** Jesmond Dene, Newcastle; tel. (091) 281 3281. Excellent, locally caught fish in candlelit surroundings, with the restaurant itself set in a steep-sided valley park just outside the city center. Smart dress preferred. Dinner is around £27 with wine. Set lunch is from £10 without. AE, DC, MC, V.

**Jade Garden,** 53 Stowell St., Newcastle; tel. (091) 261 5889. Solid, good-value Cantonese cooking in Newcastle's bustling Chinatown. City's best selection of roast and barbecued meats and noodle dishes. Dinner is around £12 with wine. Set dinner is from £4.20 without. Set lunch is £3. AE, DC, MC, V.

**Ramblers Country House,** Farnley, near Corbridge; tel. (043471) 2424. Fine, consistent German menu in Victorian house high above the Tyne. Smart dress preferred. Dinner is around £18 with wine. Set dinner is £9.85 without. AE, DC, MC, V.

**General Havelock Inn,** Radcliffe Rd., Haydon Bridge; tel. (043484) 376. Plain, reliable English cooking in an old inn by the Tyne. Pies and roasts are particularly good. Dinner is around £18 with wine and extras. Set dinner is £12.50 without. Set lunch is from £5. No credit cards.

# 12

# THE
# NORTHWEST

As a region, the Northwest begins much farther south than what is called the North Country on the other side of the Pennines. It stretches from the lush dairy farming area of the Cheshire plain to the Lake District. Its boundaries to the west are the Welsh border and then the Irish Sea and to the east the long rib of the Pennines. To the south, Cheshire rolls into Shropshire and Staffordshire, two shires whose northern parts have very similar countryside to Cheshire but which are nonetheless perceived to be part of the Midlands rather than the Northwest. Try telling the difference between Blue Cheshire cheese and its Shropshire counterpart! And much of the western part of Cheshire, with its many half-timbered buildings, would seem to have more in common with other counties on the Welsh marches, like Shropshire or Herefordshire, than it does with Lancashire. But what Cheshire and Lancashire do have in common is that both are part of the hinterland of the two great commercial centers of Liverpool and Manchester. And this fact points to another distinctive feature of the region. The conurbations around Liverpool and Manchester are some of the most densely populated and urbanized parts of Britain. Northern Lancashire is one of the least densely populated parts of the country. Cheshire, meanwhile, has lush, rich farming land and villages and market towns, which signal a wealth and affluence far more typical of southern counties like Berkshire or Suffolk.

In British terms Liverpool and Manchester are new cities. In their present form they do not date back much before the end of the 18th century, yet they form the core of the Northwest rather than do the old county towns of Chester and Lancaster. Manchester, of course, was the world's first industrial city, the "cottonopolis" of the 1830s and 1840s, and Liverpool its greatest port. Indeed Liverpool's fortunes were originally made on the intertwined trades of slavery and cotton in the early 19th century. Today Liverpool is no longer Britain's great seaport. With British membership in the EEC, the country's economic orientation is increasingly toward Europe rather than the Atlantic, and the ports of East Anglia have inherited Liverpool's mantle. And since the Second World

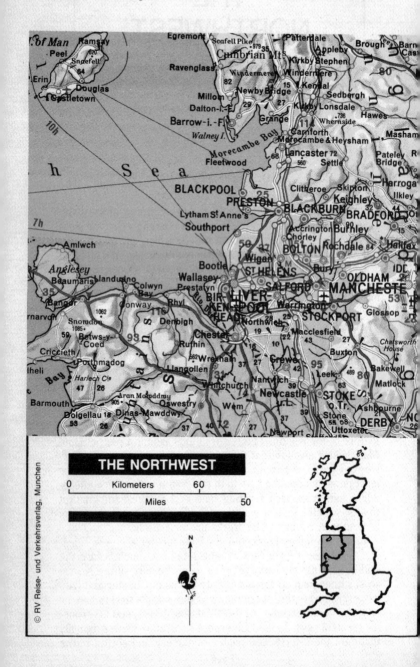

THE NORTHWEST

0    Kilometers    60

Miles    50

N

© RV Reise- und Verkehrsverlag, Munchen

War, many of the cotton mills of the Manchester area have fallen victim to competition from the Far East.

Liverpool and Manchester both suffered badly in the recession of the early 1980s, but both now have the feel of cities starting to "come up" again. The decline of the old industries has improved dramatically the environment of the cities. The Mersey at Liverpool is increasingly a clean river; and with factory and mill chimneys no longer belching out smoke, the magnificent Victorian architectural heritage of the mercantile patricians who built up Liverpool and Manchester can now be more fully appreciated. In common with other old ports like Cardiff and Glasgow, or Baltimore in the United States, Liverpool's waterfront is being renovated to be a center of service and leisure, rather than manufacturing industries, and the real estate boom of the south of England is starting to hit Manchester.

To many, however, the image of the Northwest is still firmly fixed in football, fish and chips and beer—the staple pastimes of the British working class; and the football, fish and chips and beer remain as good as ever. Manchester United, Everton, and Liverpool, England's most glamorous soccer clubs, are here with their legend-soaked grounds and their armies of supporters; but so too are a host of other legendary clubs like Manchester City, Blackpool, Bolton Wanderers, and Tranmere Rovers. A fish-and-chips supper after the match, washed down with a few pints of Boddington's, Higson's, or one of the many other real ales of the area, is a seminal Northwestern experience. And that's to say nothing of other culinary traditions like black pudding or Lancashire hot pot. Furthermore, Liverpool and Manchester are two of the most cosmopolitan areas for food outside of London. Both cities have old established Chinatowns, and for Indian food Manchester offers an exciting variety of regional cuisines.

The cosmopolitan nature of Manchester and Liverpool also comes out in their continued preeminence in British pop music. Liverpool is the city of the Beatles, but long before they were playing the Liverpool clubs the towns of the Northwest were turning out music hall singers and comedians like George Formby or "the lassie from Lancashire" herself, Gracie Fields. In the sixties it was in Manchester clubs like The Twisted Wheel that the working class subculture of "northern soul"—dancing in mohair suits to the music of Detroit and Philadelphia—began, and in recent years Manchester has been a great producer of indie music with bands like The Smiths and New Order, and the Factory Records label. No fan of indie music visiting Manchester should miss Factory's Hacienda club on Whitworth Street.

For such large cities, Liverpool and Manchester are incredibly friendly, particularly in comparison to London. Liverpudlians, or "scousers," have a quick-witted repartee and style whose only equals are to be found in Glasgow and Dublin; and, like Glasgow and Boston, Liverpool has strong claims to being the capital city of Ireland outside Ireland. A few days' immersion in it, and in Manchester, makes a refreshing urban interlude between the wild fastnesses of north Wales and the Lake District. Cheshire and Lancashire too are full of beautiful countryside, pretty villages, castles, and stately homes; and the old cathedral city of Chester, right on the Welsh border, is a *must* for anyone interested in the remains of Roman and medieval Britain.

A word about geographical designations. Local government changes in recent years have created an administrative entity called Merseyside, encompassing the conurbation around Liverpool and therefore including areas formerly part of Lancashire or Cheshire. Traditionally, the northern boundary of Cheshire was the river Mersey. So Birkenhead and Port Sunlight, across the Mersey from Liverpool, were actually in Cheshire. Likewise the Wirral Peninsula. This chapter will observe these traditional designations and will use "Merseyside" only as a descriptive term.

Chester makes a good starting point for the region, especially if you have been in north Wales. It's worth several days' exploring on foot, taking in the famous medieval "Rows" of shops, the old city walls, and the cathedral, and it also makes a perfect base for trips into the Cheshire countryside. From Chester go up through the picturesque Wirral Peninsula to Liverpool or travel across the county to Manchester. There is much to see and do in both cities and from them you can head north toward the Lake District. If you want to spend time in Lancashire itself—it is the second largest county and is full of fine country laden with history—then the seaside resort of Blackpool has an extremely wide range of hotel accommodation.

# TRAVEL

The Northwest has excellent road and rail links with the rest of Britain and within the region boasts the country's best motorway network. The M6 runs through north to south, and the M62 from east to west. Chester, Liverpool, Manchester, and Blackpool have Inter-City express rail services from London Euston, all with journey times of less than three hours. At Ringway, Manchester has an international airport, the main one after the London airports, with direct daily flights from the United States, Canada, and many European cities. There are passenger boat services from Liverpool to Dublin and Belfast, and from Heysham, in north Lancashire, to the Isle of Man. From the Northwest you are in easy reach of north Wales, the Peak District, the Yorkshire Dales, and the Lake District.

# ☙ HOTELS

Credit card abbreviations used in hotel and restaurant listings are as follows: AE for American Express, CB for Carte Blanche, DC for Diner's Club, MC for MasterCard, and V for Visa.

## Chester

**Chester Grosvenor Hotel,** Eastgate St., Chester CH1 1LT; tel. 0244-324024, telex 61240, fax 0244-313246, U.S. toll free 800-223-5581, Canada toll free 800-346-8480. Grosvenor is the family name of the Duke of Westminster, and the hotel is part of the Grosvenor estate, along with much of the rest of Chester and the Mayfair area in London. The Chester Grosvenor itself is very much the hotel of county society in Cheshire. The Princess of Wales stayed here when she was Lady Diana Spencer, and her former room is now called the Lady Diana. In the spacious days of transatlantic passenger ships, American travelers like the novelist Henry James would often pause here on their journey between Liverpool and London. Other famous guests after whom suites are named are James Mason, Prince Rainier of Monaco, and King Constantine of Greece. The Grosvenor is situated in a prime location within the city walls next to the ancient East Gate Tower and a short stroll from the Rows, the cathedral, the river, and the racecourse. The present building was built in 1866 and underwent extensive and costly refurbishment during the winter of 1987–88. There has been an inn on this site since Tudor times, and the Grosvenor family, who have held lands in the area for over nine hundred years, acquired it in 1800. Suites at the Grosvenor fall into two categories: luxury ones such as the Rainier or the Constantine, with separate sitting rooms; and junior ones with sitting room and bedrooms combined. All suites have dining-room tables on which meals can be served. Some rooms have yew wood or mahogany balustrades, and Capellini furniture is featured throughout the hotel. Bathrooms are of Italian marble and also have small dressing areas adjacent to them. All suites and rooms have ice buckets and computerized minibars. A residents' drawing room can be found on the first floor as well as an exclusive leisure suite with exercise equipment. The club atmosphere is maintained in the book-lined, deep-carpeted Library cocktail bar. Morning coffee and afternoon tea can also be had in here, and a pianist plays in the evenings. The Library leads into the Arkle restaurant. Of the Grosvenor's two restaurants, the Arkle is the more formal and opulent. The other, La Brasserie, caters rather more to the city trade. (See "Restaurants," Chester, below.) In a roof adjacent to the hotel lobby is a room called the Secretariat, where business facilities are available. Above the door of the Secretariat and the lobby stairwell hangs the Grosvenor chandelier. This contains 28,000 pieces of crystal, weighs half a ton, and was originally from a club in St. James's, London. Room rates: from £95 for a deluxe single to £290 for a luxury suite (prices exclude breakfast); weekend breaks: £135 per person. A Continental breakfast in La Brasserie costs £5.95; a full English breakfast is £7. Parking is available for 600 cars. All major credit cards.

**Lime Tree Guest House,** 1 Bridge Pl., Lower Bridge St., Chester CH1 1SA; tel. 0244-325892. On Lower Bridge Street just up from the river Dee and the city walls, a few minutes' walk from the Rows and the city center, Mrs. Sylvia Thompson offers a friendly welcome to a cozy guest house that is open all year round. Of the four rooms, two contain a double and a single bed with shared bathroom, and there is another family room and also a single room, each of which have private bathrooms. Room rates: £9–10 per person per night. Continental breakfast costs £1; a full English breakfast costs £2. Street parking is available overnight. No credit cards.

**Queen Hotel,** City Rd., Chester CH1 3AH; tel. 0244-28341, telex 617101, fax 0244-318483, U.S. toll free 800-223-5672. Located across the road from the railway station and a short distance from the city center, this is your traditional Victorian station hotel. Queen Victoria's statue greets you as you enter the marble-columned entrance, and there's a sizable, secluded, and leafy private garden, onto which the Garden Room restaurant opens. The Garden Room offers a set dinner of three courses and coffee for £10.75. The 90 rooms all have en suite facilities. Victoria's most celebrated prime ministers, Gladstone and Disraeli, give their names to two function rooms. The hotel has an arrangement with a nearby health club for those who wish to work out or unwind. Room rates: from £53 single to £74 for a superior room with garden view. Continental breakfast runs £4.50, and a full English breakfast costs £6.50. Parking is available for 100 cars. All major credit cards.

**Riverside Recorder Hotel,** 19–22 City Walls, off Lower Bridge St., Chester CH1 1SB; tel. 0244-326580. The Riverside is in a beautiful position on the old city walls, overlooking the river Dee and close to Chester's ancient center. You approach it from the city walls through its pretty garden. Try to get a room facing the river. The £42 rooms have four-poster beds and river views. Edgar's Restaurant does a three-course set dinner for £8.25, including coffee. À la carte, when in season, there is fresh Dee salmon poached in white wine with a hollandaise sauce. Room rates: from £20 for a single to £42 for a double; family rooms, £44–48. (Rates include breakfast.) Parking is available for 25 cars. All major credit cards.

# Liverpool

**Aachen Hotel,** 89–91 Mount Pleasant, Liverpool L3 5TB; tel. 051-709-3477/1126. A small hotel at the top end of Mount Pleasant with its own lounge bar. Bedrooms are equipped with facilities that you would not expect in a hotel in this price category. Also the staff is very friendly and helpful. Room rates: from £15 for a single with shared bathroom to £36 for a double with private bathroom. Family room for two adults and one child, £36;

half price for children sharing. Garage space for parking. All major credit cards.

**Antrim Hotel,** 73 Mount Pleasant, Liverpool L3 5TB; tel. 051-709-9212. Also well-situated, a few doors down from the Aachen on Mount Pleasant. In many respects this is the most interesting part of Liverpool in which to stay: you are both ten minutes' walk from the city center and at the top of the hill near the cathedrals (with magnificent views over the city), the Mersey, and many of the city's best restaurants and pubs. Room rates: from £18.50 for a single without shower to £30 for a double with shower. Limited parking in garage. All major credit cards.

**Atlantic Tower Hotel,** Chapel St., Liverpool L3 9RE; tel. 051-227-4444, telex 627070, fax 051-236-3973. A modern building across the street from Liverpool's original parish church and near the Pier Head, Custom House, and Albert Dock complex. It has two restaurants, one of which is modeled after a ship's stateroom and overlooks the Mersey. À la carte main dishes are £8. On the second floor, the Club Car restaurant offers a set meal of three courses for £10.50. Room rates: from £57.50 for a single to £95 for a suite. An English breakfast costs £6; Continental breakfast costs £4.50. Parking for 150 cars. All major credit cards.

**Britannia Adelphi Hotel,** Ranelagh Pl., Liverpool L3 5UL; tel. 051-709-7200, telex 629644, fax 051-708-8326. The Adelphi is one of Liverpool's great landmarks. Previously a hotel for wealthy voyagers, the Adelphi continues to be the focal point for the mammoth round of socializing that surrounds the Grand National horse race held at Liverpool's Aintree racecourse. Harry MacDonald, the hotel's chief porter, has many fascinating tales with which he can regale followers of racing folklore. From the moment you enter the hotel lobby with its marble columns, mirrored ceiling, and Art Deco wall lamps the impression is that you have stepped onto a cruise liner, an impression that is further enhanced as you walk through into the huge high-ceilinged lounge with its French windows leading off into the various function rooms. One of these, the Empire Room, is based on Napoléon's dining room. Another, the Sefton Room, was used as the ship's restaurant in the film *Chariots of Fire.* What used to be the boardroom of the old Midland Railway Company (which built the hotel) can also be hired for meetings. The hotel has two restaurants. The more informal Jenny's has a carvery and offers a dinner of three courses and coffee for £8.95. This restaurant has its own discotheque and dance floor and can be turned into a self-contained nightclub. Crompton's French restaurant is more formal and traditional. A set dinner menu is £14.50 (three courses), and main courses à la carte are around £8. What is now Jenny's bar used to be a Masonic suite, and Masonic symbols can still be seen on the walls. The Adelphi's original American Bar is still upstairs next to the lobby. Spindles health club contains the hotel's original Edwardian swimming pool and has a poolside lounge and health-food bar. Room rates: from £25 (Saver) to £75 (Executive Suite); Weekend Supersavers,

£12–50; £10 extra for double occupancy of suite and executive rooms. Parking is available for 2,000 cars. All major credit cards.

**St. George's Hotel,** Lime St., Liverpool L1 1NQ; tel. 051-709-7090, telex 627630, fax 051-709-0137. A new building located near the Lime Street station and the architectural splendors of the St. George's Hall area. The Carvery has a set meal for £9.25. Pre- and postprandial refreshments can be had in the adjacent Dragon Bar, and for snacks the Lime Street Parlour is open 10 A.M.–10 P.M. except Sun. For conferences there are four suites, the largest of which, the Gladstone, will take up to 25 people theater-style; the smaller suites are ideal for groups of around 20. Room rates: from £53 for a single to £80 for a suite (excluding breakfast); weekend rates (including breakfast) are from £34 for a single to £65 for a suite. A Continental breakfast costs £4.50; an English breakfast is £6.50. Ample parking. All major credit cards.

**Shaftesbury Hotel,** Mount Pleasant, Liverpool L3 5SA; tel. 051-709-4421. Featured in the film *Letter to Brezhnev* is a medium-size hotel in the center of Liverpool, near the Adelphi and at the foot of Mount Pleasant, the street leading up to the cathedrals and the Philharmonic Hall. The hotel restaurant does a set lunch for £3.75 and dinner for £6.50. There are two bars. Room rates: from £17 for a single on weekends to £34.50 for a double in midweek. Parking is available for 40 cars. All major credit cards.

**Trials Hotel,** 62 Castle St., Liverpool L2 7LQ; tel. 051-227-1021. Housed in an 1867 bank building, Trials is so called because it faces Liverpool's law courts across Derby Square. At night it commands an impressive view of the floodlit monument to Queen Victoria in the middle of the square, and it's also near the Pier Head and the Albert Dock development. What used to be the banking hall, complete with cupola dome and classical pillars, is now a large and stately bar and lunchtime brasserie. Trials is privately owned and is one of the first suites-only hotels in Britain. Luxurious accommodation is the main emphasis in a hotel whose owner—a local boy made good—began his hotel career as a dishwasher. Each suite has a Jacuzzi in the bathroom, a refrigerated drinks cabinet, and an extensive range of complimentaries including boxes of chocolates and fresh fruit. The cocktail lounge and restaurant are on the first floor. The latter serves lunch and dinner: four courses and coffee for £10.95; main courses à la carte are between £8.95 and £9.95. Room rates: from £60 for single occupancy of suite to £80 for double occupancy (breakfast included). Reduced rates at weekends. All major credit cards.

# Manchester

**Britannia Hotel,** Portland St., Manchester M1 3LA; tel. 061-228-2288, telex 665007, fax 061-236-9154. Another impressive Victorian conversion, this one from the 1850s Watts warehouse, in its day the largest mercantile building in Manchester. Centrally located on Portland Street, the Britannia is near Manchester's

Chinatown and the City Art Gallery, but also has extensive leisure facilities of its own. Crompton's Restaurant and cocktail bar uses shelving and panelling from a Victorian tobacconist's shop. Like its sister hotel, the Liverpool Adelphi, there are Saturdays and Kick's discotheques as well as Spindles health club. There is also a Jenny's diner and a pizza restaurant offering meals at bargain prices. Jenny's has split-level views into the hotel swimming pool. Some of the 315 bedrooms do not have an external window, since they are in what was the middle of the warehouse. All are opulent and comfortable. There are two suites with four-poster beds. Room rates: from £57 for a standard room to £85 for a four-poster suite and £225 for the Royal Suite. Weekend Supersavers: from £22 for a standard room to £50 for four-poster suites and £125 for the Royal Suite. Double occupancy of suites and executive rooms is £10 extra. Free mini-bus service to and from Manchester airport. Parking is available for 1,500 cars. All major credit cards.

**Portland Thistle Hotel,** Portland St., Piccadilly Gardens, Manchester M1 6DP; tel. 061-228-34000, telex 669157, fax 061-228-6347, U.S. Sales Office 212-689-0217, 800-847-4358. Farther up Portland Street from the Britannia and overlooking Piccadilly Gardens, the Portland is another imposing Victorian building with a luxurious interior. Its ground floor champagne bar has a mirrored ceiling and boasts the world's largest champagne list (199 entries). It also offers 120 different malt whiskies. The Carver's Table offers a variety of fork buffets from £10.95 per person. There is also a very fine dining room—à la carte main courses here go from £8.50 to £13.25. With a French catering manager there is naturally an extremely good wine list. An Art Deco style Leisure Spa has a full range of exercise facilities. There are four small suites named after four of Manchester's great soccer figures, Joe Mercer of Manchester City and Sir Matt Busby, Bobby Charlton, and Dennis Law of Manchester United. Soccer, cricket, and horse-racing fans should take note of the Portland's Classic Hospitality Packages. The soccer package, for instance, provides for a drinks reception on match day at the hotel, a four-course lunch with liquor, coach transportation from the hotel to the United ground at Old Trafford, and a reserved seat in the main stand for the match. Afterward you get to meet manager and players over coffee and discuss the match with them. Depending on the match, the soccer package is £65–85, and overnight accommodation at the Portland is offered at the special rate of £30 per night including breakfast. Comparable packages are available for a day's cricket watching Lancashire at Old Trafford (£115), a day's racing at Haydock Park (£70), the Grand National (£172.50), and a tour package for the Granada Studios (£98, including overnight accommodation). The Portland can also arrange evenings of aristocratic hospitality at stately homes in the Manchester area! Room rates: from £69 for a Standard Club single to £275 for the Presidential Suite (rates exclusive of breakfast). Some rooms are designated no-smoking. Limited parking. All major credit cards.

**Ramada Renaissance Hotel,** Blackfriars St., Manchester M3 2EQ; tel. 061-835-2555, telex 669699, fax 061-835-3077, U.S. reservations 800-228-9898. Recently opened at the center of Manchester on Deansgate, the Ramada Renaissance manages the difficult feat of creating a genuine local ambience within a new building. The tone is very much set by the paintings of old Manchester on the walls of the lobby, which were specially commissioned from the Parisian painter Pierre Gogoi. On a split level with the lobby are the Deansgate bar and restaurant. Fairbairn's lounge is on the first floor, and the hotel has its own health club. Because the building was originally designed for apartments, there are no small rooms. All are mini-suites with two large windows offering impressive views of Manchester's Victorian skyline and the hills beyond. No-smoking rooms and rooms specially equipped for the disabled are available. In common with other Renaissance hotels, the top three floors are set aside for exclusive Renaissance Club accommodation. There is a Renaissance Club lounge, set aside from other public areas, where members can entertain or hold small business meetings in the atmosphere of a gentleman's club. Room rates: from £67.50 for a single to £85 for a double; Renaissance Club from £87.50 for a single to £145 for a double; the Renaissance Suite is £300. Weekend breaks for £24 per person sharing twin room (includes breakfast and welcoming half bottle of champagne). Parking is available for 409 cars. All major credit cards.

**Sacha's Hotel,** Piccadilly, Manchester M4 1PQ; tel. 061-228-1234, telex 668504, fax 061-236-9202. Also part of the Britannia chain and converted from the old C. and A. department store building, the emphasis here is very much on style, informality, and the breaking down of the old hotel boundaries and traditions. Sacha's aims to offer both up-market seclusion and a place where you can go for a beer and a pizza, with entertainment costing anywhere from £3 to £30. Indeed, the stuffed polar bear, crocodile, and hammerhead shark that greet you in the entrance tell you you're somewhere rather . . . different. Sacha's also claims to be the only hotel in Manchester with complete air-conditioning and heat control in all its rooms. All bedrooms have full facilities, but Saver and City rooms are windowless. One wall is decorated like the New York skyline, with nets and drapes over a nighttime glow effect that greets you as you walk into the room. The hotel also contains both a discotheque and a health club with pool. Room rates: from £39 (Saver) to £69 (suite with Jacuzzi); Weekend Supersavers, £18–45. The Presidential Suite is £125 at all times. Add £10 to suite and executive room rates for double occupancy. English breakfast costs £6.95; Continental breakfast, £4.75. Public car parking is available for three hundred cars. All major credit cards.

## Blackpool

**Pembroke Hotel,** North Promenade, Blackpool FY1 2JQ; tel. 0253-23434, telex 677469, fax 0253-27864. On Blackpool's North Promenade looking out onto the beach and the Irish Sea, the Pembroke is an ideal base or stopover place on your way to the Lake District, the Yorkshire Dales, or for exploring the Lancashire countryside in the nearby Trough of Bowland. There is also the first-rate golf facilities of Royal Lytham and St. Annes. Nearby is Blackpool's renowned tower, the only serious rival to Paris's Eiffel Tower. There are two restaurants, one attached to the hotel's nightclub, a cocktail bar, and an indoor swimming pool. A three-course lunch is £6–8; dinner, £10–12. In addition to a sauna and solarium there is a games room and a children's playground. Room rates: from £75 for a single to £85 for a double (including breakfast). Parking is available for 300 cars. All major credit cards.

# Chester

For the historically minded traveler, Chester must rank as one of the main British cities to visit. It has the remains of a Roman amphitheater, numerous medieval churches including a cathedral, stately Georgian houses, and a Victorian neo-Gothic extravaganza of a town hall. The city walls survived a parliamentary siege during the civil war, and it has England's oldest racecourse. And shopping in Chester is a unique experience due to the Rows, with their two tiers of shops—there are walkways and shop entrances at the upper floor level as well as along the street. They were originally built so that the ground floor could be sealed off from attack by Welsh raiding parties!

## A Walking Tour
The best starting point for a walking tour of Chester is underneath the **Eastgate Clock** (1897) in front of the Grosvenor Hotel. This is where the city's Eastgate stood in the Middle Ages. From here you can take the steps up onto the walls or join the Rows beyond the Grosvenor. **Chester Cathedral** is just around the corner on St. Werburgh Street.

Joining the walls you reach the King Charles Tower in one direction or the river Dee in the other. But whichever direction you take, keeping to the walls will eventually bring you back to the Eastgate clock. The **King Charles's Tower** (open April through October, Monday through Saturday from 10 A.M. to 5 P.M., Sunday from 2 to 5:30 P.M.; 35 pence admission) dates from around the 13th century, and it was from here on the afternoon of September 24th, 1645, that Charles saw the defeat of his army at the Battle of Rowton Moor. Inside the tower are displays on the civil war and the siege of Chester. Taking the opposite direction, you will shortly see to your left the excavated remains of a **Roman amphitheater** and garden surrounded by Georgian houses. Moving along you reach the river, with the Georgian Riverside hotel to your right. Immediately after the Riverside you may descend from the walls at Bridge Gate to admire the old **Dee Bridge.** For two thousand years this was the only route into

Wales from Chester and was the scene of many a border skirmish. The famous Jolly Miller of Dee also had his mill by the bridge. If you are thirsty at this point, you may want to pause at one of the Lower Bridge Street pubs. If not, then get back on the walls and make for **Chester Castle.** Here too you should leave the walls to look at the castle. The original medieval castle was given various Greek revival additions during the 18th century and now houses the Cheshire Regimental Museum (open daily from 9 A.M. to 5 P.M.,) the Crown Court, and the Cheshire Regiment Officers' Mess. Of the original castle, the Norman Agricola Tower is the most impressive survival. From the top of the tower there are panoramic views of the city. Farther along to your left after the castle is the **Roodee Racecourse.** This is where the Romans had a massive harbor. Since then the river Dee has silted up, and Chester lost its ascendancy as the main port for Ireland to Liverpool. "Roodee" means a rood or cross in an "eye," or meadow. The earliest recorded horse race took place here in 1540, and Chester's two annual meetings are landmarks of the flat-racing season. To your right after the racecourse are some fine Georgian terraces around the city's Watergate. Should you not wish to go all the way to King Charles's Tower, you can head back toward the city center along Watergate Street.

Watergate Street is the most medieval part of the Rows and contains the headquarters of the Cheshire Historical Society.

## PUB STOPS

By Watergate itself is the **Old Custom House pub.** This serves Border Ales, formerly brewed at Wrexham in north Wales, although now part of Marston's, the Burton-upon-Trent brewers. The pub also serves a martial sounding lager called Marcher, advertised as "the lager with the edge from Marston's." Look out for the carved woodwork under the public bar and around the front fireplace.

There are many other great old pubs in the middle of Chester, some, like the **Deva** (the Roman name for Chester) on Watergate St., built into the upper tier of the Rows. On Northgate St. beyond the Town Hall and market square is a lovely old inn called the **Pied Bull.** Off Northgate St. up an alley behind St. Peter's Church is the **Commercial Hotel,** a comfortable, authentic residential pub with four small bars, one of which has an interesting sliding window. On the corner of Lower Bridge St. and Grosvenor St., near both the Grosvenor Museum and the Heritage Center, stands the **Falcon.** This pub, which serves Sam Smith's Yorkshire Ale, has had its sandstone columns and exposed beams carefully restored with the aid of a Europa Nostra grant. At the bottom of Lower Bridge St. by the Bridge Gate is the black and white half-timbered **Bear & Billet.** This dates from 1664, has continuous window bands on the first and second floors, and was the original town house of the earls of Shrewsbury. Also on Lower Bridge St. is a friendly server of Boddington's Ale called the **Cross Keys,** with its late Victorian glasswork intact.

On a more spiritual note, **St. Werburgh's Cathedral,** located on St. Werburgh St. between Eastgate and Market Square, should not be missed. This became a cathedral in the 1530s and is very much the cathedral of a shire—the Cheshire Regiment chapel is to your right as you enter; the cathedral's red sandstone matches that of parish churches throughout the diocese. Two interesting plaques are on the wall just before the choir stalls. The upper of the two is dedicated to Frederick Philips, born 1720 in the "Province of New York," died Chester 1785. An American loyalist, Philips had owned one of the largest estates in New York until its confiscation by "the usurped legislature of that province." Underneath this is a wooden plaque and display case commemorating H.M.S. *Chester,* sunk on May 31st, 1916, during the Battle of Jutland. One of those lost then was 16-year-old John Travers Cornwell. Although mortally wounded, he stood at his post until the end of the action with his gun crew dead and wounded around him. At the site of St. Werburgh's shrine to the right of the Lady Chapel are the headless figures of Mercian saints and kings, and on the corner is a carving of a dog scratching his ear with his leg.

Material on Chester's past from Roman times onward can be found in the **Chester Heritage Centre,** housed in the former St. Michael's Church at the end of Bridge Street Row, and in the **Grosvenor Museum** on Grosvenor Street. The museum is open Monday through Saturday from 10 A.M. to 5 P.M., Sunday from 2 to 5 P.M.

## RESTAURANTS

In addition to the pubs mentioned above, the **Jigsaw Cafe** at 21–23 Northgate St. is a good place for coffee, hot food, salads, and sandwiches throughout the day (closed 5:30 P.M.). **Il Gabbiano Fish Restaurant,** across from the cathedral entrance at 13 St. Werburgh St., offers a cold buffet lunch with dishes like the local delicacy Dee salmon for £4.95 and an impressive à la carte menu in the evenings. Poached skate wings served with black butter and capers, for instance, is £5.95 (tel. 0244-314663). Credit cards; AE, MC, V. In an old house in a courtyard off Northgate Street is the **Abbey Green Restaurant** (2 Abbey Green, Northgate St., tel. 0244-313251). This won the 1988 National Vegetarian Restaurant of the Year award and is definitely haute cuisine vegetarian. During the day, main dishes are around £3. Evening meals are more elaborate, with main dishes like courgette roulade with a mushroom and sherry filling for £6.85. Non-dairy dishes are highlighted on the menu for the benefit of vegetarians. MC.

Going seriously up-market in Chester involves a visit to the Grosvenor Hotel. **La Brasserie,** the more informal of its two restaurants with its polished wood and glass, is based on a Parisian original. A three-course lunch is £8.95; dinner is £12.50. There's also an interesting à la carte menu with main courses like veal sausage with grated, fried potatoes in an onion sauce (£6.25). La Brasserie serves food throughout the day. All major credit cards. Its neighbor, the stately **Arkle,** is named after Ann, duchess of Westminster's race horse. A specially commissioned painting of Arkle decorates one wall of the restaurant, and the horse is also featured on the plates. Set lunch (three courses) is £15; dinner (six courses), £32. At lunchtime a roast of the day is served from a trolley, and a strong emphasis is given to local produce like Parkgate shrimps and Dee salmon. For the Grosvenor's address see "Hotels" above. All major credit cards.

# Liverpool

The center of Liverpool is one of the most visually stunning townscapes in England. Your best first impression is to see it from the steps coming out of Lime Street station. Ignore the 1960s St. John's shopping mall to your left and look to the magnificent neoclassical sweep of buildings to your right: first, the Grecian columns of St. George's Hall fronted by the Wellington column, and then, along William Brown Street, the old County Sessions House, the Walker Art Gallery, and the Public Library Building. Equally memorable is the view over the city, the docks, and the river Mersey from St. John's Gardens, by the Anglican cathedral. And no trip to Liverpool is complete without standing at the Pier Head, where the Ferry across the Mersey that Gerry and the Pacemakers sang about in the 1960s still runs. Behind you stands the Royal Liver Building, topped by the famous Liver birds, and the Custom House. To your left, upstream, are the newly restored Canning and Albert docks. A Mersey cruise on the *Royal Iris* will give you a great river view of the Liverpool waterfront. In the middle of town on Matthew Street, meanwhile, you are in the heart of the Beatles' Liverpool, where the Cavern Club used to be.

**For a map of Liverpool, see atlas pages 18–19.**

## A Walking Tour
**St. George's Hall** is where a walking tour of Liverpool should start. Walk along from Lime Street station with the hall to your left, and to your right, the only Gothic building on this great classical square, **Alfred Waterhouse's North Western Hotel** (1868–71), fronting the station. The 1920s

**Empire Theatre** adjacent to the North Western resumes the classical theme. London Road, running off Lime Street to the right, is rather shabby these days but with pub names like the Legs of Men (the Isle of Man ferries used to sail from Liverpool) and Dixie Dean's that are redolent of old Liverpool. Between 1925 and 1938 Dixie Dean was Everton football club's most prolific goalscorer. Also on London Road is the **Odeon cinema.** This is now divided up into multiple screens, but in 1963, when it was one theater, it was the scene of one of the Beatles' greatest concerts ever. After London Road, Lime Street becomes Commutation Row as it leads up to the County Sessions building. The Court House pub echoes the legal theme.

**St. George's Hall** was built to be both law courts and a concert hall. Its Great Hall is said to be based on the Baths of Caracalla in Rome, and has a magnificent floor and ceiling. Try to be there during an organ recital to hear the superb acoustics. Around the sides of the Great Hall are statues of eminent figures from Liverpool's 19th-century heyday: politicians like William Gladstone and Robert Peel; Sir William Brown, the Liverpool merchant whose firm of Brown, Shipley and Company controlled the Lancashire cotton trade at the time of the American Civil War; William Roscoe, another local merchant, who was also elected Liberal MP for the city in 1806. Roscoe was a great campaigner against slavery and for religious equality, and his art collection became the core of the Walker Art Gallery. George Stephenson, designer of the world's first steam engine, the *Rocket,* is here. He was chief engineer to the Liverpool and Manchester Railway Company, and their opening of a line to Manchester in 1830 heralded the start of the railway age. The former Crown and Civil courts are at opposite ends of the Great Hall. Although no longer in use, these have been preserved as they were when functioning. The 1851 Crown Court was where one Florence Maybrick in 1889 was convicted of poisoning her husband by soaking flypaper in his drinking water. (St. George's is open from the end of April through August, Monday through Saturday from 10 A.M. to 5 P.M., Sunday from 2 P.M.; 60 pence admission.)

The **County Sessions House,** across William Brown Street from the north entrance hall to St. George's, now houses the **Museum of Labour History** (open Monday through Saturday from 10 A.M. to 6 P.M., Sunday from 2 to 6 P.M.). This has extensive photomaterial and artifacts on working-class lifestyles and employment in one of the traditionally strongest bastions of the Labour movement. There is a reconstruction of a Victorian elementary schoolroom, and the ornate woodwork and ceiling of the former Magistrates' Room is worth a visit in itself.

Next door is the **Walker Art Gallery.** Though the gallery contains Rembrandt's *Self-portrait as a Young Man,* its great strength is in 19th-century narrative paintings. On the stairs to the left of the entrance hall is Benjamin Haydon's monumental *Wellington on the Field of Waterloo* and Henry Holiday's *Dante and Beatrice.* The opposite stairs have Solomon J. Soloman's *Samson* being bound while a voluptuous Delilah gloats. Here also are Paul Delaroche's *Napoleon Crossing the St. Bernard,* Edward Lear's *Bethlehem,* and M. A. Shee's *William Roscoe*—portraying the merchant as philosopher–prince. Old favorites inside include *And When Did You Last See Your Father?, The Death of Nelson,* and Sir E. J. Poynter's *Faithful Unto Death*—showing a Roman centurion at Pompeii standing his ground as lava falls all around him. At the time of this writing the galleries holding the Walker's extensive Pre-Raphaelite collection were closed for structural renovations, but the **Lady Lever Art Gallery** at Port Sunlight in the Wirral also houses an impressive array of their work. A free shuttle bus service operates every Sunday from the Walker Art Gallery—departing 1:30 P.M. (returning 3:30 P.M.) and 3:30 P.M. (returning 5:30 P.M.). This includes a guided tour of Port Sunlight, built early this century as a model village for his work force by industrialist the 1st Viscount Leverhulme. The gallery itself has a great collection of Georgian and Victorian paintings—Reynolds, Turner, and the Pre-Raphaelites being particularly strong—and also Chinese and Wedgwood porcelain. The Port Sunlight athletics ground is where the Paris Olympics scenes in *Chariots of Fire* were filmed. (Both the Walker Art Gallery and the Lady Lever Art Gallery are open Monday through Saturday from 10 A.M. to 6 P.M., Sundays from 2 P.M. to 6 P.M.)

## A BEATLES AND PUB TOUR

After a morning spent at the above you should head into the main shopping area to Matthew St. and the **Grapes Pub,** where you can recharge your batteries with a pint of Higson's and a cheese and onion sandwich. This is Beatles country, and the Fab Four themselves would frequently pop into the Grapes before playing at the Cavern Club, which was then next door. The Cavern has sadly gone, but apart from the Cavern Walks shopping precinct the street is much as it was in the sixties. On the wall of where the Cavern stood is a bronze sculptured Lady Madonna with a dedication below it to "four lads who shook the world." Next to it is a bronze bambino with a guitar, above it the inscription "Lennon lives," and some lines from his song "Imagine." At 23 Matthew St. is the **John Lennon Worldwide Memorial Club,** and No. 31 is a Beatles shop selling memorabilia. Across the road on the wall of the **Flanagan's Apple pub** is a 1927 bust of C. J. Jung citing the great psychoanalyst on how "Liverpool is the pool of life."

For Beatles fans there is a "Beatles Magical History Tour." This is a two-hour coach tour, departing 2:30 P.M. daily from outside the Lime Street Tourist Information Centre, by the station. It costs £3.50 and visits their birthplaces, where they played, Penny Lane, and Strawberry Fields—and is accompanied with Beatles recordings. For further information call 051-709-2444.

From Matthew Street you can stroll to the bracing and perennially breezy **Pier Head.** Mersey Cruises offers two-hour trips on the Royal Iris from May to September for £2.00 (adults) and £1.00 (children). Call (051) 630 1030 for information. After admiring the view, you should head for the nearby Canning and Albert docks. These were formerly at the heart of the dock area before most trade moved downstream to a container port. Here you will find **Granada Television,** which is closed to the public but has an architecturally impressive facade, the **Merseyside Maritime Museum,** and the **Tate Gallery** of the north. The Maritime Museum has permanent exhibitions on Liverpool's evolution as a port, shipbuilding on the Mersey, and on emigration from Liverpool to America and the colonies. There are models, videos, and tapes of emigrants' experiences, and reconstructions of an 1850s Liverpool street and of the interior of an emigrant ship. A computerized display shows ways in which emigrant ancestry can be traced. The museum is open daily from 10:30 A.M. to 5:30 P.M.; £1 for adults, 50 pence for children.

The Tate, housed in what was the largest of the Albert Dock warehouses, has the London gallery's Surrealist collection, Mark Rothko's Seagram Mural Project, and sculpture by Henry Moore, Jacob Epstein, Barbara Hepworth, and others. The gallery is open Tuesday through Sunday, from 11 A.M. to 7 P.M. Elsewhere in the dock complex is a former pilot boat, the *Edmund Gardner;* the Piermaster's House, with a reconstructed Edwardian interior; the Cooperage; and the Old Pump House, now a pub. There are also various shops and cafés within the docks.

## The Cathedrals

To get from the dock to the two cathedrals and St. John's Gardens you should head back to Lime Street and the Adelphi Hotel, at the end opposite the railway station. Ascend **Mount Pleasant,** pausing in the small park next to the Shaftesbury Hotel for the memorial to Joseph Blanco White, early 18th-century Spanish writer and political exile. At the top of the hill the 1960s wigwam-shaped Roman Catholic Metropolitan Cathedral of Christ the King is to your left. This is a remarkably hideous concrete and glass affair, but the stone crypt was designed by Lutyens and was to have been the base of a grand domed affair that would have dwarfed St. Paul's in London and St. Peter's in Rome. At the opposite end of Hope Street is the **Anglican cathedral.** Work on this massive, traditional edifice began in 1904 and only finished a few years ago. It towers over the city and river and is surrounded by Georgian merchants' houses and the romantically overgrown cemetery of St. John's Gardens. Behind the cathedral lies **Toxteth.** Despite the notoriety this area acquired during the riots of the early 1980s, the streets in this vicinity—mostly Georgian, some Victorian—are architecturally delightful.

Strolling back from the Anglican cathedral you should take a detour down Rice St. to your left. Here is **Ye Crack,** the pub favored by Liverpool bohemians. There are sketches of old Liverpool pubs in the interior and some early Beatles pictures; a beer garden with real ale is at the back. Try a pint of Oak Brewery, from Ellesmere Port, "across the water" in Cheshire. Up to 7:30 P.M. you can also get vegetable curry and rice for a mere £1.25. Farther along Hope Street are the Victorian splendors of the **Philharmonic Hotel.** Real ale and food are served at lunchtimes, and a stained-glass window in the Liszt Room bears Longfellow's adage "Music is the universal language of mankind." The universal language is particularly well represented on Hope Street with the Philharmonic Hall, home of the Royal Liverpool Philharmonic Orchestra. Here is the **Everyman Theatre** with its vegetarian bistro, and around on Hardman Street is **Antoni's Greek Restaurant** (See "Restaurants" below). Descending from the Anglican cathedral to where Berry St. meets Nelson St. brings you to Liverpool's Chinese district, with its many excellent restaurants.

## Entertainment

In addition to the Everyman, Liverpool also has the **Playhouse and Empire theaters,** both near Lime Street station. Jazz can be heard at the **Philharmonic Hotel** and in the bar of the Hardman House Hotel on Hardman Street. For nightclubbing try **Snobs** and **The Continental** on Seel Street off Bury Street. Also don't miss the **Bluecoats Chambers** in School Lane in the city center. A 17th-century orphan school, this is now an arts center.

Soccer fans will want to go to a match at either or both Liverpool's ground at Anfield or Everton's at Goodison Park. See the national or local press for details.

## RESTAURANTS

For good Chinese food check out the Berry St./Nelson St. area. At the **Orient Restaurant** (54 Berry St.; tel. 051-709-2555; MC, AE) banquets run £8.50–12.50 per person. Main dishes are mostly £3.50–4.20. Vegetarian courses are available. The **Jung Wah** (36 Nelson St.; tel. 051-709-1224; no credit cards) has set meals from £5.90 to £9.90 and main dishes like Roast Duck Cantonese style, £4.80.

The restaurant in **Trials Hotel** (see "Hotels") is elegant and stylish. **Antoni's Greek Restaurant** (37 Hardman St.; tel. 051-709-1574; no credit cards) is delightful and a good value. The owner provides a fulsome welcome to all and considerate, jolly attention during the meal. Try afelia as a main course. It's made from pork or lamb marinated in wine overnight and then panfried in coriander and more wine. Vegetarians get good value at the **Everyman Bistro,** and many pubs do lunch. The Philharmonic Hotel is especially recommended.

# Manchester

The city has put on a clean face since its mill chimneys stopped smoking, and its Victorian stylishness stands out more than ever. At Castlefield, near Deansgate and the city center, is Britain's first urban heritage park, where a whole day can be spent tracing the history of Manchester from Roman times to today. On the site of the world's first passenger railway station you will find the Greater Manchester Museum of Science and Industry, with the world's largest collection of working steam engines. And at "Burbank on the River Irwell," the Granada television studios take you onto the set of the world-famous soap *Coronation Street,* not to mention Sherlock Holmes's Baker Street. The city has also got serious claims to being both the culinary and the real ale center of the Northwest.

**For a map of Manchester, see atlas pages 20–21.**

## A Walking Tour

Start your tour with the giddy Gothicness of Alfred Waterhouse's **Town Hall.** Completed in 1877, it took nine years to build. In Albert Square are statues of Gladstone and John Bright, Victorian Manchester's Liberal heroes, and an Albert Memorial to rival that in London. Two Victorian captains of industry, James Joule and John Dalton, are on either side of the Town Hall entrance, and other Victorian worthies are represented around its cavernous Sculpture Hall. The thing to see above all are the Pre-Raphaelite murals by Ford Madox Brown in the Great Hall on the first floor. They represent 12 scenes from the city's history, from the building of a Roman fort to John Dalton collecting marsh gas in the research that eventually led him to his atomic theory. Access to the Great Hall is by guided tour only. Call (061) 234-3157/8 for details.

From Albert Square walk round through Southmill Street to the **Free Trade Hall** on Peter Street. This is on the site of the 1819 Peterloo Massacre when several people were killed by the local yeomanry during a rally about parliamentary reform. The Free Trade Hall was built to commemorate the triumph of "Manchester economics" in the 19th century, when they helped make Britain the world's greatest trading center. Behind the Free Trade Hall is the former Central Railway Station with its 210-foot single-span roof. This is now the G-Mex Centre, and its huge pillarless floor space (over one hundred thousand square feet) is used for staging exhibitions and other events.

Return now to Southmill Street and take a left off Albert Square onto Brazenose Street. Here you will find a **statue of Abraham Lincoln,** which was presented to the city in 1919 in honor of the support given to the North during the American Civil War by the Lancashire cotton weavers and spinners. Many of them nearly starved with the collapse of the cotton trade. Walking through the Dalton Alley off Brazennose Street brings you to the 1794 Roman Catholic Church of St. Mary's the Hidden Gem. The altar and the stone carvings behind it are impressive. To the right of the altar is the **Shrine of Our Lady of Manchester.** Reproductions of the portrait of Our Lady by local artist Harold Riley can be purchased at the church, as can copies of R. S. Lowry's painting of the exterior of the church.

Back to Albert Square and Cross Street is your next route.

On Cross St. a pit stop may be made at **Mr. Thomas's Victorian Chop House.** This pub was built in 1867, and it serves sandwiches and also hot dishes with a local flavor, such as hot pot with red cabbage (£2.10).

To your right, a little farther down the street, is the **Cross Street Unitarian chapel.** This was founded at the end of the 17th century, but the original building was destroyed in the war. Cross Street chapel was the focal point of Manchester's radical dissenting middle classes in the 18th and early 19th centuries.

Turning left across from the chapel will bring you down to **St. Ann's Square** with its Renaissance-style church built under Queen Anne in 1712. John Wesley preached there in 1733. Look for the Lady Chapel with the only Queen Anne altar known to exist, and a 17th-century oil painting of *The Descent from the Cross* by Annibale Carracci. The nave of the church is surrounded by a gallery over which are the original plain windows. Below the gallery are Victorian stained-glass windows and the original box pews, still bearing the names of their original owners.

Also in St. Ann's Square is **Ronnie's Cafe Bar,** where you might pause for coffee, tea, or something more substantial (see "Restaurants" below).

At the opposite end of the square from the church is the **Royal Exchange Theatre.** This opened as Manchester's

Cotton Exchange in 1809 and gained the prefix "Royal" after an 1851 visit by Queen Victoria. Trading ceased on December 31st, 1968, and the international cotton prices on that day have been preserved on the display board high over the old trading floor. A theater space has now been enclosed within the latter, at one time the world's largest enclosed space. It opened on a theater for the Royal Exchange Company in 1976. The predecessor of this was the 69 Company, founded by Albert Finney, Tom Courtenay, and Edward Fox. There is now a new production every six weeks. Food is available before and after performances, and there is a licensed bar, also open for coffee. Special tours of the building can be arranged.

Across from the Royal Exchange Theatre is the **Barton Arcade** (1871) of shops. From the Deansgate side of the arcade you can reach **Manchester Cathedral** by walking toward Victoria station past the Ramada Renaissance Hotel. The cathedral was founded as a collegiate church in the 15th century and became a center of High Church Jacobite Toryism in the 18th century, promoting the local Low Church contingent to found St. Ann's as an alternative place of worship. Across Fennel Street from the cathedral is another medieval building, **Chetham's Hospital School and Library.** Built in the 15th century, it was endowed as a school by Humphrey Chetham in 1653. It now houses Britain's first national school for talented young musicians.

If thirst beckons while in this area, it is necessary to brave the concrete fastnesses of the Arndale Centre from Cathedral Square in order to reach Shambles Square. Here supermarkets and chain stores surround two ancient inns, **Sinclair's Oyster Bar,** serving Sam Smith's Yorkshire Ale, and the **Old Wellington Inn,** which pours Bass Beer. The Old Wellington was the home of the poet John Byron (1692–1763), who wrote the hymn "Christians Awake" as a Christmas present for his daughter, Dolly. He also invented phonetic shorthand. Sinclair's was the site of John Shaw Punch House (1738), the first gentleman's club in Manchester. Oysters were introduced in 1845, and at lunchtimes, when in season, half a dozen can still be had for £4.20. There's also a beef and lobster pie for £3.20.

Retracing your footsteps from here to Albert Square can lead you to Princess Street and the **City Art Gallery.** This was designed in 1824 by Sir Charles Barry, architect of the Houses of Parliament. The gallery possesses Gainsborough's *A Cart Receding Down a Woody Lane,* Turner's *Thomson's Aeolian Harp* with its view of the Thames from Richmond Hill, and Norwich School painter John Crone's *Woodland Scene with Sheep.* Its Pre-Raphaelite room is superb: Arthur Hughes's *Ophelia,* Dante Gabriel Rossetti's *The Bower Meadow,* Holman Hunt's *Lady of Shallott,* Millais's *Autumn Leaves.* Spencer Stanhope's *Eve Tempted* has a spooky Satan leering round the tree of knowledge, while Ford Madox Brown's huge canvas homily on the dignity of labor, *Work,* very much sets the Victorian tone for this great Victorian city. The gallery is open Monday through Saturday from 10 A.M. to 6 P.M., Sunday after 2 P.M.

Back to Deansgate, take a left off John Dalton Street to another Victorian Gothic treasure, the 1890 **John Rylands Library.** Now part of Manchester University, its collection of early printed books and manuscripts is open to the public. There are several Caxtons and, with the 1423 St. Christopher woodcut, the library has the earliest dated Western print.

# Castlefield Urban Heritage Park

Proceeding off Deansgate to the right onto Liverpool Road you enter the environs of the Castlefield Urban Heritage Park. The Castlefield Visitors Centre is on the corner here, so stop in to get maps and other material. With the Greater Manchester Museum of Science and Industry (open Monday through Saturday from 10 A.M. to 5:30 P.M., Sundays from 2 P.M. to 6 P.M.; £1 for adults, 50 pence for children) within the area on the site of the 1830 railway station and goods yard, and the Granada Television Studios just beyond Castlefield, you can easily spend an entire day here. The Granada Studios stay open later than Castlefield and the museum, so plan accordingly. Within the museum there's a licensed restaurant called Chuffers in an old railway carriage, and at the Salford Station end of Castlefield the Mark Addy is a riverside pub and terrace. The museum's Air and Space Gallery has a collection of Spitfires and other airplanes, and in Underground Manchester you can walk through an actual Victorian suburb.

In the Granada Television Studios on Water Street you watch the various stages of a television production and walk around sets for Downing Street, the House of Commons, and Sherlock Holmes's Baker Street. The high spot is the set for the long-running soap of Manchester life, *Coronation Street.* Here you can sip a pint in its world-famous local, the Rover's Return. In the Telestars Studio on Grape Street you can appear on *Coronation Street* and take home the video. The studio complex contains an ice cream parlor, a hamburger restaurant, and a carvery. The guided tour takes about ninety minutes, after which you can roam around as you like. There's a film on the history of the moving image and a *Coronation Street* shop, where you can buy souvenirs like flying ducks from Hilda Ogden's wall. (Grounds are open daily from 8:30 A.M. to 10:30 P.M., during summer; first and last tours are at 10 A.M. and 7:30 P.M. Winter times are more restricted; call Tourist Information at 061-234-3157/3158 for details; adults £5.50; children £3.50.)

## Other Museums

Also worth visiting are the **Manchester Museum** (great collection of Egyptian mummies!) on Oxford Road in the university area and, in the heart of the old Jewish quarter, the **Manchester Jewish Museum** on Cheetham Hill Road. This is housed in a former Spanish and Portuguese synagogue and has photographs, documents, and tape recordings on the history of one of the largest Jewish communities in Britain. The museum also organizes guided walks around the area (call 061-834-9879 for details). The Tourist Information Centre organizes various guided walks around the city, including an Elizabeth Gaskell tour in which you are taken around the Manchester of the 1840s and 1850s, about which Gaskell wrote in her "Condition of England" novels *Mary Barton* and *North and South.* Tourist information is located in the St. Peter's Square extension of the Town Hall (tel. 061-234-3157/8). There is also a Manchester Ticket Shop for productions at the Opera House, the Royal Exchange Theatre, and other venues (tel. 061-236-7076). (The Manchester Museum is open Monday through Saturday from 10 A.M. to 6 P.M., Sundays from 2 P.M. to 6 P.M.. The Jewish Museum is open Monday through Thursday from 10:30 A.M. to 4 P.M., Sundays til 5 P.M.; closed on Jewish holidays; 60 pence)

## Football, Pubs, and Other Entertainment

At Old Trafford, the Lancashire County Cricket Club has one of the great English county grounds. To see northern cricket between the two traditional rivals Lancashire (the Red Rose county) and Yorkshire (the White Rose one) go to the annual "Roses" match. Football fans can see Manchester United and Manchester play and also get free guided tours of their grounds at Old Trafford and Maine Road, respectively (Old Trafford, tel. 061-872-1661; Maine Road, tel. 061-226-1191). Old Trafford also has a Manchester United Museum (admission £1.00; closed Saturdays).

Manchester has many traditional real ale pubs. The Campaign for Real Ale publishes a book, *Vintage Pubs and Real Ale in the Manchester Area* (£2.50 from local bookstores), and the pubs to look out for especially are the ones serving Boddington's beer. In the city center, and handy for its restaurants, is the **Coach and Horses.** This is on London Road across from Piccadilly railway station. About as basic a Manchester working man's pub as you will find. In the Rusholme section of the Wilmslow Road, where many of the best Indian restaurants are located, is the **Clarance.** Draft Bass, traditional Irish music live and across the road from the Shere Khan Restaurant (see below).

Live music in pubs and clubs is another of Manchester's strong points. **Ganders Go South,** below the Barton Arcade, St. Ann's Square, has live jazz most evenings with the emphasis being on traditional, Dixieland, and honky-tonk. The band leader Don Long puts together different bands on different nights with the idea of re-creating New Orleans in Manchester. On Sundays two bands play in the Barton Arcade while a brunch is served. **The Band on the Wall pub** on Swan Street off Piccadilly also features jazz and blues. It gets its name from having a stage halfway up the wall to protect the band from rowdy audiences of U.S. Army deserters during World War II! Northern soul still flourishes with "all nighters" at one of its spawning grounds, the **Twisted Wheel** (now renamed Rockies) at 6 Whitworth Street (tel. 061-228-3078). You will find the **Hacienda Club** at 11–13 Whitworth Street West (tel. 061-236-5051) on the corner of City Road near the G-Mex Centre. It is open till 2 A.M. Wednesdays to Saturdays. Admission is £2 before 11 P.M.; £2.50 after. Wednesday night is Acid House; Thursday, Indie Pop; Friday, House; and Saturday, Dance Music. For the performing arts try the **Green Room**, 54–56 Whitworth Street West (tel. 061-236-1677), near Oxford Road railway station (pâté or cheese with salad is served).

## ❧ RESTAURANTS

The two main clusters of restaurants in Manchester are the Faulkner St. area for Chinese, and Wilmslow Rd. in Rusholme for Indian. Manchester's Chinatown, between Albert Sq. and Portland St., even has its own Chinese imperial arch. The **Yang Sing** at 34 Princess St. (tel. 061-236-2200) is Manchester's best known Chinese restaurant, but its popularity makes booking in advance an absolute necessity. Credit cards: AE, M. **Woo Sang,** 19 George St. (tel. 061-236-3697) has a range of Cantonese set dinners for £11.65. So too does **Pearl City** at 33 George St. (tel. 061-236-2574), where a set meal for two is £20 and most main dishes à la carte are around £5. Both Woo Sang and Pearl City take all major credit cards.

Out on Wilmslow Rd., just beyond Manchester University, a variety of regional Indian restaurants begins. Across from the Clarence pub is the **Shere Khan,** 52 Wilmslow Rd. (tel. 061-256-2624). Here Karahi specialties go from £2.80 to £3.50. All major credit cards. The **Tandoori Kitchen,** 131 Wilmslow Rd. (tel. 061-224-2329) has Persian dishes for around £3.90; and the **Sanam Sweet House and Restaurant,** 149–151 Wilmslow Rd. (tel. 061-224-1008) does Sanam specialties for £3.50. Credit cards: MC, V. Near there the **Minar** offers a combination of East African and south Indian dishes for £3. No credit cards.

In the city center near the red-brick Gothic crown court building is the **Assam Gourmet,** 17A Bloom St. (tel. 061-236-6836). Assam specialty dishes are around £5, and, when available, Hurranka Gosht Kebab: grilled venison in a lemon sauce

(£6.95). Credit cards: AE, DC, MC. For Korean food the **Koreana,** behind Kendal's department store on Deansgate, 40A King St. West (tel. 061-832-4330) does an excellent-value three-course special lunch for £3.90, Mon.–Fri., but really comes into its own in the evenings with its Bulgogi banquet of five courses for £11 per person. Although the Korean emphasis on beef is apparent on the menu, there is also a vegetarian special for £8.50. All major credit cards.

**Ronnie's Coffee Bar** in St. Ann's Square offers a choice of hot roast joints or fish dishes at lunchtimes for around £4 in surroundings of Art Nouveau tiling and stained glass. Credit cards: MC, V. At **Ganders Go South** in the Barton Arcade the food has a New Orleans flavor to go with the live jazz: chef's special jambalaya, £7.15; beef Louisiana, £6.95. All major credit cards. The **Armenian Taverna** in Albert Square can help you out if you want to eat fast, with a salad of humous, aubergine, beans, and buckwheat for £3.15, but it specializes in a wide range of classic Armenian dishes. All major credit cards.

# Cheshire and Lancashire

The Cheshire countryside is pretty rather than beautiful. There are well-kept farms and villages, great estates, and everywhere old churches built out of the distinctive red sandstone of the area. North Cheshire and the Wirral Peninsula are very much commuter areas for Manchester and Liverpool, but most of the county remains agricultural and contains some of the best farming land in England. Cheshire dairies do produce, after all, one of the most famous and popular English cheeses. County high society also continues to flourish in Cheshire. Prince Charles is a frequent participant in polo matches.

## South of Manchester and the Cheshire Plains

Just outside Manchester, at Quarry Bank Mill in **Styal** is a factory village preserved from the days of the Industrial Revolution. The mill was one of the first water-powered cotton spinning mills and is located in the middle of the National Trust's Styal Country Park. For details of opening times call 0625-527468. You get there by a short walk from Styal railway station or by driving off the M56 at exit 5. Styal is also near Alderley Edge and one of the best views in Cheshire.

**Alderley Edge** is adjacent to Manchester's plush southern suburb of Wilmslow. It has spectacular views over the rolling Cheshire plain below it, and locals claim it has a cave in which Merlin, King Arthur's wizard, is sleeping until he is called for in Britain's direst hour of need! The **Cheshire meres** between Alderley Edge and Knutsford are small lakes caused by subsidence over the centuries. The countryside around them is classic fox-hunting territory. Cheshire is basically a plain between two ranges of hills, those of Wales and of the Peak District. This makes for a lot of rainfall, which is why the county is so lush and green. It's said that if you can see the distant settlement of Mow Cop in the Derbyshire hills, that means it is going to rain. If you can't see it, then it is raining already!

## Beeston and Peckforton Castles

The only significant interruptions to the rolling Cheshire plain come in the west of the county with the hills on which are to be found the castles of Beeston and Peckforton. Beeston is a medieval castle built along the Welsh and English border to keep an eye on the Welsh, and the view from its ruins at the top of a five hundred-foot crag are phenomenal. It was built on a glacial outcrop and was largely demolished by the Roundheads during the English Civil War. King Richard II is said to have left his treasure buried at the foot of the castle's deep well. Beeston is 11 miles southeast of Chester on a minor road off the A9. (Open from mid-March to mid-October, Monday through Saturday from 9:30 A.M. to 4 P.M., Sundays from 2 P.M. to 4 P.M. £1.25 for adults, 95 pence for children.) Nearby you can sometimes see a Cheshire cattle market in progress. Peckforton, a short distance away, is a Victorian folly built at the end of the long outcrop of Peckforton Hill. Both hills are visible for miles around. The castle itself is closed to the public.

## The Cheshire Country Houses

Cheshire has many fine country houses, reflecting the long-standing wealth of its gentry. Especially worth visiting are **Little Morton Hall** and **Tatton Park.** Both are within easy distance of Manchester. Little Morton Hall, outside Congleton, is 16th-century with black and white half-timbered walls, a moat, and a geometrically designed knot garden. Tatton Park, just off the M6 motorway near Knutsford, is Georgian with Italian and Japanese gardens. Some of *Brideshead Revisited* was filmed there. Little Morton Hall is open March and October, Saturday and Sunday from 1:30 P.M. to 5:30 P.M., April through September daily except Tuesdays from 1:30 P.M. to 5:30 P.M.; £2.00 on weekends, £1.60 weekdays. Tatton Park is open end of May to beginning of September, Monday through Saturday from 10:30 A.M. to 7 P.M., Sundays from 10 A.M. to 7 P.M.; .90 pence admission.)

## The Wirral Peninsula

One of the most beautiful parts of the county is the Wirral Peninsula between the estuaries of the rivers Dee and Mersey. Traveling by either road or train from Chester to Liverpool takes you through the heart of the Wirral.

## The Northern Areas

North of Liverpool and Manchester are Wigan and Preston, two Lancashire towns steeped in the literature of industrial Britain. George Orwell visited Wigan in 1936 to write about the effects of unemployment on the town. His book *The Road to Wigan Pier* was the result. Wigan Pier itself was an old music hall joke popularized by the likes of George Formby. Piers were what seaside towns like Blackpool were supposed to have, not grimy industrial places like Wigan. Today the postindustrial pier has become the center of an industrial heritage museum that includes the world's largest working steam engine used to power the nearby cotton mill. Charles Dickens based Coketown in his 1854 novel *Hard Times* on Preston and he himself visited the town during a prolonged labor dispute between mill workers and their bosses. His oafish self-made man Josiah Bounderby created a vivid caricature of a blunt northern mill owner.

## Blackpool

The industrial workers of the Northwest took their holidays at Blackpool in the days before cheap package holidays in Spain. Blackpool remains something of a mixture of Coney Island and Atlantic City. Its tower rivals Paris's Eiffel Tower and its huge fun fair, the Pleasure Beach, claims more visitors annually than any other tourist attraction in Britain. Whatever you think of buckets and spades, donkey rides on the beach, and other seaside traditions, Blackpool does have an extensive selection of hotels across the price range and so is an excellent stopping-off place on the way to or from the Lake District.

## The Lancashire Witch Country

Near Blackpool is some splendid countryside, particularly in the Forest of Bowland, and to the east of the county, by the Ribble Valley and the old market town of Clitheroe, is Pendle Hill. In Elizabethan times Pendle Hill became notorious as the haunt of alleged witches. Harrison Ainsworth's 1849 book, *The Lancashire Witches. A Romance of Pendle Forest,* tells the story. This is wild, rugged country, stretching over from Lancashire toward the Skipton area of Yorkshire. The isolation of this region and much of the rest of the county at the time of the Reformation, together with the conservatism of many of the Lancashire gentry, helped the survival of the old Catholic religion to a far greater extent than anywhere else in England. This, combined with massive Irish immigration into the industrial areas, continues to make Lancashire the most Catholic part of Britain, and in rural Lancashire traces of the world of Evelyn Waugh's novel *Brideshead Revisited* can still be found.

## Lancaster

Although smaller and more isolated geographically than Chester, its Cheshire counterpart, the county town of Lancaster should be on your itinerary. There is a cluster of different historical styles of architecture on the hill around the medieval castle and grim relics of olden times such as the Crown Court's branding iron. And a little to the north of Lancaster you start to approach the Lake District.

# 13

# CUMBRIA: THE LAKES

William Wordsworth walked the fells in all weathers at all hours. He tossed his verses out onto the howling winds because he liked to hear the effects of his words on the breeze or gale. His sister, Dorothy (who is only now beginning to receive her due credit as co-author of William's poetry), was usually by his side taking down his stanzas, encouraging, amending, the two of them returning to Dove Cottage hours later, well after nightfall, often soaked to the skin and shivering. Thus the whole of 19th-century Romanticism, from Wordsworth's own circle to the American transcendentalists, was born along the high ridges and deep waters of the Cumbrian Mountains as the 18th century was coming to a close.

Hiking alone on the fells is not recommended today, even with swift channels of communications and helicopter rescue teams, let alone in 18th-century gear and with total lack of a fail-safe system. One would have to be mad to attempt such a thing. And so the Wordsworths and their set probably were slightly mad. Yet there is a distinct and undeniable allure to the high, sheep-strewn, stream-thundering mountains of the Lake District. It only takes a tiny stretch of the imagination to picture William and Dora, he in his greatcoat, she in her long skirts, spending most of their waking hours exploring, observing, absorbing the dignity and mystery of Nature at her most powerful.

A recent survey revealed that there is barely a man, woman, or child in Britain who has not made his or her way to the Lake District at least once, and often half a dozen times. The popularity of the area attests to its delights; it also accounts for weekend traffic jams in Ambleside, hikers crowding out sheep on the Derwent Fells, and the necessity of making reservations in advance at the hotels and many of the restaurants we suggest. But despite the crush of visitors during July and August, the Lake District has managed to retain its identi-

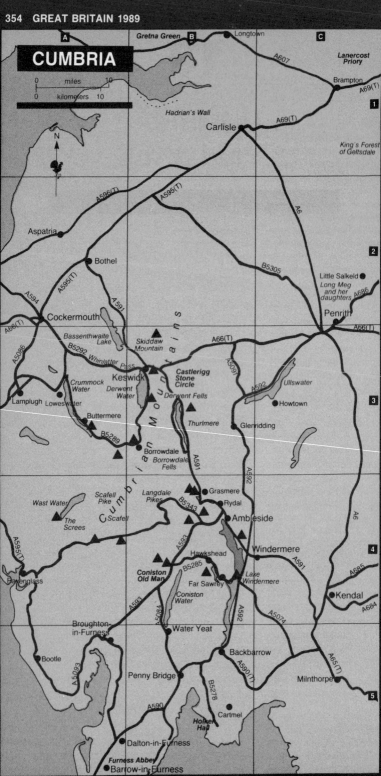

# CUMBRIA

miles
0 ———————— 10
kilometers
0 ———————— 10

N

Gretna Green

Longtown

A607

Lanercost
Priory

Brampton

A69(T)

1

Hadrian's Wall

A69(T)

Carlisle

King's Forest
of Geltsdale

A596(T)

A595(T)

A6

Aspatria

2

Bothel

B5305

Little Salkeld

Long Meg
and her
daughters

A594

A595(T)

A686

Cockermouth

A591

Penrith

A66(T)

A66(T)

A66(T)

A5086

Bassenthwaite
Lake

B5292

Skiddaw
Mountain

Whinlatter Pass

Castlerigg
Stone
Circle

A591

A592

Ullswater

A595(T)

Keswick

Derwent
Water

Derwent Fells

Howtown

Lamplugh

Loweswater

Crummock
Water

3

Buttermere

B5289

Thirlmere

Glenridding

Borrowdale

Borrowdale
Fells

A591

A592

Wast Water

Scafell
Pike

Langdale
Pikes

Grasmere

B5343

Rydal

The
Screes

Scafell

Ambleside

A593

Windermere

4

A595(T)

Hawkshead

Lake
Windermere

A591

A685

Ravenglass

Coniston
Old Man

B5285

Far Sawrey

Kendal

Coniston
Water

A592

A5074

A684

Broughton-
in-Furness

A5084

Water Yeat

A592

A65(T)

Bootle

A5093

Backbarrow

Milnthorpe

Penny Bridge

B5278

A590(T)

5

A590

Cartmel

Holker
Hall

Dalton-in-Furness

Furness Abbey

Barrow-in-Furness

A  B  C

ty and spirituality largely due to the fact that most of the land in its most beautiful, grandiose reaches—some 880 square miles—is part of the Lake District National Park, and of this the National Trust owns two-hundred thousand hectares of countryside, including forests, fells, houses, farms, villages, and lakes.

Undoubtedly Cumbria manages the 12 million annual visitors with such ease and aplomb because it's been doing so for two centuries. In 1778 Thomas West tapped into Britons' growing interest in the area by producing his *Guide to the Lakes,* a project later repeated by Wordsworth and more recently and thoroughly by fell-walker and artist Alfred Wainwright.

The country each was commenting on encompasses some of the most ancient lands in Britain; indeed, many geologists speculate that the five-hundred-million-year-old Skiddaw Mountain is the oldest in Europe, considerably predating the Alps. The teal-to-silver slates and shales characteristic of the northwest fells date from this period. The next important period and type of rocks are the volcanic, which comprise the lava crags and ash screes of the central pikes around Borrowdale and Langdale. Southern Cumbria is largely composed of sedimentary rock laid over volcanic, and affected by eras of submersion under saltwater seas. Relatively recently, up to twenty thousand years ago, all of this other activity was further tempered by the last Ice Age, whose receding glaciers carved crags more sharply and valleys more deeply, putting the finishing touches on Cumbria's stupefying scenery.

As did the various waves of geological history, so have the various waves of human history made their mark on the landscape. The earliest known evidence of man dates back to the postglacial Paleolithic period on through the Bronze Age's beaker and food-vessel peoples, whose tools are on display at the Carlisle Museum and whose monuments include the Castlerigg Stone Circle near Keswick and Long Meg and Her Daughters near Penrith. The Romans arrived around A.D. 71, built roads and fortresses and finally Hadrian's Wall, much of which is still visible, from the Solway Firth near Carlisle all the way east to Newcastle by the North Sea. The wall served as defense against the raiding tribes from the north, a task that proved too much for the Cumberlanders alone after the Romans withdrew in 410. During the Middle Ages, the border districts were the scene of sorties back and forth between Cumbrian and Scottish brigands who had a taste for cattle rustling, church looting, and farm-wife violating. The Scottish raiders were joined by Viking raiders from Ireland and Scandinavia in the eighth and ninth centuries and finally by the Normans from southern Britain in the late ninth century. Scottish independence in the 14th century increased attacks from that quarter, and the centuries of fighting took their toll on Cumbrian commerce, leaving the area ravaged and impoverished. This situation was not finally resolved until James VI of Scotland became James I of England in 1603. By the late 18th century, quarrying, mining, farming, and a growing tourist trade had become Cumbria's primary industries, and these continue to provide the locals' livelihood to this day.

We have devoted an entire chapter to the county of Cumbria, not only because it covers a large area, but primarily because it is so popular a destination and because it contains such a plethora of things to see and do. We have divided the county into four parts to ease you in orienting yourself and in getting around. While one area is not very far from the next as the crow flies, time stretches out in the Lakes, drives are long and beautiful, and unfortunately traffic can be a problem in centers like Windermere, Grasmere, and Ambleside. And each area offers such a long list of activities that you'll want to (and easily can) devote several days to each of the four. They are as follows: Kendal and the south; Windermere and the central Lakes; Penrith, Keswick, and the northern Lakes; and Carlisle and the Roman north.

## TRAVEL

The nearest **airports** with scheduled service are at Newcastle to the east and Manchester to the south. Neither are convenient enough to warrant the trouble and expense of flying. Rather we suggest coming by **train**. The four-hour journey from London's Euston Station (tel. 01-278-2477) runs up the Glasgow line to either Penrith or Carlisle, with local trains running to Kendal and Windermere. Other fetching rail options are the **steam trains** which ply the area. They mostly provide diversion, not serious transportation from here to there, but are fun, popular, and cruise through some lovely scenery. The Carlisle-Settle Railway runs north to south between the two towns (tel. BritRail in Carlisle, 0228-44711). The Lakeside and Haverthwaite Railway runs for 3½ miles up the Leven Valley (tel. 05395-31594). The Ravenglass and Eskdale Railway is narrow-gauge service over seven miles from the coast into the hills (tel. 06577-226). The South Tynedale Railway is England's highest narrow-gauge line, operating from Alston into Northumberland (tel. 0498-81696). Most of these railways are seasonal, so be sure to call in advance for timetables.

When you're in Cumbria, you'll need to have **a car** to enable you to get away from the more crowded areas into the high fells. Brantfell Garage at Bowness (09662-2000), Lakes & Dales Self Drive at Kendal (053-9-29311), and Scotts Europcar at Windermere (09662-5910) are local, reliable rental agencies.

Although we don't usually recommend **bus tours** in countryside areas, the Lake District offers a very attractive option in Mountain Goat Holidays (tel. 09662-5161/2/3). This company runs tours to more out-of-the-way destinations in minibuses that hold a maximum of only 15 passengers, allowing you to concentrate on the scenery rather than on your road map.

The other great go-nowhere-and-have-a-great-time-while-you're-doing-it form of transportation in the Lakes is **boating**. There are boats on Windermere run by the Iron Steamboat company (tel. 05395-31188), but this is the busiest and not the prettiest of lakes. Given a stated preference, we suggest The Motor Yachts of Ullswater (tel. 0539-21626 or 03532-229); boats travel between Glenridding, Howtown, and Pooley Bridge daily during the summer season. Also on Ullswater is the Glenridding Sailing School (tel. 03532-541); any of their 15 different classes of sailboats can be hired from an hour to a week. A final favorite is the *Gondola,* a Victorian Steam Yacht operated by the National Trust on Coniston Water (tel. 05394-41288).

Naturally the most worthwhile mode of transport is **by foot:** Fell walking has become what amounts to a national pastime. Yet despite the well-marked trails, the presence of other hikers and the availability of good maps, people are careless and set out unprepared. In the spring of 1988 two hikers on separate expeditions were killed on the same day by lightning in flash thunderstorms. This is not to be alarmist but to warn you that the Lakes' weather is notoriously changeable: storm systems blow in and out. You must set out on any expedition armed with proper shoes, foul-weather clothing, a water and food supply, and a detailed map. Some of the best surveys are the work of Alfred Wainwright, whose *Pictorial Guides to the Lakeland Fells* (see below) are brilliantly written, drawn, and filled with amusing tidbits of information.

## Alfred Wainwright

In the 1960s a passion among the back-to-nature folks was a series of quixotically clever books photocopied (more or less) from the journals of the borough treasurer of Kendal. The *Pictorial Guides to the Lakeland Fells,* however, were not the usual gushing rhapsodies on Cumbria's scenic pulchritude. And their creator, the elusive Wainwright, was not the usual travel-brochure purple proser. Alfred Wainwright, who for a long time declined to disclose his Christian name, was born in 1907 in Blackburn, Lancashire. He was hired by the town of Kendal to be its treasurer in 1948, and four years later the first of seven guides appeared.

Wainwright's approach is unabashedly subjective: he grouses about the annual invasion of tourists, complains when his favorite pubs are overrun with strangers, and lambasts the tour groups that dash around from one famous photo site to the next without taking time, as he prefers to do, to walk at a leisurely, solitary pace with frequent stops to enjoy the view along the way. This is all done in Wainwright's neat, restrained penmanship and liberally illustrated with drawings cum diagrams cum cartoons.

The seven volumes, each devoted to a particular geographical area of the Lakes, are still very much in print and available at most bookstores in Cumbria, along with *Fellwalking with Wainwright,* a sort of "best of" in which Wainwright chooses 18 of his favorite fell walks.

Since the Lakes have been in the tourism game for lo these many years, there are literally hundreds of hotels, guesthouses, and B&Bs from which to choose. One of the nicest options is to stay at one of the eighty fell-side farms owned by the National Trust. The trust owns the land and leases it to working farmers, some of whom then open their doors to overnight guests. For information on Trust farmhouse accommodations, write to The Booking Secretary, Fell Foot Park, Newby Bridge, near Ulverston, Cumbria LA12 8NN (tel. 05395-31273).

On a more luxurious scale, some of Britain's best country house hotels and restaurants are nestled in valleys or beside lakes with spectacular scenery without and spectacular cuisine within. In fact, the prototype for all country house hotels the country over, the stellar-as-always Sharrow Bay shimmers on the southern shores of Lake Ullswater, this year in its forty-first season. With one or two very special exceptions, the hotels we have chosen are not situated in the center of major towns. You come to Cumbria to get away from crowds and congestion, so it only makes sense to select a hotel that will assist in the quest for solitude and serenity. Although not smack dab in the center of town, most of these hotels are located in the Central Lakes region—the Windermere/Ambleside Grasmere area—and make good bases for touring the entire area. Exceptions are Farlam Hall in Brampton just east of Carlisle in the north, Sharrow Bay on Ullswater near Penrith and Uplands in Cartmel and the Old Vicarage in Witherslack, both near Kendal in the south. All four of these hotels are near enough to plenty of activities and are extraordinary enough to warrant a little extra driving time to the farther-away areas of interest.

Some points to keep in mind: As mentioned, the Lakes are a tremendously popular destination; during summer and bank-holiday weekends these hotels fill up weeks, if not months, in advance. Additionally, many are open seasonally, so in any case be sure to call as early as possible to book your room, and be sure to request one with a lake or fell view whenever possible. Also note that many hotels require a minimum stay of two or more nights and request that you dine at their restaurant—with no refund of money if you eat elsewhere—so try two or three hotels if you're here for a week or more.

**Credit card abbreviations used in hotel and restaurant listings are as follows: AE for American Express, CB for Carte Blanche, DC for Diner's Club, MC for MasterCard, and V for Visa.**

## Ambleside

**Rothay Manor Hotel,** Rothay Bridge, Ambleside, Cumbria LA 22 EH; tel. (05394) 33605. The Nixons run a comfy operation of 15 rooms and three suites in this 1836 former private home set beside a stream amid flower gardens just off the main road into Ambleside. Rooms are bright with floral fabrics, lots of white, and vivid carpets. The dining room is men's clubby in browns and golds, and it serves up local favorites like roast leg of lamb with fresh mint jelly or poached char (a deep-water lake fish) in white wine and court bouillon. Rothay has an intriguing and unusual program of special dinners with cuisines from around the world, and week-long courses in music appreciation during the winter season (write for details). A double room including breakfast is £34–42 per person per night. All major credit cards.

## Brampton

**Farlam Hall Hotel,** Brampton, Cumbria CA82NG; tel. (06976) 234/357/359). The house dates back to the late 17th century and is set on lovely grounds by a pond with fountain, weir, and ducks—perfect for an after-dinner stroll in the moonlight. The rooms have been refurbished by local craftsmen and are decorated with antiques and silk moiré fabrics; some have four-posters and Jacuzzis. But undoubtedly the best reason to stay here is the Quinion family, who are everything country house hosts should be: warm, solicitous—and, above all, able to make all their hard work seem effortless. One of the Quinions presides over this Relais & Château kitchen, whose output is among the best in Cumbria. Everything about the family establishment is truly exceptional. Double room per person including dinner and breakfast ranges from £45–65. All major credit cards. Closed February.

## Cartmel

**Uplands Country House Hotel,** Haggs Lane, Cartmel, Cumbria LA11 6HD; tel. (044854) 248/9. Uplands is set atop one of the gentle hills of the southern Lakes and is run by Miller Howe Hotel alumni, Tom and Diana Peter. This bright, optimistic 19th-century house is decorated with posters from the Metropolitan Museum in New York. The four guest rooms are named for rivers and are done in Bakers & Warners fabrics. Tom, who worked for 13 years with John Tovey, is full of energy and imagination, and his dining room, with a picture-window view of the Cartmel valley, serves up such delights as baked fillet of fresh sea bass with chive and Noilly Prat sauce and roast saddle of hare with wild French mushrooms and Madeira sauce. Double rooms are £40–48 per person, including dinner and breakfast. AE, MC. Closed January and February.

## Grasmere

**Michael's Nook,** Grasmere, Cumbria LA22 9RP; tel. (09665) 496. Jake the Great Dane will come loping out to greet you, a substantial beast for a substantial house, built in 1859 by a Lancashire industrialist. The Michael in question is Mr. Wordsworth's shepherd, whose tale was penned just down the road at Dove Cottage. There are nine doubles and two luxury suites maintained in a rather formal style by Reg Gifford. Previously an antiques dealer, Mr. Gifford has furnished his hotel with some magnificent pieces. Guests have access to the heated indoor pool, sauna, and solarium at the Wordsworth Hotel nearby. The dining room is under the supervision of head chef Heinz Nagler and features local game, seafood, and lamb. The per-person rate for a double room including breakfast and a five-course dinner ranges from £60–96. All major credit cards.

**White Moss House,** Rydal Water, Grasmere, Cumbria LA22 9SE; tel. (09665) 295. Wordsworth bought this 18th-century gray stone cottage, and although he never lived here some of his descendants did. White Moss has the reputation of serving some of the finest food in the Lake District thanks to the inspired work of Peter Dixon. The no-choice menu might include crispy roast mallard with sage and onion stuffing, plum port, and Pinot Noir sauce, preceded by two courses and finished with famous Guardsman's pudding with hot strawberry sauce and a selection of fine English farmhouse cheeses. The five bedrooms in the main house and the two in the charming Brockstone Cottage (rented as a suite) are decorated with chintz and fresh flowers, and several have Rydal Water views. Although all have en suite facilities, check out the upstairs painted porcelain loo. Double rooms per person including breakfast and five-course dinner are £45 or £55. Closed Nov.–March. No credit cards.

## Great Langdale

**Langdale Hotel,** Great Langdale, near Ambleside, Cumbria LA22 9JB; tel. (09667) 302; telex 65188 LANGDL G, fax 09667 694. Langdale is a hotel and time-sharing condos based very much on the model of many American self-contained resorts. It's a great place to stay if you have kids because there are plenty of activities and facilities. You can swim in the indoor pool; relax in the sauna, solarium, and steam bath; play squash, take lessons in riding, sailing, windsurfing, or waterskiing. Rooms range from country chintz to clean-line modern. The resort is built of stone and timber and is set around a millstream in the woods. Double rooms are £44 per person, including breakfast. Self-catering condos are also available on a weekly basis. All major credit cards.

## Ullswater

**Sharrow Bay,** Lake Ullswater, Penrith, Cumbria CA10 2LZ; tel. (08536) 301/483. Dinner on the veriest edge of Ullswater, the lake lapping at the foot of the terrace: A courtly gentleman in a dove gray suit makes his way around the dining room inquiring after your meal and your state of contentedness. Despite his decades on the job, he seems genuinely pleased to find you are reduced to a state of bliss. Forty-one years ago, Francis Coulson found himself with an 1840s house, £500, and a harebrained scheme to open a hotel in this faraway spot, but to run it more like a private house party than a public inn. Guests paid a guinea a day, which entitled them to lunch, dinner, and a drink before bed. Thus Brian Sack, Mr. Coulson's equally charming eventual partner, relates the modest beginnings of this, England's first and firmly still one of her finest country house hotels. Sharrow Bay, as beautiful as its name, has gone from glory to glory, and although Mr. Coulson is no longer at the helm in the kitchen, both he and Mr. Sack try to be sure at least one of them is there at all times to oversee the staff, whom they consider family. The rooms are filled with treasures gathered over the years and all the extra touches you would find if you were staying in some-one's home—flowers, sherry, books and magazines, and views unsurpassed in the lakes. You have your choice of staying in the main hotel or at any of several houses and cottages near-by—none of which are anything less than tip-top. Mr. Coulson's Relais & Château legacy in the kitchen is a tradition of finely fla-vorful English cooking with an emphasis on local game and fish. The menu is long and interesting, encompassing five or six courses depending on how you call it. The only imperative is Sharrow's Sticky Toffee Sponge for dessert; otherwise you're on your own. Afterward stroll through the Italian gardens or down by the lake—heaven. Dinner, bed, and breakfast per per-son from £58. No credit cards, but personal checks are accept-ed. Closed Dec.–Feb.

## Windermere

**Langdale Chase Hotel,** Windermere, Cumbria LA23 1LW; tel. (05394) 32201. Langdale Chase is a rambling old dear built around the turn of the century, with more corners and gables and wings than you can make sense of. Among the guest rooms, the turret rooms are the most coveted, with 270-degree views of Windermere, and also a very special bedroom and bath right atop the boathouse. You can amuse yourself waterskiing, swim-ming, rowing, playing tennis or croquet, or sitting down to a lake-view meal. Double room with private bath (some less expensive rooms don't have them, so be sure to request a bath if you want one) and breakfast is £31.50–39. All major credit cards.

**Miller Howe,** Windermere, Cumbria LA23 1EY; tel. (09662) 2536. Dining at Miller Howe isn't so much a meal as it is an event: lights flicker to announce the arrival of courses, and the main dish is paraded through the dining room for everyone's ap-proval. Some purists may sniff at former theatrical director John Tovey's flamboyant approach to dining, but it's hard to argue with the deliciousness of his results—as the continuing populari-ty of his cookbooks as well as his restaurant attests. The guest rooms at Miller Howe house some of Tovey's collection of an-tiques and glass; many have canopy beds and field glasses for keeping an eye on activity on the lake or birds in the vicinity. Request one with a private terrace on the water side. Weekend cookery courses are always fun and popular. Dinner, bed, and breakfast per person per night begins at £54. All major credit cards.

## Witherslack

**The Old Vicarage,** Witherslack, Grange-over-Sands, Cumbria LA11 6RS; tel. (044852) 381. The Old Vicarage is cradled in a vale of green just below the Whitbarrow Scar in the extreme south of the region about 15 minutes from Kendal. The Burrington-Browns have been at it for years: providing R&R off the beaten track in this lovely old house (hard by the church, of course) filled with antiques and painted landscapes no prettier than the views from any of the homey, amply equipped guest rooms. Dining is by candlelight on fresh-from-the-garden produce and fresh-from-the-market meat and game. A double room including dinner and breakfast begins at £46 per person. All major credit cards.

# Kendal and the South

## Kendal

Kendal made its fortune in the 14th and 15th centuries on the wool trade, whose most famous staple was known as Kendal Green or, mistakenly, as Kendal "Cotton." Most of Kendal's older buildings are gone; however, to give you an idea of what the place was like, visit **Abbot Hall Art Gallery and Museum of Lakeland Life and Industry,** set in a Georgian house amid 18th-century gardens beside the river Kent. The gallery is in the house; the museum is in the stable block. Artists featured include Lake District devotees Turner, Romney, and Reynolds. The museum tells you all you need to know about people's lives in Cumbria through the ages. (Open Monday through Saturday from 10:30 A.M. to 5 P.M., Sunday from 2 to 5 P.M.; closed Saturday mornings in winter.) While you're here, check out the museum shop, which features the best of Cumbrian crafts. Another favorite museum in town is that of **Natural History and Archeology.** It presents specimens of local wildlife and traces the coming and disposition of man in the mountains.

If you're feeling a bit weak from all this history, there are two good cafés in town. The **Lord Ted** at 21A Stramongate features somewhat fancy food at fair prices. **The Moon,** 129 Highgate, is a whole-food restaurant that does cater to carnivores, serving vegetables, fish, and meats, and is a local standard. The Moon is right across from the Brewery Arts Center; occupying, as you might suspect, an old brewery, it is probably the Lakes' best venue for music (pop, folk, classical), drama, film, and the fine arts. Call (0539) 25133 for information and reservations.

Just outside of Kendal there are two terrific stately homes, Sizergh Castle and Levens Hall. The former is run by the National Trust, and the latter is still owned by the Bagot family, who have been residents for over seven hundred years. **Sizergh Castle's** (at the A6 and A591 intersection) massive pele tower is demonstrative of its historical connection to the border wars between England and Scotland. The castle's owners, the Stricklands, were Stuart sympathizers and as such maintained some rather unpopular (and ultimately ill-fated) loyalties in this area. The interior's treasures include carving and paneling from the late 16th century. Outside there are a rock garden, water garden, rose garden, and wildflower banks. (Open April through October, Sunday, Monday, Wednesday, and Thursday from 2 to 5:45 P.M.; admission to house and grounds is £2.)

**Levens Hall,** just off the A6, is most famous for its 17th-century topiary garden. The oldest part of the house is a 13th-century pele tower, but most of the livable wings were completed in the late 16th century. The house's interior is truly rich, with intricate plasterwork ceilings, heavily carved paneling, paintings by Lely and Rubens (among others), and some unusual Jacobean hand-tooled and painted leather wall coverings. The topiary gardens were laid out by Colonel Grahme, who won Levens in a poker game from his cousin, in the late 17th century. Walking through its boxwood pompons and spirals and popsicle designs, one feels transported in space as well as time, not just to another era but somehow to another planet. Horticultural operations are overseen by Chris Crowther, famous in Britain for his frequent appearances on the telly. (Open Easter through mid-October, Sunday through Thursday from 11 A.M. to 5 P.M.; admission is £2.20.)

# Cartmel Peninsula

West of here on a peninsula is Cartmel, a little town reached by unmarked roads off the B5278. The town's principal attraction is **Cartmel Priory,** "The Cathedral of the Lakes." In 1188 Augustinian canons were instructed in a vision to build between two rivers, one flowing north and one flowing south, so this site was chosen. The local people persuaded the authorities to spare the church during Henry VIII's Dissolution of the Monasteries because, they argued, it had an altar for their use and was therefore a parish church. The interior is gained through a Norman doorway, the nave dates back to the 14th century, and the choir is graced with a 17th-century screen depicting the "true vine" and a 15th-century misericord with fanciful carvings to keep the priests from dozing off. The changes are rung on the church's three-hundred-year-old bells twice on Sunday and on Wednesday evening.

Just outside the Cartmel Gatehouse, a shop and craft center run by the National Trust, is the **Cavendish Arms,** Cartmel's oldest pub, serving Bass on draft and good food at lunch or dinnertime.

Around the tip of the peninsula about five miles from the center of Cartmel is **Holker Hall.** The hall itself is best appreciated by lovers of the Victorian, having been rebuilt in 1874 after a terrific fire. No expense was spared; the rebuilding incorporated lavish wood carving and fireplaces, including one of Wedgwood design. Also on the grounds is a motor museum, craft and countryside museum, a group of turn-of-the-century kitchens, and 22 acres of parkland. Holker boasts a busy schedule of events, from a hot-air balloon rally to horse trials, on weekends during the summer; call for a schedule (044853-328). Open Easter through October, daily except Saturday, from 10:30 A.M. to 6 P.M.; there are separate admission charges for each area).

## Seaside Cumbria

At the tip of another, larger peninsula to the west off the A590 is **Furness Abbey.** Furness was founded in the 12th century by monks and it grew to be the wealthiest and most powerful in the area. Naturally it became an obvious target during the Dissolution, and today only its ruins remain. They are, however, formidable—of red sandstone and including a still-standing transept and choir, tower, dormitory, and chapter house. (Open March through October, Monday through Saturday from 9:30 A.M. to 6:30 P.M., Sunday from 2 to 6:30 P.M., winter hours till 4; 75 pence.) On the other side of town jutting out into the Irish Sea is the Isle of Walney, whose seaward side is a long, lovely stretch of beach.

In fact, these southern lands of Cumbria owe more allegiance and interest to the sea than to lakes or fells. The topography is moderate and soothing here, rolling down to estuaries and bays that play host to a whole roster of permanent and migratory waterfowl. It is a quieter, less crowded region than the more northerly parts of Cumbria, with a maritime character all its own.

# Windermere and the Central Lakes

This is home to the tourist legions through the Lakes, headquartered in Windermere and forging northward thence on the Wordsworth trail to Ambleside, Rydal, and finally Grasmere. The roads are so thickly littered with cars, gas stations, guesthouses, and souvenir shops that the main attractions (the lakes and mountains) are often effectively obscured. There are definitely ways around this—routes on the opposite shores that initially look longer; but when you consider the congestion on the A roads, the minor roads may not take much longer and certainly are much pleasanter. On the western shore of Windermere stick to the B5285 and unmarked roads farther south. If you need to cut back across to the eastern shore, there is a five-minute car ferry that shuttles from

Far Sawrey to Bowness just about midway up the lake. Likewise, the unmarked road running along the eastern shore of Coniston Water is preferable to the A593 on the western. The Ambleside to Grasmere stretch of the A591 is probably the worst for traffic in Cumbria; stick to the unmarked roads that connect with the A593 west of the towns.

## In the Footsteps of Wordsworth

If you're here on Wordsworthian business the best place to begin is at **Dove Cottage** in Grasmere. Just off the A591 (parking is always a problem) is Wordsworth's home between the years of 1799 and 1808, coupled with the excellent Wordsworth Museum out back. Dove Cottage began its life as an inn, The Dove and the Olive, and is therefore considerably larger than the cottages of Wordsworth's farmer neighbors would have been. The Wordsworths rented it for £5 per annum and were to run it practically as an inn themselves: a steady stream of Wordsworth's coterie, including Coleridge, Southey, Scott, and De Quincey, joined the family for nights or years at a time. Small groups are shown through the house by guides, each of whom is truly professional and able to answer virtually any questions you might have. The house was preserved practically from the start, bought by devotees of the poet's work; it has been open to the public 99 years this year, and therefore most of what it contains is original to the time when the Wordsworths lived here.

### William Wordsworth

It is difficult to overestimate William Wordsworth's effect on the English-speaking world. Wordsworth may not have been the first poet to extol the majesty of nature, or to celebrate the life of the simple, rural man, or to assume the role of the independent genius; but he collated these elements, perfected, and ultimately legitimized them to a global audience. Hence he is quite rightly credited with the germination and flowering of 19th-century English Romanticism.

One of the primary reasons Wordsworth's accomplishments are difficult to assess is the very fact of their tremendous and all-pervasive impact on British (and hence American, Australian, and Canadian) culture. His ideas about nature, the good life, and the poetic vision are taken for granted today. It's easy to forget that previous to the Lake Poets (including Wordsworth cronies Robert Southey and Samuel Taylor Coleridge), most people didn't think this way; these ideas were radical and revolutionary when first elucidated in *Literary Ballads,* a joint publication of Wordsworth and Coleridge, in 1798.

Born April 7, 1770, at Cockermouth, Wordsworth lost his mother at the age of 8 and his father at 13. He was sent by relatives to the school in Hawkshead where he flourished, then studied at St. John's College, Cambridge from 1787 to 1791. In this final year he traveled to France, eager to witness for himself the effects of the Glorious Revolution. While there he met Annette Vallon, who became pregnant and bore Wordsworth a daughter, Caroline; but he was forced to leave the country and did not marry Annette, consideration of which apparently dogged him all his life. Returning to England, Wordsworth was reunited with his beloved sister, Dorothy, and in 1795 they settled in Dorset, where they met Coleridge, who was living in Bristol. Coleridge suggested that they move to Somerset together, thus beginning an intense, productive, albeit stormy, intimacy among the trio. After the surprise success of *Lyrical Ballads,* the group decided to move operations back to Cumbria, and the Wordsworths took up residence at Dove Cottage in 1799.

Critics agree that Wordsworth's "great decade" fell between 1796 and 1806, most of which was spent at Grasmere, and during which Wordsworth produced his finest poems and married Mary Hutchinson (in 1802). After this time, the quality of Wordsworth's work and his productivity dropped off significantly. He was, however, named poet laureate in 1843, a post he accepted on the condition that he never be required to write poems for official occasions. He died at Rydal in 1850.

"The Prelude," Wordsworth's multi-chapter magnum opus, is essentially an epic autobiographical poem which celebrates, rather than flaunts, the importance of one individual's life experience. If you don't have time to get through the entire "Prelude," try "Tintern Abbey," a shorter poem that manages to include most of Wordsworth's essential principles; and the aforementioned preface to *Lyrical Ballads,* a prose exposition and clarification of the poet's tenets. The Oxford University Press edition of Wordsworth, edited by Stephen Gill, is highly recommended.

Behind Dove Cottage is the **Wordsworth Museum,** primary installation of the Wordsworth Trust, which has done a bang-up job of collecting the poet's manuscripts, cloaks, portraits, and other items pertaining to him, his family, his friends and colleagues. Headsets offer readings of poems by Dr. Robert Woolf, an officer of the Trust whose northern accent goes very well indeed with Wordsworth's words. (Open daily from 9:30 A.M. to 5:30 P.M.; admission to cottage and museum, £2.50.) For those interested in a more scholarly pursuit, the Trust runs residential courses in the summer and winter; call (09665) 544/547 for more information. Also do take advantage of the book and gift shop, which of course stocks copies of the Lake Poets' works.

Just south of here on the A591 is Wordsworth's final home, **Rydal Mount.** Quite a handsome house, the poet and company lived here for the last 32 years of his life, although his best work was produced during the eight short years at Dove Cottage. The 16th- to 18th-century building contains more family memorabilia but is considerably less interesting than Dove Cottage. The spot is best admired for its little garden, laid out by the man himself and maintained as he originally envisioned.

(Open March through October, daily from 9:30 A.M. to 5 P.M., till 4 in the winter; £1.50.)

The last of the Wordsworth associations in this area is actually the first, chronologically, in the poet's life. He spent much of his childhood in the town of Hawkshead, a wee village now largely owned by the National Trust. Hawkshead is reached by the B5285 on the western side of Windermere and is still sweet, with cobbled streets and Cumbrian cottages. **Ann Tyson's Cottage** served as young William's lodgings; the schoolhouse, founded in 1585, still contains the desk with his name carved in it; and the **Courthouse,** a 15th-century edifice, is currently a museum for local life and crafts. Phone the National Trust office in Hawkshead (09666-355) for opening times and admission charges.

Also just opened in the town is the **Beatrix Potter Gallery,** showing original drawings. Miss Potter lived in a tiny 17th-century house called **Hill Top** farther along the B5285 in Near Sawrey. The house is on such a tiny scale, it's small wonder she chose to concentrate on rabbits, mice, and squirrels for her drawings. Hill Top is open April through October, Monday through Saturday from 10 A.M. to 5:30 P.M., Sunday from 2 to 5:30 P.M., closed all day Friday; admission is £2. Try to come early because it gets very crowded when the bus tours begin arriving around noon.

## Coniston

Another literary light who chose to settle in this area was 19th-century painter, author, and art critic John Ruskin. Ruskin chose a sumptuous site on the eastern shore of Coniston Water to build, or rather to enlarge, a fine house called **Brantwood.** The house is now essentially a gallery for Ruskin's watercolor studies; Ruskin devotees will be delighted, but the uninitiated may be a bit disappointed. For those not that keen on the man, check out the Wainwright at Brantwood exhibit, celebrating the work of the fell-guide author, or take the nature walk through the woods with great views of the Coniston Old Man across the lake.

Everyone will certainly enjoy the **Jumping Jenny Tea Room.** You can eat in the stable tables set up in former stalls or outside on the patio overlooking Coniston.

Brantwood is open daily from 11 A.M. to 5:30 P.M.; in winter, only Wednesday through Sunday from 11 A.M. to 4 P.M.; £1. Also on the grounds are the **Lakeland Guild Craft Gallery** and the **Brantwood Bookshop.**

## Central Hikes

The Coniston Old Man is just one of the many good hikes available in this central band of the Lakes. Some favorites are here, including the highest peak in England. The Coniston group of fells includes the Coniston Old Man, accessible from the town of Coniston and from paths leading from the A593, and Harter Fell to the west, reached by paths beginning on either of two unmarked roads that swing westward from the A593 to Little Langdale. Along the east-west road from Little Langdale to Eskdale is Hardknott Castle, a Roman fort known as Mediobogdum that defends a mountain pass. (Open all reasonable times; admission is free.)

## The Scafells

To the north of the Coniston Mountains are the Langdale and Scafell pikes. It is here that you will encounter Scafell itself, at 3,210 feet, the highest in England. The Scafells can be approached from the south along the Hardknott Road or from the east off the B5343. On the western border of Scafell are the Screes, a cliff and precipitous tumble of loose rock that runs at a dizzying angle straight down into Wast Water, what some consider to be the most beautiful of Cumbria's lakes. It is indisputably the deepest (250 feet at some points). Non-climbing types can reach Wast Water by unmarked roads off the Hardknott Road or off the A595 to the east—a bit out of the way but a most worthwhile detour.

An easy hike is that to Stockghyll Force approached from the center of Ambleside by foot or along an unmarked road leading to the Kirkstone Pass and thence to Ullswater. The largest of the falls drops sixty feet, and footpaths and bridges are perfect for picture taking.

## ❧ RESTAURANTS

Not surprisingly, some of Cumbria's best restaurants call this popular area home. We recommend the following:

**The Burn How,** Belsfield Rd., Bowness-on-Windermere; tel. (09662) 6226. Don't be put off by having to drive up past the motel; the dining room is surprisingly elegant, with 19th-century tables and chairs, silver candle holders, and a lake view. The three-course table d'hôte menu is a steal at £12.50, or order à la carte. Food is fresh and simple: roast leg of lamb cooked on a bed of root veggies and seasoned with crushed peppercorns, plaice wrapped around a stuffing of radicchio and prawns and poached. Maggie Gill oversees the kitchen duties, and Mr. Robinson is the manager/host. AE, MC, V.

**The Porthole,** 3 Ash St., Bowness-on-Windermere; tel. (09662) 2793. The year 1989 is chef Michael Metcalfe's 13th at this restaurant with decidedly Italian leanings and a wine list considered one of the best in England. Wrought-iron tables topped with waxed-warm wood and drippy candles fill this tiny, crowded dining room. Upstairs is a lounge with fireplace and walls lined with bottles that tempt. Sample the baked Scottish salmon with dill, Chablis, Campari, and lemon juice served with a red-pepper sauce; or supreme of chicken sautéed with roasted almonds, bacon, mustard, white wine, and cream; or grilled sirloin with oregano, tomato, garlic, and red wine. Try a dish of homemade ice cream with homemade liqueur and/or seasonable fruit sauce for your dessert. All major credit cards.

**Roger's,** 4 High St., Windermere; tel. (09662) 4954. Roger and Alena Pergl-Wilson run a comfy, well patronized establishment that consistently turns out thoughtful, flavorful food such as tartare of sea trout gravlax with cucumber salad or mousseline of pigeon with morel sauce filling, to start; fillet of veal with a saffron cream sauce or salmon and monkfish with an herb sauce, as entrée; and handmade farmhouse cheese or Norfolk treacle tart, for dessert. The lace-curtained, strawberry-and-floral dotted and pink-damask dining room fills up fast, so reservations are a must. Dinner with wine is about £20 per person. All major credit cards.

# Penrith, Keswick, and the Northern Lakes

The northern lakes—Ullswater, Thirlmere, Derwent Water, Buttermere, Crummock Water, and Bassenthwaite Lake—are easily the most beautiful and thankfully the least pored over in Cumbria. Once you've done your Wordsworthing duties, beat a hasty retreat to the stunning, lonely fells and dales stringing from Penrith in the east to Cockermouth in the west, with Keswick roughly halfway in between.

## Penrith and Vicinity

Penrith's best attractions are outside of town: to the northwest on the B5305 is **Hutton-in-the-Forest,** whose 14th-century pele tower is reputed to be the site of the Green Knight's castle in the Arthurian legend. The tower has been aggrandized by 17th- to 19th-century additions. The building features a Jacobean Gallery and Cupid Staircase. Outside is a 17th-century dovecote, gardens, and woodland walks. (Open May through September, Thursday, Friday, and Sunday from 1 to 4 P.M.; admision to house and grounds is £2.)

South and west of Penrith on the A592 is **Dalemain,** an 18th-century house built around a Norman pele tower. The interior's fine points include a Tudor room and the Drawing Room, with original 18th-century Chinese wallpapers. (Open daily except Friday and Saturday from 11:15 A.M. to 5 P.M.; £2.) Nearby in Dacre is a Norman church mentioned by the Venerable Bede; inspect the stone "bears" in the churchyard.

North and east of town is a terrific stone circle known as
**Long Meg and Her Daughters** off the A686 on an unmarked road near Little Salkeld. Cows crop the grass quietly;
and the curious one will come lick your fingers, the others
scratch up against the sixty-odd upright stones, the tallest of
which—pink and standing somewhat aside overseeing
things—is Long Meg herself, keeping a maternal eye on her
gray progeny. Meg is decorated with spiral carvings.

Although Penrith itself is a bit disappointing and inexplicably
crowded, it is a good place for pubs, and the best is probably
the **Gloucester Arms** on the square between Corn Market
and Princes Street. The Duke of Glouchester, later Richard III,
lived here circa 1471, and some of its fittings date back to the
17th century. Food is hearty and cheap, with nothing much over
£3. Vegetarian and lo-cal choices are available.

## Ullswater

West of Penrith on the A592 is **Ullswater,** whose varying
aspects range from the calm to the epic. There is a lovely walk
around the southern verge beginning at Howtown and following the shore to Glenridding; from here you can take a steam
yacht back to Howtown (see "Travel," at the beginning of this
chapter). On the northern shore of the lake, take time out to
visit Aira Force, some of whose cascades plummet seventy
feet. A loop of trails crosses bridges above and below the
falls—fairly easy walking.

The next lake to the west is Thirlmere, almost too picture-
perfect to be real, and actually it is not real, not exactly. The
lake is partially man-made and the pine forest surrounding is
man-planted. Don't let this deter you, but take the drive along
the western side by turning left off the A591 onto a road
marked to Armboth—you'll be hanging out the windows to
catch the views.

## Keswick

Continue north to Keswick, a pleasant town and the center
for hiking journeys in the Lakes; its streets are strewn with
mountaineering-gear shops, and its Tourist Information Centre at Moot Hall in the center of town is a great resource.
Moot Hall is also the place to buy theater and film tickets for
all the local groups during the summer; call the information
center for schedules (07687-72645).

To the east of town (follow signs from the A66) is
Castlerigg Stone Circle. At the hub of a half-dozen exquisite
valleys stands a ring of stones with a smaller oval of stones
inside pointing east to the sunrise. Indeed, scholars have
noted that the positioning of the stones in relation to the sun
indicates that the circle was perhaps used as a calendar to
gauge the coming and going of the seasons. In any case, the

stone configuration on the brow of the hill, guarded by curly-horned sheep, has obviously been a site of great power and significance since its Bronze Age construction fifteen hundred years ago.

🐾 Keswick's favorite eatery is undoubtedly the **Dog and Gun** on Lake Rd. Sit in the room with the fireplace, wedged between whose stones you can probably find enough pennies to pay for your pint—but don't try it; the bartenders are wise to people who come to them with a handful of change. The food is excellent: hearty, rib-sticking local fare at very low prices.

## Must-Do Drive

A Lake District must is the day-long round-trip drive from Keswick through Honister Pass to Cockermouth and back to Keswick again. The journey starts southward on the B5289 past Derwent Water. A road off to the left marked to Watendlath passes over Ashness Bridge, a little stone arch that has figured in more snapshots than probably any other scene 🐾 in the neighborhood. Farther up the road is **Ashness Cottage,** a great little B&B with views down of Derwent and the fells opposite (tel. 0596-84244 for information and reservations). At the very top of the road (it dead-ends) is a network of paths the westerly ones of which lead down the mountain past the Lodore Cascades, a paean to which was penned by Robert Southey.

Back on the B5289, the road twists up into the Derwent and Borrowdale fells through the brooding, forbidding Honister Pass, overshadowed by the Honister crags of loose stones and impossibly sized boulders. As you continue down the valley, stop and have a holler to enjoy the remarkable sonic effects. The road passes by Buttermere and Crummock Water, just beyond which is a left-hand turn marked to Loweswater. Continue on this road up a hill, then turn left again toward Lamplugh. Drive through this tiny village, turn right at the sign for Cockermouth, then right again onto the A5086, which will take you into that town.

On Main Street in Cockermouth is the **Wordsworth House,** where the poet was born in 1770 and spent his early childhood, so fondly recalled in the opening chapters of *The Prelude.* The Georgian house, now owned by the National Trust, was originally built in 1745 for Joshua Lucock, the sheriff of Cumberland, who sold it to John Lowther, who in turn left it to his estate and law agent, John Wordsworth. The furniture, although not original to the house, is typical of that which an 18th-century Cumberland town house would have contained. The kitchen is put to good use and offers gingerbread studies of the house, soup, light lunches, and teas. Musical events are held at the house as well as poetry and prose readings (call 0900-824805 for information; open April through October, Monday through Saturday from 11 A.M. to 5 P.M., Sunday 2 to 5 P.M., closed Thursday; £1.50).

Leave Cockermouth via the B5292 and drive through Whin-latter Pass, portions of which are bordered by Thornthwaite Forest, through which webs a series of trails interesting because the forestry service has erected signs indicating the various plantings of trees made throughout the woods. Just before you reach Keswick, another pleasant detour to the right off the B5292 leads to **Lingholm Gardens** on the western side of Derwent Water. There are formal begonia and gentian gardens, acres of woodland gardens ablaze with rhododendrons and azaleas in the spring, and of course the daffodils Mr. Wordsworth admired so much. (Open daily, April through October from 10 A.M. to 5 P.M.; £1.50.)

Superb hiking abounds in this area. Some of the best is along the ridge on the western shore of Derwent Water south and west into the fells. Skiddaw Mountain, accessible by the A66, A591, and a circle of unmarked roads that ring the Skiddaw group, is the centerpiece of a collection of high fells whose Ordovician slates are some of the oldest rocks in Europe and have been weathered to a mellow, hulking skyscrape.

# Carlisle and the Roman North

Carlisle is a great little city about twenty miles south of the Scottish border. If you plan to do any shopping, or want to see a film or visit a pretty Cumbrian town of considerable size that isn't completely overrun by tourists, Carlisle is the place to be. Given its proximity to Scotland, the city's history is a complicated, often brutal story of warring back and forth—of Scottish rule, then English rule, then Scottish rule, and so on. The first conquerers were, however, the Romans, who governed this northernmost reach of their empire from the late first to the fourth century. Carlisle Castle is thought to be built on the site of a Roman fort, and Hadrian's Wall with its string of forts is still very much apparent across the countryside east and west of Carlisle, as we shall discuss anon.

## Carlisle

Carlisle is a compact city, and most of its points of interest can be visited in any easy day's walking tour. The best place to start is at the Tourist Information Centre in the Old Town Hall just by the Market Cross where Scotch, English, and Castle streets come together to, form a pedestrian square. The office will provide you with maps of the town and suggestions of where to eat, shop, and generally disport yourself.

Start your tour down St. Cuthbert's Lane, at the end of which you will find the **Parish Church of St. Cuthbert's,** believed to have been dedicated by the saint himself in 685.

The present church dates back to 1779. It is light and airy, with robin's-egg blue trim and berry blue carpet and pews topped with mahogany bordered by two stories of neat white Doric pillars. The mayor's pew, the first on the left, is marked with the city coat of arms. Across the courtyard is the **Tithe Barn,** built to store the tithes, or taxes, extracted from local farmers in the form of grain or other crops. Now coffee is served here Friday and Saturday from 10 A.M. to 12 P.M., there are tea dances Wednesday afternoons and sequence dancing Monday nights—to all of which guests are most welcome.

Next door to the barn is the **Sportsman Inn,** an inviting pub with flip-down benches, sporting prints and fishing tackle in the decor, and a conveniently low wall outside for sunny-day imbibing.

Backtracking to the town center and thence down Castle Street brings you to Carlisle's principal treasure, the **Cathedral Church of the Holy and Undivided Trinity**—known familiarly as Carlisle Cathedral. The cathedral was built as an Augustinian priory in the early 1120s by order of Henry I so as to have a stronghold of English church rule against that of the Scottish bishops hard by. The interior is rife with work of the finest craftsmen. Probably the most striking feature is the wagon roof painted with stars and supported by vaults cantilevered from which are carved angels. The roof, restored in the mid-19th century, soars above the choir, whose carved misericords and canopies were each wrought entirely from a single piece of wood in the 15th century. On the outside of the choir stalls are paintings depicting the lives of St. Augustine, St. Anthony of Egypt, and St. Cuthbert, and the Apostles' Creed. The upper portion of the great eastern window contains some of its original glass from the 14th century.

Across from the church in the 13th-century undercroft is **The Buttery Tea Room** and the **Cathedral Bookshop.** Also on the property is the **Prior's Tower Museum,** located in the 13th-century pele tower, containing historical and ecclesiastical exhibits and most importantly a marvelous painted ceiling circa 1510. The cathedral is open daily from 7:30 A.M. to 6:30 P.M.; the Prior's Tower, from 10 A.M. Concerts are held here regularly; inquire at the shop in the cathedral.

Down Abbey Street from the cathedral is the **Carlisle Museum and Art Gallery,** installed at Tullie House, a 1689 dean's house with an 1893 extension. The museum traces Cumbrian history from geologic time onward through the Roman, Viking, and Scottish invasions to the present. (Open April through September, Monday through Friday from 9 A.M. to 7 P.M., Saturday till 5, Sunday from 2:30 to 5 P.M.; winter hours are from 9 A.M. to 5 P.M. Monday through Saturday; free.)

Crossing Castle Way by the subway brings you to **Carlisle Castle** (open daily from 9:30 A.M. to 6:30 P.M., till 4 in winter; £1). Carlisle Castle has seen more sieges than any other in Britain, hence it never became a stately home but has always been a fortress, considered the key to England. Its rooms incorporate a well-produced exhibit tracing the castle's bellicose history and the fates of those who ruled (Edward I) here, or who were imprisoned (Mary, Queen of Scots) here. Of special interest is a preserved cell door with carvings originally thought to be the work of prisoners but now postulated to have been done by soldiers under siege.

Returning to the town center via Castle St., you'll pass the **Board Room,** another of Carlisle's recommended pubs dressed up in a Victorian manner. A block to the east is Fisher St., on the east side of which you'll find Treasury Court, on which you'll find **Hudson's Coffee Shop,** another great place to stop for a bite, a cream tea, or perhaps a scoop of their own ice cream—all of which you can enjoy outside under a striped tent or at a table in the sun. If you prefer to picnic—and even if you don't, stop in anyway—down Fisher St. is the **Carlisle Market;** here you can buy cheese at the Cheese Board, lunch meats from Alex Watson, or smoked mackerel pâté from Bells in the fish market next door. Continue your shopping at the Lanes, an indoor mall one street again to the east, cleverly disguised behind some antique-looking façades on Scotch St.

## Hadrian's Wall

After you have done Carlisle to your heart's content, head eastward on the A69 till you see roads marked to Lanercost Priory, just beyond Brampton. Stop in at **Lanercost Priory** (open April through September, daily from 9:30 A.M. to 6:30 P.M., from 2 on Sunday; 75 pence) to admire its Morris and Burne-Jones stained glass. Continue on, following signs to **Hadrian's Wall.** Built between A.D. 120 and A.D. 130, it stretches 73½ miles (80 Roman miles) and follows the course of what was originally a turf wall with a fort built every Roman mile and turrets halfway between each. About two miles west of Gilsland is **Birdoswald,** an important fort now undergoing extensive excavation. There are an exhibition, museum, shop, and various finds on display as they are unearthed. For those further interested, continuing eastward across the county line into Northumberland there is a **Roman Army Museum** located on the B6318 just east of Greenhead (open daily from 10 A.M. to 5 P.M.; £1.20); which displays figures dressed as they would be when patrolling the wall and explains the life of the average Roman soldier. Farther east off the B6318 near Once Brewed is **Vindolanda** (same hours and admission fee), a fort and civilian settlement with recorded information and a museum displaying various articles excavated in the area.

# 14

# WALES

Wales is not just a region of Britain. It is the original Britain, the mountain fastness to which the Romano-British withdrew following the incursion of Saxon invaders in the Dark Ages after the Roman armies left. With Brittany in France, Cornwall in England, the Highlands and islands of Scotland, and Ireland, it is part of the Celtic Fringe of Western Europe. It is a remnant of an ancient civilization, of the sun-worshiping pagan religion of the druids, and subsequently of Christian saints and scholars. English invasion and occupation during the Middle Ages gave it a magnificent chain of castles along its border and around its coastline, but the ancient Welsh language survives and indeed remains the first language of the rugged interior and of the northwestern coast. And Wales gave to England its great Renaissance dynasty the Tudors, the royal house of Henry VIII and his daughter Elizabeth I.

Geographically, Wales is a land of sharp and beautiful contrasts. Behind the spectacular coastline are soft hills and forests, rivers and valleys, mountains and lakes. A land of sheep, it is estimated that there are three sheep to every one person. Although there has been mining in Wales since at least Roman times, the Industrial Revolution in the early 19th century transformed large parts of south Wales into mining and later iron- and steel-producing communities, while in north Wales the slate that covered the roofs of houses throughout the British Empire was quarried from the mountains. The Welsh slate-mining industry had collapsed by the 1920s, the former miners and their families mostly either emigrating or moving to the industrial south. Apart from the huge quarries themselves, the narrow-gauge railways that once brought slate down from the hills and now ferry tourists up to them are the chief visible remnant of the age of slate. After the collapse of the slate industry, Wales became economically divided between the relatively impoverished hill farmers of the north and the more prosperous English-style farmers of the southwest along with the mining and smokestack industries of the

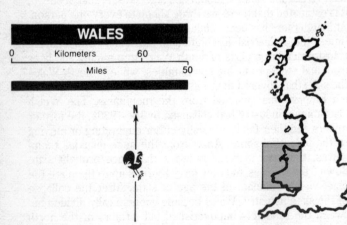

## WALES

| 0 | Kilometers | 60 |
|---|---|---|
| | Miles | 50 |

N

© RV Reise- und Verkehrsverlag, München

south. This north–south division also approximately corresponds to the linguistic division; English speakers are prominent in the wealthier, southern areas. This is no historical accident. Wales south of the mountains was conquered and settled by the Normans shortly after their conquest of England and assimilated into their Anglo-French civilization. Those of the native Welsh who resisted assimilation were forced up into the more barren heartland to the north.

In the 1930s and again in the 1980s, the industrial areas of south Wales, the mining valleys north of Cardiff, and the steelworks of Bridgend and Port Talbot plunged massively into recession. Unemployment continues to be a huge problem, with the decimation of Welsh mining and steel production. Attempts to turn former industrial areas into a service economy by attracting tourists can be of limited use to most of the population of those areas. It recently has been estimated that there are now more museums of mining in the "Valleys" than there are working coal mines! Nevertheless, industrial south Wales is rich in history: of the British working class, of its labor unions, and of the Labour Party. It has long been a center of political radicalism, from the Chartists of early Victorian times to the anarcho-syndicalists in the 1900s and the Communist Party in the 1930s. The Labour Party has also had a strong Welsh tinge. Anneurin Bevan, the great hero of the postwar Labour left, was from the Valleys, as is the current party leader, Neil Kinnock. The religion of the Welsh working class has been similarly antiestablishment, overwhelmingly "chapel" rather than "church." Because the Anglican church was perceived to be the religion of anglicized landowners, the Welsh, a nation of hymn-singers, flocked instead to gaunt Baptist, Methodist, and Presbyterian chapels. Nowadays, however, the place to hear Welsh hymn-singing at its lustiest is at Cardiff Arms Park during a Rugby International, when the crowd gives out with "Bread of Heaven." With some justification, the game of rugby has been called Wales's first sport and second religion! Unlike English rugby, with its tweedy middle-class and public-school following, Welsh rugby is *the* mass spectator sport (and soccer definitely takes second place). Cardiff Arms Park during an International between Wales and England is one of the world's seminal spectator-sport experiences, but the whole area in and around Cardiff is dotted with superb club rugby played by the likes of miners and policemen.

Wales is a particularly good place for a traveler with literary interests. The medieval Welsh monk Giraldas Cambrensis (Gerald of Wales) wrote an account of the journey he made around Wales stumping up recruits for the First Crusade, and in the 19th century the Romany folklorist George Borrow published his account of rambling Wales's length and breadth in *Wild Wales*. The writings of Dylan Thomas are full of echoes of his native Swansea, of the Gower Peninsula, and of the area around Laugharne and the Teifi estuary, where he lived in his boathouse. There is also much writing on the perennial question of Welsh identity, Gwyn Williams's *When Was Wales?* being a good, recent example. Finally, Wales has in the border town of Hay-on-Wye the world's greatest collection of secondhand bookstores. So, epicures of the printed word, go there and gorge yourselves!

Wales is only two hundred miles from north to south, but those two hundred miles are crammed with areas of outstanding natural beauty. A rough breakdown in terms of landscape would be to emphasize the Pembrokeshire coast and the Gower Peninsula in the southwest, the Usk and Wye valleys in the Black Mountains along the southeast border or marches, the Brecon Beacons in the center, and Snowdonia in the north. For the traveler who is also a railway buff, it should be said that much of Wales is accessible by rail and that the Heart of Wales line from Swansea to Shrewsbury, the West Wales line from Swansea to Pembroke Dock, and the Cambrian Coastline from Machynlleth to Pwllheli are not to be missed. In addition there are "the great little trains of Wales," the eight narrow-gauge railways with their steam locomotives.

Road and rail links between London and south Wales are excellent, and for this reason we recommend that someone intending to tour the whole of Wales go to the south first and then travel up through the center to the mountains and lakes of Snowdonia in the north. Traveling east along the north Wales coast from Conwy by either road or rail brings you into Chester and the northwest of England, so by following this route you are nicely set up for the next stage of your tour of Britain. Alternatively, you can double back from south Wales to the sylvan delights of the Usk and Wye valleys, with the Tintern Abbey of William Wordsworth's poem being your focal point, and then either head west into the Black Mountains and the Brecon Beacons before going north or hit the secondhand bookshops of Hay-on-Wye and return to London through Hereford.

## TRAVEL

There are several special BritRail passes for travel through Wales: Freedom of Wales Pass (seven days unlimited travel throughout Wales, £35); Coasts and Peaks Pass (unlimited travel through north Wales, the northwest of England around Liverpool and Manchester, and the Derbyshire Peak District, £19); Mid-Wales Explorer, £25 (seven days; includes train travel from either London Euston or Puddington station to Wales, unlimited rail and bus travel in mid-Wales); Pass Cambria £36 (eight days unlimited rail and bus travel through mid-Wales).

All are available from the Wales Centre, 34 Piccadilly, London) W1.

For guided sightseeing tours of north Wales call 0492-3206 or 48090.

# ❧ HOTELS

**Credit card abbreviations used in hotel and restaurant listings are as follows: AE for American Express, CB for Carte Blanche, DC for Diner's Club, MC for MasterCard, and V for Visa.**

## Tenby and the Pembrokeshire Coast

**Castle Mead Hotel,** Manorbier, Tenby, Dyfed, Wales SA70 7TA; tel. (0834) 82358. Approximately five miles from Tenby on the A4139 followed by the B45485, surrounded by the Pembrokeshire National Park with its bird sanctuaries and nature reserves, the Castle Mead Hotel offers delightful, uninterrupted views from its lawns and gardens of Manorbier Bay. Situated at the head of the valley, the hotel is some 500 yards from the beach between the 12th-century castle and the 11th-century Parish Church of St. James. The bay itself is good for both bathing and surfing.

Priding itself on shielding its guests from the outside world, Castle Mead's nine rooms, all with bathrooms en suite, have full facilities *except* for telephones. Room rates run from £19 for bed-and-breakfast to £26 for bed, breakfast, and dinner. Weekly, three-night, and five-night rates are also available. The hotel is open March–Sept. Parking available within grounds. No credit cards.

**Clement Dale Hotel,** South Cliff Gardens, Tenby, Dyfed, Wales SA70 7DS; tel. (0834) 3165. This is one of Tenby's many guest houses—small, friendly, central, family-run, one block from South Beach. Open April–Oct. Parking nearby. Room rates run from £10 per person for bed-and-breakfast. No credit cards.

**Harbour Heights Hotel,** 11, The Croft, Tenby, Dyfed, Wales; tel. (0834) 2132. A delightful family-run hotel set in a Regency terrace overlooking Tenby's North Beach with almost Mediterranean views on a sunny day. Chris and Anne Taylor are aiming Harbour Heights at older couples in the 35+ age range. All rooms have en suite bathrooms with beautiful tiling, but the ones to go for are the attic rooms with views of the beach (Rooms 10 and 11). The rooms have pretty much everything except for telephones. Harbour Heights prides itself on being a haven from the outside world, but a portable phone is available if requested. Most rooms have their original windows, but with double glazing on the outside.

With its plush carpeting and stylish decorations within an elegant terrace, Harbour Heights has something of the feel of a Regency town house or one of the smaller gentlemen's clubs. This level of intimacy and comfort is maintained in its restaurant, which serves dinner exclusively to residents. It boasts a new chef, Simon Sharpe, who is keen to establish his reputation at Harbour Heights. The menu changes daily, but there are normally three or four types of appetizers, such as Stilton and cauliflower soup, and two or three main dishes, like skate wing with black butter or chicken braised in cognac. A four-course meal including cheese costs £9.50 and can be booked as a daily option by bed-and-breakfast guests.

Non-driving travelers should note that Chris Taylor owns a Renault Espace, a kind of luxury minibus, and he is happy to drive guests to places along the coastal footpath and collect them later from some other agreed-upon point. Connoisesurs of the macabre should note that while a murder once took place in the kitchen of Harbour Heights—a French husband stabbed his wife with the kitchen knife—the hotel is sadly deficient in the area of ghosts! Room rates run £16–30, bed, breakfast and/or dinner inclusive. Credit cards: AE, DC, MC, V.

**Imperial Hotel,** The Paragon, Tenby, Dyfed, Wales, SA70 7HR; tel. (0834) 3737; fax: 0834-4342. A two hundred-year-old hotel, the Imperial is located on the Paragon, one of Tenby's maze of medieval streets. Very much the place where Agatha Christie's Miss Marple or Dorothy L. Sayers's Harriet Vane would stay should their detective work take them to Tenby. It's built on top of a cliff, with a sheer drop down to the sea below. Around the turn of the century there was a suicide from Room 3. The balcony of this room leads onto one of the turrets of the medieval town wall, and it was from this that the unfortunate woman threw herself. Room 6 also has an Executive Suite bathroom built into one of these medieval turrets. All other rooms have either bathrooms or showers en suite. Rooms start at £26 (for a single with breakfast) and run to £90 (for the Executive Suite with breakfast and dinner). Executive Suite Balcony Supplement, £5 per night. Parking is available. Credit cards: AE, DC, MC, V.

**Waterwynch House Hotel,** Narbeth Rd., Tenby, Dyfed; tel. (0834) 2464. Waterwynch House is an ideal retreat for the writer, the artist, or the walker. At the end of a turning on the right as you drive out of Tenby along the A478, it is set in 27 acres of woodland and garden, facing southeast onto a former smuggler's cove. An old cannon juts out from the terrace toward the cove, and the beach, to which guests have access, can also be reached from Tenby along the Pembrokeshire Coastal Path. The core of the building is an 1820 family house built by the Tenby artist Charles Norris, and the hotel has retained an atmosphere of intimacy and seclusion for the selective professional clientele to which it caters. It has 12 individually designed en suite luxury rooms. Three lounge suites have patio doors, and one of these can function as a family room. In the Honeymoon Suite you can lie in bed watching the sea or sit in the bay window. Room 6 also has a bay window facing the sea. Five rooms—ranging from an ordinary standard to a lounge suite—have garden views. The remaining seven are balcony suites overlooking the sea.

Given the location and the quality of its accommodation, Waterwynch House is superb value for the middle of the hotel price range. Its other facilities are equally excellent. There is a sun lounge with a view of the sea and an adjacent bar lounge. The Recreation Room contains a full-sized snooker table. The room is also suitable for bridge games. In the main lounge there are grand and upright pianos, and a nonsmoker's lounge is heated with a gas fire. There are two dining rooms; the smaller of these can accommodate up to 15 people, the larger 54. It should be noted that non-residents may use the bar only if they are eating in one of the restaurants. Waterwynch House boasts one of the foremost chefs in south Wales, and fish is his specialty. There are a wide range of starters, such as oysters creole, and main courses à la carte, such as baked lemon sole with shrimp and dill sauce (served with green beans, mange toute, rutabaga, and boiled potatoes) for £7. Closed Jan. and Feb. Room rates: £17–50 (for a standard suite with garden view during Nov., Dec., and March), £35 (for a sea-view suite with separate lounge March 28–September 30). These rates include dinner and breakfast. For bed-and-breakfast rates, deduct £7 from the above rates. No children under six years permitted. Reduced rates for children six to 14 years. Parking for thirty cars. No credit cards.

## The Gower Peninsula

**Mumbles Hotel,** 650 Mumbles Rd., Swansea, Wales SA3 4EA; tel. (0792) 367147. On the seafront overlooking Swansea Bay, the hotel is on the "Mumbles mile" of pubs much beloved of Dylan Thomas. From here it's a short drive onto the Gower Peninsula. Rates run from £13 (for a single with shared bathroom) to £25 (for a double with private shower). Rates include breakfast. Credit cards: MC, V.

**Oxwich Bay Hotel,** Oxwich Bay, Gower, West Glamorgan, Wales SA3 1LS; tel. (0792) 390329/390491. The Oxwich Bay is in a stunningly beautiful position right next to one of the most beautiful beaches in this unspoiled peninsula. Facilities for windsurfing are also nearby. Oxwich village, with its thatched cottages and shop, is reached by leafy lanes running through wooded hills and a nature reserve. The hotel is excellent value both for location and for accommodation. Parking is available. Rates: from £13.50 per person per day (bed-and-breakfast during low season) to £22.50 (bed, breakfast, and dinner during July and Aug., with a £3 single-room supplement during those months). Credit cards: AE, DC, MC, V.

**Woodside Guest House,** Oxwich, Gower, West Glamorgan, Wales SA3 1LS; tel. (0792) 390791. This hotel, also in Oxwich, just up from the beach in the center of the village, offers an attractive restaurant in a three hundred-year-old restored cottage with three guest rooms. Owners Diane and David Workman also live in the cottage. Lovely old rooms all with central heating and wash basins. Go especially for Room 2, with its original Welsh beam exposed in the ceiling. The Woodside's bar also has an exposed inglenook. Its restaurant is also excellent value, with a choice of two set three-course menus—at £3.75 and £6, respectively. Afternoon tea (there are tables outside) for £2 per person. Homemade cakes! Restaurant is closed in Dec. and Jan. Parking nearby. Rooms cost £11 per person, bed-and-breakfast (£12 during August). Discounts for children and for bookings over five nights. No credit cards.

## Cardiff

**Walton House,** 50 Ryder St., Pontcanna, Cardiff CF1 9BU, Wales; tel. (0222) 220222. In the Victorian conservation area of Cathedral Road and a short walk from the city center and the Canton area. Rooms cost £10 per person, breakfast included. There is parking nearby. No credit cards.

## Mid-Wales

**La Fosse,** Oxford Rd., Hay-on-Wye, Herefordshire HR3 5AJ; tel. (0497) 820613. On a lovely stretch of the Wye Valley, on Offa's Dyke, the ancient border between England and Wales, and nestling beneath the Black Mountains and Brecon Beacons, Hay claims to be the world mecca of secondhand book junkies. Handy for all these goodies is this 160-year-old guest house with oak-beamed ceilings. It's centrally heated, has TVs in all rooms, and offers a choice of traditional and whole-food breakfasts. Rates run from £12 for a single room to £20 for a double; breakfast is included.

## North Wales

**Bodysgallen Hall,** Llandudno, Gwynedd, LL30 1RS Wales; tel. (0492) 84466, telex: 617163, *fax:* 0492-82519. You approach Bodysgallen Hall uphill through its wooded grounds along a private road, which leads off the main A470. At the top of the hill the superb stone house awaits you. Entering through the main door you find yourself in a wood-paneled entrance hall. Eighteenth-century portraits observe you as you sink into the deep comforts of its couches and armchairs, surrounding its large, open wood fire.

The oldest part of the building is the tower. This was built in 1320 as a lookout for Conwy Castle. Jonathan Thompson, Bodysgallen's general manager, will be glad to show you up the winding stair of the tower so that you can see the commanding view of the castle below, of the river, and the mountains beyond. As a house, Bodysgallen has developed with the fortunes of the Mostyn family since 1620. In 1720 the library was built; the dining room, in 1894. Bedroom wing extensions were added in 1905 and 1917. All of these extensions were done with stone from the same quarry, so there is a sense of organic growth over the centuries like the continuities of a family. The house stands in 47 acres of parks and gardens. Seven acres of formal gardens include the 17th-century knot garden. There are also lily ponds, rose gardens, and kitchen gardens. The extensive parklands have marked walks. The 18th-century Lady's Walk leads to the edge of an escarpment with a grand view across to Conwy Castle.

Bodysgallen Hall was purchased by Historic House Hotels in 1980 and, having been skillfully restored, reopened as a country house hotel in 1983. There are 19 bedrooms in the main building and nine cottage suites within the gardens of the hotel. Formerly the cottages of estate workers, these have been refurbished with sitting rooms, bedrooms, and bathrooms. The success of the restoration work can be measured by the number of awards received by the owners and their architects. These include a 1983 British Tourist Authority Heritage Award, a Prince of Wales Award, and a 1987 Queen's Award for Export Achievement in attracting foreign business. Above all, the owners pride themselves on their running a small country house hotel noted for the luxuriousness of the house and its grounds and the overall standard of service to the guests. Guests arriving by train can be picked up at the station by a chauffeur, or a rented car can be sent to await their arrival. The hotel also has two very good guides who can drive guests' cars for them around the dauntingly narrow country roads of north Wales. Within the grounds are tennis courts and croquet lawns; horse riding is available at the home farm. Picnic hampers can be arranged for guests to take with them on outings.

On the first floor the library has been completely restored, with a splendid fireplace and stone-mullioned windows. There are numerous other seating areas around the house, including comfortable alcoves on the staircases. Each bedroom also has its own small library of books and magazines, in addition to all the usual accoutrements. All the rooms are spacious and restful, with their own sitting areas, fresh flowers, and bottles of Decantae (Welsh mineral water). Bathrooms are lavishly Edwardian: great, deep baths with brass taps and fitments, and wood loo seats. All rooms have either double or twin beds. One room has a four-poster bed. For views from windows, rooms at the front have the best, and the higher up you are the better the view. There are two adjacent dining rooms. One, a morning room, has French windows opening onto a garden terrace where, weather permitting, preprandial drinks may be taken. The other dining room faces south. Details of Bodysgallen's magnificent food are given in the section below on "Tasting Wales." Conference facilities are extensive. Rates run from £63 for a single room to £138 for a room with a four-poster bed; cottage suites run from £73 (single) to £173 (quadruple). Credit cards: AE, DC, MC, V.

**Hotel Portmeirion,** Portmeirion, Gwynedd, Wales LL48 6ET; tel. (0766) 770457, telex: 61540, fax: 0766-771331. Details of the superb cuisine can be found below in the restaurant section. The emphasis here is on accommodation facilities. These are to be found in cottages throughout the village as well as in the hotel building itself. The village bedrooms have proved particularly popular with the various celebrities who have stayed at Portmeirion. Noel Coward stayed in the Fountain during the week in which he wrote *Blythe Spirit,* and the Anchor was used by Patrick McGoohan during the filming of *The Prisoner*. Visitors who particularly like seclusion should try to book White Horses, next to the Camera Obscura on the coastal footpath and isolated from the rest of the village. All the rooms in the main building are magnificently furbished. With the exception of House 1 they all have straight views over the estuary to the mountains beyond. House 4 has a delicately painted bedside cabinet and luxurious drapes on the ceiling above the twin beds; House 5 is designed to an Indian theme, House 1 to a Chinese one. House 1 compensates for its lack of a frontal view by its exquisite Chinese cabinet, its circular, blue stained-glass window, and the blue fish-tiling in the spacious bathroom. Village bedrooms have self-catering facilities. Provisions can be obtained from the village shop.

On arrival at the village you can check in at the main hotel by the tollgate. There is also a reception desk in the main building. The latter has recently reopened after a catastrophic fire in 1981, and the restoration work—£1.2 million of it—is remarkable. In the lobby as you enter is a big open fireplace in which logs are burned. On the mantelpiece above it is a row of carved cats. The originals of these were 1930s American fairground prizes, but all of those, save two, were destroyed in the fire. Fortuitously, a few months before the fire two of the cats had been knocked down and smashed by a drunk swinging his walking stick. The broken cats were taken away to be repaired, and so replacement models could be made from them. To the left of the lobby, as you enter, is the Mirror Room, with its blue walls and views over the estuary. Adjacent to this is the library, with newspapers, deep armchairs, writing facilities, and a large bay window. The Elephant's Bar next door is entirely furnished from India, right down to the shutters over the bar. As elsewhere in the building, everything was replaced or restored after the fire. Evening drinks are accompanied by music from the grand piano, strains of which can also be heard in the neighboring restaurant.

Guests also can avail themselves of the outdoor heated swimming pool on the terrace near the main building and free golf at Porthmadog Golf Club. Room televisions have a video channel on which can be seen episodes of *The Prisoner* and a film about Portmeirion and its founder, Clough Williams-Ellis. Rates run from £45 for a village bedroom in early and late seasons to £100 for the Peacock Suite in the main building from May 20th through Sept. 23rd. Room rates are for two persons sharing; deduct £10 for single occupancy. Credit cards: AE, DC, MC, V.

**Leamore Hotel,** 40 Lloyd St., Llandudno, Gwynedd LL30 27G, Wales; tel. (0492) 7552. As you enter the Leamore one of the first things to catch your eye is the word *Croeso* over the top of the bar. *Croeso* is the Welsh word for "Welcome," and a very Welsh welcome, including a glass of Welsh wine on arrival, is certainly what you get from proprietors Beryl and Fred Owen.

The Leamore is, then, a genial and cozy small hotel—stamped with Beryl and Fred's personal touch. One of the nicest rooms is the attic. Breakfast not only extends to kippers but also to the increasingly rare haddock with poached egg on top. Barabrith (currant loaf) and griddle cakes are also available. Rooms run from £13 to £16 per person, including breakfast; £19–22 for bed, breakfast, and evening meal.

**St. Tudno Hotel,** North Parade, Llandudno, Gwynedd, Wales LL30 2LP; tel. (0492) 74411. The St. Tudno is the stylish pride of Llandudno. It occupies a prime position in one of the Victorian terraces that line Llandudno's promenade. Lewis Carroll's Alice, the Alice Liddell upon whom *Alice in Wonderland* was based, stayed in this house during her visit to the resort at the age of eight. More recently the St. Tudno has acquired the justified reputation of being one of Britain's most beautiful and luxurious seaside resort hotels.

In the lobby and coffee lounge, wicker chairs and lots of greenery provide a pleasingly relaxed but stylish introduction to the building. Beyond the lounge lies the green and airy Garden Room Restaurant (see "Tasting Wales" below). At the front of the hotel, on either side of the entrance hall the guest finds the Victorian solidities of the Sitting Room and the Bar Lounge, both of which afford views of the seafront. Nonsmokers should note that both the Garden Room Restaurant and the Sitting Room are designated nonsmoking areas.

On arrival in their room guests are welcomed with a half-bottle of sparkling wine. Each of the rooms is individually designed and furnished in authentic Victorian tones. Room 2, facing the seafront, is particularly recommended. Breakfast buffs might note that grilled kippers are an option for breakfast; since they come filleted, they make an ideal initiation into the delights of kippered herring. Health-conscious guests can avail themselves of the hotel's indoor heated swimming pool. Rock'n'roll addicts can get MTV on satellite in their rooms.

In recent years the St. Tudno has received various prestigious awards, including the Good Hotel Guide César Award for Best Seaside Hotel in Great Britain and Ireland. Rates run from £28 (for room at rear of hotel) to £37.50 (for room with superior seafront view); breakfast is included. Special rates for long, short, and weekend visits. Passenger lift. Small parking lot; also garage for £2.50. Credit cards: AE, DC, MC, V.

# A Tour of Wales

Particular emphasis in this chapter will be given to the Pembrokeshire coast and the Gower Peninsula. They are areas of great natural beauty and of considerable historical and literary interest, easily accessible by road and rail from London and great for walking in. From them you can easily get to mid- and north Wales, but they are a holiday in themselves. They would make an ideal four- or five-day tour from London. You could also fit them into a trip to the west of England.

The M4 motorway and the superb Inter-City 125 train service from Paddington now make Pembrokeshire much nearer to London in terms of traveling time. By train **Swansea** is only two and a half hours from London, leaving from Paddington and traveling on the Great Western through BritRail's showpiece region. Zooming through Thomas Hardy's Wessex and then the Severn Tunnel, you change trains at Swansea onto a snug little train that takes you into the different, slower, greener world of the west of Wales. By car there's a similar transformation just before Swansea. The power-driving experience of the M4 and the spectacular crossing of the Severn Bridge into Wales gives way to the A48. Make for **Tenby,** medieval port and Victorian resort with plenty of good hotels in a wide price range. The train from Swansea will also take you to Tenby in a lovely journey around the "heron-priested shore" of the Towy estuary near Laugharne and Dylan Thomas's boathouse. Using Tenby as your base, you can make further excursions into west Wales or you can be energetic and go walking on the Pembrokeshire coastal footpath.

After Tenby head back east to Swansea and the **Gower Peninsula.** Base yourself either at the Mumbles, the little Victorian resort just south of Swansea where Dylan Thomas did much of his Swansea drinking, or in the hamlet of Oxwich out on Gower itself, near Three Cliffs Bay. Having gotten suitably relaxed and healthy in Gower, you may feel in need of some urban dissipation. You may also be interested in rugby, opera, or Victorian architecture at its most imposing. For any or for all of these reasons, the Welsh capital of **Cardiff** is worth several days of your time.

In mid-Wales **Hay-on-Wye, Brecon,** and **Llandrindod Wells** all make excellent bases for exploring the **Marches** along the border, the **Black Mountains,** and the **Brecon Beacons,** but we would especially recommend the Victorian spa resort of Llandrindod Wells. Bibliophiles can pay a visit to the university town and seaside resort of **Aberystwyth,** where the Welsh National Library is located. If Cardiff is the administrative and commercial capital of Wales, Aberystwyth is very much the cultural capital, especially with regard to the Welsh-speaking parts of the country. Prince Charles, whose title as heir to the throne is Prince of Wales, spent a year at the University College here after he came down from Cambridge. The only BritRail steam line still in existence runs on the narrow-gauge railway from Aberystwyth to the wooded gorge and waterfalls of **Devil's Bridge.** (The other Welsh narrow-gauge railways are privately owned.)

From Llandrindod Wells and/or Aberystwyth, go north up the **Cambrian Coast** through **Harlech** and its medieval fortress to **Porthmadog.** By either the coast road or the Cambrian Coast railway, the mountain ranges of Cader Idris and then **Snowdonia** will form brooding backdrops to your view inland. Train travelers who wish to concentrate on north Wales have two routes from London's Euston Station: to **Shrewsbury** and thence through the middle of Wales to **Machynlleth,** joining the Cambrian coastline there for the spectacular journey to **Porthmadog;** the more northerly route through **Chester** to Llandudno Junction for either **Llandudno** or taking the Conwy valley line inland to **Blaenau Ffestiniog** and then the narrow-gauge railway, with its various scenic stopping-off points en route to Porthmadog.

**Porthmadog,** nearby the birthplace of Lawrence of Arabia, has plenty of reasonably priced bed-and-breakfast guest houses and is well placed for exploring the **Lleyn Peninsula,** the Gower of north Wales, to its west, and Snowdonia and the Vale of Ffestiniog to its east and north. Not to be missed is the late Sir Clough Williams-Ellis's spectacular fantasy village of Portmeirion. This is located on a wooded peninsula between Portmadog and Harlech.

**Portmeirion** is usually described as an Italian village, and its original core was put together in the 1920s and 1930s with Portofino very much in mind. Postwar additions, however, were far more eclectic: the hall of a Jacobean Welsh country house, a Georgian colonnade from Bristol, and statues of Buddha resting on the tops of Doric columns. Think of it as its founder did, as an experiment in architecture, color, and landscape, and you will get the picture. Calling it his "light opera" approach to architecture, he wanted to demonstrate that you could develop a naturally beautiful site without spoiling it. (Ironically, modern planning laws would prevent such eclecticism.) The son of the main house's previous owner had imported a number of exotic plants into the surrounding woods, known in Welsh as the Gwyllt ("the Wild"), and these plants have flourished in the microclimate created by the combination of the Gulf Stream and the secluded peninsula. In the 1930s and 1940s many writers and artists, including Bertrand Russell, Frank Lloyd Wright, and Noel Coward, stayed at Portmeirion. Edward, Prince of Wales, also resided here during his Investiture. Portmeirion is where the 1960s cult television series *The Prisoner* was partly filmed. The village contains a Prisoner Shop, and each September the Prisoner Society holds its annual worldwide convention here. Max Hora in the Prisoner Shop is an expert on the series. So the hotel and village bedrooms of Portmeirion are far more than up-market alternatives to Porthmadog. They are outstanding and unique in themselves, a magical part of any visit to Britain, and if you go nowhere else in Wales, then this is where you should visit.

Driving through the **Snowdonia National Park** takes you through some of the most majestic and wildest mountain scenery in Europe. It is also a journey through the heart of the ancient Wales of druids, bards, and warriors. Traveling northwest through the **Vale of Ffestiniog** brings you to **Blaenau Ffestiniog** and the **Llechwedd Slate Caverns.** From there you ascend the 1,263-foot Crimea Pass in order to descend the forested **Lledr Valley** to the lovely village of **Betws-y-Coed.** There are then two alternatives for the next stage of your trip.

The first of these takes you due north on the A470 through the Conwy Valley to Conwy and Llandudno. **Conwy** is an intact medieval and Tudor coastal town with an extensive waterfront and some surviving medieval walls. Inside the town is Aberconwy House, the town house of a medieval merchant, and at its edge, guarding the estuary of the Conwy and the mountains of Snowdonia behind it, is Edward I's castle of Conwy, built in 1283. At the foot of the castle walls the A55 coastal road passes across the river on a suspension bridge, designed by Thomas Telford in 1822. The railway from Chester to Holyhead, along which the Irish Mail travels en route to the Dublin ferry, also passes by here. Llandudno justly claims to be Wales's premier resort. Llandudno Bay, flanked by the twin mountains of the Great and Little Ormes, faces out into the Irish Sea. The town itself is one of the best British examples of an intact, planned, 19th-century seaside resort. It was planned by the Mostyns, one of the great gentry families of north Wales since Tudor times, and one of the Mostyns' country houses, the 17th-century Bodysgallen Hall, just outside of Llandudno, on a ridge below the Great Orme, has recently been restored to become Wales's top hotel. Within Llandudno there is a wealth of good hotels at all prices. Among these, the St. Tudno stands out as one of *the* luxury seaside hotels of Britain. It was also where Lewis Carroll's Alice stayed at the age of eight, when she first visited Llandudno in 1861. The country outside of Llandudno was also where Evelyn Waugh located Llanabba Castle, the private school at which Paul Pennyfeather, the hero of *Decline and Fall,* went to teach. Your alternative route takes you along the A5, the old London-Holyhead road for the Irish Mail coaches in the 18th century. Your ultimate destination here is the castle town of **Caernarfon** with its Roman and medieval remains, scene of the Investiture of the Prince of Wales, televised for the first time in the 1960s. On the way, however, you can stop overnight in the village of **Llanberis.** Llanberis is at the foot of the 3,560-foot Mt. Snowden, and the officially designated mountain footpath starts from there.

Train travelers can follow a variation on the first of these two routes. The independent narrow-gauge Ffestiniog railway runs from Porthmadog to Blaenau Ffestiniog, where it connects with BritRail's Conwy Valley line down to Llandudno Junction, where there are connections for both Llandudno and Conwy. From Llandudno Junction you can also pick up the main London-Holyhead line as far as Bangor, where there is a bus service to and from Caernarfon and Llanberis.

When you are sated with Snowdonia, your home run by either road or rail takes you east along the coast, again with a backdrop of mountains on the landward side. Beyond these you pass by the spacious sands of the Dee estuary across which the cattle were called home to the farm in Charles Kingsley's poem "The Sands of Dee." Soon you will be in Chester with the northwest of England before you.

# Pembrokeshire and Gower

## Tenby

Tenby is a Victorian seaside resort built in the street pattern of a medieval town. All the winding streets eventually take you to the seafront and one of the town's two beaches. Castle Hill juts out on a promontory dividing the north and south beaches. Take the footpath to the top of this hill for great views of the harbor and the nearby islands of St. Catherine's and Caldy. Caldy Island has a 12th-century church with a leaning spire and a functioning monastery. There are daily sailings out to it from Tenby harbor on summer weekdays (adults £3, children £1.50), and the monastic peace and calm will relax you.

In Tenby itself the Victorian façades of many of the buildings belie their true age. To get an idea of pre-Victorian Tenby, go to the **Tudor Merchant's House** (open March through September, Monday through Friday from 10 A.M. to 1 P.M., 2:30 to 6 P.M., Sunday from 2 to 6 P.M.; £1 admission) next to Plantagenet's Restaurant, off Tudor Square. This is actually medieval, the oldest house in Tenby, but the first reference to it is in an Elizabethan town chronicle. The interior wall decorations are 13th century, and upstairs there is a Georgian four-poster bed with a 15th-century oak cradle at its foot. Where Boots stands on the High Street was Jasperley House, where Henry Tudor hid with his Uncle Jasper before fleeing to France after the Battle of Tewkesbury (1471). This was part of a cluster of houses that went up to the two medieval gable ends by the Sun Inn. The **Five Arches** and the town walls date from the end of the 13th century, but they were shored up against the Spanish Armada in 1588. **Little Rock House** on St. Julian Street is where Emma Hamilton stayed while Lord Nelson was stationed at nearby Milford Haven. The Globe Theatre, where she acted for Nelson, was once in Fry Street by the walls. **St. Mary's Parish Church** (13th century) is the largest medieval parish church in Wales. Gerald of Wales, the great scholar, was its first parish priest. To the left of the nave, in the Lady Chapel, is Thomas Rees's memorial to his wife, Margaret. She died in childbirth in 1610 at the age of 30, having borne 10 children over 12 years of marriage, 7 of whom survived. On the west side of the north door is a 15th-century effigy of a decomposing corpse, a reminder of man's mortality. For Victorian Tenby at its best see the **Medical Hall,** across from St. Mary's. Still in operation, its interior remains that of a Victorian pharmacy, colored bottles and all.

A short distance from Tenby is the **Norman Manorbier Castle** (open March through September, daily from 10:30 A.M. to 5:30 P.M.; £1 for adults, 30 pence for children). This is a beautiful location at the head of a bay. Inside the castle there are life-size models of Gerald of Wales working in the cell he used as a study, and of prisoners chained in a dank dungeon. On the other side of the Castlemartin peninsula from Manorbier stands the great Norman castle of **Pembroke,** where Henry Tudor was born. This, like Manorbier and Tenby, is on the 167-mile-long Pembrokeshire Coastal Footpath, which is signposted through the National Park that stretches from Amroth to Cardigan. (Pembroke is open April through September, daily from 9:30 A.M. to 6 P.M., in March and October from 10 A.M. to 5 P.M., November through February, Monday through Saturday from 10 A.M. to 4 P.M.; £1.20 for adults, 60 pence for children.)

## Dylan Thomas Tour

Traveling east from Tenby to **Swansea** takes you through the Dylan Thomas country of **Camarthen Bay** and the **Teifi Valley.** Here you will find the Fern Hill where he was "young and easy among the apple boughs" in the poem of that name, and the village of **Laugharne,** where he lived in the boathouse with his wife, Caitlin. This is now a **Dylan Thomas museum** (open from Easter to November, daily from 10 A.M. to 6 P.M., 90 pence for adults). Also in the village are the **Cross House Inn** and **Brown's Hotel,** both of which Dylan patronized, and the **Town Hall clock tower** with the chiming bell and weathercock that are so central to *Under Milk Wood.* Dylan is buried in **St. Martin's churchyard** in the town.

Fans of Dylan Thomas should also visit Swansea, taking in his childhood home in Cymdonkin Dr. and the pubs he frequented on the Mumbles Rd. at Oystermouth. The Mermaid Hotel, from which he was frequently ejected, ironically now has a rather garish Dylan's Tavern, but the **Antelope** is well worth the price of a few pints. In Swansea itself, near the French-provincial–looking railway station, is an authentic, unspoiled 1940s workingman's bar, the **Adam and Eve,** which serves the formidable Brains S.A.

## The Gower Peninsula

The Gower Peninsula is a short drive or busride from Swansea along the A4118. Gower was saved from development as a holiday area by the outbreak of World War II. It has miles of unspoiled coast punctuated by a cluster of pretty villages, which you reach on narrow country lanes shielded by hedge-rows. Its farthest point is **Worm's Head** at Rhosili Bay, an-other source of inspiration for Dylan Thomas. Nearer to Swansea, with a glorious beach that is surrounded by a nature reserve, lies the hamlet of Oxwich. At the **Gower Boardsail-ing Center** here you can hire mountain bikes, which will en-able you to explore parts of the peninsula inaccessible by car. Between June and the end of August, bike tours are available for £10. The center also provides facilities for windsurfing and has a staff of qualified Royal Yachting Association instructors who can teach you the five levels of skills comprising the Na-tional Windsurfing Scheme. It is located a few yards from the beach next to the Oxwich parking lot. (Oxwich Bay Car Park, Oxwich, Gower, West Glamorgan SA3 1LS, Wales; tel. (0792) 390774).

# Cardiff

Rugby and Cardiff Arms Park apart, why visit Cardiff when your time is limited and there are the beauties of Pembroke-shire, Gower, and Snowdonia to explore? The short answer to this question is that Cardiff is one of the great Victorian cities of Britain. Although Cardiff Castle and Llandaff Cathe-dral are medieval buildings, the city's great surge of growth was in the 19th century as the port of the south Wales coal mines. At one time 13 million tons of coal a year were passing through Cardiff, and its Coal Exchange, the coal industry's trading center, had a direct telegraph link with the London Stock Exchange. The Coal Exchange has been restored, and the restoration continues apace in the rest of the historic area of Bute Town, the *Tiger Bay* of the famous film. Cardiff's Vic-torian fortunes were crucially bound up with the fortunes of the immensely wealthy Bute family. The 3rd marquis of Bute hired the great Gothic revival architect William Burges to re-store **Cardiff Castle.** Burges's interior designs are exotic and Pre-Raphaelite in style. The roof garden, the Arab Room, and the library are particularly impressive. (Open daily from 10 A.M. to 5 P.M.; £2.20 for adults, £1.10 for children.) Out-side Cardiff, Burges also built Castell Coch for the marquis. This is a complete Gothic fantasy extravaganza, comparable only to the castles of Mad King Ludwig in Bavaria. Castle Coch is open from mid-March to mid-October, Monday through Saturday from 9:30 A.M. to 6:30 P.M., Sundays from 2 P.M. to 6:30 P.M., mid-October to mid-March open only till 4 P.M.; £1 for adults, 50 pence for children.

As Wales's capital, Cardiff offers the **National Museum of Wales** (open Tuesday through Saturday from 10 A.M. to 5:30 P.M., Sundays from 2:30 P.M. to 5 P.M.; £1 for adults, 50 pence for children), which has a good collection of Post-

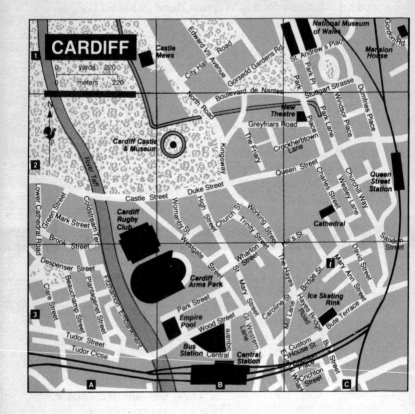

impressionist paintings; the **New Theatre,** now home to the Welsh National Opera; and St. David's Hall, an internationally renowned concert center. Avant-garde drama productions can be seen at the **Sherman Theatre** and the **Chapter Arts Centre.** The Chapter, located in Canton, the new hip area of Cardiff, also has three cinemas, three galleries, and various workshops. More traditionally, out at St. Fagan's, is the open-air **Welsh Folk Museum** (open April through September, Monday through Saturday from 10 A.M. to 5 P.M.; £2 for adults, £1 for children). And down at the end of Bute Street in the old dock area is the **Welsh Industrial and Maritime Museum** (open Tuesday through Saturday from 10 A.M. to 5 P.M., Sundays from 2:30 P.M. to 5 P.M.; £1 for adults, 50 pence for children), its three buildings housing the Shipping Transport and Railway galleries. The **Railway Gallery** is in the former Bute Street railway station. Nearby in Mount Stuart Square, named after local Victorian bigwig, Lord Ninian Creighton Stuart, stands the magnificent old **Coal Exchange.** The basement of this is now given over to television companies and the upper galleries above the exchange floor are now offices, but it remains gloriously Victorian. At the entrance there is a tidal clock, and at one end of the exchange floor another clock is surrounded by carved dragons. Had de-

## The Arts in Cardiff

For free up-to-date information write to Cardiff Arts Marketing, FREEPOST, Cardiff CF1 1YT, Wales (no stamp needed) or phone the 24-hour Entertainment Hotline, (0222) 36244. The Cardiff Visitor Center, 8–14 Bridge Street, provides tourist information, car hire, theater tickets, and accommodation bookings throughout Wales. Open all year from 9 A.M. to 7 P.M. (6 P.M. on Saturday) and on Sundays, May through October from 10 A.M. to 5 P.M.

Cardiff is a good city to explore on foot, and the Visitor Centre has two "Town trail" pamphlets to assist you. There are many tiled Victorian shopping arcades and many, many good pubs. On St. Mary Street in the middle of town stands the brewery of S.A. Brain and Company, producer of Brains S.A. This is meant to stand for Special Ale, but locals invariably refer to it as "Skull Attack" on account of its potency. A wondrous pint, but some palates may prefer Brains Dark, their other draft beer. Just off St. Mary Street, the Old Arcade pub used to be the haunt of the pop singer Shakin' Stevens and continues to be the mecca both for Cardiff bohemia and for rugby supporters—it's a real local institution. On the other side of the brewery stands the Albert, on St. Mary Street, and the Duke of Wellington. Over by the Holiday Inn and the Earl of Bute's statue is the Golden Cross, with its spectacular Edwardian tiles. Across the road from Cardiff Castle on Castle Street stands the Four Bars Inn, Cardiff home of the Welsh Jazz Society, with live music upstairs every night for £1 admission. Down in Butetown many of the old rough-and-ready docks pubs continue to flourish. Handy for the Coal Exchange and the Industrial Maritime Museum are the Ship and Pilot, The Packet, The Bute Dock, and the Big Windsor. The Big Windsor was once the most famous restaurant in Wales and was visited by royalty. On its wall is a plaque to Abel Magneron, the French landlord whose "gastronomic standards contributed to the greater glory of the Entente Cordiale" in the years after World War II.

There are also many good, cheap clubs to visit after the pubs close, but they are essentially Friday and Saturday places. Cardiff is pretty quiet during the week. Followers of alternative and indie (independent label) music will want to visit Radcliffs-Square Club at 41 Westgate Street (tel. 0222-371570) near the Arms Park. Admission is between £1 and £3. The upstairs room has wall paintings of the Creature from the Black Lagoon and an octopus, projectors that "make the walls move," and a DJ's box painted like the back end of a police van, complete with flashing roof light. The DJ himself is known as "The Lizard" and was described by the club manager as being "a friendly rebel."

volution happened in the 1970s, the Coal Exchange would have been the Welsh parliament building. Now it is used as a gallery, as a location for feature films, and for dinner dances in honor of French rugby teams after they have played Internationals at the Arms Park.

## ☙ RESTAURANTS

In addition to being one of the most spectacularly scenic parts of Britain, Wales is rapidly becoming one of *the* areas in which to find good places to eat. Thanks to the efforts of a number of Welsh restaurateurs, Wales can increasingly display a cuisine to match its language and literature. As well as Welsh lamb, there is salted duck, Rhondda hotpot, Glamorgan sausages, and an abundance of seafood and fish. Foremost among the latter is sewin, a salmon trout that can be either poached or smoked. The traditional craft of cheesemaking also has undergone a great revival in recent years; there now is an impressive range of Welsh country cheeses to set alongside the famous Caerphilly. Breakfast and tea can take on a pronounced Welsh flavor with larva bread, cockles and bacon, Welsh griddle cakes, and barabrith. The vineyards of Croffta in Glamorgan and Monnow Valley in Monmouthshire produce fine wines to complement the cuisine, the Welsh Whisky Company in Brecon produces a single malt whisky called Prince of Wales, and there is now also Welsh gin, vodka, and liqueurs. And the Welsh have been producing and drinking mead for over a thousand years. Finally, Wales's capital city, Cardiff, has long boasted a cosmopolitan air to its restaurants worthy of what was formerly a great cosmopolitan port, and its Chinese restaurants are particularly worth investigating. What follows is a regional guide to some of the ways you can taste Wales.

## Cardiff

**Blas ar Gymru** (A Taste of Wales), 48, Crwys Rd., Cardiff, tel. (022) 382132.

Patricia and Meirion Dally's award-winning restaurant, a five-minute taxi ride or a 20-minute walk from the city center, gives you a taste of Wales in a carefully created old Welsh atmosphere. In the evenings waitresses wear traditional Welsh costume, and Patricia and Meirion enjoy explaining Welsh culinary traditions. Their set menu of three courses followed by coffee and Welsh cakes is excellent value at £7.95.

Among their starters, we particularly recommend the smoked sewin. This comes from the same smokery at Cennarth that is used by the *QE2*. The sewin's flavor is enhanced by having been smoked over the pure oak that comes from the oak lumber mill adjacent to the smokery. For the main course, roast lamb, cooked in ginger and honey cider, accompanied by a separate plate with lots of fresh vegetables, is an obvious choice, but the menu has other delights to match this. The crispy salted duck, cooked on a trivet and served in a port gravy, perhaps; or Glamorgan sausages, full of cheese, breadcrumbs, and herbs, with a strong flavoring of sage, and served with homemade chutney. Another local tradition is Rhondda hot pot: lean beef and smoked ham with carrots, parsnips, and brown flakes of potatoes on the top of the pot. It comes with a small, freshly baked (still warm) cracked wheat or whole-meal loaf. There is also the goose cawl, a casserole of lean goose meat, fresh vegetables, and herbs; and venison marinated in claret. A glass or a bottle of Croffta, with its interesting blend of the German Muller Thorgau and various French grapes, can accompany most of these dishes, and there is also a good house claret. The claret is also good with the splendid selection of farm cheeses from west Wales. The cheeses are named after the local farms, such as Pant-ys-gwuan near Pontypool, which is a goat cheese with peppers; or Skirrid, a ewe's cheese marinated in mead. There are also Teifi cheeses, low fat and blended with sweet pickle. AE, DC, MC, V.

# North Wales

**Portmeirion,** Gwynedd, tel. (0766) 770457.

An aperitif on the terrace of Portmeirion provides an opportunity both for perusing the menu and wine list and for taking in the stunning view across the estuary. Inside the restaurant you should try to get a table by the window so as to get more of the view. During the summer months it's particularly impressive as the sun goes down. Nonresidents should always book. If you're at Portmeirion as a day visitor, this booking can be done at the reception building near the village entrance. On Sundays and in the evenings your admission to the village as a nonresident will be refunded at the restaurant.

Hefin Williams, the head chef, is a local who was trained at Maxim's in Paris. His specialties include lamb, beef, and local seafood, especially lobster. Dinner, served on plates from Portmeirion's own pottery, is £14.95. The restaurant also serves a Continental breakfast for £2.15 and a full Welsh one for £4.25, which offers haddock, kippers, or kedgeree as alternatives to bacon, sausage, and eggs. All major credit cards.

**St. Tudno Hotel,** North Parade, Llandudno, Gwynedd, tel. (0492) 74411.

Like Portmeirion, the St. Tudno restaurant, the Garden Room, is a nonsmoking area. Airy and green, a suggestion of Hockney pastels in the coloring of the walls complementing the abundant potted greenery enhances the greenhouse effect. The green-on-white tree murals are Japanese. This stylish setting combined with a very friendly and informal staff make eating at the St. Tudno seem closer to Hollywood than Holyhead!

The menu, which is changed daily, is heavily oriented toward local produce, game, and fish. Salmon, for instance, is smoked locally. Welsh dishes are marked on the menu with a dragon symbol. Jeannette Bland very much sees the St. Tudno cheeseboard as putting a definitive Welsh stamp on the restaurant, and Jane, the restaurant manager, trains her staff in the knowledge of Welsh cheeses so that they can provide patrons with the background to each of the 12 or 13 cheeses normally on offer.

These come from all over Wales and include Maesllyn, smoked with an Austrian flavor, and Llangloffan, containing chives and comparable to a blue Cheshire. By arrangement, Jane can arrange a presentation of the hotel cheeses together with leaflets on their production. Dinner is £14.95 and after dinner you may wish to further pursue your researches into Welsh beverages in the hotel bar. Sit in the bay window overlooking the promenade sampling Prince of Wales single-malt whisky; Swn-y-mor, a blended whisky; Merlyn, a cream liqueur comparable to Bailey's Irish Cream, Welsh gin (Glen Usk), and Welsh vodka (Taffski!). All of these are products of the same Brecon company. A nonalcoholic alternative to all of this is Decantae, the Welsh mineral water. All major credit cards.

**Bodysgallen Hall,** Llandudno, Gwynedd, tel. (0492) 84466. Precede your meal at Bodysgallen Hall with a visit to the bar, where Alex the barman claims to mix the best dry martini in Wales. If the weather is good you can take your drink out through the French windows of the north dining room onto the terrace overlooking the garden. The dining rooms are open to nonresidents for both lunch and dinner.

The hotel's kitchen garden is the source of much of the vegetables, fruits, and herbs used in Bodysgallen dishes. Martin James, the chef, aims at a Welsh nouvelle cuisine. Appetizers of a Welsh character can include Anglesea crab and seaweed tart in lemon butter sauce, halibut and watercress mousse served on spinach mayonnaise, and Bodysgallen terrine of game with game jelly and hot brioche. For the main course there might be roast loin of spring lamb with onion marmalade. What is in season and fresh determines each day's menu. The menu also emphasizes that Martin James "usually cooks the vegetables lightly so that they retain their crispness and flavor better." The puddings served for dessert are renowned and the menu usefully offers advice on dessert wines to accompany them. A selection of Welsh and English cheeses follows pudding, and sweetmeats (dinner only) and coffee round off the meal. A two-course luncheon is £8.25; three courses, £10.25. Dinner (five courses and coffee) is £19.75. The house red wine, a St. Emilion, and the white, a Loire, are both £7.90 a bottle. The house claret is £9.70 and the Cellarman's Choice is £10. A wide range of Grand Cru clarets is also available, ranging £11–£150 a bottle. All major credit cards.

**The Lanterns Fish Restaurant,** 7 Church Walks, Llandudno, Gwynedd, tel. (0492) 77924.

Around the corner from the St. Tudno, on Church Walks, this is one of two Welsh specialty seafood restaurants recommended by Egon Ronay. It opens at 7:30 P.M., and last orders for food are normally at 9:30 unless by prior arrangement. Most main courses are £9–10, including a choice of fresh vegetables or salad. Special dishes are very much geared to fresh shellfish and fish—local where possible—but there are also specialty meat dishes. The broad wine list has a pronounced southern hemisphere orientation. All major credit cards.

**Craigside Manor,** Colwyn Rd., Little Orme, Llandudno, Gwynedd, tel. (0492) 45943.

Out on the Colwyn Road toward the Little Orme, David Harding does wonderful things to fish with a high-pressure steamer. His appetizers include crab with larva bread in a butter sauce (£3.75) and locally smoked salmon (£5.50). For a main course, try saddle of Welsh lamb with spinach, wrapped in puff pastry in a red wine sauce (£9.75). These prices include a choice of vegetables or a salad. The house wine is £5.75, but there is also a rather fine claret, a Château Tour Musset 1983, for £12.50. Lunch is 12:30–2 P.M.; dinner 7:30–10 P.M. All major credit cards.

**Y Bistro,** 43–45 High St., Llanberis, Gwynedd, tel. (0286) 871278.

Where the Dallys at A Taste of Wales in Cardiff specialize in south and west Walean dishes, Nerys Roberts at Y Bistro places a similar emphasis on the dishes of the north. Like the Llandudno restaurants listed above, Y Bistro is spearheading the culinary renaissance of the northwest tip of Wales.

A set dinner of four courses is £14.50 and includes canapés on your arrival. There is a choice of five dishes for each stage of the menu, and the menu changes monthly. By contrast with the nouvelle cuisine of the St. Tudno and Bodysgallen, the general flavor here is described as "Welsh with a bit of *cordon bleu.*" Starters include Welsh riblets grilled with honey and rosemary. For the main course look for poached sewin with Croffta wine. Cheeses include Pen Carreg, the Welsh brie. Y Bistro is open 7:30–9:30 P.M. Tues.–Sat. Credit cards: MC, V.

A recent spin-off from Y Bistro is Y Bistro Bach at 4, The Square, Caernarfon (tel. 0286-3075). This restaurant offers lunch noon–3 P.M., with dishes like local mackerel fried in oatmeal (£3.25), available together with a help-yourself bar. There is also an upstairs tearoom that is open all day.

Also recommended:

**Foreshore Coffee Shop, Mumbles Road, Swansea,** tel. (0792) 369054. Follow up a brisk stroll along the Oystermouth promenade, or set yourself up for a day exploring Gower with a Welsh breakfast. Larva bread, cockles, bacon, egg, tomato, and fried bread, with toast and marmalade for £2.40.

**No. 1 Bistro, Llandudno,** tel. (0492) 75424. Just down the road from the Great Orme funicular railway, this is run by two former employees of the St. Tudno. It has two cozy Victorian rooms with open fireplaces. Everything is homemade, and what is available is always what is fresh and in season. Starters are £1–3.25, main courses £3.65–6.95, a vegetarian selection £3.80–4.25. Most wine is around £5.95 a bottle. For lunch, main courses are around £2.90: lots of fresh fish. Lunch served noon–1:45 P.M., Tues.–Sat.; dinner 7–9:45, Mon.–Sat. No credit cards.

# Pembrokeshire and Gower

**The Lamb Inn, High Street, Tenby,** tel. (0834) 2154. This is a pub offering the two great Welsh real ales, Brains S.A. and Felinfoel Double Dragon. At lunchtimes in the basement a crab salad is often available for £3.70. This will have been caught the previous morning, cooked during the day, and when cooled down delivered to the hotel by the fishermen in the evening so that it will be ready for lunch the next day. No credit cards.

**Chives Restaurant, Manorbier,** tel. (0834) 871230. After visiting Manorbier Castle pause here for afternoon tea. A cream tea is £1.65 and you can get barabrith for 55 pence.

**Plantagenet's, Tenby,** tel. (0834) 2350. In part of the National Trust–owned Tudor Merchant's House, cozy and picturesque with Welsh dressers, is a 13th-century Flemish bar. Look for the organic wines. All major credit cards.

**Tim Munday's Cellar, Swansea,** tel. (0792) 55332. Situated up an alleyway called Salubrious Passage(!!) off one of Swansea's main drags, Wind St., but also accessible through the No Sign Wine Bar on Wind St. Have a drink in the wine bar first. In a refurbished Georgian building in the center of the old commercial quarter, it is redolent with the feel of 18th-century merchants sipping their sherry and port. The restaurant is in the original wine cellar, and its ceiling has a gantry formerly used for moving in barrels from boats on the river. Poached sewin is often available, and on Wed. and some Mon. there is live jazz. Hot food from £1.55 to around £7. All major credit cards.

# 15

# THE SCOTTISH LOWLANDS

The great thing about southern Scotland is that it covers a lot of territory and caters to a lot of tastes. The great thing about traveling in southern Scotland is that you can have a dozen different holidays packed into your stay. Most assuredly, you'll want to enjoy cosmopolitan Scotland (not a paradox) in one or the other, preferably both, of its great cities. Edinburgh in the east is at once a medieval royal burgh and a Georgian capital; Glasgow in the west is a Victorian merchant town blossoming into a 20th-century cultural center. You'll be intrigued by historic Scotland reposited in a mile-long list of castles and stately homes, abbeys, and battlefields. You'll need to explore natural Scotland on walks through the mountain forests of the Trossachs or on luxurious drives through the sheep meadows of the Borders. You'll want to avail yourself of sporting Scotland on the links at any of literally hundreds of courses in this, the cradle of golf, or by salmon fishing in fast-running rivers, horseback riding through the fields of Fife, or windsurfing on a mountain-ringed loch. And while you're at it, sample hedonist Scotland at hotels and restaurants and resorts of peerless quality and service.

The area we've entitled the Lowlands more properly might be called the low*er* lands, for you'll find plenty of rolling hills and even mountains on your journey. The Lowlands is a conglomeration of a half dozen regions in the southeastern and central part of Scotland—from the northern edge of England to the southern slopes of the Highlands, slammed on the east coast by the North Sea. The Lowland regions include the Borders, an oft-disputed area just north of England; the Lothians, strung along the south coast of the Firth of Forth and including Edinburgh; Strathclyde, centered in Glasgow, to the west; Central, a northern apex equidistant to Edinburgh and Glasgow, and including the Trossachs; Fife, the peninsula forming the north coast of the Firth of Forth; and Tayside, stretching north from Central and Fife until it touches the Highlands.

Most of Scotland's royal (and rollicking) history was played out hereabouts. In Pictish times the central seat of government was at the present site of Scone Palace, a tradition con-

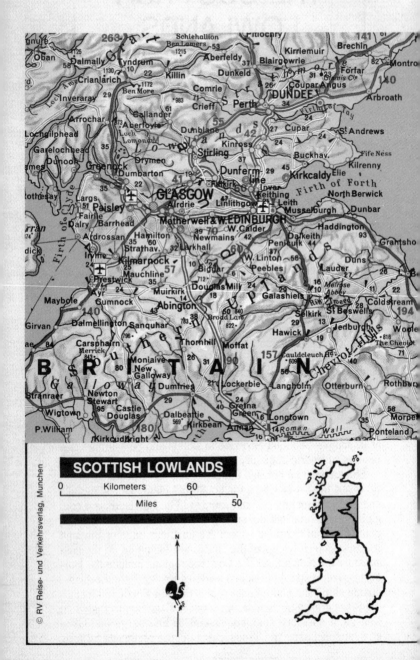

SCOTTISH LOWLANDS

0       Kilometers       60

Miles       50

N

tinued by the Irish Scots rule of Kenneth MacAlpin and later, after the wars of independence from England, by King Robert the Bruce. Eventually, Scottish royalty divided its time between the castles at Stirling and Edinburgh, the latter of which became the undisputed capital city of Scotland. Undisputed by everyone but the English.

King Edward I, Hammer of the Scots, was relentless in his quest to bring the northern tribes into the realm. His mission was first thwarted by William Wallace's decisive victory at Stirling Bridge in 1297. His son, Edward II, vowed to carry on his father's quest for union but was ultimately dissuaded by Robert Bruce's stunning victory at Bannockburn in 1314. Not content merely to pack it in and head back to London, Edward's troops burned down every abbey and home they could along the route of their retreat into Northumberland.

Thenceforth the history of the Borders was one of raiding back and forth over a constantly shifting boundary line between England and Scotland, as the number of ruined abbeys, fortified pele towers, and thrice-rebuilt manor houses attests. The most telling blow in this back-and-forth battling was dealt in 1513 at the Battle of Flodden Field in Northumberland, England, where James IV was slain along with ten thousand other Scottish warriors. The only real peace came with the advent of the Jacobean era. Queen Elizabeth I, after much speculation and debate, named the son of her cousin, Mary, Queen of Scots, her sole heir and successor, thus uniting the two kingdoms under James VI of Scotland and I of England.

Because this area is so packed with history and activity, we have divided the chapter into four sections. The first covers the city of Edinburgh and includes a list of day trips from there. The second is devoted to the Greater Glasgow area. The third is concerned with the Borders. And last—the Heart of Scotland—includes the territory north of the cities, the regions of Central, Fife, and Tayside.

While you can travel within these smaller regions in easy day trips, the distance between the extreme southern parts of the Borders and the extreme northern parts of the Heart of Scotland makes for a long day of driving back and forth. Thus, if you plan to spend a lot of time exploring both of these areas in one trip, you will have to consider spending a few nights in each of them. Both Glasgow and Edinburgh are within easy driving distance from either the Borders or the Heart of Scotland regions, and it is also a very fast and easy trip between one city and the other.

## TRAVEL

There are three major **airports** in this region: at Edinburgh, Glasgow, and Prestwick. Prestwick is on the coast about 30 miles southwest of Glasgow and offers direct transatlantic service from New York and Boston several times each week. Flight time is approximately nine hours. The Prestwick phone number is (0292) 79822. Edinburgh Airport has regular service from London, about 24 flights, daily. Flight time is approximately one hour. Call (031) 333-1000. Glasgow Airport has about 20 flights daily from London, also approximately one hour. Call (041) 887-1111.

Going by **train** is a very pleasant option indeed. The InterCity 125 network links London with both Edinburgh and Glasgow. These trains are fast, efficient, air-conditioned, offer full bar and meal services, and travel through some beautiful countryside— by far the best way to travel to Scotland. All trains to Edinburgh's Waverley Station depart from London King's Cross (tel. 01-278-2477). All trains to Glasgow Central leave from London Euston (tel. 01-387-9400). Trains to Edinburgh run every hour or so, and the journey lasts about 5 ½ hours. The round-trip Saver fare is about £50. Trains to Glasgow run every two hours and take about five hours. The round-trip Saver fare is about £55. If you'd like to save some cash (up to £20), you can take the night train to either city. These trains leave London late in the evening and arrive in Scotland first thing in the morning. Trains to the Borders are on the Glasgow InterCity line stopping in Carlisle (Cumbria, England), where you can catch a Scottish Borders Rail link bus to Hawick, Selkirk, and Galashiels. Buses can also be taken south from Waverley Station, Edinburgh, or northwest from the station at Berwick-upon-Tweed (Northumberland, England). For the Trossachs and points north, trains travel to Stirling and Perth on the Edinburgh-Aberdeen line. Service between Edinburgh and Glasgow Queen St. Station runs every half hour and takes just under one hour. Fare varies according to time of day; it is approximately £5.

For **Steam Train** fans, the Bo'ness & Kinneil Railway runs along the southern shore of the Firth of Forth on a 3 ¼-mile track from Bo'ness Station 17 miles west of Edinburgh (tel. 0506-822-298). Trains run weekends in spring and daily except Monday and Tuesday in summer. Also, Kerr's Miniature Railway runs along the southeast coast of Fife, weekend afternoons in spring and fall, daily in Jul. and Aug. (tel. 0241-79249).

The **bus ride** from London to Edinburgh and Glasgow can last up to eight hours and more. You arrive rumpled and exhausted. However, if budgeting is a primary concern, buses do provide a very inexpensive service, at £25–30. Scottish Citylink Coaches leave from Victoria Station in London and connect with St. Andrews Square Bus Station in Edinburgh (031-556-8464) and Buchanan Bus Station in Glasgow (041-332-7133).

Although both Edinburgh and Glasgow are connected to London and other points south by motorway (the M1 to the M6 to the M74 to the M8), the **car trip** is a very long and (on the motorways) dull journey indeed. We suggest you take the train (or fly if you're in a tearing hurry) and rent a car at your destination.

## TOURING

Both Glasgow and Edinburgh are best seen on foot (although in Glasgow you'll need to take a bus or Underground for the longer distances). Both cities are extremely confusing and crowded for driving, and parking is scarce and can be expensive. A great way to see either town is to take a taxicab tour. Edinburgh's greatest natural raconteur, Robert Skirving, is the man to call: 031-442-4557. In Glasgow call the Taxi Cab Association, 041-332-6666.

If you're starting in one of these cities and touring from there, pick up your rental car when you're ready to drive out of town, not first thing when you arrive. Likewise, if you're touring the countryside first and finishing your trip in a city, drop the car off as soon as you get into town and proceed on foot.

If you'd rather not be left to your own devices, it is possible to get around by bus and rail, although service tends to be between major towns and does not necessarily include major attractions nestled in the countryside. If you plan to do a lot of traveling by bus, you might like to get a bus rover ticket, at £3.50 per day for unlimited travel within a delineated region. Regional bus services are: in the Borders, Lowland Scottish, Galashiels; tel. (0896) 58484. In the Heart of Scotland, Midland Scottish, Stirling; tel. (0786) 73763.

If you'd like to go in style, you can hire a chauffeur-driven car from Small World Tours, Edinburgh; tel. (031) 666-1944. Or hire a chauffeur-driven Rolls-Royce from Heather Tours Ltd., Perthshire; tel. (0764) 63835 during business hours.

Boat Tour options: From South Queensferry, west of Edinburgh, the *Maid of the Forth* sails weekends spring and fall and daily Jul.–Aug. The *Maid* sails around the Forth Bridges to Inchcolm Island. Also evening jazz cruises Fridays only in summer. Tickets can be purchased in Edinburgh from the Ticket Centre Waverley Bridge, or call (031) 331-1454.

From Anderston Quay, Glasgow, the *P. S. Waverley*, the world's last seagoing paddle steamer, cruises up the Clyde River from Easter to Sept. Call (041) 221-8152 for details.

# ❦ HOTELS

Spending the day fishing waist-deep in the river Tweed or hiking knee-high in heather, rolling home across the waters of Loch Katrine or in from a night at the opera in Glasgow, nothing is more comforting than the thought that the day's adventuring will end at a wonderful hostelry. Be it a cosmopolitan chestnut with regal appointments or a country inn equipped with simple pleasures, you won't fail to be delighted with the array of excellent choices southern Scotland strews in your path.

Since the Lowlands of Scotland include her two most important cities, Edinburgh and Glasgow, you can choose whether you wish to base yourself in town and drive to the country, or in the country and make trips into town. Perhaps if you live in a rural area, you'd prefer the novelty and buzz of a city, but if you have no preference, we suggest choosing a country house hotel or inn because it is this kind of accommodation that conveys the truest sense of Scottish tradition and hospitality. Do keep in mind, however, that some of the most appealing events in Glasgow and Edinburgh occur at night—a ballet or military tattoo that plays until well after 10 P.M.—after which you may not be keen to drive an hour to a middle-of-nowhere hotel. If you do plan to take advantage of these kinds of citified festivals and festivities (and we strongly urge you to do so; they are as integral to the Scottish landscape as are salmon and sheepdogs), why not arrange your trip so that you can spend a few nights in one and/or the other city, and the rest of your stay cradled in the country.

If sporting is your scene, undoubtedly you already know about the joys that await you on the courses of St. Andrews, Gleneagles, and Muirfield. Perhaps you don't know that some of the best salmon and trout are pulled from the waters of the Borders, an area also duly famous for its pheasant shooting and cross-country horseback riding. The Trossachs are perfect for the quiet outdoorsman who prefers to take long, solitary walks in mountain woods by mountain streams, or the rowdier breed who enjoys windsurfing and sailboat racing. Besides the Edinburgh and Glasgow hotels below, good spots to stay over in the Borders include Gorebridge (near Edinburgh), Kelso, and Peebles. Auchterarder, Callander, Peat Inn, and St. Andrews are in the central area.

Despite the broad urban/rural dichotomy, these hotels all have a few things in common: the food, service, and furnishings are uniformly of the highest caliber, so whether you've spent the day lost in a bunker or lost in reverie, you can count on a welcome that's professional, yet warm and sincere.

**Credit card abbreviations used in hotel and restaurant listings are as follows: AE for American Express, CB for Carte Blanche, DC for Diner's Club, MC for MasterCard, and V for Visa.**

# Auchterarder

**Auchterarder House,** Perthshire, PH3 1DZ; tel. (076) 46-2939 or 46-3646/7. What a pleasure it is to introduce Scotland hotels with this splendid house, designed by William Burn and built in stages between 1829 and 1877; minutes away from Gleneagles, you can have your golf and a delicious dose of old Scotland, too. From an immense tub in the Cunningham Room, you can enjoy a sip of sherry as you watch the pheasants roaming the Ochil Hills outside your window. Audrey and Ian Brown are salt-of-the-earth Aberdonians who insist that their guests have the best of everything—from Edwardian antiques to a library stocked with Burns and Scott to fresh flowers supplied by the three gardeners and arranged by Mrs. Brown herself. All rooms have bath/shower, bidets, toiletries, TV and radio, direct-dial phones, and unobstructed views of rare beauty. A special treat is lunch in the marble and mosaic conservatory. Rates, including VAT and full Scottish breakfast, range from £85–120 for two; discounts are given in the off-season and for extended stays. All major credit cards.

**The Gleneagles Hotel,** Perthshire, PH3 1NF; tel. (0764) 62134; telex 76105; fax 0764-62134. The brochure quotes a *Morning Post* headline upon the Gleneagles's opening in 1924, "The Scottish Palace in the Glens; The Playground of the Gods." An excusable hyperbole, this is as true today as it was

75 years ago. Gleneagles is one of the outstanding resorts in the world: its 750 acres encompass the King's and Queen's courses, designed by James Braid; the Prince's and Glendevon courses, completed more recently; four all-weather and one lawn tennis court; the Jackie Stewart Shooting School for clay and skeet shooting; the Mark Phillips Equestrian Centre; jogging circuits; shooting, stalking, and fishing; and a Country Club with tropical pool, Jacuzzi, squash courts, and health center with sauna, solarium, massage, and Turkish baths. Rooms are decorated in mauves and umbers, suites feature bow windows and antiques; Eastern rooms have the best views. All rooms have private bath, TV with in-house movies, telephone, and minibar. Rates, inclusive of VAT, start at £65 for a single, £110 for a double, and climb to £215 for suites. Breakfast is not included in these prices. All major credit cards.

## Callander

**Roman Camp Hotel,** Main St., East End FK17 8BG; tel. (0877) 30003. A 17th-century manor house used by the earls of Moray as a shooting lodge, Roman Camp looks like a little château with its low lines, turrets, and bow windows. And it feels like a château, set right beside the river Teith, enveloped in brilliant, fragrant private gardens. The Swiss connection comes from the proprietors, Mr. and Mrs. Denzler, who combine Scots warmth with Swiss precision so that your wants are not so much accommodated as anticipated—somehow they know just what you want before you have to ask—the service is superb. All the rooms overlook gardens or courtyards and are furnished with antiques or good reproductions, bath, TV, phone, and a thoughtful packet of information on amusements in the area. Former satisfied customers range from J. M. Barrie to the Beatles. Aside from the roman camp (first century A.D.) just beyond the southern end of the property, the hotel is a perfect base for touring Stirling and the Trossachs and is an exceptional value, with rooms (including VAT and full breakfast) from £45. No credit cards, but will take a personal check.

## Edinburgh

**Caledonian Hotel,** Princes St., EH1 2AB; tel. (031) 225-2433; telex 72179; fax 031-225-6632. Blue-liveried footmen will usher you in through the brass and mahogany doors of Edinburgh's five-star favorite, the Caley. Try to arrange a fourth or fifth floor room overlooking Princes Street and Gardens in this 1903 grande dame originally built by the Caledonian Railroad over a train station (the track ran through where the front hall stands, and the original station doors and clock have been incorporated in the bar). With a staff of four hundred for 238 rooms, odds are you'll be fussed over and pampered to the nth degree. All rooms are decorated with reproduction antiques, have ample baths, loads of towels, TV with in-house films, minibars, and 24-hour room service. It is the Caley's stated purpose to show off the best of Scotland to the world. From £90 for a double, £225 for suites, not including breakfast. All major credit cards.

**The George,** George St., EH2 2PB; tel. (031) 225-1251; telex 72570. Behind the small hunter green sign on George Street you'll find people enjoying a delicious tea amid the pale blue trim and upholstery, the ornate, impeccably maintained cornices and moldings, and the marble floors of the George—whose west wing was part of Robert Adam's 18th-century plan for Edinburgh's New Town. The rooms in the old wing tend to have more interesting shapes and views, but standard in all 195 rooms are TV, minibar, phone, and smallish bath but well-supplied with toiletries and towels. The hotel has restaurants, bars, and 24-hour room service. Prices for doubles including VAT, excluding breakfast from £99–110, £170 and up for suites. All major credit cards.

**See also Borthwick Castle, 12 miles south of Edinburgh in Gorebridge, below.**

# Glasgow

**Babbity Bowster,** 16/18 Blackfriars St., G1 1PE; tel. (041) 552-5055. Have swashbuckler Fraser Laurie show you the "before" pictures of this recently restored, listed Robert Adam building, and you'll appreciate how hard Fraser's worked and doubly enjoy any one of the six tidy, cozy rooms upstairs over one of Glasgow's favorite cafés. The rooms are small but prettily decorated in dove gray and powder blues with lightwood furnishings. Each has private bath and phone. No TV, no radio, just the basics in bright, centrally located accommodations. Babbity Bowster refers to a traditional 17th-century wedding dance involving bobbing for a pillow; you, too, will kick up your heels at the price: £22.50 for a single, £40 for a double (not including breakfast). Because it's small, pleasant, and reasonable, it's always booked, so call well in advance. AE, MC, V.

**One Devonshire Gardens,** One Devonshire Gardens, G12 0UX; tel. (041) 339-2001. Since its opening in July 1986, Ken McCulloch's country-house-in-town hotel has developed a reputation as being The Place to stay in Glasgow. In an 1860 building in the Victorian West End, the place is pretty close to perfect: there is a unity of design in each of the eight inviting bedrooms, done over in rich navies, unobtrusive grays, deep burgundies, curtains tumbling onto the floor, milk-white pillows cocked waiting to receive your weary head; understated opulence is everywhere evident. Aside from the usual niceties, like TV and phones, there are the little things like potpourri, paisley counterpanes, fresh freesia. And the not-so-little things, like bedroom-sized baths with reproduction antique tubs from Italy. Prices for a double room including VAT and Continental breakfast begin at £95. AE, DC, MC, V.

**The White House,** 11–13 Cleveden Crescent, G12 0PA; tel. (041) 339-9375; telex 777582; fax 041-337-1430. The half-moon of houses in the West End among which the White House (no relation) sits was designed by John Burnet, who is also responsible for the Glasgow Stock Exchange. The hotel itself is an interesting hybrid: Its 32 self-catering units include full kitchens as well as TV, private bath, and phone. It's not quite a guest house, not quite a hotel, but maid service and a full menu of in-room catering service are available. The rooms themselves are cheerily decorated with a mishmash of turn-of-the century pieces and David Hockney prints. There is the occasional decorating gaffe—velour upholstery, electric fireplaces with light-up coals—but mostly things are spacious, gracious, and comfortable. You'll be welcomed with flowers and champagne by an attentive, efficient staff. Prices for a superior double begin at £66. There are also suites, and mews cottages out back sleeping up to five, from £85. Special long-term and weekend discounts are available. Prices include VAT but not breakfast. All major credit cards.

## Gorebridge

**Borthwick Castle,** North Middleton, Midlothian EH23 4QY; tel. (0875) 20514. Twelve miles south of Edinburgh, just north of the Borders, this is a great base from which to tour both city and country. To get to the castle, drive through a little glen with lambs skipping by until the twin towers of this solid 15th-century keep come into view and you (as did Mary, Queen of Scots, who came before) will know you've arrived. The queen was once married to the earl of Bothwell and probably spent the night in the elegant room, with its massive four-poster and crimson hangings, that bears her name. Aside from heating and plumbing and fresh paint, the 20th-century intrusions are kept to a minimum, and you can sense here, as nowhere else in Scotland, that you're living in a medieval castle, with its 14-foot-thick stone walls and its 40-foot vaulted great hall complete with thundering fire, suits of armor, and overhanging minstrel's gallery. History is omnipresent but not oppressive: there is a framed letter from Cromwell to the proprietor of the castle, dated 1650, giving an ultimatum—which was ignored—and the Roundheads besieged the place; there is a chapel with relics used by Mary. Including full breakfast and VAT, high-season rates range from £70–95; off-season, £50–85. The hotel is closed Jan. and Feb. AE, DC, V.

## Kelso

**Sunlaws House Hotel,** Roxburghshire, TD5 8JZ; tel. (05735) 331; telex 728147 Sunlaw G. Sunlaws' 200 acres are situated in the heart of the Borders, and 60 percent of the hotel's clientele is here for hunting and fishing. This keeps the atmosphere unstuffy and unfussy: Don't be surprised to find your fellow guests leaving their muddy boots in the entryway and striding, stocking-footed, up to the bar. The family of the present proprietors, the Duke and Duchess of Roxburgh, attest that a house (not this one) has been here for five hundred years and that Bonnie Prince Charlie was entertained here in '45 by Lady Chatto. It is also speculated that she is the Lady in Green who has occasionally been seen walking along the inner hall or out by the Chinese Bridge. The public rooms offer fireplaces and magazines such as *Stalking* and *Orvis World.* Bedrooms are large and have TV, phones, and baths (but not always showers, so request one if it's important to you). The hotel has an array of special hunting, fishing, horseback riding, and tennis packages available, as well as suggested itineraries for exploring the area's country homes, castles, antique shops, and woolen trail. Needless to say, dogs are most welcome. Prices, including VAT and full breakfast, start at £66 for a double, £90 for a room with a four-poster. AE, DC, MC, V.

# Peat Inn

**The Peat Inn,** Cupar, Fife, KY15 5LH; tel. 033484-206. We have it on the best of authority that David and Patricia Wilson were forced by their customers, some of whom drove from Glasgow and beyond to dine here, to build a residence so that they could enjoy the menu and the wine list to their hearts' content without having to worry about a two-hour drive home. Patricia drew on experiences touring the fine provincial hotels of France when buying for and decorating the eight rooms, all duplex suites except for the Marron Room, which is a suite on one level. The feel is more like staying in an elegant apartment than a hotel room: rich fabrics, loads of closet space, floor-to-ceiling windows, fresh flowers, specially designed stationery, marble bathroom with thick towels and robes, Czech and Speake 88 toiletries flown in fresh from Jermyn St. to match the brass fixtures. Although your tariff card mentions you'll be having a Continental breakfast en suite, that breakfast includes a massive dose of fresh fruit and juices, fresh-baked breads, croissants and brioche, tea or coffee. No one is surprised, but everyone is delighted that the Wilsons have created a small hotel whose comfort and beauty and service are easily equal to those of their excellent restaurant. Closed two weeks in Nov. and two weeks in the beginning of Jan. All major credit cards.

# Peebles

**Cringletie House Hotel,** the Borders EH45 8PL; tel. (072) 13233. A red-stone Victorian house set in a field of daffodils with views down the river Tweed valley toward Peebles, this hotel is under the care of Stanley and Aileen Maguire, who have furnished it with paintings and antiques from their own collection. There is a putting green, hard-surface tennis court, walled kitchen garden (where many items in the larder come from), and 28 acres of walks through sheep fields and woodlands. Bedrooms (request a turret room) are decorated with pastel flowers and antiques; some have original Victorian bathtubs, all have phone and TV. The attic rooms are wee and cozy and share a bath. Doubles are £55, including full breakfast. MC, V.

**Peebles Hotel Hydro,** EH45 8LX; tel. (0721) 20602; telex 72568. The Hydro is one of those grand old resorts to which people came when they were children and return years later with their own children and grandchildren. The clientele is almost completely English and Scottish, so you won't be overrun by "furriners." And no wonder the rate of recidivism is so high; there's lots to do—tennis, croquet, archery, putting, golf, horseback riding, squash, snooker, swimming in a heated indoor pool, sauna, solarium, and gym. Families can do things together, or the kids can be busy with supervised activities while their folks do their own thing. The first Hydro was built as an exclusive Edwardian spa in 1890, burned in 1905, and was rebuilt in 1907. Health is still a primary concern here, with the hotel's water supply piped down from the source on the hill, and the menu always has vegetarian and "health-conscious" selections which list calories and sodium content. Rooms are decorated with modern furnishings in light color schemes to match the view outside your window (southwesterly rooms are the best); all have TV, phone, and private bath. The service is seasoned and expert and practically unflappable (no matter what your kids get into). Prices vary widely according to room size and length and season of stay. Tariff per person for a twin-bed room during the summer season is £46, including full breakfast, dinner, service, and VAT—a very good value indeed. All major credit cards.

## St. Andrews

**The Old Course Golf and Country Club,** St. Andrews KY16 9SP; tel. (0334) 74371; telex 76280. The Old Course Hotel is so smack-dab in the middle of the action that the building itself is actually a hazard. Officially opened in June of 1983 by Princess Anne, it is a modern construction, over half of whose guest rooms survey the Old Course itself and the North Sea beyond. Everything the golfer—from the seasoned pro to the weekend hacker—could wish for is here: pro shop, steward, caddies, five high-profile pros, laundry and club-cleaning services, and a Leisure Club with sauna, steam, whirlpool, swimming pool, and Jacuzzi to soothe you after a taxing afternoon tackling the Road Hole—the peerless, merciless par-4 17th. Although a new facility, the place is dripping with tradition; clubs and photos of the famous line the walls, and brasses on the lockers let you know that your cleats are residing where once those of Trevino, Nicklaus, and Ballesteros did. The 150 rooms all have small but serviceable baths, TV, and lots of wardrobe space. They're comfortable, if a bit hotelish—but after all, you didn't come here to spend the day in your room. All the restaurants and bars also overlook the action, so once you're safely home you can critique the exploits of your fellows from a secure vantage point with a scotch in hand. Rates vary according to season; during the summer a double room with full breakfast is £125. Rates are considerably lower in the off-season, and weekend golfing packages offer a much better value. All major credit cards.

# Edinburgh

"I'll tell you what happens every time," barks veteran cabbie George McDonald over his shoulder, "and it's not just one time I'm talking about, it's hundreds of times. I've had hundreds of people in my cab who are just passing through. And they say to me, 'We planned to be here only for a couple of days, because we didn't know what Edinburgh was all about. If anyone had told us, we'd have spent our whole trip here.'"

Don't let yourself become another grim statistic in George's random sampling. We're here to tell you that Edinburgh is one of the fantastic cities of Europe—nay, of the world—and you should plan to devote a serious portion, if not the entirety, of your holiday here.

The history and disposition of Edinburgh is quite literally a tale of two cities. As soon as you hop off the train at Waverley Station, you'll notice that you're in a valley between two hills—where you'd expect a river to be rather than a rail terminal. To your left you'll see the majestic bulk of Edinburgh Castle, recumbent and resplendent on an ancient volcanic hill worn down by glaciers. To your right are the façades of Princes Street, and a Gothic pavilion dedicated to the pen and patriotism of Sir Walter Scott.

Edinburgh's twins—medieval Old Town and Georgian New Town—are quite different in atmosphere and scope, but each is equally fetching in its own way. And each provides a vivid contrast of backdrops for the annual Edinburgh Festival, held here from early August and nowadays spilling into September in order to accommodate the plentitude of artistry that flourishes in the fresh summer air. The city hums, buzzes, sings with everything from symphony orchestras to street artists on kazoo.

The great thing about the festival is that it isn't merely a once-a-year pop that ignites, explodes, and dies; the festival's energy permeates the city even when August has come and gone. In January and in June, there is always a vast variety of cultural activities available to give head and heart a workout.

Even as the hillside city's streets give your heart and hamstrings a workout. By all means walk everywhere. That's the best way to get the bipartite feel of the Robert Adam-inspired squares and avenues of the New Town and the steep twisted stairs and multistory medieval tenements of the Old Town. Edinburgh is an elegant, self-assured metropolis, a mysterious, romantic burgh. Romantic? Most certainly.

**For a map of Edinburgh, see atlas pages 24–25.**

## The Edinburgh Festival

There are the "official" festival offerings, for which there is print-ed a serious brochure every preceding spring. Information on this summer's festival can be obtained by writing to Edinburgh Festi-val August '89, Dept. L, 21 Market Street, Edinburgh EH1 1BW, Scotland. Or phone (031) 226-4001. Schedules are usually final-ized by early May, and some of the more popular events sell out almost instantly, so if you possibly can, do plan and write ahead. Concurrently running is the Fringe Festival, which is the venue for more risky, forward-looking theater, dance, music, et al. This is the real heart and guts of the festival. Every day the Fringe office produces a broadsheet, printed in tiny lettering and cramped spacing just chockablock with events. Listings begin usually around 8:30 A.M. and tear through the day and on into the wee hours of the next morning.

If you're at all keen, you'll realize that this annual saturnalia encompasses not one but several festivals. Here are the pertinent statistics for contacting each: Edinburgh Festival Fringe, Box CE, The Fringe Office, 170 High Street, Edinburgh EH1 1QS; tel. (031) 226-5257/5259. Edinburgh International Folk Festival; tel. (031) 220-0464. Edinburgh International Jazz Festival, (031) 557-1642. Filmhouse/Edinburgh International Film Festival, (031) 228-6382. And as if these items weren't enough to set your head spinning, by far the most popular event during festival time is the Edinburgh Military Tattoo, a Cecil B. de Mille-goes-military extravaganza starring Scotland's own massed pipes-and-drums bands and a list of special guest stars that changes annually. Infor-mation and booking forms can be obtained through The Tattoo Office, 22 Market Street, Edinburgh EH1 1QB; tel. (031) 225-1188. Tickets for most events (some Fringe offerings being the outstanding exception) can be purchased over the phone using a credit card, so whether you hail from Perth, Perthshire, or from Perth, Western Australia, you can have your tickets in hand be-fore you leave the house—or the hemisphere.

Every effort is made to accommodate the disabled at festival events. The festival publishes a leaflet describing facilities and accessibility (toilets, guide dogs, parking) at each of the principal venues. The leaflet can be obtained through the 21 Market Street address above. Also available to would-be festival goers is ARTLINK, which runs a free escort service staffed by volunteers who will drive or accompany any disabled visitors to the events and also provides information about museums, theaters, and gal-leries throughout the city and throughout the rest of the year. They can be contacted at ARTLINK (Edinburgh and the Lothi-ans), 4 Forth Street, Edinburgh EH1 3LD; tel. (031) 556-6350.

One final word: the city is jam-packed during this time, so be sure to acquire accommodations early. Information and a booking form can be had from Advance Reservations, Tourist Centre, 3 Princes Street, Edinburgh EH2 2QP; tel. (031) 557-2727.

# The Castle of Scottish Kings

The romance evolves from the history, and the history properly begins on **Castle Rock,** where you should properly begin your tour. The castle parking lot will cost you £1 for two hours (not necessarily sufficient time to see the place). The castle is open weekdays from 9:30 A.M. to 5:30 P.M., Sundays from 11 A.M. to 5:30 P.M.; admission is £2.20. There is evidence of building on the site as early as the sixth century, but nothing worthy of being dignified by the word *castle* appeared until the 11th century. At that time the group of buildings existing here was frequented by King Malcolm III and his queen, later canonized St. Margaret for her generosity and tireless efforts in promoting Catholicism. The only structure extant from that period is St. Margaret's Chapel.

It was not until the reign of James IV in the 16th century that the castle came into its own as the primary seat of Scots governance and was endowed with structures worthy of such an august position. As the castle grew more vital as a military stronghold, it grew less appealing as a royal residence, and comfort-seeking rulers decamped down the road to Holyrood.

You walk through a series of gates past an array of batteries, each constructed as deemed necessary while the castle spread its girth ever wider atop the rock. One of the batteries is still a working one. Every day from Mill's Mount Battery, looking north, is sounded the sternum-throbbing One O'Clock Gun, a modern war machine fired at this rather unorthodox hour, as the cheekier guides will tell you, because the parsimonious Scots don't want to waste all their ammo launching twelve shots at noon.

As you tour around, take advantage of the guides employed by the castle to assist you. They're extremely well-informed and extremely patient and pleasant about answering questions for the millionth time. You'll recognize them because they're wearing tartan trousers.

**Crown Square** is a tetrahedron of buildings including the **Scottish National War Memorial** (1924–27), **The Palace** (early 16th century), which contains the Crown Jewels of Scotland—much more elegant and much less fussy than the headgear displayed in London, and the **Great Hall.** The latter is paneled in oak, carved in Scottish geometrics with an oak hammer-beam roof, a structure so-called because it was constructed by drilling and pegging the timbers together. The beams are hammered together; no nails or screws are involved. The result looks like the upside-down belly of a ship, and indeed these roofs were built on many of the same principles, using some of the same craftsmen and materials. This particular ceiling was erected in 1503.

The **regimental museums** located in various buildings of the castle are best appreciated by aficionados. The general public might enjoy seeing Mons Meg, a monster of a cannon that actually blew up (fatally) in the king's face when he was showing it off to his queen. Meg, a Flemish lass, can be seen in the vaults.

## The Royal Mile

Sweeping down from the Castle is the **Royal Mile,** named because all the gentry—who wanted to have at close hand the king's ear for influence and the king's fortress for defense—settled in the tenements down the street from His Highness. Along the Royal Mile are some of Edinburgh's most important sights, along with the bevy of cashmere and shortbread hawkers that must inevitably follow when so many attractions are grouped along one thoroughfare. Unless you get up early in the morning and are hard at your touring all day, it will be difficult to fit everything worth seeing along the Royal Mile into a day. It's best to select the three or four addresses you think would appeal most to you, and include the Castle and Holyrood Palace parenthetically at either end of the street.

One item we would also urge be included on everyone's list is **Gladstone's Land** (open April through October, Monday through Saturday from 10 A.M. to 5 P.M., and Sunday from 2 to 5 P.M.; November, Saturday from 10 A.M. to 4:30 P.M., Sunday from 2 to 4:30 P.M. Closed December through March; admission £1.50). Thomas Gledstanes (as his name was originally spelled) built the house in 1620. It is full of period antiques—not necessarily those of the inhabitants. There are some fine examples of oyster-shell inlay, furniture which is made by slicing beautifully grained wood into lozenges and laying them out in a pattern of concentric, irregular circles. Most impressive is the bedchamber with its painted ceiling. Before the National Trust for Scotland took over the house, the ceiling was plastered over. Quite by accident the fruit-flocked beams were discovered, then uncovered and restored. The golden eagle hanging outside was found in pieces in the basement.

Also along the Royal Mile (whose actual street names—to make things more complicated—are Lawnmarket, High and Cannongate) in descending order from the castle you'll find the **Camera Obscura** (open Monday through Friday from 9:30 A.M. to 6 P.M.; Saturday from 10 A.M. to 6 P.M.; Sunday from 10 A.M. to 7 P.M.; admission, £1.45). As you wait to enter, you can take some snapshots of the city from the lookout. Once inside the little room, you are essentially inside the box of a camera whose lens is atop the building. Images are filtered through a series of mirrors onto a white table in the center of the room, which serves much the same purpose as would the film. The difference is that you see live-action shots, as a chipper guide tours you around the town in ten minutes. Try to go on a sunny day, or the image is apt to be a bit dark and colorless.

Across the street is the **Scotch Whiskey Heritage Centre** (open seven days). This is a recent addition to the street's attractions; an ambitious audiovisual spectacle explores the history of the making of, and the maintaining of, whisky.

**Lady Stair's House** is tucked down Lady Stair's Close on your left as you walk down the hill (open Monday through Saturday from 10 A.M. to 5 P.M., Sunday from 2 to 5 P.M.; admission, free). This museum is somewhat slavishly devoted to Scotland's triumvirate of writers—Burns, Scott, Stevenson—with model scenes from the lives of the poets, items of a household nature that belonged to the poets, portraits of the poets, and scenes from their works.

Just beyond the George IV Bridge crossing is the plaza bordered by **Parliament House** (1632–40). This building, now the supreme court, is worth a look for the hammer-beam roof of its Great Hall and the portraits of Scottish luminaries painted by Scottish luminaries hung beneath. (Open Tuesday through Friday, from 10 A.M. to 4 P.M.; admission, free.)

In the middle of the plaza is a heart set into the paving stones. The older lads refer to this as "Spittle in the Middle", and attest that if you can hit this mark on your way to work, you'll be lucky for the rest of the day.

The ecclesiastical building on the south side of the square is commonly referred to as **St. Giles' Cathedral** but is properly referred to as the High Kirk of St. Giles, named for a Greek saint, Egidius. Before you enter, enjoy the crown spire, resting delicately atop an eight-pointed joist of buttresses. There has been a church here since the 9th century, although this building, much altered in the 19th century, dates structurally from the 15th. The interior is a varied mishmash of styles and monuments to heroes. Aside from the regular order of services, most popular is St. Giles' at Six, a weekly recital of music each Sunday evening. A list of upcoming programs is available as you enter.

At 45 High Street is the **John Knox House,** built c. 1490 (open Monday through Saturday from 10 A.M. to 5 P.M.; winter hours, from 10 A.M. to 4 P.M.; £1). A video explains Knox and the house, which is of primary interest to historians, Presbyterians, and architecture buffs. The latter will enjoy the fireplaces' delft tiles and the city's finest painted ceiling, depicting a hermaphroditic devil, flowers, and animals.

Also of interest is the **Acheson House,** a 17th-century house that also served at one time as a brothel; now the wares it displays are those of local artisans, and it serves as the Scottish National Craft Centre (open Monday through Saturday from 10 A.M. to 5:30 P.M.; admission, free).

**The Huntly House** (open June through September, Monday through Saturday from 10 A.M. to 6 P.M.; winter hours, till 5; admission, free) is the museum of the City of Edinburgh, and it outlines the city's history with pictures, documents, and a collection of locally produced ceramics and silver.

Stop in the shops at 13A James Court—a close just beyond Gladstone's Land—for **Clan Bagpipes.** They make the pipes right before your very eyes or will sell you kits to do it yourself. The **Cason Clark Gallery** at 173 Cannongate has maps—antique and unusual—from all over the world. Across the street at number 172 is our favorite, **Cadenheads Whisky Shop,** where they have the produce (12 to 70 years old) from 117 distilleries (for £17 to £3,000). Cadenheads has all the major brands as well as black-and-white-labeled bottles that can't be found elsewhere. They will ship. Pop the cork on a Springback 21—divinely smooth.

## Palace of British Kings and Scottish Queens

At last, at the foot of the Royal Mile is **Holyrood Palace.** A pair of double-turreted towers overlook a courtyard that has seen much action over the centuries. Since it is still a royal residence (Her Majesty *et famille* stay here when they're city-hopping down from Balmoral), you are obliged to be breezed through on a brisk, if not brusque, tour given by quick-talking guides. This notwithstanding, pay your £1.60 (open Monday through Saturday from 9:30 A.M. to 5:15 P.M., Sunday from 10:30 A.M. to 4:30 P.M.; closed during royal visits). Enter at the Grand Staircase, where there's a portrait of the present Elizabeth looking a bit pinched. The primary glories of the palace are the ceilings of ornate, pendulous plaster designed by John Hulbert and George Dunsterfield. The most salacious palace associations are centered in the north turret and begin with Lord Darnley's bedroom, complete with a glass-encased 16th-century, ostrich-tasseled and velvet-canopied bed. Upstairs is the bedroom of his consort, Mary, Queen of Scots, with frieze and ceiling paintings including the heraldry of Mary's parents, James and Mary. In the corner is a door, only recently rediscovered, used by Darnley and several of his supporters to sneak into the queen's bedroom and into the closet of her "secretary," David Riccio, who was dragged from there and murdered before the eyes of the horrified Mary. Outside the palace are the remains of the 12th-century Holyrood Abbey, in which the Sinclairs, Mary's royal huntsmen, are buried. Have a peek at the rock garden (closed to the public) out back.

## The Museums

The Royal Mile is only the beginning of Edinburgh's amalgam of riches. A trio of museums awaits, deployed all about the town. Just off the Royal Mile on Chambers Street is the **Royal Museum of Scotland,** housed in an 1866 amassment of Victorian glass atria. Its exhibits begin with pre-history and work their way through the Middle and industrial ages. There are also natural history, geology, and visiting exhibits. (Open Monday through Saturday from 10 A.M. to 5 P.M., Sunday from 2 to 5 P.M.; admission, free.)

The **National Gallery of Scotland** is an 1850s William Playfair Classical construction on the Mound (a man-made hillock built of earth excavated as the New Town was being constructed). There is a quickie video explaining the museum and the collection, or you can just dive right into this sanely sized, comprehensive collection with works by Raphael, del Sarto, Titian, El Greco, Rubens, and Vermeer up through Courbet, Renoir, and Pissarro. Do take in the Scottish painting galleries, rich with Ramsays and Raeburns as well as lesser-known, but no less talented artists. The gallery is open Monday through Saturday from 10 A.M. to 5 P.M., Sunday from 2 to 5 P.M.; some exhibits are closed for a noon to 2 P.M. lunch break during the winter. Admission is free.

Finally there is the **Scottish National Gallery of Modern Art,** a bit tricky to get to in the northwestern suburbs; call for directions (031-556-8921). This museum lives in a splendid former school building set well back from the road behind an expanse of clovery lawn, under whose trees and amid whose squirrels are arranged objects from the sculpture collection. Inside you'll find a few examples each of Picasso, Kokoschka, Klee, and Matisse as well as important Scots moderns such as Mactaggart, James, Peploe, Bone, and Cameron. Events and special exhibits are listed on the information board to your left as you enter. (Open Monday through Saturday from 10 A.M. to 5 P.M., Sunday from 2 to 5 P.M.; admission, free.) There's a shop and restaurant/café that sells wine and beer.

## New-Town Touring, Old-Town Shopping

A tour of Georgian Edinburgh should include a walk along George Street from Charlotte to St. Andrew squares. Along the north side of the former is the **Georgian House** (1766–1840), an NTS property that re-creates the interior of 19th-century mansion. Videos explaining the Georgian House and the New Town are on view in the basement. (Open Monday through Saturday from 10 A.M. to 5 P.M., Sunday from 2 to 5 P.M.; in winter till 4:30; admission, £1.80.)

For shopping take a stroll down **Victoria Street** in the Old Town, a steep curve replete with antique stores. Check out **Pine and Old Lace,** which has camisoles and commodes. **Byzantium** is a crafts market at the Preservation Hall (where music is the rule in the evening). **Kinnells** is a good stop for picnic stuffs. Continue on down and to the right for the pubs of **Grassmarket,** or go left and up to the shops along **Candlemaker Row,** where there are secondhand clothes at numbers 58 and 62. Across the street is **Back Beat Records,** selling new and used and heavy on the blues, including Blues 'n' Trouble, Edinburgh's own R&B masters.

## Day Trips
As if there weren't enough to tax your shoe leather in town, several intriguing half- and full-day trips are easily accomplished.

### Culross and Dunfermline
Both north of the city, the former is an entire 16-to-17th-century town preserved by the National Trust, and the latter is Robert the Bruce's royal capital. Culross is an inhabited village, not a frozen-in-time museum. While it's important and fitting that the town be kept lively in this way, it also means that only a few of the buildings are open to the public. They include the **Jacobean Palace,** with fine portraits and paneling; and the **Study,** a 17th-century town house with painted ceiling and period furniture. Hours of opening vary with the mood of the somewhat cantankerous caretaker; it's wise to call in advance, (0383) 880-359, so as not to be disappointed.

Dunfermline, an otherwise gray, gritty town, is best appreciated for its **Abbey Church,** which is the Scots equivalent of Westminster Abbey (it claims to be the resting place of twenty-odd Royals, including Robert Bruce). The abbey itself is a restored Norman edifice. Also of interest is **Andrew Carnegie's birthplace** on Moodie Street. It's quite an eye-opener to see the erstwhile steel czar's humble beginnings as the son of a Fife country weaver.

### Roslin
South of the city is Roslin, where you'll find the astonishing **Rosslyn Chapel,** dedicated to St. Matthew in 1450. The chapel (open daily from 10 A.M. to 5 P.M., from 12 to 5 P.M. on Sundays; admission, £1.25) is fairly unprepossessing from the outside as you circumambulate the structure, and it's just as well because the beauty and craftsmanship of the interior come as a greater surprise and delight. Inside, under a three-foot-thick roof, is a veritable lacework of stone draped delicately about every niche and crevice. Down through the church's checkered history comes the tale of the master and the apprentice: While the former was away, the latter carved a pillar of such rare and delicate detail that when the master returned he was so consumed with jealousy that he murdered the apprentice, a crime that caused him to be hanged and the church to be reconsecrated. At the baptistry end of the church, on the three pillars by the entrance to the Baptistry, are depicted the master, the apprentice (with a gash in his forehead), and the apprentice's weeping mother. Other high-

lights include carvings of the seven vices and virtues, the Dance of Death, and various other ecclesiastical favorites.

## Linlithgow Palace and Hopetoun House

West of Edinburgh are two fine castles drenched in history. **Linlithgow Palace** was once graced by the Stewart monarchs, who liked its situation for defense and hunting. James V was born here a year before his father's death at Flodden Field, and Mary, Queen of Scots' consort, Lord Darnley, died nearby in a mysterious explosion. The present state of the palace is as a ruin, but many of the interior details and fireplaces and much of the stonework are intact.

East of Linlithgow toward the city is **Hopetoun House** (open daily May 1 to mid–September, from 11 A.M. to 5:30 P.M.; admission to the house and grounds, £2.50). The building was begun by William Bruce in 1699, was continued by William Adam until his death in 1748, and was completed in 1767 by Adam's sons, Robert, James, and John. The opulent interiors include 18th-century furniture and a respectable collection of paintings.

If you're up for spending for lunch, the **Champany Inn,** just outside of Linlithgow at the junction of the A803 and the A904, has some of Lothian's finest food—superlative steaks—and an acclaimed wine list. For simpler, lower-priced fare try some of the pubs-with-a-view under the Forth Bridge on the water in Queensferry, down the road from Hopetoun.

## THE EAST LOTHIAN COAST

To reach the coast, take the B1348 to the A198 out from Musselburgh. There's lots to do: beautiful beaches from Aberlady Bay to John Muir Country Park in Dunbar, formidable castle ruins in Dirleton and Tantallon, championship golf at Muirfield.

But all of this activity is merely a means for occupying the rest of your day before and/or after you've lunched at **La Poitiniere** in Gullane (see below)—an event that will properly keep you busy all afternoon. Do call ahead for reservations (before you leave home, if you can), but if you're unsuccessful beforehand, keep trying; there are often same-day cancellations.

## ⚜ RESTAURANTS

**The Barony Bar,** 81/83 Broughton St., tel. (031) 557-0546. On the east side of town, this is actually a pub-cum-wine bar, but they serve great food, above and beyond the call of pub grub, like Crofters Mutton Pie and Smoked Haddie Crumble. There's also a good whisky selection. Dinner with wine costs about £10. AE, MC, V.

**Café Royal Oyster Bar,** 17A West Register St., tel. (031) 556-4124. Next-door to the Café Royal Bar, the entire building has many important literary and political associations since it opened in 1862 as a gentlemen's club. It also has an incredibly beautiful decor, featuring tile murals of famous inventors and elaborately decorated ceilings and windows. The food is pricey but excellent. Of course, try the oysters—plain with lemon and brown bread, or fancy with jalapeño, cream, and nutmeg. Main courses revolve around fish, but game and steaks are also available and delicious. There are only eight tiny tables, so reservations are a must. £25 will buy a good meal with wine. MC, V.

**The Howtowdie,** 27a Stafford St., tel. (031) 225-6291. This is the name you'll get when you query locals about where to go for Scots food. Howtowdie is a dish Mary, Queen of Scots' Gallic chefs concocted in good Auld-Alliance fashion. It's still on the menu here, complete with spinach nest and drappit (poached) egg. You can, in fact, also get haggis with a creamy leek sauce, plus Cullen Skink, Scotch beef, venison, and salmon. À la carte, or a six-course Taste of Scotland menu with coffee and short-bread is £25 plus service. All major credit cards.

**Le Mange Tout,** 6 Union St., tel. (031) 558-1467. On an otherwise unremarkable street you'll find this sweet little spot—lace curtains, sparsely funished, pink and white cloths. There are a few mistakes, like a nasty green carpet and paper napkins, but the food—soup de mer with ginger and basil, rabbit in prunes, duck in cassis, salmon in red pepper—is imaginative and quite reasonable: the prix-fixe dinner costs £10.50. Closed Sun. and Mon. All major credit cards.

**Merchants,** 17 Merchant St., tel. (031) 225-4009. Merchants has raw wood floors with a smattering of sawdust, cane chairs, whitewashed stone walls, polka-dot bow-tied waiters, pots of ivy hanging from the beams, a huge overflowing basket of breads and toast as you are seated, and Pierre the parrot overlooking the action. Specialties include cream of cucumber soup with mint and sorrel, smoked duck, lamb with wild mushrooms, and shark steak on a bed of samphire with a tarragon sauce. Prix-fixe lunch costs £7.50 or dinner at £13.50, and there's also an à la carte menu. A small wine list has recommended vintages at the back. Closed Sun. and all of Nov. AE, MC.

**La Poitiniere,** Main St., Gullane, East Lothian; tel. (0620) 843-214. Plan a day trip around this magical wee place (op.cit. above)—even if you have only a few days in Edinburgh (and plan ahead; reservations are scarce). Hilary Brown, essentially self-taught, does the kitchen duties, and David Brown does everything(!) else. In the front room of a tiny cottage behind a wishing well you'll find lace curtains, an Oriental carpet, mulberry petit print wallpaper, and a little card by the door informing you of the day's offering: a no-choice, prix-fixe meal, the equal of which you'd have to swim across the Channel to find. At your place you'll find a name card and never less than three tiers of dinner-ware. Luncheon begins with a pea soup garnished with a cream daub and mint sprig. A mousseline of swirled pink salmon and white sole follows. The entrée is a *poulet à la francaise,* perfectly prepared and presented. Last is cheese or a praline soufflé. And this is only an example; the menu changes daily, and Hilary starts from scratch every morning. David has three cellars and several other rooms devoted to storing the wines on his 45-page list, which can only be described as astonishing in quality and scope, with plenty of ready-now vintages at sane prices. Luncheon begins at 1 P.M. and lasts easily till 4 and beyond. It would be unseemly to beg you to come here, but we would if we could. Lunch *only* Mon.–Fri. except Wed.; Sat. dinner. Closed all of Oct. and part of Feb. Prix-fixe dinner, £18.50. No credit cards.

**Rafaelli,** 10 and 11 Randolph Pl., tel. (031) 225-6060. The consensus is that this is Edinburgh's best Italian—*molto conoscuto*—as the dangerously charming waiters, all Tuscan imports, will inform you. A not unpleasant sense of Tuscan formality and pride hovers in the air, along with the irresistible scent of veal with sage, *ossobuco alla toscano,* fettucine with smoked salmon and vodka, *filetto* in red wine with artichokes and aubergine. They have a great wine selection, albeit pricey, properly weighted toward the Italian. However, there is a more casual wine bar next-door. Open weekdays for lunch and dinner, Sat. dinner only. Closed Sun. Dinner with wine costs £20. All major credit cards.

The next two entries are on the waterfront in Leith, an up-and-coming area worth exploring and only a cab ride from the town center.

**Skippers Bistro,** 1A Dock Pl., Leith, tel. (031) 554-1018. Menu changes daily according to the fresh catch and is 98 percent seafood. Allan Corbett (brother of one of the Ronnies whose picture is on the wall) became proprietor after breaking away from the Waterfront Wine Bar (see below) to open his own little place. The decor of this previous pub is casual nautical: straw place mats, wood tables, terrapin shells, and lanterns on the walls; the atmosphere is cluttered but cozy. Prix-fixe menu, £10.25 for two courses, £13 for three, both including coffee. Try the halibut with saffron and smoked mussel sauce, sole paupiettes with prawn mousseline, or langoustines in *beurre d'ail.* Reservations are strongly recommended. Closed Sun. AE, MC, V.

**Waterfront Wine Bar,** Dock Pl., Leith, tel. (031) 554-7427. Reds and rosés, whites and bubblies are listed in polychrome chalk on the blackboard in the front of this former waiting (for boats to dock) room. It is presently paneled with wine-case butts and set with wooden booths arranged to allow for cozy, remote corners. The bartender says the food is "Frenchy-Scots"; it includes oysters, prawns, salmon en croute with watercress mayonnaise; lamb gigot with raspberry sauce, and cheese and oatcakes for dessert. In back is a garden greenhouse with arbor by a finger of water; there are also outdoor picnic tables. Prices are terrific, with entrées £4–6. No credit cards.

## PUBS

**Athletic Arms,** Henderson and Angle Park Terraces. Better known as The Diggers. Spit-and-sawdust dive, best ale in town. It's hard to find, so take a cab.

**Bennetts,** 8 Leven St. This pub with African mahogany bar, gold moldings, painted tiles, and jug bar for women and children has been around since 1839.

**Café Royal,** West Register St. A landmark pub with 360-degree bar, narrow, slippery booths, marble floors, and a long literary and political history.

# Glasgow

"Glasgow's miles better," proclaims recent tourist board PR. "Miles better than Edinburgh," is the inevitable implication of the slogan. Yet as the capital city rests serenely—some would say smugly—on her hills and her laurels, 45 miles away, Glasgow is roaring into the 1990s. A glorious garden festival exploded onto the scene last year; for the inauguration of the decade, Glasgow has been named European City of Culture for 1990; and the annual Mayfest has been very canny about uncovering and attracting artists on the cutting edge of the cultural scene. Even the staunchest Edinburgh supporter would ruefully admit that Glasgow is charged with energy and enthusiasm and is poised to burst, supernova-wise, into competition with the centuries-celebrated artistic capitals of Europe.

And it couldn't happen to a nicer town. In all this dusting off and refurbishing, what's emerging is a beautiful Victorian city with public buildings and residential areas shamefully overlooked by the tromp of tourists through Scotland only a few short years ago. Aside from some lovely physical attributes, Glasgow's greatest assets are the Glaswegians themselves. You'd have to look far an' wee around the globe to find city folk who are as amiable, sociable, good-natured, helpful, and humorous as the sons and daughters of Strathclyde. They'll chat you up on the Underground, they'll walk you to your destination instead of merely giving directions, they'll buy you pints, they'll help you with your bags—all as if it were the most natural thing in the world to be kind and congenial, because for them it is. For them nothing is more important than that a stranger should share their own pride and excitement in being a part of Britain's biggest renaissance.

**For a map of Glasgow see atlas pages 26–27.**

## A Glance at Glasgow's History

The Glasgow coat of arms depicts a salmon and a ring, referring to a legend from the days of St. Mungo, the city's patron: A jealous husband accused his wife of infidelity. She pleaded innocence, but he pointed out that a ring he had given her was missing from her finger. The wife protested that she had not given it to a lover but merely had lost it. The husband would not be moved and sentenced his wife to death. St. Mungo saved the day by retrieving the ring from the belly of a Scottish salmon.

St. Mungo began preaching in these parts in the sixth century on land said to have been blessed by St. Ninian at the end of the fourth century. Under David I, Glasgow was established as the center of the diocese of Strathclyde, and a suitably ambitious cathedral was in the works by 1136. Completing the city's identity as an important seat of sacred and secular thought was the founding of the university in 1451.

Glasgow's ascendance to a position of might in Britain began in the late 17th century as a result of trade with the North American colonies. Although detested by patriotic Scots, the Union of 1707, incorporating the Scottish Parliament into the English, enabled Scottish ships to operate directly to the New World. Beginning with sugar and rum, culminating in tobacco and cotton, the town grew in shipping might because transit time from the Americas to Glasgow was up to twenty days shorter than to London. As shipping boomed, so did the shipbuilding industry, and when the Clyde proved too narrow and shallow to accommodate the city's grandiose schemes, the game Glaswegians merely enlarged the river, hence the ubiquitous slogan: "The Clyde made Glasgow and Glasgow made the Clyde."

Inevitably, as heavy industry in the north declined so did northern cities, and after being known as the Second City of Empire, Glasgow became famous, or rather infamous, as the home of Gorbals, a slum seething with poverty and socialism. In the 1920s the Red Clydesiders rocked the walls of the House of Commons with their tempestuous orations. To this day Glaswegian MPs shore up the Labour Party and are a perpetual thorn in the side of Thatcherism.

As the city's history is splattered across the centuries, so too are her sites splattered across the miles. While you can easily walk around the shopping streets surrounding George Square, the galleries about the university, and the vestiges of the medieval community supporting the cathedral, you'll need to use some form of public transport to get from one of these centers to the other. Buses cover the most territory and run until 11:30 P.M. Exact change is required for fares, which vary according to the distance of your journey, so keep plenty of change on hand. The Underground loops its way around the center of town and is good for getting out to the West End and the university. The Underground does not run in the evening or all day Sunday. Fare depends on destination. Information on bus and Underground stops and scheduling can be obtained from Strathclyde Passenger Transport (041-226-4826).

Taxis are cheap, plentiful, and piloted by able, amiable gents. Phone the Taxi Cab Association (332-6666) or Taxi Owners Association (332-7070). If you're stuck finding a cab downtown at night, they'll be queuing at Central and Queen Street stations. Crime is a problem in Glasgow, so don't wander around (especially unattended ladies) in unknown areas (especially along the river) after dark.

# The Burrell Collection

Glasgow's primary points of interest are spread wide about the Clyde, so it takes a bit of doing to do them all. Case in point: the Burrell (pronounced "burl") Collection. Downtown buses 10, 11, 45, 48A, and 57 service the Pollockshaws Road entrance, and jitneys shuttle you from bus stop to museum.

Despite the modicum of distance and difficulty to overcome, this unique and exquisite collection should not be missed. It is mind-boggling to consider that on amassment of treasures as fine and vast as this (there are 8,000-plus items displayed on a regular rotation) was the life's obsession of a single individual. Sir William Burrell made his fortune aggrandizing the family's ship holdings. Today, the Burrell Collection stands unrivaled as the most popular attraction in Scotland. The museum is open Monday through Saturday, from 10 A.M. to 5 P.M., Sunday from 2 to 5 P.M. Admission is free. Guided tours begin at 2:30 P.M. Wednesday nights at 7:30 there is a program of chamber music for £4. For information and schedules of events, phone (041) 649-7151. Grab a gallery plan at the information desk on your left as you enter.

Burrell's panoptic taste began with the ancient world, and the collection includes Persian, Egyptian, Greek, and Roman pottery; stone and bronze work; glassware; Oriental ceramics; medieval stained glass from France, Germany, the Netherlands, and England; European paintings including Flemish masters Hans Memling and Lucas Cranach, a Bellini *Madonna and Child,* and a froth of French: Delacroix, Daumier, Degas, Courbet, Corot, and Cézanne. There are Rembrandt oils, Dürer engravings—the list is exhaustive.

Last are three rooms from Burrell's home, Hutton Castle, disassembled and rebuilt, timber by timber, with all their 15th- and 16th-century furniture and tapestries intact.

# The City Through the Ages

The earliest monuments of Glasgow are found on the hillock in the northeastern part of the city:

At **Glasgow Cathedral** (open 9:30 A.M. to 7 P.M., and from 2 to 5 P.M. on Sundays; winter hours till 4; admission, free) services, 11 A.M. and 6:30 P.M. Sundays, begin and end with piano music. The church is dedicated to St. Mungo (the familiar name of St. Kentigern), whose remains lie in the Lower Church. It is the only medieval church in Scotland that is almost entirely intact, consecrated in 1136 and again in 1197. The building work was finished in the early 14th century, with the improvements introduced by Robert Blackadder, Glasgow's first archbishop. The 15th-century choir screen, or *pulpitum,* is the only one surviving from the period; above the entrance are carved the seven deadly sins. The carving throughout the cathedral exemplifies the 13th-century stiff-leaf style, incorporating foliage and beasts; check out the bosses in the Lady Chapel, the capitals on the pillars surrounding St. Mungo's tomb, and the area atop the choir arcade.

Across the street from the cathedral is **Provand's Lordship,** the oldest house in Glasgow, dating from 1471. It was a manse for St. Nicholas Hospital and the residence for various bishops, whose guests included James II and Mary, Queen of Scots. The building is rife with exposed distressed beams wrapped by iron bars, which have not prevented floors and ceilings from sagging in a charming way. Furnishings run the gamut from 16th through 20th century. (Open Monday through Saturday from 10 A.M. to 5 P.M., Sunday from 2 to 5 P.M.)

Bouncing blithely through the centuries you'll find central Glasgow, where the city's Victorian-era glories, financed by the tobacco lords and their ilk, are situated. Begin in **George Square,** the center of the city center. Along the eastern verge are the **City Chambers;** by all means arrange to be here to take a 45-minute guided tour (which run 10:30 A.M. or 2:30 P.M. weekdays, but schedules may vary due to civic duties, so call first, 227-4017). More than likely the Lord Provost's ample ebony Rolly will be parked out front (license, GO) of this 1888 William Young extravaganza of a building, one of the great town halls of Europe. The inside is ablaze with marble, granite, mosaics, gilt—materials gathered from around the land and around the world.

## Shoppers' Options

Now is the time to do all your shopping. The stores along St. Vincent Street (check out the **Scottish Design Centre** at number 72), and the shopping centers of Buchannan Street and Princes Mall, are loaded with knitwear, tweeds, and tartans as well as designer fashions whisked in from around the world (drop in at **Fraser's Department Store** for a facial). **The Briggait** at 72 Clyde Street is an 1873 fishmarket that is now home to Glasgow's glitteriest specialty shops for clothes, crafts, and gifts. The hippest fashions in town, however, are to be had at **ichi ni san,** 123 Candleriggs (the sign above the door is all but illegible); the small but important group of designers represented create spare, elegant styles. Not cheap.

If you need a stiffening of backbone during these spending forays, the **Potstill** at 154 Hope St. has the largest selection of whiskies in the city and, most likely, in the world. Sip a dram of any of several hundred.

You can't speak of shopping in Glasgow without mentioning **the Barras,** touted as Europe's largest flea market. Five hundred-plus vendors set up shop on weekends from around 8 A.M. to 4 P.M. in this labyrinth of stalls and street entertainers and roustabouts—twice the size of London markets, half the tourists, half the price.

It is essential when at the Barras, or merely when in Glasgow, to have a jar at the **Saracen's Head** (pronounced various ways by the locals), at 209 Gallowgate. A 1755 coaching inn, the place specializes in ciders and something they call a white tornado, decanted from an old tun with a dragon crawling up the side. It has mellowed from the old days, when it was clear white lightning; the present brew is better described as a kick-ass sherry.

## The West End

In the western reaches of the city lie the university and a marvelous conglomeration of museums. As with nearly all Glasgow's terrific collections, these museums are free except the Mackintosh rooms at the Hunterian Art Gallery, where there is a charge of 50 pence weekday afternoons and Saturdays. Besides the minor savings, it makes sense to begin here in the morning because it allows you to work your way downhill through Kelvingrove Park as you proceed.

**Hunterian Art Gallery** (open Monday through Saturday from 9 A.M. to 5 P.M.) and **Mackintosh House** (open 9:30 A.M. to 12:30 P.M. and from 1:30 to 5 P.M.; Saturday till 1). Most important here is the James MacNeill Whistler collection, bequeathed to Glasgow by the painter's sister-in-law and executrix, who upon his death sent the city essentially the contents of this provocative artist's studio. Also interesting are the Mackintosh rooms, transported from his 6 Florentine Terrace home, where he and his wife, Margaret Macdonald Mackintosh, lived between 1906 and 1914. The rooms are a study in crisp, clean-line design using base metals, basic colors, and rectilinears relieved by circles or ovoids. The effect is not stark; it manages, inexplicably, to be warm and inviting.

**The Hunterian Museum** (open Monday through Friday from 9:30 A.M. to 5 P.M., Saturday till 1; admission, free). Housed in a double barrel-vaulted room of impressive height and design, this museum began in 1807 with Dr. Hunter's eclectic collection, donated to the university in 1783. The museum includes Scottish geology and archeology, and it is best known for the Hunter coin collection, with objects from sixth century B.C. Greece on forward. If the contents of the museum don't particularly interest you, it's worth a visit just to appreciate the rooms, which are vast, stunning, and unique in Scotland. This holds true for the university buildings in general. Constructed in the 1880s by a series of architects, including George Gilbert Scott, John Oldrid Scott, and William Stark, the Gothic fantasies, set with courtyards of cherry blossoms in springtime, are worth exploring in and of themselves. Overseeing operations is the spire, with its turrets and stentorian bells. The best view in Glasgow is to be had from its pinnacle. It's a long, huff-and-puff climb that can only be made on Fridays by calling in advance (330-8855, ex. 252), but it's well worth the extra effort.

After all this culture, indulge the sybarite in you and take the long way (and perhaps a picnic) down the hill into Kelvingrove Park, through which runs the Kelvin River under bridges and over rapids.

Across the river is yet another bagatelle in the city's string of museums, the **Glasgow Art Gallery and Museum.** The 1902 edifice opens into a three-story hall with a gold, gilt, red, and azure ceiling, the height and detail of which are truly splendid, hung with ponderous brass corona lamps suspended on what appear to be very delicate wires. Along the galleries you'll enjoy works by Bellini, Lippi, Rembrandt, Millet, Monet, Dali, Picasso, and Braque. British painting is represented by several prominent Pre-Raphaelites, and local talent specifically by the Scottish colorists (Peploe, Hunter, Fergusson) and the Glasgow Boys (Henry, Hornel, Guthrie).

There's also a gallery devoted to "The Four": Charles Rennie Mackintosh and his wife, Margaret Macdonald, her sister, Frances, and brother-in-law, Herbert MacNair. The gallery incorporates entire rooms, down to embroidered shawls produced by The Four and their fellow proponents of the Glasgow Style. (Open Monday through Saturday from 10 A.M. to 5 P.M., Sunday from 2 to 5 P.M.; free guide service for British and Continental paintings from 10 A.M. to 4 P.M., Monday through Saturday, inquire at the information desk; admission, free.)

## Sport and Transport

Across Byres Road from these museums is the mammoth new **Kelvin Hall Complex,** which boasts an immense sports arena open for public use and events, and Glasgow's Museum of Transport. The sports complex, run by the Department of Parks and Recreation, is a veritable palace for athletes. All the facilities—all you could need—are available for public use for modest fees between 9 A.M. and 10:30 P.M. seven days a week. Equipment, towels, and locker space are also available for hire. Call 357-2525 for information and to book time.

The **Museum of Transport** moved from its South Clyde address to these sparkling new digs just last spring. You can stroll down "Kelvin Street," a reproduction of Glasgow storefronts as they would have looked in 1938—Friday, December 9, to be exact. The collection of cars covers the slickest (for example, Jackie Stewart's Tyrell-Ford Grand Prix, twice world champion, lent by James Young Stewart himself) to the sanest (Fords and Morrises). Upstairs is the Clyde Room, a ravishing collection of ship models—steamers, sloops, subs— in a salon as big as the *Queen Mary*. The shop has matchbox cars and railway and steamer poster postcards. (Open Monday through Saturday from 10 A.M. to 5 P.M., Sunday from 2 to 5 P.M., admission, free.)

## Elsewhere in Glasgow

**The People's Palace,** Glasgow Green (open Monday through Saturday from 10 A.M. to 5 P.M., Sunday from 2 to 5 P.M.; admission, free). A museum of Glasgow history including exhibitions explaining the tobacco link with the Americas, a punch bowl from the Saracen's Head (see above), and James Watt memorabilia. café in the Winter Garden greenhouse.

**Glasgow School of Art,** 167 Renfrew Street (open Monday through Friday from 10 A.M. to 12 P.M. and from 2 to 4 P.M.; admission, free). Still very much in the business of discovering and nurturing Scots talent, this building was designed by Mackintosh to accommodate the institution that launched him. Built between 1897 and 1909, the interiors are a nouveau tour de force (open to view are the Library, Board Room, and Directors Room). Also on display is a large collection of Mackintosh furniture.

**The Tenement House,** 145 Buccleuch Street, Garnethill (open daily from 2 to 5 P.M.; winter hours on Saturday and Sunday only, from 2 to 4 P.M.; admission, £1), is a break away from splendor into the simplicity of the working class. The 19th-century flat of a typist, Miss Toward, and her mother, a dressmaker, has been preserved almost perfectly, so you can see how this half lived.

## At Night

Don't exhaust yourself with touring during the day because by night, Glasgow's a-glitter with the best in the performing arts. Mayfest, held throughout the town throughout the month, is an international arts festival par excellence. Write to Mayfest Ltd., 46 Royal Exchange Square, Glasgow G1 3AR, or call (041) 221-9931.

The **Scottish Opera,** which performs at the Theatre Royal, Hope Street, is one of the world's most exciting young companies. Under the direction of North American import Richard Mantle, the opera blows the dust off the bel canto and provides stunning new productions of modern works. If you're at all an opera fan, and more especially if you're not, pick up some tickets (credit card phone orders: 041-331-1234 or 332-9000).

Located in the heart of a revamped slum, the **Citizens Theatre,** Gorbals, specializes in native Scottish and Fringe works. In keeping with the culture-of-the-people ambience of the Gorbals, all seats are £3—a real deal (credit Card bookings—MasterCard and Visa—041-429-0022).

The best in new, classic, and cult films trotted in from around the globe can be found at the **Glasgow Film Theatre,** Rose Street Cinema, 12 Rose Street, 332-6535. The program changes daily, if not hourly.

The **Third Eye Centre,** 350 Sauchiehall Street (332-7521) provides gallery, cinema, theater, concert hall, or performance space for artists exploring the new and unused.

Tickets for most events throughout the city can be purchased at the Ticket Centre, Candleriggs (227-5511). Daily information on events can be obtained from the Greater Glasgow Tourist Board (227-4880).

## ❦ RESTAURANTS

**Buttery,** 652 Argyle St., tel. (041) 221-8188. You'll never find it, so take a taxi. This is an old Victorian Masonic lodge decorated with church trappings—the bar is upside-down pews, and the circular section was the pulpit; plush, comfortable cranberry velvet upholstery completes the 19th-century sensation. New takes on Scottish classics; game is featured, and there's an excellent vegetarian menu. A three-course table d'hôte luncheon costs £11.50, including service. Dinner à la carte will run about £25. Only 45–50 covers; very popular. Downstairs is **The Belfry,** which has a darker, more pubby atmosphere—paper napkins, straw mats, stone walls. Half the cost of upstairs. Both accept all major credit cards.

**Cafe Gandolfi,** 64 Albion St., tel. (041) 552-6813. Modern stained-glass in rich blues and indigos of "A Flock of Fishes," capriciously carved and inlaid wood, benches, stools. The menu explains Scotland to you—in French. French menu, Belgian beer, American music, Scots cooking—more or less. They serve a variety of salads, sandwiches, and a potato soufflé. Casual and cheap, this place is frequented by students, grannies, and yuppies alike. A meal will run £6 tops. No credit cards.

**The Fire Station,** 33 Ingram St., tel. (041) 552-2929. In an old one, Deco-designed with marble and granite. Unfortunate vinyl place mats. The bar and booths are elevated around the walls. Twenty pastas, mussels, prawns in puff pastry, stir-fry, and sirloin make up the menu. Live music most weekend nights. Frequented by a young-ish, hip crowd having fun. At these prices, you will, too: £10. MC, V.

**Loon Fung,** 417 Sauchiehall St., tel. (041) 332-1477. Cantonese the way you like it: bright lights, silk flowers, panda carpet, open-plan seating, and badly spoken English. Dim sum from £1.30, great hot-and-sour soup with shrimps, pork, peas, and coarse-grated ginger. Duck is a specialty, crispy with orange or lemon sauce. Set dinners for 2–6 and more are available. Loon Fung means Phoenix and Dragon, a gold installation of which (with light-up eyes) occupies the rear wall. Meals run about £10–12. Open 12–12 daily. All major credit cards.

**One Devonshire Gardens,** 1 Devonshire Gardens, tel. (041) 339-2001. We don't like to suggest eating at a hotel in a city, but for such an exceptional place exceptions must be made. As with all rooms in this Victorian house, the dining room is decorated in deep shades—navy and brown. Your napkin is tied up with a bow, and your table is set with silver and crystal. Jim Kerr (not the pop star) commands the kitchens, which produce marinated fillet of beef with cracked pepper, supreme of salmon with lobster, and salmon mousse. The £21.50 menu allows a choice of three appetizers, a soup, three main courses, a dessert, cheese, and coffee. The wine list is exclusively French, short, but adequate. Reservations are necessary. AE, DC, MC, V.

**Rogano,** 11 Exchange Pl., tel. (041) 248-4055. Fish is the specialty in this 1935 interior with its soft light and beautiful murals painted on the burly wood paneling—the woodwork is as special as the fish. Service is sprightly and efficient. The menu consists of Rendez-vous of Native Seafood in a saffron beurre blanc, grilled halibut with pinhead oatmeal and tarragon beurre noisette, and saddle of venison with game sauce and black currants. The café downstairs has famous-folk photos on the walls with frivolous quotations. Enjoy pasta, sirloin, or grilled trout in this less fussy, less expensive café. A meal at the restaurant costs £25; at the café, £15. Open daily except Sun. All major credit cards.

**The Ubiquitous Chip,** 12 Ashton Lane, tel. (041) 334-5007. Ubiquitous is also its reputation for being among Scotland's finest. A bit tricky to get to: find the Underground station on Byers Road (Candleriggs), then ask—everyone will know. The Chip is many restaurants: pub/café upstairs, indoor dining room and courtyard garden down. The proprietor, Mr. Clydesdale, is a stickler for researching traditional Scots recipes, then giving them his own spin—oxtail ragout, fillets of St. Oban-landed chicken, halibut with green peppercorn and pine kernel crust with red wine sauce, and supreme of Perthshire pheasant with cream and scotch ale sauce. The name comes from author Arnold Wesker's comment on the number of fish-and-chip shops in town. He referred to Glasgow as one big ubiquitous chip. The wine list is among Scotland's best, and all servers are certified by the Wine and Spirit Education Trust. Not to be missed. Prices are very reasonable given the quality of ingredients and preparation. £18 will buy a meal with wine. Closed Sun. All major credit cards.

**The Willow Tea Rooms,** upstairs in Henderson's Jewelry Store at 217 Sauchiehall St., tel. (041) 332-0521. As you've undoubtedly been informed by various museums around town, many of Charles Rennie Mackintosh's most important public buildings were tearooms. And this is one of them. Much of the original 1904 work is intact, and furniture has been carefully reproduced. So much nicer to experience the atmosphere of a Mackintosh interior as it was originally intended. Open Mon.–Sat. 9:30–4:30 for brunch, lunch, and afternoon tea. Choose from sandwiches, salads, quiche, lasagne, and home-baked pastries; all are inexpensive. No credit cards.

# The Borders

Early Friday morning the Royal and Ancient Burgh of Selkirk is wall-to-wall tams and tweeds bobbing among the antique stone houses set in a verdant enfolding of hills. From the crush of horses and riders emerges the Standard Bearer. A bonnie lad indeed, he is presented with the colors and gallops out of Selkirk full tilt, a mass of bridled and beribboned horse-flesh hot on his hooves, sent crashing across the country with the entire town's lusty rendition of "Hail Smiling Morn."

Thus begins Selkirk's Common Riding, a centuries-old festival drenched in color and tradition. Caked in mud and sweat, the Standard Bearer returns to the Market Square having ridden the boundaries of the Royal Burgh with his cavalry of attendants, and as the entire town joins for a rousing chorus of "Up Wi' the Souters o' Selkirk," he casts the colors in a ritual re-enactment of a day 475 years ago when, of the eighty men sent to support James IV at Flodden, only a single Souter returned, bearing a captured English standard. Wounded, grief-stricken, speechless, when asked for news of the battle he could only raise the flag above his head, letting it fall to the ground as did the brave men of Selkirk who died beside their king.

All summer long similar days of revelry, pageantry, and history occur throughout the Borders, the conglomeration of districts in the southeast of Scotland. If you can grab a mount and stay aboard—"safe oot, and safe in"—you can join the three hundred-strong throng of riders crashing through the countryside of Scotland as perhaps your ancestors did, riding the marches, marking the boundaries of the freedoms and privileges Borders men fought and died for at Flodden.

The annual rabble-rousing round of Common Ridings, one held in a different town each weekend, is quintessential Borders, where memories of the "rough wooing" of Scotland by the English are as fresh as if it all happened half a minute rather than half a millennium ago; where the laddies and lasses grow up as comfortable in the saddle as they are in their sneakers; where the cognoscenti among sportsmen convene for their pheasant shooting, salmon fishing, fox hunting.

Since the region is relatively compact and self-contained, you can base yourself in one of the more southerly towns such as Jedburgh or Kelso, or closer toward Edinburgh, where Peebles offers a good selection of hotels. In either case, the principal points of interest are all within a half-hour's drive of one another.

For the sake of simplicity, we have listed abbeys with abbeys and stately homes with stately homes. Unless you're very keen on either type of structure, you'll probably not want to see four abbeys in one day and half a dozen homes in another. We suggest you choose a couple that interest you most from each category, pinpoint them on your map, and devise an easy tour of three to four a day.

## The Abbeys

It makes sense historically to introduce first the tetrad of abbey ruins, which attest to the unrest in the region, and which have lured famous tourists like Scott and Wordsworth with their mystery and melancholy.

### Jedburgh

**Jedburgh Abbey,** High Street in Jedburgh, makes for a good beginning in many ways: it is the southernmost of the four, its remains are among the most extensive, and it has recently opened a visitors' center, which gives a good introduction to this community particularly and the Borders abbeys generally.

This abbey, like the other three, was founded by David I as a priory for a French order of Augustinians. The foundations were laid in 1140, and building continued sporadically over the next century. Although roofless, the abbey's architectural elements, wrought in a sanguine shade of sandstone, are relatively well preserved. (Open April through September, Monday through Saturday from 9:30 A.M. to 7 P.M., Sunday from 2 to 7 P.M., winter hours, till 4 P.M., closed Thursday afternoons and all day Friday; admission, £1.50.)

While you're in town you might like to stop in at **Mary, Queen of Scots' House,** so named after a royal visit in 1566. The house itself was built earlier in that century by the Kers family. There are lots of Mary's personal effects inside, and a pretty little garden outside. (Open Easter through October, Monday through Saturday from 10 A.M. to 12 P.M., and from 1 to 5 P.M., Sundays from 2 to 5 P.M.; open Sunday mornings in July and August; admission, 75 pence.)

### Melrose

The **Abbey** is in the center of town. Another of David I's brainchildren, this time for Cictercian monks, who began building in 1136. Consistantly harassed by retreating English troops, especially by Edward II's army, a remorseful Robert the Bruce resolved to restore the abbey to its former splendor. So attached was Bruce to the place that legend has it while his body rests at Dunfermline, his heart was removed and transported here to Melrose for burial.

Aside from the abbey, Melrose is also famous for the introduction of seven-a-side rugby. A gent named Ned Haig, the butcher, invented the modern game, trimming the sides down to their present configuration. The oldest tournament in the world is held here around the middle of April; an international roster of the world's finest club teams are invited to it to challenge the local boys—who invariably prove to be more than a match for all comers.

While in Melrose for sites or sports, do drop in at **Marmions,** on Morrow Gardens just down from the abbey. This chipper, noisy, very busy brasserie is a good place to sit and chat with the locals and get their suggestions of what else to see and do. Fare is simple but tasty, perfect for lunchtime. Inexpensive sandwiches, fettucini, curry of the day, vegetarian dishes. Save room for dessert. Open 9 A.M.–11 P.M. six days, 1–6 P.M. Sun. in summer; closed Sun. in winter.

## Kelso

Of the four, the least remains of **Kelso Abbey,** abbey, ironically and tragically because of the four, it was the oldest (foundations date back to 1113) and by far the most important (Kelso Abbey was the richest, and her abbot the most senior, in Scotland). Begun as a cloister for Benedictine orders, the abbey was built primarily between 1128 and 1212. It survived through many near-disasterous battles but was finally dealt a fatal blow in 1545 by the earl of Hertford, whose troops were forced into a two-day pitched battle by 12 monks and ninety laymen barricaded inside. Although much of the abbey has vanished, its unique, ambitious double-transept design is still discernible among the stones. Sir Walter Scott attended a grammar school here on the site. (Open April through September, Monday through Saturday from 9:30 A.M. to 7 P.M., Sunday from 2 to 7 P.M.; winter hours till 4 P.M.; admission, free.)

Although Kelso's abbey is not the most striking, the town itself is one of the prettiest in the area. Take in the expanse and color of the Market Square.

The Kelso Races, "over the sticks" (steeple chasing), have been held at Berrymoss since 1883. Races run from early spring through summer on selected Wednesdays beginning at 2:15 P.M.

The **Whipman Bar** at the Cross Keys Hotel is a good choice for a bite, if 18th-century coaching inns are to your liking.

### Dryburgh

**Dryburgh Abbey** is near Newton St. Boswells on the B6356. Neither the largest nor the best preserved, but for many, the setting of russet Dryburgh stones beside an ample elbow of the Tweed River, with a roaming sun conducting a choreography of shadows through the wheel window onto the brilliant grass, make this the loveliest of all the Borders abbeys. It was built beginning in 1150 for a relatively obscure order called the Premonstratensians. The place, even as a ruin, so touched the spirit of several romantic souls that Field Marshal Earl Haig and Sir Walter Scott—an avid aficionado of mystical beauty—chose to be buried here. (Open April through September, Monday through Saturday from 9:30 A.M. to 7 P.M., Sunday from 2 to 7 P.M.; winter hours till 4 P.M.; admission, £1.50.)

## Historic Homes

Thankfully, not all Borders properties are in a state of disassembly. Commanding some of the counties' most strategic and aesthetic vistas are the homes of some of Scotland's foremost families. In ascending order according to age, the half-dozen we recommend are as follows:

### Traquair

This white fantasy of a castle's earliest incarnation was as a royal hunting lodge early in the 12th century. Necessity dictated that the residence be transformed into a pele tower during the wars of independence. The interior of the house is rich with Jacobite associations. Among the Mary, Queen of Scots connections with the house is the Baroque canary state bed, brought here from another family estate. The spread was made by the queen herself and her ladies; she used the cradle for her son, the future James VI of Scotland and I of England. Among the ancillary buildings, you'll find the brewery where Traquair ale is produced. Don't miss a sampling of this stout, frothy blend. (Southeast of Peebles at the junction of the B709 and the B7062. Open May through September, daily from 1:30 to 5:30 P.M.; July through mid-September from 10:30 A.M.; admission, £2, £2.50 during July and August.)

### Mellerstain

Most people agree that among Adam houses in Scotland, this is easily the finest. Of all the houses on your list, this should be put at the top. This is the home of the Baillies, who through marriage became the earls of Haddington. The wings were designed in 1725 by William Adam, who also had plans (which are on display in the Great Gallery) for a central structure to connect the two. His version was never realized, and the main body of the house was designed in 1770 by his son, Robert, who worked with a Baillie widow, Grisel.

The Robert Adam building is two storys with a long corridor—down which the current George Baillie likes to ride his tricycle—connecting rooms to the south to catch the sun. Mellerstain is famous primarily for its Adam details, especially the ceilings in the Library and the Music Room (originally intended as a dining room). Since the 18th century sightings of a lady dressed in black who walks along the upstairs balcony and enters the Rose Bedroom have been reported. Speculation is that it is Lady Grisel returned to check up on what has been done to her house. There is a shop and tearoom, which serves light lunches. Also, several times during the summer season, concerts are held in the Music Room. There are seats for only one hundred, so reserve early. Information is available through the ticket office at (057) 381-225. (Follow signs off the A6089, northwest of Kelso. Open May through September, from 12:30 to 5 P.M. daily, closed Saturday; admission, £2.)

## Bowhill

You'll note that the time of opening for Bowhill is frustratingly limited. If you happen to be traveling nearby, try calling to see if you can tag on with a group tour that might be scheduled for the days you're in the neighborhood, (0750) 20732. Tour guides are apologetic that the house is not more interesting architecturally, but the important asset of Bowhill is not the building but what is contained therein: a collection of art and furniture second only to the Queen's in size and quality. Indeed Bowhill is the site of a series of art courses cosponsored by Sotheby's called the Buccleuch Studies. For information write Sotheby's Art Courses, 30 Oxford Street, London W1R 1RE; tel. 01-408-1100.

The Buccleuchs have always been avid collectors and preservationists, each successive generation duly embued with a great respect and love for the family's treasures, which include Canalettos, Gainsboroughs, Van Dycks, Holbeins, and a Reynolds. The coach house is being converted into an intimate, candle-lit country restaurant, featuring local produce and recipes, tentatively to be called Philipburn at Bowhill—and run by the Hills, who are in charge of the fine kitchen at the Philipburn House Hotel in Selkirk. For reservations and information call (0750) 20732. Also available: pony trekking (0750-20192) around the grounds, mountain bike rentals (0721-22934), and the Bowhill Little Theatre Programme (0750-20732). (Off the A708, west of Selkirk. Open early July through mid-August, Monday through Saturday from 1 to 4:30 P.M.; Sundays from 2 to 6 P.M. Grounds are open May through August; admission, £2.50.)

## Floors

The castle was originally begun by William Adam in 1721 for the first Duke of Roxburgh. The 6th duke commissioned William Playfair to enlarge, modernize, and stylize the property in 1841. He did so with great imagination; the present façade is a forest of onion domes and turrets, making it the largest inhabited home in Scotland. Across the sweep of lawn is the river Tweed and a view of Kelso Bridge, used as a prototype by John Rennie for his Waterloo Bridge in London.

Inside, the rooms were revamped in the late 19th century by the 8th duke's American wife, Mary Goelet, a New York heiress who brought with her an outstanding collection of Louis XVI furniture and tapestries. The Innes Ker family still lives here, as the photographs, magazines, and telephones you'll see in the rooms attest. Perhaps His Grace may drive up in his silver BMW or Bessie, the terrier, will run out to greet you. In addition to the collection of classics, the present duchess has recently introduced some moderns from the family collection—Matisse, Bonnard, Redon in the Needlework Room, a copy of a room at Versailles with Louis XVI furniture miniaturized for the ladies. (On the A6089 leading out of Kelso. Open May through September, Sunday through Thursday from 10:30 A.M. to 5:30 P.M.; July through August also open Friday; admission, £2.20.)

## Abbotsford

Sir Walter Scott bought this farm and house from Dr. Robert Douglas. Scott demolished the existing structure and started work on Abbotsford in 1822. The name derives from a bridge over the Tweed used by Melrose monks—Abbots' Ford.

Scott worked closely with his architect, William Atkinson, to build a country manor worthy of the author's romantic fantasies and suitable for housing his vast collection of books and historic curios. Whether you've read every word of the Waverley novels or not, Abbotsford is particularly interesting because Scott was an avid collector with a taste for the quirky and unusual, and the historically important. (On the B6360 between Melrose and Galashiels. Open late March through October, Monday through Saturday from 10 A.M. to 5 P.M., Sunday from 2 to 5 P.M.; admission, £1.50.)

## Manderston

Having seen the original Adam mansions, it is interesting to see the Edwardian reproduction of the style by architect John Kinross. Manderston was one of the last of the great country houses to be built in Britain, and here no extravagance was spared. Highlights include the carved and compartmented plasterwork ceilings, the silver staircase, the marble fireplaces. The most intriguing feature of the building actually exists below the luxurious public rooms and apartments: in the basement you'll find a maze of kitchens, larders, linen rooms, and lodgings for the veritable army of servants required to maintain the house in its heyday. The 56 acres of parkland include lavishly appointed stables, a marble dairy, formal gardens, and woodland walks. (Open Thursdays and Sundays mid-May through September, and selected Bank Holiday Mondays, from 2 to 5:30 P.M.)

## Off The Abbey-and-Mansion Trail

**Border Collie and Shepherd Centre,** Tweedhopefoot, Tweedsmuir, Lanarkshire, on the A701; tel. (08997) 267. TV sheepdog handlers, Geoff and Viv Billingham run a school for working dogs, who are put through their paces for visitors daily at 10 and 11 A.M. and at 2, 3 and 4 P.M. from May through October; Saturdays by appointment; admission, £1.50.

**Scottish Borders Woolen Trail.** Border tweeds and knits are some of the finest in Scotland. You can watch them being made and buy them for rock-bottom prices at mill shops centered in Hawick and Galashiels.

**Fishing.** One of the chief diversions of the neighborhood is fishing. Be it salmon, trout, coarse or sea angling, in rivers, still waters, or the ocean, the Borders boasts some of the best sport to be had in Scotland. A detailed book, *Angling in the Scottish Borders,* is available for a small sum from the Scottish Borders Tourist Board, Municipal Buildings, High Street, Selkirk TD7 4JX (tel. 0750-20555); it explains everything you need to know about seasons, licenses, tackle shops, and accommodation.

## ❦ RESTAURANTS

**Cringletie House Hotel,** Peebles, tel. (07213) 233. Aileen Maguire's kitchen produces traditional, no-fuss food made special by its freshness (check out the kitchen garden at the back of the house) and simplicity. A £16.50 four-course menu includes fillet of sole in fresh herb custard, chicken with apples, almonds and Grand Marnier, or roast loin of lamb with courgette stuffing. MC, V.

**Sunlaws House Hotel,** Kelso, tel. (05735) 331. The dining room is a combination of equestrian oil paintings and bamboo-backed chairs. There is a large picture window overlooking the lawns of the estate. The staff is young and the occasional error may be made; however, their eagerness and attentiveness make up for any lack of finesse. Game is always a good choice at Sunlaws; on your menu you might find Berwickshire quail, oven-roasted with chestnut and apple stuffing, or roast saddle of venison served with a rich port wine sauce. Vegetarian and cold-plate choices are always available. The dessert tray will convince you that you've got just a little room for more. Dinner with wine costs £18. AE, DC, MC, V.

# The Heart of Scotland

The central regions of Scotland are the heart of golf country: St. Andrews gave the sport to the world and the world regularly returns to play and pay homage. And in the hills of Auchterarder basks the incomparable Gleneagles. Both of these resorts feature links courses—courses designed to conform to the contours of the land, not vice versa. The gentle hills, the ancient trees, the omnipresent water are a reflection of the order and beauty available naturally in these regions of Scotland. After all, it was here that the game was born close to five hundred years ago when the laddies sent the first small, dense ball sailing over the greensward with a crooked stick.

The various parts of this area are accessible to one another by day trip and are also a day trip away from Edinburgh and/or Glasgow, so if golf and the sea are your passions, hole up in Fife, a peninsula thrusting its fierce, feisty head out into the North Sea. If you prefer to take long drives winding about bens and lochs, settle down in the Trossachs. And if you want to be in the center of all these things yet in the middle of nowhere, install yourself in Auchterarder.

Stirling is the principal city in these parts, and, while it's recommended that you stay in the countryside, you should plan to spend a day or two exploring the castle and its town spilling down the hill.

## Stirling

You might as well start at the top: **Stirling Castle** tickets are available at the visitor's center for £1.50. The castle is open Monday through Saturday from 9:30 A.M. to 6 P.M., Sunday from 10:30 A.M. to 5:30 P.M.; winter hours till 5:05 P.M. and 4:20 P.M., respectively. The visitor's center has an audio-visual production explaining what you're about to see and a step-up panorama window with a taped explanation of the history of the hills and planes that can be seen from the castle. And when you hear the history of constant struggle over the area, coupled with the view of the mountains and rivers that converge here, you'll understand why Stirling has always been viewed by various armies as the key to controlling Scotland.

The castle was built, like its counterpart in Edinburgh, over a period of centuries and therefore provides a good time line of Scottish royal residential and defensive architecture. Highlights include the Queen Anne Garden, built bowling-green–style overlooking an earthworks in the valley (this was actually another formal garden, called the King's Nut, during the reign of Charles I). The exterior of the palace, built by James IV in 1496, is a study in northern Renaissance style that is exceptionally fine for Scotland. Most impressive of all are the Stirling Heads, a collection of once-painted roundels carved from Irish oak. The series, originally consisting of some forty-odd medallions, formed a magnificent ceiling depicting the kings and queens of Scotland, biblical and mythological characters, and a jester or two. The Chapel Royal is decorated with a 1628 painted frieze and was where Mary, Queen of Scots was crowned and her grandson, Henry, was baptized.

In summer the tourist office on Dunbarton Road provides guided walks of the area, or you can take yourself on a leisurely tour around the old town of Stirling, stopping in at the 15th-century **Church of the Holy Rood,** with its impressive oak roof. The **Guildhall,** now used for music and ceilidh dancing, was built in the 1630s by philanthropist John Cowane, whose statue keeps an eye on things outside. Down Broad Street you'll see the **Mercat Cross,** whose base is new but whose unicorn, known as "the Puggy" for its grotesque, monkey-like muzzle, is from the original. In August the **Stirling Arts and Ale Festival** (a winning combination indeed) centers here in the historic market square, where a medieval market is recreated complete with wenches, ox roasting, and stilt-walkers in traditional tartans. The **Smith Art Gallery and Museum** on Dunbarton Road is open during the summer daily except Monday; it contains work by local artists, visiting exhibitions, and a bit of Scottish history.

Undoubtedly, you'll have noticed the **Wallace Monument** crowning Abbey Crag just north of town. It was built in the 19th century to commemorate the glorious victory of Wallace (who was later executed at Smithfields in London for his pains) at the Battle of Stirling Bridge, September 11, 1297. There are several historical exhibitions to enjoy, but best of all is the view (362 feet of Abbey Crag and 220 feet of monument) available from the top of the tower—a long and arduous climb.

Also of major historical interest is the battle site at **Bannockburn,** an essential element in the struggle for Scottish independence, and its accompanying heritage center.

The Heritage Centre, just south of Stirling on the A872 is open daily from 10 A.M. to 6 P.M. April through October; admission, £1.50. There is an audiovisual presentation devoted to the battle and an exhibition utilizing models of battles, relics, music, and text to trace the entire history of Scottish independence. If you're at all confused by the facts and major figures, this display will straighten you out in a fun and painless way.

Outside in the field, for God and St. Andrew, is a circle of concrete and steel, open on two sides with a view to Stirling Castle from one side and to the battlefield from the other. Just beyond, looking keenly out over the Scottish landscape

## The Battle of Bannockburn

In 1307, the English king Edward I, Hammer of the Scots, with his dying breath enjoined his son, also Edward, to finish the business of conquering Scotland. So sure was Edward II of victory that before he set out on the northward journey, he had already portioned out Scottish lands among his favorites, some of whom made the trip with furniture and tapestries in anticipation of claiming their new castles after the inevitable victory.

They reckoned without the dazzling military skill and determination of King Robert the Bruce, whose brothers were hanged by the English. Bruce hoped to even the three-to-one odds against his army by careful topographical study and preparations, including booby-trapping the bogs with pits and spikes to paralyze the English cavalry. On June 23rd, 1314, the armies met in what was to become the decisive battle for Scottish independence. At the end of two fierce days of fighting, the Scots had won the day, and Edward II had quit the field and retreated south with his generals, who left enough of the loot of their overoptimism on the field to finance Scotland's return to prosperity in the ensuing years.

framed by a scuttling of clouds, is the wind-whipped equestrian statue of Robert the Bruce, commanding the view from great height mounted on his charger.

# ❧ RESTAURANTS

Stirling is best for fun, café-type fare. Here are some suggestions:

**Littlejohn's,** 54 Port St., tel. (786) 63222. Not surprisingly, this branch (there are others in Perth and St. Andrews) opened on April Fool's Day. Ceiling fans whirr, Dixieland jazz entertains. Original old junk—bicycles, golf clubs—on the walls. Burgers, pizza, steak, veggie dishes, and ice cream served in this cheap (£8 with beers), noisy, and fun place. There may be a queue at lunch. All major credit cards.

**Barnton Bar and Bistro,** 3 ½ Barnton St., tel. (786) 61698. Marble-top tables with green iron feet, woodsy wallpaper, and a mahogany bar are the decor in this café serving chicken, salads, and jacket potatoes. They have a short, reasonable wine list. Low-budget and tasty at about £6 per person. No credit cards.

**Darnley Coffee House,** 18 Bow St., tel. (786) 74468. Legend has it that Mary, Queen of Scots' husband, Lord Darnley, lived here and used a secret tunnel for intrigues in the castle. Now Mrs. Anne Cameron runs three neat little cave-like rooms, which she supplies with homemade soups, breads, lasagne, and Darnley apple cake served warm with whipped cream. Wine and beer are also available. Delightful. A meal costs about £5. No credit cards.

# The Trossachs

North and west of Stirling, the Trossachs ramble their ancient and sage way across the center of Scotland. Here you'll find mountains more accessible and inviting than their northerly brethren, the Highlands. Here, too, are a string of lovely lochs including Lomond, whose banks, unfortunately made famous by song, are crammed with tourists and consequently much less bonnie than they used to be. It's better to explore tiny Lochs Ard and Chon, or hike around the northern shore of Loch Katrine. Or better yet, cruise back in time as you skim across the surface of the latter in the steamer the *S.S. Sir Walter Scott,* the sole survivor of what was once a fleet of similar little ships. The trip one way takes about 45 minutes from one end of Loch Katrine to the other; you can then disembark and hike back, or picnic and wait for the return cruise, or take the round-trip hour-long afternoon cruises. The *Sir Walter Scott* runs from early May through late September; prices range from £1.20 to £2. Another watery voyage is the Inchmaholme Ferry, a small 12-seater that will shuttle you over from Port of Monteith on the B8034, on demand (turn the signal board on the dock so that the white "request call" side faces the island), from 9:30 A.M. to 5 P.M., April through September, Monday through Saturday and from 11 A.M. to 5:50 P.M. on Sundays. Inchmaholme Island is a wee treasure set in the middle of Scotland's only true lake. It is the site of ruins of a 13th-century priory at which Robert the Bruce prayed for victory before Bannockburn, and was a summering spot for Mary, Queen of Scots.

## Doune

As far as overland transportation goes, Scotland's greatest collection of thoroughbred motorcars is at the **Doune Motor Museum** (open daily from 10 A.M. to 5:30 P.M., winter hours till 5 P.M.; admission, £1.80). The nucleus of the museum is the private collection of the earl of Murray, a keen racing car driver himself, so the emphasis is on sports cars. Among the forty-odd cars for your inspection are Jags, Morgans, and a stunning 1938 Bugatti that could hit speeds of 105 mph—unheard of in that day. There is also the "Old Girl," a 1905 Rolls-Royce, the second-oldest still running and the second car to leave the Cook Street shop in Manchester, used as a demonstrator by Captain Rolls.

The best part about the Motor Museum is that several times during the season, it is the site of the Doune Motor Racing Hill Climb, which attracts racers throughout the land who bring their classic cars to take on one another and the 1 to 4 grades of the mile-long asphalt course. There are special events of a pertinent nature most weekends at the museum; for details call (0786) 841-203.

Down the road (more or less) is **Doune Castle,** south of the town on the A821. Doune is a castle as you would picture it: solid, heavyset, impregnable. (Open Monday through Saturday from 9:30 A.M. to 7 P.M., Sunday from 2 to 7 P.M.; winter hours till 4 P.M.; closed for lunch from 12:30 to 1:30 P.M.; admission, £1.) The present structure was built in the late 14th century by the Stewart dukes of Albany, descendants of Robert the Bruce.

### Dunblane
**Dunblane Cathedral** (open Monday through Saturday from 9:30 A.M. to 7 P.M., Sunday from 2 to 5:30 P.M.; winter hours till 4 P.M.) is where St. Blane, a Briton from Strathclyde who was educated in Ireland, established Christianity in 600. Clement, Dominican bishop of Dunblane, began building a cathedral to augment the 12th-century free-standing tower. Of special interest are the Chisholm Cannon Stalls at the rear of the nave, all rare survivors of the 15th century.

## ✻ RESTAURANTS

**Braeval Old Mill Restaurant,** near Aberfoyle, tel. (08772) 711. Previous to recent renovations, sheep were the only ones grazing at this centuries-old mill. Nick Nairn thought the navy was keeping him away from his lovely Fiona, so they sold their flat in Glasgow and set off to see what could be done with a derelict mill Nick's father had bought. Their accomplishment in resurrecting the place would have been impressive enough, but as luck would have it, Nick turned out to have the makings of a great chef—he is now one of the young Turks of Scottish cooking. Nick's menu includes items such as monkfish fillets with mussels and fresh asparagus in a saffron sauce and pigeon breasts with celery and hazelnuts. Emphasis is on fresh-from-the-hillside ingredients. The operation is small, but the mill has been converted beautifully and hung with tapestries done by Mrs. Nairn senior. Last year the Old Mill was named the Best Newcomer in the Scottish Field/Bollinger Restaurant of the Year competition. It couldn't have happened to more deserving, more delightful people. Not to miss. A meal runs about £18. Closed Mon.; reservations advisable. AE, MC, V.

**Roman Camp Hotel,** Callander, tel. (0877) 30003. A bright surprise awaits in the dining room of this hunting lodge-cum-château hotel, a combination of Alpine and Highlands. The cooking is on the lighter side, a welcome relief from the swelter of sauces. The salmon is a steak, ever so lightly cooked in butter with no additional fuss. The Swiss connection continues with spaetzle and strudel for dessert and of course with the wine list, which is brief but has many good choices under £10. Dinner runs about £23. Reservations suggested. No credit cards.

# Fife

The eastern component of central Scotland is the peninsula of Fife. At the southeastern tip is the East Neuk, a chain of fishing villages which still send their ships out into the blowsy North Sea. Crail, Pittenweem, and Anstruther are all worth traveling through. Anstruther (pronounced "anster") is the home of the Scottish Fisheries Museum; surrounding a little courtyard, it contains paintings, an aquarium, gear, and a collection of Scottish fishing tales and traditions.

While in town take time to have a meal at **The Cellar,** 24 East Green, a wee cottage overlooking the sea. The Jukes serve the freshest in local catch prepared in a sparkling, simple manner.

## St. Andrews

The approach along the southern coast is through some nasty industrial territory; it's better to drive down from the north, where most travelers will be stationed anyway—in and around that shrine of golfdom, St. Andrews. With all the reverential ink spilled over the Royal and Ancient game, the original purpose of this magic medieval city—today the ruins of **St. Andrews Cathedral** has been a bit obscured. The town was built to honor a shrine of a very different kind, housing the relics of St. Andrew, whose tooth, rib, and knucklebone were brought here by Bishop Occa in 723. Several other structures safeguarded the relics until building was begun in the late 12th century for a most ambitious edifice to become the primary cathedral of Scotland. As originally planned, it was to be the largest cathedral in Britain, but during the work, one wing fell down and was never completed. Even in its truncated form, it was second in size only to the cathedral at Norfolk. It was consecrated in 1318 in the presence of King Robert the Bruce.

During the 13th and 14th centuries the cathedral attracted annually from Britain and northern Europe 60,000 to 70,000 pilgrims—Scotland's first tourists—making St. Andrews second in pilgrimage attraction only to Canterbury, and second to none in Scotland for trade in herring, salt, coal, hides, and—Scotland's greatest export at that time—fighting men: 30,000 Scots mercenaries settled elsewhere in Europe from the 13th to the 16th centuries. The cathedral has been in ruins since 1559, when it was sacked by Reformationists, and left to rot. You can still climb up in the free-standing tower (157 steps), which slightly predates the cathedral, and survey the beaches and the town of St. Andrews and get a gull's-eye view of the medieval university as well as the famous courses. (Open from 9:30 A.M. to 7 P.M., and from 2 to 7 P.M. on Sunday, winter hours till 4 P.M. There is a small charge to ascend the tower.)

The presence of **St. Andrews University**—whose 15th-century campus you might like to explore by day—provides the town with an excellent cultural program. Primarily an institution for arts and letters, the Crawford Centre and the Byre Theatre ensure that something's always going on in the evening. Check the tourist office at South and Church streets for schedules.

## The Golf Courses

Speaking of the courses, there are four and a half presently, although there are plans to turn the half into a fifth. The four 18-hole links are called the **Old, New, Eden,** and **Jubilee,** and all are open to the public for play or spectating. Advance arrangements must be made in either case, and if you plan to pitch and putt during the high season, a year in advance is none too soon to make your reservations. This can be done (for any of the courses) by contacting the Links Management Committee, Golf Place, St. Andrews, Fife KY 16 9JA, Scotland; tel. (0334) 75757. If you're staying at any of the resort hotels in the area, take advantage of their special golf packages, which include reservations on the courses. Since the hotels make block arrangements with the Links Management Committee, they tend to be granted the best tee-off times. Traditionally, the Old Course is closed for play on Sunday, at which time the townsfolk walk the links, unhassled by midair fores, and picnic beside the sea.

## ❦ RESTAURANTS

**The Cellar,** Anstruther, See Above.

**The Peat Inn,** Peat Inn, tel. (033) 484-206. The Peat Inn is the kind of place pilgrimages are made of. David Wilson—a self-taught chef, incredible as it may seem—is one of the country's top two or three practitioners and exponents of exquisite Scottish cuisine. Not 'neeps and 'tatties, but regional cooking in the sense of developing and celebrating the best of local ingredients, sometimes along Gallic-Gaelic Auld-Alliance lines, often along lines emanating from Wilson's own fertile imagination. The Peat Inn has all the components of a classic European inn: an 18th-century structure actually built as an inn fitted with several elegant dining rooms, a wine list par excellence, a kitchen full of chefs of the highest caliber, and a host and hostess as seriously devoted to their guests as they are to their food— which is very seriously indeed. A £25 tasting menu is available; it encompasses petit portions of six courses and is a remarkable value. À la carte selections might include scallops on a bed of young leeks with an emulsion of citrus fruits or julienne of pigeon breast with brown lentils to start, followed by whole lobster in a lightly spiced sauce or fillet of beef in a Madeira sauce flavored with wild mushrooms or breast of wild duck in a sauce flavored with orange and cognac. The desserts are worth every last calorie.

The Peat Inn should be on the must-do list of anyone interested in enjoying and appreciating the absolute brilliance of modern Scottish cooking. Dinner costs £35. All major credit cards.

## To the North

North of Fife and the Trossachs, swinging into the hinterland toward the Highlands, is a locale rife with historically significant, spectacular castles. Superlative among these are the trio of Glamis, Scone, and Blair. They are relatively far apart and contain a plentitude of treasures, so you should choose only two to do in a single day.

### The Castles

**Glamis** is one of those castles that has what every traveler is looking for in a British castle: Shakespearean heritage, strong royal family links, even an in-house haunting. The castle's history hearkens back nearly a thousand years to when, as a royal hunting lodge, in 1034 Malcolm II was attacked by his enemies while sporting in the park and was carried back into the castle to die. The oldest extant part of the castle is the inner portion, which includes Duncan's Hall, where much of *Macbeth* is set (Macbeth was thane of Glamis before he became thane of Cawdor).

The main body of the building was constructed in the northern baronial style between 1675 and 1687, after falling into the hands of the Lyon family in 1372, when John Lyon married a royal princess. The lands have descended in a direct line from there ever since; the line has come to include the earls of Strathmore and Kinghorne, family of the Queen Mum, who still spends a lot of time here and whose second daughter, Princess Margaret, was born here. The 6th earl fell into disfavor with James V, who imprisoned the earl's widow here in the castle while debating how best to dispatch her. He finally hit upon burning her for witchcraft, and it is said to be she who reappears as the Grey Lady and still walks the confines of her prison.

Stunning outside and in, the castle is known for its series of 17th-century plasterwork ceilings and its collection of porcelain, Mortlake tapestries, arms, and armor. Open daily May through October except Saturday, from 1 to 5 P.M.; admission, £2.

Although the present palace at **Scone** is relatively new, the site is ancient and illustrious, tracing its importance back to the kingdom of the Picts. When Kenneth MacAlpine arrived in 843 with his band from Ireland, he chose this as the final resting place for the Stone of Destiny and here set up his throne symbolizing the union of his Irish-Scots with the native Picts. So great was the power and the mystery surrounding the stone—which came to be known as the Stone of Scone—that when Edward I was in the neighborhood hammering the

Scots, he stole it and had it sent down to Westminster Abbey, where it has remained to this day underneath the Coronation Chair. There is a story, however, that the Scots might just have gotten their own back. In 1951 some students allegedly stole it, copied it, and dutifully returned the original to London. Later, several of the culprits insisted that they had actually sent the copy south and replaced the real thing here in the chapel on Moot Hill.

The foundation of the palace, ancestral residence of the Murray family, the lords Mansfield, was laid in the 1580s. This core was gothicized in 1802 by architect William Atkinson.

The most interesting knickknacks in the house are the 17th-century elephant and walrus ivories collected from all over Europe. Artwork includes paintings by Van Dyck and Ramsay, and a bust of Homer by Bernini given to the 1st earl by his great friend, Alexander Pope.

Give yourself an extra hour or so to reconnoiter Moot Hill and to take one of a series of 15- to 60-minute walks around the magnificent Tayside grounds, which are home to the earl's celebrated highland cattle, Jacob's sheep, and a flock of albino peacocks. The house and grounds are open Easter through October, Monday through Saturday from 10 A.M. to 5:30 P.M., Sunday from 2 P.M.; Sundays in July and August from 11 A.M.; admission, £2.20.

**Blair Castle** is large, rambling, chock-full of stuff, and the most visited historic house in Scotland. Given these circumstances, plan on being here at least two hours if you've a mind to see the whole place. The house is still resided in by Iain, the 10th duke of Atholl, the only man in Britain who can boast his own private army, the Atholl Highlanders, a reminder of the days when Atholl was a little Highland kingdom unto itself.

The castle was begun in 1269 but has been renovated according to the tastes of the intervening centuries. In the Entrance Hall you'll see a stuffed red stag whose name was Tilt; just beyond in the Central Passage is an arbor of horns, ten of which belonged to Tilt from his 3rd to his 13th year. This obsessive collecting is typical of the Murrays; the castle contains an unbelievable amount of stuff, some of it priceless, some of it merely curious.

The present duke and his estate office are sanguine about maintaining revenues, pursuant to which there is a busy calendar of events most weekends during the summer. Highlights include the Atholl Gathering and Highland Games late in May, during which the Atholl Highlanders strut their stuff, and the International Sheep Dog Trials, touted as the world's most prestigious, which occur early in September. (Open Easter through mid-October, Monday through Saturday from 10 A.M. to 5 P.M., Sunday from 2 to 5 P.M., summer Sundays from 12 to 6 P.M.; admission, £2.50.)

# ❧ RESTAURANT

**Auchterarder House,** Auchterarder, Perthshire, tel. (0764) 63646. Dinner at Auchterarder House is full of wonderful little extras, beginning with complimentary cocktails and canapes in the library, where you can relax and plan your impending gastronomic sortie. The menu, priced according to the number of courses you choose (from two at £20 to five at £35), recommends a wine to complement each dish. Paul Brown's wonderful concoctions perfectly match the gracious Victorian proportions of the dining room. The wine list is long and expensive—beginning in the teens of pounds and ascending. Try the daily selection of wine by the 9-ounce glass. AE, DC, MC, V.

# 16

# THE SCOTTISH HIGHLANDS AND ISLANDS

The Highlands are not the Europe of luxurious villas, pored over by tourists since the centurions. The Highlands are not the Britain of primrosey-perfect villages and fields mapped out by neat networks of footpaths. The Highlands are wild, rugged, and real—and have always been so. Highland history is as wild and rugged as its geography, ever since the Irish kings set forth from Tara in the early ninth century, arriving in Iona, following in the footsteps of St. Columba three hundred years before. These Irish invaders, known as Scots, throttled the less sanguine Picts, many of whom threw themselves into the sea rather than live in the cacophonous, bellicose society they foresaw would be established by the Celtic invaders. In the meantime, there had also been raids from the north; Viking ships worried the inhabitants of the Western Isles from the eighth through the 13th centuries. The Shetlands and Orkney islands remained in Norse control until 1468, when they became part of Scotland as Margaret of Denmark's dowry to James III. Finally, in the 14th century, northwestern Scotland was united into a single kingdom ruled over by the Macdonald clan, who assumed the title of Lords of the Isles.

During the struggle for independence in the 14th century, Highlanders were always involved in the thick of the fray. They repeated their valorous showing four hundred years later when Bonnie Prince Charlie returned from exile to claim his right to the throne. The final disastrous battle of Charlie's campaign was fought at Culloden Moor just outside of Inverness. When the smoke cleared, the entire proud, ancient way of Highland life had perished. In reprisal, the English instituted cruel taxes and labor laws which reduced the Highland pop-

# SCOTTISH HIGHLANDS and ISLANDS

| 0 | Kilometers | 60 |
|---|---|---|
| | Miles | 50 |

Sula-Sgeir          °North Rona

N

Flannan Isles

Butt of Lewis
Port of Ness
Barvas
Lewis
Stornoway                    Scourie

O u t e r   H e b r i d e s

North Minch          Lochinver

Inchnadam

Clisham
799                Loch Broom
Tarbert                              Ullapool
Harris
Rodel                                    1062
North Uist                            Beinn Dearg
Lochmaddy       Rudha Hunish        1081
Monach Is.                           Gairloch        1109
Benbecula                                  Loch        74
                    Little Minch       Uig      Maree
South                                              1053
Uist        Dunvegan Castle    Portree      Achnasheen
       620   Ben More        Skye
              Bracadale       Raasay          G R E
              Sligachan       Kyle of
Lochboisdale   1009            Lochalsh   Stromeferry    E
Barra          Sea     Cuillin H.s  Broadford
Castlebay             Canna  Cuillin Sd          Carn Elge  Drumnadro
                            Elgol           1182
Barra Hd   Barra   of the   Rum  811  Armadale    87            660
                           Eigg              Ft Augustus
              Hebrides       Muck
                                   Glenfinnan       Glen  Mor
                   Coll           Salen        Spean Bridge  24
Tiree                     Tobermory    888   Ft William  Dalwh
         Tiree Passage        Achnalea  32° 1343
                  Salen   Lochaline Ballachulish  Ben Nevis  Drumo
                  Island  Portnacroish          Kinlochleven
                   Mull      63    1148  Rannoch Stat.
Fionphort   955  Ben More    Craignure          263
                           Oban   Dalmally  Tyndrum
         Firth of Lorne   Kilmelford       1130  10   22  Ki
                                  Crianlarich    1172
                                           Ben More

ulation to a destitute, desperate state. Many were transported or fled to the Americas during this period because their future in Scotland was hopeless.

Highlanders, like most ancient tribes, have very long memories. And for many of them, especially those in the remote parts of the west and in the islands, the old ways are not merely memories but are still their ways. If you attend church or an important national festival, the men will be wearing their kilts. Many of them still ply the trade of their great grandfathers, working as fishermen or shepherds or small-scale farmers on crofts (communal farmlands) tilled by eight generations of their ancestors. The women still tend the cows and the chickens, take care of the orphan lambs, and knit up a storm before their coal- or peat-fed fires. Stores close at noon every day for lunch hour, and each town is usually shut for an afternoon midweek and of course all day on Sunday. Gaelic is still spoken throughout the Western Isles.

Ninety-eight percent of all the land in Scotland is rural, and the percentage is even greater in the Highlands. The land is, in fact, the thing to go for. Awesome. Breathtaking. The words somehow seem too tired and tame to describe the mountains which make up the northwest portion of Scotland. Although certainly not the tallest in Europe, these mountains look extremely large because many of them—the Cuillins on Skye, for example—shoot up out of the sea to a height of well over three thousand feet. There are lots of ways to explore the mountains. The most obvious, of course, is on foot, and hiking is one of the most popular activities in the area. Trails are usually well marked and kept up; however, it is essential to have a good map and directions, and serious climbing and foul-weather gear if you plan to do any hiking in the Highlands. The best source of information is the tourist board in each area. They can suggest some routes suited to your abilities and supply you with detailed maps.

Another favorite, low-tech mode of touring is pony- or horse-trekking. There are dozens of riding centers dotted around the Highlands, and this is a terrific way to travel to the remotest parts of the country and back to civilization again in the course of a day. There are half-day, full-day, and week-long trips and beyond for experienced riders as well as the rank amateur. Destination Scotland Ltd. has published a booklet describing about thirty trekking holidays, all sanctioned by the Scottish Trekking and Riding Association. For a copy write to them at West Renfrew House, 26 Brougham Street, Greenock, Scotland PA16 8AD (tel. 0475-85220/26941).

And of course if hiking or trekking isn't your favorite sport, a slow, delicious drive through the mountains with frequent stops for picnics and photo opportunities is about the nicest way you could imagine to spend a day.

High-country scenery is not the only thing the Highlands have to offer, not hardly. We have divided the area up into three territories: the southeastern portion, including the Grampian region, where you'll find the city of Aberdeen; Royal Deeside, those areas bordering the River Dee; and Speyside, famous for its Whiskey Trail. The second territory is in the eastern part of the Highland region, just west of Grampian, and includes the city of Inverness and Loch Ness. The last territory runs along the entire northwest coast (including Western Isles) from Ullapool down into Inveraray in the northern portion of the Strathclyde region, where you'll encounter some of the starkest, most beautiful scenery in the world.

## TRAVEL

The quickest way to get to these out-of-the-way areas is **by air.** For the northeastern destinations, there are airports at Aberdeen (tel. 0224-722331) and at Dalcross near Inverness (tel. 0463-232471). For northern portions of the western Highlands and island region, use Inverness airport. For the southern portion, the Glasgow airport (041-887-1111) is closer.

As with the Lowlands, the pleasantest way to get to the Highlands is **by rail.** It is, however, an all-day affair. Trains depart from King's Cross Station in London (tel. 01-278-2477) and travel on the Edinburgh corridor, arriving in Aberdeen (0224-594222) from seven and a half to ten hours later. Trains to Inverness depart from either King's Cross or Euston (tel. 01-387-7070), arriving in Inverness (tel. 0463-238924) eight and a half to nine hours later. The overnight train to both cities is a pleasant and economical journey. Some of the most memorable rail routes run through the Highlands, the most famous of which are the northerly route to Skye from Inverness to the Kyle of Lochalsh, and the "Road to the Isles" route from Fort William (with connections south to Glasgow) to Skye at Mallaig. In the summer **steam trains** run along this line several times weekly. Call (0397-3791) for information.

Whether you go by air or rail, you will have to **rent a car** once you're in the Highlands because there is no other way to get deep into the countryside—the primary purpose for any visit. Budget Rent a Car offers the best rates of the majors, with offices at the Aberdeen airport (tel. 0224-771777), in Aberdeen (tel. 0224-639922), at the Glasgow airport (041-887-0501), and in Inverness (tel. 0463-239877). Driving up from London is a fool's errand: It's an extremely long journey even by motorway, and the scenery from the highway is not particularly interesting until you get past Glasgow/Edinburgh. Better to fly or take a train up and hire a car here. And by the time you buy gas, pay any per-mile charges, and perhaps make a necessary night's stopover on the way, it will save you money and aggravation in the long run.

Likewise with **bus travel.** Long hauls from London, while admittedly economical, are a miserable way to travel. And inter-highland transport probably does not go to all the places you want to go when you want to go.

Naturally, the primary way to get to the islands is **by ferry.** The principal carrier in the northwest of Scotland is Caledonian MacBrayne (tel. 0475-33755 for information, 0475-34531 for reservations). Cal–Mac boats run between the mainland and 23 different islands on regularly scheduled crossings. They also offer special "Island Hopscotch" and "Island Passport" packages, which give discounts for people interested in visiting several different islands on the same trip (tel. 0349-63434 for information on special packages).

## DRIVING IN THE HIGHLANDS

Cruising through the mountains of northwest Scotland is an experience unequaled elsewhere in Britain for sheer beauty and out of this worldliness. It is also an experience in tough-road driving. Most of the roads worth driving on are single-track; that is, they are just wide enough for one car to negotiate at a time. Every couple of hundred yards there are passing places, little extensions where the road widens briefly for you to pull over (always remembering to smile and raise a finger or two from the steering wheel in salute) when a car approaches from the other direction or wants to pass you from behind. Some roads are unpaved; in springtime, bridges may be washed out; you may be held up for twenty minutes while a shepherd and sheepdogs move their charges from one field to another—if this happens, just relax and enjoy the show; it's rivetting to see the man and dogs at work.

The point is that driving in the Highlands is all part of the adventure and is great fun if you approach it with this attitude. If you try to go anywhere in a hurry or get upset over what seems needless delay, you're going to be in for trouble. There simply is no fast way to get there from here, but with a landscape as spectacular as this, who cares?

This having been said, there are a few things to keep in mind to ensure that your journey isn't too "adventurous." First of all, whatever you do, don't rent a big, boaty car. As mentioned, the roads are extremely narrow and impossible to negotiate in an unwieldy auto, so stick to a nice compact—and save yourself some money, too. Second, get yourself a good road map and pay attention to it. Most roads, even those through the middle of nowhere, are extremely well marked; however, if you make a wrong turn it may be a long time till you discover your mistake and make it back to the right place again. Third, get gas whenever your tank dips below the half-empty mark. If you play chicken with your gas gauge, letting it get down to the very bottom, thinking there will be a filling station in the next town, you could be sadly mistaken. And all the hill climbing burns up more gas than you may have calculated. Finally, whenever you ask a Scot how long it takes to get from here to there, always allow for half again as much time as he tells you. It's not known whether or not the Highland people travel by rocket, but you'd have to have one to get between places as quickly as they claim to do.

# ✤ HOTELS

To say you will be pleasantly surprised by the accommodations available in this rugged, remote part of the world is the understatement of the year. *Surprised* is not the word—*dazzled* is more like it. Some of Europe's finest hotels—and best chefs—are to be found nestled in the farthest-away places you could imagine. The inns and lodges and houses and castles of the Scottish Highlands would give any London hotel a run for its money—and its clientele. What a joy it is, then, that these marvelous properties not only offer near-to-perfect service, food, and appointments but offer them in settings as far away from the dirt and congestion of city living as you can get in this country.

Highland hospitality is second to none. It is an ancient and very real ethic ingrained in the people since the days when the hills were ruled by the great clans. In Sir Walter Scott's *Waverley,* young Waverley, raised by English sympathizers, arrives at the manors and camps of the Highland lairds expecting backward, barbarous behavior. Instead he finds a most sincere, civilized code governing the clan chief's behavior to other clan chiefs, members of his clan, and guests in his home. Many of your hosts and hostesses will greet you in their clan tartan and/or preside at dinner in same. This is not picturesque posturing for the tourists, but a heartfelt expression of the dignity and pride they derive from extending the hospitality of their house. And enjoying the solicitous and attentive service of a Highland hotel is an experience you'll not find elsewhere. It is due in large measure to the fact that while Highland hosts take their work very seriously—that is, take their work very much to heart—they understand that no matter how grand or elegant their property may be, a visitor wishes to feel comfortable, not like he or she has to be minding his or her p's and q's. The hotels and inns we have included manage to strike a balance between beauty and elegance and familiarity and ease.

For those of you spending a week or two in the Highlands—and the area's variety of points of interests warrants at least that much time—we recommend that you base yourself at two or three of these hostelries—perhaps one in the east and more southerly regions around Aberdeen or Inverness, and another in the north and west on or about the islands and mountains of Rosshire. You'll need three or four days to really settle in, relax, and let the Highlands' sorcery work its way with you. If you choose a southern base and a northern base, you should easily be able to make day trips from each to see the sights that interest you particularly. And although traveling is a slow-paced process in this part of the world, the spectacular drives you'll be taking are an important part of touring Scotland.

Because almost all of these hotels are quite literally in the middle of nowhere, instead of identifying them by town, we have grouped them according to the breakdown—Grampian, Inverness, and the Northwest Highlands and Islands—used later for touring this region.

One caveat: Since many of these hotels are in remote mountain settings, some are not open all year round. We have checked their seasons of closings up through the spring of 1989; however, it is important to call in advance for reservations because schedules can change at the last minute.

**Credit card abbreviations used in hotel and restaurant listings: AE for American Express, CB for Carte Blanche, DC for Diner's Club, MC for MasterCard, V for Visa.**

# Grampian

**Craigendarroch Hotel and Country Club,** Braemar Road, Ballater, Royal Deeside AB3 XA; tel. (0338) 55858, telex 739952. Four and a half million pounds was pumped into this hotel-resort complex in 1988 to fix it up for Aberdonian oil men and the Royals from across the river at Balmoral. And indeed the Princes Harry and Wills often come with their nanny or mum for a swim in the pool. Craigendarroch is an all-inclusive resort, with condos, a hotel, a leisure club and spa, and a fine view of the river Dee from its hillside setting. Rooms are modern-hotel takes on antiques and comfort. Try to get a southern-facing one with river view. The club has an indoor pool, whirlpool, sauna, trimnasium, solarium, health and beauty salon. Outside there are tennis courts, a putting green, a dry ski slope to practice your parallel turns, and golf available nearby. There is a café by the pool and the more formal Oaks restaurant, which features Scottish and continental fare. Craigendarroch is open all year; a double room with breakfast is £80–115. All major credit cards.

**Invery House,** Banchory, Royal Deeside, Kincardineshire AB3 3NJ; tel. (03302) 4782, telex 73737. Sir Walter Scott was frequently a guest here, and the rooms are named for his novels. Perhaps he was intrigued by the ghost of the woman who was buried just by the gate when a freak snowfall forced her funeral procession to halt. Perhaps he was beguiled, as you no doubt will be, by the secluded beauty of Invery's setting beside the river Feugh. Stewart and Sheila Spence drew on years of experience, gained at their hotels in Aberdeen, to create their fantasy country house hotel here in Banchory. The rooms have satellite TV, phones in bedrooms and bathrooms, and were decorated by Sheila herself, with an eye for cheerfulness and comfort. The dining room produces some of Deeside's finest food, and Stewart's wine cellar is well stocked. Also savor a malt whisky or vintage Armagnac in the drawing room after your meal. Nearby are top-drawer salmon fishing and hunting, golf, castles, and the city of Aberdeen. Bed and breakfast for a double room begins at £85. All major credit cards are accepted. Invery House is closed for the first three weeks in Jan.

**Kildrummy Castle Hotel,** Kildrummy by Alford, Aberdeenshire AB3 8RA; tel. (03365) 288, telex 9401 2529 KCHL. Kildrummy is just beside the ruins of a 13th-century castle amid one of Aberdeenshire's loveliest gardens. The present house is full of Edwardian comforts and turn-of-the-century interpretations of an old Scottish manor house. The lobby and halls have tapestry wall coverings, the carved staircase is guarded by a brace of lions, even the light switches, doorstops, knobs, and keyholes are all in keeping with the Gothic flavor of the house. Compared to the public rooms, the guest rooms are simply furnished; their best features are, not surprisingly, the views over the castle ruins and gardens. The dining room produces some spotty selections: stick to simple preparations, others tend to be oversauced. The rates at Kildrummy are a bit less expensive than at other hotels in its category; doubles are from £64, including breakfast. The hotel is closed Jan.–Feb. All major credit cards except DC are accepted.

## Inverness

**Culloden House,** Inverness IV1 2NZ; tel. (0463) 790461, telex 75402. If Ian McKenzie ran a roadside-hut B&B it would be the best place to stay in town. Ian and his wife, Marjory, quite simply are some of the nicest people on the planet. Their property is not, however, as postulated, but rather one of the most stunning Robert Adam mansions in the land. It's a house fraught with historical associations, not the least of which is that it served as headquarters for Bonnie Prince Charlie before the battle of Culloden in 1746, and for Prince Charles a few years ago when he visited to open the Battlefield Centre nearby. Room 11 was BPC's; room 14, HRH's. Another piece of history involves a 1730 letter of a traveler who remarked that it "is the custom of that house . . . to take up your freedom by cracking his nut; that is a cocoa shell filled with champaign." And the McKenzies greet all their guests with a bit of the bubbly as they show them to any of their splendid guest rooms filled with antiques and brightened by soft floral papers. The baths are large, several with Jacuzzi, and all stocked with standard-size toiletries. The public rooms are magnificent, with Adam-style plasterwork and ceilings. The dining room, in a rich hunter green, is warm with the light of candles and the scent of Michael Simpson's Auld-Alliance blend of French and Scottish techniques. The price of a standard double begins at £100, including a delicious, massive breakfast. Culloden House is open year-round and accepts all major credit cards.

**Knockie Lodge,** Whitebridge, Inverness-shire IV1 2UP; tel. (04563) 276. Lord Lovatt built the lodge in 1789 for his hunting pleasure, and it has been the scene of many exciting displays of firearm finesse—ask your host Ian Milward to tell you the story about Lady McTaggert's gun battle with an estranged lover. Yet when you drive (and drive and drive) down the road to Knockie, you'll feel you have found the soul of calm and escape. Sitting under Beinn a' Bhacaidh, beside its own loch just south of Loch Ness, there's nothing else but sheep and streams and forest for miles. Everybody gets to know everybody else and fixes everybody else's drink while the family room discussion centers on the day's adventures. The dining room provides the best of the local larder. Rooms all have spectacular views—as do most of the bathrooms—and have some 19th-century antiques. Knockie is simple serenity—at a great price; doubles begin at £45, including breakfast. Knockie Lodge accepts MC and V. It's closed Nov.–April.

# The Northwest Highlands and Islands

**The Airds Hotel,** Port Appin, Appin, Argyll PA38 4DF; tel. (063173) 236. Eric Allen greets you, beaming through his whiskers, extending a hearty handshake as you check in to this 1740's inn on the shores of Loch Linnhe that he and his wife, Betty, have owned for ten years. Airds is a member of Relais & Château, and dinner is a delight: Betty Allen, although self-taught, is recognized as one of the best chefs in Britain, and the Allens buy all their fish, game, and meats locally. After dinner, settle into an overstuffed chair before the fire with the *Glasgow Herald* or *Country Life,* or perhaps a copy of *Rob Roy* from their well-stocked shelves. Your room will welcome you with lighted lamps, your clothes will be folded, fresh towels will have appeared in the bathroom. Decorating is done with florals and antiques. The bath is brass and mahogany with Highland Heather toiletries. The Allens have made this delightful inn truly one of Scotland's most special places to stay. Airds is closed mid-Jan.–Feb. A double room including breakfast is £60–£70. No credit cards, but personal checks are accepted.

**Alt-na-harrie Inn,** Ullapool, IV26 2SS; tel. (0854) 83230. Heretofore Ullapool was mostly known as the point of embarkation for ferries to the Outer Hebrides. Now it is becoming famous for this remarkable inn, set on the opposite shore of Loch Broom, reachable only by launch. Your homing instinct would bring you to Alt-na-harrie's door even if Mr. McKay didn't motor over in his Wellingtons to fetch you at the pier. Two chimneys puffing cheerily greet you, as does Fred Brown, who ushers you up to your room, which is simply furnished with pale wood, subdued shades, and modern tapestries on the wall. In the sitting room downstairs, the fire is bright, snapping as Mr. Brown recites the evening's menu. Gunn, his wife, is an inspired chef who has invaded the Scottish culinary scene as surely as her Scandinavian ancestors made their mark on these northern regions of Scotland. She employs ingredients she raises or gathers from the land nearby or that arrive on the daily *Red Star* from Glasgow. Alt-na-harrie is the kind of place you dream about finding—and once you've found it, you'll dream about it even more. The inn is closed the first two weeks of July and Oct.–March or April. The rate per person for dinner, bed, and breakfast is £72, including the ferry service. No credit cards are accepted, but you can pay with a personal check.

**Ardsheal House,** Kentallen, Argyll PA38 4BX; tel. (063174) 227. There's a nice swing in the tree as you drive up the long road to Ardsheal. Any of a number of dogs will run down to give you their wagging approval as you take care of business in the lobby of this long stucco house set up on a little rise commanding a spectacular view of Loch Linnhe. Jane and Robert Taylor found this place 12 years ago, instantly fell in love with it, and moved their base of operations from New York City to this, a setting that could not be farther removed from the madness of Manhattan. The rooms are comfortable, if not grand, with thick carpets, warm wallpapers, baths with Crabtree & Evelyn goat's milk soaps, and all around canine artwork from prints to bronzes—Bob is director of the Westminster Dog Show in New York. The delight of dining here is the greenhouse, full of flowers and extending out into the garden. Aside from the swing, there is a tennis court, swimming in the loch for the brave, fishing, horseback riding, and hiking nearby. Ardsheal is open April–Nov. Dinner, bed, and breakfast per person starts at £50. AE, MC, and V are accepted.

**Arisaig House,** Beasdale, Arisaig, Inverness-shire PH39 4NR; tel. (06875) 622, telex ARISAIG 777279. Arisaig is another Relais & Châteaux offering in an 1864 house on a spit of land looking out toward the Hebrides. The atmosphere is surprisingly formal for a middle-of-nowhere place such as this, silver-salver service in modulated tones: it's to preserve the stillness here that you'll find as you work your way through the woods and down by the water on their miles of nature walks. The rooms all take full advantage of the views and are provided with sitting areas with small armchairs and TV—if you can take your eyes off the entertainment out the window. There are velour robes, bidets, lily of the valley and sandalwood toiletries in the bathrooms. The kitchen, under the direction of Mr. and Ms. Steward, is duly celebrated and often draws lunchtime clients from Inverness, who arrive by helicopter at the house's private pad. A double room including dinner and breakfast begins at £60. AE, MC, and V are accepted. Arisaig is closed Nov.–Easter.

**Inverlochy Castle,** Torlundy, Fort William PH33 6SN, Highland; tel. (0397) 2177, telex 776 229. People assume a hushed, reverential tone when referring to Inverlochy Castle. It is the standard by which all other country house hotels are judged. And Inverlochy is a lot to live up to. Queen Victoria, a woman who had been around, "never saw a lovelier or more romantic spot" than the 500 acres of woods, ponds, and delicious gardens set directly below Ben Nevis, Britain's highest peak. The house was purchased in 1944 by the Hobbs family from Vancouver, British Columbia, and is presently presided over by Grete Hobbs, who attends to every detail with a quiet professionalism and assurance. Inverlochy houses much of the Hobbses' priceless collection of art and antiques, and indeed the princely proportions, frescoed ceilings, and French furniture are as reminiscent of a châteaux as they are of a Scottish manor house. Room 1 was Queen Victoria's and is regal in its rose carpeting, floor-to-ceiling draperies, pink-marble commode in the bath, mineral water, Vitabath, Jean Patou soaps, and magnificent vista. Other special rooms are in the turret; number 7 is lemony shades with prints of birds and flowers, and closets and armoires bigger than some London flats. Graham Newbould came here after quitting his culinary duties as chef at St. James's Palace; hence dining at Inverlochy is as remarkable (and costly) as is everything else about the place. A double room is £145; a suite, £172.50 including full Scottish breakfast. All major credit cards are accepted.

**Kinloch Lodge,** Sleat, Skye IV43 8QY; tel. (04713) 214. On the lawn leading down to the Sound of Sleat is a sculpture of a sea otter in ecstasy, and so too will you be when you get a gander of the view from just about anywhere on the property. Lord Macdonald (scion of the Hebrides' most illustrious clan) will come to greet you, or perhaps Lady Macdonald will, arriving from the kitchen, pearls flung around her neck, wiping her hands on her apron. Lady MacD has written several cookbooks, and the food is certainly a stellar feature of Kinloch living. The ten rooms are not large or fancy, but they are supplied with some very nice clan antiques, ample bathrooms, and of course ravishing vistas. A double room, including breakfast and dinner, is only £65 per person. MC and V accepted. The lodge is closed Dec.–March.

**Taychreggan Hotel,** Kilchrenan, by Taynuilt, Argyll PA35 1HQ; tel. (08663) 211. Evenings John and Tove Taylor mingle in the bar, make dinner suggestions for the guests, and seem to be on good terms with everybody. John is English, Tove is Scandinavian, and their inn, situated on a point thrust into Loch Awe, combines the best of those worlds and of the Scottish world. Dr. Johnson and his faithful companion, Boswell, stayed at this very inn. (The latter gives a most dramatic account of traveling Loch Awe in a terrible storm; needless to say, he was delighted to be greeted with a bright, cosy hotel in which to weather out the storm.) The dining room looks westward over the Loch, so you can enjoy the sunset while you're munching on local langoustines or Aberdeen lamb (unfortunately you'll see the parking lot first). Request a room in the older part of the hotel; those in the stable extension are a bit boxy. A double room with breakfast and dinner begins at £48 in the low season, £52 in the high (per person, per night). All major credit cards are accepted.

# Grampian—Aberdeen, Royal Deeside, and The Whisky Trail

This part of the Highlands has the most variety of all the regions. Aberdeen is a remarkable city built from the riches of the sea: first silver darling (herring), then black gold (North Sea oil). City fathers have proudly pumped their wealth back into the town: parks and galleries, theaters and monuments abound. Along the banks of the river Dee and thereabouts is a trail of some of Scotland's finest castles, and the Highland Games held at Braemar in September are the country's most celebrated—and a great place for Royal stalking. Surrounding the Spey River are dozens and dozens of distilleries where Scotland's most celebrated export, malt whisky, is produced. You can't say you've seen Scotland until you've spent a day or two visiting the heartland of whisky country and sampling some of its wares—from internationally recognized major brands to tiny, two-man operations. Probably the best place to base yourself for these tours is along the Dee. Hotels in Aberdeen and along the Whisky Trail are somewhat disappointing, whereas Royal Deeside inns are spectacular and are convenient to both Aberdeen and Speyside.

## The Silver City

The lifeblood of Aberdeen, originally two cities that have merged into one over the centuries, pumps through her two arteries, the Dee and the Don, down to her harbor and quays. Since the first settlements in 5,000 B.C., Aberdeen's economy has been water-based, beginning, of course, with fishing (for a taste of historic Aberdeen, start your day—7 to 9:30 A.M.— at the Fish Market on Market Street, a scene of congenial mayhem), which attracted settlers from the Continent, who eventually mixed with the native population. During the late Middle Ages, trade with Flanders, Germany, and the Netherlands brought goods and wealth to the city, a cathedral was

built and a university founded. Early in the 19th century Aberdeen stepped up its foreign trade and became a major center for clipper ships sailing to China. In the 20th century, wealth is again being gleaned from the sea; Aberdeen has become the major point of entry for Britain's North Sea oil.

The city's layout reflects her long history: Aberdeen is divided into old Aberdeen and new Aberdeen. The best plan of attack is to begin in the old city; although it's romantic cobbled streets are perfect for a twilight stroll, there's not much to do in the way of nightlife, so spend the morning here.

## Old Aberdeen

This is where you'll find the university, founded in 1495 by Bishop Elphinstone; schedule yourself some time to wander around its ghostly quads and gardens. Not surprisingly, the most important sights are ecclesiastic in nature. **St. Machar's Cathedral,** at the corner of Chanonry and Seaton Park, is named for the religious leader of Aberdeen's Celtic settlers. Perhaps during your visit the carillon from the cathedral's heavy-set twin towers will sound, enhancing your enjoyment of the 14th- to 15th-century structure. Not to be missed is the coffered ceiling, whose recesses are ablaze with the coats of arms of the princes and popes of Europe circa 1520—it's a history lesson in itself. The other splendid church in Old Aberdeen is **King's College Chapel.** You'll recognize its crown spire (17th century) from the similar one perched atop St. Giles in Edinburgh. The early-16th-century chapel is exuberantly Gothic, an important example of the northern expression of the style. Inside is one of the few medieval Scottish church interiors to have escaped destruction during the Reformation. While you're in the neighborhood of things medieval, have a look at the **Brig o' Balgownie,** spanning the river just off Don Street, built in the 14th century and still looking mighty solid.

## Misters Smith and Simpson's Granite City

Much of (more) modern Aberdeen was built by Archibald Simpson and John Smith, two gents of the early 19th century who traded important architectural commissions generated by the wealth provided by improvements in the harbor and its facilities. The Aberdeen granite both men preferred is largely responsible for the city's shimmery silver look (and hence the nickname Silver City). The tourist information center is a tiptop organization at St. Nicholas House, Broad Street (tel. 0224-632727).

## Galleria Gloriosa

Don't even think about coming to Aberdeen without spending several hours at the **Aberdeen Art Gallery,** Schoolhill (tel. 0224-747333; open Monday through Saturday from 10 A.M. to 5 P.M., Thursday till 8, Sunday from 2 to 5 P.M., free). Start upstairs in the Alexander Macdonald rooms—so named for a 19th-century Aberdonian granite merchant and art patron. These galleries contain Scottish masters, including Aberdonians William Dyce, John Phillip, and George Reid. Most interesting is Macdonald's collection of ninety self-portraits by important 19th-century British artists. Elsewhere on the premises you'll find the Murray Room, a collection of watercolors and prints by Monet, Brueghel, Turner, Sargent, etc. For more information on the Aberdeen arts scene call ARTLINE at 0224-632133 for daily events.

## A PAIR O' PUBS

On a little lane between Belmont St. and Back Wynd is the **Cameron Inn,** known affectionately as Ma Cameron's. Skip the upstairs and go to the snug bar down to your right as you enter. The laddies'll be there nursing their pints in the paneled bar with its tartan curtains, yellowed prints of old Aberdeen, and cribbage board at the bar. The **Prince of Wales** is at 7 Nicholas Lane, down the stairs off Union Street. One of the longest bars in the kingdom supports eight brands of ale in a pub that's generally of generous proportions. There are milk-glass Edwardian lamps, high stools, and (somewhat) more comfortable and (somewhat) more private tables in the back room. Always crowded, it's a perennial favorite that's lying in the path of a proposed shopping mall, so get here while you still can.

## More Museums

While you're here—and hopefully refreshed at one or both of the above—there is a tetrad of fun and various museums that, taken as a whole, give a very thorough picture of life in Aberdeen down through the ages:

**Provost Skene's House,** Guestrow (open Monday through Saturday from 10 A.M. to 5 P.M.; free). Each room of this 17th-century merchant's house is outfitted with antiques from a different era, beginning with the 16th century and working forward to the early 20th century. Don't miss the chapel's painted ceiling.

**James Dun's House,** Schoolhill (open Monday through Saturday from 10 A.M. to 5 P.M., free). In the house of a former rector of Aberdeen you'll find a list of changing exhibitions of special interest to children.

**Marischal College,** Broad Street (open Monday through Friday from 10 A.M. to 5 P.M., Sunday from 2 to 5 P.M.; free). The building, with the largest granite façade in the world, is itself worth a look. The museum is a mishmash of world anthropology and some interesting local history.

**Maritime Museum,** Provost Ross's House, Shiprow (open Monday through Saturday from 10 A.M. to 5 P.M.; free). In another merchant's house, this one dating to the late 16th century, the Maritime Museum is essential to understanding the city's history as it developed from the rivers and harbor.

## Bloomin' Aberdeen

Aberdeen has won so many Britain in Bloom awards that every now and then it is requested to abstain from competition to give other cities a fighting chance. The riot of color runs rampant all over town.

A favorite among the gardens is **Duthy Park,** with its pastoral Deeside setting. Here you'll find the Winter Gardens, blooming year-round in a network of tremendous greenhouses. You will also enjoy the famous Rose Hill, a tumble of bands of brilliant roses, and the stables for Aberdeen's Clydesdales.

**Hazlehead Park** is 680 acres including three golf courses—two 18-hole and one 9-hole. It also has a tremendous rose garden, rhododendrons of a hundred different varieties, and most especially a pink-to-purple heather garden.

And while we're on the subject of open spaces, the sands along the **Beach Esplanade** are most welcome on a warm summer's day or for a brisk jog on a crisp autumn morning.

## In the Evening

There are three excellent theaters in Aberdeen that offer works from classic to avant-garde: **His Majesty's Theatre,** Rosemount Viaduct (tel. 0224-64112); **Music Hall,** Union Street (tel. 0224-641122); and the **Arts Centre,** King Street (tel. 0224-635208). Another venue is 26 miles northwest of Aberdeen (take the A92 to the B9005) at **Haddo House,** an 18th-century mansion. There are musical performances from April through August indoors and out. Ticket and program information can be obtained through the Music Hall (see phone number above).

## ❦ RESTAURANTS

**Jasmins,** 25 Crown Terr.; tel. (0224) 572362. Jasmins is one of the town's favorites for Peking cuisine. Tuck yourself away at a comfy banquette in the arcade surrounding the dining room so that the Muzak won't interrupt your dining. Naturally duck is the special here; for £25 (easily serving two) you can have it any of three different ways. Accompany this with a bottle of Great Wall wine direct from the mainland. All major credit cards.

**Silver Darling,** Pocra Quay, North Pier; tel. (0224) 576229. It's very tricky to find this place from the town center: follow your map to the Aberdeen lighthouse on Pocra Quay; park and walk past the lighthouse; the restaurant is on your left and the water is on your right. There are only about a dozen tables in this little restaurant, which specializes in the freshest of Aberdeen's catch. Through the big bow windows you can see out onto the pier and watch the fishermen coming and going about their business. After your meal, take a little constitutional through the close-packed stone houses of North and Santon squares, where the fishing-village feel of old Aberdeen is still to be sensed. AE, MC, V.

# Royal Deeside

Queen Victoria wrote that at her country retreat at Balmoral, "You can walk forever, and then the wildness, the solitariness of everything is so delightful, so refreshing." Things along Royal Deeside—given its title by virtue of Victoria and her descendants, who holiday here from August through September—have remained remarkably unspoiled by the incursions of tourists attracted by its royal cachet. This is in part due to the fact that any new building within a ten-mile radius of Balmoral has to be given the sovereign's okay before it can be constructed. Although most visitors arrive from the east in the direction of Aberdeen, by far the most spectacular approach is down from the mountains of Glenshee on the A93 into Braemar. The stark, barren peaks slowly subside into the lush, welcoming Linn o' the Dee, silvery with birch and larch. The A93 is the primary drag along the north side of the Dee, where you'll find most of the important hotels, castles, and attractions; however, we recommend taking the south-side route of B-class roads, the B976, 993, 974, and 9077; it's much quieter.

Here you'll track down a pack of wonderful castles and gardens herded into a manageable touring area. It is about 65 miles from Aberdeen to Braemar at the far western end of the river, but if you want to see two or three of the castles listed and plan on several hours at each, count on spending at least a day on the drive. What we suggest is, to drive westward on the B roads out to Braemar (you'll have to cross over to the A93 just at Balmoral) and backtrack along the A93 eastward along the north side of the river where the castles are located; some of them are open only afternoons anyway, and you won't be so put off by the stop-and-go driving. For information contact the tourist office at 45 Station Road, Banchory AB3 3XX (tel. 03302-2066). Royal Deeside's castles (from west to east) are as follows:

## Braemar

The original 1628 castle was burned in 1689 and rebuilt in 1748. The present structure is unremarkably furnished but has interesting architectural features, like a traditional yett (gate) and pit prison. (Open May through early October, daily from 10 A.M. to 6 P.M.; £1.50.)

The town of Braemar is host to the most celebrated of the Highland Gatherings, complete with sword dancing, caber (tree-trunk) tossing, shot-putting, and of course plenty o' pipes and kilts the first Saturday in September.

## Balmoral

The only part of the castle open to the public is the immense ballroom lined with some of Victoria's silver and Edwin Landseer paintings of the Victorians en retrait. The gardens and exterior of the castle, however, may be enjoyed at leisure. (Open May through July, daily except Sundays; hours vary; admission £2.20.)

### The Royals at Play

Ever since Victoria and Albert bought the place sight unseen in the 1840s and built a "pretty little castle" they could call their own here in 1855, Royals young and old have breathed a hearty sigh of relief upon returning for their annual sybaritic escape to this fifty-thousand-acre sanctuary. In the beginning of their married life, the Prince and Princess of Wales had many, much-publicized spats here: he loved the peace and seclusion, she hated the boredom and dampness. But lately, Diana is beginning to come round to Charles's point of view. Seeing her sons, William and Henry, running around the woods, left to their own devices, unmolested by security guards or film crews, the Princess of Wales has been captured and convinced by the spell of Balmoral. If you're keen to catch a glimpse of royalty, it's best to come during the Braemar Gathering, when regal attendance is assured, or try the pool at the Craigendarroch Hotel in the afternoons, or the Crathie Church (of Scotland, not England, by the bye) at the 11:30 A.M. Sunday service. Shops in practically every town display the royal warrant indicating (at least) three years of service to the royal household, but daily rations are sent up from Kenneth Murdoch's bakery in Ballater.

## Craigievar

You'll have to take a little detour—the 9094 to the B9119 to the A980—to get to Craigievar. It's less difficult than it sounds, and along the way you might like to stop at the Tomnaverie Stone Circle and/or the Culsh Earth House to check out how the real ancients amused themselves. The drive is well worth it: Craigievar is often held to be Scotland's most delightful castle and its most perfect example of baronial architecture. It rises seemingly miraculously, compact, wedding-cake perfect, from the side of a little hill. Craigievar was built in 1626 by William Forbes (the lively Aberdonian merchant called Danzig Willie) on the "L" plan common to Scottish castles during the Middle Ages and copied by Forbes, who wanted a home in the old style. Throughout the house are elaborate plaster ceilings and details, massive fireplaces, and heavy carved-oak paneling, and much of the upholstery, floor coverings and incidental fabrics are various tartans important to the Forbes clan. (Open May through September, daily from 2 to 6 P.M.; £1.50.)

## Crathes

Crathes was begun in the early 16th century and completed late in the 17th by the Burnetts, who had a passion for art and gardening. If you have been overwhelmed by the French-induced finery of southern Scotland's castles, Crathes is all that you could hope for in northern highland elegance and simplicity. The walls of local gray granite are up to eight inches thick in places. The kitchen looks as it did 450 years ago. The upper rooms are remarkable for their marvelous painted ceilings; these rooms include the Nine Nobles and the Green Lady's rooms—the latter named for the ghost of a young serving woman who had a child by one of the Burnetts' manservants. Both mother and baby died mysteriously. In the last century a baby's skeleton was unearthed by workmen renovating the hearth. The castle gardens cover only a modest 3.75 acres, but they are among the loveliest in Scotland—their beauty is concentrated into a small space. The plantings are laid out according to color and you can stroll through the Blue, Red or Golden Garden, along the White Border, or among the shrubs of the Yew Borders or the bird-beguiling Aviary Borders. (Open May through September, Monday through Saturday from 11 A.M. to 6 P.M., Sunday from 2 to 6 P.M., gardens open year-round from 9:30 A.M. to dusk; admission to castle and grounds, £2.)

## Drum

Unlike the pure forms of architecture at Craigievar and Crathes, Drum is an amalgam of styles inside and out. The oldest section of the castle is a 13th-century tower whose lands were granted to the Irvine family by King Robert the Bruce. The newer section was completed in the early 17th century. Inside furnishings also range from baronial to Victorian Scottish. (Open May through September, daily from 2 to 6 P.M., grounds open year-round from 9:30 A.M. to sunset; £1.50.)

# Strath Spey: The Whisky Trail

As you drive through the gentle-to-great Grampian Mountains, you'll notice a road sign you've probably not seen before. It doesn't denote a castle or an ancient monument or a golf course; rather the black pagoda-esque structure with the pointed roof signifies "turn here for a distillery." In this part of the world the main attraction is definitely the work of the "Maltsmen of Moray," the whisky distillers of the Moray district, which runs down from Elgin through river-coursed glens to Grantown on Spey.

If you know anything about whisky production—and if you don't, you're going to—you know that to produce the finest you have to have one vital ingredient: crystal clear mountain stream water. The distillers from the tiny Tamnavulin-Glenlivet to the major-league Glenfiddich are crazy over conservation. The larger operations have bought all the land around their water sources and will allow nobody but sheep to dwell there. The Grampian Highlands and Aberdeen Tourist Board publishes a map and guide to the Whisky Trail that you can pick up free at any tourist office in the area. A good place to start your journey is Dufftown, just outside of which is the Glenfiddich distillery, certainly one of the larger operations but a good place to start because it gives continuous tours daily, and an A-V program explains the history and process before you begin. The tourist office in Dufftown is located in the clock tower right in the center of town—you can't miss it—(tel. 0340-20501) and has plenty of ideas about where to go from there.

You'll definitely want to get off the beaten track and travel south on the B9009 to the B9008 to Tomintoul, then back north on the B9136 over to the B9102, where you can turn south to Grantown-on-Spey or north and work your way back past Dufftown and northward to Elgin on the B9105.

Do try to visit at least one of the smaller, more private distilleries; this is where the process is followed in the old-fashioned, time-honored way. Most of these distilleries (although not all) welcome visitors but are not staffed for regular tours, though they will gladly accommodate you if you call in advance to arrange for an appointment. Try the **Cragganmore Distillery** in Ballindalloch (tel. 08072-202) or **Macallan Distillery** in Craigellachie (tel. 03405-471). The Scotch Whisky Association in London at 17 Half Moon Street (tel. 01-629 4384) and Lawnmarket, Edinburgh (031-229 4383) can help you with lists, suggestions, and phone numbers to plan your Whisky Trail tour ahead of time.

## Uisge Beatha

Speculation has it that early Christian missionary monks brought more than just the Good News to the Celtic tribes of Scotland. They also brought the skill of distilling spirits. A particular spirit, made from malted barley, mixed with spring water, and heated over peat fires in copper pot stills, became the specialty of the Highland tribes, who called the brew *uisge beatha,* "the water of life," and considered it a gift from God.

The making of whisky was a family affair in the ancient days: farmers would reserve some of their crop each season and make enough whisky for themselves and their neighbors, bartering the remainder if there was any. Prior to 1700, whisky production was basically a cottage industry throughout the Highlands and islands, providing a few extra quid a year for the local farmers.

The union with England brought in a foreign and largely unsympathetic legal system intent on extracting taxes from the independent distillers; and finally the Jacobite rebellion in 1745 invoked a series of punitive measures against all things considered to be uniquely Scottish. Private stills were outlawed and a hefty duty on all whisky was imposed. But the resourcefulness of the Highlanders and the mazelike network of glens ensured that an underground industry flourished—as a source of substantial revenue and also as a symbol of defiance against English oppression.

Needless to say, in recent years the British government has grown considerably better disposed toward the whisky industry, since it provides a great source of wealth and a minimum of pollution in a region whose industries tend to produce the opposite effects.

There are two types of whisky: The first type is blended whisky, which combines several different types of whisky, including malt whisky made from malted barley, and spirits made from other grains such as corn or wheat. The second type is the one we will be concerned with here—malt whisky, made exclusively from malted barley in an ancient, almost mystical process exclusive to the northern reaches of Scotland.

In the malting process, barley is steeped in water, which allows it to germinate (sprout green shoots). The malted barley is then dried in a peat-fired kiln, then milled into a mash known as grist and mixed with water—making a liquid called wort, which is drawn off and used in fermentation. Combined with yeast, the wort is fermented, then distilled twice (and often again) over peat fires in large copper stills. Many of the smaller distilleries use hand-beaten copper stills of a particular size and shape, which determine the discrete character of the whisky. The liquid, now called low wine, is distilled a final time, then matured in oak casks for a minimum, by law, of three, but usually at least eight, years before it is bottled and shipped off.

A single, unblended malt rolled around the tongue is divinely deep and silky, with just enough fire to allow you to trace its progress down your throat. It is for this reason that malt whiskys are properly drunk neat, with ice or water if you must but never with mixers, which may tarnish the lily. It is a custom in these parts to have whisky not only as a before-dinner cocktail but also as an after-dinner drink in lieu of cognac or Armagnac. Try it some evening after your salmon or venison.

## ☙ RESTAURANTS

Another great source of information is **A Taste of Speyside,** 10 Balvenie St., Dufftown (tel. 0340-20860). This simple, no-frills restaurant is carpeted with tartan and decorated with unvarnished pine furniture. The focus is on food and drink, and owner Joe Thompson knows all the local distillers and how to arrange to visit their operations. Speyside's menu is eye-poppingly inexpensive: venison pie (game cured for 19 days) is £5, rabbit casserole is also £5, wild salmon salad is £6, and the pâtés—venison with whisky, salmon, and white wine—are out of this world and only £1.50. Joe and his partner Ann McLean offer at least 55 single malt whiskys from eight years on up. Definitely drop in here.

"Gateway to the Highlands" is the Scottish Tourist Board term for this area. If you've been traveling up from Aberdeen, you have been in the Highlands for some time. However, Inverness is the beginning of the hard-core Highlands, where the countryside becomes less benevolent, less gracious. To the east of Inverness are a couple of important castles, the battle site of Culloden, and the prehistoric Clava Cairns. To the south are the Cairngorm Mountains—some of Scotland's most dramatic. To the west is Loch Ness, popular for its fjord-like scenery and of course its most famous, albeit reclusive resident, Nessie. North is a veritable no-person's land, tremendously isolated and topographically uninteresting to the tip of Scotland, John o' Groat's. West of here at Scrabster, ferries sail to the Orkney Islands, interesting but distant.

## The Highland Capital

As mentioned, some of the monickers Inverness has been clapped with over the years can be a bit deceptive. While undoubtedly the largest city in the Highlands, Inverness barely hints at the riches of the lands over which it is supposed to preside. By and large it is an unremarkable town; best to use it as a point of entry and swift departure, or for doing any department-store type shopping, which is centered along High Street. Another important factor in Inverness shopping is the **James Pringle Woolen Mill,** a mile and a half from the center of town on the A862 to Dores. This shop is probably the best place in the Highlands for all the tartan trappings, and it has warehouse selections at warehouse prices. The **Inverness, Loch Ness, and Nairn Tourist Board** is at 23 Church Street, IV1 1EZ (tel. 0463-234353).

While you are in town, you might enjoy taking a peek at the **Inverness Museum and Art Gallery,** Castle Wynd (tel. 0463-23114, open Monday through Saturday from 9 A.M. to 5 P.M. free). This pleasant little museum has to be everything to everybody under one roof, so naturally the exhibitions are brief, but they're informative. There are antique farming implements, taxidermied natural-history specimens, pictish stones, Hebridean pottery, Highland costumes, Inverness silver, and a creditable wee selection of pictures—oils of local scenes including work by Faquarharson and Naysmith. Across Castle Street, Brooke's Wine Bar at No. 75 is Inverness's best for informal imbibement (see "Restaurants," below).

Also of interest to the artistically inclined is the **Eden Court Theatre,** Bishops Road (tel. 0463-221718). The Eden Court presents ballet, drama, musicals, musicians—pop, folk, and classical. There is also a full program of film (same phone number). The Eden Court's self-serve café right beside the river Ness is another favorite lunch spot.

Inverness is also the departure point for several ferries which cruise **Loch Ness and/or the Caledonian Canal.** Jacobite Cruises (tel. 0463-241730) sails on Loch Ness for monster hunting. The Caledonian Canal runs 60 miles through the Highlands from near Inverness to near Fort William: 22 miles are man-made canal and the other 38 travel through natural lochs. For information on trips (there are no scheduled ones; you must rent a boat and crew) contact the Inverness Tourist Board on Church Street.

## Castles, Cairns, and Culloden

Across the Moray Firth east of Inverness head out the A9 to the A96 and travel just beyond the town of Nairn—a good place for golf and beaches, if you're interested—to **Brodie Castle** (open May through September, Monday through Saturday from 11 A.M. to 6 P.M., Sunday from 2 to 6 P.M.; £2). The drive is through an arcade of copper beeches planted—as you can discern from an aerial view—in the form of a wine glass, with the cup toward the castle. Brodie suffered a fire in 1645 and consequently its "Z"-plan conformation is a mixture of 17th- and 19th-century work. Among the castle's special features are the dining room ceiling, made from two tons of plaster, the most pendulous elements of which hang several feet below the plane of the ceiling and are painted to look like wood. The furnishings range from 15th-century to Victorian, with newer pieces predominating. You might see Brodie (the present laird) strolling the grounds, or Tom the retriever chasing sparrows.

Travel back toward Inverness on the B9101 to the B9090 till you reach **Cawdor Castle.** If the title of Cawdor rings a bell, remember that Macbeth, as per the prophecy of the weird sisters, became the Thane of Cawdor, and tradition has it that Duncan was murdered here at the castle. Peering out over the lower 16th- and 11th-century additions is the 1372 central tower. The interior features fine tapestries, paintings, and Jacobean architectural details. There are gardens and nature trails to be explored. (The castle is open May through September, daily from 10 A.M. to 5 P.M.; £2.)

The B9090 intersects the B9091, which intersects the B9006, along which you'll see directions to the **Clava Cairns.** The cairns are a group of Bronze Age burial chambers constructed roughly during the same period as Stonehenge. They are flanked by a group of standing stones in a little hollow of beech trees—a mysterious and mystical setting. (Open all daylight hours; admission is free.)

Farther along the B9006 is **Culloden Moor,** a heathery bog that saw an end to the Jacobite cause during the brief but disastrous battle April 16, 1746, between the Highland troops of Bonnie Prince Charlie and the English troops led by the Duke of Cumberland. There is an excellent Visitor Centre, which shows a film and has an installation giving background history on the Jacobite rebellion. Outside is the Old Leanach Cottage, with a heather-thatch roof and furnished as a peasant cottage might have been in the mid-18th century. (The cottage and center are open daily April through October, from 9:30 A.M. to 5:50 P.M.; admission is £1.20.)

The battlefield itself is always open and always free. It is

## The Battle of Culloden

The campaign of '45 was essentially a civil war. Charles II was succeeded by his brother, James VII (James II of Great Britain). James was unpopular because of his despotic practices and his promotion of the Catholic faith. He was deposed in 1633, and William and Mary, James's niece and nephew, were invited to take the English throne. James's son, James VIII (James III of Great Britain), was furious when he was passed over as lawful heir in 1714, and he sent his son, Prince Charles Edward Stewart, along on an unsuccessful invasion of England in 1715. In 1745 Bonnie Prince Charlie again sailed from France, landing at Loch nan Uamh in the northwest. The Jacobite cause gained strength and popularity, and BPC's army marched southward all the way to Derby, just over a hundred miles outside of London. Bad management, however, forced a miserable retreat, and circumstances found the Jacobite army outside of Inverness early in April of 1746, hotly pursued by the Duke of Cumberland.

The battle began on the morning of April 16. The Highlanders were outnumbered nine thousand to five thousand, and the open flat field favored the cavalry and artillery of the English army. Fighting lasted only forty minutes, during which time twelve hundred of the prince's troops were killed, compared to four hundred government troops.

But Cumberland was not content with his victory. Wounded Highlanders were killed on the field where they lay. Any that managed to escape to shelter in nearby farms were hunted down and executed, as were some of the people who had helped them. But even this was not sufficient; the English wanted to eradicate the society which had promoted the Jacobite rebellion. The wearing of tartans and playing of the pipes was proscribed. The bearing of arms was forbidden, and known Stewart sympathizers were imprisoned, executed, or sent to the colonies and sold as indentured servants. These official "Clearings" were further abetted by an economy which no longer favored the clan chiefs' retaining men to serve as soldiers. Scottish landowners realized the only feasible industry in the Highlands was sheep farming, and tenant farmers were evicted from their crofts in favor of sheep. The forty minutes of battle at Culloden Moor were a death knell tolling the end of ancient Scottish life and the beginning of a century of hardship and privation for the Highlanders—a period from which the region has never fully recovered.

marked by stones denoting the position of the troops, by the Well of the Dead, and by a large Memorial Cairn at which is held a memorial service the Saturday preceding April 16. As with all scenes of great conflict, there is something moving and inexpressibly sad about the beeches and birches and heathery moor that can't merely be explained away by the viewer's predilection for romanticism. It is a windy, sacred place and won't fail to transport you back 250 years to the day when the hopes of the Scottish nation perished here.

## Loch Ness

Monster mania has, unfortunately, not done much to enhance the beauty of this once-peaceful loch. Along the northwestern shore are motels and shops selling Nessie T-shirts, mugs, earrings, postcards—you get the idea. The road along the southeastern side is much prettier, so set off from Inverness on the B862, cut over onto the B852, which follows just beside the loch, then connects with the B862 again about ten miles outside of Fort Augustus, the loch's southwestern tip. You might stop there at **The Gallery Restaurant** for a sandwich or burger or some ice cream, or continue around to the more traveled shore of Loch Ness along the A82. At Drumnadrochit you won't be able to miss signs for the "Official Loch Ness Monster Exhibition," which is worth a visit for the kitsch value, if you're into such things. It shows photographs and videos and recorded testimonies of sitings of Nessie. (Open daily during the summer from 9 A.M. to 9:30 P.M.; £1.50.)

Just east of Drumnadrochit is Urquhart Castle, a formidable ruin of what was once one of Scotland's most formidable fortresses and the site of many pitched battles, strategically positioned as it is, guarding the approach to Inverness. The last castle to stand on this promontory was begun in the 14th century and was blown up by the English in 1692 to prevent a Jacobite takeover. It is from this site that the monster is most frequently spotted.

## ❧ RESTAURANTS

**Brookes Wine Bar,** 75 Castle St., Inverness; tel. (0463) 225662. There are between 150 and 200 wines offered at Brookes, several dozen available by the glass, along with simple, well-prepared food. Soups are warming and rich and only £1. Fresh poached trout is only £4. The pale pea-green wallpaper goes well with the parquet checkerboard floor and rattan chairs—check out the Wynken, Blynken and Nod motif in the ladies' loo—most soothing. No credit cards.

**Le Chardon,** Church St., Cromarty; tel. (03817) 471. Chardon means thistle, and Robyn and Mena Aitchison's wonderful little auberge *(sans chambres)* is a marriage of the Gallic and the Caledonian. Robin, one of Scotland's Young Turks of cuisine, serves as chef, and Mena is waitress, sommelier, bookkeeper, manager, dishwasher . . . . The plain pine floors are scattered with Oriental rugs which complement the nouveau wallpaper and the milk-glass sconces. A prix fixe five-course dinner is a mere £17 and worth every farthing to sample Robin's creations, which have included venison, apple, and pistachio terrine; mushrooms with fennel in a pastry boat; or beetroot soup with horseradish cream for starters; breast of pheasant with raspberry sauce, sole baked with pears and cream, breast of mallard with green peppercorn sauce for an entrée; and perhaps a Tia Maria soufflé or homemade ice cream for dessert. Le Chardon is about 45 minutes from Inverness; take the A9 to the A832 and follow signs for Cromarty at the end of the peninsula known as the Black Isle. Just as you get onto the A832 on your right, you'll see a riot of colored fabric tied to the branches of trees. This is a rag or a holy or a fairy well. Descended from Celtic legend, it is believed that if you tie a rag onto a branch nearby the mystic spring, you will have good fortune. AE, MC, V.

# The Northwest Highlands and Islands

The northwestern stretch of Scotland is severed from the rest of Britain by the southwesterly slicing of Lochs Ness, Oich, Lochy, and Linnhe. The lands of Wester Rosshire and the islands of the Hebrides might as well be cut off completely and drift dreamily out to sea. The landscape here bears little resemblance to any other in Britain, or any other elsewhere on earth. Driving the A835—the main "highway" from Inverness to Ullapool—or the A832 south from there, the road climbs up to rarefied mountaintop pleateaus where there is nothing—absolutely nothing—from the road to the horizon in all directions but broken rock and scree and heather and sheep. There are no buildings, no fences, no trees, no cars—nothing. Scored by the wind, scraped by glaciers, excoriated by pelting rain and sleet, the Northwest Highlands are scarred but unbroken: fierce, implacable, ferocious against the watery clouds. It is this ferocity of landscape that is the salient feature of the northwest. It is savage not like a tangled jungle but like a barren veldt. Unlike the veldt, though, this land is anything but flat: mountains thrust out of the ocean, boulders overshadow the heather, cliffs plummet vertiginously into lochs. When you bring home your photographs to show your friends, they'll stare in amazement and wonder, as if perhaps you had traveled to the moon instead of merely to another world. Once you've seen and lived among these aged and uncompromising mountains for a time, their power over your imagination cannot be underestimated. Certain bends in the road, certain vistas, a thundering gorge, will inflame your imagination and invade your dreams until you return again, and again.

There are no galleries or theaters, few castles or stately homes along this trail. If you need a constant barrage of man-made stimuli, then steer a wide berth of this region. For all intents and purposes, there is nothing to do here—absolutely nothing. Your only recourse is to take day-long walks through the heather-flocked, sheep-pocked hills and straighten out the world in your mind—you probably won't meet another soul to help you with the disentangling. There is an inexplicable peace and solace to be drawn from the wild, pitiless hills.

## From Ullapool, Plans A and B

The reason we're starting here is that Ullapool is probably about as far north as you'll want to go unless you have ambitions to attack the Orkneys and the Shetlands—interesting islands, but a very, very long journey (14 hours from Aberdeen by ferry to Lerwick in the Shetlands) when the Hebrides, Inner and Outer, offer a more accessible and equally various option. While you're in Ullapool, you should consider no other choice but to dine and/or preferably stay at Alt-na-Harrie, across Loch Broom (see "Hotels" at the beginning of this chapter). What to do from here is up to you. Plan A: You can take the ferry to the **Isles of Lewis and Harris,** home of tweed, sheep, and not much else. Lewis is flatter and less dramatic than Harris, except for the marvelous standing stones of Callanish, 22 massive slivers of rock set in a cruciform. Harris is more interesting topographically, with manic volcanic-formed mountains.

If you're stopping for the night (you'll probably have to), call in at **Scarista House** on Harris (085-985-238).

A ferry leaves from Tarbert on Harris for Uig on the Isle of Skye.

Plan B: An alternate route from Ullapool to Skye—simpler, and perhaps less adventurous, though not necessarily so—is to head south on the mainland, wending a memorable way down the A832 to the A896 to the A890 to the A87 and on to the **Isle of Skye.** If you look at your map, you'll note that this is a somewhat circuitous route, but it follows a glorious lochside path and is not significantly longer than any other approach.

## Driving the Coast

Along the way you'll find plenty of distractions to impede your progress. Just at the junction of the A835 and A832 are the **Falls of Measach** (150 feet), where the Corrieshalloch Gorge takes a dramatic tumble. The National Trust for Scotland (NTS) has set up walks and bridges. At **Inverewe Gardens** (directly on the A832 on Loch Ewe) every bee in the northwest and every thrush with any sense is buzzing and chirruping amid the wild and the cultivated. Flowers from Chile coexist with ground covering from New Zealand growing among thick Scottish moss shaded by a tree from the mountains of Russia. Peter Clough, the head gardener, gives tours Thursdays at 1:30 P.M., and oversees the 120 acres with savvy and aplomb. The shop is great (buy some seeds), the café is pretty, a visit is obligatory (open daily from 9:30 A.M. to sunset; £1.90).

Down the road a piece in Gairloch is a nice wee museum, the **Gairloch Heritage Museum** (open Easter through September, daily except Sunday from 10 A.M. to 5 P.M.; 50 pence). It has a bit of this and a bit of that and in a successful, neighborhoody way explicates the Highland way of life. The museum is not marked from the road, so follow the signs for the tourist information center.

The A832 swings inland and passes **Victoria Falls,** another worthwhile detour; flowing over steppes of rock is a wide tongue of water thundering down through red sandstone. There are well-marked trials fitted with footbridges and timber steps. The falls are on one side of Loch Maree, at the far end of which is Slioch Mountain, looking for all the world like a giant Christmas pudding with a hard sauce of snow trickling down the crevasses.

Across the loch is **Beinn Eighe,** centerpiece of a national nature reserve and favorite with hikers who want the views, but not the crowds, of Ben Nevis. Take the A896 back toward the sea and continue south till you reach **Loch Carron;** follow signs to your right (or your map) directing you toward the ruins of **Strome Castle.** It's not much to look at, but along the way you'll see the mill for **Locharron Weavers, Ltd.** They weave all their own tartan here (you're encouraged to watch) on electric hand-run looms converted from pedal looms. They stock over seven hundred varieties of tartan and will sell you a ready-made kilt or make one to order and ship it anywhere in the world. If you've been comparison shopping for just such an item, this is unquestionably the place to come (open Monday through Saturday from 9 A.M. to 5 P.M.).

At the northeast end of Loch Carron the 896 intersects with the A890; take it southwest to the A87, which leads to the **Kyle of Lochalsh.**

## Skye—The Isle of Mists

Tourism is the island's major industry, and your primary duty is to escape all vestiges of same and situate yourself as far as possible from its hotbeds in Portree, Dunvegan, and Broadford. Skye is a very large island, 48 miles long and up to 25 miles wide, so this is easily accomplished. We have suggested Kinloch Lodge—delightfully solitary—but should also mention our favorite B&B: Creagan Ban in Linicro, just north of Uig on the Trotternish Peninsula (the "Winged Isle's" northernmost avian appendage). Mrs. Macdonald and her husband, Alec, speak with a lilt that is augmented by their Gaelic, and Sporan certainly barks bilingually. Scones and tea are served at 9:30 P.M.—when there's still plenty of daylight left. Simple, immeasurably cozy, and most beautiful—sea out the front door, mountains out the back window—their home is always welcoming.

## Around Trotternish

In fact, the whole Trotternish Peninsula is a perfect day's drive (with stops) or (*very* long) walk (with no stops). Just up the road from Linicro is the **Kilmuir Croft Museum,** a cluster of houses containing objects and explanations of the crofters' life (open Easter through October, Monday through Saturday from 9 A.M. to 6 P.M.; £1). On the eastern side of Trotternish is **Quiraing;** take the road marked for Uig to the west, off the A855 at Staffin Bay. It's a crazy zigzag of a climb past some tremendously (phallic, it must be admitted) stoic outcroppings.

## Other Skye Stops

Other favorite stops are **Dunvegan Castle** (open Easter through October from 2 to 5 P.M.; summer from 10:30 A.M.; £2.50), where you can see the Fairy Flag used by the MacLeod chiefs to ward off disaster. While you're here, take a boat trip out to visit the seal colony.

Skye's most prominent features are the **Cuillins, Red and Black,** the latter reaching to 3,300 feet straight up from the sea. These mountains are truly tantalizing for the serious hiker in the southwest corner of the island. Sligachan is the best base of operations for hiking, or ponies can be hired for trekking. Keep in mind that whatever mode you choose, the weather changes oh-so-fast on Skye, so gear up accordingly and be sure to leave word of where you're headed with someone down in the valley.

Your first or last stop in Skye should be the **Clan Donald Centre,** just in from the ferry pier at Armadale on the A851. In a well-programed slide show, "The Sea Kingdom," the Lordship of the Isles is explicated. The center also explains local geology and genealogy, all in the gardens and by the ruined castle of the Macdonalds. There are woodland and seaside walks, a shop and café with Skye island baking and cooking. (Open April through October, Monday through Saturday from 9 A.M. to 5:30 P.M.; Sunday afternoons in summer; £1.50.)

# The Road to the Isles

The ferry from Armadale takes you to Mallaig on the main-land, where you pick up the A830, the "Road to the Isles" (in this case *from* the isles), a duly celebrated trip into the hinterland to Britain's most massive Ben (mountain), Nevis, which thrusts its head through the clouds 4,406 feet above Fort William. Unless you have the good fortune (or at least a small one) to be staying at Inverlochy Castle, skip touristy Fort William except to get hiking suggestions at the Tourist Information Centre—a vital resource—at Cameron Square (tel. 0397-3781).

Instead, continue south on the A82 and take an inward jag to Glencoe. The pass ramming through the high, brooding mountains is one of the Highlands' most evocative panoramas. The place still has something of a terrible solemnity about it, certainly connected to the famous massacre of Glencoe, when in 1692 a troop of Campbell soldiers, loyal to the English king, accepted the hospitality of the Macdonalds and broke bread with them. When their hosts were in bed, the soldiers slaughtered them. About fifty Macdonald clansmen died by violence or of exposure when they were forced to flee into the snowy night. There is an NTS hiking center at the western end of the glen to assist you with walking and camping plans. From here you can do a big sweeping loop through the glen on the A82 and then back west on the A85, or you can backtrack to the A828 down the coast of Loch Linnhe. If you choose this latter route, you'll pass the **Sea Life Centre** (open April through October, daily from 9 A.M.; to 6 P.M., till 8 in July and August; £2.25). In the Highland region of Argyll, as is true throughout most of Scotland, you are never very far from the sea. The seals at Sea Life Centre don't jump through hoops or balance on their flippers; they do "perform" all their usual behaviors for you so you can get an idea how they and all the other local specimens you'll see here disport themselves in the wild. Of course it's a great place for kids, but it has some very grown-up purposes as well.

# A Trinity of Islands: Mull, Staffa, and Iona

The A828 leads to the A816 into **Oban,** a crowded, cluttered resort town; therefore, the best plan is to climb immediately aboard a boat bound for one or all of these three isles. Caledonian MacBrayne (tel. in Oban 0631-63058), in conjunction with several local tour operators, runs all-day ferry tours, departing at 10 A.M., to all three of the islands. Mull is the largest, and consequently the most varied. It has a sizable mountain (Ben More), a good beach (Calgary Bay), and a port town (Tobermory). Staffa is basically a barren block of basalt west of Mull in the Treshnish Isle group; however, the basalt has been spectacularly molded by volcanos and sea into ramrod-erect high massed pillars of rock and into features like Fingals Cave, which inspired Mendelssohn's *Hebrides Overture* and unquestionably fires the imagination of even the most jaded globetrotter.

Iona is perhaps the holiest place in Scotland. It is to this tiny outcropping of land that St. Columba traveled in A.D. 563, bringing with him his religion and several of the devoted from Ireland. The island and its religious treasures were almost lost but for the efforts of an essentially religious commune, founded in the 1930s and flourishing in the 1960s, that rescued and now maintains Iona.

## Ancient Scotland Again

When you resume your journey from Oban, take a southward swing on the A816; you'll drive through an area fairly infested with the remains of various tribes. At the church in **Kilmartin,** there are three crosses dating back to the 8th, 15th, and 16th centuries—all in fine condition. In the churchyard are the Poltalloch Stones, circa 14th century, grave slabs taken from a nearby estate that depict knights and heraldry.

About a half mile out of Kilmartin, make a right, where you'll see several groups of cairns and single standing stones basking in a sheep field. Pottery dating back to 2400 B.C. has been found at this site. Farther up the road from these burial mounds are the **Temple Wood Stone Circles** (the trees were planted by some later romantics). The stones replaced earlier wooden structures and were laid sometime during the two thousand years that the Bronze Age peoples thrived in this area.

The final place to visit is **Dunadd Fort,** a natural fortress eked out of a large rock hillock. It was an important capital of Dalriada, a Celtish kingdom from the sixth to the ninth century. The people didn't need to do much to adapt the natural disposition of the rock to protect and survey the surrounding territory. At the summit of the rock (a fairly easy climb) is a basin, a boar, and a footprint carved into the stone, possibly used as part of a coronation ceremony.

## Loch Fyne and Awe

The A816 connects with the A83, which swings back up north to Inveraray. Along the way is **Crarae Glen Garden** (open from 9 A.M. to 6 P.M. all year), a good place for a picnic or a walk through the trees. Inveraray is a sweet little white town, darling of tourists, yet still manages to be honestly quaint and charming. The primary reason for visiting here is to tour **Inveraray Castle,** a silvery turreted affair, seat of the Duke of Argyll, head of the worldwide clan of Campbells. (The castle is open April through October, Monday through

Thursday, Saturday from 10 A.M. to 1 P.M. and 2 to 6 P.M., Sundays from 1 to 6 P.M. In June, July, and August, it is open all day every weekday including Friday; £1.50.) Inveraray is a formal, grand palace. Campbells especially are encouraged to sign the guest register to keep track of the clan's global peregrinations. Although the Campbells have lived on the site since the 15th century, the present castle was built in the latter half of the 18th and contains fine family portraits by Reynolds and Raeburn, Adam-designed details, a hidden china turret, and lots of Campbell momentos.

There is a cafeteria at the castle, but the best place to eat in the area is the **Loch Fyne Oyster Bar** on the A83 at the northeast end of Loch Fyne. The long, low whitewashed building used to satiate cows and sheep, but now Greta Cameron cooks for Johnny Noble and Andrew Lane, whose oyster farm's customers include Fortnum & Mason in London and the Hong Kong Hilton. Here at the Oyster Bar you can get a dozen for a mere £5.40, a half dozen langoustines for £7.15, and any manner of other aquatic goodies at equally low prices. They will also wrap and ship.

If you're still not out of breath and energy, take the A819 north out of Inveraray to **Loch Awe.** Off the A85 (after driving through a lovely glen) you'll see signs for the **Bonawe Furnace,** a most interesting restoration/re-creation of one of the Highlands' earliest and longest-lasting industries—iron smelting. Or you can tour the loch in style on the antique steamer *Lady Rowena,* departing from Loch Awe Station Pier (call 041-334-2529 in Glasgow or 08382-440 locally).

# 17

# TRAVEL ARRANGEMENTS

# For Information

Whether you're crossing the English Channel or winging halfway around the world to get to Britain, there is a veritable army of government and commercial agents waiting to assuage your every worry. The key to a successful trip is advanced planning. Because there are so many people and organizations all over the world to assist you, it is possible and it really pays to do as much of the legwork as you can before you climb onto your Britain-bound flight.

The ultimate source for information on all things British is the British Tourist Authority (BTA). BTA employees in offices all over the globe know everything there is to know about their country and have answered every question you could possibly concoct to stump them. By all means call, write, or—better yet—drop in in person at any of their offices, which are as follows:

## BTA OFFICES

### Australia
Midland House
171 Clarence St.
Sydney NSW 2000
Tel. (612) 29-8627
Telex: 20762 BTA SYD AA

### Canada
94 Cumberland St., Suite 600
Toronto, Ontario M5R 3N3
Tel. (1416) 925-6326
Telex 6104914211 BRITOURIST TOR

### Ireland
123 Lower Baggot St.
Dublin 2

Tel. 353 614188
Telex 91419 BTA EI

### New Zealand
Eighth Floor
Suite 305, 3rd fl.
Dilwich Bldg.
at the corner of Customs and Queen Sts.
Auckland 1
Tel. (649) 31 446
Telex c/o BRITN "FOR BTA"

### United States
John Hancock Center
Suite 3320
875 N. Michigan Ave.

Chicago, IL 60611
Tel. (312) 787-0490

Cedar Maple Plaza
Suite 210
2305 Cedar Springs Rd.
Dallas, TX 75201-1814
Tel. (214) 720-4040
Telex 4952106

World Trade Center
350 South Figueroa St.
Suite 450
Los Angeles, CA 90071
Tel. (213) 628-3525

40 West 57th St.
New York, NY 10019
Tel. (212) 581-4700
Telex 237798 BRA UR

New York is BTA's main U.S. office, so if you're choosing among them, call there first.

There are 12 regional tourist board offices in England, and offices for Scotland and Wales as well. If you are planning to spend a major portion of your time in one area in particular, write or phone the regional tourist board for specific information. Addresses are as follows:

**Cumbria Tourist Board**
Ashleigh, Holly Rd.
Windermere, Cumbria
Tel. (096) 62 4444

**East Anglia Tourist Board**
Toppesfield Hall
Hadleigh, Suffolk IP7 5DN
Tel. (0473) 822922

**East Midlands Tourist Board**
Exchequergate
Lincoln LN2 1PZ
Tel. (0522) 31521

**Heart of England Tourist Board**
(including **West Midlands**)
2–4 Trinity St.
Worcester WR1 2PW
Tel. (0905) 613132

**London Visitor & Convention Bureau**
26 Grosvenor Gardens
London SW1W 0DU
Tel. (01) 730-3450

**Northumbria Tourist Board**
Aykley Heads, Durham City
County Durham DH1 5UX

Tel. (091) 3846905

**Northwest Tourist Board**
The Last Drop Village
Bromley Cross, Bolton BL7 9PZ
Tel. (0204) 591511

**Southeast England Tourist Board**
One Warwick Park
Tunbridge Wells
Kent TN2 5TA
Tel. (0892) 40766

**Southern Tourist Board**
Town Hall Centre, Leigh Rd.
Eastleigh, Hampshire S05 4DE
Tel. (0703) 616027

**Thames and Chilterns Tourist Board**
Eight, The Market Place
Abingdon OX14 3UD
Tel. (0993) 778800

**West Country Tourist Board**
Trinity Court 37 Southernhay East
Exeter EX1 1QS
Tel. (0392) 76351

**Yorkshire and Humberside Tourist Board**
312 Tadcaster Rd.
York Y02 2HF
Tel. (0904) 707961

The **Scottish Tourist Board (STB)** has its head office at:

23 Ravelston Terr.
Edinburgh EH4 3EU
Tel. 031 332 2433
Telex 72272

There are 38 regional tourist boards within Scotland, information about which can be obtained from the Edinburgh office.

The **Wales Tourist Board (WTB)** has its head office at:

Brunel House
2 Fitzalan Rd.
Cardiff CF2 1UY
South Glamorgan
Tel. 0222 499909
Telex 498269

There are six regional tourist boards within Wales, information about which can be obtained from the Cardiff office.

# Information and Tours for the Disabled

Sights, hotels, restaurants, shopping centers throughout Britain are working diligently to ensure that everybody can enjoy as much of the country as possible. The umbrella group for information pertaining to the disabled is the Royal Association for Disability and Rehabilitation (RADAR). Their main office is at 25 Mortimer St., London W1N 8AB; tel. (01) 637-5400. The Automobile Association (AA) has published a book especially on the subject of holiday planning called the *AA Traveller's Guide for the Disabled*. For a copy, write to the Automobile Association, Fanum House, Basingstoke, Hampshire RG21 2EA.

In many major cities ARTSLINE is a telephone service that lists galleries, museums, theaters, and concert halls that have facilities for people with special needs. Several ARTSLINE offices will also arrange for transportation to and from special events. The ARTSLINE number in London is (01) 625-5666/7. For other cities, check local listings.

Several travel agents operate services specially designed for those who are confined to a wheelchair, are blind, or are deaf. Contact:

**Evergreen Travel Service**
19505 44th Ave. West
Lynnwood, WA 98036 USA
Tel. (800) 435 2288

**Trafalgar Tours Ltd.**
15 Grosvenor Place

London SW1X 7HH
Tel. (01) 235-7090

**Whole Person Tours Inc.**
Box 1084
Bayonne, NJ 07002–1084 USA
Tel. (201) 858-3400

William Foster, disabled himself, is the first wheelchair guide registered in the U.K., and he operates tours for other disabled visitors. His address is One Belvedere Close, off Manor Rd., Guildford, Surrey GU2 6N; tel. (0483) 575401 (24 hours).

# The Seasons in Great Britain

When to go is always a tricky question, especially when it comes to Britain, because weather always has to be counted as a factor. High season for tourism is June–Aug. with considerable spillover into May and Sept. Not only do good weather and school holidays prevail during these months, but visitors are assured all the castles, shops, hotels, galleries, and restaurants they want to enjoy will be open. Great Britain is definitely a country open to view seasonally. This means that, although you may find the countryside free of tourists during the off season, the reason nobody is around then is that many places are closed. This is often the case in the coastal resorts, in northern England, Wales, and most especially in the Highlands and islands of Scotland. The obvious exceptions to the off-season rule are major cities like London and Glasgow, and major attractions like Stonehenge and York Minster which can be seen year round. The opening times we have quoted are as up to date as possible, but if you plan to visit some of the more out-of-the-way sights and hotels Oct.–Apr., be sure to check in advance to confirm they will be operating when you arrive—nothing is more frustrating than driving two hours to a stately home only to discover its season does not begin for another three weeks.

It is no accident that Britons have a reputation for their brollies (umbrellas), Macs (Mackintosh raincoats), and Wellies (Wellington boots). It's not that it rains constantly here; rather it sprinkles, then stops, then drizzles, then stops, then the sun comes out, then the clouds roll in, then it rains, and then the sun is out again. That's why the pragmatic Londoner will take his brolly with him to the City on the most cloudless of mornings. You should follow this example and likewise be prepared for any exigency, with a brolly in your bag or a Mac in the boot of the car.

As mentioned, Britain's weather is highly capricious—even print and television meteorologists won't predict the outlook more than a day in advance—and of course varies considerably within the country itself. In very general terms, winter brings snow to the Scottish Highlands (for skiing) and the Lakes, but elsewhere rarely enough to last more than a day or two. Spring starts out chilly and wet in Mar., but dries and warms up considerably by late April into May. Summer arrives usually in mid-June and lingers often into Oct., with warmer sunny days, the occasional passing shower, and cool evenings. Autumn brings flashes of color to wooded areas and dropping temperatures by early Nov.

## Weather Information

| Climate | Jan. | Feb. | Mar. | Apr. | May | Jun. | Jul. | Aug. | Sep. | Oct. | Nov. | Dec. |
|---|---|---|---|---|---|---|---|---|---|---|---|---|
| Average daily temperature | | | | | | | | | | | | |
| °C | 4 | 4 | 6 | 9 | 12 | 15 | 16 | 16 | 14 | 11 | 7 | 5 |
| °F | 39 | 39 | 43 | 48 | 54 | 59 | 60 | 60 | 57 | 52 | 45 | 41 |
| Average rainfall | | | | | | | | | | | | |
| milimeters | 86 | 65 | 59 | 58 | 67 | 61 | 73 | 90 | 83 | 83 | 97 | 90 |
| inches | 3.3 | 2.5 | 2.3 | 2.2 | 2.6 | 2.4 | 2.8 | 3.5 | 3.2 | 3.2 | 3.8 | 3.5 |
| Average daily sunshine hours | | | | | | | | | | | | |
| | 2 | 2 | 4 | 5 | 6 | 7 | 6 | 5 | 4 | 3 | 2 | 1 |

All this means that no matter when you come, you will need to bring different weights of clothing. The time-honored formula is to bring clothes you can pile on and peel off as the thermometer yo-yos from cool to comfortable. If you come in the winter (Nov.–Feb.), bring lots of warm clothes. If you come in the summer but plan to spend much of your time in northerly regions—in the hills of England and Wales or especially in the Highlands and islands of Scotland—you should likewise prepare yourself for evening temperatures to drop into the forties. Spring, summer, autumn, pack a variety: some cool outfits to keep you fresh on hot days, and some warmer things for a passing cold front or for nighttime. If you plan to do any serious trekking, you absolutely must come prepared with sturdy footwear and clothing. While not quite the conquest of Everest, hiking Ben Nevis is serious business and should not be considered without proper gear. Even if your perambulatory ambitions take you nowhere more treacherous than the sidewalks of London, comfy shoes (that won't be destroyed by water) are a must.

As to style of dress, basically use your judgment. As every-where, cities tend to be more formal, and if you plan to step out to the theater and restaurants in London, you'll want to bring some dressy outfits. Even at some of the tonier country house hotels, while there is certainly no specific dress code, jacket and tie is usually the mode for dinner.

Similarly, if you are here on business, as you might expect, the British professional community evinces a decided conservatism in dress. The habit of wearing sneakers to work, then changing to wingtips or pumps, hasn't reached these shores yet. Tie loosening and shirtsleeve rolling should be held in abeyance, unless your hosts take the informalist lead. Rugged individuality is definitely not appreciated. Otherwise, pack for comfort, space (save room for new acquisitions to your wardrobe), and of course for a minimum of wrinkles. Do leave any jewelry you really care about at home, or if you must bring it, leave it in the hotel safe—but really, it's not worth the hassle. It's tough to impress a country when you've got the Crown Jewels to contend with.

# Formalities

Every foreign citizen will need a valid passport when entering Britain. Special visas are necessary only if you plan to stay for over six months and/or plan to be employed by a British firm. If you do not have a valid passport, you will have to apply for one, a simple, but lengthy procedure, so give yourself a good six to eight weeks to allow for processing time.

**United States:** You can get a passport at the county clerk's office in your area or at selected post offices. It's best to apply in person to save time. You will need: (1) proof of citizenship, such as a birth certificate, (2) proof of identity, such as a valid driver's license with photo, (3) two 2-inch photos, which can be taken at many camera or film-developing stores, and (4) $35 for a processing fee. The passport will be good for ten years. For further information contact the Passport Office, Department of State, 1425 K St. NW, Washington, D.C. 20524; tel. (202) 783-8200.

**Canada:** Apply to the passport office in your region (listed in the phone book), to selected post offices, or by mail to the Bureau of Passports, Complexe Guy Favreau, 200 Dorchester West, Montreal PX H2 LXA. You will need: (1) proof of citizenship, (2) two 2-inch photographs, and (3) $21 for a processing fee. The passport will be valid for five years.

**Australia:** Apply in person at your local post office with a processing fee of $30. The passport will be valid for five years.

**New Zealand:** Write to the Office of Internal Affairs in your local district or in Wellington for information and an application form, which you will return to the agency. The processing fee is $30. The passport will be good for ten years.

Arriving in Britain each passenger is permitted one liter of liquor and four hundred cigarettes. You may not bring meat or poultry (unless fully cooked) or any type of plant material into Britain.

All pets brought into Britain must have a rabies license and are subject to a mandatory six-month quarantine. This also applies to guide dogs. Unless you are moving here for a period of years, it is troublesome and uncomfortable for your pet to endure an extended time of isolation, so it is best for you and the animal to leave it at home.

# Money Matters

Nothing is more anxiety-provoking than keeping close tabs on the daily fluctuations of your national currency when you are overseas. At the time of this writing, the pound was hovering around $1.80 U.S. and $1.90 Australian, Canadian, and New Zealand. These are optimal rates; the rates at which you will be permitted to exchange money are lower because of commissions, processing fees, and other measures determined to fleece you to the max. While it's a given that every time you change money, somebody makes money on the transaction at your expense, there are ways to minimize your loss.

Rule Number One is that you should change money only once. Never buy pounds with dollars, then buy dollars back with those pounds. As mentioned, each transaction saps you of a little more cash so by the time you've made a series of exchanges you can lose up to 15 or 20 percent. If you have any pounds left over, buy something at the duty-free shop at the airport. Unless you've badly mismanaged and have large amounts of pounds, spend what you have left when you are there—this is especially true of coins, which cannot be exchanged overseas.

Rule Number Two is never change money at a bureau de change or at a hotel. Their rates are invariably the worst, and they often charge heavy handling fees on top. Banks give the best rate of exchange. They are open Mon.–Fri., 9:30 A.M.–3:30 P.M. In some cities banks may also be open Sat. mornings, and major post offices often do exchanges as well (although their rates tend to be somewhat less favorable than at banks). If you're stuck without cash on a weekend or when out in the country, use your credit card whenever possible, and change only the absolute minimum necessary to see you through till you can get to a bank.

Many banks throughout Britain will exchange currency—even in small towns. It is, however, always wise to be prepared, so you should plan on having an extra £50–100 set aside for emergencies at all times. Although most airports have extended hours of exchange service, it is best to arrive with £100 in cash and/or traveler's checks (in *pounds sterling*) to save you the bother and time when you land.

Most hotels, restaurants and shops, BritRail and the bus companies will accept traveler's checks. Probably the best kind to get are Barclay's: there are lots of Barclay's banks where they can be cashed, and the bank doesn't charge a fee (usually 1 percent with other checks) when you purchase them.

The most popular credit cards in Britain are Visa (Barclaycard here) and MasterCard (Access here), followed closely by American Express, then Diner's Club, and finally Carte Blanche. Most hotels, restaurants, shops, gas stations, and modes of transport will honor your card in major tourist centers. As you get farther out into the country the number of member establishments decreases proportionally. B&Bs do not take credit cards. Gas stations will usually take MasterCard and Visa, but much less commonly the others.

Credit cards are also useful for getting cash or traveler's checks. If you haven't done so already, get a PIN (personal identification number) for your credit cards like you have for your bank card. This will enable you to use your credit card like a bank card, and withdraw cash from automatic teller machines at the banks in Britain that honor your card. For a listing of these institutions, call the service information number for your card. Most banks that operate this service tend to be in more populous areas. Additionally, American Express offices will cash personal checks for AmEx card holders. Aside from your card you will need a photo ID (passport or driver's license). In all cases, there is a ceiling on the amount you can withdraw, and you will be obliged to pay a small service charge.

If you lose your credit card call American Express at (0273) 696933; Diner's Club at (0252) 516261; MasterCard (Access) at (0702) 352255; or Visa at (0604) 230230.

# VAT

VAT, or Value Added Tax, is basically a government tax on all goods and services. It is possible for foreign visitors to be reimbursed for VAT on goods but *not* on services, although the process is so Byzantine that it is worth pursuing only if you have spent a lot of money in one store. Not every shop has a VAT reimbursement scheme, but the ones that do usually require a minimum purchase (£50). When you pay for your package, ask for a VAT form, which they will give to you with a stamped envelope addressed to themselves. When you are leaving Britain you must carry your purchase in your *hand luggage* through British customs along with the form and receipt from the store. The customs officer will stamp your form, and you mail it in its accompanying envelope back to the store. The store will mail you a refund check in pounds sterling, so you will have to cash it at home, and will of course lose money on the transaction. As you can see, cashing in on VAT refunds is worth the bother only if you have spent a substantial sum in one place, or a substantial sum in each of several places.

# Tipping

A 15 percent tip is standard in restaurants, taxis, and for any tour guide you might engage. Tipping at hotels is, of course, at the discretion of the guest; however, a fiver (£5) for the chambermaid is suggested for stays of several days or longer. Tipping your host and/or hostess at a country house hotel or B&B is decidedly bad form. Many hotels and restaurants will add a service charge of 10–15 percent automatically, and this should be indicated on the menu and/or the bill. You are welcome to add more if the service has been particularly good, and you are within your rights to have money subtracted from this charge if the service was unsatisfactory—but be prepared to explain why.

# Transportation

## FLYING TO GREAT BRITAIN

Britain is a most fortuitous choice of destinations: Its popularity ensures a range of modes of transportation at a range of costs. Most visitors from North America and the South Pacific will be arriving by air. A general rule of thumb when sallying forth on international sorties is to fly on the airline of your destination. British Airways is unquestionably one of the best in the atmosphere: service is professional, crisp, solicitous. British Caledonian, whose specialty is Scotland, is an equally good choice, staffed by extraordinarily congenial people who are very serious about their work.

Of course if you are flying to London from North America, you have the option of doing so supersonically. The only caveat attached to traveling on the Concorde is that its speed and service are highly addictive. The three-and-a-half-hour crossing is pure pleasure, and peering down at the clouds zooming by far, far below at 59,000 feet as you scream across the Atlantic is a guaranteed kick for even the most jaded of passengers. You can leave the States at 9 A.M., read your *Financial Times* and *The Economist,* and arrive at Heathrow in time for cocktails—sharp, fresh, and in fighting form. The Concorde is perfect for a special-occasion flight, but as mentioned, once you've tried it, you'll want to come back for more.

If your expense account or trust fund just won't stretch as far as the Concorde, we recommend taking a morning rather than an evening flight from North America. Traditionally, flights to Europe depart in the early evening and land the following morning, depositing you at your destination tired and cranky. You arrive in London by mid-morning, and many hotels will not allow you to check in until noon. You can avoid this sure-fire formula for jet lag by taking a morning flight, which should arrive in Britain in the evening. You can have dinner, perhaps take a stroll around town, then go to bed for a good night's sleep so you'll be ready for action the next morning. Be sure your hotel knows you'll be arriving at night so that they save your reservation.

Since Britain is such a popular destination, competition tends to keep prices down. Some of the best prices are offered by charter companies, which buy up plane seats in bulk and can thereby pass along the savings. Most charters are perfectly reputable companies, but many impose restrictions on when you can go, how far in advance you must buy your ticket, and extract hefty (monetary) penalties for any change in plans. If you have any doubts about a particular charter company, contact your local better business bureau to see if there is anything to dissuade you from using it.

By far the cheapest way is to go as an air courier. This means that you agree to carry a package for an air-freight company from your city to Britain, and in return they agree to pay part or all of your airfare. This is a legal and legitimate business, and provided you deal with a reputable firm you will not be duped into transporting contraband materials. Most major cities have overnight courier services to London; call up the ones listed in your phone book to see if they will hire you to fly over this way. Usually there are restrictions on the amount of luggage you can bring, and restrictions on when and for how long you can go, but if you're planning a trip for a week or two, this is a very inexpensive way to fly.

# CRUISES

At the opposite end of the luxury-economy scale is a cruise to Britain. Cunard's *Queen Elizabeth 2* has regular service between Britain and North America. They even have a special package that enables you to sail one way and fly the other on the Concorde—five days and three and a half hours per crossing in the same trip. For information in the U.S. phone 1-800-5-CUNARD.

# FROM THE CONTINENT

Until the completion of the Chunnel (the tunnel beneath the English Channel), the only way to get to the British Isles from the Continent is by ferry. There are daily services from Belgium, France, and the Netherlands that are short hops, and longer journeys from Denmark, Germany, Norway, and Sweden. All of these countries have services to ports of call close to London. Additionally there are services from the Scandinavian countries to northeast England and to Scotland. The closest ports to London with connections to France are Folkestone and Ramsgate; Dover has connections to France and Belgium; and Sheerness has connections to the Netherlands. In addition to ferries, if you're in a hurry and/or you want a kick, there are hovercraft that make the usually several-hours' crossing in 35 minutes. Naturally, the cost is commensurately higher. The major ferry and hovercraft companies use British Rail as their overseas travel agents, so you can make reservations for Channel crossings through your local BritRail representative. If you are planning to ferry a car across or to take a hovercraft, advance reservations are essential. When in Britain, for information on cross-Channel services, call BritRail at (01) 834-2345.

# TRAVEL AROUND GREAT BRITAIN

The British countryside profers beauty that ranges from sweet to staggering, and traveling through it is one of the great pleasures of visiting the island. Getting around from place to place should, therefore, be an important and enjoyable component of your holiday, not an annoying chore. As we enjoin you through-out this book, don't try to cram your vacation full of as many sights as are humanly possible to see in the time you have. This completely misses the point of coming to a nation like Britain, which has an innate and unshakable reverence for its marvel-ously varied landscape. You could easily spend a month or two—or a lifetime—exploring the area covered by a single chap-ter in this book. Of course many people who haven't traveled in Britain before will be eager to see it all and do it all, but if you pursue this course, you will really only have time to feel what it's like to be a tourist in Britain, not what it's like to live here. And that would be a great shame. It is one of the more gentle, ancient, civilized, and sane ways of life devised by man.

# RAIL TRAVEL

By far the nicest way to cover long distances is by train. To those from other countries whose rail service is inefficient, run-down, and erratic, you are in for a most pleasant surprise. BritRail is almost always a delight. Trains are modern, fast, clean; they offer bar and cafeteria and sit-down restaurant service on long hauls; personnel are smart, chipper, and courteous; and for the most part, trains run on or close to schedule. If you are a stickler for comfort and spaciousness, you might prefer to travel first class.

An adult BritRail Pass costs about $240 for 15 days. This will allow you to travel throughout Britain (with the exception of Northern Ireland) on any train at any time. Passes *must* be pur-chased at home, i.e., in Australia or the United States. They *cannot* be purchased in Great Britain. Rover tickets are available in Britain for unlimited travel, usually within the confines of a par-ticular region. When this is a good option for the area you are traveling in, we have mentioned so in the text. Passes are a bar-gain if you plan to use trains as your primary means of transpor-tation. If, however, you plan, as we suggest, to take trains on long hauls (say, London to Edinburgh and back) and rent a car for local touring, it is cheaper just to buy a round-trip rail ticket. If you are planning such an expedition, be sure to buy a return (round-trip) ticket when you set out. This is considerably less ex-pensive than buying two one-way fares. Additionally, there are special days each month, blue saver days, when fares are re-duced—to encourage people to travel during off-peak times. Not only does travel on these days save you money; it also usually means that the trains will be less crowded. Saver days are post-ed at BritRail ticket offices, or you can call the nearest station for information.

In any case, *do* take the train: it allows you to take your mind off the map and take a look at the scenery; it allows you time to plan your trip as you go; and, perhaps best of all, it allows you to chat with the locals about where to go and what to do at your destination. BritRail offices in North America: New York, (212) 599-5400; Los Angeles, (213) 624-8787; Dallas, (214) 748-0860; Toronto, (416) 929-3333; Vancouver (604) 683-6896. While you are conferring with the BritRail agent, be sure to in-quire about their special rail/drive combo tours.

# BY BUS

The other prevalent form of public transportation around Britain is by bus (called "coach" when referring to extra-urban, longer-distance lines). For trips to destinations just outside London (within an hour's time), buses are a convenient and economical method of travel. Green Line coaches (tel. 01-668-7261 in London) generally service this area and depart from Victoria Coach Station, Buckingham Palace Rd.—about a quarter mile from Victoria Rail Station.

We do not recommend taking the coaches on longer hauls: they drive along the motorways, often take much longer than the train, and are considerably less comfortable. If, however, money, and not time or comfort, is the primary consideration, coach is significantly less expensive than train travel. National Express is the primary carrier for long-distance routes in Britain. They can be contacted in North America by calling 1-800-621-3405; in London on 01-437-4203; or in Birmingham on 021-456-1122.

Deep in the exurbs, buses are the only means of public transport to the remote places not serviced by BritRail. You will find, however, that most rural bus services are primarily used as transport for people going to and from work or school, and therefore run early in the morning and not frequently again until four or five in the afternoon, requiring you to be up at the crack of dawn to catch them and leaving you stranded until late afternoon to leave. It is for this reason that we encourage you to rent a car if you are planning (as we hope you are) to do extensive traveling in the countryside.

# BY BOAT

One of the loveliest, most leisurely ways to tour the country is on Britain's extensive network of inland waterways, rivers, and canals that tend to favor the more rural parts of the nation. Obviously, this mode of transport is for those interested in ease and relaxation, not for those concerned with speed and seeing as much as possible. If you are 21 or over, you are eligible to hire a self-skippered boat and pilot it wherever and for as long as you choose. If you are under 21, or prefer to be a passenger, many companies operate tours that provide you with a crew and guide. These tours may be group tours (you share the boat with other passengers) or single tours (you have the boat and skipper to yourselves). In some cases, we have listed water tours in the appropriate regional chapter. Another good source of information is the tourist board information office for each specific region. Here is a list of several companies that specialize in river and canal tours: Bargain Boating (U.S.), tel. (304) 292-8471; Canals Europe (U.S.), tel. (415) 332-9565; Horizon Cruises, Ltd. (U.S.), tel. (1-800) 421-0454; PGL Adventure Ltd. (Britain), tel. (0989) 768768; Page & Moy, Ltd. (Britain), tel. (553) 54 2000; Skipper Travel Services Ltd. (U.S.), tel. (415) 321-5658; Thames Hotel Voyages (Britain), tel. (0273) 324 72; UK Waterway Holidays Ltd. (Britain), tel. (0923) 770040/776205.

# DRIVING

If you're restricting yourself to urban areas and you are considering renting a car, there is only one word on that subject: DON'T. It simply is not worth the hassle, expense, and assorted headaches. 'Nuff said.

With the outstanding exception of cities, driving in Britain is a glorious affair. Most roads are no more than two lanes wide and cut through some of Europe's prettiest property. Of Britain's 232,400 miles of roadway, only 4 percent is motorway (express highway), yet motorways account for 30 percent of road traffic. This clues you in to the fact that if you want to avoid congestion and the anti-aesthetic of highway driving, stick to the smaller roads.

Motorways are titled with "M" route numbers (M1, M67, and so on). Trunk roads, usually two to four lanes with a median between, are designated by an "A" and a two-digit number (A46, A69, and so on). "A" roads are designated by three digits (A485, A303, and so on). "B" roads are generally minor routes, denoted by a "B" and three or four digits (B1362, B655). Local routes are unnumbered roads and are marked by signs directing you to the next town; these roads may be two-lane or single-track roads (one lane with passing places to pull over to allow oncoming or faster traffic to go by). Unless otherwise posted, speed limits are 70 mph on motorways and dual carriageways (two-lane roads), 60 on single carriageways (one-lane roads), and 30 driving through towns.

After having driven here a short time, you will realize that many of the major A roads run right through the center of small towns in their path. Regardless of your hurry, it is not only dangerous but extremely discourteous to come barreling through the center of an erstwhile quiet town. Nowhere you are going could possibly be so important that it warrants disturbing an entire village in order for you to get there a few minutes earlier.

Contrariwise, you may find it a bit unnerving to be driving on motorways whose speed limit is 70 but along which many drivers (not you of course) will be doing 80 or 90 (even in large trucks). If you don't feel like keeping up with these Mario Andrettis of the motorways, just keep calm, stay in the slower lanes, and maintain a steady 70 mph.

If you take our advice, you shouldn't be traveling on the motorways anyway. The purpose of motorways is to go long distances as quickly as possible. As we have suggested, if you are traveling long distances it is much, much better to take the train, then rent a car at your destination for local driving. Motorway driving manages to be terribly nerve-racking and terribly dull at the same time. It is nerve-racking because of the speed and the traffic; it is dull because it is cheerless, characterless, and much the same as driving a superhighway anywhere else in the world. In other words, don't bother.

If you have reserved a car wherever the train has left you off, you would do well to wait until you are ready to drive out of town before you pick up your auto. For example, if you take the train to Manchester and plan to spend a couple of nights in town before heading out to tour the Peak District, don't get a car as soon as you arrive. Use public transportation while you are in town and start your rental on the day you plan to head into the countryside. Likewise if you are starting in the country and ending up in a city, drop off your car as soon as you arrive in town and use local transport while you are there.

When you are driving around the rural reaches of Britain, as much as possible try to avoid motorways and trunk roads, and stick to B and unmarked routes. Not only are these thoroughfares immeasurably nicer; they also can be just as fast, although they might initially appear longer. You can easily get stuck behind a line of cars stuck behind an overladen lorry (truck) on a major A road when you could have had the parallel minor routes all to yourself. We have tried wherever possible to suggest some of these alternatives to the main drag through a region. But feel free to do a little exploring yourself, and strike off on any of your map's narrow little routes that seem intriguing.

It must be stressed that you wait until you are ready to leave town before you pick up your rental car. This does not mean, however, that you should wait until that moment to make arrangements for doing so. On the contrary, the further in advance you can make your reservations, the better your chances are for getting the type of car you want at the price you want. It is very, very expensive to rent a car in Britain. This is especially true if you need to rent an automatic-transmission model. To cut down on expense and precious vacation time wasted, it's a good idea to make arrangements for your car rental *before* you leave home. The major car rental companies that enable you to make reservations in your home country (and hence command a guaranteed-not-to-fluctuate rate) are Avis, Budget, Europcar-Godfrey Davis (overseas contact, National Car Rental), Hertz, and Swan National. All of these companies will be listed in your local phone book, and most have toll-free numbers, with the exception of Swan National, whose overseas office is in New York City, tel. (212) 929-0920.

One final piece of advice: Don't even *think* about renting a large barge of a car. As noted, the roads you (should) will be traveling on are narrow, sinuous, and in some cases barely have enough room for one small car. Additionally, fuel is *very* expensive in Britain, and climbing hills in a gas-guzzler is bound to make your petrol and hence your pounds evaporate at a rapid rate. Do yourself many favors: rent an economical compact. If you're bound to be extravagant, rent a convertible—you'll be much happier.

A valid driver's license from your home country will serve in Britain. If you are planning to stay over six months, you will need to get an international driver's license. Contact your local department of motor vehicles listed in the phone book for information. A driver's license is essential when renting a car.

# INTRA-CITY TRAVEL

Consult regional chapters for specific instructions on how to get around each particular city. Other than that, we will only reiterate: Do not drive in any of them unless absolutely necessary. If you've got a rental car, park it and walk around.

# Touring

Recommending package tours is a dicey business. For the most part, we emphatically do not recommend them. This book is written for the independent traveler who wants to take his or her own sweet time exploring at a sane and tranquil pace, not hitched up with a pack of other tourists. In many countries where traveling is difficult (or against government regulations) without a local guide, package tours may be just the ticket. In a country like Britain, however, tourism is a major, modern industry: the road system is well laid out and marked, public transportation is efficient and pleasant, language is (usually) no problem, and the local folk are amiable and delighted to assist. It is so supremely simple to travel on your own in Britain, we see no reason to be constrained by some tour operator's generic schedule when with just a little research you can easily plan (and amend at any time) your own customized schedule.

We enjoin you to spend most if not all of your holiday exploring one small, discrete region. Most tours, even the upper-crust, luxury ones, tend to have you bombing around the countryside at a frenetic pace, barraging you with sights and sensations so fast and furiously that after a while one abbey blends into the next stately home into the next garden. If you are planning your train journeys, laying out your driving routes, working out a restaurant strategy, you will be much more connected to and hence have a far better understanding of the country where you will be traveling. If you sit down with your schedule and your maps and your budget and this book, you will have hands-on experience debating the pros and cons of this hotel or that county. Before any trip, a good trick is to tack a map of your destination to the wall in a prominent place, and just by constant peripheral glances at the country or county or city you plan to visit, you'll begin to get a feel for the area.

## DRIVER/GUIDE TOURS

Of course, many people prefer or need to have some assistance with their traveling. A fast-developing industry in Britain, which allows you to have the convenience and security of a driver/guide while still affording a good deal of independence, is that of chauffeur-driven cars. You can rent a driver/guide when you rent the car. It is rather an expensive approach, and any of these services reflect their upscale nature by offering Mercedes', Rolls-Royces, and Jaguars to accompany their drivers. Many tour and car-rental companies are adding this to their roster of services. Try contacting the following:

**Abercrombie & Kent**
11 Sloane Sq.
Holbein Place
London SW1W 8MS
Tel. (01) 730-9600

**Boswell & Johnson Travel Services Ltd.**
Grosvenor House
4 Oriel Terr.
Chelthenham Spa
Gloucestershire GL50 1XP
Tel. (0242) 237212

**Britain Without Tears Limited**
7 Kingsdown House
Kingsdown, near Corsham
Wiltshire SN14 9AX
Tel. (0225) 742304

**Connoisseur Travel**
7 Church Lane
Nether Poppleton
York
North Yorkshire Y02 6LB
Tel. (0904) 790924

**Driver-Guides**
5 Ravenscroft Rd.
Henley-on-Thames RG9 2DH
Tel. (491) 572384

**Ghillie Personal Travel Ltd.**
64 Silverknowes Rd. East
Edinburgh EH4 5NY

Midlothian, Scotland
Tel. (031) 3363120

**Scottish Tours**
2E Commercial St.
Leith, EH6 6JE
Scotland
Tel. (031) 5550606

**Take-a-Guide Ltd.**
11 Uxbridge St.
London W8 7TQ
Tel. (01) 221-5475

**Waleslink**
City Travel
13 Duke St.
Cardiff, Wales
Tel. (0222) 395317

# SPECIALIZED TOURS

The other good reason for taking a tour is if you have a special interest such as golf or gourmet dining, wildlife, or walking. Many operators specialize in specialty tours. Of course you can easily plan your own golfing tour of Scotland with this book, or work out an itinerary for visiting the ancient monuments of the South on your own. However, often tour operators will have access to homes and parks that are otherwise closed to the public. Additionally, since they buy in bulk, they often will be able to offer you preferred rates for hotels, theater tickets, greens fees, fishing gear, etc.

# ART, ARCHITECTURE, AND ANTIQUES

Many if not most tour companies offer some sort of stately-home or gallery tour. The following are among those that specialize in this.

**Abercrombie & Kent International, Inc.**
(see above)

**The Canterbury Cathedral Trust**
2300 Cathedral Ave., NW
Washington, DC 20008 U.S.A.
Tel. (202) 328-8788

**Country Homes and Castles**
118 Cromwell Rd.
London SW7 4ET
Tel. (01) 370-4445

**Historic Houses of Britain**
21 Pembroke Sq.
London W8 6PB
Tel. (01) 937-2402

**Temple World Tours**
Randolph's Lane
Iden, near Rye TN31 7PR
East Sussex
Tel. (07978) 258

**Travel England**
25 Cockspur St.
London SW1Y 5BN
Tel. (01) 930-5022

# HAUTE CUISINE

If you would like an itinerary based on eating at only the finest restaurants and/or sampling the best local specialties (who wouldn't?), the following offer several packages:

**Abercrombie & Kent International Ltd.**
(see above)

**British Pride Tours**
484 Lake Park, 67
Oakland, CA 94610 U.S.A.
Tel. (415) 839-9874

**Connoisseur Travel**
(see above)

**International Cooking
with Polly Stewart Fritch**
One Scott Lane
Greenwich, CT 06831, U.S.A.
Tel. (203) 661-7742

**Pathfinders**
1 Bath St.
Cheltenham GL50 1YE
Tel. (0242) 515712

**Stately Home Hospitality**
8 Ashley Court, Frognal Lane
London NW3 7DX
Tel. (01) 435-2173

**Travel Concepts, Inc.**
373 Commonwealth Ave.
Suite 601
Boston, MA 02115–1815, U.S.A.
Tel. (617) 266-8450

# LITERATURE

Whether you want to scramble around the Brontës' moors, Hardy's Wessex, Herriot's Yorkshire, or Burn's Highlands, the following companies make Britain's best backdrops come alive:

**Axistour Travel Services**
21 Panton St.
London SW1Y 4DU
Tel. (01) 930-9361

**Landscape & Literature**
10 Frederick Rd.
Chichester, West Sussex PO19 3JQ
Tel. (0243) 776905

**Temple World Tours**
(see above)

**Wilson & Lake International**
One Appian Way, Suite 704–8
South San Francisco, CA 94080,
U.S.A.
Tel. (415) 589-0352

Nearly every airline and tour operator worth its salt has a full roster of theater tours to London and/or Stratford and/or the Edinburgh festival. However, there are some whose business it is to arrange tours highlighting the performing arts—including opera, concerts, ballet, modern dance as well as theater—and to dig up those hard-to-come-by tickets:

**Concertworld (UK) Ltd.**
6 Belmont Hill
London SE13 5BD
Tel. (01) 852-2035

**Dailey-Thorp Travel, Inc.**
Park Towers South
315 W. 57th St.
New York, NY 10019
U.S.A.
Tel. (212) 307-1555

**Edwards and Edwards**
Shaftesbury Ave.

London WC2
Tel. (01) 379-5822

**Guide Friday Ltd.**
The Civic Hall
14 Rother St.
Stratford-upon-Avon
Warwickshire CV37 6LU
Tel. (0789) 294466

**London Arts Discovery Tours**
15–17 Old Compton St.
London W1V 5PJ
Tel. (01) 434-9973

# SPORT

Golf, shooting, fishing—these are primary reasons many people come to Britain. Other people come for spectator purposes to Wimbledon, the races at Ascot, the regatta at Henley, cricket and football matches, and the British Grand Prix. The companies below are experts in arranging tours for the sportsman or woman and/or the serious spectator:

**Airtrack Services Ltd.**
5 Lees Parade, Uxbridge Rd.
Hillingdon, Uxbridge UB10 0PQ
Tel. (0895) 70921

**Caledonian Golf, Inc.**
9 Colquhoun St.
Luss House
Helensburgh G84 8AN, Scotland
Tel. (0436) 78680

**Capital Sport**
36 Winchester Ave.
London NW6 7TU
Tel. (01) 625-4618

**Country Pursuits of Scotland**
51 Queen St.
Edinburgh EH2 3NS, Scotland
Tel. (031) 2255442

**Golf Links International**
The Mount, Cuddington Ln.
Cuddington
Cheshire CW8 2SZ
Tel. (606) 88 3070

**Keith Prowse & Co., Ltd.**
Banda House, Cambridge Grove

London W6 0LE
Tel. (01) 741-7441

**Perry Tours**
9 Colquhoun St.
Helensburgh
Glasgow G84 8AN, Scotland
Tel. (0436) 71763

**Persona Vacations**
26 Lawrence Walk
Newport Pagnell
Buckinghamshire MK16 8RF
Tel. (0908) 612589

**Scottish Golf Holidays Ltd.**
18 Crowhill Rd.
Bishopriggs
Glasgow G64 1QY, Scotland
Tel. (041 762) 3965

**Wilfred Taylor**
Sun Court, Cromarty
Cromarty IV11 8XA
Ross-shire, Scotland
Tel. (038 17) 269

# WALKING AND WILDERNESS

For those of you who want to get off the beaten track, but don't want to lose your way while doing it, various organizations have come up with walking tours which range from roughing-it camping to hikes from deluxe inn to inn:

**British Coastal Trails Inc.**
150 Carob Way
Coronado, CA 92118
U.S.A.
Tel. (619) 437-1211

**Country Walking Holidays Ltd.**
1122 Fir St.
Blaine, WA 98230 U.S.A.
Tel. (604) 921-8304

**Elegant Ambles**
Box 6616
San Diego, CA 92106 U.S.A.
Tel. (619) 222-2224

**English Wanderer**
13 Wellington Court, Spencers Wood
Reading RG7 1BN, Berkshire
Tel. (0734) 882515

**Explore Cumbria**
Kirkstead, Cartmel
near Grange-over-Sands
Cumbria LA11 6PR
Tel. (0448 54) 225

**Outdoor Bound**
18 Stuyvesant Oval, No. 1A
New York, NY 10009 U.S.A.
Tel. (212) 505-1020

**The Wayfarers**
Breithwaite
Keswick
Cumbria CA12 5TN
Tel. (059) 682570

**Wayfinder Holidays**
83 Abbostsham Rd.

Bideford, EX39 3AQ, Devon
Tel. (02372) 78417

**Wilderness Travel**
801 Allston Way
Berkeley, CA 94710 U.S.A.
Tel. (415) 548 0420

## THE NATIONAL TRUST AND THE NATIONAL TRUST FOR SCOTLAND

In 1895 several forward-looking Britons looked about them and saw that the industrial revolution and the concurrent jump in population were encroaching on (and in some cases had already destroyed) many properties important to the nation for historic or aesthetic reasons. Their solution was to form the National Trust for Places of Historic Interest or Natural Beauty (NT), a body that has grown to be the largest conservation society in the world, granted specific powers and privileges by Parliament. Its equivalent in the north, the National Trust for Scotland (NTS), was begun in 1931. Between the two, the NT and NTS are responsible for maintaining over 710,000 acres of Britain, including vast expanses of coastline, castles, farms, forests, dovecotes, museums, waterfalls, gardens, even entire villages. Many of the places we suggest in this book are NT and NTS properties, and if you plan to travel in Britain for a week or more it's a good idea to invest in an Open to View pass. These passes, available for various periods of time, allow free entrance to all NT and NTS properties, and some additional properties, throughout Britain. If you visit eight or ten of these properties, the pass will pay for itself, and if there are a few pounds left over, you'll be contributing to a most worthwhile cause. Open to View passes can be purchased at any BTA office in your home country.

## Accommodations

How clever you are to have chosen to travel in Great Britain, and how fortunate. Perhaps more than any other country in the world, Britain offers the broadest range of places to stay, appealing to the widest spectrum of tastes and budgets. You can march up to a farmhouse in Yorkshire, pitch your tent, and watch the cows come home. You can motor up to a castle in the Chiltern Hills and dine as sumptuously as ever did its regal inhabitants. The choice of where (and how) to stay in Britain presents an embarrassment of riches, a situation that can actually prove as tricky as it is tempting. It's tricky because there are so many gradations of service—from a farmhouse B&B to a stately mansion—and because within each of the many categories there are many choices. Obviously you don't have the time or the inclination (or the postage stamps) to write away for literature on the hundreds of properties available in any one region you are interested in visiting.

When it comes right down to it, the most important consideration when you are choosing an accommodation is value. In Britain, with very few exceptions, you will find the best value for your money at either end of the price scale: the most worthwhile places to stay are either simple B&Bs or sumptuous country-house hotels. The two- and three-star establishments in between are significantly more costly than a basic B&B, but the appointments and service will not be significantly better and quite possibly may not be as good.

Bed-and-breakfasts are one of the great inventions of modern tourism. Not only is the price right, but the ladies and gentlemen who run them are almost always delighted to chat with you about local lore, to give you tips on the best pubs and restaurants to visit, to help you plan the prettiest routes possible through their territory. For the most part, we have not listed B&Bs. This is not at all because we don't fancy them; as mentioned, we think they are brilliant. There are just too many of them, most of them can handle no more than six or eight guests at a time, and many open and close when the humor suits them, so it can be tough to make reservations.

If you are traveling outside major cities, and even in some major cities, it is usually quite easy to find an acceptable B&B wherever you happen to find yourself for the evening. It can be trickier if you are traveling alone (single rooms are scarcer), are traveling on a bank-holiday weekend, or are traveling in a contained area (on an island like Skye or the Isles of Scilly). In these cases, you might want to make a reservation in advance. You can do this by writing or phoning the English, Scottish, or Welsh tourist board information center nearest to your destination. They have full listings of all sorts of B&Bs in the area and will be of great assistance in finding one to your liking in your price category. If for some reason you are dissatisfied with your lodgings, you can always find another place to set up camp the next morning, but at least you will have a bed to count on for the night of your arrival. Which brings up another important point. If you are planning to find a B&B on the road (i.e., without a reservation), plan to be at your destination by 5 P.M. After that you will find many places are filled up, or the ladies get discouraged and take down their "vacancy" signs. If you can't find a place to stay and the tourist office is closed, try stopping 'round the pub and inquiring there if they know anyone in the neighborhood who does B&B—invariably they do.

Bed-and-breakfast should run you £8–15 per person per night; singles will probably be slightly higher. Always establish the price *before* you agree to take the room, then have a look at the accommodations. If they are not to your liking, ask to see another room. Likewise, if the price is too high, inquire if there are any rooms to be had at a lower rate. Check the bathroom, too. Many houses in more remote areas do not have showers (but tubs only). If you need to have a shower, keep looking at other places until you find one. There are usually plenty of B&Bs in any given area, so you shouldn't feel constrained to stay at one that's not quite right.

Some of the most fun places to stay at are farmhouse B&Bs—working farms that offer lodgings. This usually means fresh eggs, fresh-from-the-cow milk and cream, and home-cured ham or bacon. For information about farmhouse B&Bs, write to the Farm Holiday Bureau, National Agricultural Centre, Stoneleigh, Warwickshire CV8 2LZ or tel. (0203) 696969.

When, on the other hand, you are parting with upwards of £50–100 per night for deluxe accommodations, you can and should be a stickler for detail. If you choose to stay at any of the country house hotels and inns we suggest, you are assured of not merely a worry-free visit but one that is truly peerless, even in this land of lords.

Country house hotels may need a bit of explanation. The idea began some forty years ago on Ullswater in the Lake District. A gentleman by the name of Francis Coulson, a chartered surveyor, found himself with a rambling 19th-century house on the shore of the lake and not much money to play with. He decided that he would like to open a hotel of sorts, but to keep things relatively casual as befitted the clientele likely to trek up to this out-of-the-way place in 1948 when food was still being rationed. The establishment Coulson devised became Sharrow Bay, and the formula he devised for entertaining customers as one would one's friends on one's weekend country estate became the prototype for an entirely new breed of hostelry.

Country house hotels are usually found in a stately home that's been converted to accommodate several dozen guests—although some hotels are in hunting lodges or castles or priories. Each room in the hotel is decorated individually, usually with antiques, fine wallpapers, chintz fabrics—just as you would find in a private home. And since they cater to an up-market clientele, many offer extras like four-poster beds, Jacuzzis, satellite TV. But perhaps the most important things (as is often the case) are the little things: like fresh flowers, a decanter of sherry, a basket of fruit, luxurious toiletries, books and magazines—all those extra touches you might expect when staying with friends, but usually cannot when staying at a hotel. The hotels themselves, aside from being interesting architecturally and historically, are invariably situated on magnificent grounds, with extensive gardens and always with impressive views. The final component is, of course, the gastronomic one. All of the proprietors realize that anyone demanding this level of luxury will also be wanting to enjoy a high standard of cooking—not often easy to find in the remote areas where some are situated. There are veritable battles over good chefs, rural innkeepers wooing them away from the best hotels and restaurants in London out to the Cotswolds or Cornwall, Wales, or the Scottish Borders.

In each chapter, we have selected a dozen or so establishments which fulfill every criterion for a superior inn or hotel, and we recommend every one without reservation. If you would like a more exhaustive survey, we suggest consulting *The Good Hotel Guide,* published by the Consumers' Association and Hodder & Stoughton Ltd. This annually revised volume is extremely well researched and is available at book stores throughout Britain and elsewhere in the world as well.

## Please, Sir, I Want Some More: British Cuisine

The "more" young Oliver Twist was so desperately requesting was a nasty gruel that tended to be thin and watery when it wasn't lumpy. There were days when the sophisticated traveler would have pronounced with an imperious sniff that "British Cuisine" was a contradiction in terms. There were days when "British Cuisine" meant thick porridge, kippers, roast beef and Yorkshire pudding, neeps and tatties (turnips and potatoes), and was the butt of incessant jokes.

Let it be said, once and for all, that those days are (and have been for some time) indisputably over. British chefs from Land's End to John o' Groats are among the cleverest, most energetic, most original, and most successful in Europe. Even the wildly Francophilic *Guide Michelin* has bestowed a sacre bleu and a star or two on many practitioners of the gastronomic arts on this side of the Channel. The term *Modern British Cooking* was coined by somebody somewhere and is ambiguous enough to be applicable to the many different tacks taken by chefs the country over. For all the variety of exciting experimentation and superb results bubbling around the island, there are a few basic tenets which are emerging as a credo among the men and women maintaining and extending the frontiers of Modern British Cooking.

The first commandment has to do with ingredients. The idea of using only local produce in the kitchen is hardly new or exclusive to these shores, but with modern air-freight being what it is, the idea of forsaking ingredients produced down the road for foie gras from Gascony, kiwis from South Africa, and shrimp from the Gulf of Mexico can be tempting. Most British chefs understand, however, that to ignore their local suppliers is to spurn an invaluable and irreplaceable resource which will eventually take its business elsewhere or cease to operate entirely. Most British chefs understand, as well, that visitors don't come to England to eat bouillabaisse or to Wales to eat pasta; they come to sample what the local imaginations have concocted.

And British chefs need look no farther than their own backyard. Their nation is, as one Scottish innkeeper puts it, "The larder of Europe." Aberdeen angus beef, Devonshire cream, Welsh lamb, Highland malt whisky, Cotswold berries, Cheshire cheeses, Yorkshire venison, Dover sole, Tweed River salmon: these items are shipped not just to the Continent, but around the world. In fact, many rural restaurateurs complain that the problem is getting local producers to save a portion of their stock for local restaurants before they ship it off to London or Glasgow or Paris or New York. You, the diner, benefit from the chefs' browbeating their suppliers into retaining precious local produce for local kitchens. After dinner at the White Moss House at Grasmere in the Lakes, you can sample Peter Dixon's fine list of farmhouse cheeses. Despite the fact that the Peat Inn is in the middle of nowhere in Fife, Scotland, David Wilson's policy mandates that all primary ingredients be as local as possible. On the menu at the Oakes restaurant on the outskirts of Stroud in the Cotswolds, Chris Oakes has listed all the local distributors who are his lifeline of supplies. Their diligence is your pleasure, and is largely responsible for the flowering of British cooking.

The second commandment is connected to the first: use traditional ingredients and offer traditional recipes in an innovative, updated way. One of the reasons many of these chefs are so wildly creative is because many of them are self-taught. Although they may get off to a stuttering start, having to start from scratch, once they hit their stride they are not confined by the authoritarian dictates of classic cooking. Rather they vary themes their mums cooked for them, or rework a dish they tasted on an overseas junket, or simply let their imagination go to work on what to do when the fishmonger has no shrimp and sends over halibut instead.

Many will combine the old with the new, not only within a recipe but also on the menu. If you're dining in Leeds, why not have a taste of roast beef and Yorkshire pudding? After a trying day on the links at St. Andrews, why not enjoy a wee dram of single malt with your haggis? And when in Cornwall, what better way to fortify yourself for hiking the coastal footpath than with a luscious Cornish pasty? The point is that along with these traditional—and most worthwhile—dishes you will also find new takes on time-honored recipes. The past hasn't been eschewed but rather enhanced and modernized to reflect changes in taste and disposition. Perhaps you'll be favored with a roast leg of lamb in a mustard marinade with garlic and onions, or slices of duck breast in a honey and ginger sauce, or roasted venison on a bed of vegetables with a sauce of port and red currant jelly, or mousseline of scallops with a langoustine sauce—all of this to be followed by unregenerately rich desserts: trifles, gateaux, puddings, fruit, and fresh cream. Makes your mouth water just thinking about it.

# 1989 Events

One of the best ways to get the flavor of a country is to attend a special event. Aside from the thrill of watching center court at Wimbledon or cattle judging in Kent, people-watching reigns supreme on these occasions. The following is a brief roster of some of the enticing red-letter days (or weeks or months) throughout the land. Our information is taken from British Tourist Authority listings, and of course dates are subject to change. For the most complete and up-to-date listings for a particular area, contact the regional tourist board.

## JANUARY

**Antique and Crafts Fair,** Jan. 2, 1989, Layer Marney Tower, Colchester, Essex

**London International Boat Show,** Jan. 5–15, 1989, Earls Court Exhibition Centre, Warwick Rd., London

**Whittlesey Straw Bear Festival,** Jan. 7, 1989, Whittlesey, Cambridgeshire

**Burning of the Clavie,** Jan. 11, 1989, Burghead, Grampian

**European Ice Figure Skating Championships,** Jan. 17–22, 1989, National Exhibition Centre, Birmingham, West Midlands

**Jorvik Viking Festival,** Jan. 28–Feb. 25, 1989, York, North Yorkshire

# FEBRUARY

**Crufts Dog Show,** Feb. 9–12, 1989, Earls Court Exhibition Centre, Warwick Road, London

**United Kingdom Cross Country Ski Championships,** Feb. 11–12, 1989, Glenmore Forest, Aviemore, Highland

# MARCH

**Anglo Dutch Festival of Concerts,** Mar. 3–11, 1989, Worcester Cathedral, Hereford, and Worcester

**Daily Mail Ideal Home Exhibition,** Mar. 7–Apr. 2, 1989, Earls Court Exhibition Centre, Warwick Rd., London

**Chelsea Antiques Fair,** Mar. 14–25, 1989, Chelsea Old Town Hall, King's Rd., London

**Edinburgh International Folk Festival,** Mar. 17–26, 1989, Edinburgh, Lothian

**Norfolk Easter Antiques Fair,** Mar. 22–25, 1989, St Andrew's Hall, St Andrew's Plain, Norwich, Norfolk

**Newport Drama Festival,** Mar. 22–27, 1989, Dolman Theatre, Kingsway, Newport, Gwent

**Harrogate International Youth Music Festival,** Mar. 22–29, 1989, Harrogate, North Yorkshire

**Easter Parade,** Mar. 26, 1989, Battesea Park, London

**Horse Racing:** Grand National Meeting, Mar. 30–Apr. 1, 1989, Aintree Racecourse, Aintree, Merseyside

**British International Antiques Fair,** Mar. 30–Apr. 5, 1989, National Exhibition Centre, Birmingham, West Midlands

# APRIL

**London International Book Fair,** Apr. 3–5, 1989, Olympia 2, Hammersmith Rd., London

**Edinburgh International Festival of Science and Technology,** Apr. 3–12, 1989, Edinburgh, Lothian

**Antiques Fair,** Apr. 5–8, 1989, Roxburghe Hotel, Charlotte Sq., Edinburgh, Lothian

**LEC International Clowns Convention,** Apr. 7–9, 1989, Bognor Regis, West Sussex

**Embassy World Professional Snooker Championship,** Apr. 15–May 1, 1989, Crucible Theatre, 55 Norfolk St., Sheffield, South Yorkshire

**London Marathon,** Apr. 23, 1989

**Shetland Folk Festival,** Apr. 27–30, 1989, Shetland

**Garden Heritage Week,** Apr. 29–May 7, 1989, throughout Britain

## MAY

**Glyndebourne Festival Opera Season,** May–Aug., 1989, Glyndebourne, Near Lewes, East Sussex

**Chichester Festival Theatre Season,** May–Sept., 1989, Chichester, West Sussex

**Pitlochry Festival Theatre Season,** May–Oct., 1989, Pitlochry Festival Theatre, Pitlochry, Tayside

**Horse Racing:** 1000 Guineas Stakes, May 4, 1989, Newmarket Racecourse, Newmarket, Suffolk

**Whitbread Badminton Horse Trials,** May 4–7, 1989, Badminton, Avon

**Horse Racing:** 2000 Guineas Stakes, May 6, 1989, Newmarket Racecourse, Newmarket, Suffolk

**Scottish International Gathering,** May 6–14, 1989, Inverness, Highland

**Spalding Flower Festival,** May 7–8, 1989, Spalding, Lincolnshire

**Mayfest,** May 7–27, 1989, Glasgow, Strathclyde

**Royal Windsor Horse Show,** May 11–14, 1989, Home Park, Windsor, Berkshire

**Mary Wakefield Westmoreland Festival,** May 13–21, 1989, Kendal, Cumbria

**Perth Festival of the Arts,** May 17–28, 1989, Perth, Tayside

**Scottish Kennel Club Show,** May 19–21, 1989, Ingliston Showground, Edinburgh, Lothian

**Southern Counties Craft Market,** May 19–21, 1989, The Maltings, Bridge Square, Farnham, Surrey

**Highlands and Islands Music and Dance Festival,** May 20, 1989, Oban, Strathclyde

**Chelsea Flower Show,** May 23–26, 1989, Royal Hospital, London

**Corpus Christi Carpet of Flowers and Floral Festival,** May 24–25, 1989, Arundel Cathedral, London Rd., Arundel, West Sussex

**British Interior Design Exhibition,** May 25–June 18, 1989, Chelsea Old Town Hall, King's Rd., London

**Bath Contemporary Art Fair,** May 26–29, 1989, Green Park Station, James St. West, Bath, Avon

**Dumfries and Galloway Arts Festival,** May 26–June 4, 1989, Dumfries and Galloway

**English Riviera Dance Festival,** May 27–June 10, 1989, Torquay, Devon

**Bath International Festival,** May 29–June 11, 1989, Bath, Avon

**Nottingham Festival,** May 30–June 16, 1989, Nottingham, Nottinghamshire

# JUNE

**Open Air Theatre Season,** June–Sept. 1989, Regent's Park, London

**Royal Academy of Art Summer Exhibition,** June 3–Aug. 20, 1989, Royal Academy of Arts, Piccadilly, London

**Beating the Retreat,** June 6–8, 1989, Horse Guards Parade, Whitehall, London

**Horse Racing:** including the Derby, June 7–10, 1989, Epsom Racecourse, Epsom, Surrey

**Royal Scottish Automobile Club International Scottish Rally,** June 10–12, 1989, Glasgow and throughout Scotland

**Royal International Horse Show,** June 15–18, 1989, National Exhibition Centre, Birmingham, West Midlands

**Trooping the Colour,** June 17, 1989, Horse Guards Parade, Whitehall, London

**Aberdeen Bon Accord Festival,** June 17–25, 1989, Aberdeen, Grampian

**Horse Racing:** Royal Ascot, June 20–24, 1989, Ascot Racecourse, Ascot, Berkshire

**Criccieth Music Festival,** June 22–27, 1989, Criccieth, Gwynedd

**Glasgow International Jazz Festival,** June 23–July 2, 1989, Glasgow, Strathclyde

**Northern Mystery Plays,** June 23–July 15, 1989, Sheffield, South Yorkshire

**Bournemouth Music Festival,** June 24–July 1, 1989, Bournemouth, Dorset

**450th Anniversary of the Dissolution of Whitby Abbey,** June 25–July 2, 1989, Whitby, North Yorkshire

**Lawn Tennis championships,** June 26–July 9, 1989, All England Lawn Tennis and Croquet Club, Wimbledon, London

**London International Festival of Theatre,** June 26–July 16, 1989, London

**Henley Royal Regatta,** June 28–July 2, 1989, Henley-on-Thames, Oxfordshire

# JULY

**Cheltenham International Festival of Music,** July 1–16, 1989, Chelthenham, Gloucestershire

**Llangollen International Musical Eisteddfod,** Eisteddfod Field, Llangollen, Clwyd

**Cutty Sark Tall Ships Race,** July 5–8, 1989, start from London

**Shrewsbury International Music Festival,** July 5–12, 1989, Shrewsbury, Shropshire

**St Albans Organ Festival,** July 8–15, 1989, St. Albans Abbey, St. Albans, Hertfordshire

**City of London Festival,** July 9–26, 1989, The City, London

**Lincoln Mystery Plays,** July 12–20, 1989, Lincoln Cathedral, Lincoln, Lincolnshire

**York Early Music Festival,** July 14–23, 1989, York, North Yorkshire

**Stratford-upon-Avon Festival,** July 14–30, 1989, Stratford-upon-Avon, Warwickshire

**Inveraray Highland Games,** July 18, 1989, The Games Field, Inverary, Strathclyde

**Golf: Open Championship,** July 20–23, 1989, Royal Troon Golf Club, Troon, Strathclyde

**Henry Wood Promenade Concerts,** July 21–Sept. 16, 1989, Royal Albert Hall, Kensington Gore, London

**Welsh Proms,** July 22–Aug. 6, 1989, St. David's Hall, Cardiff, South Glamorgan

**Royal Welsh Show,** July 24–27, 1989, Royal Welsh Showground, Llanelwedd, Builth Wells, Powys

**Champagne Mumm Admiral's Cup,** July 27–Aug. 6, 1989, The Solent, Isle of Wight

# AUGUST

**Welsh National Sheepdog Trials,** Aug. 3–5, 1989, Bala, Gwynedd

**Sidmouth International Folklore Festival,** Aug. 4–11, 1989, Sidmouth, Devon

**Vale of Glamorgan Festival,** Aug. 6–28, 1989, Vale of Glamorgan, South Glamorgan

**Bath Guildhall Antiques Fair,** Aug. 8–10, 1989, Guildhall, High St., Bath, Avon

**Aberdeen International Youth Festival,** Aug. 9–19, 1989, Aberdeen, Grampian

**English National Sheepdog Trials,** Aug. 10–12, 1989, Osberton, Worksop, Nottinghamshire

**Edinburgh International Festival and Fringe Festival,** Aug. 13–Sept. 2, 1989, Edinburgh, Lothian

**Scottish National Sheepdog Trials,** Aug. 17–19, 1989, Barony College, Dumfries and Galloway

**Edinburgh International Jazz Festival,** Aug. 19–26, 1989, Edinburgh, Lothian

**Port of Dartmouth Royal Regatta,** Aug. 24–26, 1989, Port of Dartmouth, Dartmouth, Devon

# SEPTEMBER

**Blackpool Illuminations,**Sept. 1–Oct. 29, 1989, The Promenade, Blackpool, Lancashire

**Sailing:** Start of Whitbread Round the World Race, Sept. 2, 1989, The Solent, Portsmouth, Hampshire

**Scottish Pipe Band Championships,** Sept. 2, 1989, Inverness, Highland

**Braemar Royal Highland Gathering,** Sept. 2, 1989, Princess Royal and Duke of Fife Memorial Park, Braemar, Grampian

**Panasonic European Open Golf Championship,** Sept. 7–10, 1989, Walton Heath Golf Club, Deans Lane, Walton on the Hill, Surrey

**Widecombe Fair,** Sept. 12, 1989, Widecombe in the Moor, Dartmoor, Devon

**Chelsea Antiques Fair,** Sept. 12–23, 1989, Chelsea Old Town Hall, King's Rd., London

**North Wales Music Festival,** Sept. 24–30, 1989, St. Asaph, Clwyd

# OCTOBER

**Swansea Festival,** Oct. 2–21, 1989, Swansea, West Glamorgan

**Norfolk and Norwich French Festival,** Oct. 5–15, 1989, Norwich, Norfolk

**Swansea Festival Fringe,** Oct. 6–28, 1989, Swansea, West Glamorgan

**Cheltenham Festival of Literature,** Oct. 7–22, 1989, Cheltenham, Gloucestershire

# NOVEMBER

**Lord Mayor's Procession and Show,** Nov. 11, 1989, The City, London

**Cardiff Festival of Music,** Nov. 15–Dec. 2, 1989, St. David's Hall, Cardiff, South Glamorgan

## DECEMBER

**Olympia International Showjumping Championships,** Dec. 14–18, 1989, Olympia, Hammersmith Road, London

**Bank holidays** in 1989 are Jan. 2, 3 (Scotland only); March 24 (Good Friday), 27 (Easter Monday, England and Wales only); May 1 (May Day), 29; August 7 (Scotland only), 28 (England and Wales only); December 25 (Christmas Day), 26 (Boxing Day).

# BUSINESS BRIEF

Business in Britain is much like British weather—predictably unpredictable. A typical British weather forecast will advise you to expect "sunshine with intermittent showers" or "rain with occasional sunshine." Only rarely will it predict a real storm.

You'll find that it's much the same when you're doing business with the inhabitants of this tight and tidy little isle. The British—be they English, Scot, or Welsh—are a polite people. Like their weather, their moods may vary between pleasant and dour, but it takes a great deal of adversity to provoke them into a noisy or disagreeable storm.

British reserve is confusing to many Americans, who are far more prone to express a current mood, whether it is delight, displeasure, or disappointment. The British, one soon begins to believe, must surely be great poker players.

This brief piece is meant to serve as an umbrella—a "brolly," if you will—for those Americans (and others) who are fortunate enough to find themselves "doing business" in the United Kingdom. In a modest way it is meant to shield you during those occasional showers and to give you a sense of security when all is sunny and bright. It may even help you avoid one of those infrequent storms.

Let's get down to business:

- Recognize first of all that the British actually *like* most Americans (whether they show it overtly or not). They respect most of us (but not all of us), they dislike some of us (but not most of us), and they are occasionally confused by the whole bloody lot of us. Try as they will, they find it difficult to fit us into a proper (that is, "British") mold. This ambiguity about "you Americans" stems from the fact that we're truly alike in many basic ways, yet we are also so very, very different.
- Keep in mind that a firm "no" will be rendered every bit as politely in Britain as an enthusiastic "yes." In other words, don't assume that your deal has been concluded until hands have been shaken or a letter of intent has been signed—either of which is worth its weight in pounds sterling or gold.
- Don't be surprised that most of them (English, Scot, or Welsh) are more class-conscious than many Americans, although this is more evident in their dealings with each other than with visiting Americans. Again, as above,

they find it difficult to catagorize the "typical" American—but they will *always* place a high value on good manners.

- Also keep in mind that many if not most of your British counterparts place an even higher value on solid experience than on university degrees. Experience, they feel, speaks for itself, while flaunting one's education is terribly bad form. Many successful British men and women hold *no* university degrees, but it would be a grave mistake on your part to assume that yours gives you any sort of superiority.
- Don't be thrown if you encounter a bit more sexism in Britain than you might find in the States. In all likelihood you will find fewer women in managerial positions, and in many meetings and conferences you'll find none at all (excepting the "tea lady," of course). Above all, don't take umbrage if your British counterpart calls to his "girl" to bring you coffee or tea—your business is *business,* not the social order of things.
- Don't be loud, either in dress or speech. Although some of the British dress rather badly, they often express surprise when an American is conservatively dressed and neatly groomed. They also believe—or *pretend* to believe—that we're much too brash, although they secretly know that's often not true. They'll deny it, of course, but many of them secretly admire us for some of the qualities they tend to deride.
- Avoid, if possible, discussing British politics—but be forewarned that the British will discuss yours. Many of them are convinced they understand American politics better than you do, and they're equally convinced that you know nothing of theirs. That may well be true—but politics, like religion, has no place in a business discussion.
- Avoid also any criticism of the royal family (even if they don't) and try to sidestep any comparison between British and American "football" or cricket and baseball—at least until your business has been concluded.
- Don't underestimate the British—*any* of them—for under that scruffy tweed jacket or Savile Row suit beats a heart that is both clever and canny. Person for person, and acre for acre, they've managed their affairs better than most—and they've been at it for hundreds of years.
- Don't mistake civility for servility, pomposity for lack of ability, or good manners for weakness. There are exceptions, of course, and broad generalities are dangerous—but British business acumen is a fact.
- Above all, consider yourself lucky if you're planning a business trip to Great Britain. The country is a constant delight, the natives are civilized, the language is almost the same as yours, and the weather is *usually* mild.

# CULTURAL TIME LINE

**Prehistoric and Ancient Britain**

| | |
|---|---|
| c. 18th–14th centuries B.C. | Stonehenge, sacrifical altar and observatory near Salisbury. |
| 5th century B.C. | Celtic invasion of British isles. |
| 55–54 B.C. | Julius Caesar's expeditions fail to subdue "Britannia." |
| c. 120–136 A.D. | Hadrian's Wall built across Britain's northern frontier. |
| 410 | Romans leave Britain. |

**5th–9th centuries: Anglo-Saxon rule. A heptarchy of seven kingdoms (Essex, Wessex, Sussex, Kent, East Anglia, Mercia, and Northumbria) arose in England.**

| | |
|---|---|
| 449 | Germanic tribal invasions (Angles, Saxons, Jutes). |
| 597 | Saint Augustine's mission arrives in Kent. |
| c. 700 | Lindisfarne Gospels. |
| 825 | King Egbert of Wessex unites England. |
| 878 | Alfred the Great defeats the Danes at Edington. |
| 1016–1042 | Danish rule of England by King Canute and his descendants. |

**1066–1485 The Middle Ages: Period of Norman and Plantagenet rule, War of the Roses between the houses of York and Lancaster.**

| | |
|---|---|
| 1066 | Battle of Hastings. Norman conquest of England. William the Conqueror crowned in Westminster Abbey. Feudal system replaces Anglo-Saxon nobility with Normans. |
| 1085 | Domesday book compiled. |
| 1152 | Henry II marries Eleanor of Aquitaine. |
| 1193 | Durham Cathedral (Norman style). |
| c. 1135 | Legends of King Arthur recorded; Geoffrey of Monmouth's *Historia Regnum Britanniae*. |
| 1167 | Oxford University founded. |
| 1170 | Thomas à Becket murdered at the altar of Canterbury Cathedral by four knights of Henry II. |

| | |
|---|---|
| 1190 | Richard I (the Lionhearted) leads the Third Crusade to retake the Holy Land. |
| 1215 | King John forced to sign the Magna Carta limiting royal powers. |
| 1245–1269 | Westminster Abbey rebuilt in Gothic style. |
| 1290 | Harlech Castle (Wales). |
| 1332 | Two houses of Parliament instituted. |
| 1337–1453 | Hundred Years War. |
| 1348 | Black Plague reaches England. |
| 1376 | Heretic John Wycliffe's English Bible. |
| c. 1387 | Chaucer begins *The Canterbury Tales*. |
| 1415 | Henry V triumphs at the Battle of Agincourt. |
| 1446 | King's College Chapel, Cambridge, begun (Perpendicular style). |
| 1455–1485 | War of the Roses between houses of York and Lancaster. |
| 1484 | William Caxton prints Malory's *Morte d'Arthur*. |

**Renaissance: Late 15th–16th centuries. Period of Tudor rule and England's ascent as major European commercial, naval, and colonial power**

| | |
|---|---|
| 1512 | Parliament destroyed by fire. |
| c. 1520 | Barrington court, Somerset (E-shaped Elizabethan style). |
| 1534 | Henry VIII excommunicated; Church of England established. |
| 1535 | Thomas More executed in the Tower of London. |
| 1536 | Wales united with England; Suppression Act transfers ownership of monasteries to the Crown. |
| 1540 | Holbein the Younger's *Portrait of Henry VIII*. |
| 1549 | Book of Common Prayer authorized by Edward VI. |
| 1553–1558 | Catholic restoration under Queen Mary. |
| 1558 | Queen Elizabeth I crowned. |
| 1577 | Sir Francis Drake begins his circumnavigational voyage. |
| 1588 | Defeat of the Spanish Armada; George Gower's Armada: portrait of Elizabeth I. |
| 1599 | Globe theater built, south bank of the Thames. |
| 1600 | British East India Company founded. |
| 1601 | Shakespeare's *Hamlet*. |
| 1605 | Gunpowder plot: Guy Fawkes attempts to blow up Parliament. |

**17th–19th centuries. England's rise to world's greatest military and commercial power, extension of the British Empire, Industrial Revolution**

| | |
|---|---|
| 1611 | King James Bible. |
| 1616 | Inigo Jones, England's first architect, introduces the Renaissance Palladian style at the Queen's House in Greenwich. |
| 1620 | Pilgrims found Plymouth Colony. |
| 1622 | Banqueting House at Whitehall completed by Inigo Jones. |
| 1637 | Van Dyck's *Children of Charles I.* |
| 1642 | English Civil War. |
| 1649 | Cromwell made Lord Protector. Charles I beheaded. End of Civil War between Royalists and supporters of Parliament. Commonwealth established. |
| 1649–1652 | Cromwell suppresses Irish and Scots revolts. |
| 1651 | Hobbes's *Leviathan.* |
| 1660–1685 | Stuart Restoration. |
| 1666 | Plague and Great Fire of London. |
| 1667 | Milton's *Paradise Lost.* |
| 1675 | Sir Christopher Wren (1632–1723) begins St. Paul's Cathedral. |
| 1688 | Glorious Revolution; James II deposed. |
| 1689 | Purcell's *Dido and Aeneas;* English Bill of Rights enacted, ending Parliamentary strife. |
| 1694 | Bank of England chartered. |
| 1705 | Sir John Vanbrugh begins Blenheim Palace, Oxfordshire (Baroque style). |
| 1707 | England and Scotland united as Great Britain. |
| 1709–1711 | *Tatler* and *Spectator* founded. |
| 1726 | Swift's *Gulliver's Travels.* |
| 1727 | Handel's *Coronation Anthem* written for George II. |
| 1735 | Hogarth's *The Rake's Progress.* |
| mid-18th century | English Industrial Revolution begins. |
| 1753 | British Museum founded. |
| 1755 | Johnson's *Dictionary.* |
| 1763 | Canada ceded to England at the Treaty of Paris ending Seven Years' War. |
| 1768 | British Royal Academy founded with Sir Joshua Reynolds as its first president. |
| 1770 | Gainsborough's portrait of *The Blue Boy.* |
| 1775–1783 | American War of Independence. |
| 1784 | James Watt invents the steam engine. |
| 1789–1794 | French Revolution; Blake's *Songs of Innocence.* |
| 1791 | Boswell's *Life of Johnson.* |
| 1798 | Coleridge and Wordsworth: *Lyrical Ballads.* |
| 1805 | Nelson's victory at Trafalgar. |
| 1813 | Austen's *Pride and Prejudice.* |
| 1815 | Napoléon's defeat at Waterloo. |

| 1816 | Elgin Marbles purchased by the British Museum; John Nash: Royal Pavilion, Brighton (Indian Gothic style). |
|---|---|
| 1821 | Constable's *The Hay Wain*. |
| 1824 | National Gallery founded. |
| 1830 | First railway from Liverpool to Manchester. |
| 1833 | Britain abolishes slavery throughout the Empire. |
| 1836 | Sir Charles Berry designs the Houses of Parliament. |
| 1837 | Queen Victoria crowned, makes Buckingham Palace the royal residence; Carlyle: *The French Revolution*. |
| 1839 | Turner's *The Fighting Temeraire*. |
| 1845–1846 | Irish famine. |
| 1848 | Pre-Raphaelite brotherhood founded. |
| 1849 | Karl Marx begins work on *Das Kapital* in the British Library; Dickens begins *David Copperfield*. |
| 1851 | Joseph Paxton designs Victorian Crystal Palace for the Great Exhibition. |
| 1858 | India transferred to British Crown; Darwin's *Origin of Species*. |
| 1862–1863 | Carroll: *Alice in Wonderland*. |
| 1886 | New English Art Club founded. |
| 1897 | Queen Victoria's Diamond Jubilee. |
| 1899–1902 | Boer War. |
| 1900 | Conrad's *Lord Jim;* Elgar's oratorio *Dream of Gerontius* premieres at Birmingham festival. |
| 1901 | Queen Victoria dies. |

---

**20th century: Modern period. British rulers from houses of Saxe-Coburg and Windsor. World wars and dissolution of Empire.**

---

| 1903 | Shaw's *Man and Superman*. |
|---|---|
| 1908 | Rolls-Royce factory opened in Derby. |
| 1912 | British ocean liner *Titanic* sinks. |
| 1913 | Vorticist movement founded by Wyndham Lewis. |
| 1914 | Vaughan Williams: *London Symphony*. |
| 1914–1918 | World War I. |
| 1918 | Women's suffrage in England. |
| 1921 | Irish free state established. |
| 1922 | Joyce's *Ulysses;* Eliot's *The Waste Land*. |
| 1924 | First British Labour government; Forster's *Passage to India*. |
| 1938 | Chamberlain signs the Munich Pact with Hitler; Orwell's *Homage to Catalonia*. |
| 1939–1945 | World War II. |
| 1940 | Churchill becomes Prime Minister, Germans bomb London. |

| | |
|---|---|
| 1944 | Francis Bacon's tryptych: *Figures at the Base of a Cross.* |
| 1947 | Independence granted to India and Pakistan. |
| 1953 | Queen Elizabeth crowned at Westminster Abbey. |
| 1967 | Beatles' *Sergeant Pepper's Lonely Hearts Club Band.* |
| 1971 | British troops sent to Northern Ireland. |
| 1973 | Britain enters the Common Market. |
| 1979 | Margaret Thatcher becomes the first woman Prime Minister. |
| 1981 | Marriage of Prince Charles and Lady Diana Spencer. |

# Chronology of Reigns
## Norman (1066–1189)

| | |
|---|---|
| William the Conqueror | 1066–1087 |
| William II (Rufus) | 1087–1100 |
| Henry I (Beauclerc) | 1100–1135 |
| Stephen | 1135–1154 |

## Plantagenet

| | |
|---|---|
| Henry II | 1154–1189 |
| Richard I | 1189–1199 |
| John (Lackland) | 1199–1216 |
| Henry III | 1216–1272 |
| Edward I | 1272–1307 |
| Edward II | 1307–1327 |
| Edward III | 1327–1377 |
| Richard II | 1377–1399 |

## House of Lancaster

| | |
|---|---|
| Henry IV | 1399–1413 |
| Henry V | 1413–1422 |
| Henry VI | 1422–1461, 1470–1471 (restored) |

## House of York

| | |
|---|---|
| Edward IV | 1461–1469, 1471–1483 |
| Edward V | 1483 |
| Richard III | 1483–1485 |

## Tudor

| | |
|---|---|
| Henry VII | 1485–1509 |
| Henry VIII | 1509–1547 |
| Edward VI | 1547–1553 |
| Mary I | 1553–1558 |
| Elizabeth I | 1558–1603 |

## United Kingdom House of Stuart

| | |
|---|---|
| James I | 1603–1625 |
| Charles I | 1625–1649 |

## Commonwealth and Protectorate

| | |
|---|---|
| Oliver Cromwell | 1653–1658 |
| Richard Cromwell | 1658–1659 |

## House of Stuart (Restoration)

| | |
|---|---|
| Charles II | 1660–1685 |
| James II | 1685–1688 |
| (Glorious Revolution) | 1688 |
| Mary II & William III | 1689–1702 |
| Anne | 1702–1714 |

## House of Hanover

| | |
|---|---|
| George I | 1714–1727 |
| George II | 1727–1760 |
| George III | 1760–1820 |
| George IV | 1820–1830 |
| William IV | 1830–1837 |
| Victoria | 1837–1901 |

## House of Saxe-Coburg

| | |
|---|---|
| Edward VII | 1901–1910 |

## House of Windsor

| | |
|---|---|
| George V | 1910–1936 |
| Edward VIII | 1936 |
| George VI | 1936–1952 |
| Elizabeth II | 1952–present |

# VITAL INFORMATION

## Emergencies

In case of disaster call 999. This is a free call from anywhere, but should only be used in an emergency when immediate action is necessary. For minor mishaps (lost property, purse snatching) call the local police department listed in the phone book.

## Medical Care

Britain's plan of socialized medicine is known as the National Health Service (NHS). If you are admitted to an emergency room or need minor medical care, most likely you will not be charged for the service. If, however, your condition warrants complicated and/or overnight care, you will be charged the private-patient rate. Call your insurance company to ascertain whether or not any of your current policies cover medical treatment overseas, and if so what type and up to how much cost. Check also with your credit card company. Several offer inexpensive programs to insure card-members when traveling abroad.

If you decide you want to take out an insurance policy just in case, do so in your home country. While not impossible to obtain insurance in Britain, it is time consuming and costly, so attend to that at home by contacting any major company listed in your phone book.

## If You Lose Your Passport

Report it to the local police—there is a large black market for free-world passports. Then report to your embassy to arrange to have a replacement. The following addresses and phone numbers are all in London:

Australia High Commission, Australia House, The Strand (tel. 438 8000)

Canadian High Commission, Canada House, Trafalgar Sq. (629 9492)

Irish Embassy, 17 Grosvenor Place (235 2171)

New Zealand High Commission, New Zealand House, Haymarket (tel. 839 4580)

United States Embassy, 24 Grosvenor Sq. (tel. 499 900)

## If You Lose Your Traveler's Checks

You will have to go for a refund at the dispensing agency for your particular checks (i.e., Barclay's Bank, American Express). Of course you remembered to keep the list of numbers for your checks SEPARATE FROM THE CHECKS. Bring the list along with you and some form of identification (a passport or photo driver's license).

## If You Lose Your Credit Card

call:
American Express 0273 69633
Diners Club 0252 516261
MasterCard (Access) 0702 352255
Visa 0604 21288

## Lost Property

Report to the nearest police station (ask a policeman on the street, or call directory assistance for the address). In many major cities, there are Lost Property Offices, also listed in the phone book.

## Tourist Board Offices in London

British Travel Centre, 12 Regent St. (tel. 730 3400)

The Scottish Tourist Board, 19 Cockspur Street (tel. 930 8661/2/3)

The Wales Tourist Board, 34 Piccadilly (tel. 409 0969).

BritRail general information 834 2345, or call the station from which your train is leaving

## Post Offices

Post Offices are open Mon.–Fri. 9–5:30, Sat. 9–12:30. You can also buy stamps from selected newsellers or tobaccanists which display the "Post Office" sign. In rural areas, post offices may be attached to private homes; these too will have the familiar post office sign hung outside, and usually a telephone box in the yard (along with the chickens and the clothesline). Post offices in cities often offer Girobank foreign currency exchange.

## Telephones

Don't even think about making calls from your hotel room. You will be scurrilously ripped off. Most hotels have public phones in their lobby, or you can find a phone box on the street or in a post office. There are two types of public telephones in Britain. The first is coin-operated using from 2p to £1. The second type is a phonecard phone. Phonecards can be purchased from post offices and selected newsagents. The cards are electronically imprinted with "units" from 10 to 200 (10p per unit). You simply insert the card into the phone's slot and start talking. When all the units are used up, you will hear several quick blips which means you have to finish your conversation quick, or insert another card. If you hang up before the units are used up, the leftover units will be saved, and the card can be reused.

For London directory assistance: 142

For directory assistance everywhere else in Britain: 192

For overseas operator assistance: 155

If you want to make an international call dial 010, then the appropriate country code, and the number. Country codes are:

for Australia: 61
for Canada and the United States: 1
for New Zealand: 64

Phone rates within Britain are most expensive weekdays 8 A.M.–1 P.M., they go down after 1 til 6 P.M., and are least expensive 6 P.M.–8 A.M. and all weekend long.

International calls are lowest 8 P.M. to 8 A.M. weekdays and all weekend. Lowest rates for Australia and New Zealand are daily midnight–7 A.M. and 2:30–7:30 P.M.

## Electricity

If you plan to bring electrical appliances (keep these to an absolute minimum; most hotels have hair dryers and irons or laundry service), you will need to buy an adapter if you are coming from North America. British electricity runs 220–240 volts, 50 cycles. Most hotels have dual plugs in the bath for electric shavers, but if you need an adapter you can buy one at a hardware store here or at home.

## Airline Offices

Air Canada, 140 Regent St. (tel. 759-2636); British Airways, 75 Regent St. (tel. 434-4600); Pan Am, 193 Piccadilly (tel. 759-2595); TWA, 200 Piccadilly (tel. 636-4090)

## London Tourist Board Information Centres

Victoria Station Forecourt

Harrods Department Store, Brumpton Road, Knightsbridge

Selfridges Department Store, Oxford St.

Tower of London, West Gate

Heathrow Terminals 1,2,3, Underground Concourse, and Terminal 2, Arrivals Concourse

For London Tourist Board Telephone Information Service, phone 730-3488

## For Travel Elsewhere in Britain

British Travel Centre, 12 Regent St. (tel. 730-3400)

Northern Ireland Tourist Board, 11 Berkeley St. (tel. 493-0601)

Scottish Tourist Board, 19 Cockspur St. (tel. 930-8661)

Wales Tourist Board, 34 Piccadilly (tel. 409-0969)

For BritRail general information (tel. 922-6632), or call the station whence your train is departing, listed in the phone book.

For Green Line (bus) coaches from Victoria Station, call 668-7261

## TOURIST INFORMATION CENTERS

Following is a partial list of tourist information centers in Great Britain. For the regional tourist boards, see the *Travel Arrangements* chapter.

# England

### Alnwick
The Shambles
Northumberland Hall
Northumberland NE66 1TN
tel. (0665) 603129

### Ambleside
Old Courthouse
Church St.
Cumbria
tel. (05394) 32582

### Avebury
The Great Barn
Wiltshire SN8 1RF
tel. (06723) 425

### Bath
Abbey Church Yard
Avon BA1 1LY
tel. (0225) 62831

### Battle
88 High St.
East Sussex TN33 0AQ
tel. (04 246) 3721

### Birmingham
The Piazza
National Exhibition Centre
West Midlands B40 1NT
tel. (021) 780 4321

2 City Arcade
West Midlands B2 4TX
tel. (021) 643 2514

Birmingham International Airport
Airport Info Desk
West Midlands B26 8QJ
tel. (021) 767 7145

### Blackpool
1 Clifton St.
Lancashire FY1 1LY
tel. (0253) 21623; 25212

(weekdays only)

87A Coronation St.
Lancashire FY1 4PD
tel. (0253) 21891

Blackpool Airport
Terminal Building
Squires Gate Lane
Lancashire FY4 2QY
tel. (0253) 43061

### Bodmin
Shire House
Mount Folly Sq.
Cornwall PL31 2DQ
tel. (0208) 6616

### Bradford
City Hall
Hall Ings
Channing Way
West Yorkshire BD1 1HY
tel. (0274) 753678

### Brampton
Moot Hall
Cumbria CA8 1RA
tel. (06977) 3433

### Brighton
Marlborough House
54 Old Steine
East Sussex BN1 1EQ
tel. (0273) 23755; 27560

Sea Front
King's Rd.
East Sussex
tel. (0273) 23755; 27560

### Bristol
Colston House
Colston St.
Avon BS1 5AQ
tel. (0272) 293891 / 260767

Bristol Airport
Bristol
Avon BS19 3DY
tel. (027587) 4441

### Burford
The Brewery
Sheep St.
Oxfordshire OX8 4LP
tel. (099382) 3558

### Burton-upon-Trent
Town Hall
King Edward Sq.
Staffordshire DE14 2EB
tel. (0283) 45454

**Bury St.-Edmunds**
6 Angel Hill
Suffolk IP31 1UZ
tel. (0284) 63233; 64667

**Buxton**
The Crescent
Derbyshire SK17 6BQ
tel. (0298) 5106

**Cambridge**
Wheeler St.
Cambridgeshire CB2 3QB
tel. (0223) 322640

**Canterbury**
13 Longmarket
Kent CT1 2JS
tel. (0227) 766567; 67744

**Carlisle**
Old Town Hall
Green Market
Cumbria CA3 8JH
tel. (0228) 25517

**Cheddar Gorge**
Somerset BS27 3QE
tel. (0934) 744071

**Cheltenham**
Municipal Offices
Promenade
Gloucestershire GL50 1PP
tel. (0242) 522878 / 521333

**Chester**
Town Hall
Northgate St.
Cheshire CH1 2NF
tel. (0244) 40144 Ext. 2111 or 2250;
49026 (evenings and weekends)

Chester Visitor Centre
Vicar's Lane
Cheshire CH1 1QX
tel. (0244) 313126

**Chichester**
St. Peter's Market
West St.
West Sussex PO19 1AH
tel. (0243) 775888

**Cockermouth**
Riverside Car Park
Market St.
Cumbria CA13 9NP
tel. (0900) 822634

**Coniston**
16 Yewdale Rd.
Cumbria
tel. (05394) 41533

**Coventry**
Central Library
Smithford Way
West Midlands CV1 1FY
tel. (0203) 51717 / 20084

**Derby**
Central Library
The Wardwick
Derbyshire DE1 1HS
tel. (0332) 290664

**Dorchester**
7 Acland Rd.
Dorset DT1 1EF
tel. (0305) 67992

**Dover**
Townwall St.
Kent CT16 1JT
tel. (0304) 205108

**Durham**
Market Place
Co. Durham DH1 3NJ
tel. (091) 3843720

**Exeter**
Civic Centre
Paris St.
Devon EX1 1JJ
tel. (0392) 265297

Exeter Services
Granada Services Area (M5) Junction 30
Sandy Gate
Devon EX2 8UJ
tel. (0392) 37581 / 79088

**Glastonbury**
1 Marchant's Buildings
Northload St.
Somerset BA6 9JJ
tel. (0458) 32954

**Grasmere**
Red Bank Rd.
Cumbria
tel. (09665) 245

**Guildford**
The Civic Hall
London Rd.
Surrey GU2 1AA
tel. (0483) 575857

**Hastings**
4 Robertson Terr.
East Sussex TN34 1EZ
tel. (0424) 722022

The Fishmarket
Old Town
East Sussex TN34 1EZ

tel. (0424) 721201; 722022

**Hawkshead**
Near Car Park
Cumbria
tel. (09666) 525

**Haworth**
2/4 West Lane
Nr. Keighley
West Yorkshire BD22 8EF
tel. (0535) 42329

**Helmsley**
Town Hall
Market Place
York
North Yorkshire YO6 5DL
tel. (0439) 70173

**Henley-on-Thames**
Town Hall
Market Place
Oxfordshire RG9 2AQ
tel. (0491) 578034

**Hereford**
Town Hall Annexe
St. Owens St.
Herefordshire HR1 2PJ
tel. (0432) 268430

**Hull**
75/76 Carr Lane
Humberside HU1 3RD
tel. (0482) 223559

Central Library
Albion St.
Humberside HU1 3TF
tel. (0482) 223344

King George Dock
Hedon Rd.
Humberside HU9 5PR
tel. (0482) 702118

**Hythe**
Prospect Road Car Park
Kent CT21 5NH
tel. (0303) 67799

**Isles of Scilly**
Town Hall
St. Mary's
Cornwall TR21 0LW
tel. (0720) 22536

**Kendal**
Town Hall
Highgate
Cumbria LA9 4DL
tel. (0539) 25758

**Kenilworth**
The Library

11 Smalley Place
Warwickshire CV8 1QG
tel. (0926) 52595 / 50708

**Keswick**
Moot Hall
Market Sq.
Cumbria CA12 5JR
tel. (07687) 72645

**King's Lynn**
The Old Gaol House
Saturday Market Place
Norfolk PE30 1HY
tel. (0553) 763044

**Lancaster**
5 Dalton Sq.
Lancashire LA1 1PP
tel. (0524) 32878

**Leeds**
19 Wellington St.
West Yorkshire LS1 4DG
tel. (0532) 462454 / 5

**Leicester**
12 Bishop St.
Leicestershire LE1 6AA
tel. (0533) 556699

25/27 St. Martin's Walk
Leicestershire LE1 5DG
tel. (0533) 549922

St. Margaret's Bus Station
Leicestershire LE1 3TY
tel. (0533) 532353

**Lichfield**
Donegal House
Bore St.
Staffordshire WS13 6NE
tel. (0543) 252109

**Lincoln**
9 Castle Hill
Lincolnshire LN1 3AA
tel. (0522) 29828

21, The Cornhill
Lincolnshire
tel. (0522) 512971

**Liverpool**
29 Lime St.
Merseyside L1 1JG
tel. (051) 709 3631

Atlantic Pavilion
Albert Dock
Merseyside L3 4AA
tel. (051) 708 8854

**Mablethorpe**
Dunes Family Entertainment Centre
Central Promenade

Lincolnshire
tel. (0521) 72496

**Manchester**
Town Hall Extension
Lloyd St.
Greater Manchester M60 2LA
tel. (061) 234 3157 / 8

Manchester International Airport
NWTB TIC
International Arrivals Hall
Greater Manchester M22 5NY
tel. (061) 436 3344

**Matlock Bath**
The Pavilion
Derbyshire DE4 3NR
tel. (0629) 55082

**New Romney**
2 Littlestone Rd.
Kent TN28 8PL
tel. (0679) 64044

**Newcastle-upon-Tyne**
Northumberland NE13 8BU
tel. Tyneside (091) 2711929

Airport Terminal Building
Woolsington

Central Library
Princess Sq.
Tyne & Wear NE99 1DX
tel. (091) 2610691

Monk Street
Tyne & Wear NE1 4XW
tel. (091) 2615367

**Norwich**
Guildhall
Gaol Hill
Norfolk NR2 1NF
tel. (0603) 666071

**Nottingham**
16 Wheeler Gate
Nottinghamshire NG1 2NB
tel. (0602) 470661

County Hall
Loughborough Rd.
W. Bridgford
Nottinghamshire NG2 7QP
tel. (0602) 823823

**Oxford**
St. Aldates
Oxfordshire OX1 1DY
tel. (0865) 726871 & 3

**Penrith**
Robinson's School
Middlegate

Cumbria CA11 7PT
tel. (0768) 67466

**Penzance**
Station Road
Cornwall TR18 2NF
tel. (0736) 62207

**Plymouth**
Civic Centre
Royal Parade
Devon PL1 2EW
tel. (0752) 264849 / 264851

12 The Barbican
Devon PL1 2LS
tel. (0752) 223806 or evenings
264850

**Portsmouth**
The Hard
Hampshire PO1 3QJ
tel. (0705) 826722

Continental Ferryport
Rudmore Roundabout
Hampshire
tel. (0705) 698111

**Ravenglass**
Ravenglass & Eskdale Railway Car
Park
Cumbria
tel. (06577) 278

**Rochester**
Eastgate Cottage
High St.
Kent ME1 1EW
tel. (0634) 43666

**Rye**
48 Cinque Ports St.
East Sussex TN31 7AN
tel. (0797) 222293

**Salisbury**
Fish Row
Wiltshire SP1 1EJ
tel. (0722) 334956

**Sandwich**
St. Peter's Church
Market St.
Kent CT14 6EY
tel. (0304) 613565

**Scarborough**
St. Nicholas Cliff
North Yorkshire YO11 2EP
tel. (0723) 373333

**Sheffield**
Town Hall Extension
Union St.

South Yorkshire S1 2HH
tel. (0742) 734671 / 2

**Shrewsbury**
The Square
Shropshire SY1 1LH
tel. (0743) 50761 /2

**Skegness**
Embassy Centre
Grand Parade
Lincolnshire PE25 2UP
tel. (0754) 4821

**Southampton**
Above Bar Shopping Precinct
Hampshire SO9 4XF
tel. (0703) 221106

**Stoke-on-Trent**
1 Glebe St.
Staffordshire ST4 1HP
tel. (0782) 411222

**Stratford-upon-Avon**
Judith Shakespeare's House
1 High St.
Warwickshire CV37 6AU
tel. (0789) 293127 / 67522

**Taunton**
The Library
Corporation St.
Somerset TA1 4AN
tel. (0823) 274785 / 270479

**Tetbury**
The Old Court House
63 Long St.
Gloucestershire GL8 8AA
tel. (0666) 53552

**Warwick**
The Court House
Jury St.
Warwickshire CV34 4EW
tel. (0926) 492212

**Wells**
Town Hall
Market Place
Somerset BA5 2RB
tel. (0749) 72552 / 75987

**Winchester**
The Guildhall
The Broadway
Hampshire SO23 9LJ
tel. (0962) 840500

**Windermere**
The Gateway Centre

Victoria St.
Cumbria LA23 1AD
tel. (09662) 6499

**Windsor**
Central Station
Thames St.
Berkshire SL4 1QU
tel. (0753) 852010

**Woodstock**
Hensington Rd.
Oxford OX7 1JQ
tel. (0993) 811038

**York**
De Grey Rooms
Exhibition Sq.
North Yorkshire YO1 2HB
tel. (0904) 21756 / 7

York Railway Station
Outer Concourse
Station Rd.
North Yorkshire YO2 2AY
tel. (0904) 643700

# Wales

Cardiff
8-14 Bridge St.
South Glamorgan CF5 2EJ
tel. (0222) 27281

# Scotland

**Aberdeen**
St. Nicholas House
Broad St.
Aberdeenshire AB9 1DE
tel. (0224) 632727 / 637353

**Anstruther**
Scottish Fisheries Museum
Fife
tel. (0333) 310628

**Auchterarder**
90 High St.
Perthshire PH3 1BJ
tel. (07646) 3450

**Ballater**
Station Sq.
Aberdeenshire AB3 5RB
tel. (0338) 55306

**Banchory**
Dee Street Car Park
Aberdeenshire AB3 3YA
tel. (03302) 2000

**Braemar**
Balnellan Rd.
Aberdeenshire AB3 5YE
tel. (03383) 600

**Callander**
Leny Rd.
Perthshire FK17
tel. (0877) 30342

**Crieff**
James Sq.
Perthshire PH7 3HJ
tel. (0764) 2578

**Dufftown**
The Square
Banffshire
tel. (0340) 20501

**Dunblane**
Stirling Rd.
Stirlingshire FK15
tel. (0786) 824428

**Dunfermline**
Glen Bridge Car Park
Fife
tel. (0383) 720999

**Edinburgh**
Waverley Market
Princes St.
EH2 2QP
tel. (031) 557 1700

Edinburgh Airport
tel. (031) 333 2167

**Fort Augustus**
Car Park
Inverness-shire
tel. (0320) 6367

**Fort William**
Inverness-shire PH33 6AJ
tel. (0397) 3781

**Gairloch**
Achtercairn
Ross & Cromarty DG7
tel. (0445) 2130

**Galashiels**
Bank St.
Selkirkshire
tel. (0896) 55551

**Glasgow**
35–39 St. Vincent Place
G2 1ES
tel. (041) 227 4880

Glasgow Airport
Inchinnan Rd.
Paisley
Renfrewshire
tel. (041) 848 4440

**Inveraray**
Argyll
tel. (0499) 2063

**Inverness**
23 Church St.
Inverness-shire IV1 1EZ
tel. (0463) 234353

**Jedburgh**
Murray's Green
Roxburghshire TD8
tel. (0835) 63435 / 63688

**Kelso**
Turret House
Roxburghshire TD5 7AX
tel. (0573) 23464

**Kyle of Lochalsh**
Ross & Cromarty
tel. (0599) 4276

**Linlithgow**
Burgh Halls
The Cross
West Lothian EH49
tel. (0506) 844600

**Mallaig**
Inverness-shire
tel. (0687) 2170

**Melrose**
Priorwood Gardens
Nr Abbey
Roxburghshire TD6
tel. (089 682) 2555

**Peebles**
Chambers Institute
High St.
Peeblesshire EH45 8AG
tel. (0721) 20138

**Pitlochry**
22 Atholl Rd.
Perthshire PH16 5BX
tel. (0796) 2215 / 2751

**Portree**
Isle of Skye
IV51 9BZ
tel. (0478) 2137

**Selkirk**
Halliwell's House
Selkirkshire TD7
tel. (0750) 20054

**Stirling**
Dumbarton Rd.
Stirlingshire FK8 2LQ
tel. (0786) 75019

Broad Street
tel. (0786) 79901

**Stornoway**
4 South Beach St.
Isle of Lewis
Western Isles PA87 2XY
tel. (0851) 3088

**Tarbert**
Isle of Harris
Western Isles
tel. (0859) 2011

**Ullapool**
Ross & Cromarty
tel. (0854) 2135

# Index

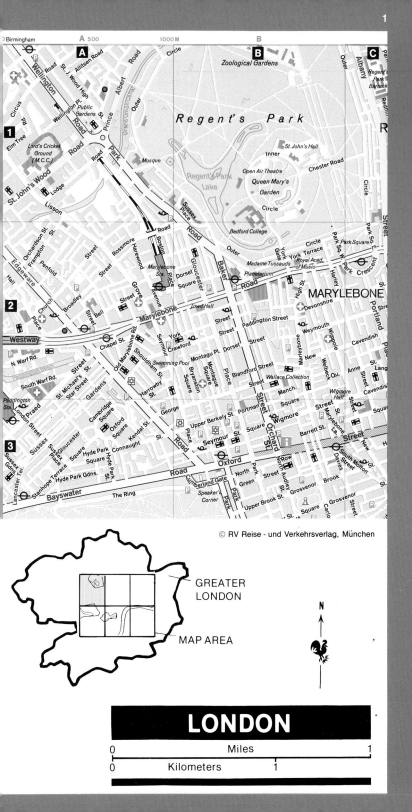

© RV Reise - und Verkehrsverlag, München

GREATER LONDON

MAP AREA

N

# LONDON

| Miles | |
|---|---|
| 0 | 1 |

| Kilometers | |
|---|---|
| 0 | 1 |

# FAST FACTS

Greater London's size (square miles) .... 609.7 square miles

Greater London population (mid-1986) ............ 6,775,000

Queen's public expenditure incurred in carrying out
official duties as head of State in 1986 .......... £ 4.3 million

The Prime Minister's salary (from Oct. 1987) ........ £ 62,698

Number of licensed taxis in London ........... about 14,200

Traffic through the
port of London in 1986 .............. 53.7 million metric tons

Passenger journeys on
the BritRail system in 1986-87 .................. 689 million

Passenger traffic at London's airports in 1986 ..... 47.6 million

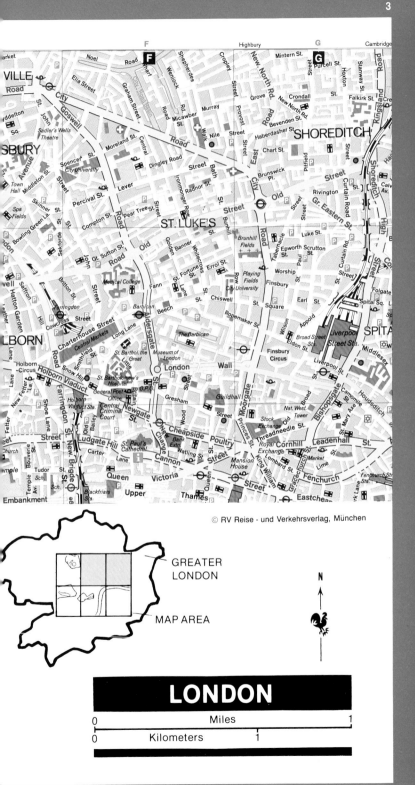

© RV Reise - und Verkehrsverlag, München

GREATER LONDON

MAP AREA

N

# LONDON

| 0 | Miles | 1 |
| 0 | Kilometers | 1 |

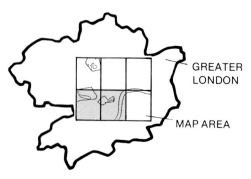

GREATER LONDON

MAP AREA

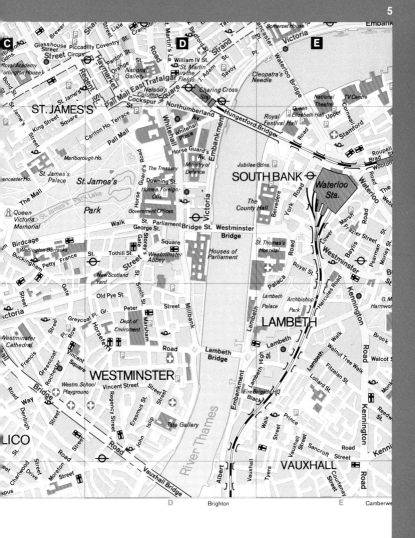

# LONDON

| Miles | |
|---|---|
| 0 | 1 |

| Kilometers | |
|---|---|
| 0 | 1 |

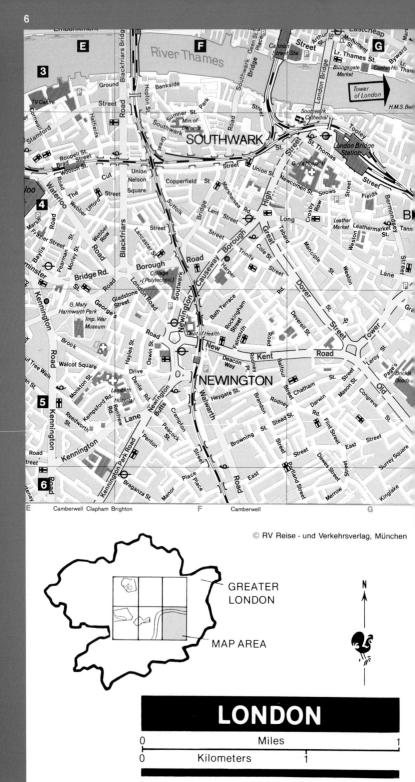

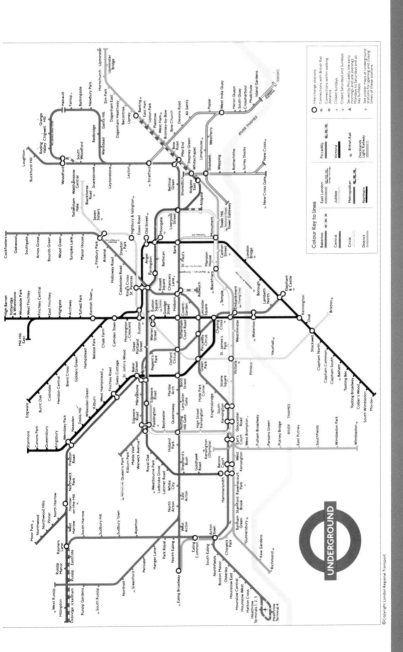

8

HERTFORDSHIRE

ESSEX

ENFIELD

BARNET

HARROW

HARINGEY

WALTHAM FOREST

REDBRIDGE

HAVERING

HILLINGDON

BRENT

CAMDEN

HACKNEY

ISLINGTON

NEWHAM

BARKING AND DAGENHAM

EALING

KENSINGTON AND CHELSEA

CITY OF WESTMINSTER

TOWER HAMLETS

HAMMERSMITH AND FULHAM

CITY OF LONDON

River Thames

HOUNSLOW

GREENWICH

BEXLEY

RICHMOND UPON THAMES

WANDSWORTH

LAMBETH

SOUTHWARK

LEWISHAM

River Thames

MERTON

KINGSTON UPON THAMES

SUTTON

CROYDON

BROMLEY

KENT

SURREY

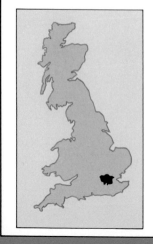

Inner London

N

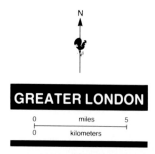

**GREATER LONDON**

0     miles     5

0     kilometers

9

# GREAT BRITAIN

| 0 | miles | 50 |
| 0 | kilometers | 120 |

N

Scrabster

Ullapool

Kyle of
Lochalsh

Mallaig

Inverness

Aberdeen

Montrose

Oban

Dundee

North Sea

Dunoon

**Glasgow**

Edinburgh

Ardrossan

✈ Prestwick

Dumfries

Blyth

Stranraer

Newcastle ○ Sunderland

Carlisle

Hartlepool

Workington
Whitehaven

Middlesborough

Scarborough

Irish Sea

Barrow

Heysham ○ Lancaster

Fleetwood

Bradford ○ York

Preston ○ Leeds

Hull

Holyhead

**Liverpool** ○ **Manchester**

Goole

Immingham ○ Grimsby

Chester

Sheffield

✈ Ringway

Stoke-on-
Trent

Derby

Nottingham ○ Boston

Shrewsbury

Kings Lynn

Great
Yarmouth

Wolverhampton

Leicester

Norwich

Aberystwyth

**Birmingham** ✈ Birmingham
International

Lowestoft

Coventry

Worcester

Stratford
upon Avon

Northampton ○ Cambridge

Fishguard

Ipswich ○ Felixstowe

Milford Haven

Swansea

Newport

Sharpness

Luton ✈

Colchester ○ Harwich

Pembroke Dock

Oxford

✈ Stansted

Port Talbot

Cardiff ○ Bristol

Reading

Heathrow ✈

Barry ○ Bath

**London**

Barnstaple

Ramsgate

✈ Gatwick

Dover

Southampton

Folkestone

Shoreham

Exeter

Poole

Brighton

Weymouth

Cowes ○ Portsmouth ○ Newhaven

Plymouth

Penzance ○ Fowey

English Channel

**1**
**2**
**3**
**4**
**5**

**A**
**B**
**C**

Slough

**A**      **B**      **C**

**1**

Pococks Lane

The Playing Fields

Eton Wick Road

Slough Road

Keats La.

**Eton College**

The Home Park

South Meadow

**Eton Parish Church**

King Edward VII Avenue

**2**

Eton Ct.

Eton Sq.

**Our Lady of Sorrow Church (RC)**

The Brocas

**The Cock Pit**

Datchet Road

Pleasure Ground

Putting Green

River Thames

Thames Side

Thames Avenue

**Windsor and Eton Riverside Rail Station**

**Old House Hotel**

Barry Ave

River St.

**King George V Memorial**

**Theatre Royal**

Alexandra Gardens

Thames St.

Coach Park

**Windsor and Eton Central Rail Station**

**Windsor Castle**

Arthur Road

**Queen Victoria Statue**

Castle Hill

Oxford Rd

**Guildhall**

St Alban's St.

**Royal Mews**

**3**

Bexley Street

**Windsor Parish Church**

High St.

Park St.

**Nell Qwynne's House**

Peascod St.

The Home Park

Clarence Road

Victoria Street

Sheet Street

Sports Ground

Goslar Way

**Victoria Barracks**

Alexandra Road

**4**

Frogmore House

Springfield Rd

Bus Station

Frances Road

King's Road

Osborne Road

**Household Cavalry Museum**

**Royal Mausoleum**

**Combermere Barracks**

Bolton Ave

St Leonard's Road

Albert Road

**5**

# WINDSOR & ETON

| 0 | yards | 440 |
|---|-------|-----|
| 0 | meters | 400 |

N

11

Alcester

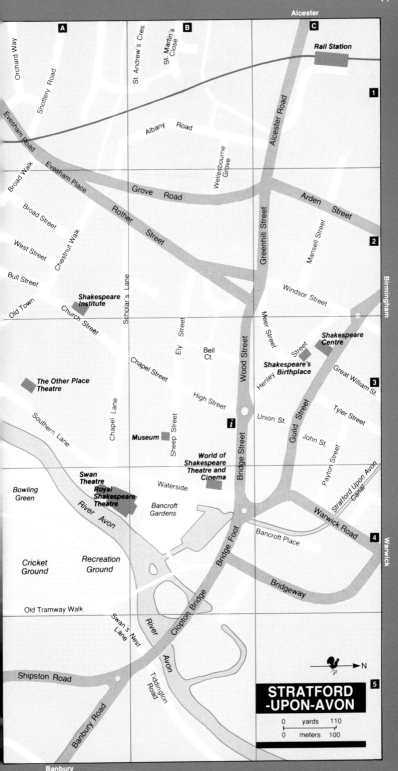

**A**  **B**  **C**

**Rail Station**

**1**

Orchard Way

Shottery Road

St. Andrew's Cres.

St. Martin's Close

Albany    Road

Alcester Road

Evesham Road

Broad Walk

Evesham Place

Grove    Road

Wellesbourne Grove

Arden    Street

Broad Street

Rother    Street

**2**

Mansell Street

West Street

Chestnut Walk

Greenhill Street

Bull Street

Windsor Street

Old Town

Church Street

**Shakespeare Institute**

Scholar's Lane

Ely Street

Bell Ct.

Wood Street

Meer Street

Street

**Shakespeare Centre**

**Shakespeare's Birthplace**

Henley

Great William St.

**3**

**The Other Place Theatre**

Chapel Street

Chapel Lane

High Street

**i**

Union St.

Guild Street

Tyler Street

John St.

Payton Street

**Museum**

Sheep Street

**World of Shakespeare Theatre and Cinema**

**Swan Theatre**

**Royal Shakespeare Theatre**

Waterside

Bancroft Gardens

Bridge Street

Stratford Upon Avon Canal

Warwick Road

**4**

Bowling Green

River Avon

Southern Lane

Bancroft Place

Bridge Foot

Cricket Ground

Recreation Ground

Bridgeway

Old Tramway Walk

Swan's Nest Lane

Clopton Bridge

River

Avon

Tiddington Road

Shipston Road

Banbury Road

N

**5**

# STRATFORD -UPON-AVON

| 0 | yards | 110 |
| 0 | meters | 100 |

Birmingham

Warwick

Banbury

# OXFORD

| 0 | yards | 440 |
| 0 | meters | 400 |

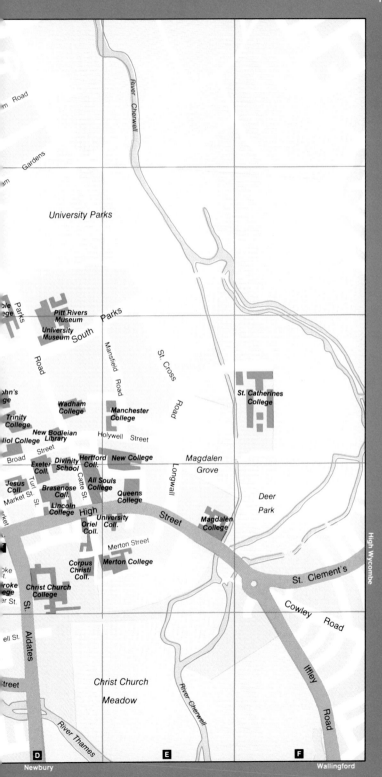

Road

Gardens

University Parks

River Cherwell

Parks

Pitt Rivers
Museum
University
Museum South

Road

Mansfield Road

St. Cross Road

St. Catherines
College

ble
ge Parks

hn's
ge

Wadham
College

Manchester
College

Trinity
College

New Bodleian
Library
iol College

Holywell Street

Broad Street

Exeter Divinity Hertford New College
Coll. School Coll.

Magdalen
Grove

Jesus
Coll.

Brasenose
Coll.

All Souls
College

Catte St.

Longwall

Deer
Park

Market St.

Turl

St.

Lincoln
College

Queens
College

High

University
Oriel Coll.
Coll.

Street

Magdalen
College

ke
t.
roke
ege
r St.

Corpus
Christi
Coll.

Merton Street

Merton College

Christ Church
College

St. Clement's

St.

Aldates

Cowley Road

ell St.

treet

Christ Church

Meadow

River Cherwell

Iffley Road

High Wycombe

River Thames

14

Huntingdon

Bedford

**1** Madingley Rd.

Lady Margaret Rd.

Castle Street

Chesterton Lane

Northampton Street

*Magdalene*

Magdalene St.

New Park Street

Bridge Street

**2** Queens Road

St. John's St.

*St. John's*

Bridge of Sighs
St. Johns Bridge

River Cam

*Trinity*

Trinity Street

Sidney

Green Street

The Backs

Trinity Bridge

Garret Hostel Br.

*Trinity Hall*

*Gonville and Caius*

Kings Parade

*University Church*

Mark

Pett
Cu

**3**

Clare Bridge

*Clare*

*King's College Chapel*

*King's*

**i**

Excha

**4** Queens Road

West Road

The Backs

King's Bridge

River Cam

*Queen's*

Kings Parade

Benet St.

*Corpus Christi*

Pembroke St

Pembr

Queen's Bridge

Silver Street

Mill Lane

Trumpington Street

N

Little St. Mary's La.

**5**

## CAMBRIDGE

*Museum*

*Peterhouse*

*Fitzwilliam Museum*

0    yards    220
0    meters   200

Queens Road

**A**      **B**      **C**

Grantchester, Newnham Rd.

River Cam

us Green

Jesus

Midsummer Common

Victoria Avenue

Victoria Avenue

Butts Green

Jesus Lane

Maids Causeway

ey ex

Short St.

Fair Street

Newmarket

King Street

Fitzroy St.

Fitzroy St.

Christ's

Christ's Pieces

Emmanuel Road

Elm Street

Eden Street

St. Andrew's Street

Drummer St.

Clarendon Street

Emmanuel St.

Melbourne Place

Prospect Row

Emmanuel St.

Emmanuel

Parker Street

Downing Street

St. Andrew's Street

Parkside

Museum

Park Terrace

Parkers Piece

Tennis Court Road

Regent Terrace

Regent Street

Gonville Place

Downing

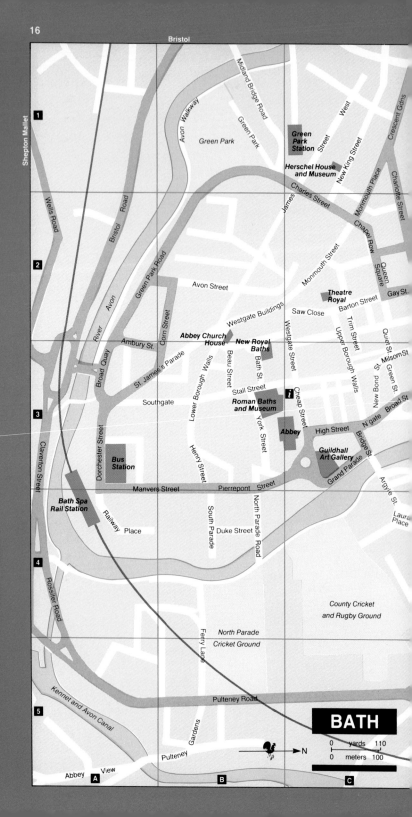

BATH

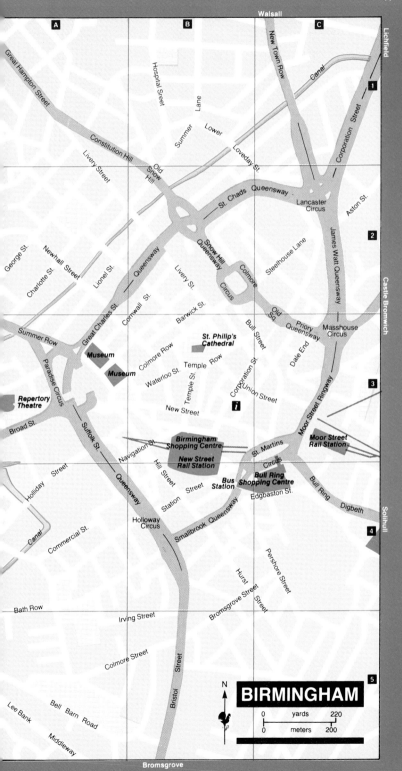

# BIRMINGHAM

| 0 | yards | 220 |
| 0 | meters | 200 |

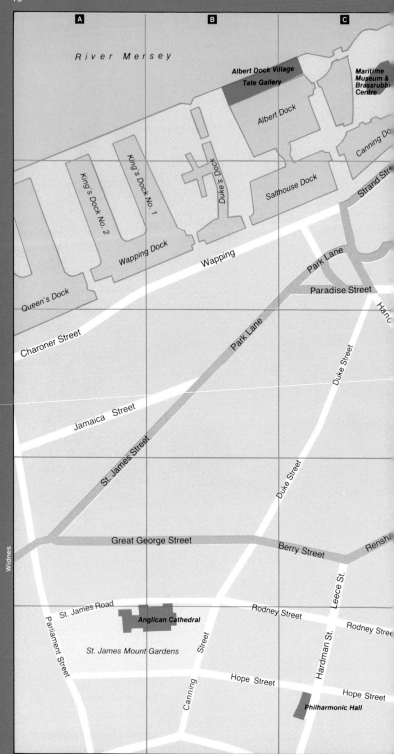

**A**  **B**  **C**

*River Mersey*

Albert Dock Village
**Tate Gallery**

Maritime
Museum &
Brassrubbi
Centre

Albert Dock

Canning Do

King's Dock No. 1

King's Dock No. 2

Duke's Dock

Salthouse Dock

Strand Stre

Wapping Dock

Wapping

Wapping

Park Lane

Paradise Street

Queen's Dock

Hanc

Charoner Street

Park Lane

Duke Street

Jamaica Street

St. James Street

Duke Street

Widnes

Great George Street

Berry Street

Rensha

Leece St.

St. James Road

Rodney Street

Parliament Street

*Anglican Cathedral*

Street

Hardman St.

Rodney Stree

*St. James Mount Gardens*

Canning

Hope Street

Hope Street

*Philharmonic Hall*

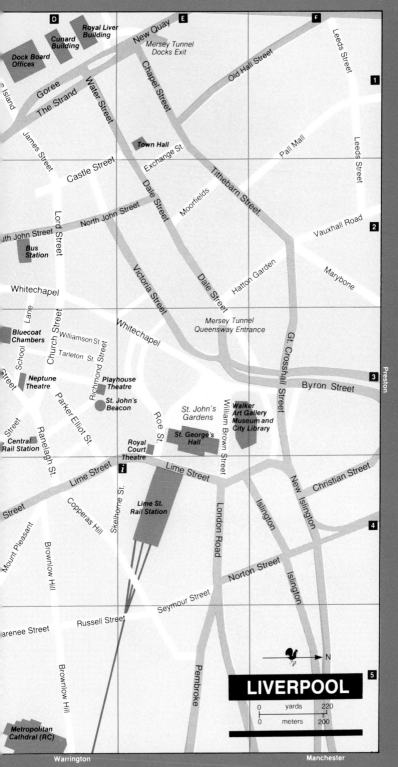

LIVERPOOL

| 0 | yards | 220 |
| 0 | meters | 200 |

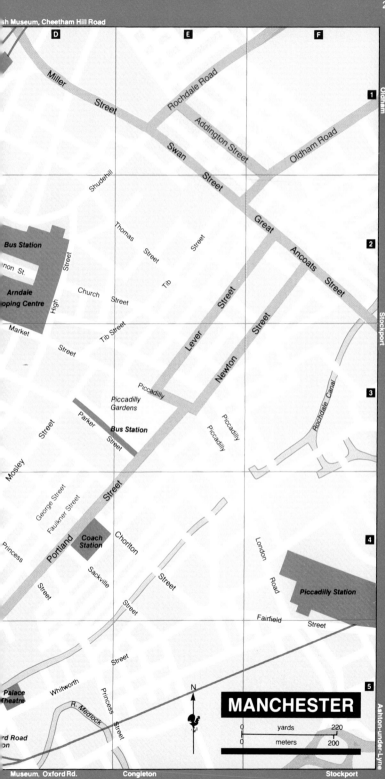

sh Museum, Cheetham Hill Road

**D**   **E**   **F**

Oldham

**1**

Miller Street

Rochdale Road

Addington Street

Swan Street

Oldham Road

Shudehill

Great

**2**

Ancoats Street

Stockport

**Bus Station**

non St.

Thomas Street

Street

Street

**Arndale
oping Centre**

Church Street

High

Tib

Lever Street

Newton Street

Rochdale Canal

Market

Tib Street

Street

**3**

Piccadilly

Piccadilly
Gardens

Piccadilly

Piccadilly

Street

Parker

**Bus Station**

Street

Mosley

Street

George Street

Faulkner Street

Portland Street

Chorlton

London Road

**4**

Princess

**Coach
Station**

Sackville

Street

**Piccadilly Station**

Street

Street

Fairfield Street

Street

**5**

**Palace
Theatre**

Whitworth

Princess

N

**MANCHESTER**

rd Road
on

R. Medlock

Street

0   yards   220

0   meters   200

Museum, Oxford Rd.     Congleton     Stockport

Ashton-under-Lyne

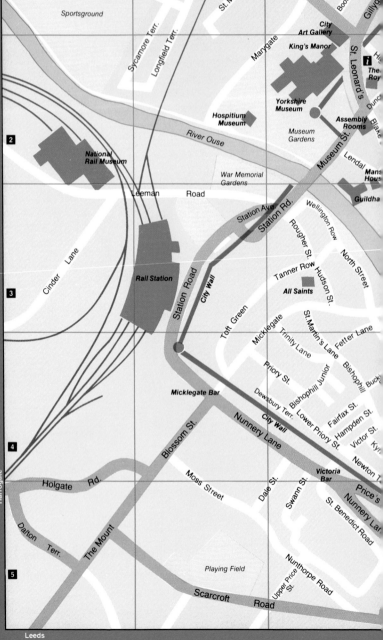

Thirsk

**A** **B** **C**

Playing Field

North Parade
Queen Anne's Road
Clifton
Bootham Terr.
Bootham
Bootham Row
Gillyga

St. Mary's

Sycamore Terr.
Longfield Terr.
Marygate

City Art Gallery
King's Manor
St. Leonard's

*i* Hi
The Roy
Dunc
Blake

Yorkshire Museum

Hospitium Museum

Museum Gardens

Assembly Rooms

River Ouse

National Rail Museum

War Memorial Gardens

Museum St.
Lendal
Mans Hous

Leeman Road

Guildha

Station Ave.
Station Rd.
Wellington Row

Rougher St.
North Street
Hudson St.
Tanner Row

Cinder Lane

Rail Station

Station Road

City Wall

All Saints

Toft Green
Micklegate
Trinity Lane
St. Martin's Lane
Fetter Lane
Bishopthill Junior
Bishophill
Buck

Priory St.

Micklegate Bar

Dewsbury Terr.
Lower Priory St.
Fairfax St.
Hampden St.
Victor St.
Kyn

City Wall
Nunnery Lane

Blossom St.

Holgate Rd.
Moss Street
Dale St.
Swann St.

Victoria Bar
Newton T.
Price's
Nunnery Lan
St. Benedict Road

Dalton Terr.
The Mount

Playing Field

Nunthorpe Road
Upper Price St.

Scarcroft Road

Harrogate

Leeds

**1** **2** **3** **4** **5**

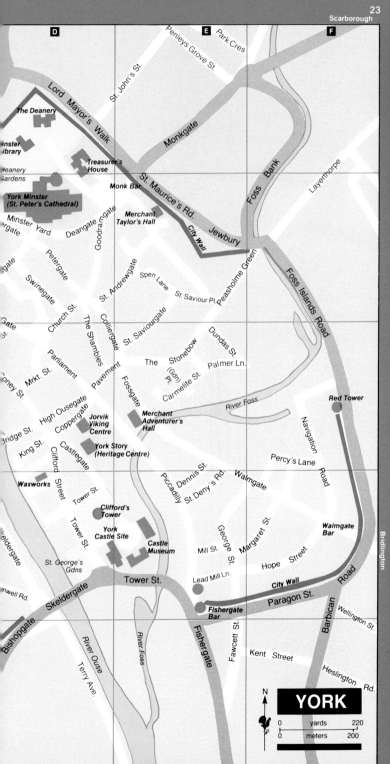

Park Cres
Penleys Grove St.
St. John's St.
Lord Mayor's Walk
The Deanery
inster
library
Monkgate
Foss Bank
Layerthorpe
eanery
Gardens
Treasurer's
House
St. Maurice's Rd.
Monk Bar
York Minster
(St. Peter's Cathedral)
Minster Yard
rgate
Deangate
Goodramgate
Merchant
Taylor's Hall
City Wall
Jewbury
Peasholme Green
gate
Petergate
Swinegate
St. Andrewgate
Spen Lane
St. Saviour Pl.
Foss Islands Road
Gate
i
Church St.
The Shambles
Colliergate
St. Saviourgate
Dundas St.
Parliament
The Stonebow
Palmer Ln.
(Grn)
Pl.
oney St.
Mrkt. St.
Pavement
Fossgate
Carmelite St.
River Foss
Red Tower
High Ousegate
Coppergate
Jorvik
Viking
Centre
Merchant
Adventurer's
Hall
Bridge St.
King St.
Castlegate
York Story
(Heritage Centre)
Navigation Road
Percy's Lane
Clifford
Street
Waxworks
Dennis St.
Piccadilly
St. Deny's Rd.
Walmgate
Tower St.
Clifford's
Tower
York
Castle Site
Castle
Museum
Mill St.
George St.
Margaret St.
Walmgate
Bar
Tower St.
keldergate
St. George's
Gdns
Hope Street
Bridlington
mwell Rd.
Skeldergate
Tower St.
Lead Mill Ln.
City Wall
Paragon St.
Barbican Road
Wellington St.
Bishopgate
River Ouse
River Foss
Fishergate
Bar
Fishergate
Fawcett St.
Kent Street
Heslington Rd.
Terry Ave.

N

YORK

0    yards    220
0    meters    200

Selby

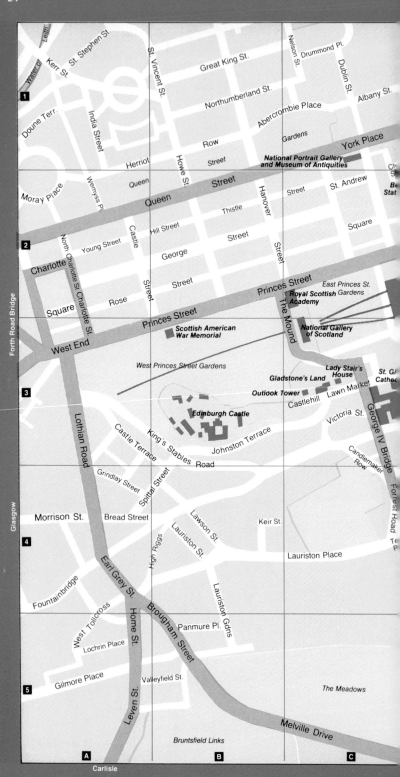

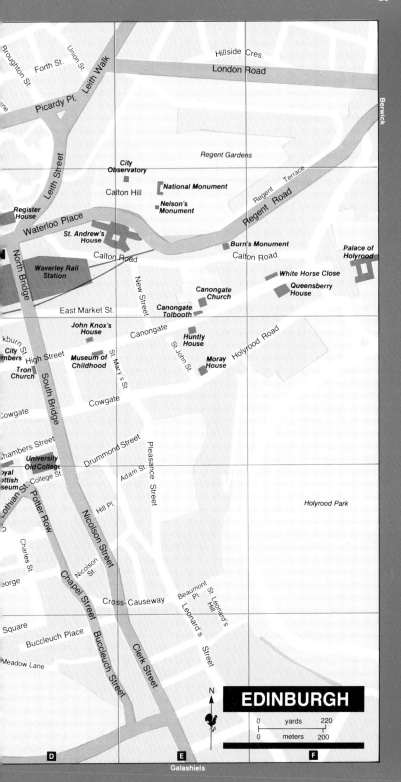

Hillside Cres.

London Road

Broughton St.

Forth St.

Union St.

Picardy Pl.

Leith Walk

Berwick

Regent Gardens

Leith Street

City Observatory

National Monument

Calton Hill

Nelson's Monument

Regent Terrace

Register House

Waterloo Place

St. Andrew's House

Calton Road

Burn's Monument

Calton Road

Regent Road

Palace of Holyrood

North Bridge

Waverley Rail Station

New Street

White Horse Close

Queensberry House

East Market St.

Canongate Church

Canongate Tolbooth

John Knox's House

Canongate

Huntly House

Holyrood Road

kburn St.

City St. mbers

High Street

Museum of Childhood

St. Mary's St.

St. John St.

Moray House

Tron Church

South Bridge

Cowgate

Cowgate

Chambers Street

University Old College

Drummond Street

Pleasance Street

oyal ottish seum

College St.

Adam St.

Holyrood Park

Lothian St.

Potter Row

Hill Pl.

Nicolson Street

Charles St.

Nicolson St.

eorge

Chapel Street

Cross- Causeway

Beaumont Pl.

St. Leonard's Hill

Square

Buccleuch Place

Buccleuch Street

Clerk Street

Leonard's Street

Meadow Lane

N

EDINBURGH

0 yards 220

0 meters 200

D

E

F

Galashiels

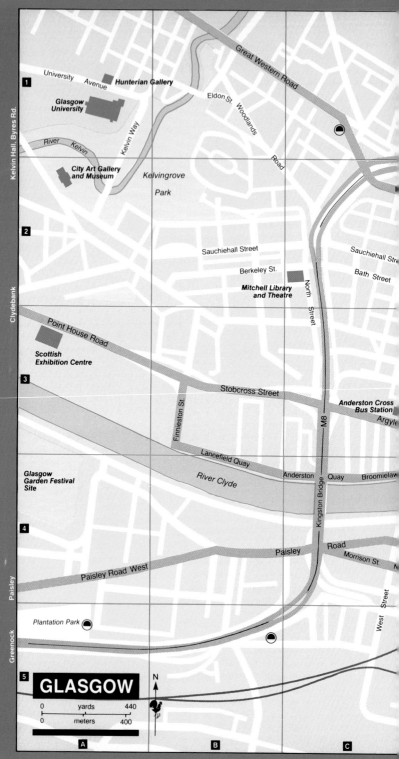

University Avenue
**Hunterian Gallery**
**Glasgow University**
Eldon St.
Woodlands
Great Western Road
River Kelvin
Kelvin Way
Road
**City Art Gallery and Museum**
Kelvingrove Park

Kelvin Hall: Byres Rd.

**1**

**2**

Clydebank

Sauchiehall Street
Sauchiehall Stre
Berkeley St.
Bath Street
**Mitchell Library and Theatre**
North Street

Point House Road
**Scottish Exhibition Centre**

**3**

Stobcross Street
Finnieston St.
**Anderston Cross Bus Station**
Argyle
M8
Lancefield Quay
**Glasgow Garden Festival Site**
River Clyde
Anderston
Quay
Broomielaw
Kingston Bridge

**4**

Paisley
Road
Morrison St.
Paisley Road West
N

Street

Plantation Park
West
Street

Greenock

**5**

# GLASGOW

N

0 — yards — 440
0 — meters — 400

**A**
**B**
**C**

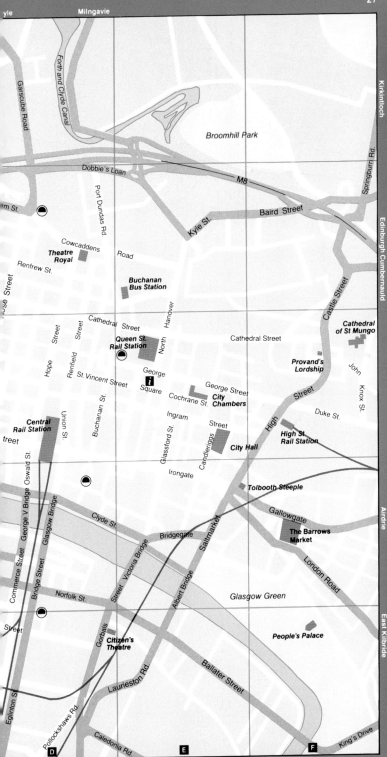

yle
Milngavie

Forth and Clyde Canal

Garscube Road

Broomhill Park

Kirkintloch

Spingburn Rd.

Dobbie's Loan

M8

m St.

Baird Street

Kyle St.

Edinburgh Cumbernauld

Cowcaddens

Theatre Royal

Road

Port Dundas Rd.

Renfrew St.

Castle Street

Cathedral of St Mungo

ose Street

Buchanan Bus Station

Cathedral Street

North Hanover

Cathedral Street

Street

Queen St. Rail Station

Street

Provand's Lordship

John

Hope

Renfield

St.Vincent Street

North

George

George Street

City Chambers

Knox St.

Square

Cochrane St.

Street

High

Duke St.

Buchanan St.

Ingram

Street

Central Rail Station

Union St.

Glassford St.

Candleriggs

City Hall

High St Rail Station

treet

Oswald St.

Irongate

Tolbooth Steeple

George V Bridge

Glasgow Bridge

Clyde St.

Gallowgate

The Barrows Market

Airdrie

Commerce Street

Bridge Street

Street

Victoria Bridge

Bridgegate

Saltmarket

London Road

Norfolk St.

Albert Bridge

Glasgow Green

East Kilbride

Street

Gorbals

Citizen's Theatre

People's Palace

Eglinton St.

Laurieston Rd.

Ballater Street

Pollockshaws Rd.

Caledonia Rd.

King's Drive

**D**

**E**

**F**

Burrell Collection    Cathcart

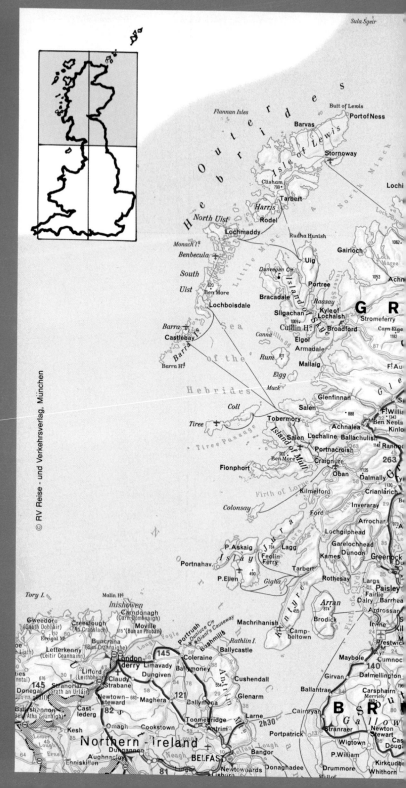

Sula Sgeir

Flannan Isles

O u t e r   H e b r i d e s

Butt of Lewis
Port of Ness
Barvas
Isle of Lewis
Stornoway
North Minch
Lochi

Clisham 799

Tarbert
Harris
Rodel

North Uist
Lochmaddy

Rudha Hunish

Monach I$
Benbecula

South
Uist
Ben More 620

Little Minch

Gairloch
Loch Maree
1062

Uig
Island of Skye
Portree
1053
Achn

Dunvegan C$e

Bracadale
Raasay

Lochboisdale
Sligachan
1009
Kyle of
Lochalsh
G R
Stromeferry

Barra
Castlebay
Canna

Cuillin H$s
Broadford
Carn Eige
1182

Elgol
Armadale

Barra H$d
Rum 811

Mallaig

Ft Au

Sea
of the
Eigg

Muck

H e b r i d e s

Glenfinnan
Gle

Coll
Salen
Ft Willie
888
Ben Nevis
1343
Kinlo

Tiree
Tobermory
Achnalea
Lochaline Ballachulish

Tiree Passage
Salen
Island of Mull
Portnacroish
1148 Rannoc

Ben More 966
Craignure
263

Fionphort
1125
Oban
58
Dalmally G

Firth of Lorne
Kilmelford
1130
Crianlarich
Be

Colonsay
Ford
Inveraray 29

Arrochar
973

Lochgilphead
Garelochhead
35

P. Askaig
784
Lagg
Kames
Dunoon
Greenock
Du

Portnahav.
Islay
Feolin
Ferry
Tarbert
Rothesay
Largs
Paisley
St Fairlie

P. Ellen
490
Gigha
356
Arran
874
Dalry
Barrhea
Ardrossan
S

Tory I.
Malin H$d
Inishowen
Carndonagh
(Carn Domhnaigh)
Machrihanish
Brodick
Irvine

Gweedore
(Gaoth Dobhair)
Creeslough
(An Craoslach)
515 (Bun an Phobail)
Camp-
beltown

Errigal M$
Letterkenny
(Leitir Ceanainn)
Portrush
Dunluce C$e
Giant's Causeway
Bishmills
Rathlin I.
Ballycastle
Frestwic
Ayr

152

Lifford
Leithbhe$
London-
derry
Limavady
Coleraine
Ballymoney
Cushendall
Maybole
140
Cumnoc

145
Stranorlar
(Srath an Urláir)
Newtown-
steward
Claudy
Strabane
Dungiven
Ballymena
Glenarm
Girvan
Dalmellington

Donegal
676
Castle-
derger
82
Maghera
121
Ballantrae
Carsphairn
Merrick
786
B S R

Ballyshannon
Kesh
Omagh
Cookstown
Toomebridge
Antrim
Larne
Cairnryan 2h30
Stranraer
Newton
Stewart
Galloway

Lower
Erne
64
Aughnacloy
Dungannon
Neagh
BELFAST
Portpatrick
Wigtown
Cas
Doug

Enniskillen
Northern-Ireland
Newtownards
Bangor
Donaghadee
P.William
Kirkcud
Whithorn

81
Lisbura

© RV Reise- und Verkehrsverlag, München

Fair Isle

North Ronaldsay
Westray
Sanday
Sule Skerry
Rousay
Stack Skerry
Stronsay
Mainland
Stromness
Kirkwall Shapinsay
Hoy 477
Scapa Flow
Orkney
St.Margaret's
Hope
South Ronaldsay
Dunnet Hd.
Bettyhill
John o'Groat's
Duncansby Hd.
Tongue
Melvich Thurso
Ben Hope
927
Altnaharra
Kinbrace
Wick
961
Ben Klibreck
Latheron
Lairg
705
Lybster
254
Helmsdale
Golspie Brora
Bonarbridge
Dunrobin Cle.
Dornoch
Dornoch Firth
Alness
Tain
Moray Firth
Dingwall
Burghead Lossiemouth
Nairn
Elgin Buckie
Inverness
Forres
Fochabers Banff
Dores Moy
Craigellachie
Keith
Turriff
Fraserburgh
Carrbridge
Grantown-
o.-Sp.
Dufftown
172
Huntly
New Deer
Peterhead
Aviemore
Tomintoul
Oldmeldrum
Ellon
Kingussie
1245
Alford
Inverurie
Newburgh
Ben Macdhui
1310 1172
Balmoral Cle.
Echt
ABERDEEN
Linn of Dee
Braemar
Aboyne
Crathie
Ballater
Peterculter
Mountains
Lochnagar
Banchory
1119
Braedownie.
Stonehaven
Pass of
Killiecrankie
Dunnottar Cle.
Pitlochry
141
Inverbervie
Aberfeldy
Kirriemuir
Brechin
Dunkeld
Blairgowrie
Montrose
Coupar
Angus
Glamis Cle.
140
Perth
Forfar
DUNDEE
Arbroath
Cupar
St.Andrews
Kinross
Buckhav.
Fife Ness
stirling
Kilrenny
Dunferm-
line
Inver-
keithing
Kirkcaldy Elie
North Berwick
Falkirk
Leith
Firth of Forth
Linlithgow
Musselburgh
Dunbar
E.& W.EDINBURGH
W.Calder
Haddington
wmains
Dalkeith
Grantshouse
Penicuik
W. Linton
Duns
Berwick-u.-Tw.
Peebles
Lauder
iggar
Melrose
Abbey
uglas Mill
Galashiels
Coldstream
194
Broad Law
Selkirk St.Boswells
Belford
822
Hawick
Jedburgh
Wooler
Moffat
157
Cauldcleuch Hd.
The Cheviot
Alnwick
606
Lockerbie
Langholm
Otterburn
Rothbury
Alnmouth
Gretna
Green Longtown
Newbiggin-
by-the-Sea
bean Annan
Roman Wall
Morpeth
Ponteland
Blyth
oth Wigton
Brampton
93
Carlisle
Hexham
NEWCASTLE Tynemouth

Herma Ness
Bluemull Sd.
Haroldswick
Unst
Isbister
Ronas Hill
440
Yell
Fetlar
The Faither
Hillswick
Burravoe
St.Magnus
Bay
Firth
Out Skerries
Papa Stour
Voe
Melby
Mainland
Whalsay
Shetland
Vaila
Lerwick
(Zetland)
Foula
Bressay (Gr. Br.)
I. of Noss
Scalloway
West Burra
Mousa
Fitful Hd.
Grutnes
Sumburgh Hd.

N

**GREAT BRITAIN**

Kilometers
0    30    60    90
0    20    40    60
Miles

# GREAT BRITAIN

### Kilometers
0 — 30 — 60 — 90

### Miles
0 — 20 — 40 — 60

Craigavon
Lurgan
Newtownards
Lisburn
81
79
Armagh
Banbridge
Keady
Downpatrick
Portaferry
Monaghan
(Muineachán)
Ards Pen.
Mull of Galloway
Whithorn
Maryport 57
Cockermouth
Workington
Whitehaven
Egremont
Scafell Pike 979
Cumbria
Ravenglass
Keswick
Millom
Dalton-i-F.
Newby B
Barrow-i.-F.
Walney I.
Gr
Morecambe B.

I. of Man
P. of Ayre
Ramsay
Peel
Snaefell
Douglas
Castletown

Irish Sea

Fleetwood
BLACKPOOL
PRESTO
Lytham St. Anne's
Southport
50
Wiga
ST HE

Balbriggan
(Baile Brigin)
82
Innfield
(An Bothar Buidhe)
DUBLIN
(BAILE ÁTHA CLIATH)
66 D
Lambay I.
Naas (Nás)
Kingstown
(Dún Laoghaire)
Bray
(Brí Chualann)
Wicklow Mts.
Wicklow
(Cill Mhanntáin)
Arklow
(An tInbhear Mór)
137
Gorey
(Guaire)
rford
(rman)
slace
's Láire)
Carnsore Pt.

7h
3h30'
Carmel Hd.
Amlwch
Holyhead
Holy I.
Anglesey
Beaumaris
Llandudno
Colwyn Bay
Rhyl
Prestatyn
Bootle
Wallasey
Conway
116
LIVER
KEN POOL
BIR HEAD
Bangor
Denbigh
Chester
North
Snowdon
1085
Betws-y-Coed
Ruthin
Wrexham
31
Caernarvon
1062
Nefyn
Criccieth
Porthmadog
Llangollen
Whitchurch
Nan
14
Pwllheli
Lleyn Pen.
Harlech Cle
Aran Mawddwy
905
Oswestry
Wem
72
Bardsey
Barmouth
Dolgellau
Dinas-Mawddwy
Shrewsbur
Tel
Tremadoc Bay
Tywyn
Machynlleth
Welshpool
Montgomery
Wellington
WOLVER
Cardigan Bay
Aberystwyth
752
Newtown
Bishop's Castle
Bridgnorth
546
Aberaeron
New Quay
Tregaron
Rhayader
Knighton
Ludlow
Kid
mins
Fishguard & Goodwick
Cardigan
Newcastle Emlyn
Lampeter
Llandrindod Wells
660
Leominster
St. David's Hd.
St David's
537
Haverfordwest
Redstone Cross
Carmarthen
Builth Wells
Llandovery
Talgarth
Bromyard
Worcest
Milford Haven
Begelly
St Clears
Llandeilo
Brecon
Hereford
37
Pembroke
Kidwelly
Tenby
Llanelly
225
Brecon Beacons
886
Abergavenny
Ross-o-W.
Ledbury
St Govan's Hd.
Carmarthen Bay
SWANSEA
Neath
Merthyr Tydfil
Tredegar
Monmouth
26
Gloucest
Symonds Yat
Gower Pen.
Mumbles
Port Talbot
Aberdare
Rhondda
Risca
Tintern Abbey
71
Bridgend
Caerphilly
Chepstow
69
198
NEWPORT
Thornbury
Mal
bur
Barry
CARDIFF
BRISTOL
65

Bristol Channel
Ilfracombe
Lynton
Weston-s.-M.
Clevedon
Congresbury
Bath
Dev
Barnstaple
Exmoor Forest
520
Minehead
Wells
Beckington
Trowb
Bideford
493
Sth Molton
Bridgwater
Glastonbury
Shepton Mallet
Frome
Warr
Stone
Gt Torrington
Bampton
Taunton
Wincanton
149
Sa
Bude-Stratton
Holsworthy
Hatherleigh
Tiverton
Cullompton
Ilminster
Ilchester
Yeovil
58
Sherborne
Shaftes
Boscastle
Okehampton
Crediton
Honiton
Chard
Crewkerne
Sturminster
Camelford
DEVON
Launceston
High Willhays
621
Moreton hampstead
Axminster
Blandford Forum
Ring
Padstow
Wadebridge
Dartmoor Forest
Tavistock
516
Exeter
27
Sidmouth
Lyme Regis
Bridport
Wimborne M.
Newquay
CORNWALL
190
Bodmin
Callington
Liskeard
Newton Abbot
Exmouth
Teignmouth
Dorchester
14
POOLE
St Ives
Redruth
55
Lostwithiel
53
Fowey
Saltash
Totnes
Lyme Bay
Wareham
B
Hayle
St Austell
Looe
TORBAY
Portland
Weymouth
M
Penzance
Truro
PLYMOUTH
Paignton
Dart mouth
Brixham
Bill of Portland
St Michael's Mount
Helston
Falmouth
Kingsbridge
Lizard

St Ives R
St Just
252
Pen
St Michael's Mount
Lundy I.
Hugh Town
Land's End
Gwennap Hd.
Isles of Scilly
Liz

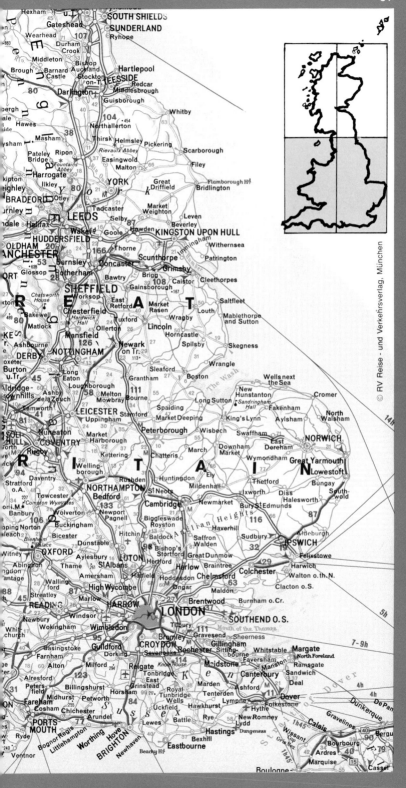

**Signs Giving Orders** *These signs are mostly circular and those with red circles are mostly prohibitive*

Maximum speed

National speed limit applies

Stop and Give Way

No entry for vehicular traffic

No overtaking

*Signs with blue circles but no red border are mostly compulsory*

No motor vehicles

Give way to traffic on major road

No right turn

Ahead only

Turn left (right if symbol reversed)

Roundabout

Cross roads

Traffic merges from left

Dual Roadway ends

Right-hand lane closed (symbols may be varied)

**Warning Signs** *Mostly triangular*